Intellectual Property Protection for Multimedia Information Technology

Hideyasu Sasaki
Ritsumeikan University, Japan

INFORMATION SCIENCE REFERENCE

Hershey · New York

Acquisitions Editor:	Kristin Klinger
Development Editor:	Kristin Roth
Senior Managing Editor:	Jennifer Neidig
Managing Editor:	Sara Reed
Copy Editor:	Angela Thor
Typesetter:	Jamie Snavely
Cover Design:	Lisa Tosheff
Printed at:	Yurchak Printing Inc.

Published in the United States of America by
Information Science Reference (an imprint of IGI Global)
701 E. Chocolate Avenue, Suite 200
Hershey PA 17033
Tel: 717-533-8845
Fax: 717-533-8661
E-mail: cust@igi-global.com
Web site: http://www.igi-global.com

and in the United Kingdom by
Information Science Reference (an imprint of IGI Global)
3 Henrietta Street
Covent Garden
London WC2E 8LU
Tel: 44 20 7240 0856
Fax: 44 20 7379 0609
Web site: http://www.eurospanonline.com

Library of Congress Cataloging-in-Publication Data

Intellectual property protection for multimedia information technology / Hideyasu Sasaki, editor.

    p. cm.

  Summary: "This book provides scholars, management professionals, researchers, and lawyers in the field of multimedia information technology and its institutional practice with thorough coverage of the full range of issues surrounding multimedia intellectual property protection and its proper solutions from institutional, technical, and legal perspectives"--Provided by publisher.

  Includes bibliographical references and index.

  ISBN 978-1-59904-762-1 (hardcover) -- ISBN 978-1-59904-764-5 (ebook)

  1. Multimedia systems. 2. Information technology--Management. 3. Intellectual property. 4. Copyright infringement. I. Sasaki, Hideyasu.

  QA76.575I235 2007

  006.7--dc22

                    2007022234

British Cataloguing in Publication Data
A Cataloguing in Publication record for this book is available from the British Library.

Table of Contents

Section II
Solutions

Section III
Surveys

Detailed Table of Contents

Section I
Frameworks

In this chapter, we present a formulation for protecting digital library as intellectual property, especially image digital library. The entire content of digital library assembled by database designers is to be differentiated from its individual contents. The digital library community demands an innovative approach for protecting digital library associated with content-based retrieval that dynamically generates indexes to its contents. The entire content with dynamically assigned indexes goes beyond the scope of the conventional copyright protection of the database with statically assigned indexes. The proposed formulation uses the patent of content based retrieval process, and protects its object digital library in the specified domain without any excessively exclusive protection in general domains. That formulation determines whether the problem retrieval process identifies a classification of the entire content stored in its object digital library as a single and unique collection or its equivalents within the scope of its specified domain. The similar collection realized in other digital libraries evidences unauthorized use of the problem retrieval process or its equivalents as far as it is patented. The patent of content-based retrieval process works as a catalyst of digital library protection, and restricts any other assembling of equivalent digital libraries in the scope of its specified domain. We provide mathematical foundation and reasoning of the proposed formulation, and confirm its feasibility and accountability in several case studies.

This chapter presents some foundational concepts and issues in intellectual property. We begin by defining intellectual objects, which we contrast with physical objects or tangible goods. We then turn to some of the normative justifications that have been advanced to defend the granting of property rights in general, and we ask whether those rationales can be extended to the realm of intellectual objects. Theories of property introduced by Locke and Hegel, as well as utilitarian philosophers, are summarized and critiqued. This sets the stage for reviewing the case against intellectual property. We reject that case and claim instead that policy makers should aim for balanced property rights that avoid the extremes of overprotection and under-protection. Next we examine four different kinds of protection schemes for intellectual property that have been provided by our legal system: copyright laws, patents, trademarks, and trade secrets. This discussion is supplemented with a concise review of recent U.S. legislation involving copyright and digital media and an analysis of technological schemes of property protection known as digital rights management. Finally, we consider a number of recent controversial court cases, including the Napster case and the Microsoft antitrust suit. Many of the issues and controversies introduced in this chapter are explored and analyzed in greater detail in the subsequent chapters of this book.

The principal concern of this chapter is to provide those in the multimedia or content protection community with an overview of multimedia content encryption technology. Multimedia (image, audio, or video) content encryption technologies are reviewed, from the background, brief history, performance requirement, to research progress. Additionally, the general encryption algorithms are classified, and their performances are analyzed and compared. Furthermore, some special encryption algorithms are introduced. Finally, some open issues and potential research topics are presented, followed by some conclusions. The author hopes that the chapter will not only inform researchers of the progress of multimedia content encryption, but also guide the design of practical applications in the industry field.

Chapter IV

Many audio watermarking techniques presented in the last years make use of masking and psychological models derived from signal processing. Such a basic idea is winning because it guarantees a high level of robustness and bandwidth of the watermark as well as fidelity of the watermarked signal. This chapter first describes the relationship between digital right management, intellectual property, and use of watermarking techniques. Then, the crossing use of watermarking and masking models is detailed, providing schemes, examples, and references. Finally, the authors present two strategies that make use of a masking model, applied to a classic watermarking technique. The joint use of classic frameworks and masking models seems to be one of the trends for the future of research in watermarking. Several tests on the proposed strategies with the state of the art are also offered to give an idea of how to assess the effectiveness of a watermarking technique.

In this chapter, we propose a new information hiding and extracting method without embedding any information into the target content by using a nonlinear feature extraction scheme trained on frequency domain. The proposed method can detect hidden bit patterns from the content by processing the coefficients of the selected feature subblocks to the trained neural network. The coefficients are taken from the frequency domain of the decomposed target content by frequency transform. The bit patterns are retrieved from the network only with the proper extraction keys provided. The extraction keys, in the proposed method, are the coordinates of the selected feature subblocks and the neural network weights generated by the supervised learning of the neural network. The supervised learning uses the coefficients of the selected feature subblocks as the set of input values, and the hidden bit patterns are used as the teacher signal values of the neural network, which is the watermark signal in the proposed method. With our proposed method, we are able to introduce a watermark scheme with no damage to the target content.

The idea of embedding some information within a digital media, in such a way that the inserted data are intrinsically part of the media itself, has aroused a considerable interest in different fields. One of the more examined issues is the possibility of hiding the highest possible amount of information without affecting the visual quality of the host data. For such a purpose, the understanding of the mechanisms underlying Human Vision is a mandatory requirement. Hence, the main phenomena regulating the Human Visual System will be firstly discussed and their exploitation in a data hiding system will be then considered.

Section II
Solutions

We propose a new technical and legal approach, called online personal data licensing (OPDL), for responding to concerns about the privacy of personal data. Unlike traditional privacy-enhancing technologies that typically aim to hide personal data, OPDL enables individuals to concretize their consent to allow others to use their personal data as licenses. Service providers must obtain licenses before legally collecting, processing, or using a person's data. By allowing individuals to issue their own licenses and to determine the content of the licenses, OPDL brings the control of personal data back to their owner, and ensures that the use of the data is strictly under the owner's consent. In contrast, most Web-based service providers today use passive consent, which usually results in situations in which users have inadvertently given the providers the authorization to use their personal data. Besides, users generally do not have information on who still owns a copy of their data, and how their data have been, or will be, used.

Chapter VIII

Authentication is the way of identifying an individual. The techniques used to accomplish such practice strongly depend on the involved parties, their interconnection, and the required level of security. In all cases, authentication is used to enforce property protection, and may be specifically intended for the copyright protection of digital contents published on the Internet. This chapter introduces the basic concepts of authentication, explaining their relationship with property protection. The basic functionalities of challenge-response frameworks are presented, together with several applications and the future trends.

Chapter IX

The mobile Internet has been used widely in Japan. If we use a cellular phone with the Q-R (Quick Response) code reader function (a two-dimensional code developed by Denso-Wave Corporation), we can very easily access a Web site. However, though the existence of Q-R code reader function in the cellular phone is well-known, not many people use the function. The reason is that the Q-R code is not intuitive because it was developed to be read by machines. Our idea to solve the problem is to combine the Q-R code with a designed particular picture or graphic. We propose a method to produce the designed Q-R code and we develop its production system. This chapter describes the proposed method, the production system, and evaluation results using some designed Q-R codes produced by the system.

Chapter X

Web applications, which are computer programs ported to the Web, allow end-users to use various remote services and tools through their Web browsers. There are an enormous number of Web applications on the Web, and they are becoming the basic infrastructure of everyday life. In spite of the remarkable development of Web-based infrastructure, it is still difficult for end-users to compose new integrated tools of both existing Web applications and legacy local applications, such as spreadsheets, chart tools, and database. In this chapter, the authors propose a new framework where end-users can wrap remote Web applications into visual components, called pads, and functionally combine them together through drag-and-drop operations. The authors use, as the basis, a meme media architecture IntelligentPad that was proposed by the second author. In the IntelligentPad architecture, each visual component, called a pad, has slots as data I/O ports. By pasting a pad onto another pad, users can integrate their functionalities. The framework presented in this chapter allows users to visually create a wrapper pad for any Web application by defining HTML nodes within the Web application to work as slots. Examples of such a node include input-forms and text strings on Web pages. Users can directly manipulate both wrapped Web applications and wrapped local legacy tools on their desktop screen to define application linkages among them. Since no programming expertise is required to wrap Web applications or to functionally combine them together, end-users can build new integrated tools of both wrapped Web applications and local legacy applications.

Chapter XI

Symbolic Computation for DS-CDMA Code Acquisition Using First Order Logic /

CDMA (code division multiple access) is widely used because of its effectiveness to send multiple signal and confidentiality of career signal. We present a formulation of state-space problem of which solution is directed by redundant reasoning control method for semiheuristic and lightweight DS-CDMA code acquisition. The reasoning of the state-space problem provides us with the way to find a K bit synchronized sequence among K dephased sequences with less calculation cost, compared with serial search and matched filter. In this process, redundancy-restriction method, called weighting strategy, enhances the searching ability of FOL (first order logic) reasoning for the faster and lightweight code acquisition. The combination of weighting strategy and correlator enables us to achieve the peak-detection within K/3 times of calculating inner products and its measurement. Our system is evaluated by the reduced cost of proving state-space problem using weighting strategy and its robustness of using the proposal code acquisition framework. Experiment shows that the proposal method is robust if K/N sequences are grouped with N ranging from 3 to 5.

Chapter XII

Device Driver Based Computer in Broadband Age /

In this chapter, we present a device-driver-based computer that realizes the reduction of mode (domain or vertical) switching overheads between user and kernel mode with innovative attributes, including shared keyboards and mice, access-controlled files, and timed files. Experimented results show that old personal computers can revive again with the proposed Driverware technology. The proposed Driverware can improve the CPU resource utilization by three times.

Section III
Surveys

Chapter XIII

Cultivating Communities Through the Knowledge Commons:

In recent years, impacts of information and communication technologies, market enclosures, and the struggle to retain public goods have had significant impacts on the nature of interactions of communities. This chapter examines communities in the context of the knowledge commons—a space by which "a particular type of freedom" (Benkler, 2004) can be practised. It is also an appropriate concept applied to the discussion of communities and the ways they work. As Castells (2003) noted, self-knowledge "is always a construction no matter how much it feels like a discovery," and this construction is enabled when people work, or associate themselves with each other. In particular, the chapter is concerned about the structure of open content licenses operating within such domains. The chapter first explores the concept of the knowledge commons to understand the types of intellectual property that are distinctive to communities (public, communal, and private). Thereafter, licenses, as a structure, are examined as they may apply within such contexts. A significant influence on the discussion is the contemporary media environment operating in today resulting in the breaking down of boundaries, the blurring of distinctions between an original and a copy, and shifting the nature of production in communities. These debates lead to a case for open content licenses as appropriate structural mechanisms for communities.

Chapter XIV

Until recently, digital libraries have provided free access to either limited resources owned by an organization or information available in the public domain. For digital libraries to provide access to copyrighted material, an access control and charging mechanism needs to be put in place. Electronic commerce provides digital libraries with the mechanism to provide access to copyrighted material in a way that will protect the interest of both the copyright owner and the digital library. In fact, many organizations, such as the Association for Computing Machinery (ACM) and the Institute of Electrical and Electronics Engineers (IEEE), have already started to make their collections available online. The subscription model seems to be the favourable option at this point of time. However, for many ad hoc users, the subscription model can be expensive and not an option. In order to cater to a wider range of users, digital libraries need to go beyond the subscription models and explore other possibilities, such as the use of micro payments, that appear to be an alternative logical solution. But, even before that can happen, digital libraries will need to foremost address a number of outstanding issues, among which including access control, content management, information organization, and so on. This chapter discusses these issues and challenges confronting digital libraries in their adoption of e-commerce, including e-commerce charging models.

Chapter XV

This chapter presents the first attempt at analyzing the relationship between strategies to protect intellectual property rights and their impact on the likelihood of joining formal standardization processes, based on a small sample of European companies. On the one hand, theory suggests that the stronger the protection of one's own technological know-how, the higher the likelihood to join formal standardization processes in order to leverage the value of the technological portfolio. On the other hand, companies at the leading edge are often in such a strong position that they do not need the support of standards to market their products successfully. The results of the statistical analysis show that the higher the patent intensities of companies, the lower their tendency to join standardization processes, supporting the latter theoretical hypothesis.

This chapter uses citations to patents disclosed in the standard setting process to measure the technological significance of voluntary standard setting organizations (SSOs). We find that SSO patents are outliers in several dimensions and importantly, are cited far more frequently than a set of control patents. More surprisingly, we find that SSO patents receive citations for a much longer period of time. Furthermore, we find a significant correlation between citation and the disclosure of a patent to an SSO, which may imply a marginal impact of disclosure. These results provide the first empirical look at patents disclosed to SSO's, and show that these organizations both select important technologies and play a role in establishing their significance.

Multiple cases have been reported in which patents have posed dilemmas in the context of cooperative standard setting. Problems have come to the fore with regard to GSM, WCDMA, and CDMA standards, for example. Furthermore, JPEG and HTML standards, as well as VL-bus and SDRAM technologies, have faced patent-related difficulties. Nevertheless, it could be argued that complications have arisen in only a small fraction of standardization efforts, and that patents do not therefore constitute a real quandary. This article assesses the extent and the causes of the patent dilemma in the ICT sector through a brief analysis of how ICT companies' patent strategies and technology-licensing practices relate to standard setting and by exemplifying and quantifying the problem on the basis of relevant articles, academic research papers, court cases and on-line discussions. Particular attention is paid to so-called submarine patents, which bear most significance with respect to the prevailing policy concern regarding the efficacy of the patent system.

Nowadays the Web page is one of the most common medium used by people, institutions, and companies to promote themselves, to share knowledge, and to get through to every body in every part of the world. In spite of that, the Web page does not entitle one to a specific legal protection and because of this, every investment of time and money that stays off-stage is not protected by an unlawfully used. Seeing that no country in the world has a specific legislation on this issue in this chapter, we develop a theory that wants to give legal protection to Web pages using laws and treatment that are just present. In particular, we have developed a theory that considers Web pages as a database, so extends a database's legal protection to Web pages. We start to analyze each component of a database and to find them in a Web page so that we can compare those juridical goods. After that, we analyze present legislation concerning databases and in particular, World Intellectual Property Organization Copyright Treatments and European Directive 96/92/CE, which we consider as the better legislation in this field. In the end, we line future trends that seem to appreciate and apply our theory.

In the digital environment, steganography has increasingly received attention over the last decade. Steganography, which literally means "covered writing," includes any process that conceals data or information within other data or conceals the fact that a message is being sent. Though the focus on use of steganography for criminal and terrorist purposes detracts from the potential use for legitimate purposes, the focus in this chapter is on its role as a security threat. The history of stenography as a tool for covert purposes is addressed. Recent technical innovations in computerized steganography are presented, and selected widely available steganography tools are presented. Finally, a brief discussion of the role of steganalysis is presented.

The Grid environment is rapidly emerging as the dominant paradigm for wide-area-distributed application systems. The multimedia applications demand intense problem-solving capabilities, and Grid-computing makes it possible to share computing resources on an unprecedented scale among geographically distributed participants. In a Grid environment, virtual organisations are formulated and managed from a computing resource point of view. The Grid provider allows for the dynamic discovery of computing resources, the immediate allocation and provision of the resources, and the management and provision of secure access. Although the security problem in Grid environment is being addressed from the technological point of view, there is no work to identify the legal issues that are arising in Grid multimedia transactions.

With the rapid advance in digital network, digital libraries, and particularly WWW (World Wide Web) services, we can retrieve many kinds of images on personal and mobile computer anytime and anywhere. At the same time, secure image archiving is becoming a major research area because the serious concern is raised about copyright protection and authority identification in digital media. A more sophisticated technique is required for future multimedia copyright protection. In this chapter we propose a secure image archiving using novel digital-watermarking techniques. Firstly, a nonlinear adaptive system (neural network) is applied for frequency-based digital watermarking. Secondly, we discuss application-oriented watermarking method for GIS image archiving. This chapter is divided into two parts. First section is about the way to apply nonlinear adaptive system for frequency-based image watermarking. We propose a new asymmetric technique employing nonlinear adaptive system trained on frequency domain. Our system uses two public keys to prevent removal attack and archive more fragile watermarking. In embedding, location information of frequency domain, where adaptive system is trained, is binalized, expressed in hexadecimal number, and encrypted in asymmetric cryptosystem. Encrypted location information is embedded in several parts of digital host contents. In generating key, supervised neural networks learn to assign the array of coefficients to teacher signal corresponding to the message to insert. This is one kind of transform-based method to generate public key from private key. In extracting, we use key matrix created by one-way signal processing of adaptive system. Proposal method is tested in still image, and we have empirically obtained the results that the proposal model is functional in implementing more secure and fragile watermarking compared with previous techniques, such as correlation and transform-based asymmetric watermarking. Several experiments are reported to validate the effectiveness of our watermarking method. Second section is about the application of GIS image archiving using digital watermarking technique. Recently, the utilization of GIS (geographical information system) is becoming rapidly pervasive. Consequently, new methodology of archiving and managing images is a pressing problem for GIS users. It is also expected that as the utilization of GIS becomes widely spread, protecting copyright and confidential images will be more important. In this chapter, we propose a three-layer image data format that makes it possible to synthesize two kinds of related images and analysis information in one image data size. To achieve the confidentiality of one hidden image, we apply the private watermarking scheme, where the algorithm is closed to the public. In the proposal model, encoder netlist embedded in the third layer is generated by FOL prover to achieve more secure and less information to decode it, compared with one operation of another block cipher such as RSA. Proposal system users can process two images without the cost of maintaining key and decoding operation.

Preface

INTRODUCTION

Intellectual property protection is a hot issue on the globe in the twenty first century, because the recent expansion of network connectivity to the Internet known as ubiquitous allows people to enjoy a number of contents and software stored in the digital forms which are fragile to unauthorized electric duplication or copyright and/or patent infringement. Institutional protection against digital infringement of multimedia intellectual property has been practically supported by technical solutions to digitally maneuver multimedia contents and software in the Internet. The advent of new solutions in the area of information technology is to allow easy access to the tools for protection against multimedia intellectual property infringement that is negative side effect of innovation in the information industry.

Facing the digital infringement of intellectual property of contents and software, those in the fields of multimedia information engineering and its institutional operations have been aware of a need for a complete reference of past, current and future trends of multimedia intellectual property protection from technological fields to institutional aspects. This book, all twenty one chapters of which have been double-blind reviewed by leading scholars, is to offer a first reference on multimedia intellectual property protection with multidisciplinary intellectual property knowledge and analyses which are given by twenty three leading researchers and practitioners with the technical backgrounds in multimedia information engineering and the legal or institutional experiences in intellectual property practice.

PURPOSE

The principal concern of this book is to provide those in the multimedia information technology and its institutional practice including law and policy with a series of concise and thorough references on a variety of issues of multimedia intellectual property protection and its proper solutions from the technical and legal aspects. We discuss both technical and institutional solutions to protect copyrighted material and patentable software for multimedia intellectual property protection.

The first object of our discussion is digital copyright protection. We study its past, current and future technology: digital watermark and its innovative idea like steganography on digital copyright, and infringement or misappropriation of digital contents and their protection by peer-to-peer technology. The second object of our research is the protection of multimedia databases or digital libraries, and their infringement and counteraction from the point of network security. In the advent of multimedia digital libraries, the protection of their rights as intellectual properties is an urgent issue to offer an instrument for recouping investment in their development. A new scheme for the protection of multimedia digital libraries should be studied. The third object of our research is institutional analysis on multimedia intellectual property protection. It includes information management issues on intellectual property protection of multimedia contents, international intellectual property protection and standardization.

We thoroughly discuss those institutional and technical issues, and provide their solutions on multimedia intellectual property protection from legal to technological analyses. The goal of this book is to design a complete reference in the area of multimedia intellectual property protection which is demanded by those in the areas of law and technology. Already published intellectual property law and business books just discuss institutional analyses without interdisciplinary insights by technical experts. Meanwhile, technical references only talk about engineering solutions without the social impact to institutional protection of multimedia digital information. This book should fill in the gap between law and technology, and to fulfill a great mission under which people in the field of multimedia intellectual property protection discuss all the related issues and their solutions from both institutional and technical aspects.

AUDIENCE

This book is a first guidance or introductory reference to graduate students and students in professional schools, researchers and practitioners in the areas of law and policy, engineering and education, and provides them with mandatory knowledge bases on intellectual property protection of multimedia information engineering. This kind of complete reference has not been available in the previous research publication. The readers may enjoy the brand new aspects of legal analyses of engineering solutions for multimedia intellectual property protection.

The content of the book is also useful to the academia in which those concerned about intellectual property management need to acquire sound techniques for intellectual property protection and fundamental knowledge on intellectual property rights in the frontiers of IT outbursts. Meanwhile, this book works as a technical milestone for research trends of multimedia intellectual property protection engineering in the target of the next ten years. Both practitioners with technical agendas and IT engineers of institutional agendas may appreciate the content of this book with a variety of interdisciplinary topics. Multimedia information engineering or technology per se has not been discussed from any legal or technological aspects. In the previous publications, *both legal and technical aspects* on the multimedia intellectual property protection have not been analyzed in any single titles in the world.

ORGANIZATION AND OVERVIEW OF THE CHAPTERS

The book is organized three sections into twenty-one reviewed chapters with the following major themes:

1. Frameworks
2. Solutions
3. Surveys

Section I is concerned with **Frameworks** on the intellectual property protection.

Chapter I, **Digital Library Protection Using Patent of Retrieval Process**, presents a technical formulation for protecting digital library as intellectual property, especially image digital library. The chapter identifies an innovative approach for protecting digital library associated with content-based retrieval that dynamically generates indexes to its contents.

Chapter II, **Intellectual Property Rights: From Theory to Practical Implementation**, presents foundational concepts and issues in intellectual property, and examines each IP right with a concise review of recent U.S. legislation and court cases, including the Napster case and the Microsoft antitrust suit.

Chapter III, **Multimedia Encryption Technology for Content Protection**, presents an overview of multimedia content encryption technology with the general encryption algorithms, and introduces the special encryption algorithms.

Chapter IV, **Masking Models and Watermarking: A Discussion on Methods and Effectiveness**, describes the relationship between digital right management (DRM) and Intellectual Property on the watermarking techniques and masking models. The chapter also presents two strategies that make use of a masking model, applied to a classic watermarking technique.

Chapter V, **Damageless Watermark Extraction Using Nonlinear Feature Extraction Scheme Trained on Frequency Domain**, presents a new information hiding and extracting method without embedding any information into the target content by using non-linear feature extraction scheme trained on frequency domain.

Chapter VI, **Perceptual Data Hiding in Still Images**, presents steganography that embeds some information within a digital media, in such a way that the inserted data are intrinsically part of the media itself without affecting the visual quality of the host data, using the mechanisms underlying Human Vision.

Section II is concerned with **Solutions** for the intellectual property protection.

Chapter VII, **Online Personal Data Licensing: Regulating Abuse of Personal Data in Cyberspace**, presents a new technical and legal approach, called online personal data licensing (OPDL), for responding to the concerns about the privacy of personal data. The OPDL enables individuals to concretize their consent to allow others to use their personal data as licenses.

Chapter VII, **Property Protection and User Authentication in IP Networks Through Challenge-Response Mechanisms: Present, Past, and Future Trends**, introduces the basic concepts of authentication explaining their relationship with property protection. The basic functionalities of challenge-response frameworks are presented, together with several applications and the future trends.

Chapter IX, **Q-R Code Combined with Designed Mark**, introduces a method to produce the designed Q-R code and its production system, which allows a cellular phone with the Q-R (Quick Response) code reader function (a two dimensional code developed) to be easily accessed to web-sites.

Chapter X, **Visual Environment for DOM-Based Wrapping and Client-Side Linkage of Web Applications**, introduces a new framework where end-users can wrap remote Web applications into visual components called pads, and functionally combine them together through drag and drop-paste operations by using new media architecture, "IntelligentPad"

Chapter XI, **Symbolic Computation for DS-CDMA Code Acquisition Using First Order Logic**, introduces a formulation of state-space problem of which solution is directed by redundant reasoning control method for semi-heuristic and lightweight DS-CDMA code acquisition.

Chapter XII, **Device Driver Based Computer in Broadband Age**, introduces a device-driver-based computer, which realizes the reduction of mode (domain or vertical) switching overheads between user and kernel mode with innovative attributes including shared-keyboards and mice, access controlled files, and timed files.

Section III is concerned with **Surveys** on the intellectual property protection.

Chapter XIII, **Cultivating Communities Through the Knowledge Commons: The Case of Open Content Licenses**, surveys the communities in the context of the knowledge commons about the structure of open content licenses operating within such domains. The chapter explores licenses as a structure from the concept of the knowledge commons.

Chapter XVI, **E-Commerce and Digital Libraries**, surveys the access control model and system on the electronic commerce in digital library service.

Chapter XV, **Intellectual Property Protection and Standardization**, surveys the standardization strategies to protect intellectual property rights based on a small sample of European companies.

Chapter XVI, **The Performance of Standard Setting Organizations: Using Patent Data for Evaluation**, surveys the technological significance of voluntary standard setting organizations (SSOs) using citations to patents disclosed in the standard setting process.

Chapter XVII, **Patents and Standards in the ICT Sector: Are Submarine Patents a Substantive Problem or a Red Herring?**, surveys the cooperation on standard setting in the Information Communication Technology sector.

Chapter XVIII, **Legal Protection of the Web Page as a Database**, surveys legal issues on the institutional protection of intellectual property related to the WebPages from the points of database protection. The chapter identifies each component of database that is found in individual web page, and presents legislative concerns on databases.

Chapter XIX, **Steganography and Steganalysis**, surveys steganography in the context of security threat and discusses steganalysis.

Chapter XX, **Intellectual Property Protection in Multimedia Grids**, surveys the legal issues on the Grid computing environments and multimedia content transactions with immense volume of multimedia content from the point of computing resource.

Chapter XXI, **Secure Image Archiving Using Novel Digital Watermarking Techniques**, surveys and introduces secure image archiving techniques using novel digital watermarking techniques.

USE AS A COURSE TEXT

This book is designed to offer a reference in the communities on multimedia information technology and intellectual property studies. The main target of prospective academic audience is graduate students who study information studies, management of information technology, library science, computer science, information engineering, system engineering. Another target is students who work for professional degrees in business schools, management schools, MOT programs, public policy schools, law schools, or their equivalents. The book has twenty one chapters, which are materials for assignment in class at junior or senior engineering of the undergraduate lectures, and master-level graduate schools of management, or law schools. Lectures may commence with all the chapters in the Section I, and select some chapters from the Section II and/or III to complete one semester.

The other target is not a small number of practitioners including lawyers who counsel to IT companies as in-house counsels or at firms, chief information officers (CIOs), chief technology officers (CTOs) and chief risk management officers (CROs) in enterprises and the consultants in those related fields. Not the last but an important part of prospective audience is found in a large number of intellectual property related staff or administrators in universities and librarians. Instructors of business administration programs and information management curricula may follow the above instructions in their classes.

Acknowledgment

The editor would like to thank all the authors who have submitted chapter proposals, and all accepted authors and reviewers from a variety of fields for their excellent contributions and insights, without which this book would not have been possible. I particularly appreciate Professors Drs. Yasushi Kiyoki and Yoshiyasu Takefuji. Both of them were my doctoral supervisor and advisor at Keio University. I definitely appreciate Professor Dr. Gregory Silverman at Seattle University School of Law. In his cyberlaw class of 1999 at the University of Chicago Law School, an idea to publish this kind of book flashed in my mind. Special thanks go to the excellent staff at IGI Global for the opportunity to publish this book focusing on the multidisciplinary studies of intellectual property and multimedia information technology. I am grateful to the Microsoft Research Trust for Intellectual Property Studies, for its generous financial grant on my study. I am very happy and proud to have the great chance to publish this book with the marvelous friends and fellows around me this time.

Again, thank Lord and all of you who have helped and supported me.

I dedicate this book to my best friends, Dr. Terrence C. Bartolini, his wife, Dr. Carol Braun, their children: Alyssa, Lindsay, and Kyle, and, Jim Wyse, and all the Rotarians of Omiya (Japan) and Oak Lawn (Illinois) Rotary Clubs, who have helped and supported my stay of happiness and joy in Chicago with their kindness and gentleness, generosity, and patience.

Hideyasu Sasaki, PhD &Esq.
Attorney-at-law, admitted to practice in NY
Associate Professor of Computer Science, Ritsumeikan University, Kyoto, Japan
November, 2007

Section I
Frameworks

Chapter I
Digital Library Protection Using Patent of Retrieval Process

Hideyasu Sasaki
Attorney-at-Law, New York State Bar, USA & Ritsumeikan University, Japan

Yasushi Kiyoki
Keio University, Japan

ABSTRACT

In this chapter, we present a formulation for protecting digital library as intellectual property, especially image digital library. The entire content of digital library assembled by database designers is to be differentiated from its individual contents. The digital library community demands an innovative approach for protecting digital library associated with content-based retrieval that dynamically generates indexes to its contents. The entire content with dynamically assigned indexes goes beyond the scope of the conventional copyright protection of the database with statically assigned indexes. The proposed formulation uses the patent of content-based retrieval process, and protects its object digital library in the specified domain without any excessively exclusive protection in general domains. That formulation determines whether the problem retrieval process identifies a classification of the entire content stored in its object digital library as a single and unique collection, or its equivalents within the scope of its specified domain. The similar collection realized in other digital libraries evidences unauthorized use of the problem retrieval process, or its equivalents, as far as it is patented. The patent of content-based retrieval process works as a catalyst of digital library protection, and restricts any other assembling of equivalent digital libraries in the scope of its specified domain. We provide mathematical foundation and reasoning of the proposed formulation, and confirm its feasibility and accountability in several case studies.

INTRODUCTION

In this chapter, we present a formulation for protecting digital library as intellectual property,
especially image digital library (Sasaki & Kiyoki, 2002, 2003). Digital library integrates cultural or educational, academic or professional knowledge that takes the various forms of multimedia docu-

ments including images, pictures, films, video streams, and so forth. Content-based retrieval enables database designers to store and use a tremendous amount of multimedia contents in digital libraries.

Its technical advancement, however, grows with the burden of investment in research and development by digital library community. Digital library protection as intellectual property is indispensable for the successive investment in collection of multimedia contents, implementation of retrieval processes, and design of digital libraries (Samuelson, 1996). The Asia-Pacific region is catching up with the digital library initiative that originated from the Western countries in the nineties. An innovative approach for protecting digital library associated with content-based retrieval is to be its command that promotes knowledge integration to keep up with the foregoing countries.

The advent of that new retrieval technology demands a new approach for digital library protection. A digital library consists of its individual contents and database. Those contents are copyrightable for content creators, as the database is so for database designers. The essential problem on copyright is that different people, both content creators and database designers, have copyrights over digital libraries. The entire *content* of digital library assembled by database designers is to be differentiated from its individual *contents*. A digital library with statically assigned indexes for keyword-based retrieval is copyrightable for its database designers. Content-based retrieval, however, *dynamically* generates indexes to the entire content of the digital library that goes beyond the scope of the conventional copyright protection of the database with statically assigned indexes.

Digital library protection must be, however, fair to both the foregoing and the followers in the digital library community. The proposed formulation for digital library protection should not allow any circumvention over a number of digital libraries just by changing the small portion of databases or retrieval processes.

The goal of this chapter is to present a formulation that uses the patent of content-based retrieval process, and protects its object digital library in the specified domain without any excessively exclusive protection in general domains. That formulation determines whether the problem retrieval process identifies a classification of the entire content stored in its object digital library as a single and unique collection or its equivalents within the scope of its specified domain. The similar collection realized in other digital libraries evidences unauthorized use of the problem retrieval process, or its equivalents, as far as it is patented. The patent of content-based retrieval process works as a catalyst of digital library protection, and restricts any other assembling of equivalent digital libraries in the scope of its specified domain.

In Section 2, we discuss the advent of content-based retrieval in digital library, and identify limitations of the conventional copyright protection of database. We then describe the background of an innovative approach for protecting digital library associated with content-based retrieval. In Section 3, we propose the formulation of digital library protection. In Section 4, we confirm its feasibility and accountability in several case studies of image retrieval systems. In Section 5, we provide mathematical foundation and reasoning of the proposed formulation. In Sections 6 and 7, we conclude with discussion on the scope of the proposed formulation.

BACKGROUND

In this section, we discuss the limitations of copyright protection in the advent of content-based retrieval in digital library, and then describe the background of an innovative approach for protecting digital libraries.

Copyright Protection and Digital Library

As the referent of copyright protection, we should have a component that identifies the entire content of digital library that is differentiated from its individual content.

Keyword-based retrieval approach is a well-known technique of document and image retrieval in Web search engines, for example, Google (Brin & Page, 1998). In assembling a digital library with keyword-based retrieval operations, database designers assign *static* indexes to its individual contents as retrieval objects stored in databases. Those indexes integrate and identify the entire content of digital library as is different from its individual contents.

An assembling or compilation of individual contents, that is, preexisting materials or data, is to be a copyrightable entity as an original work of authorship fixed in tangible form (Gorman & Ginsburg, 1993; Nimmer, Marcus, Myers, & Nimmer, 1991; U.S. Copyright Act, 1976). Figure 1 outlines that the collection of static indexes and individual contents constitutes a component of "contents-plus-indexes" that identifies the entire content of digital library as a referent of copyright protection, that is, the copyrightable static compilation in digital library.

After elaboration in keyword-based retrieval, content-based retrieval was introduced, and has been receiving more attention as the latest promising technology. The component of contents-plus-indexes no longer identifies the entire content of digital library that is associated with content-based retrieval.

Content-based retrieval systems classify contents, for example, images using automatic solutions of feature extraction and indexing based on their structural or color similarity. Figure 2 outlines its retrieval operations in the case of content-based image retrieval (CBIR): Every time sample images are requested for retrieval, the feature extraction process extracts visual features, for example, shape, color out of the sample, and candidate images stored in a database; The indexing process groups the extracted features and then *dynamically* generates indexes to those images; finally, the classification process determines which class of candidate images is structurally similar to the requested sample images.

In the application of content-based retrieval, copyright has two limitations on digital library protection, as outlined in Figure 3: First, a component of contents-plus-indexes, that is, a collection of individual contents with *dynamic* indexes does not identify the entire content of any digital library.

Figure 1. A digital library associated with keyword-based retrieval

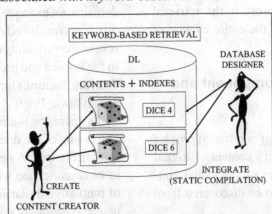

Figure 2. Content-based retrieval operations

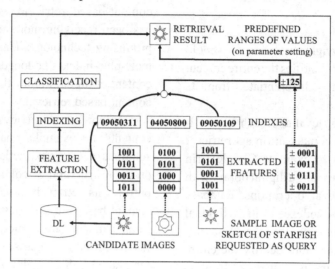

Every time new sample images are requested as queries, the order of similarity-rate changes in the collection of respectively rated and displayed individual contents. That collection is a copyrightable static compilation, but not to identify the entire content of digital library with *dynamically* assigned indexes. Second, any proposed frameworks do not remedy that problem at the present. The European Union legislated the *sui generis* right of database protection in the case of commercial databases (Reinbothe, 1999). That framework does not protect the digital library with content-based retrieval because its protection is based on the property of copyrightable compilation.

An only remaining resort is the retrieval process that is to identify the entire content of digital library.

Parameter Setting Component and Digital Library

We should find a component in retrieval process that is to identify the entire content of digital library as is different from its individual contents. That component is to be discovered from consulting the technical property of content-based retrieval.

Content-based retrieval, especially, CBIR has two types of approach regarding its object domain: the domain-general approach and the domain-specific approach (Rui, Huang, & Chang 1999). The domain general approach deals with various kinds of visual features in broad domains, for example, Virage Image Retrieval (Bach, Fuller, Gupta, Hampapur, Horowitz, Jain, & Shu, 1996) and QBIC (Flickner, Sawhney, Niblack, Ashley, Huang, Dom, Gorkani, Hafner, Lee, Petkovic, Steele, & Yanker, 1995). The domain-specific approach focuses in the narrower or specified domains, for example, the field of brain images. As different from broad domains, specified domains restrict the variability on type of extracted features in the limited and predictable scope (Smeulders, Worring, Santini, Gupta, & Jain, 2000; Yoshitaka & Ichikawa, 1999).

Its operation is almost the same with the data processing of the domain-general approach outlined in Figure 2. A significant difference is found in its classification where representative classes of mutually similar images are identified in its object domain. A component for thresholding

Figure 3. A digital library associated with content-based retrieval

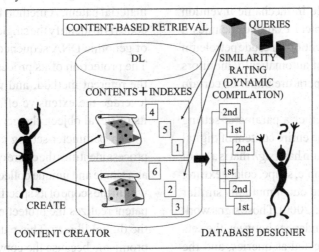

Figure 4. Parameter-setting component for thresholding operations

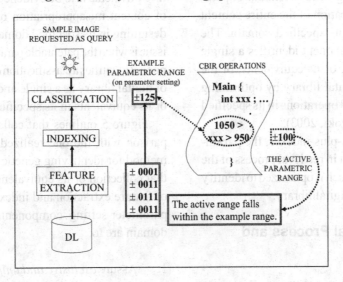

is to evaluate structural similarity of extracted features, and is to identify the entire content stored in a database. That component consists of the means for "parameter setting" that selects or adjusts parametric values on operating parameters for feature extraction and index classification in the domain-specific approach.

Figure 4 outlines its thresholding operations. A set of certain parametric ranges determines, as thresholds, which candidate image is mutually similar to a requested sample image, based on the computation result of their structural similarity. That set of parametric ranges is to be selected as identifies the representative classes of mutually similar images in its specified domain. Those classes represent the classification of the entire content of a digital library.

The parameter-setting component is to be computer-related invention in the form of computer program (European Patent Office, 2001;

U.S. Patent and Trademark Office, 1996). That is familiar as patentable in mechanic invention (Merges, 1997). Its typical example includes a patented thermostat invention for crude petroleum purification process that automatically monitors and fixes crude oil temperature under its certain explosive point.

The problem is whether a parameter-setting component identifies the entire content of digital library. A specified domain has a *sign* that is a set of visual features, for example, shape, color, texture, region, that are extracted out of mutually similar images (Smeulders, et al., 2000). Those signs work to identify the correspondences between the sets of sample images requested as queries, and the classes of mutually similar candidate images in each specified domain. When a parameter-setting component identifies signs, its thresholding operations realize a classification of the entire content of a digital library in its specified domain. The parameter-setting component identifies a single and unique collection, or its equivalents, of the entire content of a digital library by optimizing content-based retrieval operations in its specified domain (Sasaki & Kiyoki, 2003).

Instead of contents-plus-indexes, the parameter-setting component in retrieval process of the domain-specific approach is optimized to identify the entire content of digital library.

Patent of Retrieval Process and Digital library

We should realize the digital library protection using the intellectual property of its retrieval process in the form of parameter-setting component. The practice in the field of bioinformatics offers an exemplary approach that uses the patent of retrieval process and protects its objects.

The methods for identifying genetic codes have been yielded with process patent as means/step-plus-function (MPF) in the form of computer program, even before the admission of the pat-

entability of genomic DNA sequences *per se* as material patent. A method for identifying genetic codes is to identify the single and unique collection of genomic DNA sequences encoding a protein. The protection of its process patent goes beyond the referent method, and works as a catalyst to leverage the extensive effect of protection over its retrieval object, the gene *per se*.

If a parameter-setting component in retrieval process identifies the entire content of digital library as a single and unique collection, or its equivalents within the scope of its specified domain, its process patent realizes the protection of its object, that is, the digital library. This patent-based approach is promising because the copyright infringement of database content is difficult to be proven, though the unauthorized use of its patented retrieval process or its equivalents is to be evidenced by the discovery of content misappropriation or similar database designing in its specified domain. The remaining issue is when the patentable parameter-setting component identifies a classification of the entire content of digital library as a single and unique collection or its equivalents in its specified domain.

Figure 5 outlines that collection in the comparison with the one realized in the patentable method for identifying genetic codes. To identify that collection or its equivalents in the processes of feature extraction and index classification, the parameter-setting components in its specified domain are to:

1. Assure *exclusive and uniform classification* among individual contents requested as queries, classes of mutually similar candidate contents and their signs in an authentic digital library.

2. Assure *identical classification* among sets of sample contents requested as queries, sets of classes of mutually similar contents, and sets of their signs in the same field of that digital library, respectively.

Figure 5. Single and unique collection

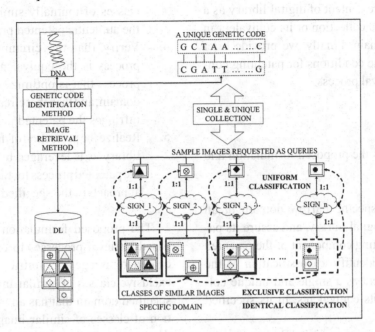

The exclusive classification is to assure that a digital library always has several representative sets of extracted features, that is, signs of mutually similar contents in its specified domain. Its typical example is a brain image retrieval system in which a specific number of visual features always identify representative signs of brain disease images, while any image is not simultaneously classified into both brain tumor and stroke classes (Liu, Dellaert, & Rothfus, 1998). The uniform classification is to assure that the signs of the contents always uniformly identify the sample contents and their corresponding classes of mutually similar contents in the same domain.

The identical classification determines the scope of the specified domain, that is, the selection of a set of predefined parametric ranges, and restricts the scope of an identical combination of the signs in that domain. In this brain image retrieval system, a set of three brain symptom groups (tumor, stroke, and normal) constitutes

a complete finite set of classification that corresponds to a finite set of signs as a specific number of representative elements of visual features (Liu, et al., 1998). When a parameter-setting component is optimized to identify a single and unique collection or its equivalents of the entire content of digital library in its specified domain, its patent protection leverages the extensive protection of its entire content.

DIGITAL LIBRARY PROTECTION

In this section, we present the formulation of digital library protection that uses patent of content-based retrieval process as a catalyst to leverage the extensive protection over the entire content of digital library with dynamic indexes. First, we outline the proposed formulation and its application to digital libraries, especially image digital libraries. Second, we formulate the conditions on parameter-setting component, that is, to identify the entire content of digital library as a single and unique collection or its equivalent in its specified domain. Finally, we provide brief description on the conditions for patenting content-based retrieval process.

Overview

Figure 6 outlines the proposed formulation and its application:

1. Identify a specific narrow domain of an authentic digital library, and assure its parameter-setting component of the patented process to identify a classification of the entire content as a single and unique collection, or its equivalents, in its specified domain.
2. Find other forgery digital library in the same or equivalent domain by duplicating, otherwise, restoring images that are similar or equivalent to the contents of that authentic digital library.
3. Discover that forgery digital library to implement a circumventing process that clas-

sifies and identifies the same or equivalent classes of mutually similar contents with the authentic patented process.
4. Verify that the circumventing retrieval process is the equivalent to the patented process that is optimized in the discussed domain, and then that circumventing process infringes the patented process.
5. Realize the protection of the authentic digital library as is leveraged by the protection of the patented process for the domain-specific approach in the specified domain.

The proposed formulation assures content-based retrieval processes to uniformly classify candidate images for retrieval into mutually exclusive classes of similar images in a certain specified domain that has an identical combination of classes of similar images. By patenting those retrieval processes, then any other digital libraries could not be implemented without the equivalents to the retrieval processes. Any digital library assembling by equivalent content collection in the specified domain evidences direct misappropriation, that is, infringement of the equivalents to those patented retrieval processes.

Figure 6. The proposed formulation and its application

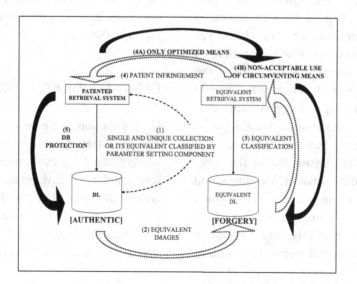

The retrieval processes contain parameter-setting components that define the scope of the equivalents to those retrieval processes with clear boundary. Consequently, the patent enforcement over those retrieval processes restricts any other digital library assembling as a catalyst of protection over the entire content of their target digital library in specified domains, without any excessively exclusive protection in general domains. The predefined parametric ranges must satisfy both the exclusive and uniform classification, and the identical classification in the specified domain, and then the parameter-setting components must be patentable in the form of computer program.

An advantage of that patent-based approach is to use the registered right for leveraging the extensive protection of its referent, digital library. The other merit is to restrict its protection leveraged by patent protection in the modest scope of specified domains. The problem is that parametric values are easy to modify and adjust in the applications. In the case of claiming parameter-setting components as computer-related inventions, exemplary parametric values must be specified to define clear boundary of the scope of equivalent modification of the claimed process. As suggested from exemplary parametric values, the scope of modification is restricted within respectively specified domains. Especially, in the domain-specific approach of CBIR, a claimed invention must distinguish itself with those exemplary parametric values from other improved formulas for parameter setting that are often based on prior disclosed means. The proposed patent-based approach is not to have any excessive protection over a number of image digital libraries in general domains.

Conditions on Single and Unique Collection

Content-based retrieval processes are implemented in parameter-setting components with predefined parametric ranges. Those ranges could be selected to assure both the exclusive and uniform classification and the identical classification in specified domains.

We formulate the conditions on parameter-setting components that are to identify the entire content of digital library as a single and unique collection, or its equivalent, in its specified domain. That collection is realized by satisfying the exclusive and uniform classification among individual candidate images as queries, classes of similar images and signs, and the identical classification among sets of candidate images as queries, sets of classes of similar images, and sets of signs, respectively. Later, we deduct and mathematically formulate the conditions on parameter-setting components from the mathematical definitions of the classifications, as described in Section 5.

Exclusive and Uniform Classification

The parametric ranges define the similarity metrics for classification of candidate images for retrieval in the spaces of images, classes of similar images and signs, and realize the exclusive and uniform classification by detecting signs of similar images.

Step 1 determines the selection of parametric values for similarity metrics, and assures that a certain specified domain should always have several sets of representative visual features, that is, signs of similar images.

Step 2 determines the parametric ranges, and assures that a certain specified domain should always have several signs that identify the correspondences between the candidate images for retrieval and the classes of similar images via signs in exclusive and uniform classification.

- **Step 1:** Conditions on parametric values of similarity metrics for detection of representative signs:

a. Let the Euclidean distance be applied to any similarity metrics for classification of candidate images for retrieval in the spaces of images, classes of similar images and signs.

b. Let any parametric value of parameter-setting components follow transitive law.

c. Let any parametric range of parameter-setting components take a bounded-close set.

d. Let any bounded-close parametric range be a nonempty set.

e. Let any bounded-close parametric range be formed as nonnegative or nonpositive, entirely.

- **Step 2:** Conditions on parametric ranges for classification of candidate images and classes of similar images:

  Let any parametric range take a bounded-close set in satisfaction of the following conditions:

  a. Any set of classes of similar images is exclusive to any other classes.

  b. Any sign is uniformly mapped to its corresponding class of similar images.

  c. Any class of similar images is uniformly mapped to each corresponding sign.

Identical Classification

Step 3 assures that a certain specified domain should always have a finite set of signs and its corresponding finite set of classes of similar images in identical classification. The step determines the selection of a domain, that is, a selection of a set of predefined parametric ranges. The predefined ranges determine the scope of the specified domain that has an identical combination of signs.

- **Step 3:** Conditions on domain selection:
  Let us define the scope of a certain specified domain with the following conditions:

a. There exists a finite set of classes of similar images.

b. There exists a finite set of signs.

c. The set of classes of similar images has the same number of finite set of signs.

d. Any combination of the classes of similar images converges to a certain identical combination of those classes. (Consequently, any combination of signs converges to a certain identical combination of those signs as the finite set of signs.)

Conditions on Patenting Parameter-Setting Component

The retrieval processes have several combinations of means/step-plus-function claims, and comprise parameter-setting components to which specific formulation is indispensable for their patent application.

Step 4 consists of the conditions for patenting content-based retrieval processes as computer-related inventions in the form of computer programs, based on our study (Sasaki & Kiyoki, 2002, 2005). We have followed the *Guidelines* issued by the United States Patent and Trademark Office (USPTO) (1996) and the European Patent Office (EPO) (2001). Those conditions formulate three requirements for patentability: patentable subject matter (entrance to patent protection), nonobviousness/inventive steps (technical advancement) and enablement/clarity of claims (specification), respectively (Merges, 1997).

- **Step 4:** Requirements for patentability on combined computer programs consisting of parameter-setting components:

a. **Patentable subject matter:** Claim the means for parameter setting that performs a certain content-based retrieval function.

b. **Nonobviousness or inventive steps:** Claim a content-based retrieval process that is nonobvious from the prior arts when:
1. It comprises a combination of prior disclosed means to perform a certain function as is not predicated from any combination of the prior arts.
2. It also realizes quantitative and/or qualitative advancement.

c. **Enablement or clarity of claims:** Claim a content-based retrieval process that fulfills enablement requirement by satisfying the following conditions in the descriptions of its patent application:
1. Its description specifies some formulas for parameter setting. Otherwise, its copending application describes the formulas in detail.
2. Its claimed process performs a new function by a combination of the prior disclosed means. And, the claimed process has improved formulas for parameter setting based on the prior disclosed means also with exemplary parametric values on its parameter-setting component.

CASE STUDY

In this section, we clarify the feasible and infeasible cases of the proposed protection. We have applied the formulated conditions to digital libraries as instances of its case study: several medical image retrieval systems that are formed based on the domain-specific approach of CBIR. We present four typical cases of medical image retrieval systems that are developed by the following institutes, respectively: The University of Maryland in images of abdomen tumor (Korn,

Sidiropoulos, Faloutsos, Siegel, & Protopapas, 1998), UCLA in images of brain tumor (Chu, Hsu, C'ardenas, & Taira, 1998), Purdue University with the University of Wisconsin Hospital in images of lung disease subgroups (Dy, Brodley, Kak, Shyu, & Broderick, 1999) and Carnegie Mellon University in images of brain stroke and tumor (Liu, et al., 1998).

Infeasible Cases

Abdomen Tumor Image Retrieval System (developed by Universit of Maryland)

The instant system focuses on contours of images and applies hierarchical-modeling CBIR to abdominal images with multiscale distance function and nearest-neighbor queries. The instant system offers translation/rotation-invariant similarity comparison of target images. Its distance metrics is based on the morphological distance and the general p-th normalization formulation. The instant system is not purported to offer exclusive or uniform classification in its specified domain (Step 1). Its query relaxation approach is not designed to detect certain parametric ranges that determine the ranges of mutually exclusive classes of similar images and signs because the detected ranges overlap with other ranges.

Brain Tumor Spatial and Temporal Image Retrieval System (Developed by UCLA)

The instant system applies knowledge about visual features known as user-defined "type abstraction hierarchy" (TAH) to content-based spatial and temporal classification of brain disease images. [*See* U.S. Pat. # 5,956,707, database system with query relaxation using type abstraction hierarchy (TAH) as query condition relaxation structure, invented by *W. W. Chu*, filed on Feb. 13, 1997.]

The instant system focuses on contours of visual features for its model-based feature extraction. A certain instance-based conceptual clustering technique is introduced to sign detection and classification of similar images. The knowledge base relaxes query conditions by using TAH's with expert-involved parameters for spatial relationship definitions.

In the instant system, any class of similar images is not always mutually exclusive to each other class. Those query relaxation operations, for example, "Nearby" and "Far Away," are not purported to make boundaries of classes of similar images mutually exclusive. Its knowledge-based approach is not purported as an application to the specified domain of exclusive classification of classes of similar images and signs (Step 2).

Lung Disease Image Retrieval System (Developed by Purdue Univ. & Univ. of Wisconsin Hospital)

The instant system is a typical infeasible case of the proposed protection. That system applies customized-query approach using expectation maximization (EM) algorithm, which classifies visual features of radiological images of lung diseases into hierarchical classification from major classes to minor subclasses mainly based on visual textures. Primarily, the system classifies those visual features that the major classes of similar disease images contain. Those major classes have their corresponding signs that are obvious in medical practice. Secondarily, the system classifies minor subclasses of visual features

Table 1. Infeasible case: Lung disease image retrieval system (developed by Purdue Univ. & Univ. of WI Hospital)

Step	#	Determination
1	*	**Conditions on parametric values of similarity metrics for detection of representative signs:**
	a	The Euclidean distance is applied to any similarity metrics in its normalization.
	b	Any parametric value of parameter-setting components follows transitive law.
	c	Any parametric range of parameter-setting components takes a bounded-close set as a clustered set.
	d	Any bounded-close parametric range is a nonempty set.
	e	Any bounded-close parametric range is not negative, entirely, from its definition.
2	*	**Conditions on parametric ranges for classification of candidate images and classes of similar images: Its EM algorithm-based approach finds appropriate parametric ranges from major classes to minor subclasses in the lung disease domain.**
	a	Any set of major classes and subclasses of similar images is mutually exclusive to any other classes because its approach repeats iterative search for the minor subclasses of lung disease images and classifies them into several distinct clusters.
	b	Any sign is uniformly mapped to its corresponding class of similar images because its discovered minor subclasses are clustered as exclusive to each other.
	c	Any class of similar images is uniformly mapped to its corresponding sign with the previous reason.
3	N/A	Conditions on domain selection:
	[a]	The instant system is not purported to find any finite set of classes of similar images because discovered minor subclasses do not always constitute identical classification of lung disease classes by unsupervised clustering.
	[b]	The instant system is not purported to find any finite set of signs with the previous reason.
	[c]	The instant system is not purported to determine whether the set of classes of similar images has the same number of the finite set of the signs from their experimental result.

Table 2. Feasible Case: Brain Stroke & Tumor Image Retrieval System (developed by Carnegie Mellon Univ.)

Step	#	Determination
1	*	**Conditions on parametric values of similarity metrics for detection of representative signs:**
	a	The Euclidean distance is applied to any similarity metrics.
	b	Any parametric value of parameter-setting components follows transitive law.
	c	Any parametric range of parameter-setting components takes a bounded-close set, based on its EM stochastic approach with a finite set of three classes of similar images.
	d	Any bounded-close parametric range is a nonempty set.
	e	Any bounded-close parametric range is not negative, entirely, based on its stochastic approach that determines clear parametric ranges.
2	*	**Conditions on parametric ranges for classification of candidate images and classes of similar images:**
	a	Any set of classes of similar images is mutually exclusive to any other classes because the three classes of similar images (normal, tumor, & blood) are exclusive in nature.
	b	Any sign is uniformly mapped to its corresponding class of similar images with the previous reason.
	c	Any class of similar images is uniformly mapped to its corresponding sign based on the classification rule of its stochastic approach.
3	*	**Conditions on domain selection:**
	a	There exists a finite set of three classes of similar images as brain disease classes.
	b	There exists a finite set of the corresponding signs of visual features that consist of 9 representative visual features among candidate 11 visual features.
	c	The set of the classes of similar images has the same number of finite set of the signs, as shown in their experiments.
	d	Any combination of the classes of similar images converges to a certain identical combination of those classes, so does any combination of the signs, consequently.
4	*	**Requirements for patentability on combined computer programs consisting of parameter-setting components:**
	a	The means for parameter-setting components could be claimed as content-based retrieval processes.
	b	Disclosed combined means are not predicated from any combination of the prior arts and realize an inventive brain domain-specific approach of content-based retrieval.
	c	The instant invention or its copending application should specify improved formulas for parameter setting with more precise working examples of parametric values.

within the once-classified major classes. Each set of visual features in those minor subclasses is similar to each other but does not have its *a priori* corresponding sign. The system customizes queries by its EM algorithm every time users request a search for hierarchical classification from major classes to minor subclasses of similar disease images.

The instant system is focused on a certain domain in which the visual features most effective in discriminating among images from different classes may not be the most effective for retrieval of visually similar images within a subclass. This type of domain has uniform and exclusive classification during the course of its iterative search, which detects a certain number of classes of similar images and signs. The instant system is not purported to find any finite set of classes of similar images or signs as a certain converged set (*see* Step 3). The identical classification in our conditions is not applicable to the instant system, as outlined in Table 1.

Feasible Case

Brain Stroke and Tumor Image Retrieval System (Developed by Carnegie Mellon Univ.)

The instant system is a typical feasible case of the proposed protection. That system applies an EM stochastic computation process that dynamically customizes queries every time new queries are requested for brain images, and detects signs without a given set of supervised visual features into three classes of brain diseases: normal, stroke, and blood images. That system is applied to a certain domain that has a finite number of possible distinct classes of similar images, and is designed to realize exclusive and uniform classification in its specified domain. In its experiment, that system has found 9 visual features that constituted an identical combination of signs in 3 classes of similar images, that is, disease classes: normal, brain stroke, and brain blood, from given 11 features. The instant system has a specified domain of identical classification that contains constant and finite numbers of classes of similar images and signs. It also has potential to be patentable as a computer-related invention, as well as its related techniques invented by its staff member. [*See* U.S. Pat. # 5,784,431, matching X-ray images with reference images, invented by *Kalend, et al.* including T. Kanade, filed on Oct. 29, 1996.] The parameter-setting components with working exemplary parametric values that represent signs more clearly enough should assure the proposed protection of digital libraries in its specified domain by patenting content-based retrieval processes, as outlined in Table 2.

MATHEMATICAL FOUNDATION AND REASONING

In this section, we provide mathematical foundation to the proposed formulation, and prove that certain parameter-setting components satisfying the proposed formulation is to identify the single and unique collection or its equivalents of its object content, as is equivalent to the exclusive and uniform classification with identical classification of the entire content.

The discussed exclusive and uniform classification consists of two types of classification:

1. All the respective sets of most mutually similar images are exclusive to each set; All the respective sets of candidate images as queries are exclusive to each set; and both the respective sets of most mutually similar images and the respective sets of candidate images as queries have their representative elements inside the sets, respectively.

2. Both the representative elements of all the respective sets of most mutually similar images and the representative elements of all the respective sets of candidate images as queries have been linked by representative sets of signs.

In topologic formulation, the former classification should assure existence of maximal elements in respective sets of images, classes of similar images, and signs. The maximal elements are the representative elements to which any other elements in their neighborhood converge and form compact sets. The latter classification should assure that the representative elements in compact sets are linked to each other in respective compact sets of images, classes of similar images, and signs. Those classifications are equivalent to exclusive and uniform classification between the retrieval process and its object content.

Any categorization or combination of the representative elements in respective compact sets of images, classes of similar images, and signs should be identical in a certain specified domain. The identical categorization or combination is equivalent to identical classification of the sets of the representative elements inside the respective sets of candidate images as queries, classes of similar images, and signs. Those classifications are to be equivalent to the single and unique collection, as described next.

Definition on Classifications

In the course of definition and proof, we apply topologic formulation to the relations of images, signs, and classes of images of structural similarity. We have two reasons that justify introduction of topology into the definition and proof.

First, topologic formulation simplifies problems by giving logically uniform foundations on both similarity metrics and normalization that are implemented in parameter-setting components for retrieval.

Second, topologic approach is extensive to any practical experiments on adjustment of parameter-setting components in a variety of specified domains.

Exclusive and Uniform Classification

Definition 1. Let define exclusive and uniform classification in a certain specified domain as the following four correspondences: ψ, ψ^{-1}, ϕ, and $\phi \circ \psi^{-1}$;
If $m = n$, for $\forall$ i, j, s (a variety of signs converge to a static number of set that corresponds to a set of classes of similar images) then there exists exclusive classification that retrieval processes assure in the domain: (see Box 1).

Identical Classification

Definition 2. Let define identical classification in a certain specified domain as the following homeomorphic structure subject to the correspondences; ψ, ψ^{-1}, ϕ, and $\phi \circ \psi^{-1}$: (see Box 2).

Related Sets of Images, Signs, and Classes of Similar Images

We simply define the related sets of images, classes of similar images, and signs as sets of discrete point

Box 1.

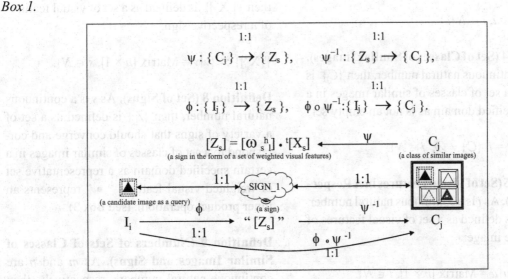

Box 2.

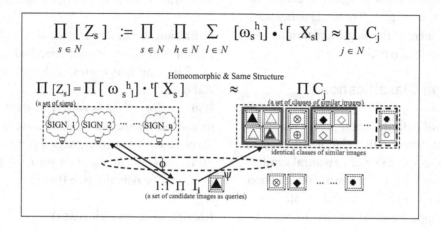

sequences, for the brevity. Individual elements of the defined sets represent respective images, classes of similar images, and signs. Each image, class of similar images, or sign is an entity that is independent of each other, so that each entity is to be simply presented as a discrete point in a set, that is, a discrete point sequence.

Definition 3 (Set of Images). As i is a continuous natural number, then $\{I_j\}$ is defined as a set of images:

$$\{I_j\} := \{y \,|\, y = i, i \in N\}.$$

Definition 4 (Set of Classes of Similar Images). As j is a continuous natural number, then $\{C_j\}$ is defined as a set of classes of similar images in a certain specified domain as is not an empty set:

$$\{C_j\} := \{x \,|\, x = j, \{C_j\} \neq \varnothing, j \in N\}.$$

Definition 5 (Set of Visual Features in A Respective Image). As i is a continuous natural number, then ${}^t[X_i]$ is defined as a set of visual features of a respective image:

$$\{{}^t[X_i]\} := \{u \,|\, u = \text{Matrix } [n \times 1], i \in N\}.$$

Definition 6 (Set of Weighing Values to Visual Features in A Respective Sign). As s, h, l are continuous natural numbers, respectively, then $\{\omega_{s\,l}^{\,h}\}$ is defined as a "h" set of weighting values that should be assigned to the "l-th" visual features of the "s-th" sign, respectively:

$$\{\omega_{s\,l}^{\,h}\} := \{w \,|\, w = \text{Matrix } [m \times n], s, h, l \in N\}.$$

Definition 7 (Set of Visual Features in A Respective Sign). As s is a continuous natural number, then $\{{}^t[X_s]\}$ is defined as a set of visual features of a respective sign:

$$\{{}^t[X_s]\} := \{v \,|\, v = \text{Matrix } [n \times 1], s \in N\}.$$

Definition 8 (Set of Signs). As s is a continuous natural number, then $\{Z_s\}$ is defined as a set of a variety of signs that should converge and correspond to a set of classes of similar images in a certain specified domain as a representative set of weighted visual features "$\bullet$" represents an inner product operation): (see Box 3).

Definition 9 (Numbers of Sets of Classes of Similar Images and Signs). As m and n are continuous natural numbers, respectively, then

Box 3.

$$\{ Z_s \} = \{ [\ \omega_{s\,1}^{h}] \bullet {}^{t}[\, X_s] \}$$

$$:= \{ z \mid z = [\omega_{s\,1}^{h}] \bullet {}^{t}[\, X_s], \ \{ Z_s \} : \neq \varnothing, s \in N \ \},$$

$$\{ I_i \} \to {}^{t}[\, X_i] \subset \{[\omega_{s\,1}^{h}] \bullet {}^{t}[\, X_s] \}\} \ .$$

$\# \{C_j\}$ and $\# \{Z_s\}$ are a number of a set of classes of similar images and a number of a set of signs, respectively:

$$m := \#\{C_j\}, \ n := \#\{Z_s\}.$$

Formulation of the Proposed Conditions on Classifications

We mathematically formulate the conditions on the parameter-setting components that satisfy exclusive and uniform classification with identical classification.

Exclusive and Uniform Classification

Step 1. Conditions on parametric values of similarity metrics for detection of representative signs:

a. The Euclidean distance on similarity metrics for classification of candidate images;
$d(distance \ metrics) = ||\,d\,||_2 : d(x,y) = \{(x_1 - y_1)^2 + \ldots + (x_n - y_n)^2\}^{1/2}$
$(x := {}^{t}[X_s], [\omega_s]; y := {}^{t}[X], [\omega_s], respectively)$.
b. Parametric values follow transitive law;
$R_y = x > \sim y.$
c. Parametric ranges take bounded-close sets;
$inf[\omega_s] \leq [\omega_s] \leq sup[\omega_s]$.
d. Parametric ranges take nonempty sets;
$\sum_{s \in N} [\ \omega_s] \neq 0, \ \sum_{s \in N} {}^{t}[X_s] \neq 0$

e. Parametric ranges take nonnegative/positive.
$[\omega_s] \geq (\leq) \, 0, \ {}^{t}[X_s] \geq (\leq) \, 0$.

Step 2. Conditions on parametric ranges for classification of candidate images and classes of similar images: Parametric ranges satisfy the following conditions; $inf[Z_s] \leq [Z_s] \leq sup[Z_s]$.

a. Set of exclusive classes of similar images;
$C_j \cap C_{j'} = \varnothing$ for ${}^{\forall} j.$
b. Uniform mapping from sign to class of similar images;
$$\{ Z_s \} \xrightarrow{1:1} \{ C_j \} \ for \ {}^{\forall} j, s .$$
c. Uniform mapping from class of similar images to sign.
$$\{ C_j \} \xrightarrow{1:1} \{ Z_s \} \ for \ {}^{\forall} j, s .$$

Identical Classification

Step 3. Conditions on domain selection: The scope of a certain specified domain is defined with the following conditions:

a. A finite set of classes of similar images;
$\# \{C_j\} < \infty$.
b. A finite set of signs;
$\# \{Z_s\} < \infty$.
c. The set of classes of similar images has the same number of finite set of signs;
$\# \{C_j\} = \# \{Z_s\}$.

d. Convergence of any combination of the classes of similar images and the signs to certain identical combinations;

for $^\forall j$; $\prod \{\{C_j\} \cap \{C'_j\}\} = \prod \{\{C_j\} \cup \{C'_j\}\}$
$= \prod \{C_j\} = \prod \{C'_j\}$
(*for* $^\forall s$; $\prod \{\{Z_s\} \cap \{Z'_s\}\} = \prod \{\{Z_s\} \cup \{Z'_s\}\}$).

Mathematical Reasoning

Finally, we provide the brief proof of the formulated conditions.

Exclusive and Uniform Classification

Steps 1 and 2 constitute the conditions on parametric values of similarity metrics and normalization. The purpose of this part is to prove that the conditions satisfy exclusive and uniform classification.

Existence of Representative Elements

Here, we have a purpose to prove the following thesis: A certain specified domain realizes exclusive and uniform classification when each set of images, classes of similar images, and signs has at least a representative element inside each set, respectively.

That thesis should be restated as a simplified problem in topologic representation. We introduce a generally accepted proposition that simplifies all the related sets in the form of point sequences.

Proposition 1.

Any set of elements existing in a distance space forms a point sequence while it is well ordered by a certain rule of order.

Suppose any set of images, classes of similar images, and signs should form a set of point sequences, respectively. This thesis is restated as follows:

Let prove existence of each representative element in each set of images, classes of similar images, and signs.

The instant problem accepts this brevity of topologic formulation without any loss of generality.

Steps 1 and 2 assure that these simplified point sequences have their representative elements inside their sets of point sequences, respectively. Existence of representative elements is equivalent to existence of maximal elements in the point sequences. Any other elements in their neighborhood of the point sequences should converge to the maximal elements. In that case, existence of representative elements is equivalent to existence of compact sets of images, classes of similar images, and signs in the form of point sequences when convergence of point sequences is evaluated as identical to formation of compact sets. We hereby introduce Bergstrom's theorem, Heine-Borel's theorem, and its equivalent Bolzano-Weierstrass' theorem to prove that any point sequences with maximal elements form compact sets when convergence of the point sequences is equivalent to the formation of compact sets.

Theorem 1. (BERGSTROM (1975)).

Any topologic space of the property of compact set under completeness always includes some sets of maximal elements.

Theorem 2.

A certain compact set in any distance space is always equivalent to a certain compact set of a certain point sequence.

Theorem 3. (HEINE-BOREL).

Any bounded-close set always forms a compact set only when the said bounded-close set exists in the Euclidean distance space and vice versa.

Theorem 4. (BOLZANO-WEIERSTRASS).

Any bounded-close point sequence always forms

a compact point sequence only when the said bounded-close point sequence exists in the Euclidean distance space and vice versa. (Heine-Borel's theorem is applicable to point sequences.)

To satisfy these theorems, we have to prove that there always exist some compact sets in the problem spaces of sets of images, classes of similar images, and signs. We should prove that the conditions given in Step 1 (a) & (d)–(e) assure that some compact sets always exist in the non-zero and nonnegative (or nonpositive) Euclidean (distance) space. We hereby introduce another generally accepted proposition that supports the existence of compact sets of images, classes of similar images, and signs.

Proposition 2.
Any open set as a nonempty set has at most n-dimension kernel in the n-dimensional Euclidean space.

Based on this proposition, the Euclidean distance space always constructs compact sets inside the space when it has some bounded-close sets. Step 1 (c) assures that any bounded-close sets of point sequences always form compact sets inside the Euclidean distance spaces of images, classes of similar images, and signs, respectively. We hereby introduce transitive law to the Euclidean distance spaces, and Step 1 (b) assures that any compact set always has some maximal elements as the representative set of elements inside the compact set. After all, these conditions assure that each representative element exists in each set of images, classes of similar images, and signs in the Euclidean distance space of completeness under transitive law.

Correspondence of Representative Elements

Here, we have a purpose to prove the following thesis: A certain specified domain realizes exclusive and uniform classification when sets of images, classes of similar images, and signs are mutually exclusive, and when representative elements of those sets are uniformly mapped into the representative elements of the corresponding sets. That thesis should be restated as a simplified problem in topologic representation. We introduce a generally accepted proposition and an important theorem that simplifies the uniform correspondence issue as convergence of point sequences to the maximal or representative elements inside the sets.

Proposition 3.
Any distance space should form a point sequence under the first countability axiom.

Theorem 5.
In any space, a mapping from any set of elements as preimage sets to any set of its corresponding direct image sets forms a continuous mapping under the first countability axiom, subject to the following convergence:

Any direct image set of any certain point sequence inside the preimage sets converges into any direct image set of the preimage sets; and

Any point sequence inside those preimage sets converges into the preimage sets.

Based on the proposition and the theorem, convergence of point sequences is equivalent to a uniform correspondence between any elements in compact sets of point sequences when any point sequence has a compact set, respectively. That convergence is applicable to any set of images, classes of similar images, and signs that have a compact set in a point sequence, respectively.

Step 2 (c) assures three things: a continuous mapping exists from any class of similar images of $\{C_j\}$ to any sign of $\{Z_s\}$; any class of similar images converges to its corresponding and representative element in the set of signs; and any element in the set of signs converges to its representative element inside the set of signs.

Meanwhile, uniform correspondence is restated in the form of convergence of point sequences, though we have an open question how to link the relations or mappings between each class of similar images of $\{C_j\}$ and each sign of $\{Z_s\}$, each image of $\{I_j\}$, and each sign of $\{Z_s\}$.

We hereby introduce a proposition on mapping between compact sets and a theorem on inheritance of the property of compact set.

Proposition 4.

Suppose there exist some topologic spaces in which any inside element as a preimage has a continuous mapping among those spaces of fundamental system of neighborhood. Any neighborhood of the preimages always includes any inverse images inside the neighborhood of any direct images of those preimages.

Theorem 6.

Suppose the Euclidean spaces have a continuous mapping between them. In those spaces, compact set property in one space should be inherited to the other space and vice versa.

Thus, when any set of images, classes of similar images, and signs forms a well-ordered point sequence subject to natural numbering in respective sets, existence of continuous mappings between respective sets is equivalent to convergence of elements of respective sets into maximal or representative elements of compact sets in any distance space.

Step 2 (b) assures that there always exists a continuous mapping between any class of similar images and any set of signs: a mapping from any sign of $\{Z_s\}$ to any class of similar images of $\{C_j\}$. The step also assures that any class of similar images converges to its representative element and forms a compact set and that any set of signs converges to its representative element and forms a compact set.

Assurance of Real Existence of Representative Elements in Related Sets

Here, we have a purpose to prove the following thesis: A certain specified domain should always have exclusive classification of representative elements that exist in real related sets. We introduce a generally accepted axiom as a basis for topologic formulation.

Axiom 1. (Axiom of Order)

Any set of elements in a domain or space should form a certain well-ordered set, subject to a certain rule of ordering.

Step 2 (a) represents the axiom that is introduced to form representative elements in each set of images, classes of similar images, and signs. Thus, a certain specified domain always has exclusive classification of classes of similar images with well-ordered parametric values on the parameter setting for similarity metrics, under the axiom of order (reflexive, antisymmetric, and transitive laws) and the axiom of choice. Here, the reflective law (for $\forall x \in X, x \sim x$) and the antisymmetric law ($x \sim y \Rightarrow y \sim x$) satisfy linear rank order of the similarity of elements that leads to exclusive classification.

Steps 1 and 2 always assure exclusive and uniform classification of any representative element in each set of images, classes of similar images, and signs.

Identical Classification

Step 3 constitutes the conditions on domain selection. The purpose of this part is to prove that the conditions satisfy identical classification.

Assurance of Identical Categorization or Combination

Here, we have a purpose to prove the following thesis: A certain specified domain always has identical categorization or combination on the compact sets of images, classes of similar images, and signs. Based on Steps 1 and 2, any set of images, classes of similar images, and signs has representative elements under the Euclidean distance metrics, respectively. Here, suppose any set of images, classes of similar images, and signs have certain *finite* compact sets, respectively. The finite compact sets cover infinite combinations of representative elements inside sets of images, classes of similar images, and signs in a certain specified domain.

First, we introduce two generally accepted propositions to simplify and restate this thesis: The finite compact sets of images, classes of similar images, and signs in a certain specified domain should inherit the property of compact sets between sets of images, classes of similar images, and signs.

Proposition 5 (Inheritance of homeomorphic property in the Euclidean space).
Suppose the Euclidean distance space is of homeomorphic property. Its subspace has the same topologic structure with the distance space of homeomorphic property.

Proposition 6 (Homeomorphic property on mapping between compact sets).
Suppose some compact sets have a continuous mapping between them. The mapping forms a mapping of homeomorphic property.

Based on these propositions, a certain specified domain of finite boundary has a mapping of homeomorphic property among any inside compact sets of images, classes of similar images, and signs. We introduce another proposition that assures that a certain specified domain has bijective and continuous mappings between any combinations of classes of similar images and signs inside the spaces of images, classes of similar images, and signs.

Proposition 7 (Mapping of homeomorphic property in the Euclidean distance space).
The Euclidean distance space has a mapping of homeomorphic property when the mapping is bijective and continuous and when its inverse mapping is continuous.

We also introduce a final proposition that assures that the sets of classes of similar images and signs have not only uniform mappings between them, but also respective finite sets of identical combination in a certain specified domain. That domain has the mappings of homeomorphic property and the same topologic structure on the sets of the classes of similar images and the signs because of inheritance of homeomorphic property.

Proposition 8 (Inheritance of homeomorphic property by mapping of homeomorphic property).
Suppose some spaces have a mapping of homeomorphic property that corresponds between the compact sets in those spaces. Those spaces construct the same topologic structure in preimage space and in its corresponding direct image space.

Based on the propositions, respective finite sets of identical combination of the classes of similar images and the signs represent representative classes of similar images and signs in a certain specified domain. It is because not infinite but finite combination provides the domain with clear boundary of the respective sets of those classes of similar images and signs.

Step 3 assures identical classification on the combination of representative images, classes of similar images, and signs.

DISCUSSION

In this section, we discuss the contributions and limitations of the proposed digital library protection.

First, the proposed formulation presents right protection to the digital library community, which demands a means for recouping investment in digital library designing and assembling. Patents as registered rights work as catalysts to protect the entire digital library against any other assembling of equivalent forgery digital libraries in certain specified domains.

Furthermore, the proposed formulation realizes substantial protection of the digital library with dynamically assigned indexes by content-based retrieval, while that kind of digital library has not been fully protected in the form of copyrightable compilation or *sui generis* of database right protection.

Third, our formulation does not have any excessively exclusive protection on digital libraries in general domains. Although parametric values in parameter-setting components are easy to modify and adjust in the applications, exemplary parametric values are indispensable for patent application, and then define clear boundary on the scope of equivalent modification of the problem digital library in specified, that is, narrow domains. That domain-specific protection enables the followers of the digital library initiative in the Asia-Pacific region to find remaining resorts for their research and development, though a number of general domains explored by the foregoers are excluded from the proposed protection.

Meanwhile, the proposed formulation has its own limitations as follows; First, it is applicable to just digital libraries that comprise patentable content-based retrieval processes at the present. Second, the scope of the proposed digital library protection is restricted within certain specified domains with clear definition of classification, that is, *a priori* finite and exclusive classification of content. A domain of an infinite combination of classes of similar images is excluded from the proposed formulation. Finally, that formulation is restrictive while its mathematical foundation determines explicitly which digital library is protected using patentable content-based retrieval process in its specified domain.

The proposed digital library protection, however, provides database designers in the digital library community with systematic protection, which any legal institution has not realized as indispensable incentive in their intellectual investments at the present.

CONCLUSION

In this chapter, we have formulated the digital library protection using patent of content-based retrieval process, especially on image digital libraries in specified domains, without any excessively exclusive protection in general domains. We have revealed the limitations of copyright protection of digital libraries that are associated with content-based retrieval. We have provided the proposed formulation with its mathematical foundation and reasoning. We have confirmed its feasibility and accountability with several case studies in the area of medical image digital libraries associated with content-based retrieval.

Our formulation is based on the technical property of the domain-specific approach of content-based retrieval, especially on its parameter-setting component. That patent-based protection is to satisfy the needs in the digital library community through the deployment of the latest patent practice in the area of bioinformatics into the image retrieval engineering. Its potential application grows as the expansion of networked digital libraries with content-based retrieval. That proposed protection promises the enhanced incentives for investing in collecting visual contents and designing digital libraries as a fair command for both the Western forgoers and Asian-Pacific followers in the digital library community.

REFERENCES

Bach, J. R., Fuller, C., Gupta, A., Hampapur, A., Horowitz, B., Jain, R., & Shu, C. F. (1996). The Virage image search engine: An open framework for image management. In *Proceedings of SPIE Storage and Retrieval for Still Image and Video Databases IV* (pp. 76-87).

Bergstrom, T. C. (1975). Maximal elements of acyclic relations on compact sets. *Journal of Economic Theory, 10*, 403-404.

Brin, S., & Page, L. (1998). The anatomy of large-scale hypertextual Web search engine. In *Proceedings of the Seventh International World Wide Web Conference* (pp. 107-117).

Chu, W. W., Hsu, C. C., C'ardenas, A. F., & Taira,R. K. (1998). A knowledge-based image retrieval with spatial and temporal constructs. *IEEE Transactions on Knowledge and Data Engineering, 10*(6), 872-888.

Dy, J. G., Brodley, C. E., Kak, A., Shyu, C.-R., & Broderick, L. S. (1999). The customized queries approach to CBIR.In *Proceedings of SPIE Storage and Retrieval for Image and Video Databases VII* 3656 (pp. 22-32).

European Patent Office. (2001). *Guidelines for examination in the European Patent Office.*

Flickner, M., Sawhney, H., Niblack, W., Ashley, J., Huang, Q., Dom, B., Gorkani, M., Hafner, J., Lee, D., Petkovic, D., Steele, D., & Yanker, P. (1995). Query by image and video content: The QBIC system. *IEEE Computer, 28*(9), 23-32.

Gorman, R. A., & Ginsburg, J. C. (1993). *Copyright for the nineties: Cases and materials* (4th ed.). Contemporary Legal Education Series. Charlottesville, NC: The Michie Company.

Korn, P., Sidiropoulos, N., Faloutsos, C., Siegel, E., & Protopapas, Z. (1998). Fast and effective retrieval of medical tumor shapes. *IEEE Transactions on Knowledge and Data Engineering, 10*(6), 889-904.

Liu, Y., Dellaert, F. D., & Rothfus, W. E. (1998). Classification driven semantic based medical image indexing and retrieval. *Technical Report.* Pittsburgh, PA: The Robotics Institute, Carnegie Mellon University.

Merges, R. P. (1997). *Patent law and policy: Cases and materials* (2nd ed.). Contemporary Legal Education Series. Charlottesville, NC: The Michie Company.

Nimmer, M., Marcus, P., Myers, D., & Nimmer, D. (1991). *Cases and materials on copyright* (4th ed.). St. Paul, MN: West Publishing.

Reinbothe, J. (1999). The legal protection of non-creative databases. In *WIPO/EC/CONF/99/ SPK/22-A* WIPO, Geneva, Switzerland. Presented Chapter to Protection of Database Workshop at International Conference of Electronic Commerce and Intellectual Property. Retrieved from http://ecommerce.wipo.int/meetings/1999/chapters/pdf/reinboth.pdf

Rui, Y., Huang, T. S., & Chang, S. F. (1999). Image retrieval: Current techniques, promising directions and open issues. *Journal of Visual Communication and Image Representation, 10*(4), 39-62.

Samuelson, P. (1996). Legally speaking: Legal protection for database content. *Communications of the ACM, 39*(12), 17-23.

Sasaki, H., & Kiyoki, Y. (2002). A methodology to protect multimedia databases by patentable programs of indexing and retrieval based-on semantic similarity. *IPS of Japan Transactions on Databases, 43*(13), 108-127. (*in Japanese*).

Sasaki, H., & Kiyoki, Y. (2002). Patenting the processes for content-based retrieval in digital libraries. In E.-P. Lim, S. Foo, C. Khoo, H. Chen, E. Fox, S. Urs, & T. Costantino (Eds.), *Proceedings of the Fifth International Conference on Asian Digital Libraries (ICADL)*, Digital Libraries: People, Knowledge, & Technology, LNCS, 2555 (pp. 471-482).

Sasaki, H., & Kiyoki, Y. (2003). A proposal for digital library protection. In *Proceedings of the Third IEEE-CS/ACM Joint Conference on Digital Libraries (JCDL)* (p. 392).

Sasaki, H., & Kiyoki, Y. (2005). A formulation for patenting content-based retrieval processes in digital libraries. *Journal of Information Process-ing and Management, 41*(1), 57-74.

Smeulders, A. W. M., Worring, M., Santini, S., Gupta, A., & Jain, R. (2000). Content-based image retrieval at the end of the early years. *IEEE Transactions on Pattern Analysis and Machine Intelligence, 22*(12), 1349-1380.

U.S. Copyright Act. (1976).17 U.S.C. sec. 101, & 103.

U.S. Patent and Trademark Office. (1996). *Examination guidelines for computer-related inventions, 61 Fed. Reg. 7478 (Feb. 28, 1996)*.

Yoshitaka, A., & Ichikawa, T. (1999). A survey on content-based retrieval for multimedia databases. *IEEE Transactions on Knowledge and Data Engineering, 11*(1), 81-93.

Chapter II
Intellectual Property Rights:
From Theory to Practical Implementation

Richard A. Spinello
Boston College, USA

Herman T. Tavani
Rivier College, USA

ABSTRACT

*This chapter presents some foundational concepts and issues in intellectual property. We begin by defining **intellectual objects**, which we contrast with physical objects or tangible goods. We then turn to some of the normative justifications that have been advanced to defend the granting of property rights in general, and we ask whether those rationales can be extended to the realm of intellectual objects. Theories of property introduced by Locke and Hegel, as well as utilitarian philosophers, are summarized and critiqued. This sets the stage for reviewing the case against intellectual property. We reject that case and claim instead that policy makers should aim for balanced property rights that avoid the extremes of overprotection and underprotection. Next we examine four different kinds of protection schemes for intellectual property that have been provided by our legal system: copyright laws, patents, trademarks, and trade secrets. This discussion is supplemented with a concise review of recent U.S. legislation involving copyright and digital media and an analysis of technological schemes of property protection known as digital rights management. Finally, we consider a number of recent controversial court cases, including the Napster case and the Microsoft antitrust suit. Many of the issues and controversies introduced in this chapter are explored and analyzed in greater detail in the subsequent chapters of this book.*

INTRODUCTION

It is now a common refrain that the ubiquity of the Internet and the digitization of information will soon mean the demise of copyright and other intellectual property laws. After all, "information wants to be free," especially in the open terrain of cyberspace. John Perry Barlow and other information libertarians have argued this case for years, and there may be some validity to their point of view. Perhaps Negroponte (1995) is right when he describes copyright law as a vestige of another era, a mere "Gutenberg artifact" (p. 58). Even many of those who concede that this vision of cyberspace as a copyright free zone is too utopian argue for a system of intellectual property protection that is as "thin" as possible, just enough to encourage creativity (Vaidhyanathan, 2001).

The digital revolution has already thrown the music industry into chaos and the movie industry will probably be next. Both of these industries have been struggling with piracy, and peer-to-peer (P2P) networks, such as Gnutella, KaZaA, and Morpheus, are the primary obstacle in their efforts to thwart the illicit sharing of files. These P2P networks continue to proliferate, and users continue to download copyrighted music and movie files with relative impunity. Everyone knows, however, that the content industry will not sit idly by and lose its main source of revenues. It will fight back with legal weapons such as the Digital Millennium Copyright Act and technological weapons such as trusted systems.

Of course, debates about intellectual property rights are not confined to digital music and movies. There is apprehension that the Internet itself will be swallowed up by proprietary technologies. Currently, developing countries argue that they can never surmount the digital divide if intellectual property rights remain so entrenched. Governments debate the pros and cons of endorsing open source software as a means of overcoming the hegemony of Microsoft's control of certain technologies. And some claim that the impending "enclosure movement" of intellectual objects will stifle creativity and even threaten free speech rights. Hence, they argue, we must abandon our commitment to private ownership in the digital realm.

The result of these public and controversial squabbles is that the once esoteric issue of intellectual property rights has now taken center stage in courses and books on cyberlaw and cyberethics. The economic and social stakes are quite high in these disputes, so they should not be regarded in a cavalier manner or dismissed as inconsequential. The centrality of the property issue becomes especially apparent when one realizes that other social issues in cyberspace (such as speech and privacy) are often closely connected to the proper scope of intellectual property rights. For example, Diebold Election Systems, a manufacturer of voting machines, has pursued college students for posting on the Internet copies of internal communications, including 15,000 e-mail messages and other memoranda, discussing flaws in Diebold's software. The company claims that this information is proprietary and that these students are violating its intellectual property rights, while the students say that their free speech rights are being unjustly circumscribed. They contend that copyright law is being abused to stifle free speech.

This tension between intellectual property rights and the First Amendment has been addressed by many commentators on the law. As Volokh (1998) has pointed out, "Copyright law restricts speech: it restricts you from writing, painting, publicly performing, or otherwise communicating what you please."

One could easily use the intellectual property issue as a lens to examine the expanding field of cyberethics since the most salient issues seem to have a property dimension. In addition to speech, personal privacy is another issue closely connected with intellectual property. Employers, for example, often invoke property rights to justify monitoring the e-mail communications of their employees. Since the IT systems and e-mail software are the property of employers, they assume the prerogative to ensure that their property is being used in accordance with company rules and regulations.

Given the breadth of the intellectual property field, it is impossible to review all of the current topics and controversies. Our purpose in this introductory essay is merely to provide a comprehensive overview of the nature and scope of intellectual property rights. This overview will include a discussion of intellectual objects, the normative justification of these rights, the philosophical and ethical case made against property rights, the legal infrastructure, and some enumeration of the major cases that are reshaping the legal and social landscape of cyberspace. Our objective is twofold: to provide some important background that will make the remaining in-depth essays in this book more intelligible, especially to the novice reader, and to defend the need for a moderate and balanced regime of intellectual property protection. An ancillary purpose is to shed some light on several hotly debated issues from a moral as well as a legal perspective.

We contend that *information socialism*, where all intellectual objects are "unowned," is an impractical and unworkable alternative to the current system. But we also argue that *information capitalism*, which promotes strong rights and thick protection that can impair the intellectual commons, is also misguided. Policy and law should neither overprotect rights nor underprotect them, but instead should seek the Aristotelian mean or intermediate position between these two deficient policy options. It is difficult, of course, to determine the "right" amount of protection that rewards creators for their efforts and stimulates creativity while not impairing the intellectual commons, but in the course of this analysis we offer some suggestions.

Along the way, we hope to offer reasoned answers to some important questions. For example, how do we assess the validity of the normative justifications for intellectual property rights? Can a case be made for a "natural" intellectual property right, or can this right be grounded only on a more pragmatic, utilitarian foundation? Can cyberspace accommodate intellectual property rights (and the laws that protect those rights) without losing its most attractive features? What are the costs and benefits of relying on technology to protect

digital content? Under what circumstances should secondary liability for copyright infringement be invoked? And finally what can moralists bring to this debate that so far has been dominated by legal scholars? We begin with a conceptual background on the nature of intellectual objects.

INTELLECTUAL OBJECTS

Property is a dynamic concept, which has evolved dramatically since the 18th Century. Originally, it referred exclusively to land but eventually it was extended to include things or physical "objects" such as farms, factories, and furniture (Hughes, 1989). The kinds of objects that count as property now include entities that reside in the non-tangible or intellectual realm as well. Different expressions have been used to refer to the kinds of objects or entities at stake in the intellectual property debate. Sometimes these objects are referred to as *ideal objects* or *non-tangible goods* (Palmer, 1997). Following Hettinger (1997), however, we use the expression *intellectual objects* to refer to various forms of intellectual property. Unlike physical property, intellectual property consists of "objects" that are not tangible. These objects are creative works and inventions, which are the manifestations or expressions of ideas.

Unlike tangible objects, intellectual objects (such as software programs or books) are public goods. Public goods are both non-rivalrous and nonexclusive. An object is non-rivalous if consumption by one person does not diminish what can be consumed by others. So if *A* owns a desktop computer, which is a physical object, then *B* cannot own that computer, and vice versa. However, consider the status of a word-processing program that resides in *A*'s computer. If *B* makes a copy of that program, then both *A* and *B* possess copies of the same word-processing program. *B*'s use of this non-rivalrous intellectual object does not take away from *A*'s use.

A good is nonexclusive if it is impossible to exclude people from consuming it. For example, the national defense and protection of the United States is a public good that covers all citizens regardless of whether or not they pay taxes. Since public goods are non-exclusive as well as non-rivalrous, there is a tendency that they will be underproduced without some type of protection or government intervention that will provide some measure of exclusivity. This has critical implications for intellectual objects. As Gordon (1992) explains, important intellectual property markets will remain uncultivated where the up-front investment cost is high, copying is simple, and free riders threaten to undercut the innovator's prices and thereby appropriate that innovator's created value.

The characteristic of *scarcity* that applies to many physical objects—which often has caused competition and rivalry with respect to those entities—need not exist in the case of intellectual objects. Consider that there are practical limitations to the number of physical objects one can own, and there are natural and political limitations to the amount of land that can be owned. However, most kinds of intellectual objects are easily reproducible and shareable. For example, countless digital copies of a Microsoft Word program can be reproduced and distributed at a marginal cost of zero.

Intellectual objects are also distinguishable from physical objects by virtue of what exactly it is that one can legally claim to own. It is impossible to "own" an abstract idea or concept, at least in the same (legal) sense that one can own a physical object. One cannot exclude others from using that idea once it is revealed, as one can exclude people from using land or some other physical object.

As a result, abstract ideas and algorithms are not the kinds of things for which governments have been willing to grant ownership rights to individuals. Instead, legal protection is given only to the tangible *expression* of an idea that is creative or original. If the idea is literary or artistic in nature, it must be expressed (or "fixed") in some tangible medium in order to be protected. Such a medium could be a physical book or a sheet of paper containing a musical score. And if the idea is functional in nature, such as an invention, it must be expressed in terms of a machine or a process. Whereas authors are granted copyright protections for expressions of their literary ideas, inventors are given an incentive in the form of a patent for their inventions. Both copyright law and patent law, along with other legal schemes for protecting intellectual property, are discussed in detail in later sections of this chapter.

Finally, even if an intellectual object, such as a novel or musical composition, "belongs" to its author in some way, should it be described as that author's "property?" Are other characterizations more suitable? While references to "intellectual property" have become commonplace, many scholars regret the ill-effects of the ascendancy of this form of "property rhetoric." One such effect is the tendency to regard the unauthorized use of intellectual objects as "piracy" or "theft," with all of the negative connotations of those words. The popularity of the term "intellectual property" can be traced back to the foundation of the World Intellectual Property Organization (WIPO) by the United Nations in 1967. To be sure, this term appeared prior to the founding of WIPO, but according to Lemley (1997), these previous uses "do not seem to have reflected a unified property-based approach to the separate doctrines of patent, trademark, and copyright ... "

NORMATIVE JUSTIFICATIONS FOR INTELLECTUAL PROPERTY RIGHTS

What is the basis for the claim that intellectual property (or, for that matter, any kind of property) ought to be protected? The current legal system offers such protection in a web of complex statutes. But we must inquire on what philosophical grounds are these laws based?

From a legal standpoint, intellectual property rights specify the ownership privileges for intellectual objects. Normative approaches to intellectual property (IP) are focused on the justification of intellectual property rights. What is the moral ground for giving an author or publisher a "right" to possess and control an intellectual object? Is the genesis of intellectual property rights to be found in instrumentalist theories or in a natural rights perspective? Normative theory also encompasses the perspective of distributive justice, which compels us to ponder the scope of these rights. In this section, we sketch out some primary justifications for intellectual property rights, drawing heavily upon the resources of philosophers such as Locke and Hegel, who attempt to set forth some defensible rationales for determining the boundaries of those rights.

It must be said at the outset that no single theory presented here is comprehensive enough to withstand critical scrutiny. Each is subject to interpretation and each has certain flaws and shortcomings. Nonetheless, the ultimate indeterminacy of these theories should not discourage this endeavor. At a minimum, these theories are useful as avenues of reflection that can provide a more orderly method of thinking through the moral implications of intellectual property policy decisions. They can also help to resolve specific disputes when the law is unclear or ambiguous. According to Fisher (1998), while these theories may not always persuade us with inexorable logic, they can be used to "strike a cord of sympathy" and evoke a response, such as "that rings true to me."

Locke and the Labor Desert Theory

John Locke, in *The Second Treatise of Government*, was one of the first philosophers to thematize the issue of property in a comprehensive man-

ner. Locke's theory of property has undoubtedly been one of the most influential in the entire philosophical tradition. Locke's main thesis is simple enough: people have a natural right or entitlement to the fruits of their labor. In general terms, labor establishes the boundaries of one's property before civil society even exists. Thus, property is a natural right because it precedes civil society, which comes into being in part in order to protect property. But how do the specific elements of Locke's argument unfold?

Labor belongs to the laborer and when that laborer takes an object from the bountiful commons and mixes that object with her labor, it can be said that she has appropriated that object. Thus, if someone takes common, unusable land and through the sweat of the brow transforms it into valuable farm land that person deserves to own this land, which has been "mixed" with her hard work. According to Locke (1952), "As much land as a man tills, plants, improves, cultivates, and can use the product of, so much is his property. He, by his labor does, as it were, *enclose it from the common*" (p. 20; emphasis added).

As the preceding citation implies, if labor is to engender a property right, it must be useful and purposeful. Moreover, such labor often involves infusing one's very being or personality into the object in question. According to Olivecrona (1974), one's labor is an extension of one's personality and "when the object appropriated has been included within [an individual's] sphere [of personality], it will be an injury to the possessor to deprive him of it."

Locke's argument for a property right is partly based on the premise that labor is an unpleasant and onerous activity. Hence, people engage in labor not for its own sake but to reap its benefits; as a result, it would be unjust not to let people have these benefits they take such pains to procure. In short, property rights are required as a return for the laborers' painful and strenuous work. As Locke (1952) maintains, one who takes the laborer's property "desire[s] the benefit of another's pains, which he has no right to" (p. 20). Appropriation of this property against the laborer's will inflicts an unjustifiable harm on this laborer. If someone comes along and takes from you what you have worked for, that person has done something immoral. For example, if someone takes wood from a common forest in order to build a useful object such as a chair, that person would be harmed by the theft of that chair. As Gordon (1993) argues, Locke espouses a nonconsequentialist natural right to property based on this simple "no-harm principle."

In summary, then, Locke provides two reasons for his normative claim that a person's labor entitles that person to the thing constructed by means of that labor: (1) the right is derived from a prior property right in one's body and the labor that emanates from that body; (2) a property right is deserved as a just return for the laborer's pains (Becker, 1977). Hence, for Locke, an unowned item appropriated through the activity of labor is "just property" (p. 28).

Locke insists on an important condition limiting the acquisition of property that has come to be known as the Lockean proviso. According to this moral principle, one can only appropriate an object from the commons through labor when "there is enough, and as good left for others" (Locke, 1952). Thus, individuals should not be greedy or wasteful and take from the commons more than they can use "to any advantage of life before it spoils" (p. 17). One must have a need and a use for what one appropriates from the commons.

Although Locke had in mind physical property such as land, it would seem logical that this theory is applicable to intellectual property as well. An author or creator owns her labor and therefore must own the creative product of that labor. After all, should not those who expend intellectual labor be rewarded by ownership in the fruits of their labor and be allowed to "enclose it from the common"? In this case, the relevant common resource is not land or unowned physical objects but common knowledge or the "intellectual commons" (that is, unowned facts and other raw material such as ideas, algorithms, musical scores, or general plot lines). And the Lockean inspired argument is that one's intellectual labor should entitle one to have a natural property right in the finished product of that work, such as a novel, a computer program, or a musical composition.

This application of Locke's theory to intellectual property seems plausible enough. As Easterbrook (1990) remarks, "Intellectual property is no less the fruit of one's labor than is physical property." Thus, a person has a legitimate claim to ownership in works to the extent that they have been created by that person's labor. If it is the case that people deserve a property right in tangible objects through their labor, why shouldn't they deserve a property right in the intellectual objects which they have created?

Of course, the Lockean proviso must also be applied to the appropriation of intellectual property. If that appropriation impairs the commons and interferes with the public good, there is a conflict. This proviso would seem to preclude the propertization of abstract ideas such as laws of physics that may be discovered by ingenious individuals. If those ideas became enclosed and off limits to others, the public good would undoubtedly suffer. As Nimmer (2001) observes, "To grant property status to a mere idea would permit withdrawing the ideas from the stock of materials that would otherwise be open to other authors, thereby narrowing the field of thought open for development and exploitation" (pp. 13-60). Although there are different interpretations of this proviso, many scholars tend to favor ones that are more protective of the public domain (Gordon, 1993; Yen, 1990).

How might the Lockean theory with its proviso be applied to cases where there is a potential threat to the integrity of the public domain? Gordon (1993) cites the example of the U.S. Olympic Committee's (USOC) successful efforts to trademark the word "Olympic." The USOC took legal action against another group seeking to use the term "Gay Olympic Games." She describes this as a conflict between a prima facie right to an "unimpaired commons" and the USOC's prima facie right to be "free of interference" in its use of the term "Olympics" to describe its games. Gordon (1993) contends that the right of the public to an unimpaired commons must take priority, and she criticizes the Supreme Court's judgment, arguing that this word cannot be "owned" without "violating both concerns—equality and harm—found in the proviso."

At the same time, if I write a novel about star-crossed lovers and a tragic interracial marriage set in 21st Century Alabama, a copyright for this novel will not hurt the commons. Since U.S. copyright protects expression and not ideas, others can still make use of the general plot line, the setting, and the themes of this novel as long as they do not copy the "web of the authors' dramatic expression" (Hand, 1936). If the law is applied correctly, my limited property right in this novel should not impair the intellectual commons or prevent others from writing similar stories or from being inspired by this story to develop works with related themes.

Critics of Locke's thesis contend that his emphasis on labor as a grounding for property rights is misplaced. According to Drahos (1996), "labor is either too indeterminate or too incomplete a basis on which to base a justification of property." Labor works in some cases (e.g., writing a long novel) but not in others (e.g., discovery of a creative idea that can be put into concrete terms and yet consumes little time). The primary problem seems to revolve around determining an appropriate criterion for intellectual labor. Does it depend simply on time and energy expended, or is it any activity that results in social benefits? What do we do about intellectual objects that can be created with little or no labor? And does this labor have to be some sort of creative activity that yields an original work?

We cannot resolve these issues here, but how one determines the parameters of intellectual la-

bor deserving of a property right will be decisive for deciding how such rights should be awarded. We cannot deny that the application of Locke's basic theory to intellectual property is subject to conflicting interpretations. Nonetheless, the core idea that intellectual labor is deserving of some sort of property right as long as the public domain is not impaired by the granting of such a right seems to be an important consideration for any all-encompassing theory of intellectual property rights.

To some extent, modern copyright law strives to be consistent with the Lockean paradigm because it limits intellectual property rights to concrete expression instead of ideas and allows creative works to be accessed or utilized on a "fair use" basis. The law is seeking to reward the deserving individual creator while fostering the augmentation of the public domain. For example, the idea/expression dichotomy recognizes that property rights should only be extended to concrete expressions but not to abstract ideas or algorithms. According to Yen (1990), the English natural law of property, rooted in the Roman doctrines of possession along with the Lockean principle of labor, strongly suggests that property rights cannot be awarded unless the author creates things that are "capable of possession under the law." English natural law, therefore, along with Locke's important proviso, can be interpreted to support a robust public domain along with individual property rights in concrete intellectual objects. We can affirm that a creator's mental labor leads to the production of intellectual objects that deserve some sort of property right, as long as we also affirm that this right must be prudently limited in scope and duration.

Hegel on Property and Personhood

Another normative justification centers on the intimate relationship between property and personhood. It assumes that, in order to become a person, one needs some control over the resources in one's environment. If this theory provides an adequate account for the granting of property rights in general, then it is plausible to assume that the personality theory could be extended to justify intellectual property rights as well.

This theory has its roots in the philosophy of Hegel. Despite a certain wariness about property in his earlier political writings, Hegel consistently argued for the importance of property rights. In several of those works, such as "The Spirit of Christianity and its Fate," he developed an ontology of life and evaluated Judaism and Christianity according to their fidelity to the spirit of life. In this context, Hegel criticized the teachings of Jesus because they renounced self-expression of the individual achieved through property and family. But according to Hegel (1948), "The fate of property has become too powerful for us … to find its abolition thinkable" (p. 221). The abolition of property is a denial of life, since life requires free self-expression, and so individuals must be able to invest themselves in things. Hence, individuals need private property as a vehicle of self-expression. On the other hand, property must be restricted since excessive property is also opposed to life. The Greek πolis under Solon developed the correct model, since it limited the acquisition of property among the Greeks. For Hegel (1948), the virtue appropriate to property is honesty—people must manifest enough integrity and restraint to develop (or acquire) property only when necessary for the sake of self-expression. But they should not acquire goods and wealth for their own sake, since those things merely "tacked on to life … cannot be its property" (p. 221).

In later writings such as *The Phenomenology of Spirit,* Hegel (1944) develops the notion of objectification, and in language reminiscent of Locke, he describes labor as an "outer expression in which the individual no longer retains possession of himself *per se,* but lets the inner get right outside of him, and surrenders it to something else …" (p. 340). Hegel (1952) continues to emphasize the importance of property rights in works such

as the *Philosophy of Right,* where he argued with insistence that "property is the first embodiment of freedom and so is in itself a substantive end" (§ 45). One cannot be free without property, since property allows one to overcome the opposition between self and world and to freely put one's personality into external objects beyond the inner self.

Hegel elaborates on the theme anticipated in his earlier works: selfhood is achieved by self-expression, by objectifying or embodying one's will in external objects and thereby appropriating those objects into the sphere of one's possessions. Acting upon things is necessary for self-actualization (or self-expression). Without property there can be no self-expression, and without self-expression there can be no freedom. And once we accept that self-actualization is manifest in physical objects, property rights take over to prevent people "from forever being embroiled in an internecine conflict of each individual trying to protect his first forays at self actualization from the predation of others" (Hughes, 1997, p. 144).

The core insight of Hegel is this notion of "embodied will," a reminder that we have intimate relationships with objects that give our lives meaning and value. And these relationships justify ownership, since without ownership there will be no continuity in the way we relate to these valuable objects. According to Merges, Mennell, and Lemley (2000), "one's expectations crystallize around certain 'things,' the loss of which causes … disruption and disorientation" (p. 9).

Hegel has consistently maintained, then, that property is an expression of personality, a mechanism for self-actualization. This theory seems particularly apposite for intellectual property. If physical property is the "embodiment of personality" (Hegel, 1952, § 51), then the same can surely be said for intellectual property. As human beings freely externalize their will in various intellectual objects such as novels, works of art, or poetry, they create "property" to which they are entitled because those intellectual products are a manifestation or embodiment of their personality. Each of these creative works is an extension of their being and as such belongs to them. If a person has invested or "poured" himself or herself into an intellectual object, then it follows that the object should belong to that person.

To be sure, not all types of intellectual property entail a great deal of personality or self-expression. But the more creative and expressive are one's intellectual works—the greater one's "personality stake" in that particular object—the more important the need for some type of ownership rights and the stronger the justification for those rights (Hughes, 1997). Perhaps in keeping with Hegel's early views on property we should add that the creator who aspires to honesty should not seek absolute control but rather seek enough control over his or her work to prevent its unfair alienation (or exploitation).

Like the Lockean framework, a Hegelian approach to intellectual property has notable shortcomings. Once again we are confronted with the difficulty of defining and quantifying self-expression if we want to use it as a basis for granting intellectual property rights. To what extent does expression of one's personality justify increased property protection? What happens if inventions, reflecting the personality of their respective inventors, are developed simultaneously? When does imitative artwork or music manifest sufficient unique personality to qualify for a copyright? What should be done about computer software programs that rarely manifest the personality traits of their authors? On the other hand, what about works that are highly expressive and infused with personality and yet are deemed to be derivative according to current U.S. copyright law? For example, *The Wind Done Gone*, a clever takeoff on Margaret Mitchell's classic novel, *Gone with the Wind,* initially ran afoul of that copyright law due to its lack of literary originality. Yet this work would seem to qualify under an Hegelian approach, since it is a highly personal, revisionistic portrayal of the main characters in *Gone with the Wind* that borrows from the original text for the sake of parody and criticism.

In summary, then, Hegel espouses the principle that property is a natural right or end in itself because it provides freedom for the self, which, through the exercise of that freedom, objectifies itself in the external world—that is, gives its personality a reality outside of itself. And Hegel's notion that property is an expression of personality is well suited for intellectual property, since abstract objects can also be invested with personality.

Hughes (1997) has suggested that the theories of Locke and Hegel are complementary, especially if we consider the biggest weakness of each paradigm: Locke's theory cannot account for "the idea whose inception does not seemed to have involved labor," and the Hegelian personality theory is hard to apply to "valuable innovations that do not contain elements of what society might recognize as personal expression" (p. 164). But if an intellectual property right is construed as a right to the fruit of one's labor *and* individual expression, it may find a more sympathetic audience even among some intellectual property skeptics.

Utilitarianism

In contrast to intellectual property rights defended from a natural-rights perspective, we find the utilitarian approach, which assumes that the utility principle—often expressed as "the greatest good of the greatest number"—should be the basis for determining property entitlements. Intellectual property rights, according to this paradigm, are justified on the basis of their contribution to social utility.

The utilitarian argument for property rights in general is based on the premise that people need to acquire, possess, and use things in order to achieve some degree of happiness and fulfillment. Since insecurity in one's possessions does not provide such happiness, security in possession, use, and control of things is necessary. Furthermore, security of possession can only be accomplished by a system of property rights. Also, utilitarian philosophers such as Bentham justified the institution of private property by the related argument that knowledge of future ownership is an incentive that encourages people to behave in certain ways that will increase socially valuable goods.

The utilitarian argument for intellectual property rights is equally straightforward: those rights are necessary to maximize social utility by providing authors, inventors, and other creators with rewards for their work. Without those rewards, which in the Anglo-American system take the form of heavily protected monopolies of limited duration, there would be fewer such creations or inventions. This version of utilitarianism—known as incentive theory—has been articulated in many works, including those of Nordhaus (1969), who sought to demonstrate that an increase in the longevity or robustness of patents would stimulate more innovations.

Following Moore (2001) and others who have explicated this theory, it can be summarized as follows:

1. Society should adopt legal regimes or institutions if and only if they are expected to yield the optimization of aggregate social welfare.
2. A legal regime that provides authors, creators, and inventors with limited rights or control over their productions is expected to act as a strong incentive for the creation of intellectual works.
3. Stimulating the production and creation of intellectual works contributes to the maximization of aggregate welfare.
4. Therefore, a legal regime for intellectual property protection should be adopted.

The presumption, of course, is that the development of scientific, literary, and artistic works will promote general utility or social welfare. This seems to be reasonable, since it is hard to quar-

rel with any culture's need for such intellectual works. And it was precisely this need that was recognized in the U.S. Constitution that confers upon Congress the power "to promote the Progress of Science and the useful Arts, by securing for limited Times to Authors and Inventors the exclusive Right to their respective Writings and Discoveries" (Article I, § 8, clause 8).

In contrast to Locke and Hegel, utilitarian philosophers argue that intellectual property rights are not a natural entitlement or a matter of natural justice. Rather, they should be awarded purely for pragmatic purposes as a means of inducing creative or inventive activity. This line of reasoning is echoed in influential cases such as *Wheaton v. Peters* (1834), which denies that an author's intellectual property rights in published works are a matter of common law. Such a right is based purely on statute and is contingent on the consensus of lawmakers. Western societies, of course, have provided an ample level of intellectual property protection in order to promote future innovation and creativity. They have tended to presume that without such protection creators would not always be able to recover their initial investment and thus would refrain from creative activity. If society wants quality movies and technological innovation, it will have to protect those items from free riders. Precisely how that level of protection is calibrated in order to maximize productivity, however, is a matter of debate.

The primary problem with utilitarianism is the lack of empirical data available that will support those policy choices aimed at maximizing social welfare (measured as society's total wealth). To what extent will an increase or change in copyright or patent protection stimulate greater productivity of intellectual objects? Can we be sure of the effects of extending the duration of copyright protection or increasing the life of a patent from 17 to 20 years? What impact will these policy changes have on authors, inventors, and consumers? Consider Priest's (1986) trenchant observation about this problem:

[t]he inability of economists to resolve the question of whether activity stimulated by the patent system or other forms of protection of intellectual property enhances or diminishes social welfare implies...that economists can tell lawyers very little about how to enforce or interpret the law of intellectual property. (p.27)

Given these problems, one wonders whether copyright or patent jurisprudence should be based solely on utilitarian considerations. But despite its shortcomings, the utility argument should not be discounted. There are, for example, credible studies citing empirical evidence that strongly suggests a link between patent protection and innovation (Mansfield, 1986; Merges, 1992). However, a more stable basis for intellectual property rights might come from the *deontic* (or duty based) moral principles articulated in the philosophies of Locke and Hegel.

But rather than privilege one theory over another, a pluralistic approach seems more sensible. These normative theories should be seen as mutually supporting one another as they offer guiding principles for determining intellectual property policy and the validity of specific entitlements. The theories are not competitive, but complementary. A corollary principle that also emerges in these normative frameworks (especially Locke's) is the need to respect the intellectual commons or public domain. All of these prescriptive principles—utility, labor-desert, self-expression, and respect for the commons—should function in our reasoning and deliberations about intellectual property issues as a system of checks and balances.

THE CASE AGAINST INTELLECTUAL PROPERTY RIGHTS

So far, we have focused on normative justifications of intellectual property rights, which some see as morally inviolable and economically essential.

But what about the case against assigning these rights? There is a strong tradition supporting a radical skepticism about property rights that deserves our careful consideration. Antipathy to private property often springs from opposition to the capitalist market system on the grounds that it sometimes leads to gross inequities in the acquisition of property.

Some philosophers such as Karl Marx have expressed great uneasiness about the notion of private property. Marx regarded such property in the capitalist context as a form of alienation and a blunt instrument of the ruling class to protect its interests. According to the Marxist tradition, private property is the end result of alienated labor. Marx agreed with Hegel that labor was an expressive activity. For laborers in a capitalist economy, however, while the object produced embodies their personality and nature, this object is sold by the producer, and hence is not under the laborer's control. These objects, therefore, are reduced to the status of mere commodities.

While Marx did not explicitly consider intellectual property, his theory has relevance for it. For those sympathetic to Marx, there is abundant evidence that in capitalist economies, creative labor is another instance of exploited labor. According to Drahos (1996), "it is capitalists rather than workers that end up owning most of the intellectual property that is produced within a capitalist economy" (pp. 99-100). A Marxist perspective then would not regard intellectual property rights in a benign light, as a socially useful instrument to stimulate creativity. Rather, those rights are regarded as yet another sinister means by which one class organizes and controls the production undertaken by another class. Hence, intellectual property rights, which give corporate producers sovereignty over many intellectual objects, should be repudiated or at least radically revised.

Furthermore, Marx subscribed to the Hegelian idea that labor could be part of the subject's self-actualization and thereby can be viewed as a means to achieve freedom. But for Marx (unlike Hegel), production and property do not always lead to authentic self-realization. Some individuals, for example, freely create music or art as a means to express their deepest emotions. In the capitalist system, however, this type of labor becomes easily commodified and thereby alienated. As Drahos (1996) explains, "capitalism seeks out creative labor and integrates such labor into its system of production, [and] the task of integration is achieved through intellectual property law" (p. 105). Capitalism assimilates creative labor in order to gain control over these desirable intellectual objects. Intellectual property law, therefore, performs a disservice by commodifying intellectual objects and creative labor and by integrating them into the capitalist structure. According to this line of reasoning, society would be better off with a system that avoided the commodification of intellectual and creative works, so that they are not alienated from their actual creators and openly available to anyone. This system would encourage and reward the sharing of information and the advancement of scientific knowledge.

Contemporary critics of intellectual property rights such as Martin (1995) argue that these rights lead to unjustifiably harmful consequences such as the exploitation of developing countries, which are at the mercy of companies holding patents for pharmaceutical products or copyrights for important software technologies. Moreover, many plants and microorganisms found in developing countries are key starting ingredients for new drugs and crops, but these substances are usually patented by companies from developed countries. In India, the neem tree has been used by that country to develop medical products, yet U.S. and Japanese companies have patented neem-based material. Some critics argue that, because intellectual property rights such as patents only exacerbate present inequities, it would be fairer if intellectual products produced in privileged countries be made available to poor countries at no cost.

The alternative to intellectual property rights is to ensure that all intellectual products remain unowned, either by individuals or organizations. Language, for example, can be freely used by anyone, and most scientific research is public knowledge. Proponents of this view, which we might label "information socialism," argue that the elimination of intellectual property rights will lead to the expansion of the intellectual commons and the fostering of creativity.

The justification of intellectual property rights has also been questioned by recent post-modern scholarship, which has expressed doubts about the true origin of intellectual objects. There are echoes of Marx in the writings of some post-modernists, who describe a crisis of human subjectivity and who see the structures of social and economic domination inscribed in that human subject. These doubts about the immediacy of the self have led to philosophical questions about authorship. Locke never questioned the unitary self that was the source of labor and the bearer of the property right. Similarly, the assumption had always been that the correlate of the creative work (such as the novel or poem) is the creative subject, who is responsible for his or her work. But is it not arbitrary to assume that this isolated subject is the ultimate responsible source? Why not revert to something more primordial such as social or familial antecedents?

Many post-modern philosophers and their followers now contend that the notion of authorship is "socially constructed" and that we must be wary of associating any creative work with a single, discrete, individual "author." Despite the author's labor, that work is not a product of this one individual but of the community's intellectual forces, which have mightily contributed their ideas and thoughts to the author's work. Halbert (1999), for example, argues that our notions of "literary work" and the "author function" must be thoroughly deconstructed: "[t]he author is so embedded in our thought processes that we look to the author as owner instead of looking behind the role of authorship to the production of discourses in society" (p. 126). Similarly, Vaidhyanathan (2001) claims that "authorship is theoretically suspect, texts are unstable, and originality is more often a pose or pretense than a definable aspect of a work" (p. 8).

Of course, if the notion of authorship is so inchoate, and if the author is more illusory than real, it makes no sense to award "rights" to this fictional entity. And if originality is a "pretense," there would be no valid copyrights, at least as the copyright statute is currently configured. But is there any plausibility to these unorthodox viewpoints?

In order to answer this question we must consider the reflections of the philosopher Michel Foucault (1969) who describes how the "author function faded away" in the 18th Century, replaced by scientific discourses "received for themselves … in anonymity." For Foucault and other post-modern thinkers, the process of deconstruction or *différance* exposes the multiplicity of "differences" or different elements of reality that cannot be organized into categories or classified according to metaphysical species. It is the reader of a text who puts different elements together in order to create his or her own meaning. This process of *différance* represents "acategorial" thinking and has no center or author. And if a text is without an author, it must be without a unitary subject: "the subject is constituted only in being divided from itself, in becoming space, in temporizing, in deferral" (Derrida, 1981, p. 29). Thus, this questioning of authorial identity is part of the larger post-modern endeavor to raise doubts about the existence or continuity of the stable self.

It was Nietzsche who first saw the self as a *dividuum*, lacking unity and coherence, where one force temporarily dominates. Nietzsche (1962) described the self as "a plurality. . .a war and peace, a herd and a shepherd" (p. 27).[1] Following the philosophy of Nietzsche, Foucault (1969) and

Derrida (1981) also regarded the human self not as a unified being but as fissured and divided. For the post-modern tradition, then, the self is not an immediate unity nor the ultimate source of activity.

Yet behind the discourses and the narrative must there not be such a stable self, an "I" who perdures through the evolving narrative in order to provide its coherence? Without a unitary subject as a personal focal point, how can there be serious and sustained engagement with an important topic or artistic theme? Moreover, in telling the tale of how he came to propound this or that view about the nonexistent self, isn't the post-modern narrator forced "to fall back into a mode of speech in which the use of personal pronouns presupposes just that metaphysical conception of accountability which [postmodernism] disowns?" (MacIntyre, 1990, p. 210). Discourse or narration requires an efficient cause, an author who may be deeply indebted to multiple sources but who nonetheless engages the topic at hand as an intentional subject and who is ultimately accountable for what is said or done.

When Foucault (1969) refers to the impersonality of these discourses, he assumes the presence of an individual who takes on the authorial function and who is contingently related to that discourse (MacIntyre, 1990). But Foucault fails to consider the intentions of this individual (author) as he or she actively expresses meaning through preexisting linguistic structures and endows that discourse with some measure of originality and uniqueness. When, for example, Jane Austen narrates a tale about marriage and love in early 19th Century England, this "discourse" has distinct qualities thanks to her intentional use of language in a certain way and with a certain style. The true artist or great novelist could never be reduced to an impersonal or passive purveyor of shapeless, amorphous discourse where the relationship of the author to that discourse involves only an unintentional dependence on or use of language.

We concede that the concept of "author" has been overly romanticized, as Boyle (2004) claims, and is surely subject to some degree of revision or re-conceptualization. Yet it seems impossible to emancipate the literary text or musical composition from the intentionality of a stable, originating author in the way that some post-modern legal scholars have proposed.

At the same time, cultural history and common sense should prevent us from accepting the spurious notion that all creative works lack originality. While it is undoubtedly true that even the giants have stood on the shoulders of their predecessors and borrowed from their cultural heritage, they have still produced works of remarkable freshness and novelty that opened up great possibilities and new perspectives for others. Can anyone deny the native talent or artistic genius of a Mozart or a Shakespeare? Can we gaze at a VanGogh painting depicting a pair of farm shoes without recognizing that this artist has created a profound and luminous truth out of bare materials in an ingenious way that sets him apart from ordinary artisans? Yet if we accept the claims of Vaidhyanathan (2001) and others, if we insist that the author is no more than a vague "cultural entity" (p. 10), it will not be possible to give true creators like VanGogh their due or to distinguish them from those who simply imitate and appropriate the works of others.

Thus, we conclude that while the critics of strong intellectual property rights have valid concerns, the case against intellectual property rights is unpersuasive for both practical and theoretical reasons. Let us first consider the practical problems. While patents can hurt developing countries, there is another side to this issue. Without those rights, developing countries would not be able to optimize their innovations. In India, for example, biotech entrepreneurs have developed innovative products, but they have not been successful at commercialization. The reason is that Indian patent law does not adequately cover pharmaceuticals, so "the fruits of their costly research are hard to protect from copycats" ("Patents and the Poor,"

2001). The world intellectual property system needs revision to deal with biopiracy and clear-cut cases of exploitation, but while new property models are called for, the entire system should not be abandoned. Most developing countries perceive the need for a proper patent system that suits their needs. If configured fairly and managed properly, intellectual property rights can be an opportunity even for developing countries, since they will incentivize key domestic industries and enhance foreign investment ("Patents and the Poor," 2001).

From a theoretical standpoint, it is worth noting that Marx's idealistic philosophy cannot solve the incentive problem. Will people produce great quantities of intellectual work without the incentive of a tangible reward as Marx and his followers presumed? Can they risk investing in creative projects (such as big budget movies or biotech innovations) without the assurance of being able to safeguard their end products from free riders? It is no coincidence that most major innovations come from countries like the U.S. where the market system is strong and the incentive system is so generous. In addition, as we have argued, the notion that there is no discrete author and hence no basis for awarding intellectual property rights is incoherent. In our view, one is on firmer ground in proposing that property rights be moderate and balanced, recognizing the need to reward creative effort in a measured way that avoids impairment of the public domain.

LEGAL INFRASTRUCTURE TO PROTECT INTELLECTUAL PROPERTY RIGHTS IN THE UNITED STATES

To protect the rights and interests of "owners" of intellectual property, including computer software programs and applications, many nations have enacted specific laws and statutes. To some extent, the inspiration for these laws can be found in the normative frameworks. In an allusion to the Lockean paradigm, the U.S. Supreme Court indicated that "the immediate effect of our copyright law is to secure a fair return for an 'author's' creative labor" (*Harper & Row Publishers v. Nation Enterprises*, 1985). In this section, we examine four different types of schemes for protecting intellectual property rights in the U.S.: *copyright law, patents, trademarks,* and *trade secrets*. We begin with a look at copyright law.

Copyright Protection

The protections covered under U.S. copyright law are often referred to as a "bundle of rights" (Moore, 1997; Warwick, 2004) whose aim is to protect limited monopoly for certain kinds of intellectual objects. Section 106 of the U.S. 1976 Copyright Act (Title 17 of the U.S. Code) defines the set of exclusive rights granted to copyright owners under the law. Copyright holders have the exclusive right to make copies of the work and to produce derivative works, that is, translations into other languages, movies based on the book, and so forth. They also have the exclusive right to make and distribute copies of their works, display their works in public (for example, art works), and perform works in public (musicals, plays, and so forth).

In effect, a copyright is a form of legal protection given to an *author*. The author can be an organization or a corporation (such as Disney) or an individual person. Copyright protection is given to an author for the *expression* of an idea, which can be manifested in a book, poem, musical composition, photograph, dance movement, motion pictures, audiovisual works, or computer software. For a literary or artistic work to be protected under copyright law, it must satisfy three conditions. First, the work must be *original* in the sense that it "owes its origins to the author." Second, it must be *nonfunctional* or non-utilitarian in nature. Functions and processes, including inventions, are protected by patents, and, typically,

are not eligible for copyright protection. Third, in order to qualify for a copyright, the work must be *fixed* or expressed concretely in the form of some *tangible medium* such as a book, poem, or musical score. So ideas, concepts, facts, processes, and methods are not, in themselves, protected by copyright law. The distinction between an idea and its expression is not always obvious. As Justice Hand (1930) observed, "Nobody has ever been able to fix that boundary [between idea and expression], and nobody ever can."

A Short History of Copyright Law in the United States

Copyright law in the Anglo-American world generally traces its origins to the Statute of Ann, passed by the English Parliament in 1710. The first copyright law in the United States, enacted in 1790, applied primarily to books, maps, and charts. Later, the law was extended to include newer forms of media such as photography, movies, audio recordings, and so forth. The duration of copyright protection was 14 years with the possibility of renewal for another 14 years.

In 1909, the copyright law was amended to include any "form that could be seen and read visually" by humans. This modification was motivated by a challenge involving a new technology—namely, the player piano. In particular, the change was prompted by a case in 1908 involving a song that was copied onto a perforated piano music roll. Since the musical copy could not be read visually (by humans) from the piano roll, the copy was not considered a violation of the song's copyright. The "machine readable" vs. "human readable" distinction would later have implications for decisions about whether software programs could qualify for copyright protection. Although a program's source code can be read by humans, its "executable code," which "runs" on a computer, cannot. The 1909 Act also extended copyright protection to an initial term of 28 years along with 28 additional years on renewal.

Copyright law was modified once again in 1976. This Act expanded the scope and duration of copyright protection. Any work that could be "fixed in a tangible medium of expression" was eligible for a copyright. At the same time, the 1976 Act codified the idea-expression dichotomy. In addition, copyright's duration became the life of the author plus 50 years for individual authors and 75 years for corporate authors.

Under the 1976 Copyright Act, computer programs still did not clearly satisfy the requirements necessary for making them eligible for copyright protection. The Copyright Act was amended again in 1980, specifically to address the status of software programs. That year, the concept of a literary work was extended to include programs, computers, and databases that "exhibit authorship." A computer program was defined under the U.S. Copyright Act as a "set of statements or instructions to be used directly in a computer in order to bring about certain results." To be granted a copyright for a computer program, however, the author had to show that the program contained an original expression (or original arrangement) of ideas and not simply the ideas themselves.

The Copyright Act of 1976 has since been amended on a number of occasions, primarily to keep pace with significant changes involving digital technology. For example, it was amended in 1984 with the Semiconductor Chip Protection Act. That Act was enacted to protect proprietary rights in semiconductor chips, specifically protecting the design layout of these chips.

There have been many controversies involving the role of copyright protection for computer programs, but the most noteworthy of these concerned the status of the "look and feel" of computer software. Some argued that, in addition to the software code itself, the "look and feel" of a software program—that is, the user interface, which consists of features such as icons and pull-down menus — should also be protected by copyright law. Initially, Lotus Corporation won a copyright infringement suit against Paperback Software

International and Borderland International Inc., whose user interfaces included menus and buttons that resembled Lotus' 1-2-3 product. However, this decision was reversed on appeal in 1995. In a somewhat similar case, Apple lost its suit against Microsoft and Hewlett Packard for using features that Apple believed were similar to its icon-based, graphical user interface. In ruling against Apple and Lotus, the courts determined that icons and menus in a computer interface were analogous to buttons on a VCR or to controls on a car.

In 1998, two important amendments were made to the 1976 Copyright Act: the Copyright Term Extension Act (CTEA) and the Digital Millennium Copyright Act (DMCA). Both Acts have been regarded as controversial and both are examined in detail in a later section of this chapter.

Balancing Schemes in Copyright Law: Fair Use and First Sale Principles

Principles have been developed to balance the exclusive controls given to copyright holders against the broader interests of society. Two such principles are *fair use* and *first-sale*. Fair use means that every author or publisher may make limited use of another person's copyrighted work for purposes such as criticism, comment, news reporting, teaching, scholarship, and research. There are four factors that help the court determine fair use: (1) the purpose and character of the use [for example, commercial use weighs against the claim of fair use]; (2) the nature of the copyrighted work [for example, creative works receive more protection than factual ones]; (3) the "amount and substantiality of the portion used" in relation to the work as a whole; and (4) the effects of the use on the market for the work ("fair use, when properly applied, is limited to copying by others which does not materially impair the marketability of the work which is copied" [*Harper & Row v. Nation Enterprises*, 1985]). All of these factors are weighed together and decisions are made on a case-by-case basis.

Thus the fair use principle restricts the total control that the copyright holder would otherwise enjoy. The fair use principle has also been invoked to defend the practice of "reverse engineering." This practice has been very important in the computer industry in particular and in engineering in general, because it allows someone to buy a product for the purpose of taking it apart to see how it works.

Another balancing scheme in copyright law has been the principle of first sale, which applies once the original work has been sold for the first time. At that point, the original owner loses rights over the work of art. For example, once you purchase a copy of a book, audiotape, painting, etc., you are free to transfer (resell, give away, or even destroy) the copy of that work. It is not clear, however, that one can give away software that is licensed for use but not owned, strictly speaking, by a user. Some argue that the fair use and first sale principles are now threatened because of recent legislation such as the Digital Millennium Copyright Act along with growing reliance on technological schemes of protection known as digital rights management. We examine these arguments in detail in a later section of this chapter.

Software Piracy as a Form of Copyright Infringement

When personal computers became widespread in the 1980s, many users discovered how easy it was to copy software programs. Concerns about the amount of unauthorized copying of proprietary software rose as personal computer use proliferated. Some software manufacturers claimed to have lost millions of dollars of potential revenue because of software piracy. On the face of it, these software companies would certainly seem to be justified in their concerns regarding the pirating of proprietary software by individuals and organizations, both nationally and globally. However, some critics have responded by maintaining that claims made by American software manufacturers about

the loss of revenue involving the use of pirated software in developing countries are either greatly exaggerated or altogether bogus. They point out, for example, that many people and organizations in developing countries who currently use American software products would not be able to pay the high prices for these products that have been set by American pricing standards. So, in this case, American software companies have not lost any (real) revenues because their software would not be sold on the open market in most developing countries. And worse yet, these critics argue, individuals and organizations in those nations would not have access to software, if it were not for the unauthorized copies that have become available to them.

Corporations also worry about revenues lost in developed nations, including the United States, through the practice of copying software illegally. Some people believe that a distinction should be drawn between cases in which an individual makes an unauthorized copy of a friend's software program for personal use and practices in which corporations and criminals pirate software in a systematic way for profit. In terms of the economic and social consequences that can result from these two different modes of software piracy, the differences are materially significant. From a moral point of view, however, this factor may not make much of a difference.

Jurisdictional and International Challenges for Copyright Law

The copyright laws and amendments described in this section apply specifically to intellectual property in the United States. However, their implications are global because of the use of American-manufactured software products internationally. One obvious problem, of course, is how to enforce U.S. copyright law, or for that matter any nation's copyright laws, in an international arena. Some international treaties pertaining to intellectual property and copyright have been signed in recent years. For example, the Trade Relationship Aspects of Intellectual Property Standards (TRIPS) agreement implemented requirements from the Berne Convention for the Protection of Literary and Artistic Works. This international agreement is recognized by signatories to the World Intellectual Property Organization (WIPO), and it enunciates minimal standards of legal protection for intellectual property.

Nonetheless, intellectual property laws have been very difficult to enforce not only at the international level, but even within certain countries, such as the U.S., where different states can have different laws affecting the sale of goods and contracts involving goods and services. This has become especially apparent in e-commerce activities, where laws applicable to the sale of goods as well as to contracts involved in those sales, often vary from state to state. Recently, some legislative attempts have been made to improve uniformity across states in the U.S. One attempt has been through the Uniform Commerce Code (UCC), a law aimed at clarifying the rights and obligations of parties to the "sale of goods and contracts" and to the "lease of goods." Two other important pieces of legislation that could also significantly affect contracts are the Uniform Computer and Information Transactions ACT (UCITA) and the Uniform Electronic Transactions ACT (UETA). Whereas UCITA is designed to govern computer information transactions, UETA applies to electronic contracts in general. We discuss UCITA in greater detail in a later section of this chapter.

Patents

How is patent protection different from the kind of protection granted by copyright law? A patent is a form of legal protection given to individuals who create an invention or process. Patent protection is covered in Title 35 of the U.S. Code. As in the case of copyright law, the basis for patent protection can be found in Article 1, Section 8 of the U.S. Constitution. Unlike copyright protection,

patents offer a 20-year exclusive monopoly over an expression or implementation of a protected work. Patent law provides "thicker" protection than copyright protection, but for a shorter period. The first explicit U.S. patent law, the Patent Act of 1793, was passed when Thomas Jefferson was the administrator of the patent system. The present U.S. patent statute is based on the Patent Act of 1952, as amended in 1995.

Patent protection applies to inventions and discoveries that include utilitarian or functional devices such as machines, articles of manufacture, or "compositions of matter." The Patent Act requires three conditions to be satisfied for a patent to be granted. First, an invention must have a certain *usefulness* or utility in order to be awarded a patent. Inventing a machine that does nothing useful would not merit the inventor of such a machine a patent. Second, the invention must be *novel* or new in order to qualify for a patent. One cannot simply modify an existing invention and expect to be given a patent for it. The modification would have to be significant enough to make a "qualified difference." Third, the invention or process must be *non-obvious*. For example, it is possible that no one has yet recorded directions for how to travel from Ithaca, New York to Montreal, Canada, via Columbus, Ohio. However, describing the process for doing this would not satisfy the condition regarding non-obviousness.

Three different kinds of patents have been distinguished: design patents, utility patents, and plant patents. Only the first two of these, however, are of particular interest for computers and computer software. Whereas design patents protect any new, original, and ornamental design for an article of manufacture, utility patents protect any new, useful, and non-obvious process, machine, or article of manufacture. Patent protection provides a firm or individual inventor with the right to exclude others from making, using, or selling or importing the claimed invention for a twenty-year period.

The goal of the patent system's exclusionary, output-restricting monopolies is to reward and stimulate inventive efforts, which often require considerable investment. The presumption is that tight (or "thick") property protection will give the innovator the incentive to invent and provide an environment "conducive to securing the complementary assets, capital, manufacturing, marketing and support" that are necessary in order to bring that invention to the marketplace (Kieff, 2000).

Patenting Computer Programs

While computer hardware inventions clearly satisfied the requirements of patent law, this was not initially the case with computer software. In the 1960s, discussions involving the protection for software focused mainly on patents (Snapper, 1994). However, the U.S. Patent Office and the courts established a strong opposition to patents, beginning with the *Gottschalk v. Benson* (1972) decision. Benson had applied for a patent for an algorithm he developed that translated the representation of numbers from base 10 to base 2. Such an algorithm is an important feature of all programs. If granted a patent for his algorithm, however, Benson would have controlled almost every computer in use for 12 years. The patent was denied to Benson on the basis of a policy that bars the granting of patents for mere mathematical formulas or abstract processes, which are such that they can be performed by a series of "mental steps" with the aid of pencil and paper.

In the controversial court case *Diamond v. Diehr*, whose outcome was the result of a 5-4 decision, a patent was finally awarded in the case of a computer program. In this instance, the program assisted in a process of converting rubber into tires. On the one hand, Diehr had developed a new process that physically transformed raw rubber into rubber tires. On the other hand, it seemed that Diehr had only a new computer program, since all of the parts of the machine used

in the conversion process consisted of traditional technology except for the computer program. Initially, Diehr's request for a patent was denied by Diamond, the director of the Patent Office. Diehr appealed, and this case was then taken to the U.S. Supreme Court. Although the Court ruled in favor of Diehr, the justices, in their decision, continued to affirm the view that computer algorithms themselves are not patentable. They pointed out that the patent awarded to Diehr was not for the computer program but for the rubber tire transformation process as a whole.

Since the decision reached in the Diehr case, patents have been granted to computer programs and software applications. Some fear that patent protection has now gone too far. Consider that the U.S. Patent and Trademark Office (PTO) currently issues approximately 20,000 new software patents every year. Aharonian (1999) points out that between 1993 and 1999, the number of patents issued represented a tenfold increase. He also points out that between 1979 and 1999, more than 700,000 patents had been issued for electronics inventions, including software products.

Because of what some critics believe to be an overly generous granting of patent protections in the case of computer programs and user interfaces, many have recently expressed concerns about how far patent protection should be extended in this area. For example, some specific concerns have recently been raised about which kinds of features in the user interfaces should be eligible for patent protection. Should the "look and feel" of the interface or other amorphous features be eligible for protection?

Proliferation of Patents

It should be underscored that the scope of patent protection has been steadily expanding. In addition to software, it is now possible to obtain patents for gene fragments, biological material, and living organisms (see *Diamond v. Chakrabarty*, 447 U.S. 303, 1980). Even mundane "business methods," such as a hub-and-spoke mutual fund accounting system, have become patentable subject matter. These patents have been particularly popular for online businesses. We consider the possible abuse of such patents in the context of reviewing the Amazon.com case in the section on current controversies.

Given the steady growth in the number of patents awarded, it is no surprise that patents have come under increasing criticism in recent years. The patent system's detractors argue that the patent monopoly and the right to exclude gives the patent owner control over price, which normally creates a deadweight loss for society. While these detractors recognize the need for rewards as incentives, they propose other possibilities besides a property right. For example, Shavell and van Ypersele (1999) propose a system of government-sponsored cash payouts as an alternative to awarding patents. According to this system, inventions would immediately become part of the public domain. The amount of the reward would depend on the demand for the innovation as ascertained by its sales or other relevant data. But as Kieff (2000) observes, this reward system runs the risk of neglecting commercialization activities subsequent to the actual invention; these activities include raising capital for production facilities, creating distribution channels, marketing to consumers, and so forth. A limited property right and the exclusivity that it engenders, however, provides the incentive for both the invention and commercialization. According to Kieff (2000):

The patent right to exclude competitors who have not shared in bearing these initial costs provides incentives for the holder of the invention and the other players in the market to come together and incur all costs necessary to facilitate commercialization of the patented invention. (p.715)

The U.S. patent system is not perfect and there are valid concerns about the expanding scope of patent protection. However, the case for alternatives to the current system that confer a property right of limited duration must adequately deal with critical post-invention issues such as commercialization.

Trademarks

Trademarks are a form of intellectual property protection that differs in key respects from both patents and copyrights. A trademark is a word, name phrase, or symbol that identifies a product or service. The Lanham Act, also referred to as the Trademark Act of 1946, was passed to provide protection for owners of registered trademarks. One purpose of this Act was to help ensure that the quality associated with a certain logo or symbol used by a business actually represents the quality that consumers expect. So for example, when a consumer sees a Mercedes Benz or a BMW emblem, he or she can expect that the product will live up to the standards of the Mercedes Benz or the BMW industry. Some common trademarks in the United States are the golden arch-like "M" that has come to symbolize McDonald's restaurants, and the expression "coke" that symbolizes Coca-Cola. A corporation, or for that matter an individual, can typically acquire a trademark when it either: (a) is the first to use the word or expression publicly, or (b) explicitly registers the trademark with the U.S. Patent Office.

In order to qualify for a trademark, the "mark" or name is supposed to be *distinctive*. However, Halbert (1997) points out that a trademark for "uh-huh" was granted to Pepsi. Because of decisions such as this, Halbert and others have argued that trademark protections are being expanded in ways that are inappropriate and potentially damaging to the market place. A recent example that tends to support such a concern can be found in a case involving America On-Line (AOL), a major Internet Service Provider (ISP). AOL attempted to register as official trademarks a number of its symbols, including the following expressions:

"You've Got Mail," "Buddy List," and "IM" (for Instant Messenger). If granted these trademarks, other ISPs who used these expressions could be charged with infringing on AOL's registered trademarks. When AT&T challenged AOL, however, the court decided that the expressions in question were not unique to AOL and thus could not qualify for registration as trademarks.

Trademark Controversies Involving Internet Domain Names

One particularly contentious issue concerning trademark disputes in cyberspace has involved the registering of Internet domain names. A *domain name* is an alphanumeric string of characters that identifies a unique address on the Web. The domain name is included in the address of a Universal Resource Locator (URL), e.g., http://www.usersite.net. The actual domain name itself immediately follows the hypertext transfer protocol (http://) and the Web (www) portions of the URL. Google.com, stanford.edu, and ABC.org are examples of domain names. Before 1998, the registration of domain names in the United States was administered by the National Science Foundation (NSF). This organization set up a network division (NSFNET) to oversee certain aspects of Internet governance. When Congress approved commerce on the Internet in 1992, it charged NSFNET with the task of working with Network Solutions, a private organization, to develop a scheme for determining how domain names would be assigned in the future. In the original NSF system, domain names were typically registered on a first-come, first-served basis. There was neither a clear nor a systematic policy for deciding which domain names one was eligible or ineligible to register. And this practice resulted in some confusion for Web users, especially those who assumed that there would be a correlation between a Web site's domain name and its corresponding content. However, if a user wished to access the Web site for the White House (in Washington, DC) via the URL www.whitehouse.com, he or she would connect to a pornographic site (since the White House site is www.whitehouse.gov.).

At first glance, one might assume that the confusion that resulted over Internet domain names was little more than a minor nuisance. From the perspective of property rights and commerce, however, a serious issue arose when certain individuals registered domain names containing key phrases or symbols that were previously registered as legal trademarks in physical space, such as the words "Disney," or "Playboy." One controversial case involved the domain name "candyland." It turned out that the first applicant for the candyland.com domain name was not Hasbro, the toy manufacturer who marketed the Candyland game, but instead was the operator of a pornographic Web site. Many trademark owners were outraged by the ways in which their registered trademarks were being co-opted and "abused" in cyberspace, and some filed trademark infringement suits against owners and operators of Web sites whose domain names included symbols identical to their trademarks.

In the early 1990s, there were no explicit laws in place to prevent an individual or an organization from registering a domain name that potentially conflicted with a registered trademark in physical space. Nor was it altogether clear that trademarks registered in physical space necessarily applied to cyberspace. Because there were no laws or policies governing domain name registration, there was also nothing to prevent some individuals and companies from registering as many domain names as they could afford. A few individuals who did this became wealthy when they later sold the rights to their registered domain names to corporations who wished to procure domain names that were either identical to or closely resembled the trademarks they had registered in physical space. However, not all individuals and corporations were willing to pay an exorbitant price for the right to use a domain names, especially since they believed they already had the legal right to own the name by virtue of their registered trademarks in physical space. In the legal disputes that ensued, those who had registered domain names that were either identical to or closely resembled the names of trademarks previously registered in physical space were referred to as "cybersquatters." Many trademark owners argued that these cybersquatters were unfairly using a mark that already had been registered, and they petitioned Congress for legislation to protect their trademarks. In 1999, the Anticybersquatting Consumer Protection Act was passed, which enables trademark holders to file suit against anyone who uses or registers a domain name that is identical to or "confusingly similar" to their trademark.

Arguably, trademark owners had a legitimate concern about the ways in which certain symbols or "marks" with which they had come to be identified by millions of people were now being abused. Among these concerns was the issue of "trademark dilution," where a trademark becomes less effective because of similar sounding marks used by competitors and adversaries. This was especially apparent in a case involving Amazon.com, who claimed that its trademark would be diluted if some variation of the "Amazon" trademark were allowed to be registered by a "bricks-and-mortar" bookstore that had also used the "Amazon" name. Initially, one would assume that Amazon.com would have a good case for registering "Amazon" both as a trademark and a domain name. Before the Amazon.com e-commerce site had been developed, however, a bookstore named Amazon had been operating in Minneapolis, Minnesota. This bookstore was fairly well known to many people who lived in the Minneapolis area. In April 1999, the Amazon bookstore sued Amazon.com for trademark infringement. It is important to note that the "bricks-and-mortar" Amazon bookstore had never formally registered the "Amazon" trademark. However, in the U.S. there is also the concept of a "common law" trademark, which would apply to the physical bookstore as long as the store simply used the "Amazon" mark. Because

the Amazon bookstore had not formally applied to register the "Amazon" trademark, it is quite conceivable that Amazon.com was unfamiliar with the existence of this store. Defenders of Amazon.com questioned why the Amazon bookstore waited so long in filing its suit. In litigation involving trademark disputes, "delay in filing a suit" can be a relevant factor in determining the suit's legal outcome.

We should note that the policy for assigning domain names has tightened considerably since 1998, when the Federal Government directed the Commerce Department to supervise the administration of the Domain Name System. The Internet Corporation for Assigned Names and Numbers (ICANN) has since become responsible for assigning and registering domain names. However, ICANN has been criticized for implementing policies that some believe to be heavily biased towards those who owned trademarks previously registered in physical space.

Trade Secrets

Trade secrets as a form of property protection are significantly different from trademarks, patents, and copyrights. A trade secret is usually defined as information used in the operation of a business or other enterprise that is "sufficiently valuable and secret" to afford an actual or potential economic advantage over others. Included in the kind of data that trade secrets can be used to protect are: *formulas* (such as the one used by Coca-Cola), *blueprints* for future projects, *chemical compounds*, and *process of manufacturing*.

Trade secrets are generally recognized as "secrets" on which a company has expended money and energy and that are shown only to a select few major persons within an organization. Owners of a trade secret have exclusive rights to make use of a secret. However, they have this right *only as long* as the secret is maintained.

Many states in the U.S. have adopted the Uniform Trade Secrets Act (UTSA). According to this Act, a trade secret is defined as "information, including a formula, pattern, compilation, program, device, technique, or process" that (1) derives independent economic value from not being generally known to … other persons who can obtain economic value from its disclosure or use, and (2) is the subject that are reasonable under the circumstances to maintain its secrecy.

A major problem with protecting trade secrets is that trade secret law is difficult to enforce at the international level. Not only have corporate spies in the U.S. tried to steal secrets from their corporate rivals, but there is evidence to suggest that international industrial espionage has become a growing "industry." Recently, the world community has acknowledged the need for member states to protect against the disclosure of trade secrets. The Agreement on Trade-Related Aspects of Intellectual Property Rights (TRIPS), which was part of the World Intellectual Property Organization (WIPO) agreements (described in a preceding section), provides a platform for protecting trade secrets at the international level. Specifically, Article 39 of the TRIPS Agreement protects trade secrets by stating explicitly that disclosure of trade secrets "comes within the meaning of unfair competition in the global community."

RECENT LEGISLATION

In the previous section we noted that two recent amendments to United States copyright law, the Copyright Term Extension Act (CTEA) and the Digital Millennium Copyright Act (DMCA), have been highly controversial. In this section, we consider critical aspects of each act in more detail. We also examine recent legislation involving the No Electronic Theft (NET) Act and the Uniform Computer and Information Transactions Act (UCITA), which also have been subject to controversy.

Copyright Term Extension Act (CTEA)

The Copyright Term Extension Act represents the fourth major extension of the duration for copyright protection. This Act, passed by Congress and signed by President Clinton in 1998, maintained the general structure of the 1976 Copyright Act as it expanded the term for copyrights by 20 years. For creative works created by identifiable persons, the term is now 70 years after the author's death. For anonymous works and works "made for hire" (usually commissioned by corporations), the term is now 95 years from publication or 120 years from creation, whichever expires first (17 U.S.C. § 302 (c)).

Critics of the controversial CTEA did not fail to note that the law was passed just in time to keep "Mickey Mouse" from entering the public domain. Many of these critics have also pointed out that the Disney Corporation lobbied very hard for the passage of this act. In a subsequent section we examine a recent case that illustrates one way in which the CTEA threatens the communication of information that once had been in the public domain but is now protected by copyright law. The case (*Eldred v. Ashcroft*) involves Eric Eldred of Derry, NH, who operated a personal (non-profit) Web site on which he included electronic versions of classic books that have been in the public domain. With the passage of the CTEA in 1998, some of the books that were previously included in the public domain and also included on Eldred's site came under copyright protection. So Eldred found himself in violation of the new copyright law. Rather than remove books from his site, however, Eldred decided to challenge the legality of the amended Copyright Act, which he argued is incompatible with the fair-use provision of copyright law and in violation of Article 1, Section 8, Clause 8 of the U.S. Constitution (see above).

At issue is whether or not Congress exceeded its legislative authority as bestowed upon it by the

Copyright Clause of the Constitution. Does the CTEA violate the Copyright Clause's "limited Times" restriction? Another concern is whether the CTEA conflicts with First Amendment rights. We will consider these issues in more depth in the next section which treats the *Eldred v. Ashcroft* case.

Digital Millennium Copyright Act (DMCA)

We noted in a previous section of this chapter that the DMCA has been a heavily disputed piece of legislation, particularly because of its "anti-circumvention" clause (1201(a)). This anti-circumvention provision prohibits the circumvention or bypassing of any technological measure (such as encryption mechanisms) that controls access to protected works. The DMCA (1998) also forbids the manufacturing, providing, distributing or otherwise "trafficking in" any software or hardware technology that is designed to facilitate *circumvention* of a protected work (§1201 (a) (2)). While the DMCA prohibits the circumvention of *access* control measures, it does not prohibit the circumvention of *use* control measures. Access controls deter unauthorized access to a protected work, but use controls help prevent unauthorized use. A user might have legitimate access to a work, but a "use control" may limit that user's ability to print or copy that work. Paradoxically, however, it is also forbidden to manufacture, distribute, or traffic in devices that circumvent use control measures (§1201 (c)).

There are exceptions to these provisions. Reverse engineering in order to achieve interoperability is allowed (subject to certain conditions). The DMCA also incorporates an exception for "good faith encryption research" or for security research. The researcher must make every effort to obtain permission from the copyright holder before implementing the circumvention device.

Despite these exceptions, critics have highlighted many problems with the DMCA, such as its implicit subversion of the fair-use exemption. The DMCA makes it virtually impossible to circumvent encryption measures for fair use of protected works. For example, it threatens our ability to use electronic books in many of the same ways that we have been able to use physical books. Consider the case involving Dimitri Sklyarov. While working for a Moscow-based company called ElcomSoft, Sklyarov had written a program that was able to decrypt the code for an electronic book reader ("e-book reader") developed by Adobe, an American-base software company. Adobe's Acrobat e-Reader product was designed so that computer users could read digital books. Adobe was very concerned that with Sklyarov's program, users would be able to read e-books for free.

The United States Government was eager to test the DMCA, especially the Act's anti-circumvention clause. Although the Act was passed in 1998, it was not enforceable as a law until 2000. So the Sklyarov incident in the summer of 2001 provided an opportune time for law officials to prosecute a case under the provisions of the DMCA. When Sklyarov attended a computer security conference in Las Vegas, Nevada in July 2001, he was arrested by federal authorities who immediately seized his briefcase containing the controversial program. Sklyarov's arrest sparked considerable controversy and protest, especially among software engineers who realized, perhaps more than most ordinary users, the significance of the controversy at issue. A "Free Sklyarov" movement developed on the part of some protesters. Even some conservatives, who tend to be proponents of strong copyright protection, believe that the DMCA may have gone too far. While many protesters in the Sklyarov case believed that Adobe had a legitimate concern, they were also troubled by the fact that the principle of fair use was being technologically undermined by Adobe and legally undermined by the DMCA.

Some critics also pointed out the DMCA violates the principle of first sale, another element in the balancing scheme embodied in current copyright law. These critics correctly pointed out that in the case of a physical (paper and glue) book, one could do whatever one wishes after purchasing it. For example, one could lend the book or parts of the book to a friend. Also, one could make a photocopy of a chapter in that book. And, finally, one could resell that book in compliance with the first-sale principle provided under copyright law. In the case of e-books, however, one does not have the right to sell or even to give away the digital book because of the kind of protection granted to copyright holders of digital media under the DMCA. Adobe eventually dropped its charges against Sklyarov. However, most critics believe that the fundamental principles underlying the Sklyarov incident have not yet been challenged and ultimately will need to be resolved through future litigation.

The No Electronic Theft (NET) Act

The NET (No Electronic Theft) Act makes the dissemination of copyrighted information by electronic means a criminal act. In other words, it criminalizes behavior involving the distribution of copyrighted material, which traditionally could only be contested in a civil court. This Act was passed, in part at least, in response to an incident involving MIT student Robert LaMacchia who had facilitated the distribution of copyrighted software over an electronic bulletin board system in the Spring of 1994. When authorities tried to prosecute LaMacchia, they found that they were unable to do so because no explicit laws existed that made the unauthorized distribution of copyright material over a computer network a criminal act.

Prior to the NET Act, a person had to "infringe a copyright willfully and for purposes of commercial or financial gain" in order to be punished under the criminal provisions of the Copyright Act. The NET Act, however, has made criminal the "reproduction or distribution, including by electronic means...of one or more copies or phonorecords of one or more copyrighted works, which have a total retail value of more than $1,000." Grosso (2000) believes that the meaning of "copyright infringement" has been expanded under this act. For example, he points out that in addition to a copyright infringement occurring in "fixation" (in print or paper), an infringement can now occur in virtual space as well. In other words, a possible infringement can occur by means of a mere electronic distribution, regardless of whether that work is ever printed on paper or downloaded onto a diskette or CD. According to the NET Act, the mere viewing of a copyrighted work posted on the Internet can be interpreted as a violation of copyright that is criminal. In one possible interpretation, a "fixation" occurs in online viewing, because a temporary copy is "fixed" in the memory (i.e., in RAM) of the host computer, no matter how briefly the information may be stored. While many agree with the spirit of the Net Act, others believe that it goes too far.

UCITA

Earlier in this chapter we noted that in the United States, the various states have different laws affecting the contracts that govern the sale of goods and services. Electronic commerce and software licenses have been directly affected by this lack of uniformity. We also noted that recently some legislative attempts, such as UCITA (the Uniform Computer and Information Transactions Act), have been designed to improve uniformity across states and to govern computer/information transactions, including contracts for the development, sale, licensing, maintenance, and support of computer software. This Act, which extends to all shrink-wrap and "click-wrap" agreements, is an attempt to develop a single national framework that would help states address issues such as warranties and software licenses. For example, the law would turn the consumer license that comes with shrink-wrapped software into a binding contract.

To date, UCITA has been enacted into law only in the states of Virginia and Maryland. Even though UCITA is not law in most states, its effects can be felt in all states because contracts involving electronic goods and services can span multiple states and thus potentially involve Virginia and Maryland law in the process. Although there is general agreement that a uniform law across states pertaining to electronic contracts would be desirable, many worry about the effects that universal passage of the current version of UCITA would have for consumers in the United States.

UCITA's critics are concerned that the further enactment of this law by additional state legislatures will have negative consequences for consumers and for the general public. Thus far, UCITA has been criticized by the Software Engineering Ethics Research Institute and the American Library Association, as well as by many consumer advocacy groups. Many critics believe that this act overreaches because it would (a) give software vendors the right to repossess software by disabling it remotely if the vendor perceived a violation of the licensing agreement, and (b) prevent the transfer of licenses from one party to another without vendor permission. Some critics also worry that UCITA would undermine existing consumer protection laws and would threaten current copyright exceptions for the principles of fair use and first sale (Tavani, 2004).

UCITA's defenders, however, which include companies such as Microsoft and AOL, have lobbied hard on behalf of UCITA. They have tried to persuade lawmakers that UCITA would be good for e-commerce and would create more jobs, especially in the computer industry. Critics, however, believe that these companies simply want increased control over the products they license—controls that UCITA's opponents argue would further ensure that these products cannot be passed along from one party to another without

vendor approval. Other critics of UTICA point to a certain irony by noting that at the same time software vendors argue for the need for greater control over the licensing of their products, they have lobbied for the right to be exempt from responsibility and liability for those products.

DIGITAL RIGHTS MANAGEMENT AND TRUSTED PLATFORMS

Intellectual property can be protected by other means than the law. There are the community's social norms that inhibit copying another's original work. And there is what Lessig (1999) calls "code." In this context, code refers primarily to software programs (such as an encryption mechanism) that limit access and use of a protected work. It is instructive to consider the implications of the more widespread diffusion of these software architectures.

DRM Technology

Copyright and patent law may be difficult to enforce especially in cyberspace, but a code-based solution has the potential to be a more powerful substitute for the law. The content industry believes that Digital rights management (DRM) systems can be an important tool for preventing copyright infringement by imposing restrictive rules on end users.

As noted earlier, the music and movie industries need new business models since their traditional way of doing business has been disrupted by digital technology. Effective DRM will enable those new models by allowing digital content to be sold and distributed on a more secure basis. DRM encompasses a range of technologies that will give content providers varying degrees of control over how content will be accessed and utilized. At a most basic level, DRM will prevent access to creative works, usually by means of encryption.

Access is enabled for legitimate users through the use of passwords or similar mechanisms.

Thus, DRM can lock up content and prevent unauthorized access. It can also control how that content is used once it is legitimately accessed. DRM systems can embed rules that restrict the user's ability to copy that content and to transmit it to someone else. For example, a DRM technology might be configured so that it allows a user to make only a single copy of a CD. Or in the case of digital books, it may allow viewing of the book but forbid printing and transmission to another user. According to McSwain (1999), DRM (or "trusted") systems perform two basic functions: first, these systems make sure that the content is maintained "in a secure 'container,' either hardware or software, which performs encryption and decryption on the digital software"; and second, this container "stores precise instructions detailing which uses to permit, which uses to deny, and how much to charge for each, thereby 'managing' the rights relationship between the user and content provider."

A DRM application can run on an ordinary operating system such as Windows or Macintosh, but it's also possible to incorporate this functionality directly into the operating system itself. In 2002, Microsoft announced that it was working on a new operating system known as Palladium, a trusted computer platform that provides a secure environment for other applications. A machine running an OS such as Palladium would obey instructions of the programs that forward data to this machine. If an online music store sends a song with an instruction "play this one time," the Palladium OS would ensure that this command was automatically followed.

DRM technology can work hand-in-hand with the Digital Millennium Copyright Act, which bans circumvention of access controls along with the production of technologies that facilitate circumvention. Since all code is prone to attacks by hackers, the DMCA serves as a legal fallback in case DRM code is penetrated. Those who dare to bypass these DRM controls will run afoul of § 1201 of the DMCA, which gives victims the opportunity to sue for damages and to seek injunctive relief.

Standardizing DRM Controls

A universal DRM standard for computers systems can emerge in one of several ways. In one scenario, the PC industry and its complementors (for example, the content providers) could simply agree on the adoption of a single de facto standard. This process took place in the late 1990s when the movie industry settled on content scrambling system (CSS) as a standard for DVDs and DVD players. Encrypted DVDs could only be played on CSS-compliant machines. If this type of industry consensus fails to occur, it's possible that federal legislation will be enacted to demand the implementation of a standard DRM technology.

If there are multiple versions of DRM technology, the end result will be consumer confusion and chaos. Thus, agreeing upon or mandating a standard for DRM would undoubtedly overcome this chaos and hasten its acceptance. One U.S. senator has proposed the Consumer Broadband and Digital Television Promotion Act that would require the relevant industries to reach such a standard. That bill would also require digital media devices to include DRM architecture. Under this law, failure to make a digital media device without DRM would constitute a felony (Samuelson, 2003).

But without government intervention, a de facto standard could still quickly emerge, given the potential for significant network effects. Manufacturers of DVD and similar equipment will have a big incentive to make their systems compliant with the emerging standard, or they may find themselves excluded from major content markets. Once the content and entertainment equipment industries begin "tipping" toward such a standard, it will rapidly dominate the marketplace as more and more companies rush to adopt that standard.

Critical Concerns

Despite the fact that DRMs will undoubtedly be susceptible to countermeasures, this scheme for automation of copyright enforcement is unsettling. For one thing, "DRM permits content owners to exercise far more control over uses of copyrighted works than copyright law provides" (Samuelson, 2003). For example, DRM systems prohibit access even for fair use purposes.

One way to resolve this problem is to construct DRMs that incorporate provisions such as fair use. The legal conception of fair use, however, is fuzzy and open to subjective interpretation. Hence it will be difficult to develop mathematical models that will allow for fair-use exceptions to protected works. However, despite the vagueness of fair use, it may be possible to develop a subset of fair-use possibilities that can be embedded in DRM code, such as allowing for the creation of single copy of a digital work expressly for personal use. Fox and LaMacchia (2003) explain that this set of "always available" licenses (that is, fair-use rights expressed in a policy language) becomes "the first safe harbor for DRM implementers."

In addition, some DRM technologies are designed to report back to content providers, especially in pay-per-use contexts. Other systems might be set up to collect data regarding user preferences for content provided. There is some danger, therefore, that DRM could threaten privacy rights by invading a user's private space and recording his or her intellectual interests.

Finally, some economists contend that DRM technology could potentially harm innovation. These economists maintain that a considerable amount of innovation comes from the users themselves, who will be less able to experiment on a trusted platform. Thus, user-based innovation is apt to be curtailed if software usage is restricted and monitored after the software has been purchased.

CONTROVERSIAL ISSUES AND LEGAL CASES

We have so far considered normative theories defending property rights along with theoretical questions about the moral viability of these rights which, for some scholars, threaten the intellectual commons. We have also reviewed the legal infrastructure, recent legislation, and new technologies designed to safeguard those rights. We turn now to the more practical dimensions of intellectual property issues.

The commercialization of the Internet along with challenges to recent legislation have led to a number of important legal cases regarding intellectual property protection. In this section we will review some of the more significant cases and thereby highlight several major current controversies.

Napster and Peer to Peer Networks

The meteoric rise of digital music has been made possible by a standard known as MP3, an audio-compression format that creates near-CD-quality files that are as much as 20 times smaller than the files on a standard music CD. Thanks to MP3, digital music can now be accessed and transmitted over the Web without the need of a physical container such as a compact disk.

Napster was one of the first companies to take advantage of this new distribution method. This software, created by a young college student, functioned by allowing a Napster user to access the computer systems of other Napster users to search for a particular piece of music as long as they had installed Napster's free file-sharing software. Once that music was located, it could be downloaded directly from that system in

MP3 format and stored on the user's hard drive. Napster did not store or "cache" any digital music files on its own servers, and it was not involved in any copying of music files. Napster's role was confined to the maintenance of a central directory of the shareable music available among all Napster users.

In December 1999, the Recording Industry Association of America (RIAA) claimed that Napster was culpable of secondary liability for all of the copyright violations taking place on its system. Secondary liability refers to liability for acts of copyright infringement performed by another person. It can encompass contributory liability, which occurs when one party encourages or assists the infringement of another party, and vicarious liability, which occurs when one party has the ability to control the infringer's activities and enjoys direct financial benefits as a result of those activities.

The RIAA sued Napster for both vicarious and contributory copyright infringement, demanding $100,000 each time a copyrighted song was downloaded by a Napster user. In the summer of 2000, a federal district court granted the RIAA's request for a preliminary injunction ordering the company to shut down its file-sharing service. But two days later the U.S. Court of Appeals for the Ninth Circuit stayed the injunction so that Napster could have its day in court.

At trial, the plaintiffs argued that a majority of Napster users were downloading and uploading copyrighted music and that these actions constituted direct infringement of the musical recordings owned by the plaintiffs. And since Napster users were culpable of direct copyright infringement, Napster itself was liable for contributory copyright infringement, that is, for materially contributing to the direct infringement.

In its defense, Napster presented several key arguments, invoking the protection of the 1998 Digital Millennium Copyright Act (DMCA), which provides a "safe harbor" for Internet Service Providers (or search engines) against liability

for copyright infringement committed by their customers (§ 512). Napster also argued that its users often downloaded MP3 files to sample their contents before making a decision about whether or not to make a CD purchase. Napster cited the precedent of *Universal City Studios* v. *Sony Corp. of America* (1979) litigation. In that case, Universal had sued VCR manufacturer Sony for copyright infringement, but the Supreme Court ruled in favor of the defendant, reasoning that a VCR is capable of substantial noninfringing uses and that its manufacturers should therefore be immune from secondary liability when infringement does occur. One such noninfringing use would be "time-shifting," that is, taping a movie or television show so that it could be viewed at a different time. Thus, manufacturers of "staple articles of commerce" (like VCRs) that have "commercially significant noninfringing uses" cannot be held liable for contributory infringement just because they have general knowledge that some of the purchasers of that equipment might use it to make unauthorized copies of copyrighted material. Napster analogized itself to a VCR—since Napster could also be used for noninfringing purposes (e.g., downloading non-copyrighted music), the company should be immune from liability when its users infringe copyrights.

But in the end, all of these arguments were to no avail. Napster's lawyers failed to persuade the U.S. Court of Appeals for the Ninth Circuit, which found that "the district court did not err; Napster, by its conduct, knowingly encourages and assists the infringement of plaintiffs' copyrights" (*A&M Records, Inc. v. Napster*, 2001).

The demise of Napster, however, did little to impede the rapid growth of file sharing as the Napster service was replaced by true peer-to-peer (P2P) networks. Unlike server-based technology, with peer-to-peer software such as KaZaA, any computer in the network can function as the distribution point. In this way, one central server is not inundated with requests from multiple clients. P2P systems, therefore, enable communications among individual personal computers relying on the Internet infrastructure. For example, a user can prompt his or her personal computer to ask other PCs in a peer-to-peer network if they have a certain digital file. That request is passed along from computer to computer within the network until the file is located and a copy is sent along to the requester's system.

Thus, peer-to-peer networks differ from Napster technology in several salient respects. There is no central server that maintains a list of files that users can download. In addition, these networks allow for the exchange of a wide range of material in addition to MP3 music files, including movie files, books and other text files, and even photographs. This fact has been seized upon by defenders of P2P who insist that its proprietors should be protected by the Sony ruling, since these networks are capable of significant noninfringing uses.

KaZaA is the most popular music sharing software with approximately 275 million users (as of September 2003) and about three million new users added each week (Delaney, 2003). The software was created under the leadership of Niklas Zennstrom who cofounded a Dutch company called KaZaA, BV in order to distribute the KaZaA software. Zennstrom sold the software to Sharman Networks (located on a South Pacific island called Vanuatu) in early 2002, partly out of concern over impending lawsuits. Sharman's servers are in Denmark and its employees are contracted through an Australian company called LEF.

KaZaA, BV was sued in a Netherlands court for contributory copyright infringement. In the U.S., liability for contributory infringement can be imposed on anyone who "with knowledge of the infringing activity, induces, causes, or materially contributes to the infringing conduct" of the guilty party (*Gershwin Publishing v. Columbia Artists Mgmt*, 1971). KaZaA, BV lost the first round of the case, but in March 2002, a Netherlands court of appeals overturned the lower court

ruling and held that KaZaA should not be held liable for the unlawful acts of those who use its software. According to the Amsterdam Appellate Court (2002),

The KaZaA application does not depend on any intervention by KaZaA, BV. The program is expanded and functions even better by means of the services provided by KaZaA plus it can be better controlled that way. These services, however, are not necessary for the locating and exchanging of files. . . With the present state of standardization, it is not possible to technically detect which files are copyrighted and which are not. Thus, it is not possible for KaZaA (or any other software) to incorporate a blockage against the unlawful exchange of files.

This ruling seems generally consistent with the U.S. *Sony* decision, which appears to immunize the manufacture and distribution of technologies like P2P networks for which there are substantial noninfringing uses.

In addition, in the United States, the music and movie industries have also filed suit against Grokster and StreamCast for contributory and vicarious copyright infringement. Grokster uses the FastTrack networking technology that it has licensed from KaZaA, and StreamCast uses a variation of the Gnutella P2P network. The plaintiffs (which include MGM, Disney, Universal City Studios, Warner Music, Motown Records, Arista Records, et al.) contended that both of these networks were employed for the purpose of swapping copyrighted music and movie files: "90% of the works available on the FastTrack network demonstrably were infringing, and over 70% belonged to Plaintiffs" (Plaintiffs' Joint Excerpts of Record, 2003). The plaintiffs lost the first round of this case when a California district court granted the defendants' motion for summary judgment. The case has been appealed to the Ninth Circuit and a decision is pending.

At issue in this case is the applicability of previous rulings in the Napster and Sony cases. The defendants argue that the Sony precedent works strongly in their favor; i.e., they are immunized from liability since they are simply providing a "staple article of commerce." In *Sony v. Universal* (1984), the Supreme Court had concluded that a judgement in favor of Universal would give copyright holders some measure of control over non-copyright markets: "It seems extraordinary to suggest that the Copyright Act confers upon all copyright owners collectively, much less the two respondents in this case, the exclusive right to distribute [VCRs] simply because they may be used to infringe copyrights."

It is instructive to review why the *Sony* standard did not rescue Napster from secondary liability. The District Court ruled that Napster could not be construed as a "staple article of commerce" because of Napster's ongoing relationship with its users. According to the Court, "Napster's primary role of facilitating the unauthorized copying and distribution [of] established artists' songs renders *Sony* inapplicable" (*A&M Records v. Napster*, 2000). The Ninth Circuit, however, was not so quick to dismiss the *Sony* precedent: "The *Sony* Court declined to impute the requisite level of knowledge where the defendants made and sold equipment capable of both infringing and 'substantial noninfringing uses' … We are bound to follow *Sony* and will not impute the requisite level of knowledge to Napster merely because peer-to-peer file-sharing technology may be used to infringe plaintiffs' copyrights" (*A&M Records v. Napster*, 2001). However, since Napster had actual notice of infringing activities and made no effort to prevent those activities, the Ninth Circuit found that this rule for "imputing knowledge" did not apply.

One critical question for the *Grokster* case is the applicability of the *Sony* case. In an Amici Curiae Brief, forty law professors argued that the standard set by the Sony case should immunize from secondary liability those who develop technologies that have the capability for substantial noninfringing uses. They argue for the soundness of this "mere capability rule," since it accommodates the fact that uses of a technology "may evolve significantly over time" (Amici Curiae Brief, 2003). According to this simple rule, if the technology has or is capable of having substantial noninfringing uses, there should be no secondary liability regardless of what the purveyor of that technology knows or should have known about infringing uses of that technology. The Brief goes on to criticize the Napster decision because the Ninth Circuit made the mistake of "subordinat[ing] the substantial noninfringing use requirement to the knowledge requirement," and it urges that the courts separate "the substantial noninfringing use inquiry" from the "knowledge inquiry." One can infer that the presence of substantial noninfringing use should not be trumped by the knowledge of current infringement on the part of the technology provider.

This Brief, however, fails to consider some of the unresolved issues that linger from the *Sony* decision and make it a problematic standard. How should we define a "staple article of commerce"? Does it only apply to sales of physical equipment such as VCRs or DVD players? Can we be so sure that the court intended to include in this category software programs such as Napster and peer-to-peer programs such as KaZaA? What level of noninfringing use is enough to qualify as "substantial?" (see Dogan, 2001).

The vagueness of the *Sony* standard also manifests itself in other aspects of this ruling. For example, according to the Amici Curiae Brief, if a technology is merely *capable* of substantial noninfringing uses, it passes the *Sony* test, which virtually immunizes purveyors of that technology from liability for copyright infringement. But what if a technology is being used predominantly or perhaps even exclusively for infringement, yet it is recognized that the technology has the capability for noninfringing use on a significant scale in the future? Given the plasticity of computer software, it would not be hard to envision such a use for almost any single technology. That technology may *never* in fact be used in a noninfringing way by a substantial number of people, but as long as the possibility for such use is present, it passes the *Sony* test. Can we really predict how technology will be used and differentiate between hypothetical uses and ones that are likely to occur on a significant scale? This reasoning would have us prescind from *actuality,* the present use of this technology, and focus instead on nebulous potentialities, that is, the *possible* noninfringing uses for future adopters of this technology and how substantial such uses are apt to be. In this case, those who argue against the plaintiffs contend that the *Sony* precedent cannot be ignored, and, as a consequence, the fact that 90% of the files available on the FastTrack network are copyrighted should be overlooked. Should the fact that there is minimal noninfringing use with the potential for an increase in the future immunize the defendants from dealing with a massive level of current infringing use? If this is so, any purveyor of technology will be able to promote piracy unencumbered by law as long as it can point to the possibility of some substantial noninfringing use at some future time.

In addition, there are certainly some asymmetries between *Sony* and *Grokster.* In the latter case, the Plaintiffs are not trying to undermine peer-to-peer technology; they are merely seeking to deter the infringing uses of that technology. Deterring infringement on these networks does not necessarily imply that the networks will be shut down, only that they will be used for legitimate purposes. Even Napster has not disappeared but has reinvented itself as a law-abiding service providing access to music tracks by charging a fee for each download. Moreover, in *Sony* (1984), the "only contact between Sony and [its] users … occurred at the moment of sale," but developers of peer-to-peer networks maintain a more ongoing relationship with users. This relationship does not enjoy the same level of proximity as the relation-

ship between Napster and its users, but it is far more than merely incidental. First-time users on FastTrack must register and provide a username and password. That username and password is checked in every subsequent login so that servers can block access to unregistered users or to users who have violated the rules. Also, as soon as the user logs in, the software sends to an index the list of digital files on the user's computer that are available for downloading by other FastTrack users. And Grokster continues to interact with users after they have installed this software by sending messages about software upgrades and by disseminating ads and other web content that users encounter when they exchange files. Grokster also reserves the right to terminate users and to block files that contain viruses or "bogus" content.

This ongoing relationship is much different from the onetime, mediated relationship established when a customer makes a purchase of a Sony VCR from one of many retail stores where these products are sold. It is worth noting that in similar cases the court has concluded that *Sony* is inapplicable when the defendant "went far beyond merely selling" a staple article of commerce (*A&M Records, Inc. v. Abdallah*, 1996).

The District Court acknowledged that the defendants "clearly know that many if not most of [their users] who download their software subsequently use it to infringe copyrights" (*Metro-Goldwyn-Mayer Studios, Inc. v. Grokster*, 2003). The court ruled–that the defendants' liability hinges on actual knowledge of specific infringing acts occurring at a time when the infringement can be deterred. Plaintiffs contend, however, that this standard raises the bar too high, since it precludes from liability a wide range of conduct that facilitates and even encourages infringement. Moreover, in the Napster decision no such evidence of specific knowledge was required.

Space constraints prevent us from considering many other nuances of this complicated case. Our key concern has been trying to find the right standard for secondary (i.e., contributory and vicarious) liability in a dynamic networked environment. Should we follow the *Sony* precedent and drop or mitigate the knowledge requirement for these technologies with substantial noninfringing uses? If not, how specific does knowledge have to be and does one need to know about infringement *ex ante*? We tend to agree that the district court in this case has raised the bar too high. If Grokster and StreamCast know that 90% of the file sharing on their respective networks involves copyrighted files, if the magnitude (in terms of lost revenues) is material enough, there is at the very least a firm moral obligation to take action and prevent continuance of harm to the music and recording industries. Such action might require reconfiguring the architecture of these networks so they can block the sharing of infringing material once the network provider has been informed by the copyright holder of the impermissible sharing. As mentioned, these networks already block certain files (such as those that contain pornography or viruses), so they have the general capability to block infringing content.

Before concluding this discussion of peer-to-peer networks, we should reiterate that the legality of sharing copyrighted material over these networks is still a murky area. Some forms of file sharing that are "noncommercial" and do not harm the potential market for the work being shared would most likely constitute fair use. On the other hand, there is a strong case to be made that placing a large quantity of music or movie files on one's computer system for many others to copy (via a P2P network) is tantamount to direct copyright infringement. The music and movie industries have made this assumption, and they are most likely on solid legal ground. Certainly, rulings in relevant cases would tend to confirm that assumption: "[d]efendants … apparently believe that the ongoing, massive, and unauthorized distribution and copying of Plaintiffs' copyrighted works by Aimster's end users somehow constitutes 'personal use'; this contention is specious" (*In re Aimster Copyright Litigation*, 2002).

But even if peer-to-peer file sharing on this scale were perfectly legal, it would still be morally problematic. From a normative standpoint, the sharing of a large volume of these files to people all over the Internet is difficult to justify, since the creators and producers of movies, music, and other copyrighted material are not being compensated for their creative efforts. As we have observed, the design of these networks is especially troublesome, since once a user downloads a file onto his or her computer, that file is made available for other users in a widening cycle of viral distribution. Given the harm to creators caused by this rampant copying, it is difficult to absolve those engaged in this level of file sharing of any moral culpability.

Property Disputes over Cyberpatents

As observed above, the scope of patent protection has been steadily expanding, leading some legal analysts to justifiably complain about dense "patent thickets" (Shapiro, 2001). In one benchmark patent case, *State Street Bank & Trust Co. v. Signature Financial Group* (1998), the court ruled in favor of business method patents. In that case, the U.S. Court of Appeals for the Federal Circuit ruled that an innovation or invention was patentable as long as it achieves "a useful, concrete and tangible result," even if such a result amounts to no more than a "the transformation of data." Thus, patent protection for new systems or methodologies for conducting business were now possible. This opened the floodgates for many new patents, especially in cyberspace where new methods of online business were being devised in this unfamiliar terrain. These patents became known as *cyberpatents*.

One such patent that has been particularly controversial was granted for Amazon's "one-click" ordering system, which was introduced by Amazon.com in September 1997. As the name connotes, one-click ordering enables a consumer to complete a transaction over an electronic network by utilizing only a "single action." Amazon.com, the leading purveyor of online books, videos, music, and many other products, developed this model to improve upon its shopping-cart model of making online purchases whereby users would add items to the virtual shopping cart, proceed to a checkout screen, fill in (or check) billing and credit card information, and then click to execute the order. The one-click system reduces these final steps to one step after the user has selected the items for purchase. The user, of course, must have previously visited the Amazon site in order to provide necessary shipping and credit card data.

Shortly after Amazon introduced one-click, Barnes & Noble (BN), Amazon's main competitor in the online book business, followed suit with its own expedited ordering system known as "Express Lane." Like Amazon's model, only one single action needs to be taken in order for the consumer to complete his or her order.

Amazon immediately took Barnes & Noble to court and sought a preliminary injunction preventing the bookseller from using this Express Lane functionality since it was in violation of Amazon's patent. Barnes & Noble claimed that there were serious questions about the validity of the Amazon patent, and it argued that the injunction was not warranted since there was not a reasonable likelihood of Amazon's success based on the merits of its case. But to the surprise of many in the industry, the U.S. District Court for the Western District of Washington granted the preliminary injunction sought by Amazon. As a result, Barnes & Noble was forced to add a second step to its checkout process in order to preserve the Express Lane feature, pending the outcome of the trial.

There was considerable backlash against Amazon, but the company persisted in defending business-method patents. According to one unsympathetic account of the one-click patent: "When 21st Century historians look back at the

breakdown of the United States patent system, they will see a turning point in the case of Jeff Bezos and Amazon.com and their special invention" (Gleick, 2000).

Barnes & Noble immediately appealed this ruling, and the Federal Circuit concluded in February 2001 that Barnes & Noble had indeed raised substantial questions concerning the validity of the Amazon patent. One-click may not have the requisite novelty to qualify for a patent. According to the Court, "When the heft of the asserted prior art is assessed in light of the correct legal standards, we conclude that BN has mounted a serious challenge to the validity of Amazon's patent" (*Amazon.com v. Barnesandnoble.com*, 2001). Consequently, it vacated the injunction and it remanded the case for trial to U.S. District Court. One year later, the parties settled the case out of court with a confidential agreement. However, the Barnes & Noble Express Lane option still requires two clicks instead of one.

The obvious question raised by this case is the validity of cyberpatents. Do companies like Amazon.com truly deserve patent protection for developing business methods like the "one-click" system? The normative frameworks considered above might be of some assistance in addressing this question. First, it is unlikely that the development of these minor innovations would entail a substantial investment of labor and money. Developing this sort of software innovation takes a fraction of the time required to build a full software application or an operating system, which do deserve some type of intellectual property protection. The Lockean rationale, therefore, is not so strong in this case. Second, companies are probably inclined to make this type of incremental service improvement without the stimulus of a patent, as they strive to provide better service to their customers in a competitive marketplace. Consequently, it is hard to argue that such patent protection is necessary on utilitarian grounds. Third, when considered from the Hegelian perspective, it seems hard to claim that this simple new methodology is imbued with the "personhood" or personality of its creator(s). The theories strongly suggest the invalidity of such patents from a purely normative viewpoint. Cyberpatents represent a form of overprotection, and if possible, the law should be swiftly modified so that minor innovations like "one-click" are no longer patentable.

Copyright Extension

Eldred v. Ashcroft

This case was a challenge to the 20-year copyright term extensions enabled by the CTEA. The CTEA was relatively uncontroversial when it unanimously passed the Senate, but its nullification has become a *cause celebre* for some legal activists, who saw the Eldred case as an opportunity to challenge this law on constitutional grounds.

The main petitioners were Eric Eldred, founder of Eldritch Press, and Dover Publications, which both publish works in the public domain. Eldred had set up a Web site (www.eldritchpress.org) for online versions of classic books so that individuals interested in accessing these kinds of books could avoid the frustration that he experienced in helping his daughters locate some older and out-of-print books for a high school literature project. Among the works included on his site are the complete works of Nathaniel Hawthorne. It was perfectly legal for Eldred to include these books on his site because their copyright protection had expired or they had always been in the public domain. With the passage of the CTEA in 1998, some of the books that were previously included in the public domain and also included on Eldred's site came under copyright protection and their inclusion on that site was in violation of the law.

The main argument of these plaintiffs was that the CTEA hurts individuals and corporations who leverage works in the public domain. Popular culture itself also depends heavily on a public domain that is being renewed with new creative

works for others to fully draw upon as source material. Eugene O'Neill's great play, *Morning Becomes Elektra*, would have been impossible without the inspiration of *The Oresteia* written by the Greek playwright, Aeschylus. And Disney, which advocated passage of the CTEA, has benefited immensely from works in the public domain such as Hans Christian Andersen's *Little Mermaid*. Without a natural flow of enhancements to the public domain, certain types of future creativity is impaired, since works like this fairy tale cannot become the basis for new creative projects.

The case was first heard by the U.S. District Court for the District of Columbia which ruled in favor of the defendant, the U.S. Government. The case was then appealed to the D.C. Circuit Court and this court also ruled that the 20-year extension did not exceed Congress's power. Finally, appeal was made to the U.S. Supreme Court, and in early 2003 that court also upheld the 20-year extension. The Court reasoned that the CTEA "complies with the limited Times prescription" and that it "[is] not at liberty to second-guess Congressional determinations and policy judgments of this order, however debatable or arguably unwise they may be" (*Eldred v. Ashcroft,* 2003).

It may be that, based purely on the law, the Supreme Court's 7-2 decision represents a reasonable resolution of this case. Congress apparently has the prerogative to extend copyright protection, and, although the duration is excessive, the term is still "limited." One wonders, however, where is the breaking point to this authority to extend copyright duration in accordance with the "limited Times" restriction? In addition, even if the CTEA is not unconstitutional and the extension is within the authority of Congress, this law is bad policy. When one examines the CTEA through the lens of intellectual property theory, its justification is dubious. The current term seems like an ample reward for one's work, and utilitarian reasoning is unlikely to yield positive arguments on behalf of the CTEA. It is difficult to argue that this retrospective increase in copyright protection will provide a further inducement to creativity and innovation. According to one Court decision, "[a] grant of copyright protection after the author's death to an entity not itself responsible for creating the work provides scant incentive for future creative endeavors" (*United Christian Scientists v. Christian Science Board of Directors,* 1987). Further, the weakening of the public domain by delaying the introduction of creative works for a 20-year period seems to far outweigh any of the meager incentives engendered by this law. Arguably, the Hegelian personality theory also does not seem to warrant this extension. Individuals surrender property when they die and no longer require it for the exercise of freedom. There may be other reasons why we want property rights to extend beyond someone's death, but this theory intimates that intellectual property rights are only essential for free, living beings. A creator who has objectified himself or herself has no reason to expect the ability to control that objectification beyond death.

The CTEA, therefore, is an unambiguous example of Congress's failure to discern the proper level of intellectual property protection, since this law overprotects property and is not in the public interest. This legislation appears to be the result of capture by the entertainment industry's most powerful players, such as Disney. Some have called it a "hijacking of technology policy by lobbyists" ("Free Mickey Mouse," 2002). As a result, this copyright extension should be repudiated by Congress.

Challenging the DMCA

Universal City Studios v. Corley

The next controversy for consideration involves a major challenge to the DMCA, which thus far has been resolved in favor of the content and entertainment industries. This case involves the encryption system used to protect DVDs from illicit copying. This system is known as the Content Scramble System or CSS. Manufacturers of DVD players along with the major content providers (i.e., the movie studios) have jointly adopted this standard. All movies in this digital format are distributed on DVDs protected with CSS.

Personal computer users can also view DVD movies as long as they are running a Mac or Windows operating system. CSS does not support any other operating system at the present time. In the fall of 1999, Jan Johansen of Larvik, Norway, created a software program that would play DVDs on a Linux system. In order to write this software, Johansen had to crack the CSS encryption code. The resultant decryption program was called DeCSS (or *De*code *CSS*), and it allows a user to decode a DVD disk. Johansen immediately posted the executable object code of DeCSS on the Web. As both the DeCSS source code and object code proliferated through cyberspace, the movie industry decided to seek injunctions against certain offenders.

The industry filed a lawsuit against Eric Corley and others responsible for the 2600 "hacker" Web site associated with the print magazine, *2600: The Hacker Quarterly.* Corley had written a piece for the Web site about DeCSS, and he included copies of the source code and object code of DeCSS. The 2600 Web site also contained links to other Web sites with DeCSS. Corley contends that the code and the links were incorporated in his story because "in a journalistic world, ... you have to show your evidence, ... and particularly in the magazine that I work for, people want to see specifically what it is that we are referring to" (Trial Transcript, 2000).

The movie industry demanded the immediate removal of the DeCSS code and sought an injunction against Corley (along with two other defendants, Remeirdes and Kazan). In January 2000, a Federal District Court issued a preliminary injunction preventing the 2600 Web site from posting the DeCSS code. The defendants complied, but they continued to post links to other Web sites where the DeCSS code could be found. At the plaintiff's request, the scope of the preliminary injunction was broadened to include those hyperlinks, which were then removed from the 2600.com Web site by the defendants (Spinello, 2004).

A trial was held in the summer of 2000. The plaintiffs argued that DeCSS was the equivalent of a "digital crowbar" that could be used to decrypt copyrighted DVDs. The movie industry's case centered on its claim that DeCSS violated the anti-trafficking provision of the DMCA, which prohibits the dissemination of technologies that allow for the circumvention of encryption technologies (§1201(a)).

In their defense against these accusations, Corley's lawyers claimed that the DMCA was unconstitutional. The defense team argued that computer programs like DeCSS, including both object and source code, represent a form of expressive free speech that deserves full First Amendment protection. The defense also argued that the ban on linking was tantamount to suppressing another important form of First Amendment expression. Hyperlinks, despite their functionality, are a vital part of the expressiveness of a Web page and therefore their curtailment clearly violates the First Amendment.

The District Court, however, was unmoved by these arguments, and ruled in favor of the movie industry. According to the court, DeCSS "was created solely for the purpose of decrypting CSS" and its distribution was tantamount to "publishing a bank vault combination in a national newspaper" (*Universal v. Remeirdes*, 2000). The court also asserted that by linking to sites with DeCSS code the defendants were "trafficking" in DeCSS, so that the defendants were also liable for these linking activities. A permanent injunction was issued prohibiting the defendants from posting DeCSS or linking to Web sites containing DeCSS code.

The case was appealed by Corley and 2600 Enterprises (the other defendants dropped out). The appeal was based on two constitutional arguments: (1) the DMCA violates the First Amendment since computer code such as DeCSS is a form of protected speech; and (2) it violates both the First Amendment and the Copyright Act by restricting fair use of copyrighted works. But in November 2001, the U.S. Court of Appeals for the Second Circuit affirmed the judgment of the District Court. The Appeals Court agreed that posting DeCSS or hyperlinking to sites with DeCSS violated the DMCA, and it left the permanent injunction in place.

Like the District Court, the Second Circuit Court did not disagree with the categorization of the DeCSS code as a form of speech, but it reasoned that this code also has a functional component. The purpose of the DMCA is to regulate the functionality of DeCSS. Thus, any restriction on the dissemination of DeCSS is content-neutral because the intent is not to suppress the content of the expression but to advance a particular government interest, that is, the protection of copyrighted material. According to the Appeals Court:

As a communication, the DeCSS code has a claim to being "speech" and as "speech," it has a claim to being protected by the First Amendment. But just as the realities of what any computer code can accomplish must inform the scope of its constitutional protection, so the capacity of a decryption program like DeCSS to accomplish unauthorized—indeed, unlawful—access to materials in which the Plaintiffs have intellectual property rights must inform and limit the scope of its First Amendment protection. (Universal City Studios v. Corley, 2001)

The Appeals Court also agreed with the restrictions on linking to other sites containing DeCSS on the same grounds: "The linking prohibition is justified solely by the functional capability of the hyperlink" (*Universal City Studios v. Corley*, 2001).

The DeCSS case illustrates the difficulty of resolving conflicts between property and free speech rights. While the courts were undoubt-edly constrained by the language of the DMCA, there is something disconcerting about this ruling, especially the prohibition on linking to other Web sites. The defendants have a right to critique the DMCA without fear of retribution, even if part of that critique is pointing to Web sites that contain rogue code such as DeCSS. Expressiveness on a web page is inextricably connected with hyperlinks that are interwoven with textual matter, and such expression would be incomplete without links. Therefore, liability against linking under these circumstances is a major burden for free speech in cyberspace. The defendants rightly argued that the court failed to adequately consider whether the DMCA "burdens substantially more speech than is necessary to further the government's legitimate interests" (Appellant's Brief, 2001).

If Congress intended to suppress links to Web sites with decryption code, since links are a form of "trafficking" in anti-circumvention code, it has erred on the side of overprotecting property rights to the detriment of free expression. If not, the DMCA needs revision and more precise language to guide the courts in cases like this one.

Intellectual Property and Anti-Trust

U.S. vs. Microsoft

Intellectual property rights confer monopoly power, but to what extent should those rights supersede or compromise antitrust laws? Grant-ing a property right appears to give a company an exclusive prerogative to exclude competition, yet antitrust law exists to ensure that competition is fair and that monopoly power is held in check. What happens when companies like Microsoft aggressively leverage their intellectual property rights? Does this type of competitive behavior ful-fill copyright law, which bestows property rights in software, or does it undermine that law?

This was one of the key questions at the core of the Microsoft antitrust case. Because of the phenomenon of "network effects," Microsoft's proprietary Windows platform became the stan-dard for PC operating systems (OS). Network theory applies when the value of a product for each user increases with the number of users. The more people using the same operating system, the easier to communicate with other users and the more software applications such a platform will attract (the so-called complement effect). These network effects bias industries (such as operating systems) to monopoly status. Intellectual property rights strengthen that power by giving monopolies like Microsoft the right to exclude others from use of their property. But can antitrust law be invoked to curtail core intellectual property rights? Where is the appropriate balance between an intellectual property holder's right to exclude and the public's right to fair competition?

Microsoft sought to leverage its dominance in the OS market in order to strengthen its position in the browser market. A Web browser enables personal computer users to navigate the World Wide Web and to display or scan various Web pages. Netscape's Navigator browser had gained momentum in this new market, and Microsoft was anxious to fight back with its own Internet Explorer (IE) browser. Navigator was a threat to its operating system monopoly because a browser is a type of *middleware,* which exposes its own application programming interfaces (APIs). This means that applications can be written to run on the browser platform instead of the OS platform. If third-party vendors began writing applications for Navigator and users could get many of their key applications through a browser (instead of an operating system), the Windows OS would be effectively commoditized.

In its zeal to defeat Navigator, Microsoft en-gaged in several exclusionary acts that were later determined to be anti-competitive. One such act involved the company's exclusionary dealings with its Original Equipment Manufacturers (OEMs), such as Dell and Compaq, that distribute that operating system. Microsoft imposed restrictions on OEMs that prevented them from removing desktop icons, Start menu entries, etc. This prohibition precluded the distribution of a rival browser because OEMs could not remove visible access to IE. And OEMs were loath to install another browser in addition to IE since "pre-installing more than one product in a given category ... can significantly increase an OEM's support costs, for the redundancy can lead to confusion among novice users" (*U.S. v. Microsoft*, 2001). OEMs were also forbidden to modify the initial "boot sequence" that occurs the very first time a user turns on his or her computer. In the Microsoft-approved boot sequence, users were given a chance to choose a Microsoft-approved Internet Access Provider that used IE (but not Navigator) for Web site access.

The Justice Department argued with some insistence that these restrictions were anti-competitive. But Microsoft contended that the restrictions were justified since the company was "exercising its rights as the holder of valid copyrights" (Appellant's Opening Brief, 1998). Microsoft was arguing for the right to dictate how its property would be used, and this might appear to be a reasonable imposition for a property holder. According to Microsoft's lawyers, "[I]f intellectual property rights have been lawfully acquired, their subsequent exercise cannot give rise to antitrust liability" (Appellant's Opening Brief, 1998). But the Appeals Court unequivocally rejected this line of reasoning, as it cited the Federal Circuit's conclusion in a similar case: "Intellectual property rights do not confer a privilege to violate antitrust laws" (*In re Independent Service Organization*, 2000).

Thus, the Court affirmed this clear constraint against leveraging intellectual property rights in a reckless fashion that suppresses fair competition and yields anti-competitive consequences. The problem is that such leveraging could easily

stifle innovation by preventing competitors from distributing their competitive products. The essential conclusion of the Microsoft case is that intellectual property rights do not give copyright holders immunity from obeying antitrust law. Microsoft's anti-competitive actions, which it defended by citing its copyright protection for Windows, had the effect of denying the interoperability of the Navigator program and this helped defeat Navigator in the marketplace.

Windows is a gateway to the Internet, and left unanswered in this dispute is the extent to which Microsoft must share control of that gateway by licensing or opening its code so that complementary applications (such as a browser or Internet access software) are assured equal access. The Microsoft case highlights the sharp distinction between two competing visions of the Internet and its extensions. One approach sees the Internet as an information commons built primarily on open technologies that encourage access and support interoperability. Consider the open communication protocols of the Internet itself: "No one owns the Internet protocol [IP], no one licenses its use, and no one restricts access to it" (Oxman, 1999). Indeed, these open protocols have been critical to the Internet's success as an "innovation commons" (Lessig, 2001). The other approach favors the proprietary development model adopted by companies like Microsoft. Lessig argues that the Internet must continue to function as a commons built on open technologies such as TCP/IP, and avoid being held captive by the proprietary systems of companies like Microsoft. And one antidote to proprietary control is open source software, where users are free to use the software as they see fit and modify its source code. If Windows were an open source code platform, Microsoft's bundling strategy for Internet Explorer would have been futile, since users (and OEMs) could easily have removed this functionality and substituted another browser. As Lessig (2001) writes, "the source code for open source projects is therefore a check on the power of the project; it is a limit on the power of the project to behave strategically against anything written to the platform."

The primary problem with mandating open access (that is, interoperability between a platform and complementary or rival applications) *or* open source code is that it directly conflicts with intellectual property rights, which have been instrumental in stimulating software development. Such a policy would neglect the need to provide adequate incentives for investment. A law, for example, requiring that all software be "open" (with freely available source code) would destroy the market-based incentives that induce software developers to create innovative new software products. Such a requirement could have an adverse effect on future software development with a corresponding net loss for consumer welfare.

But perhaps a middle ground between the proprietary and the commons models is possible. Weiser (2003) proposes the model of a "limited commons." This model calls for proprietary standards where there is rivalry between different platform standards (for example, an operating system or browser), but favors open standards when a single standard wins and reaps "sufficient rewards." Weiser recognizes that property rights will stimulate investment while network effects will encourage the development of a standard that permits interoperability. This model "respects the need to provide incentives for investment and permits access when necessary to facilitate competition and innovation" (Weiser, 2003).

CONCLUSION

At this point we draw this overview to a close. Our purpose has been to illuminate theories underlying intellectual property rights, while exposing the difficulties involved in implementing those rights fairly and responsibly. The primary problem that has preoccupied us is the proper scope of intellectual property rights in a digital environment and a networked world. We have critiqued laws and court decisions that tend to underprotect or overprotect those rights. We have argued instead for a prudent level of protection that approximates the ideal of the Aristotelian mean, that is, property rights that are measured and proportionate to the need to reward and induce creative effort. Property rights, properly constructed, should mediate two polarities. One polarity overemphasizes the exclusive, private ownership of intellectual objects, while the other polarity is represented by the radical viewpoint that all intellectual objects should belong to the "commons" or public domain from the moment of their creation.

We began with theory. Locke was the first philosopher to seriously thematize the problem of property. For many intellectual property scholars, Locke's meditation on labor is the key to comprehending the meaning of property and the normative justification for a right to own property. The importance of property rights is also discernible in the writings of Hegel, as well as in utilitarian philosophers such as Bentham and Mill. While these philosophers did not explicitly discuss intellectual property rights, their insights have laid the foundation for those rights. For Locke and Hegel, intellectual property rights are natural entitlements, necessary as a reward for labor or as a means to achieve free self-expression. This approach contrasts with utilitarian reasoning where those rights are regarded as useful social instruments with a rationale grounded in the need for incentives to spur the steady production of intellectual objects. But both approaches demand that rights be limited by concern for the public domain and the common good. As we have seen, Lockeans may insist on the need for a property right as a just dessert of one's labors, but the bestowal of such a right cannot harm the commons by depriving it of intellectual objects (such as ideas and algorithms) that others will need as raw material for their own creations. Property rights should be neither thick nor thin, but hale and sound.

But what about the case against intellectual property—why should intellectual objects be "owned" by anyone, especially given their non-rivalrous nature? We find the case against property rights to be weak. Even if one rejects the notion of a "natural" property right, there is compelling evidence that intellectual property protection is crucial stimulus for the economy. There is also evidence that developing countries could optimize their own resources more efficiently if they had stronger property systems, albeit ones suited to their particular needs.

We reviewed the legal infrastructure that protects intellectual property, noting that the law's validity depends to some extent on the normative frameworks. We also highlighted more recent controversial laws such as the DMCA and the CTEA, and we briefly considered technological solutions such as digital rights management (DRM), which could be more efficacious than the law in protecting digital content. If enforcement of copyright law continues to be sporadic and expensive, content providers will turn to technological schemes that offer a more Draconian solution that could absolutize property rights by ignoring user rights and "safety valves" such as fair use and limited term.

Finally, we discussed some of the more prominent current controversies. These cases enabled us to perceive how the issue of intellectual property is closely interconnected with issues such as free speech, secondary liability, and even fair competition. We saw some examples of intellectual property's vulnerability in certain contexts, because of ingenious software architectures and inadequate enforcement. At the same time, several other case studies made apparent the problems and social costs that ensue when intellectual property is overprotected.

In the case of peer-to-peer networks, intellectual property is too vulnerable if precedents such as *Sony* are strictly applied and users are allowed to share files on a massive scale. On the other hand, cyberpatents and arbitrary 20-year extensions of the copyright term have no justification, especially when objectively evaluated in light of the normative frameworks. In addition, the Microsoft case revealed some of the problems with the proprietary model for software development, which, for certain critics, threatens to *enclose* the Internet commons. Open source code and open access have been proposed as possible alternatives.

As our discussion of the Microsoft case demonstrated, there are two basic property models in cyberspace. There are some content providers and software developers who seek almost absolute control (proprietary model) over intellectual objects. On the other hand, some legal scholars and cyberspace libertarians advocate a dissipation of property controls since the current system of rights is so disadvantageous to the robustness of the public domain (commons model). Those who embrace the commons model see an enclosure movement "fencing off" intellectual objects. They also worry about how the insistence on application of property rights in cyberspace will interfere with the evolution of the Internet and related technologies like peer-to-peer networks.

What the commons model and its adherents downplay is the dynamic incentive effects of intellectual property rights. As the Supreme Court has observed, the "ultimate aim" of copyright and similar protections is "to stimulate [the creation of useful works] for the general public good" (*Harper & Row Publishers v. Nation Enterterprises*, 1985). Critics of intellectual property rights also fail to fully appreciate the concept of "incomplete capture," that is, "an intellectual property owner cannot possibly appropriate all of the information (and thus social value) generated by her creation" (Wagner, 2003). Even if an intellectual object is copyrighted, there can never be complete control of that object. A protected intellectual object is not hermetically sealed off from public access. Rather, there is usually a positive spillover effect as this information is disseminated throughout society. Copyrighted works, once they are disclosed to the public, convey information, ideas, and suggestions to many others who can utilize those ideas or follow up on these suggestions without violating that copyright. Some of the information stimulated may be only indirectly or obliquely affiliated with the new creation. For example, a successful novel (and subsequent movie) like *Cold Mountain* engenders new investigations and discussions of the civil war. Thus, even "fully propertized intellectual goods" can contribute to the spiraling growth of information resources and thereby enhance in some limited way the public domain (Wagner, 2003).

But while this fixation on control and enclosure may be exaggerated, flawed legislation such as the DMCA and particularly the CTEA remind us that policy makers are subject to capture. This leads to the unwarranted expansion of intellectual property rights that is not in the public interest. In their zeal to thwart piracy and to protect fragile digital content, there is also a threat that content providers will insist on greater control than the intellectual property system has tolerated in the past. Policy makers must find that elusive middle way that balances legitimate concerns about protecting intellectual objects with the need for a robust and renewable public domain.

We admit that discerning and legislating the "right" or proportionate amount of intellectual property protection is a difficult process. A full exposition of what a moderate protection scheme would look like is beyond the scope of this chapter. But we have offered some recommendations in the course of this analysis: software platforms as a limited commons under certain conditions, shorter duration for copyright protection, more limited scope of patent coverage, thick patent protection for genuine inventions that are costly to commercialize, and so forth. Finally, as we have been at pains to insist here, while the normative frameworks may be indeterminate, they can still guide policy makers in making prudent choices

that will reward creative labor and stimulate creativity while avoiding further erosion of the intellectual commons.

REFERENCES

Aharonian, G. (1999). Does the Patent Office respect the software community? *IEEE Software, 16*(4), 87-89.

Amazon.com v. BarnesandNoble.com. (2001). 239 F. 3d 1343 [Fed. Cir.].

Amici Curiae Brief. (2003). *Metro-Goldwyn-Mayer Studios, Inc. v. Grokster, Ltd.* 259 F. Supp. 2d [C.D. Cal], on appeal.

Amsterdam Appellate Court (2002). *BUMA & STEMRA v. KaZaA*, March 28.

Appellant's Opening Brief. (1998). *United States of America v. Microsoft Corporation* 253 F 3rd [D.C. Cir.].

A&M Records, Inc. v. Abdallah, (1996). 948 F. Supp 1449 [C.D. Cal.].

A&M Records, Inc. v. Napster, (2001). 239 F. 3d 1004 [9th Cir].

Becker, L. (1977). *Property rights.* London: Routledge and Kegan Paul.

Boyle, J. (2004). A politics of intellectual property: Environmentalism for the Net. In R.A. Spinello & H.T. Tavani (Eds.), *Readings in CyberEthics* (2nd ed.), pp. 273-293. Sudbury, MA: Jones and Bartlett Publishers.

Delaney, K. (2003). KaZaA founder peddles software to speed file sharing. *The Wall Street Journal*, (September 8), B1.

Derrida, J. (1981). *Positions.* Trans. A. Bass. Chicago: University of Chicago Press.

Diamond v. Diehr (1981). 450 U.S. 175.

Digital Millennium Copyright Act (DMCA), (1998) U.S.C., § 103, Title 17, § 1201.

Dogan, S. (2001). Is Napster a VCR? The implications of Sony for Napster and other Internet technologies. *Hastings Law Journal*, 52, 939.

Drahos, P. (1996). *A philosophy of intellectual property*. Aldershot, UK: Dartmouth Publishing.

Easterbrook, F. (1990). Intellectual property is still property. *Harvard Journal of Law and Public Policy*, 3, 110.

Eldred v. Ashcroft (2003). 123 U.S. 769.

Fisher, W. (1998). *Theories of intellectual property*. Available at: http://cyber.law.harvard.edu/ipcoop/98fish.html.

Foucualt, M. (1969). Qu'est-ce qu'un Autuer? In *Textual Strategies*. Trans. J.V. Harari. Ithaca, NY: Cornell University Press.

Fox, B., & LaMacchia, B.A. (2003). Encouraging recognition of fair uses in DRM systems. *Communications of the ACM*, 46(4), 61-63.

"Free Mickey Mouse." (2002). *The Economist*, (October 12), 67.

Gershwin v. Columbia Artists Management (1971). 443 F. 2d 1150 [2d Cir.].

Gleick, J. (2000). Patently absurd. *New York Times Magazine*, (March 12), 44.

Gordon, W.J. (1992). Asymmetric market failure and prisoner's dilemma in intellectual property. *University of Dayton Law Review*, 17, 853.

Gordon, W.J. (1993). A property right in self-expression: Equality and individualism in the natural law of intellectual property. *Yale Law Journal*, 102, 1533.

Gottschalk v. Benson (1972). 409 U.S. 63.

Grosso, A. (2000). The promise and the problems of the No Electronic Theft Act. *Communications of the ACM*, 43(2), 23-26.

Halbert, D. (1999). *Intellectual property in the information age*. Westport, CT: Quorum Books.

Hand, L. (1930). Opinion in *Nichols v. Universal Pictures* 45 F. 2d 119, [2nd Cir.].

Hand, L. (1936). Opinion in *Sheldon v. Metro-Goldwyn Pictures Corp.* 81 F. 2d 49, [2nd Cir.].

Harper & Row Publishers, Inc. v. Nation Enterprises. (1985). 471 U.S. 539, 85 L. Ed. 2d 588.

Hegel, G.W.F. (1944). *The phenomenology of mind*. Trans. J. Baille. New York: MacMillan & Co. (Original work published 1806).

Hegel, G.W.F. (1948). *Early theological writings*. Trans. T. Knox. Chicago: University of Chicago Press. (Original work published 1800).

Hegel, G.W.F. (1952). *Philosophy of right*. Trans. T. Knox. London: Oxford University Press. (Original work published 1821).

Hettinger, E.C. (1989). Justifying intellectual property. *Philosophy and Public Affairs*, 18, 31-52.

Hughes, J. (1997). The philosophy of intellectual property. In A. Moore (Ed.), *Intellectual property*, (pp. 107-177). Lanham, MD: Rowman & Littlefield.

In re Aimster Copyright Litigation, (2002). 252 F. Supp 2d 634 [N.D. Ill], aff'd No 01 C 8133 [7th Cir, 2003].

In re Independent Service Organization's Antitrust Liability. (2000). 203 F. 3d 1322 [Fed. Cir.].

Kieff, F.S. (2000). Property rights and property rules for commercializing inventions. *Minnesota Law Review*, 85, 697.

Lemley, M. (1997). Romantic authorship and the rhetoric of property. *Texas Law Review*, 75, 873.

Lessig, L. (1999). *Code and other laws of cyberspace*. New York: Basic Books.

Lessig, L. (2001). *The future of ideas*. New York: Random House.

Locke, J. (1952). *The second treatise of government*. Indianapolis, IN: Bobbs-Merrill. (Original work published 1690).

MacIntyre, A. (1990). *Three rival versions of moral enquiry*. Notre Dame, IN: University of Notre Dame Press.

Mansfield, E. (1986). Patents and innovation: An empirical study. *Management Science, 32,* 783.

Martin, B. (1995). Against intellectual property. *Philosophy and Social Action, 21*(3), 7-22.

McSwain, W. (1999). The law of cyberspace. *Harvard Law Review, 112,* 1574.

Merges, R. P. (1992). Uncertainty and the standard of patentability. *High Technology Law Journal, 7*(1), 10-12.

Merges, R. P., Mennell, P., & Lemley, M. (2000). *Intellectual property in the new technological age*. New York: Aspen Law.

Metro-Goldwyn-Mayer Studios, Inc. v. Grokster, Ltd. (2003). 259 F. Supp. 2d [C.D. Cal].

Moore, A. (2001). *Intellectual property and information control*. New Brunswick, NJ: Transaction Publishers.

Negroponte, N. (1995). *Being digital*. New York: Alfred A. Knopf.

Nietzsche, F. (1962). *Also Sprach Zarathustra*. Stuttgart: Philipp Reclam. (Original work published 1892).

Nimmer, D. (2001). *Nimmer on copyright*. New York: Matthew Bender.

Nordhaus, W.D. (1969). *Invention, growth and welfare: A theoretical treatment of technological change*. Cambridge, MA: MIT Press.

Olivecrona, K. (1974). Appropriation in the state of nature: Locke on the origin of property. *Journal of the History of Ideas, 35,* 211-235.

Oxman, J. (1999). *The FCC and the unregulation of the internet*, OPP Working Paper, No. 31. Available at: http://www.fcc.gov/Bureaus/Opp/working_papers/oppwp31.txt

Palmer, T. (1997). Intellectual property: A non-Posnerian law and economics approach. In A.E. Moore (Ed.), *Intellectual property: Moral, legal, and international dilemmas,* (pp. 179-224). Lanham, MD: Rowman and Littlefield.

"Patents and the Poor" (2001). *The Economist,* June 23, 21-23.

Plaintiffs' Joint Excerpts of Record (2003). *Metro-Goldwyn-Mayer Studios, Inc. v. Grokster,* Ltd. 259 F. Supp. 2d [C.D. Cal].

Priest, G. (1986). What economists can tell lawyers. *Research in Law and Economics, 8,* 19.

Samuelson, P. (2003). DRM {and, or, vs.} the law. *Communications of the ACM, 46*(4), 41-45.

Shapiro, C. (2001). Navigating the patent thicket: Cross licenses, patent pools and standard-setting. [Unpublished manuscript, on file with *Columbia Law Review*.].

Shavell, S., & van Ypersele, T. (1999). *Rewards versus intellectual property rights*. National Bureau of Economics Research Working Paper, No. 6956.

Snapper, J. (1995). Intellectual property protections for computer software. In D. G. Johnson & H. Nissenbaum (Eds.), *Computing, ethics and social values,* (pp. 181-189). Englewood Cliffs, NJ: Prentice Hall.

Sony Corp of America v. Universal City Studios, Inc. (1984). 464 U.S. 417.

Spinello, R. (2004). Note on the DeCSS Case. In R. A. Spinello & H. Tavani (Eds.), *Readings in cyberethics* (2nd ed.), pp. 264-268. Sudbury, MA: Jones and Bartlett.

State Street Bank & Trust Co. v. Signature Financial Group (1998). 149 F. 3d 1368 [Fed. Cir.].

Tavani, H. (2004). *Ethics & technology: Ethical issues in an age of information and communication technology.* Hoboken, NJ: John Wiley & Sons.

Trial Transcript (2000). *Universal City Studios v. Remeirdes* 111 F. Supp. 294 [S.D.N.Y.].

United Christian Scientists v. Christian Science Board of Directors (1987). 829 F.2d 1152 [D.C. Cir.].

Universal City Studios v. Corley (2001). 273 F. 3d 429 [2d Cir.].

Universal City Studios v. Remeirdes (2000). 111 F. Supp. 294 [S.D.N.Y.].

Universal City Studios v. Sony Corp of America (1979). 480 F. Supp. 429 [C.D. Cal.].

U.S. Constitution, Article I, § 8, clause 8.

United States of America v. Microsoft Corporation (2001). 253 F. 3d 34 [D.C. Cir.].

Vaidhyanathan, S. (2001). *Copyrights and copy-wrongs: The rise of intellectual property and how it threatens creativity.* New York: New York University Press.

Volokh, E. (1998). Freedom of speech and injunctions in intellectual property cases. *Duke Law Journal, 48,* 147.

Wagner, R. P. (2003). Information wants to be free: Intellectual property and the mythologies of control. *Columbia Law Review, 103,* 995.

Warwick, S. (2004). Is copyright ethical? In R.A. Spinello & H.T. Tavani (Eds.), *Readings in cyberethics* (2nd ed.) (pp. 305-321). Sudbury, MA: Jones and Bartlett Publishers.

Weiser, P. (2003). The Internet, innovation, and intellectual property policy. *Columbia Law Review, 103,* 534.

Wheaton v. Peters (1834). 33 U.S. 591.

Yen, A. (1990). Restoring the natural law: Copyright as labor and possession. *Ohio State Law Journal, 51,* 517.

ENDNOTE

[1]   Eine Vielheit, . . . ein Krieg und ein Frieden, eine Herde und ein Hirt.

This work was previously published in Intellectual Property Rights in a Networked World: Theory and Practice, edited by R.A. Spinello and H.T. Tavani, pp. 1-66, copyright 2005 by IGI Publishing, formerly known as Idea Group Publishing (an imprint of IGI Global).

Chapter III
Multimedia Encryption Technology for Content Protection

Shiguo Lian
France Telecom R&D Beijing, China

ABSTRACT

The principal concern of this chapter is to provide those in the multimedia or content protection community with an overview of multimedia content encryption technology. Multimedia (image, audio, or video) content encryption technologies are reviewed, from the background, brief history, performance requirement, to research progress. Additionally, the general encryption algorithms are classified, and their performances are analyzed and compared. Furthermore, some special encryption algorithms are introduced. Finally, some open issues and potential research topics are presented, followed by some conclusions. The author hopes that the chapter will not only inform researchers of the progress of multimedia content encryption, but also guide the design of practical applications in the industry field.

INTRODUCTION

With the development of computer technology and Internet technology, multimedia data (images, videos, audios, etc.) are used more and more widely, such as video-on-demand, video conferencing, broadcasting, and so on. Now, multimedia data are in close relation with daily life, such as education, commerce, politics, military, and so forth. In order to keep privacy or security, some sensitive data need to be protected before transmission or distribution. Originally, access right control method is used, which controls media data's access by authenticating the users. For example, in video-on-demand, the pair of user name and password is used to control the browsing or downloading operations. However, in this method, multimedia data themselves are not protected, and may be stolen in transmission process. Thus, to keep secure, multimedia data should be encrypted before transmission or distribution.

Till now, various encryption algorithms have been proposed and widely used, such as DES, RSA, or IDEA (Mollin, 2006), most of which are used in text or binary data. It is difficult to use them directly in multimedia data, for multimedia data (Furht, 1999) are often of high redundancy, of large-volumes, and require real-time operations, such as displaying, cutting, copying, bit-rate conversion, and so forth. For example, the image Figure 1(a) is encrypted into Figure 1(b) by DES algorithm directly. As can be seen, Figure 1(b) is still intelligible in some extent. This is because the adjacent pixels in an image are of close relation that cannot be removed by DES algorithm. Besides security issue, encrypting images or videos with these ciphers directly is time consuming and not suitable for real-time applications. Therefore, for multimedia data, some new encryption algorithms need to be studied.

During the past decades, various multimedia encryption algorithms have been studied. In the following content, the basic knowledge, brief history, and intellectual property investigation are introduced. Additionally, the general requirement, general encryption schemes and special

encryption schemes are analyzed and compared in detail. Finally, some open issues are presented, and conclusions are drawn.

THE BASICS OF MULTIMEDIA CONTENT

Multimedia content encryption refers to adopting cryptographic techniques to protect multimedia content. Thus, the basics include both cryptographic techniques and multimedia techniques.

Cryptography

In cryptography, cryptosystem design and cryptanalysis are two closely related topics. Cryptosystem includes traditional ciphers and some new ciphers. Traditional ciphers are often based on the computing difficulty of attack operations. For example, RSA is based on the difficulty to factor a large prime number, ellipse curve cipher is based on the difficulty to solve a discrete logarithm, and such block ciphers as DES and AES are based on the computing complexity caused by iterated confusion and diffusion operations. Besides traditional ciphers, some new ciphers have been studied in the past decade. The typical one is chaotic cipher (Dachselt & Wolfgang,

Figure 1. The image is encrypted by DES directly. (a) Original image, and (b) Encrypted image

(a)   (b)

2001; Fridrich, 1997), which uses chaotic dynamic systems to construct stream ciphers or block ciphers. Cryptanalysis (Mollin, 2006) is the inverse process of cryptosystem design, that is, to break a cryptosystem. Generally, the security of a cryptosystem depends on the key. For a secure cryptosystem, it should survive such attacks as brute-force attack, statistical attack, differential attack, linear analysis, and so forth.

Multimedia Technology

Multimedia technology (Furht, 1999) includes multimedia compression, transmission, retrieve, analysis, and so on. Here, multimedia compression is focused. Generally, multimedia data are transformed into frequency domain that benefits the compression operation. Based on the transformation, multimedia compression codecs can be classified into several types: fast Fourier transformation (FFT) based codec, discrete cosine transformation (DCT) based codec, and wavelet-based codec. For example, MP3 (MPEG Layer 3) is the codec based on FFT; DCT-based codec includes JPEG (Pennebaker & Mitchell, 1993), MPEG1/2/4, H.263/4, and so forth;, and wavelet-based codec includes EZW (Shapiro, 1993), SPIHT (Said, 1996), JPEG2000, and so forth.

BRIEF HISTORY OF MULTIMEDIA CONTENT ENCRYPTION

Multimedia encryption technology is first reported in the 1980s (Matias & Shamir, 1987), and becomes a hot research topic in the second half of the 1990s. According to the development, it can be partitioned into three phases, for example, raw data encryption, compressed data encryption, and partial encryption.

Before the 1990s, few multimedia-encoding methods are standardized. More of multimedia data, such as image or video, are stored or transmitted in the raw form. In this period, multimedia encryption is mostly based on pixel scrambling or permutation, that is, the image or video is permuted so that the result is unintelligible. For example, Space Filling Curves (Matias & Shamir, 1987) are used to permute image or video data that confuse the relation between adjacent image pixels or video pixels. European TV network adopts the Eurocrypt standard to encrypt TV signals, which permutes each TV field line by line. These methods are of low-computing complexity and low cost. However, the permutation operation changes the relation between adjacent pixels, which will make the followed compression operation out of work. Thus, these encryption algorithms are only suitable for the applications that need no compression.

In the first half of the 1990s, with the development of multimedia technology, some image, audio, or video encoding standards are formed, such as JPEG, MPEG1/2, and so forth. Generally, multimedia data are compressed before being stored or transmitted. Thus, the permutation algorithms for raw data encryption are not suitable for these applications. Alternatively, novel algorithms that encrypt the compressed data directly are preferred. For example, Qiao and Nahrstedt (1997) proposed the VEA algorithm that uses the DES algorithm to encrypt video data, Romeo et al. (Romeo, Romdotti, Mattavelli, & Mlynek, 1999) proposed the RPK algorithm that combines a stream cipher and a block cipher. These algorithms focus on the system security. However, since they encrypt all the compressed data, the computing cost is high, which makes it difficult for large volume data. Additionally, the file format is changed by the encryption algorithm, which means the encrypted data cannot be played or browsed directly. Thus, these algorithms are more suitable for secure multimedia storing than for real time transmission.

Since the second half of the 1990s, with the development of Internet technology, multimedia applications put more requirements for real-time operation and interaction. By encrypting only parts of the media data, the encrypted data volumes can be greatly reduced, which improves the encryption efficiency. For example, Cheng and Li (2000) proposed the algorithm that encrypts only parts of the data stream in wavelet-transformed images or videos, Lian et al. (Lian, Liu, Ren, & Wang, 2005) proposed the algorithm that encrypts only parts of the parameters in Advance Video Coding, Servetti et al. (Servetti, et al., 2005) proposed the algorithm that encrypts only the bit allocation parameters in MP3 files. These algorithms encrypt few parts that are significant in human perception, while leaving the other parts unchanged. Thus, the real-time requirement can be met. Additionally, the file format can be kept unchanged, which benefits the transmission process.

INTELLECTUAL PROPERTY INVESTIGATION

As a hot topic, multimedia content encryption has attracted many researchers. In some well-known international academic conferences, such as IEEE International Conference on Image Processing (ICIP), IEEE International Conference on Multimedia & Expro (ICME), IEEE International Conference on Audio, Speech and Signal Processing (ICASSP), IFIP Conference on Communications and Multimedia Security (CMS), SPIE International Conference on Security and Watermarking of Multimedia Contents, and so forth, it is an important topic. Some well-known international journals also publish the research results on multimedia content encryption, such as IEEE Transaction on Multimedia, IEEE Transaction on Circuits and Systems for Video Technology, IEEE Transaction on Consumer Electronics, and so forth.

The paper and patent publications in the past decades are listed in Figure 2. The papers are indexed by Compendex database, and the patent publications are indexed by the European Patent Office. The research topics include image encryption, audio encryption and video encryption, and so forth. The applications include TV program encryption, digital video encryption, broadcast encryption, satellite encryption, speech signal encryption, music encryption, color image encryption, and so forth.

GENERAL REQUIREMENTS OF MULTIMEDIA CONTENT ENCRYPTION

Multimedia data are often of high redundancy, large volumes, real time operations, and the compressed data are of certain format. All these

Figure 2. Statistics of published papers and patents on multimedia content encryption

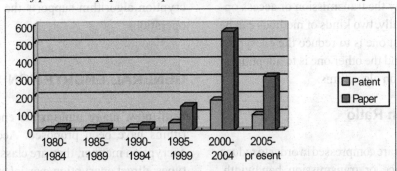

properties require that multimedia encryption algorithms should satisfy some requirements.

Security

Security is the basic requirement of multimedia content encryption. Generally, for multimedia encryption, an encryption algorithm is regarded as secure if the cost for breaking it is no smaller than the one paid for the authorization of multimedia content. This is different from traditional cipher for text/binary data encryption. For example, in broadcasting, the news may be of no value after an hour. Thus, if the attacker cannot break the encryption algorithm during an hour, then the encryption algorithm may be regarded as secure in this application. Different from text/binary encryption, multimedia encryption requires both cryptographic security and perception security. The former one refers to the security against cryptographic attacks (Mollin, 2006), and the latter one means that the encrypted multimedia content is unintelligible to human perception. According to perception security, knowing only parts of the multimedia data may do little help to understand multimedia content. Thus, encrypting parts of the multimedia data may be reasonable if the cryptographic security is satisfied.

Efficiency

Since real-time transmission or access is often required by multimedia applications, multimedia encryption algorithms should be efficient so that they do not delay the transmission or access operations. Generally, two kinds of methods can be adopted: the first one is to reduce the encrypted data volumes, and the other one is to adopt light-weight encryption algorithms.

Compression Ratio

Multimedia data are compressed in order to reduce the storage space or transmission bandwidth. In this case, multimedia encryption algorithms should not change compression ratio or at least keep the changes in a small range. This is especially important in wireless or mobile applications in which the channel bandwidth is limited.

Format Compliance

Multimedia data are often encoded or compressed before transmission, which produces the data streams with some format information, such as file header, time tamp, file tail, and so forth. The format information will be used by the decoders to recover the multimedia data successfully. For example, the format information can be used as the synchronization information in multimedia communication. Encrypting the data except the format information will keep the encrypted data stream format compliant. This will support the decoding operations and improve the error robustness in some extent.

Direct Operations

In some applications, it will save some cost to operate directly on the encrypted multimedia data, but not to do the triple operations of decryption-operation-encryption. For example, the encrypted multimedia data can be recompressed, the bit-rate of the encrypted multimedia data can be controlled, the image block or frame can be cut, copied, or inserted, and so forth. If the encrypted multimedia data can be operated by certain operations, then the corresponding encryption algorithm supports the corresponding operations.

GENERAL ENCRYPTION SCHEMES

Until now, many multimedia encryption algorithms have been proposed. According to the encryption manner, they are classified into three types: direct encryption, partial encryption, and compression-combined encryption. In the following content, they are summarized, analyzed, and compared, respectively.

Direct Encryption

Direct encryption algorithm, as shown in Figure 3, encrypts raw data or compressed data directly with traditional or novel ciphers under the control of an encryption key. The decryption process is symmetric to the encryption process. The performances of the encryption system depend on the adopted cipher and the relation between encryption and compression. Generally, direct encryption algorithm is classified into two types: raw data encryption and compressed data encryption.

Raw Data Encryption

Raw data encryption algorithm encrypts raw data directly, which does not consider the compression process. Generally, two kinds of method are often used: permutation algorithm and permutation-diffusion algorithm.

Permutation algorithms permute the uncompressed multimedia data with the control of an encryption key. For example, a pay-per-view TV program is scrambled by the permutation algorithm, based on pseudorandom number. This algorithm permutes the TV field line by line, and assigns each field a unique key. Alternatively, Pseudorandom Space Filling Curves are used to change the scanning order of image or video pixels (Matias & Shamir, 1987), which

reduces the intelligibility of image or video. In the algorithm, the scanning order is controlled by an encryption key that determines the space-filling curves' shape. Additionally, chaotic maps are used to permute images or videos (Pichler & Scharinger, 1996; Scharinger, 1998). Taking the image or video pixels' coordinates as the initial value of a chaotic map; the coordinates are changed into another one by iterating the chaotic map. The control parameters of the chaotic map act as the encryption or decryption key. Furthermore, some mathematical transforms are used to permute image or audio data, such as the magic cube (Ye, Yang, & Wang, 2003) or Fibonacci transform (Qi, Zou, & Han, 2000), that change the pixels' position in the order controlled by the key. These permutation algorithms are of low cost in computing cost or power cost, and often make the permuted images unintelligible, as shown in Figure 4. However, they are not secure enough in cryptographic viewpoint; for example, they are not secure against select-plaintext attacks (Li, Li, Chen, & Bourbakis, 2004).

Permutation-diffusion algorithms not only permute the pixels of multimedia data but also change the amplitudes of the pixels. For example, the block ciphers based on chaotic maps (Fridrich, 1997; Mao, Chen, & Lian, 2004) firstly permute the pixel's position and then change the pixel's amplitude by diffusing the changes from one pixel to another adjacent one. These algorithms are often of higher security than permutation algorithms, while of lower efficiency than permutation algorithms.

Figure 3. Architecture of direct encryption

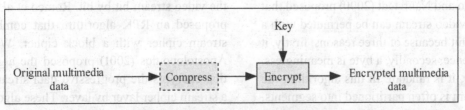

Figure 4. Examples of some permutation algorithms. (a) original image, (b) line permutation, (c) SFC permutation, (d) chaotic map permutation and (e) Fabonacci permutation.

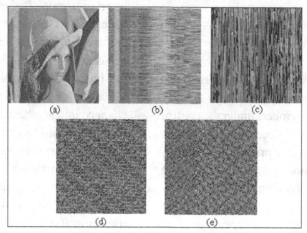

In general, these raw data encryption algorithms decrease multimedia data's understandability through changing the adjacent relation among image pixels. They are of low cost in computing or power. However, they often change the statistic properties of multimedia data, which will affect the following compression operation. Therefore, these algorithms are often used to encrypt the multimedia data that need no compression, such as TV signal, BMP image, audio broadcasting, and so forth.

Compressed Data Encryption

Compressed data encryption algorithm, as shown in Figure 3, encrypts the compressed data stream directly. The existing algorithms can be classified into two types: data stream permutation algorithm and data stream encryption algorithm.

Data stream permutation algorithms permute the compressed data stream directly. For example, Qiao and Nahrstedt (2000) proposed that MPEG1/2 video stream can be permuted with a byte as a unit because of three reasons: firstly, it is convenience, secondly, a byte is meaningless, and thirdly, it is random. In this algorithm, the video stream is often partitioned into segments, and then permuted segment by segment. The segment size determines the security level. That is, the bigger the segment is, the higher the security is, otherwise, on the contrary. This kind of algorithm is of low cost while also of low security. Thus, it is more suitable for the applications that require real-time operation and low security.

Data stream encryption algorithms encrypt the compressed data stream with modified or novel ciphers. For example, Qiao and Nahrstedt (1997) proposed video encryption algorithm (VEA) that encrypts only the even half of plaintext with DES and obtains the odd half through XOR-operation on the even half and the odd half. Thus, the encryption time is reduced to nearly 46% compared with DES. Tosun and Feng (2001) extended the algorithm by partitioning the even half into two halves again, and decreased the encryption time to nearly a quarter. Agi and Gong (1996) proposed the video encryption algorithm that uses the key stream produced by DES algorithm to modulate the video stream bit by bit. Romeo et al. (1999) proposed an RPK algorithm that combines a stream cipher with a block cipher. Wee and Apostolopoulos (2001) proposed the algorithm that encrypts the progressive data stream with a stream cipher layer by layer. These algorithms are often of high security that benefits from the adopted traditional ciphers. However, they change the file format, which means the encrypted data cannot be operated without decryption. Additionally, since all the compressed data are encrypted, the efficiency is not high enough.

Partial Encryption

Partial encryption algorithm, as shown in Figure 5, encrypts only a part of the multimedia data with the control of an encryption key while leaving the other part unchanged. The performances of the encryption system depend on the encrypted data part and the adopted cipher. For efficiency, the smaller the encrypted data part is, the lower the cost is. To obtain high security, three points are required: firstly, the encrypted data part should be independent from the unencrypted part; secondly, the encrypted data part should be significant to human perception; and thirdly, the adopted cipher should be of high security. According to the type of multimedia data, the existing partial encryption algorithms can be classified into audio encryption, image encryption, and video encryption.

Audio Encryption

Audio data are often encoded before being transmitted in order to save transmission bandwidth. Thus, audio encryption is often applied to the encoded data. For example, the speech data are encrypted by encrypting only the parameters of Fast Fourier Transformation during the speech encoding process (Sridharan, Dawson, & Goldburg, 1991). In decryption, the right parameters are used to recover the encrypted data. For MP3 (Gang, Akansu, Ramkumar, & Xie, 2001) music, only the sensitive parameters of MP3 stream are encrypted, such as the bit allocation information. For encrypting only few data, this kind of encryption algorithm is often of high efficiency.

Image Encryption

A straightforward partial encryption algorithm for images is bit-plane encryption (Podesser, Schmidt, & Uhl, 2002). That is, in an image, only several significant bit-planes are encrypted while the other bit-planes are left unchanged. By reducing the encrypted bit-planes, the encryption efficiency can be improved. However, the security cannot be confirmed, especially against replacement attacks. In replacement attacks, the encrypted data part is replaced by other data that may make the encrypted image intelligible. For example, two most significant bit-planes of an image are encrypted, as shown in Figure 6 (a) and (b), and the image (c) can be recovered from (b) by replacing the most significant bit-plane with zeros.

For compressed images, the algorithms based on DCT and wavelet codecs attract more researchers, such as JPEG or JPEG2000. In JPEG, an image is partitioned into blocks, and each block

Figure 5. Architecture of partial encryption algorithm

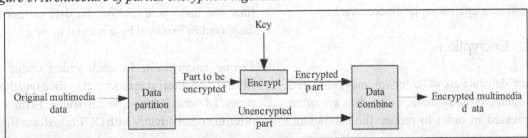

Figure 6. Examples of bit-plane encryption and replacement attack (a) original image, (b) encrypted image, and (c) replacement attack

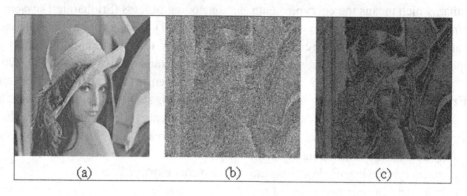

is transformed by DCT followed by quantization, run-length code, entropy code, and so forth. The algorithm proposed in Pfarrhofer and Uhl (2005) encrypts only some significant bit-planes of DCT coefficients, which obtains high perception security and encryption efficiency. In JPEG2000, an image is transformed by wavelet transformation and partitioned into blocks, and then each block is quantized, encoded by run-length code, entropy code, and so forth. The algorithms proposed in Norcen and Uhl, (2003) and Fukuhara, et al. (Fukuhara, Ando, Watanabe, & Kiya, 2002) encrypts only the significant streams in the encoded data stream that is selected according to the progressiveness in space or frequency. Generally, no more than 20% of the data stream is encrypted, which obtains high efficiency. Another algorithm (Lian, Sun, Zhang, & Wang, 2004a) encrypts different numbers of significant bit-planes of wavelet coefficients in different frequency bands, which obtain high security in human perception and keeps secure against replacement attacks.

Video Encryption

Since video data are of larger volumes compared with image or audio data, video data are often compressed in order to reduce the bandwidth.

Generally, the compressed video data stream is composed of such parts as format information, texture information, or motion information. Taking MPEG1/2/4, for example, texture information refers to DCT coefficients. Thus, according to the data parts, video partial encryption algorithms are classified into several types: format information encryption, frame encryption, motion vector encryption, texture encryption, and both motion vector and texture encryption.

Format information encryption. Since format information helps the decoder to recover the multimedia data, encrypting the format information will make the decoder out of work (Agi & Gong, 1996; Ho & Hsu, 2005). However, it is not secure in cryptographic viewpoint to encrypt only format information. This is because the format information is often in certain grammar that can be broken by statistical attacks (Agi & Gong, 1996). These algorithms change the format information, and thus, the encrypted multimedia data cannot be displayed or browsed by a normal browser.

Frame encryption. In such video codec as MPEG1/2/4, the frame is often classified into three types: I-frame, P-frame, and B-frame. I-frame is often encoded directly with DCT transformation, while P/B-frame is often encoded by referencing to adjacent I/P-frame. Thus, I-frame is the referenced frame of P/B-frame. Intuitively, encrypting only I-frame will make P/B-frame unintelligible. However, experiments (Agi & Gong, 1996) show that this is not secure enough. The reason is that some macroblocks encoded with DCT transformation in P/B-frame are left unencrypted. For some videos with smart motion, the number of this macroblock is high enough to make the encrypted video intelligible. As an improved method, SEC-MPEG algorithm (Tang, 1996) encrypts all the macroblocks encoded with DCT transformation in I/P/B-frame. In these algorithms, the motion information is left unencrypted, which makes the motion track still intelligible.

Texture encryption. The coefficients in DCT or wavelet transformation determine the intelligibility of the multimedia data. Encrypting the coefficients can protect the confidentiality of the texture information. For example, Shi and Bhar-

gava (1998) proposed the algorithm that encrypts the signs of DCT coefficients. If the coefficient is positive, then the sign bit is "1," otherwise, the sign bit is "0." The sign bits are encrypted with a cipher and then returned to the corresponding coefficients. In AVC codec, the intraprediction mode of each block is permuted with the control of the key (Ahn, Shim, Jeon, & Choi, 2004), which makes the video data degraded greatly. These algorithms are efficient in computing, but not secure enough. Firstly, the motion information is left unencrypted, which makes the motion track still intelligible. Secondly, the video can be recovered in some extent by replacement attacks (Lian, et al., 2005). For example, the encrypted intraprediction mode in the scheme (Ahn, et al., 2004) can be replaced by a certain one, and thus, the decoded video is intelligible, as shown in Figure 7.

Motion vector encryption. In most video codecs, motion vector represents the motion information.

Figure 7. Examples of replacement attacks on texture encryption. (a) original video, (b) encrypted AVC video, and (c) replacement attack.

Thus, encrypting motion vector will make the motion track unintelligible. For example, Yen and Guo (1999) proposed the algorithm that encrypts motion vectors in MPEG1/2 stream with the pseudorandom sequence generated by a chaotic map. However, if there is little motion in a video, then few motion vectors are encrypted, and thus, the video is still intelligible. Therefore, encrypting only motion vector is not secure enough.

Both motion vector and texture encryption. To keep secure, it is necessary to encrypt both DCT/wavelet coefficient and motion vector. Considering that these two kinds of information occupy many percents in the whole video stream; they should be encrypted partially or selectively. Generally, two kinds of partial encryption method are often used; for example, coefficient permutation and sign encryption. For example, in the algorithm

proposed by Shi et al. (Shi, Wang, & Bhargava, 1999), both the coefficient's sign and motion vector's sign are encrypted with DES or RSA [1]. Zeng and Lei (2003) proposed the algorithm that permutes coefficients or encrypts the signs of coefficients and motion vectors in DCT or wavelet transformation. Lian et al. (Lian, et al., 2005; Lian, Ren, & Wang, 2006a) proposed the algorithm that encrypts the DCT coefficients and motion vectors in AVC codec with sign encryption. These algorithms encrypt both the texture information and motion information, and thus, obtain high security in human perception, as shown in Figure 8. Additionally, the partial encryption operation, such as coefficient permutation or sign encryption, is often of low cost, which makes the encryption schemes of high efficiency. Furthermore, these partial encryption algorithms keep the file format unchanged.

Figure 8. Examples of both coefficient and motion vector encryption (a) original video, (b) encrypted MPEG2 video, and (c) encrypted AVC video (Lian, et al., 2006a).

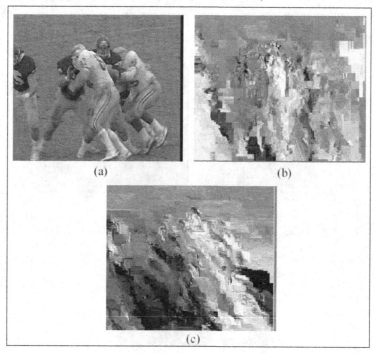

Compression-Combined Encryption

Compression-combined encryption, as shown in Figure 9, combines encryption operation and compression operation, and implemented encryption and compression simultaneously. According to the compression operations, the existing algorithms can be classified into several types: entropy-code-based algorithm and coefficient encryption algorithm.

Entropy-Code-Based Algorithm

Entropy-code-based algorithm combines encryption operation with entropy encoding and realizes secure entropy encoding. For example, Wen et al. (Wen, Sevra, Luttrell, & Jin, 2001) proposed the algorithm based on Fixed Length Code and Variable Length Code. This algorithm permutes the codeword table or encrypts the index of the codeword. Tosun and Feng (2001) proposed the algorithm based on forward error correction code. This algorithm makes the encrypted data stream have the ability of error correction. Wu et al. (Wu & Kuo, 2000; Wu & Kuo, 2001) proposed Multi-Huffman Tree algorithm and Multistate Index algorithm based on Huffman encoding and arithmetic encoding, respectively. These two algorithms realize secure Huffman encoding and arithmetic encoding by changing the codeword or the index randomly. These algorithms often obtain high security by losing some compression efficiency because some redundancy should be introduced into the original codec in order to confirm enough brute-force space.

Coefficient Encryption Algorithm

During image/video compression, DCT or wavelet transformation is often applied, which produces the coefficients in frequency domain. These coefficients are then quantized, scanned, and encoded. By changing the scanning manner or coefficient sign, the decoded data become unintelligible. For example, Uehara (2001) proposed the algorithm that combines compression and encryption. In this algorithm, the wavelet coefficients of the transformed image are permuted in different frequency bands that produce the images with different quality. This algorithm is of low cost and supports such direct operations as displaying, recompression, or bit-rate conversion. However, the algorithm is not secure against replacement attack and changes compression efficiency greatly. As an improvement, Lian et al. (Lian, Sun, & Wang, 2004b) proposed the algorithm based on SPIHT codec, which reduces the effect on compression efficiency by permuting the coefficients in trees. The examples of these encryption algorithms are shown in Figure 10. For DCT-based codec, Tang (1996) proposed the algorithm that permutes DCT coefficients completely in each block. Tosun and Feng (2000) improved the algorithm by partitioning each block into three segments and permuting DCT coefficients in each segment. Furthermore, Lian et al (Lian, Wang, & Sun, 2004c; Lian, Sun, & Wang, 2004d) improved the algorithm by introducing sign encryption and intrablock permutation. The examples of these algorithms are shown in Figure 11. These coefficient encryp-

Figure 9. Architecture of compression-combined encryption algorithm

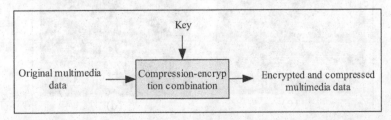

tion algorithms are often of low cost, produce unintelligible data, and support such direct operations as displaying, recompression, or bit-rate conversion. However, the compression efficiency is often changed, and the cryptographic security is to be studied. Compression-combined encryption algorithms are of low cost, keep file format unchanged, and support some direct operations. Thus, they are more suitable for such real-time applications as mobile or wireless multimedia communication.

Performance Comparison

Comparisons between the proposed three types of encryption algorithms are done to show the security (cryptographic security and perception security), compression ratio, efficiency, format compliance, and direct operations (displaying, browsing, bit-rate conversion, recompression, etc.). As shown in Table 1, Table 2, and Table 3, several typical algorithms in each type are ana-

Figure 10. Examples of coefficient encryption in wavelet domain (a) original image, (b) frequency band permutation, and (c) tree permutation

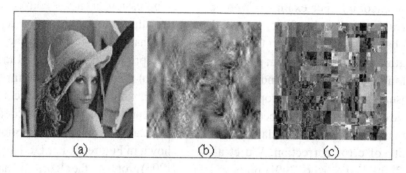

Figure 11. Examples of coefficient encryption in DCT domain (a) original video, (b) complete permutation, (c) segment permutation, and (d) inter/intrablock permutation

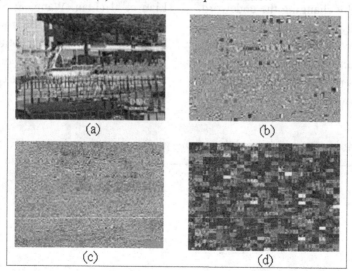

lyzed and compared. Generally, direct encryption algorithms are independent on file format; partial encryption algorithms often obtain a tradeoff between security, efficiency, and format compliance; and compression-combined encryption algorithms often support more direct operations than other algorithms. Thus, direct-encryption algorithms are more suitable for data encryption without considering the file format, partial encryption algorithms are more suitable for real-time transmission, and compression-combined encryption algorithms are more suitable for mobile or wireless multimedia transmission.

SPECIAL ENCRYPTION SCHEMES

Besides the general encryption schemes that aim at multimedia confidentiality protection, some special encryption schemes are also reported that aim at special applications, such as secure multimedia preview, scalable transmission, secret communication, or secure content distribution, and so forth.

Perceptual Encryption

In some applications, multimedia data's quality may be reduced before being used for free preview. If the customer is interested in the data, he will pay for the copy of high quality. To reduce the quality, perceptual encryption algorithm is used, which is first reported by Torrubia and Mora (2002, 2003). In the proposed perceptual encryption algorithms, two parameters are used to control the encryption or decryption operation; for example, the key K and the quality factor Q. Here, K is the encryption key, and Q controls the quality of the encrypted multimedia data. Generally, the bigger Q is, the higher the quality

Table 1. Performance comparison between different direct encryption algorithms

The algorithms		Security		Efficiency (high, middle or low)	Compression ratio (no change, slight change or great change)	Format compliance (Yes or No)	Direct operations (Enabled or Disabled)			Some applications
		Cryptographic security (high, middle or low)	Perception security (high, middle or low)				Display, browse	Bit-rate change	Recompression	
Direct encryption	Raw data permutation	Low	Middle or high	High	No change	No	Enabled	Disabled	Disabled	Broadcast encryption TV program encryption
	Permutation-diffusion	Middle	High	Middle	No change	No	Enabled	Disabled	Disabled	Secure image transmission
	Data stream permutation	Low	High	High	No change	No	Disabled	Disabled	Disabled	Not secure
	Data stream encryption	High	High	Low	No change	No	Disabled	Disabled	Disabled	Secure storage
	Significant image stream encryption	High	High	High	No change	Yes	Enabled	Partially enabled	Disabled	Internet or mobile image encryption
	Format encryption	Low	High	High	No change	Yes	Disabled	Disabled	Disabled	Not secure
	Texture encryption	Low	Low	High	No change	Yes	Enabled	Disabled	Disabled	Not secure
	Motion encryption	Low	Low	High	No change	Yes	Enabled	Disabled	Disabled	Not secure
	Texture + motion encryption	High	High	Middle or high	No change	Yes	Enabled	Disabled	Disabled	Wireless multimedia encryption
	FLC/VLC based encryption	Middle	High	Middle	Slight change	Yes	Disabled	Disabled	Disabled	Real time communication
	Coefficient permutation	Low	High	High	Great change	Yes	Enabled	Enabled	Enabled	Not secure
	Coefficient permutation + sign encryption	Middle	High	High	Slight change	Yes	Enabled	Enabled	Enabled	Secure mobile or wireless communication

Table 2. Performance comparison between different partial encryption algorithms

The algorithms		Security		Efficiency (high, middle or low)	Compression ratio (no change, slight change or great change)	Format compliance (Yes or No)	Direct operations (Enabled or Disabled)			Some applications
		Cryptographic security (high, middle or low)	Perception security (high, middle or low)				Display browse	Bit-rate change	Recompression	
Partial encryption	Significant audio parameter encryption	Middle	High	High	No change	Yes	Enabled	Disabled	Disabled	Real time Music or speech encryption
	Significant image stream encryption	High	High	High	No change	Yes	Enabled	Partially enabled	Disabled	Internet or mobile image encryption
	Format encryption	Low	High	High	No change	Yes	Disabled	Disabled	Disabled	Not secure
	Texture encryption	Low	Low	High	No change	Yes	Enabled	Disabled	Disabled	Not secure
	Motion encryption	Low	Low	High	No change	Yes	Enabled	Disabled	Disabled	Not secure
	Texture + motion encryption	High	High	Middle or high	No change	Yes	Enabled	Disabled	Disabled	Wireless multimedia encryption
	FLC/VLC based encryption	Middle	High	Middle	Slight change	Yes	Disabled	Disabled	Disabled	Real time communication
	Coefficient permutation	Low	High	High	Great change	Yes	Enabled	Enabled	Enabled	Not secure
	Coefficient permutation + sign encryption	Middle	High	High	Slight change	Yes	Enabled	Enabled	Enabled	Secure mobile or wireless communication

Table 3. Performance comparison between different compression-combined algorithms

The algorithms		Security		Efficiency (high, middle or low)	Compression ratio (no change, slight change or great change)	Format compliance (Yes or No)	Direct operations (Enabled or Disabled)			Some applications
		Cryptographic security (high, middle or low)	Perception security (high, middle or low)				Display browse	Bit-rate change	Recompression	
Compression-combined encryption	FEC based encryption	Middle	High	Middle	Slight change	Yes	Disabled	Disabled	Disabled	Secure mobile multimedia
	FLC/VLC based encryption	Middle	High	Middle	Slight change	Yes	Disabled	Disabled	Disabled	Real time communication
	Coefficient permutation	Low	High	High	Great change	Yes	Enabled	Enabled	Enabled	Not secure
	Coefficient permutation + sign encryption	Middle	High	High	Slight change	Yes	Enabled	Enabled	Enabled	Secure mobile or wireless communication

is, while the smaller the encryption strength is, otherwise, on the contrary. To control the quality of JPEG image and MP3 music, a variable number of coefficients in each data block are encrypted. However, for the proposed algorithms to encrypt the compressed data stream, they do not support such direct operations as bit-rate control or recompression. Alternatively, Lian et al. (Lian, Sun, & Wang, 2004b; Lian, et al., 2004c; Lian, et al., 2004e) proposed the algorithms combined with JPEG/MPEG2, JPEG2000, and SPIHT encoding. These perceptual encryption algorithms permute a certain number of coefficients in certain frequency band and encrypt a certain number of coefficient signs under the control of both the key and the quality factor. The examples based on JPEG and JPEG2000 are shown in Figure 12, where (a), (b), (c), and (d) are JPEG images, (e), (f), (g), and (h) are JPEG2000 images. For the encryption operations to be implemented during compression operations, they realize encryption and compression simultaneously, keep file format unchanged, and support such direct operations as bit-rate control or recompression. Thus, they are suitable for secure multimedia preview in wireless or mobile environment.

Scalable Encryption

Scalable video codecs often generate a scalable data stream that is composed of a base layer and several enhancement layers. The data stream is more suitable for time-varying channels. For example, if the channel bandwidth becomes smaller, then the data stream can be cut short directly in order to adapt the channel. In this case, special encryption methods are expected, which are named scalable encryption methods here. Until now, several scalable encryption algorithms have been proposed. Tosun and Feng (2000) proposed the algorithm that encrypts only the base layer and middle layer in the three layers (base layer, middle layer, and enhancement layer) of an MPEG video stream. In this algorithm, the enhancement layer is left unencrypted, which can be cut off directly. Yu and Yu (2003) proposed the algorithm that encrypts the pixel's bits from the most significant one to the least significant one

Figure 12. Perceptual encryption of JPEG or JPEG2000 images (a), (b), (c), and (d) are JPEG images, (e), (f), (g), and (h) are JPEG2000 images. (a) Q=100, (b) Q=90, (c) Q=50, (d) Q=30, (e) Q=100, (f) Q=80, (g) Q=60, and (h) Q=30.

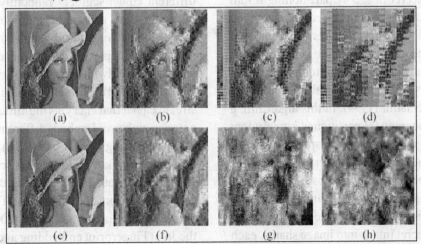

selectively. Kunkelmann and Reineman (1997) proposed the algorithms that encrypt a particular subset of important DCT coefficients in scalable MPEG video streams. Wee and Apostolopoulos (2001, 2003) proposed the algorithms for secure scalable streaming enabling transcoding without decryption. In these algorithms, the scalable stream is partitioned into segments, and then encrypted segment by segment. To change the bit-rate, some segments at the end of the stream are cut off directly. Grosbois et al. (Grosbois, Gerbelot, & Ebrahimi, 2001) proposed the encryption algorithm for JPEG2000 images, which supports the scalable property of the data stream. Yuan et al. (Yuan, Zhu, Wang, Li, & Zhong, 2003) proposed the encryption algorithms for MEPG-4 fine granularity scalability (FGS) that encrypt the base layer, and also the sign bits of DCT coefficients in the enhancement layer to enable full scalability for the encrypted video.

Visual Cryptography

Visual cryptography is based on secret sharing (Blakley, 1979; Shamir, 1979). Secret sharing refers to the method for distributing a secret among a group of participants. Each participant is allocated a share of the secret, and the secret can only be reconstructed when the shares are combined together. Visual cryptography refers to sharing a secret image by partitioning it into image shares. The secret image can be recovered only when all the image shares are combined together. Since each image share is meaningless in this case, they can be transmitted secretly. The first visual cryptographic algorithm is proposed by Naor and Shamir (1994). In this algorithm, a secret halftone image is partitioned into random halftone images printed on transparencies, each of which is meaningless. In decryption, the image is recovered by superimposing the proper transparencies. Nakajima and Yamaguchi (2004) proposed a visual cryptographic algorithm that partitions a secret image into image shares, each

of which is a prespecified image instead of a random noise. To make each image share meaningful, more redundancy is added, which reduces the quality of the recovered secret image. Fu and Au (2004) proposed the algorithm combining visual cryptography and watermarking. In this algorithm, each image share is embedded into a carrier image with watermarking technology, which produces a new image share. The secret image is visible when all the new image shares are combined together.

Joint Decryption and Fingerprint Embedding

Joint decryption and fingerprint embedding is a technique to embed such fingerprint information as user ID (identification) into multimedia data during data decryption, which produces different copies to different users. By detecting the fingerprint in an illegal copy, the illegal distributor can be traced. Thus, this technology is often used for secure multimedia content distribution. Until now, some algorithms have been proposed; for example, the multicast media distribution method (Parnes & Parviainen, 2001) is constructed based on the broadcast encryption scheme (Macq & Quisquater, 1995). In this method, a different watermark is embedded into the two cipher-segments before encryption, and the decryption process selects a different cipher-segment randomly, which produces the copy containing a unique watermark sequence. The main disadvantage of this method is that double copies need to be transmitted, which wastes the bandwidth. Anderson and Manifavas (1997) proposed the Chamloen method based on a stream cipher that encrypts multimedia data with a stream cipher and embeds different watermarks into the least significant bits (LSB) by changing the decryption key slightly. This scheme is efficient, but cannot survive such signal processing as recompression, adding noise, A/D conversion, and so forth. Kundur and Karthik (2004) proposed the Joint Fingerprint embedding and Decryption

(JFD) method based on partial encryption, which confuses the sign bit of the DCT coefficients in encryption and decrypts only part of the sign bits in decryption. This scheme can survive some signal processing operations. However, the encrypted media data are still intelligible (perception security is not high enough), and the decrypted media data's quality is reduced greatly by sign encryption. Lian et al. (Lian, Liu, Ren, & Wang, 2006b) proposed the watermarking-based algorithm that encrypts the multimedia data by increasing the embedding strength and decrypts them by reducing the embedding strength under the control of both the key and the fingerprint. This algorithm is time efficient, and keeps the decoded multimedia data of high quality. But, the method's security needs to be confirmed.

OPEN ISSUES

During the past decades, multimedia content protection has been studied in depth, and some means have been reported that satisfy various applications. However, though multimedia technology itself is in development, multimedia content protection is still not mature. In this field, there are still some open issues.

Security Analysis

Due to the difference between multimedia encryption and traditional encryption, the security analysis methods may also be different. Take partial encryption, for example. Not only such cryptographic attacks as brute-force attack, differential attack, and statistical attack, but also some other attacks should be considered, such as replacement attacks (Lian, et al., 2005), and other unknown attacks. Even now, it is still difficult to get a suitable metric on the intelligibility of multimedia content, which increases the difficulty to analyze a partial encryption algorithm.

Communication-Compliant Encryption

In practice, it is difficult to avoid transmission error or delay in multimedia communication. Thus, making the encrypted data robust to transmission error is necessary. Until now, few solutions have been reported. Lian et al. (2006a) proposed the solution based on segment encryption. In this algorithm, the data stream is partitioned into segments and then encrypted segment by segment, with each segment independently encrypted. However, it is difficult to determine the size of the segment because segment size often contradicts the security.

Format Independence or Format Compliance

In order to keep format compliance, the encryption algorithm often varies with the compression codec. In some cases, format independence is more attractive. Taking digital rights management (DRM), for example, it is required that all the content encoded with various codecs should be protected equally. Thus, there is a contradiction between format compliance and format independence.

Key Management

Key management is important in multimedia encryption systems. For example, to improve the security, multimedia data are often partitioned into blocks, and each block is encrypted with a subkey. In this case, the generation and storage of the subkeys are problems. Generally, the tradeoff between the security and the computing cost should be determined. In another case, key synchronization in transmission delay or transmission error is a challenging topic.

Combining Encryption and Watermarking

Encryption and watermarking realize different functionalities in multimedia content protection. Combining them together may bring some conveniences, such as saving time cost or increasing the security. Although it is a challenging field, some prior works have been done, that is the commutative encryption and watermarking (Lian, Liu, Ren, & Wang, 2006c) and joint fingerprint embedding and decryption (Kundur & Karthik, 2004).

Special Operation-Supported Encryption Method

In some applications, it is beneficial to operate on the encrypted multimedia content directly because of the large data volumes, such as multimedia database index, information retrieval, or data mining in patent search. In these applications, the partial encryption methods suitable for the special requirements should be designed. For example, in multimedia database encryption, the key field is left for indexing while the other fields in a record are encrypted. In patent encryption, the patent file is encrypted word by word according to a secret dictionary, and the patent file is indexed by translating the keywords. Generally, according to different applications, the corresponding encryption methods can be designed, while the performances, such as security, efficiency, or compliance need also to be evaluated.

CONCLUSION

In this chapter, the history and research progress of multimedia content protection are reviewed, and the existing schemes are classified, analyzed, and compared. Additionally, some special encryption algorithms are presented, and some open issues are given. According to the urgent demand of mul-

timedia content protection, multimedia content encryption will still be a hot research topic.

ACKNOWLEDGMENT

The author wants to thank Professor. Wang for his great help and the reviewers for their valuable advice.

REFERENCES

Agi, I., & Gong, L. (1996). An empirical study of MPEG video transmissions. In *Proceedings of the Internet Society Symposium on Network and Distributed System Security* (pp. 137-144), San Diego, CA, Feb.

Ahn, J., Shim, H., Jeon, B., & Choi, I. (2004). Digital video scrambling method using intra prediction mode. PCM2004. *Springer LNCS, 3333*, 386-393.

Anderson, R., & Manifavas, C. (1997). Chameleon —A new kind of stream cipher. In *Lecture Notes in Computer Science, Fast Software Encryption* (pp. 107-113) Springer-Verlag.

Blakley, G. R. (1979). Safeguarding cryptographic keys. In *Proceedings of the National Computer Conference, 48*, 313–317.

Cheng, H., & Li, X. (2000). Partial encryption of compressed images and videos. *IEEE Transactions on Signal Processing, 48*, 2439-2451.

Dachselt, F., & Wolfgang, S. (2001). Chaos and cryptography. *IEEE Trans. Circuits Syst. I, 48*(12), 1498-1509.

Fridrich, J. (1997). *Secure image ciphering based on chaos* (final Technical Report RL-TR-97-155). Rome, NY: Rome Laboratory.

Fukuhara, T., Ando, K., Watanabe, O., & Kiya, H. (2002). *Partial-scrambling of JPEG2000 images for security applications.* ISO/IEC JTC 1/SC29/WG1, N2430.

Fu, M. S., & Au, A. C. (2004). Joint visual cryptography and watermarking. In *Proceedings of the International Conference on Multimedia and Expro (ICME2004)*, (pp. 975-978).

Furht, B. (1999). *Handbook of Internet and multimedia systems and applications.* CRC Press.

Gang, L., Akansu, A. N., Ramkumar, M., & Xie, X. (2001). Online music protection and MP3 compression. In *Proceedings of International Symposium on Intelligent Multimedia, Video and Speech Processing*, Hong Kong, China, May, 13-16.

Grosbois, R., Gerbelot, P., & Ebrahimi, T. (2001). Authentication and access control in the JPEG 2000 compressed domain. In *Proceedings of SPIE 46th Annual Meeting, Applications of Digital Image Processing XXIV, 4472*, 95-104. San Diego, July 29th-August 3rd, 2001.

Ho, C., & Hsu, W. (2005). *Image protection system and method* (US Patent: US2005114669).

Kundur, D., & Karthik, K. (2004). Video fingerprinting and encryption principles for digital rights management. *Proceedings of the IEEE, 92*(6), 918-932.

Kunkelmann, T., & Reineman, R. (1997). A scalable security architecture for multimedia communication standards. In *Proceedings of the 4th IEEE International Conference on Multimedia Computing and Systems* (pp. 660-663). Thomas Kunkelmann. Darinstadt Univ. of Technology. IT0. D-64283 Darmstadt, Germany.

Li, S., Li, C., Chen, G., & Bourbakis, N.G. (2004). A general cryptanalysis of permutation-only multimedia encryption algorithms. *IACR's Cryptology ePrint Archive*: Report 2004/374.

Lian, S., Sun, J., Zhang, D., & Wang, Z. (2004a). A selective image encryption scheme based on JPEG2000 codec. 2004 Pacific-Rim Conference on Multimedia (PCM2004). *Springer LNCS, 3332*, 65-72.

Lian, S., Sun, J., & Wang, Z. (2004b). Perceptual cryptography on SPIHT compressed images or videos. In *Proceedings of IEEE International Conference on Multimedia and Expro (I)* (ICME 2004) (pp. 2195-2198), Taiwan, China, June 2004.

Lian, S., Wang, Z., & Sun, J. (2004c). A fast video encryption scheme suitable for network applications. In *Proceedings of International Conference on Communications, Circuits and Systems* (pp. 566-570), Chengdu, China.

Lian, S., Sun, J., & Wang, Z. (2004d). A novel image encryption scheme based on JPEG encoding. In *Proceedings of the Eighth International Conference on Information Visualization* (IV04) (pp. 217-220), London.

Lian, S., Sun, J., & Wang, Z. (2004e). Perceptual cryptography on JPEG2000 encoded images or videos. In *Proceedings of International Conference on Computer and Information Technology*, (pp. 78-83).

Lian, S., Liu, Z., Ren, Z., & Wang, Z. (2005). Selective video encryption based on advanced video coding. In Proceedings of 2005 Pacific-Rim Conference on Multimedia (PCM2005), Part II. *Springer LNCS, 3768*, 281-290.

Lian, S., Liu, Z., Ren, Z., & Wang, H. (2006a). Secure advanced video coding based on selective encryption algorithms. *IEEE Transactions on Consumer Electronics, 52*(2), 621-629.

Lian, S., Liu, Z., Ren, Z., & Wang, H. (2006b). Secure distribution scheme for compressed data streams. Accepted by *2006 IEEE Conference on Image Processing (ICIP 2006)*.

Lian, S., Liu, Z., Ren, Z., & Wang, H. (2006c). Commutative watermarking and encryption for media data. *International Journal of Optical Engineering, 45*(8), 101-103.

Macq, B. M., & Quisquater, J. J. (1995). Cryptology for digital TV broadcasting. In P*roceedings of the IEEE, 83*(6), 944-957.

Mao, Y. B., Chen, G. R., & Lian, S. G. (2004). A novel fast image encryption scheme based on the 3D chaotic Baker map. *International Journal of Bifurcation and Chaos, 14*(10), 3613-3624.

Matias, Y., & Shamir, A. (1987). A video scrambling technique based on space filling curves. In Proceedings of Advances in Cryptology-CRYPTO'87, *Springer LNCS, 293,* 398-417.

Mollin, R. A. (2006). *An introduction to cryptography.* CRC Press.

Nakajima, N., & Yamaguchi, Y. (2004). Enhancing registration tolerance of extended visual cryptography for natural images. *Journal of Electronics Imaging, 13*(3), 654-662.

Naor, M., & Shamir, A. (1994). Visual cryptography. In A. De Santis (Ed.), *Advances in Cryptology-Eurocrypt '94, Lecture Notes in Computer Science, 950,* 1-12. Berlin: Springer-Verlag

Norcen, R., & Uhl, A. (2003). Selective encryption of the JPEG2000 bitstream. IFIP International Federation for Information Processing, *Springer LNCS, 2828,* 194-204.

Parnes, R., & Parviainen, R. (2001). Large scale distributed watermarking of multicast media through encryption. In *Proc. IFIP Int. Conf. Communications and Multimedia Security* (pp. 21-22), Issues of the New Century, Darmstadt, Germany.

Pennebaker, W. B., & Mitchell, J. L. (1993). *JPEG still image compression standard.* New York: Van Nostrand Reinhold.

Pfarrhofer, R., & Uhl, A. (2005). Selective image encryption using JBIG. *Communications and Multimedia Security 2005,* 98-107.

Pichler, F., & Scharinger, J. (1996). Finite dimensional generalized Baker dynamical systems for cryptographic applications. *Lect. Notes in Comput. Sci., 1030,* 465-476.

Podesser, M., Schmidt, H. P., & Uhl, A. (2002). Selective bitplane encryption for secure transmission of image data in mobile environments. In *Proceedings of the 5th IEEE Nordic Signal Processing Symposium (NORSIG 2002)* (CD-ROM) Tromso-Trondheim, Norway, October.

Qi, D., Zou, J., & Han, X. (2000). A new class of scrambling transformation and its application in the image information covering. *Science in China—Series E (English Edition), 43*(3), 304-312.

Qiao, L., & Nahrstedt, K. (1997). A new algorithm for MPEG video encryption. In *Proceeding of the First International Conference on Imaging Science, Systems and Technology (CISST'97)* (pp. 21-29). Las Vegas, NV, July.

Qiao, L., & Nahrstedt, K. (2000). Comparison of MPEG encryption algorithm. *International Journal on Computers and Graphics, 22*(4), 437-448.

Romeo, A., Romdotti, G., Mattavelli, M., & Mlynek, D. (1999). Cryptosystem architectures for very high throughput multimedia encryption: The RPK solution. In *Proceedings of the 6th IEEE International Conference on Electronics, Circuits and Systems, 1,* 5-8 Sept., 261 -264.

Said, A. (1996). A new fast and efficient image codec based on set partitioning in hierarchical trees. *IEEE Transactions on Circuits and Systems for Video Technology, 6*(3), 243-250.

Scharinger, J. (1998). Kolmogorov systems: Internal time, irreversibity and cryptographic applications. In D. Dubois (Ed.), *Proceedings of the AIP Conference on Computing Anticipatory Systems, 437.* Woodbury, NY: Amer. Inst. of Phys.

Servetti, A., Testa, C., Carlos, J., & Martin, D. (2003). *Frequency-selective partial encryption of compressed audio.* Paper presented at the International Conference on Audio, Speech and Signal Processing, Hong Kong, April, 5, 668-671.

Shamir, A. (1979). How to share a secret. *Communications of the ACM, 22*(1), 612-613.

Shapiro, J. M. (1993). Embedded image coding using zerotrees of wavelet coding. *IEEE Transactions on Signal Processing, 41*(12), 3445-3462.

Shi, C., & Bhargava, B. (1998). A fast MPEG video encryption algorithm. In *Proceedings of the 6th ACM International Multimedia Conference* (pp. 81-88). Bristol: UK, September.

Shi, C., Wang, S., & Bhargava, B. (1999). MPEG video encryption in real-time using secret key cryptography. In *Proceedings of PDPTA'99* (pp. 2822-2828). Las Vegas, NV: Computer Science Research, Education and Application Press,.

Sridharan, S., Dawson, E., & Goldburg, B. (1991). Fast Fourier transform based speech encryption system. *IEE Proceedings of Communications, Speech and Vision, 138*(3), 215-223.

Tang, L. (1996). Methods for encrypting and decrypting MPEG video data efficiently. In *Proceedings of the Fourth ACM International Multimedia Conference (ACM Multimedia'96)* (pp. 219-230), Boston, November 1996.

Torrubia, A., & Mora, F. (2002). Perceptual cryptography on MPEG Layer III bit-streams. *IEEE Transactions on Consumer Electronics, 48*(4), 1046-1050.

Torrubia, A., & Mora, F. (2003). Perceptual cryptography of JPEG compressed images on the JFIF bit-stream domain. In *Proceedings of the IEEE International Symposium on Consumer Electronics* (pp. 58-59), ISCE, 17-19 June 2003.

Tosun, A. S., & Feng, W. C. (2000). Efficient multi-layer coding and encryption of MPEG video streams. In *Proceedings of IEEE International Conference on Multimedia and Expo, 1,* 119-122.

Tosun, A. S., & Feng, W. C. (2001). Lightweight security mechanisms for wireless video transmission. In *Proceedings, International Conference on Information Technology: Coding and Computing* (pp. 157-161), 2-4 April.

Tosun, A. S., & Feng, W. C. (2001). On error preserving encryption algorithms for wireless video transmission. In *Proceedings of the ACM International Multimedia Conference and Exhibition* (pp. 302-308), IV, Ottawa, Ont.

Uehara, T. (2001). *Combined encryption and source coding.* Retrieved from http://www.uow.edu.au/~tu01/CESC.html

Wee, S. J., & Apostolopoulos, J. G. (2001). Secure scalable video streaming for wireless networks. In *Proceedings of the IEEE International Conference on Acoustics, Speech, and Signal Processing* (pp. 2049-2052), Salt Lake City UT, May, 4.

Wee, S. J., & Apostolopoulos, J. G. (2003). Secure scalable streaming and secure transcoding with JPEG-2000. In *Proceedings of IEEE International Conference on Image Processing, 1,* 205-208, Sept. 14-17.

Wen, J., Sevra, M., Luttrell, M., & Jin, W. (2001). A format-compliant configurable encryption framework for access control of multimedia. In *Proceedings of the IEEE Workshop on Multimedia Signal Proc.* (pp. 435-440), Cannes, France, Oct.

Wu, C., & Kuo, C. C. (2000). Fast encryption methods for audiovisual data confidentiality. In SPIE International Symposia on Information Technologies 2000. Boston, USA, Nov. 2000, *Proceedings of SPIE, 4209*, 284-295.

Wu, C., & Kuo, C. C. (2001). Efficient multimedia encryption via entropy codec design. In SPIE International Symposium on Electronic Imaging 2001. San Jose, CA, USA, Jan. 2001, *Proceedings of SPIE, 4314*, (pp. 128-138).

Ye, Y., Yang, Q., Wang, Y. (2003). Magic cube encryption for digital image using chaotic sequence, *Journal of Zhejiang University of Technology, 31*(2), 173-176.

Yen J. C., & Guo, J. I. (1999). A new MPEG encryption system and its VLSI architecture. *IEEE Workshop on Signal Processing Systems* (pp. 430-437), Taipei.

Yu, H., & Yu, X. (2003). Progressive and scalable encryption for multimedia content access control. *Proceeding of IEEE International Conference on Communications* (pp. 547-550).

Yuan, C., Zhu, B., Wang, Y., Li, S., & Zhong, Y. (2003). Efficient and fully scalable encryption for MPEG-4 FGS. *IEEE Int. Symp. Circuits and Systems*, May, 620-623.

Zeng, W., & Lei, S. (2003). Efficient frequency domain selective scrambling of digital video. *IEEE Trans on Multimedia, 5*(1), 118-129.

Chapter IV
Masking Models and Watermarking:
A Discussion on Methods and Effectiveness

Mirko Luca Lobina
University of Cagliari, Italy

Luigi Atzori
University of Cagliari, Italy

Davide Mula
University Chair of Juridicial Informatics at LUISS Guido Carli, Italy

ABSTRACT

Many audio watermarking techniques presented in the last years make use of masking and psychological models derived from signal processing. Such a basic idea is winning because it guarantees a high level of robustness and bandwidth of the watermark as well as fidelity of the watermarked signal. This chapter first describes the relationship between digital right management, intellectual property, and use of watermarking techniques. Then, the crossing use of watermarking and masking models is detailed, providing schemes, examples, and references. Finally, the authors present two strategies that make use of a masking model, applied to a classic watermarking technique. The joint use of classic frameworks and masking models seems to be one of the trends for the future of research in watermarking. Several tests on the proposed strategies with the state of the art are also offered to give an idea of how to assess the effectiveness of a watermarking technique.

INTRODUCTION

Ownership is one's right to possess something and decide what is to be done with it. The concept of ownership is distinct from possession, intended as having something in one's custody. Such demarcation, very easy to understand and prove in case of a material good (e.g., as a house or a car), becomes particularly ephemeral in case of digital data. First of all, the diffusion and movement of digital content cannot be practically traced: as an example a collection of songs can be published on a Web site, a CD, or a DVD, and once it is legally distributed for the first time, there is no way to control its following circulation. Then, there are many ways to reproduce digital content and obtain copies identical to the original. Starting from a copy, a malicious person can alter or manipulate the original content and present himself/herself as the owner. This can result in great damage for the rights' genuine owner since an image or a song in a digital format are esteemed on the whole respect to their origin, which is a proof of quality, source, and content integrity. From this introduction it seems, and it is definitely true, that the encountering problems in ownership for digital content is the digital nature itself of the content: an image, printed on photopaper, can be copied with more difficulty without the original matrix (e.g., the negative, in case of a photo; or the master registration in case of an audio sample) and, in every case, the copy can be easily distinguished from the original. Furthermore, a photopaper image could not be present on millions of instances at the same time as happens to an image published on the Web. For all these reasons, different ap-

proaches have been developed for proving an origin's copyright information of digital content. On the whole, digital rights management (DRM) is any of these technologies when used to control access to digital data. DRM is not a technical protection measure (TPM). Actually, such technology controls or restricts the use and access of digital media content on electronic devices with such technologies installed, acting as components of a *DRM* design (See Figure 1). The objective of this chapter is to provide a comprehensive explanation of the crossing use of masking threshold and *watermarking* as one of the most effective *DRM* strategies.

This chapter is organized as follows. The first section provides an overview of *DRM*, discusses the distinction between cryptography and *watermarking* (explaining the relevant applicative fields in a *DRM* context of both solutions), describes *watermarking* in general, and introduces the *masking model*s. The second part is a description of the crossing use of the *masking model*s and *watermarking*. The third presents two works from the authors of audio *watermarking* schemes based on the use of the psychological masking threshold. Finally, some conclusions on the trade-off robustness/fidelity, and more generally on the use of *masking model*s in watermark schemes, are drawn.

Figure 1. DRM and TPM

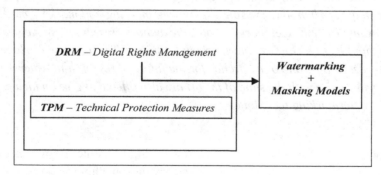

BACKGROUND

Digital Rights Management (DRM) and Intellectual Property (IP)

As already stated, digital rights management (DRM) is any technology used to control access to digital data. Such a term has been created to individuate the whole set of technical measures, where applied to digital media, or analog media released in digital format. The term "digital" is here repeated many times to underline that, while quality diminishes every copy with analog media, digital media may be copied a limitless number of times without degradation in the quality. That is, there is no difference in quality between the "master" and "copies." The last years have been characterized by a large pressure for legislation and regulation of DRM schemes' usage (specifically to publish the detailed functionalities of some of the most diffused DRM frameworks). An example of this will of regulation is the Digital Millennium Copyright Act (DMCA). That is, a United States copyright law that criminalizes creation and broadcasting of technology that can avoid measures taken to protect the owner's rights. An early example of *DRM* is the content scrambling system (i.e., CSS), based on a simple encryption algorithm (this last term is clearly explained when cryptography is introduced in the following). CSS has been used in DVDs since

1996 and requires DVD device manufacturers to sign a license agreement restricting the inclusion of certain features in their players that could be used to extract a high-quality digital copy disk. Approaching the problem of protecting the owner's rights from a legal point of view, we meet the term intellectual property (IP). IP defines how the holder of a legal entitlement (respect to ideas/information) can exercise his rights to the "subject matter" of the IP. Where, the term "subject matter" is used to reflect the idea that it is the product of the mind or the intellect. Thus, DRM and IP are complementary aspects of the same context (See Figure 2). DRM approaches the problem of protecting copyrights from a technical point of view. The legal basis of DRM is linked to IP and the underlying idea that the subject matter is the product of the mind or the intellect.

Cryptography and Watermarking

Cryptography and watermarking can be effective solutions for the distribution problem and rights management. In the following, the featuring factors of both techniques will be analyzed and discussed. Cryptography is the study of converting information from its comprehensible form into an incomprehensible format, rendering it unreadable without a secret knowledge (i.e., usually a numeric key). The field of cryptography has mainly expanded in two ways. The first one comprises

Figure 2. DRM and IP

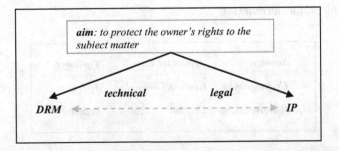

mechanisms for more than just keeping secrets as schemes for digital signatures and digital cash. Cryptography finds a second application in secure protocols, used in infrastructure for computing and telecommunications. In many cases, such protocols are applied without the users being aware of their presence. Cryptography is concerned more with this second field, and it is used mainly in tenable communications. De facto, once digital data is widely distributed also via a protected channel (Macq & Quisquater, 1995), cryptography does not preclude its further storage or illegal actions such as copying. Digital *watermarking*, also referred to as simply *watermarking*, is an adaptation of paper watermarks to the digital milieu. That is, a pattern of bits is inserted into a digital content, identifying the origin's copyright information. Like printed watermarks, the purpose is to provide copyright protection for intellectual property in digital format. This implies robustness and capacity of the *watermarking* technique. Robustness measures the digital watermark ability to resist intentional/unintentional attacks, while capacity reflects the ability of conveying useful information embedded in the original signal. But unlike printed watermarks, which are intended to be somewhat visible, digital watermarks are designed to be completely, or at most partially, inaudible/invisible. This feature is referred to as fidelity, that is, a measure of the similarity (or of the antonym distance) between original and watermarked signal. Transparency implicitly means that fidelity has been attained.

From what has been said, it is clear that cryptography and watermarking are complementary aspects and solve different classes of problems with unlike approaches. On one hand, there is cryptography that provides more than simple content encryption/decryption (i.e., message/content confidential), but it is also involved in the distribution of a secret key in a secure manner to all the involved parties (i.e., secure channel). In this sense, cryptography provides the necessary protocols for communicating parties to steadily authenticate themselves with each other, and can be considered as an "active" solution to global security. In addition, the use of digital signatures and message authentication codes provides a means for verifying that the content has not been manipulated in any way (See Figure 3). While on the other hand, watermarking for copyright protection is useful for tracking illegally copied content, although this is a very "reactive" approach to content security.

Watermarking in Detail

The first aim of this part is to provide the reader a very general overview of what is watermarking. Petiticolas, Anderson, and Kuhn, in their survey (1999), published at the end of the nineties on information hiding, introduce watermarking as a subcategory of copyright marking (See Figure 4). This is a very important account since, with this classification, they consider the robustness against possible attacks as one of the additional and mandatory requirements.

Figure 3. Cryptography and watermarking

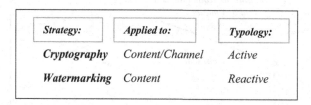

Strategy:	Applied to:	Typology:
Cryptography	*Content/Channel*	*Active*
Watermarking	*Content*	*Reactive*

Figure 4. Information hiding and watermarking

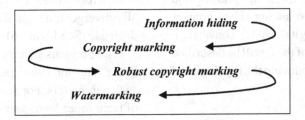

Really, watermarking has three main means: monitoring (i.e., tracing of illegal copies), copyright protection (i.e., authentication of the copyright owner by the knowledge of the secret key to read the secret watermark), fingerprinting (i.e., during the phase of authentication to a secure network). Information carrier and indication of content manipulation will be discussed in detail in the following. All these possible applications are included in two main possible watermarking schemes: secret and public. Secret watermarking is used as authentication and content integrity mechanisms. This implies that the watermark is readable/understandable only by authorized persons with the knowledge about the existence/position of the embedded secret. On the other hand, public *watermarking* means that the watermark is just an information carrier.

As it has been introduced before, *watermarking* is the insertion of a pattern of bits identifying the origin's copyright information into a signal. The righteousness of the *watermarking* technique is measured in terms of robustness, capacity, transparency, and fidelity (See Figure 5).

A good *watermarking* technique should achieve these features as much as possible. Let us see briefly, in the following, the implications of such attributes:

- The host signal should be nondegraded and the embedded data be minimally perceptible; that is, the embedded data has to remain hidden to an observer of the watermarked signal.
- The host signal and the data to be embedded must be coherent in terms of embedding dominio. That is, the *watermarking* must be inserted, taking into account the features of the original signal (as compression or encoding). In this sense, it is very important to retrieve as much information as possible on the signal to be watermarked and on its use.
- The embedded data should be resistant to intentional/unintentional modifications. That is, the original signal is modified to try a removal of the *watermarking*. The possible modifications are wide and include chan-

Figure 5. Watermarking features

> *Robustness:* measure of the digital watermark's ability to resist to intentional/unintentional attacks
>
> *Capacity:* ability of conveying a number of useful information embedded in the original signal
>
> *Fidelity:* distance between original and watermarked signals
>
> *Transparency:* inaudibilityy/invisibility of the digital watermark

nel noise, filtering, resampling, cropping, encoding, lossy compressing, printing and scanning, digital-to-analog (D/A) conversion, analog-to-digital (A/D) conversion, and so forth. Most of these will be described in detail when introducing the typologies of possible attacks.

Let us analyze the problem of nondegrading the original signal. Obviously, trade-offs exist between almost three factors: total amount of data that can be embedded (i.e., "bandwidth"), transparency respect to the host signal, and robustness/resistence to modifications. A technique can be planned that, constraining the host signal

degradation, tries to reach high embedding data, or high robustness. The two last factors are mutually divergent: as one increases, the other must decrease (See Figure 6).

The previous statement cited three factors as being true for every possible configuration of such parameters. For this reason, different kinds of techniques have been developed for different applications and requirements (See Figure 7). That is, the application fixes the requirements, the three factors' trade-offs and consequently, the technique itself.

In Bender (Bender, Gruhl, Morimoto, & Lu, 1996), another classification of *watermarking* techniques is proposed, depending on the applica-

Figure 6. Robustness vs. bandwidth

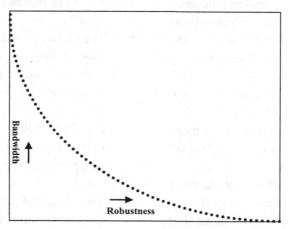

Figure 7. Requirements and watermarking's trade-offs

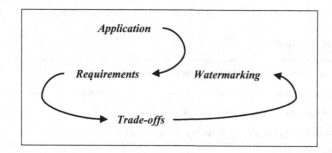

tion in terms of the amount of information that is embedded in the host signal. In this sense, the simpler technique implies the embedded data are used to place an indication of ownership in the host signal; the position is the copyright indication itself. A second category is the tamper-proof, while the third is the feature-location. Tamper-proof frameworks can be effectively included in two categories as "fragile" or "semifragile," as proposed in Kazakeviciute (Kazakeviciute, Januskevicius, Rosenbaum, & Schumann, 2005). Fragile means that watermarks act as a digital signature, allowing the detection of any modifications of the content. Instead, semifragile frameworks allow one to detect and localize any modification of the content changes. The second category is more effective respect to the set of functionalities from the digital signature. In Wu and Liu (1998), a set of desired features for tamper-proof frameworks is presented as follows:

- Determination whether a host signal has been altered or not.
- Integration of authentication data with a host signal rather than as a separate data file.
- Invisibility of the embedded authentication data under normal viewing/auditing conditions.
- Localization of the alteration that was made on the signal.
- Storage of the watermarked signal in lossy compression format.

Feature-location watermarks enable one to identify individual content features by introducing a certain degree of modification in the host signal. Generally, it requires a large amount of information respect to the other two previous techniques. Always referring to Figure 7, the "application" level includes also the case the signal to be marked is an audio or an image signal. The aim here is to exploit the main traits in the methods, considering both contexts (i.e., audio/image signals) and low/high bandwidths (always refer to Figure 7).

Blind audio *watermarking* (Eggers, Su, & Girod, 2000) techniques are first described in detail as follows. The term blind is here used to indicate that the watermarking scheme can detect and extract watermarks without nonwatermarked/original audio signal. Obviously, the blind methods need an effective method for watermark's self-detection. Compared to nonblind techniques (which implies the original signal for comparing purposes), there is a saving of *50%* for storage and bandwidth.

To give the reader a comprehensive and simple overview, five categories (See Figure 8) of frameworks are described. Of course, much more techniques are accessible (take also into account that a watermarking method must be obligatory to be published). This section does not introduce methods based on psychological models since they will be described in detail in the following.

Wikipedia introduces the term quantization as the procedure of constraining something to

Figure 8. Blind-audio watermarking technique

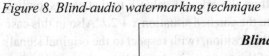
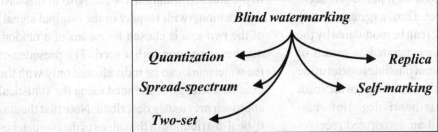

a discrete set of values. In the specific field of audio signals, it is the process of approximating a continuous range of values (or a very large set of possible discrete values) by a relatively small set of discrete symbols or integer values. Thus, a quantization method quantizes a value of the original signal (let us say χ), and assigns it a new value based on the quantized sample value D and function $q(\chi, D)$, in a way $y = q(\chi, D) \pm D$, where the signs $\pm$ depend on the value of the value of the binary watermark message {0,1}. This scheme is quite robust (Chen & Wornell, 1999) and resistant to several types of attack. The detection method is exactly the inverse with respect to the embedding process.

Spread spectrum was originally developed for military applications. Since its declassification, it has found civilian use, particularly in communications for cellular telephony. Spread spectrum is one of the most diffused and discussed schemes in state of the art (Cox, Kilian, Leigton, Shamoon, 1996; Cvejic, Keskinarkaus, & Seppanen, 2001; Kim, 2000). Several implementations have been proposed in the past, but in this chapter, the basic idea is presented. In spread spectrum, a narrowband signal (the message to be transmitted) is modulated by a broadband carrier signal that spreads the original spectrum. Spread spectrum is a correlation method that inserts a pseudorandom sequence into the original signal, in time or transform domain, and detects the watermark by calculating the correlation between the watermarked signal and the pseudorandom sequence. The carrier is the pseudorandom sequence (i.e., with statistical properties similar to a truly random signal) obtained with a random-number generator that has been initialized with a particular seed, known only to the owner. Thus, a generic binary message (the watermark) can be modulated by the pseudorandom sequence generated by means of the seed. Obviously, it is not possible to determine the watermark without the knowledge of the seed. Generally, such a factor is the privileged information that the sender and an authorized receiver

possesses. Apart form the seed, spread spectrum presents another element of robustness. That is, a large signal power is distributed over the entire frequency spectrum, so only a small amount of power is added at each frequency.

The two-set watermarking scheme marks two sets from the original signal differently. Thus, the presence of the difference itself between the two sets allows one to understand if a signal is marked or not. Also, in this case, the state of the art has been very rich and purposeful (Arnold, 2000; Bender et al., 1996; Yeo & Kim, 2003). Many variations have been proposed. In this section, we will be deep in analysis to a particular approach, that is, the patchwork approach, as in the following section "Future Trend," the crossing use of the audio *masking model* and two-set patchwork approach is described. Original patchwork approach works in embedding phase in two steps using a statistical approach: first of all, two sets, or patches, of the original signal are chosen in time/transform domain; then, a small constant value (let us say d) is added to one patch and subtracted from the other. Obviously, the patch in is composed by more than one element so that it is possible to evaluate the mean value of the elements composing each of the two patched sets (let say $\overline{\beta}^*$ and $\overline{\alpha}^*$). It is also possible to evaluate the mean value of the difference of the single mean values of the elements of the two patched sets (let say $E(\overline{\beta}^* - \overline{\alpha}^*)^1$), while the corresponding mean value of the difference of the single mean values of the elements of the two original sets can be indicated with $E(\overline{\beta} - \overline{\alpha})$. This change in $E(\overline{\beta}^* - \overline{\alpha}^*)$ and $E(\overline{\beta} - \overline{\alpha})$ is very useful in the detection phase as the value itself changes from the original value $\overline{x}$ to that corresponding to the patched situation $\overline{x} + 2d$. Also in this case the position, (with respect to the original signal) of the two sets is chosen by means of a random number generator with a seed. The presence of the watermark can be individuated only with the exact knowledge of the seed using the statistical approach previously described. Note that the statistical distribution of the values of the two patches does not change (because the same quantity is added and subtracted); it is the difference in the mean values that allows a detection (See Figure 9). The detection is performed by means of a hypothesis test. That is, given the null hypothesis (denoted H_o) against the alternative hypothesis (denoted H_1), the outcome of a hypothesis test is "reject H_o" or "do not reject H_o." In this case, the null hypothesis can be formulated as "the signal is not watermarked." Thus, the aim is to reject the null hypothesis. The performance of the patchwork

scheme strongly depends on the distance between $E(\overline{\beta}^* - \overline{\alpha}^*)$ and $E(\overline{\beta} - \overline{\alpha})$, which is function of d. Obviously, the greater the factor d corresponds to a lesser probability of failure in the detection phase, but also to a minus transparency of the watermark in the original signal. Thus, also in this case, the trade-off robustness vs. transparency must be carefully evaluated.

The idea behind replica method is that the original signal itself can be used as a watermark. Echo hiding (Bender et al., 1996) is a good example of a replica scheme. An echo is characterized by

Figure 9. Comparison between watermarked and un-watermarked distributions of the mean differences

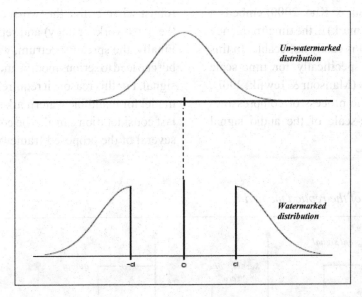

Figure 10. Replica method

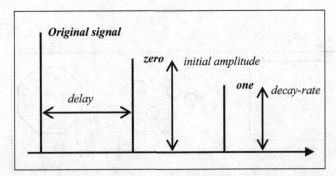

three factors: initial amplitude α, delay (offset), and decay rate (See Figure 10).

The echo is perceived as added tone with respect to the original signal (See Figure 11).

The detection phase can be considered as a decoding process involving the evaluation of the cepstrum of the echoed signal. The "cepstrum" can be used to separate the excitation signal (which contains the pitch of an audio signal) and the transfer function (which contains the audio quality). Without offering too many technical aspects (see Bender et al., 1996) the basic idea behind detection in a replica scheme is to determine the spacing between the echoes.

Finally, the self-marking method (Mansour & Tewfik, 2001; Wu, Su, & Kuo, 2000) embeds a signal (a self-evident mark) in the time/frequency domain in a way that is easily noticeable. In this chapter, we report specifically for time-scale modification strategy (Mansour & Tewfik, 2001), which basically is the process of compressing/ expanding the time-scale of the audio signal

between salient points. In Mansour and Tewfik (2001), such points are selected extrema of the wavelet decomposition, and the length of the interval is chosen according to the watermark to be embedded. In the last decade, the study of audio watermarking has been characterized by a huge improvement. This first part surveys the main five categories of audio *watermarking* apart from the use of masking and psychological models. A series of general thoughts can be expressed on such methods. Quantization approach is simple, but at the same time not very robust to several kinds of attack. In this sense, it is better than echo hiding, which is more complex but presents the same lacks in robustness. On the other hand, we have robust schemes like the two-set (and specifically the patchwork strategy) and replica approaches. Finally, the spread spectrum, which is effective, but can lead to serious modifications of the original signal. For this reason, it requires a psychological model for inaudible watermark embedding. This last consideration can also be considered true for several of the proposed frameworks.

Figure 11. Outcome of the replica method

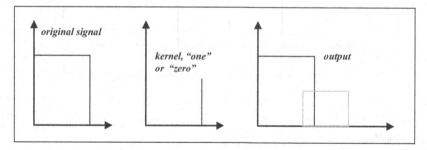

Figure 12. Patch shapes

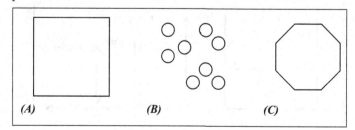

Most of the described strategies can be applied both for images and audio signals. As an example, the patchwork strategy, a low bandwidth strategy, is applied on the same way for image and audio. The difference is about the importance of the patch shape (See Figure 12) and its visibility within the image. The optimal choice of patch shape depends upon the expected image modifications, that is, if a JPEG image is considered, it is preferable to use a patch that embeds the energy in low frequencies. A comprehensive description of such a relation is proposed in (Bender et al., 1996).

The patchwork strategy is obviously an example, but the main differences between implementations of watermarking frameworks of image and audio signals are about two factors. That is, on one hand the human visual/auditory systems (HVS/HAS), and on the other the nature of the original signal itself. In the following, a brief explanation of both such factors is proposed (Bender et al., 1996).

A still image (the original signal to be watermarked) is typically an 8-bit 200×200 pixel image. Furthermore, it is also realistic to suppose that an image will be subject to many kinds of operations, such as filtering, lossy compression, and blurring. At the same time, the HVS presents sensitivity to contrast as a function of spatial frequency and the masking effect of edges (both in luminance and chrominance). The HVS is not very sensible to small changes in luminance. This is the first "hole" of the HVS. The second is the HVS's insensitivity to very low spatial frequencies such as continuous changes in brightness across an image. Many texts can be cited that propose a comprehensive description of human eye and visual system. In this chapter, we quote from Tovèe (1996), Marr (1982), and Delaigle (Delaigle, Devleeschouwer, Macq, & Langendijk, 2002). High-quality audio is usually a 16-bit 44.1 KHz signal (as Windows Audio-Visual (WAV)). A compressed audio (i.e., from (ISO MPEG-AUDIO) perceptual encoding standard, originally described in Brandenburg and Stoll (1992), presents statistics of the signal

drastically changed with respect to the original, while the characteristics that a listener perceives are the same. Many documents and much information can be retrieved about audio standards and HAS, but for a base knowledge the authors suggest one read the original standard (Brandenburg & Stoll, 1992; Pan, 1995), while the HAS will be described in the following sections.

Masking Models

Psychological and *masking model*s are usually inherited from data compression mechanisms and are very difficult to understand and explain in detail. Thus, the idea of the authors is to provide the reader with general key information and some references to find detailed information. First of all, independently from the nature of the signal itself, a masking model determines the levels of intensity (as a function of time or frequency) of a signal, to be perceived in presence of another signal. The masking model is usually a function or a set of data called simply, mask. The mask modulates the watermark to ensure its transparency, or to increase the watermark's energy for a given fidelity/transparency constraint. The main problem is specifically due to the fidelity feature; in fact, while concentrating on the increase of the trade-off energy/fidelity, little attention has been paid to the potential vulnerability of the masked watermark to a malicious attack. The scope of this chapter is to provide the reader a comprehensive description of watermark methods based on masking models, evaluate their effectiveness with respect to an intentional attack, and draw some conclusions for future trends. The concept of mask, as employed in *masking model*s, is used to signify a set of values (i.e., a matrix) that is computed on individual processing blocks (i.e., a block of 20 ms of an audio trace, or 8 × 8 pixel of an image) of the original signal. The original signal is defined as stationary in its temporal and spectral features, in an individual block. This is quite important for the definition of a correct mask. The reading of the mask leads one to understand in which regions of the transform domain a signal can be suitably inserted in a way its energy remains lower than the energy-threshold fixed by the mask, and thus can be as inaudible as possible. That is, the mask shapes the message (i.e., the sequence of bits to be inserted in the original signal to prove its copyright) to obtain the watermark. The shaping could involve all, or a portion of the transform domain: the mask can be spread over the entire transform domain (i.e., an identity matrix, multiplied by a small constant), or can be selectively embedded in particular regions of the transform domain (i.e., a matrix with all null values except from specific regions with no-zero coefficients). The retrieval of the mask differs from audio to image samples. Let us consider first of all the audio context. The psychoacoustic model is based on many studies of human perception. These studies have shown how an average human responds to sound near in frequency and/or time. The main two properties of human perception are absolute threshold of hearing (ATH) and auditory masking.

ATH means that humans can hear frequencies in the range from 20 *Hz* to 20,000 *Hz*. However, this does not mean that all frequencies are heard

in the same way. This consideration divides the range 20 *Hz* to 20,000 *Hz* in critical bands that are nonuniform, nonlinear, and dependent on the heard sound. Signals within one critical bandwidth are hard to separate for a human observer. Without introducing the relationship between Hertz and Bark (for a deeper investigation the authors quote Smith & Abel, 1999), ATH has been defined as a function of frequency, and represents the threshold of audibility of a sound at a certain frequency (see Figure 13).

The second property, auditory masking, means that humans do not have the ability to hear minute differences in frequency. This inability can be determined as the function of three factors: tone and noise maskers, and masking effect. A tone has a sharp peak in the frequency spectrum, which indicates that it is above the ambient noise of the signal. When a tone is very near to another in frequency, there is high probability that the first should mask the second (see Figure 14).

Humans have difficulty discerning signals within a critical band; the noise found within each of the bands can be combined to form one mask. Thus, the idea is to take all frequency components within a critical band that do not fit within tone

Figure 13. ATH, absolute threshold of hearing

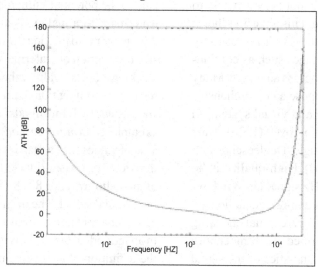

Figure 14. Frequency masking

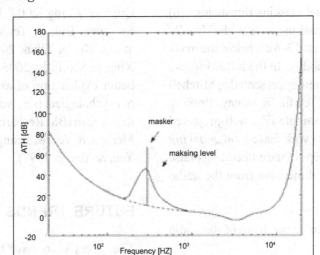

neighbourhoods, add them together, and place them at the geometric mean location within the critical band. Finally, the masking effect is related to the fact that the maskers, previously determined, affect not only the frequencies within a critical band, but also in surrounding bands: this results in a spreading of the effects of the masker (tone/noise). Apart from this straightforward introduction, if there are multiple noise and tone maskers, the overall effect is a little harder to determine. Several references can be quoted to provide the reader an idea of how the audio *masking models* and ATH work. First of all, the standard (ISO MPEG-AUDIO; Pan, 1995), which represents a good starting point also to nonspecialized people. Then, to understand the anatomy and functionalities of the HAS: (Probst, 1993; Robinson & Hawksford, 1999). Campbell and Kulikowski (1966) and Pantle and Sekuler (1969) presented masking effects in the visual domain in their works in late 1960s, and later in Tovèe (1996). Such effects, selective for bands of spatial frequencies and orientations, are the basis for the HVS and, as for the audio context, result in visual masking (Ferweda, Pattanaik, Shirley, & Greenberg, 1997). The reader can find an exhaustive description of the parameters for masking in Legge and Foley

(1980). This last article is also the reference for many of the proposed image data hiding strategies presented in the last years. The authors also suggests Pennebaker and Mitchell (1993), Lambrecht and Verscheure (1996), and Lubin (1993) and an important study on appearance colour pattern (Poirson & Wandell, 1993).

Watermarking Framework Based on Masking Models

A consistent number of watermark frameworks have been developed that control the trade-off between robustness and inaudibility by means of masking models. The approach is similar for audio and image watermarking. As an example, the audio masking model is here shortly presented as previously stated; the spectral audio masking model is based on a very simple observation. Given a tone at a certain frequency, humans do not hear this tone, and all the others below/above it, if its intensity is below the energy-threshold fixed by the mask. The most widely used audio masking model can be detailed as follows: (1) divide the signal in 20 *ms* nonoverlapping blocks; and for each block: (2) compute short-term power spectrum; (3) evaluate noise and pure-tones components; (4) remove all the masked components[2]; (5) compute the individual masking thresholds[3]; (6) compute the global masking thresholds. Usually the watermark is inserted 3-6 dB below the mask to enhance its inaudibility. In the following, we briefly describe the strategy presented in Mitchell et al. (Mitchell, Bin, Tewfik, & Boney, 1998) to give the reader an example of a well-projected *watermarking* framework based on *masking model*s. The macrosteps of the embedding phase (for a block of fixed dimension from the audio signal) are:

- Compute the power spectrum of the audio segment.
- Compute the frequency mask of the power spectrum.
- Use the mask to create the shaped author-signature.
- Compute the inverse FFT (IFFT) of the frequency shaped noise.
- Compute the temporal mask.
- Use the temporal mask to further shape the frequency shaped noise creating the watermark of that audio segment.
- Create the watermarked block.

That is, the temporal/spectral masking models are applied (Steps 2/5) to create a signal-shaped watermark. We have described this strategy also because it is probably the most representative and simple to be valued for nonspecialized readers. The detection phase, without describing too many technical aspects that can be found in (Mitchell et al., 1998), is always based on a hypothesis test as described in a previous section. The basic idea at the base of detection phase is that, as the embedded watermark is noise-like, a pirate has insufficient knowledge to directly remove the watermark. The state of the art is very prosperous of techniques based on *masking model*s. In this chapter, we quote several papers both for the novelty of the presented strategy and the results and comparisons. The reader should examine in

particular: (Herkiloglu, Sener, & Gunsel, 2004; Quan & Zhang, 2004; Robert & Picard, 2005; Swanson, Bin, & Tewfik, 1998; Tovèe, 1996; Wang, Xu, & Qian, 2005; Xie & Shen, 2005; Xing & Scordilis, 2005). The reader can find a better explanation of aspects related to the use of psychological (i.e., masking) models in watermarking in IBM Research CyberJournal (Craver, Memon, & Yeo, & Yeung, 1996; Craver, Memon, Yeo, & Yeung, 1997).

FUTURE TRENDS

The recent years have been characterized by a growing diffusion in the fruition of digital audio contents and consequently in the need for copyright and ownership property. The watermarking techniques represent a good solution for these supplies: a mark is opportunely inserted in a host signal in a way so that its ownership is provable. Lots of strategies have been presented in the recent past with this purpose. Several of these techniques inherited their core from image watermarking; more in general, this legacy was not always possible due to the differences in sensibility and perception between human ear and eye. A set of basic features for a reliable watermarking strategy was presented in Arnold (2000). Two characters are most significant and, apparently, contradicting: inaudibility and robustness to signal processing. Inaudibility means that the differences between the original and the watermarked signal should not be perceivable by the human ear. Second, the watermark must be robust against intentional or unintentional attacks. One of the most impairing attacks is the signal processing, specifically, lossy compression. Such a compression guarantees enhanced portability of digital information, but can have an undesirable effect on the embedded watermark. The development of our strategy is accomplished by referring constantly to these two features. In this section we propose two watermarking frameworks for audio contents, based on the use of a psychoacoustic model. Both works are based on the patchwork strategy, originally described in Bender (1996), for image watermarking. Further adaptations have been proposed to improve its efficiency when applied to audio contents. Such changes are mainly based on the right dimensioning of the patch in order the introduced noise that should not be perceivable by the end-user. The core of the proposed technique is the shaping of the patch so that two optimality criteria (i.e., inaudibility and robustness to lossy compression) can be satisfied. The inaudibility is guaranteed by shaping the patch vs. the minimum masking threshold, obtained with the psychoacoustic model 2. For both the proposed frameworks, the original signal is not needed for the detection of the watermark. The first strategy is an adaptive approach of the patchwork algorithm. The patchwork is originally presented in Bender (1996) for image *watermarking*. The original implementation of this technique presents several limitations when applied to audio samples. Quite a few adaptations have been proposed to improve considerably its performance (Arnold, 2000; Bassia, Pitas, & Nicholaidis, 2001; Kim,

2003; Yeo et al., 2003). From these studies, the work-dominion and the adaptive patch shaping appear as the key points for the applying of the original strategy to audio samples such as for its perfection. The proposed strategy works on an assumption introduced in Bender (1996): treating patches of several points has the effect of shifting the noise to low frequencies, where there is lower probability to be filtered by lossy compression techniques. This concept has also been introduced previously in this chapter. The problem is the dimension of the patch. Such a factor is fixed by comparing the spectrum of watermarked signal to the minimum masking threshold, as obtained referring to the psychoacoustic model 2 (ISO MPEG-AUDIO). The patch shaping is performed in the Fourier dominion. The proposed technique is applied to audio samples and compared with the adaptive patchwork state of the art, referring to the framework proposed in Gordy and Bruton (2000). As previously described, the patchwork strategy is a two-set method, that is, it makes two different sets from a host signal (Yeo et al., 2003). This difference is used to verify, or not, a hypothesis H_o (e.g., the watermark is embedded).

Figure 15. Distribution of the mean difference of the samples in un-watermarked and watermarked signals

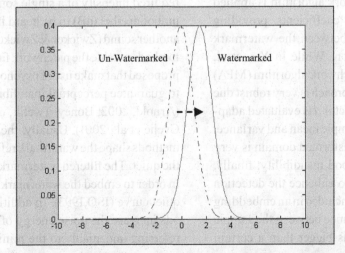

The original strategy (Bender, 1996) is applied to sets with more than 5,000 elements. The samples of each subset are considered uniformly distributed and with equal mean values. The elements are modified by adding and subtracting the same quantity *d*. Thus, the detection of a watermark is related to the condition $E[A_{marked} - B_{marked}] = 2d$. Several of these statements must be reassessed when working with audio samples (Arnold, 2000). In particular, the distribution of the sample value is assumed as normal (See Figure15). Recent approaches modify the original strategy to better take into account the human ear's sensibility to noise interferences. These methods can be classified in temporal and spectral approaches, depending on the domain where the watermark is embedded. In Bassia et al. (2001) a technique is proposed that is based on the transformation of time-domain data. A set of *N* samples, corresponding to 1*sec* of stereo audio signal, is modified by a watermark signal w(i). Arnold (2000), Kim (2003), and Yeo et al. (2003) propose spectral patchwork approaches. In particular, Arnold (2000) works with a dataset of 2*N* Fourier coefficients. The relationship between *d* and the elements of the dataset is multiplicative. The parameter *d* is adaptively chosen to prevent perceptual audibility, basing on the characteristics of the audio signal (i.e., it introduces for the first time the concept of power density function in the hypothesis tests). In Kim (2003), the patchwork algorithm is applied to the coarsest wavelet coefficients, providing a fast synchronization between the watermark embedding and detection. While in Yeo et al. (2003), the modified patchwork algorithm (MPA) is presented. Such an approach is very robust due to three attributes: the factor *d* is evaluated adaptively and is based on sample mean and variance; the patch size in the transformed domain is very little: this guarantees good inaudibility; finally, a sign function is used to enhance the detection rate. These features are included in an embedding function so that the distance between the sample means of the two sets is bigger than a certain

value d. The temporal approaches are easier to implement than the spectral ones; at the same time, they present several weaknesses against general signal processing modifications (Kim, 2003). The association between a watermarking algorithm and a noisy communication system is not new (Muntean, Grivel, Nafornita, Najim, 2002). Actually, a watermarking strategy adds a mark (i.e., the noise) in a host signal (i.e., the communication channel). In this sense, the watermark embedding can be considered as an operation of channel coding: the watermark is adapted to the characteristics of the transmission channel (i.e., the host signal in which the watermark should be embedded). In case of audio contents, where it is usually considered as an impairment, the sensibility of the human ear can be used as a way to spread and dimension the watermark. The human auditory system (HAS) is well known, that is, it is sensitive to specific frequencies (i.e., from 2*KHz* to 4*KHz*) and reacts to specific events (i.e., frequency and temporal masking). Given a signal *S*, it is possible to recover its minimum masking threshold. The minimum masking threshold of audibility represents a limit between the audible and inaudible signals for *S* at different frequencies. Independently from *S*, it is also possible to recover the absolute threshold of hearing (ATH). Such a curve (i.e., referred to as quiet curve (Cvejic et al., 2001) is different than the previous and defines the required intensity of a single sound expressed in unit of decibel (dB) to be heard in the absence of another sound (Zwicker & Zwicker, 1991). Several methods outside the patchwork fashion have been proposed that make use of psychoacoustic models to guarantee perceptual inaudibility of the mark (Arnold, 2002; Boney, Twefik, & Hamdy, 1996; Cvejic et al., 2001). Usually, the state-of-the-art methods shape the watermark referring mainly to the quiet. The filtered watermark signal is scaled in order to embed the watermark noise below the quiet curve (ISO,1993). In addition, other methods increase the noise energy of the watermark, referring undeniably to the minimum threshold of audibility. Such a threshold can be recovered through a well-defined psychoacoustic model. The MPEG/audio standard provides two example implementations of the psychoacoustic model. Psychoacoustic model 1 is less complex than psychoacoustic model 2 and has more compromises to simplify the calculations. Either model works for any of the layers of compression. However, only model 2 includes specific modifications to accommodate Layer III. In this chapter, we refer to model 2 differently from the past approaches.

As already stated, the proposed patchwork strategy modifies two sets of N elements/coefficients from the original signal (i.e., signalUn-Marked). The signalMarked strongly belongs to the correspondent signalUn-Marked. The core of our strategy is the shaping of the frequency-response of the mark signal using psychoacoustic model 2. The algorithm proposed in this chapter embeds the watermark in the frequency domain by modifying $2N$ Fourier coefficients. The choice of this transform domain is justified by the use of the psychoacoustic model. The embedding steps (see Figure 16) can be summarized as follows:

1. Evaluate the threshold of minimum audibility for the signalUn-Marked, referring to psychoacoustic model 2.

2. Map the secret key and the watermark to the seed of a random number generator. Next, generate two N-points index sets $I_N^A = \{a_1, a_2, ..., a_N\}$ and $I_N^B = \{b_1, b_2, ..., b_N\}$.

3. Let $X = \{X_1, X_2, ..., X_{2N}\}$ be 2N DFT coefficients of the signalUn-Marked, corresponding to the index sets I_N^A and I_N^B.

4. The original amplitude of the patch and the number of retouched coefficients, starting from the generic elements of index a_i or b_i, have respectively standard values (δ, θ). Such values are modified iteratively to verify that the spectrum of the watermark signal is under the minimum audibility threshold (i.e., obtained from point 1). Iteratively means a constant referring to the block of model 2 from the block shaping (see the dotted loop in Figure 16).

5. The time-domain representation of the output signal is found, applying an Inverse DFT to the signalMarked .

The phase of detection is as follows:

1. Define two test hypotheses: H_o (the watermark in not embedded) and H_1 (the watermark is embedded).

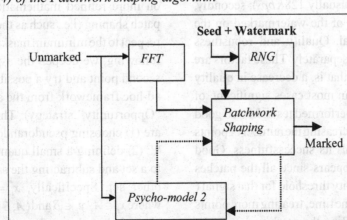

Figure 16. Steps (1-4) of the Patchwork shaping algorithm

2. Map the seed and the watermark to a random number generator and generate two sets $I_N^{A'}$ and $I_N^{B'}$.

3. Fix a threshold Δ for the detection, and evaluate the mean value (i.e., $\overline{z} = E(\cdot)$) of the random variable $z = a_i' - b_i'$, for $a_i' \in \{I_N^{A'}\}$ and $b_i' \in \{I_N^{B'}\}$.

4. Decide for H_o, or H_1, depending on $\overline{z} < \Delta$, or $\overline{z} \geq \Delta$.

We tested the proposed algorithm on 16-*bit* stereo audio signals, sampled at Fs = 44.1KHz. The size of each patch (i.e., N) was fixed to 50 points, while the default values for (δ, θ) were set to (0.5, 10). Higher values for θ were also tested only for robustness evaluation, regardless of quality aspects. The state of the art proposes a framework for the evaluation of audio watermarking techniques (Gordy & Bruton, 2000). In this chapter, we referred to this framework and considered, in particular, two key factors: quality of the watermarked signal and robustness to mp3 compression. The evaluation of quality is an essential part in testing our strategy, since the basic idea was to guarantee the maximum rate of inaudibility of the patch. The tests were performed using a subjective score (i.e., a *MOS*) and the *SNR* of the watermarked signal vs. the host signal. The robustness of the proposed strategy was tested in two steps: at first, coding and decoding the watermarked signal with a commercial MP3 encoder at different rates (e.g., usually 128*Kbps*); secondly, trying the detection of the watermarked on the uncompressed signal. Quality and robustness cannot be evaluated separately. These factors are strongly correlated, that is, a decrease in quality causes an increase, in most cases significant, of robustness. All the performed tests showed good results. The idea of increasing the number of points of the patches reveals its successfulness. Good subjective quality appears since all the patches are below the audibility threshold for that signal ($SNR \leq 26$). At the same time, treating more points has the effect of shifting the patchwork-noise to

low frequencies, where it has a lower probability to be filtered by the mp3 compression. Figure 17 shows different probability density functions (i.e., introduced as empirical probability density function (*Pdf*) in Bassia et al., 2001) of the random variable z, as described in the detection phase. The density function of z before the mp3 compression is compared with different behaviours (i.e., varying the dimension of the patch). This test shows clearly that higher dimensions of θ lead to lower alterations in the detection values. This results in a *Pdf* nearer to that of the uncompressed signal. We have also evaluated the error probability at different rates of compression (i.e., 128, 96 and 64 *Kbps*). Two kinds of errors can be individuated. The state of the art refering to them is terms of Type I (Rejection of H_o, when H_o is true) and Type II (Nonrejection of H_o, when H_1 is true) (Yeo et al., 2003). Type II errors seem to be the most impairing (the watermark is inserted (i.e., quality degradation) but the ownership cannot be proven). Figure 18 presents the Type II errors for a test audio signal. Clearly, the probability of rejection of H_o, when H_1 is true, decreases correspondently with the mp3-rate of compression.

The proposed strategy can be improved in two points: the modelling of the patch and the possibility of a wrong detection (that is, increasing the distance d, both the wrong detection and the inaudibility decrease). Actually, these step are quite coarse. Further studies have been centred on more refined mathematical mechanisms of patch shaping (i.e., such as the curve fitting) with respect to the minimum masking threshold. In the following, we deepen the aspects related to the second point and try a possible solution with an ad-hoc framework from the authors (i.e., named "Opportunity" strategy). The embedding steps are (1) choosing pseudorandomly two sets from Ψ; (2) defining a small quantity d; (3) adding d to a set and subtracting the same value from the other set. Specifically, $x_i^* = x_i + d, y_i^* = y_i + d$, where $x_i \in A$, $y_i \in B$ and $(A, B) \in \Psi$. The detection phase is based on a hypothesis testing, that is,

Figure 17. Probability density function of detection for the random variable z, varying the dimension of the patch with SNR = 26.

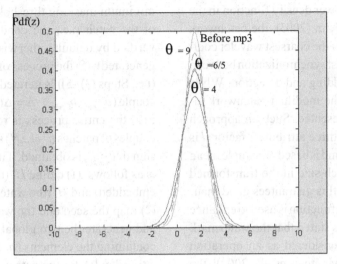

Figure 18. Error Probabilities for lossy compression at different rates

Type II Errors(%)	
MPEG I Layer III (128Kbps)	0.1
MPEG I Layer III (96Kbps)	0.7
MPEG I Layer III (64Kbps)	1.6

defined on a test statistic z and a test hypothesis H. The basic theory is as follows: let us suppose the *Pdf* of a random variable z (i.e., the test statistic) is a known function $f(Z, \theta)$ depending on the parameter θ. We wish to test the assumption $\theta = \theta_0$, against $\theta \neq \theta_0$. The assumption $\theta = \theta_0$ is denoted with the null hypothesis H_o, where $\theta \neq \theta_0$ is signified by the alternative hypothesis H_1. The purpose is to establish whether experimental evidence supports the rejection of H_o. Referring to the watermarking context: (1) the test statistic z is defined as a function of elements from A and B: $z = \bar{x} - \bar{y}$; (2) the distribution of z (e.g., $\Phi(z)$) is normal (Arnold, 2000), with an expected mean value $\bar{z} = 0$ in the unmarked and $\bar{z} = 2d$ in the marked case (i.e., in this case, $\Phi(z) = \Phi_m(z)$); (3) the test hypotheses (H_o, H_1) are defined and

verified: H_o (i.e., the watermark is not embedded) and H_1 (i.e., the watermark is embedded and $\Phi(z) = \Phi_m(z)$). The main problem is the definition of d: the probability of a wrong decision remains, although the distribution in the watermarked case is shifted to the right (see Figure 15). A possible solution could be increasing the distance factor d, with the effect of having a lower probability of false rejection, but also a greater impairment on the audibility of the watermark in the host signal. The literature tries to solve this problem in several ways. In this sense, the idea that seems to work better is the spectral patchwork (Arnold, 2000; Kim, 2003; Yeo et al., 2003), with a dataset of *2N* Fourier coefficients. The relationship between d and the elements of the dataset is multiplicative. The parameter d is adaptively chosen to prevent perceptual audibility, based on the characteristics of the audio signal (i.e., it introduces for the first time the concept of power density function in the hypothesis tests). In Kim (2003), the patchwork algorithm is applied to the coarsest wavelet coefficients, providing a fast synchronization between the watermark embedding and detection. While in Yeo et al. (2003) the modified patchwork algorithm (MPA) is presented. Such an approach is very robust due to three attributes: factor d is evaluated adaptively and is based on sample mean and variance; the patch size in the transformed domain is very little: this guarantees good inaudibility; finally, a sign function is used to enhance the detection rate. It is stated that the watermark embedding can be considered as an operation of channel coding (Muntean et al., 2002): the watermark should adapt to the characteristics of the transmission channel (i.e., the host signal in which the watermark should be embedded). In case of audio contents, what is usually considered as an impairment, the sensibility of the human ear, can be used as a way to spread and dimension the watermark. Given a signal S, it is possible to recover its minimum masking threshold and use it to opportunely shape the watermark-noise. Several methods, outside the patchwork fashion, have been proposed that make use of psychoacoustic models to guarantee perceptual inaudibility of the mark. Opportunity refers and applies this approach in a patchwork schema, maximizing a cost function that represents how much the watermark impairs the original signal. The minimum masking threshold is recovered using the *psychoacoustic model 2* (ISO MPEG-AUDIO). The proposed strategy works as follows (see Figure 19): (1) the value of d is fixed *a priori* to minimize the possibility of false rejection; (2) given Ψ, its minimum masking threshold is recovered; (3) the secret key and the watermark are mapped to the seed of a random number generator (RNG) to find a couple (a_i, b_i); (4) the patchwork approach is applied to the DFT coefficients of the host signal corresponding to (a_i, b_i), using the distance fac-

tor d; (5) a cost function $\Delta = \Delta(a_i, b_i)$ if defined, that represents the global distance between the minimum masking threshold and the amplitude of the patch (i.e., the condition $\Delta > 0$ must be verified by default, otherwise a new set (a_i, b_i) is generated); (6) the process of generation of (a_i, b_i) (i.e., Steps (3)–5)) is iterated N' times to find the couple $(a_{i\_min}, b_{i\_min}) : \Delta = \Delta(a_{i\_min}, b_{i\_min}) = \Delta_{MAX}$; (7) the entire process is repeated to embed N couples of patches ($i = 1...N$) and the watermarked signal Ψ_{marked} is obtained. The phase of detection is as follows: (1) define H_o (the watermark in not embedded) and H_1 (the watermark is embedded; (2) map the seed and the watermark to an RNG and generate the two global sets $I_N^{A'}$ and $I_N^{B'}$ (e.g., containing the elements $(a_i, b_i), i = 1...N$); (3), fix a threshold Δ for the detection, and evaluate the mean value (i.e., $\overline{z} = E(\cdot)$) of the random variable $z = a_i' - b_i'$, for $a_i' \in \{I_N^A\}$ and $b_i' \in \{I_N^B\}$; (4) decide for H_o, or H_1, depending on $\overline{z} < \Delta$, or $\overline{z} \geq \Delta$.

We tested the proposed algorithm on 16-bit stereo audio signals, sampled at $Fs = 44.1 KHz$. The size of the patch (i.e., N) was fixed to 100 couple of points while the default value for d was set to 0.25 (e.g., where the original algorithm (Bender et al., 1996) selected a fixed value 0.15 in the experiments). Higher values for d were also tested only for robustness evaluation, regardless of quality aspects, to test the rate of probability rejection. The performed investigations on the proposed strategy have the aim of showing *good audio quality* (e.g., inaudibility of the mark) of the watermarked signals and, at the same time, *low probability of false rejection* when the audio signal is subjected to postprocessing. In the following, the results of such tests are presented. The evaluation of quality is an essential part in testing our strategy, since the basic idea was to guarantee the maximum rate of inaudibility of the patch. Good subjective quality appears since all the patches are below the audibility threshold for that signal ($SNR \leq 26$). We also compared the marked/unmarked signals using the PEAQ strategy (ITU-R BS.1387-1): Opportunity shows a

Figure 19. "Opportunity" strategy

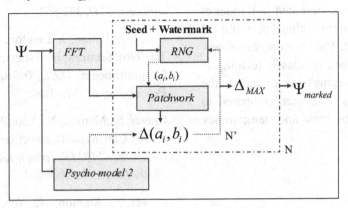

better performance with respect to the other tested strategies with default parameters (see Figure 20). The second aim of the tests was to verify a decreasing in the probability of false rejection. Two kinds of errors can be individuated. The state of

Figure 20. PEQ—MOS rating

Opportunity	4.77
MPA [YK03]	4.00
Arnold [A00]	3.23

Figure 21. Error probabilities for non-compressed signal (test1.wav)

Type II Errors(%)	
Opportunity	0.1
MPA [YK03]	0.7
Arnold [A00]	1.6

Figure 22. Error probabilities for lossy compression at different rates (test1.wav)

Type II Errors(%) -Opportunity-	
MPEG I Layer III (128Kbps)	0.32
MPEG I Layer III (96Kbps)	0.68
MPEG I Layer III (64Kbps)	0.81

the art refers to them in terms of Type I (Rejection of H_o, when H_o is true) and Type II (Nonrejection of H_o, when H_i is true) (Yeo et al., 2003). Type II errors seem to be the most impairing (the watermark is inserted (i.e., quality degradation) but the ownership cannot be proven). Figure 21 presents the Type II error for a noncompressed test audio signal (test1.wav). We also prove the efficiency of Opportunity when compressing-decompressing (i.e., at different rates of compression (i.e., 128, 96 and 64 *Kbps*)) and resynchronizing the same test signal (see Figure 22).

CONCLUSION

This chapter has presented an overview of the use of masking models in watermarking techniques, which is a relatively novel and very interesting field of research. The aim of such techniques is to guarantee a high level of robustness and bandwidth of the watermark, as well as fidelity of the watermarked signal. The general scheme for audio content has been presented both in the embedding and the detection phase. The approach is very similar both for audio and image contents. To also give an idea on how to design, implement, and verify techniques based on such an approach, two techniques on audio *watermarking* are proposed in the last section. Such strategies are both based on a two-set method, as presented in Bender et al. (1996) for image watermarking, but combined with a masking model. The development of new techniques jointly based on classic techniques and masking models seems to be a trend for the future. The strategies have been compared to others in terms of robustness and transparency of the watermark.

REFERENCES

Arnold, M. (2000). Audio watermarking: Features, applications and algorithms. *IEEE International Conf. Multimedia and Expo, 2*, 1013-1016.

Arnold, M., & Schiltz, K. (2002). Quality evaluation of watermarked audio tracks. *SPIE Electronic Imaging, 4675*, 91-101.

Bassia, Pitas, I., & Nicholaidis, N. (2001). Robust audio watermarking in the time domain. *IEEE Transaction on Multimedia, 3*, 232-241.

Bender, W., Gruhl, D., Morimoto, N., & Lu, A. (1996). Techniques for data hiding. *IBM SYSTEMS JOURNAL, 35*(3-4).

Boney, L., Twefik, A.H., & Hamdy, K. N. (1996). Digital watermarks for audio signal. *International Conference on Multimedia Computing and Systems*, 473-480.

Brandenburg, K., & Stoll, G. (1992). *The ISO/MPEG-audio codec: A generic standard for coding of high quality digital audio.* 92nd AES-Convention, preprint 3336.

Campbell, F. W., & Kulikowski, J. J. (1966). Orientation selectivity of the human visual system. *Journal of Physiology, 187*, 437- 445.

Chen, B., & Wornell, G. W. (1999). Dither modulation: A new approach to digital watermarking and information embedding. *Proceedings of the SPIE – Security and watermarking of multimedia contents, 3657*, 342-353.

Cox, I. J., Kilian, J., Leigton, F. T. & Shamoon, T. (1996). Secure spread spectrum watermarking for multimedia. *IEEE Transactions on Image Processing, 6*, 1673-1687.

Craver, S., Memon, N., Yeo, B.-L., & Yeung, M. (1996). Can invisible watermarks resolve rightful ownerships? *IBM Research Technical Report RC 20509 IBM CyberJournal.*

Craver, S., Memon, N., Yeo, B.-L., & Yeung, M. (1997). Resolving rightful ownerships with invisible watermarking techniques: Limitations, attacks and implications. *IBM Research Technical Report RC 20755 IBM CyberJournal.*

Cvejic, N., Keskinarkaus, A., & Seppanen, T., (2001). Audio watermarking using m-sequences and temporal masking. *IEEE Workshops on Applications of Signal Processing to Audio and Acoustics*, 227-230.

Delaigle, J. F., Devleeschouwer, C., Macq, B., & Langendijk, L. (2002). Human visual system features enabling watermarking. *Proceedings of Multimedia and Expo*, ICME02, 489-492.

Eggers, J. J. Su, J. K., & Girod, B. (2000). A blind watermarking scheme based on structured codebooks. *Secure Images and Image Authentication-IEE Colloquium*, 4/1-4/6.

Ferwerda, J. A., Pattanaik, S. N., Shirley, P., & Greenberg, D. P. (1997). *Computer Graphics, 31*, 143-152.

Gordy, J. D., & Bruton, L. T. (2000). Performance evaluation of digital audio watermarking algorithms. In *Proceedings of the 43rd Midwest Symposium on Circuits and Systems.*

Herkiloglu, K., Sener, S., & Gunsel, B. (2004). Robust audio watermarking by adaptive psychoacoustic masking. In *Proceedings of 12th IEEE*

Conference on Signal Processing and Communications Applications, 29-32.

Huang, J., & Shi, Y. Q. (2002). Adaptive image watermarking scheme based on visual masking. *Electronic Letters*, *34*(8), 748-750.

ISO/IEC Joint Technical Committee 1 Subcommittee 29 Working Group 11. (1993). *Information technology-coding of moving pictures and associated audio for digital storage media at up to about 1.5 Mbit/s, Part 3:Audio.* ISO/IEC 11172-3.

Kazakeviciute, G., Januskevicius, E., Rosenbaum, R., & Schumann, H. (2005). Tamper-proof image watermarking, based on existing public key infrastructure. *INFORMATICA*, *16*(1).

Kim, H. (2000). Stochastic model based audio watermark and whitening filter for improved detection. *IEEE International Conference on Acoustics, Speech, and Signal Processing*, *4*, 1971-1974.

Kim, H. J. (2003). *Audio watermarking techniques.* Pacific Rim workshop on Digital Steganography.

Kim, H. O., Lee, B. K., & Lee, N. Y. (2001). *Wavelet-based audio watermarking techniques: Robustness and fast synchronization.* Research Report 01-11, Division of Applied Mathematics-Kaist.

Kim, H. J., & Yeo, I. (2003). Modified patchwork algorithm: A novel audio watermarking scheme. *Transactions on Speech and Audio Processing*, *11*(4), 381-386.

Lambrecht, C., & Verscheure, O. (1996). Perceptual quality measure using a spatio-temporal model of the human visual system. *Proceedings of the SPIE*, *2668*, 450-461.

Legge, G. E., & Foley, J. M. (1980). Contrast masking in human vision. *Journal Optical Society*, *70*, 1458-1470.

Lubin, J. (1993). The use of psychophysical data and models in the analysis of display system performance. In A. B. Watson, *Digital images and human vision* (pp. 163-178).

Macq, B., & Quisquater, J. (1995). Cryptology for digital TV broadcasting. *Proceedings of the IEEE*, *83*, 944-957.

Mansour, M. F., & Tewfik, A. H. (2001). Audio watermarking by time-scale modification. *International Conference on Acoustics, Speech, and Signal Processing*, *3*, 1353-1356.

Marr, D. (1982). *Vision: A computational investigation into the human representation and processing of visual information.* San Francisco: W. H. Freeman.

Mitchell, D. S., Bin, Z., Tewfik, A. H., & Boney, L. (1998). Robust audio watermarking using perceptual masking, *IEEE Signal Processing*, *66*(3), 337-355.

Muntean, T., Grivel, E., Nafornita, I., & Najim, M. (2002). Audio digital watermarking for copyright protection. *International Workshop on Trends and Achievements in Information Technology.*

Pan, D. (1995). A tutorial on MPEG/audio compression. *IEEE MultiMedia*, *2*(2), 60-74.

Pantle, A., & Sekuler, R. W. (1969). Contrast response of human visual mechanisms sensitive to orientation and direction of motion. *Vision Res.*, *9*, 397-406.

Pennebaker, W. B., & Mitchell, J. L. (1993). *JPEG: Still image data compression standard.* Van Nostrand Reinhold.

Petitcolas, F. A. P., Anderson, R. J. & Kuhn, M. G. (1999). Information hiding—A survey. *Proceedings of the IEEE—special issue on protection of multimedia content*, *87*(7), 1062-1078.

Poirson, A., & Wandell, B. (1993). Appearance of colored patterns. *Journal of the Optical Society of America*, *10*(12), 2458-2470.

Probst, R., Lonsbury-Martin, B. L., & Martin, G. K. (1991). A review of otoacoustic emissions. *Journal of Acoustic Society, 89*, 2027-2067.

Quan, X., & Zhang, H. (2004). Audio watermarking for copyright protection based on psychoacoustic model and adaptive wavelet packet decomposition. *Proceedings of 2004 International Symposium on Intelligent Multimedia, Video and Speech Processing*, 282-285.

Recommendation ITU-R BS.1387-1, 11/01.

Robert, A., & Picard, J. (2005). On the use of masking models for image and audio watermarking. *IEEE Transaction on Multimedia, 7*(4), 727-739.

Robinson, D. J. M., & Hawksford, M. J. (1999). Time-domain auditory model for the assessment of high-quality coded audio. *107th Convention of the Audio Engineering Society*—preprint 5071.

Smith & Abel (1999). *Bark and ERB Bilinear Transforms*.

Swanson, M. D., Bin, Z., & Tewfik, A. H. (1998). Multiresolution scene-based video watermarking using perceptual models. *IEEE Journal on Selected Areas, 16*(4), 540-550.

Tilki, J. F., & Beex, A. A. (1996). Encoding a hidden digital signature onto an audio signal using psychoacoustic masking. In *Proceedings 1996 7th International Conference on Signal Processing* (pp. 476-480).

Tovée, M. J. (1996). *An introduction to the visual system.* Cambridge University Press.

Trichili, H., Bouhlel, M.-S., Solaiman, B., & Kamoun, L. (2003). Exploitation of the HVS features for the enhancement of image watermarking techniques. *ISPA03, 2*, 1076-1081.

Wang, R. D., Xu, D. W., & Qian, L. (2005). Audio watermarking algorithm based on wavelet packet and psychoacoustic model. *PDCAT 2005*, 812-814.

Wu, M., & Liu, B. (1998). Watermarking for image authentication. *Proceedings of 1998 IEEE International Conference on Image Processing, 2*, 437-441.

Wu, C. P., Su, P. C., & Kuo, C. C. J. (2000). Robust and efficient digital audio watermarking using audio content analysis. *Security and Watermarking of Multimedia Contents (SPIE), 3971*, 382-392.

Xie, G., & Shen, H. (2005). Toward improved wavelet-based watermarking using the pixel-wise masking model. *ICICP2005, 1*, 689-692.

Xing, H., & Scordilis, M. S., (2005). Improved spread spectrum digital audio watermarking based on a modified perceptual entropy psychoacoustic model. *Proceedings of IEEE Southeast Conference*, 283-286.

Yeo, I. K., & Kim, H. J. (2003). Modified patchwork algorithm: A novel audio watermarking scheme. *IEEE Transaction On Speech and Audio Processing, 11*(4).

Zwicker, E., & Zwicker, U. T. (1991). Audio engineering and psychoacoustics: matching signals to the final receiver: The human auditory system. *Journal of Audio Engineering Society, 39*(3), 115-126.

ENDNOTES

[1] The expression $E(o)$ indicates the operation of mean value in statistics.

[2] Including components below the absolute hearing threshold, or components too close to others to be heard.

[3] This step involves the human auditory system.

Chapter V
Damageless Watermark Extraction Using Nonlinear Feature Extraction Scheme Trained on Frequency Domain

Kensuke Naoe
Keio University, Japan

Yoshiyasu Takefuji
Keio University, Japan

ABSTRACT

In this chapter, we propose a new information hiding and extracting method without embedding any information into the target content by using a nonlinear feature extraction scheme trained on frequency domain. The proposed method can detect hidden bit patterns from the content by processing the coefficients of the selected feature subblocks to the trained neural network. The coefficients are taken from the frequency domain of the decomposed target content by frequency transform. The bit patterns are retrieved from the network only with the proper extraction keys provided. The extraction keys, in the proposed method, are the coordinates of the selected feature subblocks and the neural network weights generated by the supervised learning of the neural network. The supervised learning uses the coefficients of the selected feature subblocks as the set of input values, and the hidden bit patterns are used as the teacher signal values of the neural network, which is the watermark signal in the proposed method. With our proposed method, we are able to introduce a watermark scheme with no damage to the target content.

INTRODUCTION

In this chapter, we present a new model of digital watermark that does not embed any data into the content, but is able to extract meaningful data from the content. This is done by processing the coefficients of the selected feature subblocks to the trained neural network. This model trains a neural network to assign predefined secret data, and use the neural network weight and the coordinates of the selected feature subblocks as a key to extract the predefined code. This means that it would not damage the content at all. The proposed method is an improvement from the paper of our research project, which was published before (Ando & Takefuji, 2003).

In Section 2, we discuss the background surrounding digital watermarks, frequency transformation, and neural networks. We demonstrate the characteristics, and discuss what techniques are useful for implementing digital watermarks. In Section 3, we propose the method of damageless watermark embedding and extraction for still image. In Section 4, we provide experiment results for testing its robustness and fragileness. In Section 5 and 6, we conclude with a discussion of the proposed method, and indicate some future works of the proposed method.

BACKGROUND

In this section, we discuss the background surrounding digital watermarks, and we go deeply to the backgrounds and researches in frequency transformation and neural networks, which consist of important modules for the proposed method.

General Background Surrounding Digital Watermarks

Recently, with the rapid progress of information technologies and the emergence of the Internet, digital multimedia contents are easily distributed on the network. This circumstance helped to open digital contents to the public without difficulty, even for ordinary computer users, but also helped illegal distribution and copying of contents. Due to the characteristics of digital contents, digital contents are easy to make an exact copy and to alter the content itself. This became a main concern for authors, publishers, and legitimate

owners of the contents. Therefore, digital watermark became a key technology for protecting the copyrights. Digital watermark protects unauthorized change of the contents and assures legal uses for its copyright.

There are several ways to protect digital content. One example is to encrypt the content and to share the decryption key between the author and the observer. But this method prevents other observers without a decryption key from accessing the content. This feature avoids a free distribution and circulation of the content through the network, which, most of the time, is not desirable to the author of the content. Digital watermark only embeds data to the content, and this feature does not avoid the distribution of the content.

Watermarking techniques are one technique of information hiding techniques (Katzenbeisser & Petitcolas, 2000). The research in information hiding has a history (Kahn, 1996), namely, the researches in digital watermark and steganography have been active. Both are very similar, but the applications are different (Reither & Rubin, 1998). Digital watermark can be classified in several ways. The first classification is by the perceptibility of the watermark signal to humans. A perceptible watermark has various usages but because it limits the utility of the content, most of the research in this area has focused on imperceptible watermarking techniques. Digital watermark is often embedded imperceptibly to human receptors to avoid contaminating the content. For imperceptible images, the human visual system (HVS) model is often used. There are many still image watermark researches that make use of HVS model (Delaigle, De Vleeschouwer, & Macq, 1998; Kim, Byeong, & Choi, 2002; Reither & Rubin, 1998; Swanson, Zhu, & Tewfil, 1996; Westen, Lagendijk, & Biemond, 1996). For imperceptible audio, a psychoacoustic model is often used. The basic idea of the psychoacoustic model is that human ears are insensitive to the change in phase and amplitude, but very sensitive to the change in the time domain. Also, humans have a limitation to high frequency domain and low frequency domain (Cox, Miller, & Muttoo, 2002). There are many researches for audio watermark and many of them use a psychoacoustic model for implementations (Baumgarte, Ferekidis, & Fuchs, 1995; Boney, Tewfik, & Hamdy, 1996; Gruhl, Lu, & Bender, 1996; Wolfe & Godsill, 2000).

Most imperceptible still image watermark methods use the HVS model in order to embed data into frequency domains after the frequency transformation of multimedia content, such as DFT, DCT, and DWT. Perceptible watermarks are sometimes used, but it limits the use of the images. Therefore, main concern in this research area has focused on imperceptible watermarks. In general, digital watermark is a technique to conceal a code imperceptibly to the content to anybody who observes it, and it is also difficult to remove from the content to protect its intellectual property rights.

The second classification of watermark technique is based on whether the original content data is used during the watermark extraction process. A watermark method that needs original content to extract a watermark from embedded content is called nonblind detection watermark. A watermark method that does not need original content and only needs the embedded content to extract a watermark is called blind detection watermark. This characteristic raises the difference between the extraction method and its robustness.

The third classification of watermark is based on its robustness to the attacks. Robust watermark is normally strong against illegal alteration of the content and it is difficult to remove watermark data from the content. Even if the attacker was able to remove the watermark data, the damage to the content is very intense. Therefore, robust watermark is often used for copyright protection. A watermark method using spread spectrum is widely known for its robustness (Cox, Kilian, Leightont, & Shamoon 1997). Spread spectrum has been deployed in many researches to strengthen the robustness of the watermark. There are many researches of robust watermarking techniques (Bender, Gruhl, & Morimoto, 1995; O'Ruanaidh & Pun, 1998) and watermarks for other media such as motion picture (Echizen, Yoshiura, Arai, Himura, & Takeuchi, 1999) and text data (Brassil, Low, Maxemchuk, & O'Gorman, 1994; Brassil & O'Gorman, 1996).

To the contrary, a method called fragile watermark is a watermark method that is usually weak to alteration of the content. The watermark data will be broken or diminished when the content data is damaged. Therefore, fragile watermark is often used for an integrity check of the content. Another watermark, known as semifragile watermark, has a characteristic of both robust and fragile watermark.

Recently, a watermark method using neural network has been spreading widely. Commonly seen methods in this area are the ones that use either DCT or DWT for decomposition of the image, and a back propagation neural network is used for embedding the watermark (Davis & Najarian, 2001; Hong, Shi, & Luo, 2004; Lou, Liu, J.L. & Hu, 2003; Zhang, Wang, N.C. & Xiong, 2002). Beside that, watermark methods using generalized Hebb (Pu, Liao, Zhou, & Zhang, 2004), RBF neural network (Liu & Jiang, 2005; Zhang, et al., 2003), full counterpropagation neural network (Chang & Su, 2005), Hopfield neural network (Zhang & Zhang, 2004; Zhang, & Zhang, 2005), and many more are introduced. The use of neural network can be used to achieve both robust and fragile watermarking method.

But many of the methods that use neural network embed a watermark into the content data, which will alter the quality of data. Our method does not embed any data in the target content, which does not damage the content data at all. This characteristic is the biggest difference between the conventional methods.

Background for Frequency Transformation

In the research area of information hiding, including digital watermark, orthogonal transformation is used for the watermark embedding process to embed a watermark signal into the frequency domain of the image. Embedding in the frequency domain is commonly used because this method is able to limit the damage to the content rather than embedding the signal to the image directly. Frequency analysis is a useful tool because with the analysis, it is able to understand which range of frequency band is the important frame of the image and which is not. According to human visual system (HVS), humans are sensitive to the changes in the low frequency domain and insensitive to the changes in the high frequency domain. Consequently, watermark signals are embedded in the higher frequency domain to achieve imperceptible watermarking. But embedding a watermark signal to the high frequency band has a risk of data loss in case of image compression that uses the feature of HVS systems, like JPEG compression.

There are several methods to transform an image to frequency domain, such as discrete Fourier transform (DFT), discrete cosine transform (DCT), and discrete wavelet transform (DWT). In our proposed method, DCT is used, so we will discuss it in more detail.

Discrete cosine transform is one method of orthogonal transformation. The image compression using DCT orthogonally transforms the small blocks in the image. Compression using discrete cosine transform is known to be very effective, and is employed in MPEG format and JPEG format.

Discrete cosine transform divides an image into $N*N$ pixel small blocks. The transformation will be processed independently to the individual $N*N$ blocks. When expressing the coefficients after the discrete cosine transform as $F(u,v)$, the discrete cosine transform function, and inverse discrete cosine transform function to the $N*N$ block of two dimensional image signal $f(x,y)$ is as follows.

DCT function of $N*N$ two dimensional image:

$$F(u,v) = \frac{2}{N}c(u)c(v)\sum_{x=0}^{N-1}\sum_{y=0}^{N-1}f(x,y)\cos\left\{\frac{(2x+1)u}{2N}\pi\right\}\cos\left\{\frac{(2y+1)v}{2N}\pi\right\}$$

$$\text{if } u=0 \text{ then } c(u)=\frac{1}{\sqrt{2}} \qquad \text{if } v=0 \text{ then } c(v)=\frac{1}{\sqrt{2}}$$

$$\text{if } u\neq0 \text{ then } c(u)=1 \qquad \text{if } v\neq0 \text{ then } c(v)=1$$

Inverse discrete cosine transformation function of $N*N$ two dimensional image:

$$f(x,y) = \frac{2}{N}\sum_{u=0}^{N-1}\sum_{v=0}^{N-1}c(u)c(v)F(u,v)\cos\left\{\frac{(2x+1)u}{2N}\pi\right\}\cos\left\{\frac{(2y+1)v}{2N}\pi\right\}$$

The relation between the image signal and the frequency coefficients are shown in Figure 1.

When the size of N is the bigger, the less inferior the image will be, but the calculation cost will increase proportional to N^2; ideal number of N is known to be 8. When the image is 512*512 pixels in size, the amount of 8*8 blocks will be 64*64, total of 4096 of 8*8 subblocks. Generalized discrete cosine transform function of $N = 8$ is:

Figure 1. Relation of pixel value and DCT coefficients

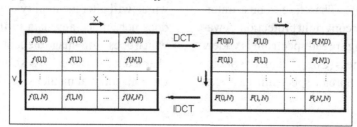

$$S(u,v) = \frac{1}{4}C(u)C(v)\sum_{m=0}^{7}\sum_{n=0}^{7}P(m,n)\cos\frac{(2m+1)u\pi}{16}\cos\frac{(2m+1)v\pi}{16}$$

$$C(u)C(v)\begin{cases} \frac{1}{\sqrt{2}} & \text{if } \quad u,v=0 \\ 1 & \text{if } \quad u,v\neq 0 \end{cases}$$

$(u,v=0,1,2,\cdots,7)$

As shown in Figure 1, the coefficient of $F(0,0)$ is the direct current and the other $F(u,v)$ is the alternate current. Coefficients closer to the direct current will be lower frequency value and closer to $F(N,N)$ will be higher frequency value. In general, low frequency values have more energy than high frequency values, and are known to be more affective to the composition of an image. In case of image compression, the region of high frequency band is omitted or quantized more strongly than the lower frequency band. Hence, embedding watermark signals to the high frequency band has a possibility of being omitted during the compression process, while embedding watermark signals to the lower frequency band will damage the frame of the original image. Considering the robustness of watermark, watermark signals are often embedded in the midfrequency band. The proposed method needs feature values from low to high frequency values, so values are taken diagonally from $F(0,0)$ to $F(N,N)$ as feature input values to the neural network.

Background for Neural Network

A neuron is a nerve cell and the brain consists of many nerve cells. The neuron itself only has simple function of input and output of electric signal. But when these neurons organically connect to form a network, the network is capable of complex processing. Mathematical models of these networks are called neural networks, and processing these artificial neural networks on computers is called neural computing. Neural computing is a classic research topic and neural networks are known to be capable of solving various kinds of problems by changing the characteristics of neuron, synaptic linking, and formation of the network.

Figure 2. DCT coefficients chosen diagonally in proposed method

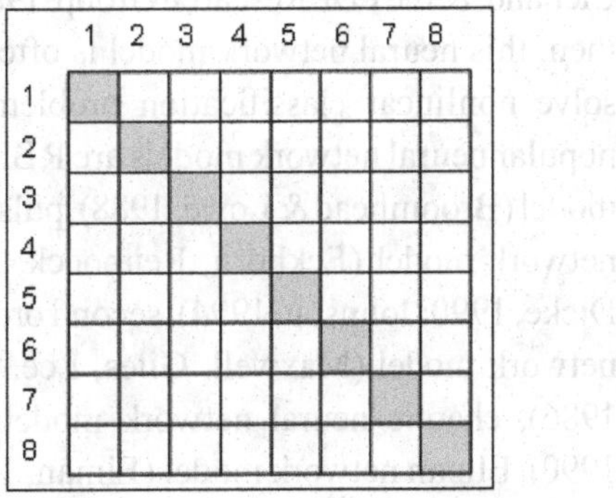

Binary model (Hopfield & Tank, 1985), sigmoid model (McCulloch & Pitts, 1943), radial basis function model (Moody & Darken, 1989; Poggio & Girosi, 1990), and competitive neuron model (Kohonen, 1982; Kohonen, 1995; Takefuji, Lee, & Aiso, 1992) are some of the models classified by the model of neuron units itself. A neural network can also be classified by its network formation. Recurrent model is a model in which neurons are connected mutually. Feed forward model is a model in which neurons are connected in a layer and signals are transmitted simply from input layer to output layer, whereas feedback model is a model similar to feed forward model, but it has a backward or recursive synaptic link. Both feed forward and feedback model sometime has a bias synaptic link.

The proposed method uses a multilayered perceptron model as a network model which has a feedforward synaptic link. Multilayered perceptron model was introduced by Rosenblatt (Rosenblatt, 1985). Two layer perceptron can classify data linearly but cannot classify data nonlinearly. Multilayered perceptron with more than three layers are known to have an approximation ability of a nonlinear function if properly trained, but then there was no ideal learning method for this kind of training. This model became popular when a training method called back propagation learning, which uses generalized delta rule, was introduced by Rummelhart (Rummelhart, Mc-Clelland, & the PDP Research Group, 1986). Since then, this neural network model is often used to solve nonlinear classification problems. Other popular neural network models are RBF network model (Broomhead & Lowe, 1988), pulsed neural network model (Eckhorn, Reitboeck, Arndt, & Dicke, 1990; Johnson, 1994), second order neural network model (Maxwell, Giles, Lee, & Chen., 1986), chaotic neural network model (Aihara, 1990), Elman network model (Elman, 1994), and many others.

Background for Multilayered Perceptron Model

Multilayered perceptron basically has a synaptic link structure with neurons between the layers but no synaptic link among the layer itself. Signal given to the input layer will propagate forwardly according to the synaptic weight of the neurons connected, and reaches to the output layer as shown in Figure 3.

For each neuron, input values are accumulated from a former layer, and outputs a signal value according to a certain function; normally sigmoid

function is used. Sigmoid function has a graph like Figure 4, and this function is expressed as:

$$y = \frac{1}{1 + \exp(-x)}$$

Each network connection has a network weight. The network weight from unit i to unit j is expressed as W_{ij}. The output value from the former layer is multiplied with this value. These output values of the former layer are summed and connected to the upper layer. Therefore, the output values for the output layer are determined by the network weight of the neural network, as shown in Figure 5. Consequently, to change the output value to a desired value, adjustment of these network weights is needed. Learning of the network is a process of conditioning the network weight with the corresponding teacher values.

Background for Back Propagation Learning

Back propagation learning is the process of adjusting the network weights to output a value close to the values of the teacher signal values.

Figure 3. Example of multilayered perceptron model

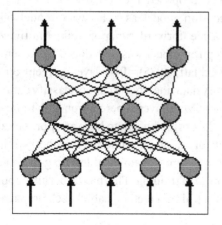

Figure 4. Graph of sigmoid function

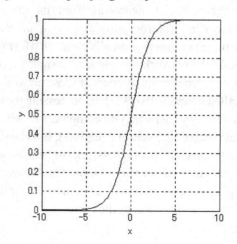

Figure 5. Input values and network weights determinate the output value

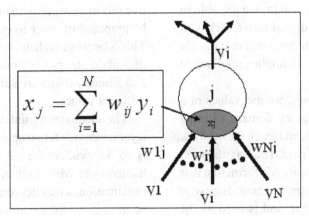

Back propagation learning is a supervised learning. In back propagation learning, teacher signal values are presented to the network. This training tries to lower the difference between the teacher signal values and the output values by changing the network weight. This learning is called back propagation because the changes of the network weight according to the difference in the upper layer propagate backward to the lower layer. This difference between the teacher signal values is called as error and often expressed as delta (δ).

When teacher signal t_j is given to the unit j of output layer, the error δ_j will be the product of the differential for sigmoid function of output unit y_j and difference between the teacher signal t_j and output value of unit y_j. So the function for calculating the error value for the output unit is:

$$\delta_j = (t_j - y_j)f'(y_j) = (t_j - y_j)(1 - y_j)y_j$$

On the other hand, calculation of error value for the hidden neurons is more complicated. This is because the error value of the output unit affects the error value for the hidden neuron. The error value for the hidden unit varies with the network weight between the hidden layer and output layer. In order to calculate the error value δ_i for hidden unit, error value δ_j of the output unit is used. So

the function to calculate the error value δ_i for hidden unit i is:

$$\delta_i = f'(y_i)\sum_{j=1} W_{ij}\delta_j = (1 - y_i)y_i\sum_{j=1} W_{ij}\delta_j$$

After calculating the error values for all units in all layers, then network can change its network weight. The network weight is changed by using the function:

$$\Delta W_{ij} = \eta\,\delta_j y_i$$

η in this function is called learning rate. Learning rate normally has a value between 0 and 1, and generally represents the speed of learning process. The lower the learning rate is the more gradual the learning process will be, and the bigger the learning rate is the more acute the learning process will be. Sometimes this parameter must be tuned for stable learning.

Proposed Method

In this section, we present the hidden bit patterns embedding method to the neural network using the selected feature values from the image, and extraction method using the network weight from the trained network with the selected feature values. With this algorithm, we are able to implement a function of digital watermark with no embedding of data into the content data. No embedding into the content implies no damage to the content data.

To accomplish our goals, we use values of a certain area in the frequency domain as input data to the neural network, and teach the network with a classification set of data. The classification data set will be the identification information that acts as watermark data. A trained neural network will have a network weight, and is used as the extraction key for the output data that is trained to approximate the watermark signal. With this model, the attacker cannot reproduce a watermark signal if he has only one of the input data set or network weights. The extractor must have both proper input data and network weights to induce a watermark signal from neural network.

With the proposed embedding method, we must decide the structure of neural network. The amount of neurons for input layer is decided by the number of pixels selected as feature values from the content data. The proposed method uses the diagonal values of the frequency domain from the selected feature subblock of the content data. For example, if the image is 512*512 pixels in size and the frequency transform is done by 8*8 DCT, then there will be 4096 subblocks being produced, and the neurons in the input layer will be 8. We select a unique feature subblock in obedience to the teacher signal. Diagonal 8 pixels of the selected subblock will be taken as input values for the neural network. In our proposed method, one bias neuron is added for better approximation also. Therefore, we will have nine neurons in the input layer for proposed method.

The output layer will be trained to output 1 or 0 as an output value. The amount of neurons for output layer is decided by the number of identification values or patterns to be embedded into the network. In the case where 32 unique identifica-

tion values are to be embedded into the network, five sets of network with one output neuron must be prepared in order to embed five bits of data. This is because each network represents, for each digit of the binary watermark signal, respectively, and 5 binary digits are sufficient to represent 32 different values.

The adequate amount of neurons in the hidden layer necessary for an approximation, in general, is not known. So the number of neurons in the hidden layer will be taken at will. For better approximation, a bias neuron like in input layer can be introduced for the hidden layer too. After the neural network structure is decided, the process is moved on to the back propagation learning procedure.

This learning process uses watermark signal data as teacher signal, which is either 1 or 0, corresponding to the digit of the watermark. After the learning process, the network weights are converged to certain values. We use these network weights and the coordinates of selected feature subblocks as the extraction keys of the embedded watermark data.

For the extraction process, we will take the same neural network structure with the network weights generated in the embedding process. Only the proper input values of the selected feature subblocks will output the proper watermark signal. Proper input values are induced only when you know the proper coordinates of the subblocks for the corresponding watermark signal.

Necessary Parameters for the Proposed Method

For embedding, there are two parameters to decide on. First is the number of class patterns, which are the identifier in the extraction process. The more the number of class patterns, the more data to be embedded, but a large number of class patterns will have a high calculation cost. Second parameter is the coordinate of the subblock that you associate the patterns to. Coordinates determine the input values for the learning process, which generates a neural network weight that acts as an extraction key for watermark in the extraction process. These two parameters are stored as the extraction keys and handed to extractor of the watermark.

For extracting, two parameters are needed to extract a proper watermark signal. First is the neural network weights created in the embedding process. Second is the coordinates of the subblocks that were associated with the patterns. These network weights and coordinates of the subblocks are the extraction keys for the watermark signal. These parameters are handed as an extraction key from the proper user who embedded the watermark. Only with the presence of the proper network weights and the proper coordinates is one able to output the proper watermark signal.

We will discuss both embedding process and extraction process in detail in the following subsections.

Embedding Process

Embedding steps consist of the following procedures:

1. Frequency transform of the image
2. Selection of the feature subblocks
3. Backpropagation learning process
4. Save the coordinates of the selected feature subblocks and converged network weights

Frequency Transform of the Image (Process 1)

This procedure simply performs a frequency transformation of the image. If DCT is used for frequency transformation method, it transforms value in each pixel into DCT coefficient values.

Selection of the Feature Subblocks (Process 2)

If user desires to embed 32 different identification patterns, then the same amount of unique subblocks must be chosen from the image. The feature subblocks can be selected randomly, or voluntarily by the user. Besides, sufficient number of networks must be prepared, which will be the number of binary digits to satisfy the identification values. In this case, five networks are enough to represent 32 different identification values.

Backpropagation Learning Process (Process 3)

A set of learning processes for each network is constructed by the training of input data set for corresponding teacher signal value, respectively. If identification patterns are 32, a set of learning processes for the network is training the network with 32 different sets of input values of the corresponding teacher signals. This learning process is repeated until the output value satisfies a certain learning threshold value. This threshold value can be set flexibly according to the usage of the watermark. This learning must be done for all five neural networks.

Save the Coordinates of the Selected Subblocks and Converged Network Weights (Process 4)

After the learning process for all the networks have converged, the coordinates of the selected feature subblocks and the values of network weights are saved. Extractor will use this information to extract a watermark signal in the extraction process.

Extraction Process

Extraction step consists of the following procedures:

1.   Frequency transform of the image.
2.   Load the coordinates of selected feature sub-blocks and the values of network weights.
3.   Feed forward the network with the input values from the selected feature subblocks.

Frequency Transform of the Image (Process 1)

This procedure is an equivalent process as the frequency transform of the image in the embedding process. We simply perform a frequency transformation of the image. If DCT is used for frequency transformation method, it transforms the value of each pixel into DCT coefficient values.

Load the Coordinates of Selected Feature Subblocks and the Values of Network Weights (Process 2)

Before the process, extractor must receive the coordinate data from the embed user. Extrac-

tor will use the coordinates of selected feature subblock and network weights as the extraction keys to extract the watermark signal. Knowing the coordinates of the feature subblocks will lead user to the proper input values for the embedded watermark signal. By knowing the network weights value, we can induce the structure of the network, and only proper network weights are able to output the proper watermark signal.

Feed Forward the Network with the Input Values from the Selected Feature Subblocks (Process 3)

After constructing the neural networks with proper network weights, we examine the output value of the network with the input values induced from the feature subblocks. Each network is to output either 1 or 0 with the aid of threshold value for output unit. If the network weights and the input values are properly set, the trained network must be able to output the corresponding watermark

Figure 6. Image of Lena

Table 1. Coordinates of feature subblocks and corresponding teacher signal

x-axis	y-axis	coordinate	teacher signal
58	64	(58,64)	00000
34	7	(34,7)	00001
43	30	(43,30)	00010
44	9	(44,9)	00011
61	46	(61,46)	00100
40	20	(40,20)	00101
30	5	(30,5)	00110
42	12	(42,12)	00111
63	13	(63,13)	01000
27	43	(27,43)	01001
63	25	(63,25)	01010
34	5	(34,5)	01011
35	44	(35,44)	01100
25	55	(25,55)	01101
55	7	(55,7)	01110
35	26	(35,26)	01111
53	25	(53,25)	10000
32	33	(32,33)	10001
8	58	(8,58)	10010
10	42	(10,42)	10011
51	14	(51,14)	10100
18	5	(18,5)	10101
36	52	(36,52)	10110
9	28	(9,28)	10111
28	58	(28,58)	11000
4	64	(4,64)	11001
51	26	(51,26)	11010
36	22	(36,22)	11011
50	21	(50,21)	11100
64	24	(64,24)	11101
6	40	(6,40)	11110
47	39	(47,39)	11111

signal. We will use an example to explain these processes in the next subsection.

Embedding of Watermark Signal

In this example, we will use TIFF format Lena image as in Figure 6, which is 512*512 pixels in size, as the target content data. We will embed 32 different identification values as a watermark signal. Therefore, five different neural networks must be prepared because 32 can be defined with five digits of binary numbers.

First, frequency transformation of DCT will be processed to the Lena image. 8*8 pixels sub-blocks are produced for 512*512 pixels Lena image. There will be a total of 4,096 subblocks produced. In terms of subblocks, it will be 64*64 subblocks are produced. Feature subblocks are selected randomly with the teacher signals correspondingly, and those coordinates of subblocks are saved as Table 1.

For example, before performing DCT, the original pixel values in subblock (47, 39) are as Table 2.

When DCT is processed, the transformed DCT coefficients values of the subblock (47, 39) are as Table 3.

For all 32 subblocks, eight diagonal DCT coefficient values are taken as feature values and treated as input values to the network. These values are then trained to a corresponding watermark signal value, which is the teacher signal of the

Table 2. Value of R in subblock (47, 39)

	1	2	3	4	5	6	7	8
1	223	215	221	223	220	213	217	216
2	218	219	221	222	218	217	217	217
3	224	223	221	220	216	216	219	215
4	221	224	220	217	218	214	215	214
5	220	222	221	217	217	213	214	212
6	221	222	222	218	218	217	211	210
7	222	224	219	221	219	219	213	202
8	220	221	221	220	220	214	212	201

Table 3. Value of DCT coefficients in subblock (47, 39)

	1	2	3	4	5	6	7	8
1	1.742125	0.026497	−0.00791	0.001626	−0.00213	0.002284	−0.00308	0.001961
2	0.006479	−0.01078	0.007188	−0.00681	0.005884	0.002945	0.00139	0.00083
3	−0.00066	0.000533	−0.00721	0.002397	0.002546	0.004778	−2.8E−05	0.000525
4	−0.00084	−0.00105	−0.00086	−0.00084	0.002695	−0.00046	0.002963	0.000518
5	−0.00313	0.000609	0.000147	−0.00168	0.002625	3.5E−05	−0.00128	0.003985
6	0.001678	0.002373	0.000715	0.003409	0.00036	0.00064	−0.00122	−0.00074
7	0.000681	0.001202	0.001972	−0.00063	0.001246	0.001165	0.001456	0.001745
8	0.000664	0.001202	0.000994	0.001249	−0.00041	0.002797	−0.00142	−2.5E−05

neural network. For this training, the number of hidden neurons of neural network is set to 10.

Back propagation learning process is repeated until the output values converge to a learning threshold. For this learning, the threshold value for the learning is set to 0.1. This means if the input values are trained to output 1, training stops if output unit outputs a value more than or equal

Table 4. Values of the DCT coefficients for all 32 subblocks

	value1	value2	value3	value4	value5	value6	value7	value8
pattern1	1.046	−0.01417	0.005203	0.005085	0.00225	0.006173	−0.00045	−0.00109
pattern2	1.90625	0.001313	0.001914	−0.00166	0.00125	0.000207	−0.00091	−0.00136
pattern3	1.737625	−0.00106	0.001597	−5.2E−05	−0.00188	0.002027	−0.00035	−0.00192
pattern4	1.257125	0.04542	0.008758	0.001642	−0.00513	−0.00034	−0.00026	0.000781
pattern5	1.91425	−0.0027	0.001082	0.000317	0.0005	2.36E−05	−0.00033	−0.00014
pattern6	1.047625	0.033841	−0.02533	0.043072	−0.00163	−0.00329	0.003834	0.004879
pattern7	1.836875	0.000575	−0.00058	−0.00099	0.001125	0.000356	0.002076	0.000559
pattern8	0.89225	−0.00841	−0.0159	−0.00392	−0.0015	−0.00533	−0.00635	0.005165
pattern9	0.773625	0.041021	0.028334	0.004469	−0.00063	−0.00257	−0.00083	−0.00342
pattern10	1.5535	0.022212	0.018848	0.003559	−0.00375	−0.00299	−0.0006	−0.00078
pattern11	1.47675	−0.0186	0.00353	3.42E−06	0.00175	0.0035	0.00247	0.001598
pattern12	1.839125	−0.00126	0.000808	0.001392	0.000875	−0.00161	0.001692	−1.8E−05
pattern13	0.990625	−0.05766	0.000265	0.00908	−0.00363	−0.00211	−0.00027	−0.00431
pattern14	1.6185	−0.0325	−0.00097	0.002016	0.007	0.003119	−0.00203	0.000866
pattern15	1.906625	−0.0051	−0.00087	0.00148	−0.00263	−0.00029	0.000369	0.002401
pattern16	0.740875	0.14334	−0.01397	−0.01949	−0.00013	−0.0079	0.006716	−0.00244
pattern17	0.852125	−0.01074	−0.00097	−0.0027	0.000375	−0.00178	0.000972	−0.00328
pattern18	1.624875	0.005121	0.016029	−0.01111	−0.00263	−0.00123	0.007721	0.000218
pattern19	0.69225	0.052677	0.013786	−0.00015	−0.00075	−0.00249	0.006715	0.001961
pattern20	1.518125	−0.00257	0.007749	0.003048	0.001125	−0.00082	0.000501	−0.00015
pattern21	1.02175	0.014577	−0.03787	0.029608	−0.00675	0.001834	0.001372	−0.00152
pattern22	1.83775	0.001225	−0.00216	0.003583	−0.002	0.001319	−0.00109	−0.00163
pattern23	1.65075	−0.0077	0.003828	0.001929	−0.00025	−0.0005	−0.00183	0.002772
pattern24	1.616625	0.011404	−0.00435	0.003599	0.003625	0.000409	−0.0024	0.001089
pattern25	1.688125	0.001867	−0.00336	−0.00125	−0.00163	0.000259	0.000356	−0.00038
pattern26	0.801125	−0.01131	0.003799	−0.00825	0.000125	−0.00029	0.006451	0.001357
pattern27	0.761125	−0.00989	−0.0026	−0.00261	0.000125	−0.00042	−0.00065	0.001919
pattern28	0.871375	−0.00438	0.067719	−0.03157	0.011125	−0.00072	0.001781	−0.00634
pattern29	1.261875	0.005028	−0.03984	−0.05209	−0.01413	−0.01511	−0.00041	−0.00434
pattern30	1.43275	0.002375	−0.00365	0.003301	−0.00275	0.000992	0.001652	0.003332
pattern31	1.528375	−0.00235	0.002131	0.002747	0.004125	0.002819	0.003369	−0.00022
pattern32	1.742125	−0.01078	−0.00721	−0.00084	0.002625	0.00064	0.001456	−2.5E−05

to 0.9, and if the input values are trained to output 0, training stops if output unit outputs a value less than or equal to 0.1. Also, the output threshold in this example is set to 0.5. This means if the output value is larger than 0.5, output signal is set to 1, and if the output value is smaller than 0.5, output signal is set to 0. This training process is repeated for all five neural networks. Eventually, networks are trained to output values for the subblock (47, 39), for example, as Figure 7.

Examples of the output values for each trained network for 32 input values are shown in Figures 8, 9, 10, 11, and 12.

Finally, the network weights of the networks are saved as extraction keys, as well as the coordinates of the selected feature subblocks. Here, network weights between the input layer and hidden layer are named $W1$, and network weights between the hidden layer and output layer are named $W2$. Network weights $W1$ and $W2$ for the five networks of the training are shown in Tables 5, 6, 7, 8, 9 ,and 10. For $W1$, the table has 11*9 values that represent a network weight between the 11 hidden layer units and 9 input layer units. For $W2$, the table has 1*11 values that represent a network weight between the output unit and 11 hidden layer units.

Figure 7. Converged networks and the flow for output values of subblock (47, 39)

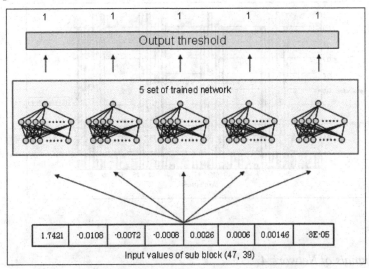

Figure 8. Output signals of network 1

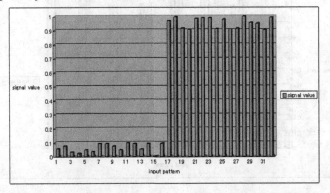

Figure 9. Output signals of Network 2

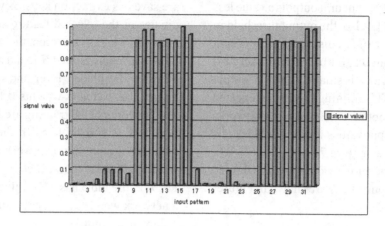

Figure 10. Output signals of Network 3

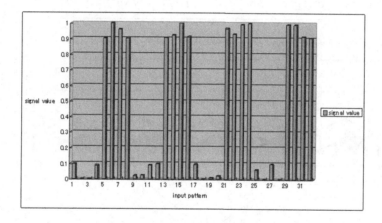

Figure 11. Output signals of Network 4

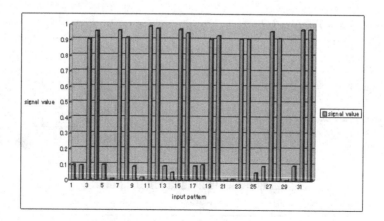

Figure 12. Output signals of Network 5

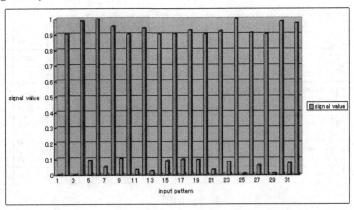

Table 5. Values of W1 in network 1

	1	2	3	4	5	6	7	8	9	10	11
1	-0.545	0.1053	-0.318	-0.409	-0.849	-0.253	-0.329	-0.638	-2.816	-0.8447	-2.2851
2	-6.243	4.2957	1.6684	-0.057	-2.049	5.7934	-2.131	2.4219	-0.212	-0.279	-1.5509
3	1.1761	-2.775	-2.683	0.2241	2.895	-8.455	7.7772	0.0238	8.9507	0.69486	-0.0214
4	-0.838	0.9695	-3.346	0.2575	-0.603	-2.367	1.6415	-1.375	-0.17	0.78862	0.17302
5	2.7196	0.7128	0.9428	0.085	-0.073	2.6079	2.3858	0.5399	-2.515	-0.0892	0.04078
6	2.0686	0.1655	0.5588	-0.618	-2.737	3.1482	-4.191	-0.942	-4.895	-0.0161	-0.7824
7	-0.642	-2.027	3.1139	-0.099	-0.362	7.2715	2.698	1.7409	-1.547	-0.2812	-0.9968
8	-0.072	-0.405	-1.32	-0.546	-0.4	-4.601	-0.374	1.0797	1.1151	-0.5249	-1.394
9	-0.415	-0.317	0.2238	-0.175	-0.737	0.1087	-0.432	-0.732	-1.891	-0.6687	-1.307

Table 6. Values of W1 in network 2

	1	2	3	4	5	6	7	8	9	10	11
1	-1.367	1.8037	-0.946	-2.038	-0.974	-0.293	-0.662	0.776	-1.044	-2.1545	-1.411
2	-0.084	9.9794	0.4168	3.9	2.8618	1.3901	-0.426	2.0642	-3.191	7.2107	-2.9311
3	1.0003	3.2476	0.2048	2.8046	2.85	-0.915	0.069	-2.509	-2.042	6.2208	-1.2299
4	-1.126	-1.968	-1.147	2.8229	1.7002	1.5579	-0.148	2.0128	0.4605	6.0481	1.7382
5	0.123	-2.412	0.4961	0.6458	0.0802	-2.341	-0.113	-4.172	1.7989	-1.6866	-3.881
6	0.5489	1.7829	-1.183	4.6794	3.1993	-0.254	0.1961	0.2275	5.3526	-3.9023	2.8114
7	-2.184	-6.115	0.1148	0.3638	-0.356	0.4263	-0.416	-1.566	2.8082	-6.332	-2.5444
8	0.0054	-0.448	1.0357	2.7707	2.3143	0.6939	0.0399	1.0644	6.0917	-2.4388	0.31353
9	-1.015	0.9244	-0.235	-1.366	-0.828	0.0797	-0.675	0.3011	-0.596	-1.6262	-0.668

Table 7. Values of W1 in network 3

	1	2	3	4	5	6	7	8	9	10	11
1	-0.52	0.5308	-1.014	0.3395	0.102	-0.991	-3.071	-0.549	-0.597	-0.5042	-1.1414
2	-0.031	-0.135	0.7059	0.8381	-0.678	0.3264	1.32	2.5973	-0.817	-1.4803	-0.6406
3	-0.699	-2.534	1.6019	0.9982	-0.058	0.7466	10.143	1.9797	1.3283	-1.1433	-3.5568
4	0.2164	1.9005	-4.163	2.2266	-5.457	-1.904	-0.588	4.3478	0.5493	1.9031	1.2143
5	0.3312	-1.035	-3.48	0.5962	-2.432	-1.026	3.1225	0.377	0.8562	0.01517	0.9234
6	0.1945	-1.733	8.6322	-1.513	4.644	1.1497	-7.22	-2.22	2.5815	0.36396	-0.1429
7	-0.239	-1.795	-3.367	0.4196	-0.65	-0.153	1.9698	0.0928	1.4199	-0.638	-0.4532
8	-0.004	-0.189	0.7364	-0.044	0.3327	0.1784	-6.282	0.9476	0.7248	0.41934	0.33366
9	-0.396	-0.006	-0.285	0.3719	-0.042	-0.431	-2.437	-0.668	-0.269	-0.4198	-0.4709

Table 8. Values of W1 in network 4

	1	2	3	4	5	6	7	8	9	10	11
1	-0.188	-0.842	-6.098	-0.282	-0.605	-0.387	1.7103	0.4583	0.8019	-0.8733	-1.5495
2	-0.391	-1.071	2.6207	-0.202	0.4143	-0.056	-2.921	0.0196	-0.21	-0.7724	-1.3532
3	-0.763	1.1549	0.2007	0.784	-2E-04	-0.483	3.7897	1.9257	1.3404	1.8556	-1.1434
4	-0.331	-7.813	-1.796	0.2511	0.2833	-0.8	-3.725	1.8876	2.0319	1.8928	-1.8213
5	2.3896	-4.29	4.4608	1.3475	4.3159	1.6742	6.0958	-2.256	-3.004	-0.2381	0.97661
6	-0.477	-0.485	-4.867	-0.465	-2.008	-0.885	1.166	1.297	1.5709	2.0531	-0.9452
7	0.9288	2.6817	7.8704	1.4954	2.2435	2.025	-1.197	-0.304	-0.643	-1.8457	0.62916
8	1.9688	1.4654	9.6635	-0.771	0.2419	2.4045	1.2159	1.8784	2.8279	-1.3986	1.0164
9	-0.153	-1.01	-4.002	-0.083	-0.558	0.011	1.0589	0.0689	0.7535	-0.6896	-0.7693

Table 9. Values of W1 in network 5

	1	2	3	4	5	6	7	8	9	10	11
1	-0.44	-0.135	-3.037	-0.515	1.164	-2.161	-1.541	0.6785	-0.706	-1.0659	-3.1528
2	-0.327	0.9845	4.3372	0.0297	1.9898	3.7382	-6.918	-4.225	-1.315	-2.6792	0.26183
3	0.1797	0.255	2.014	0.4605	7.1733	3.9717	0.8953	3.2146	0.7123	-0.3898	-0.9424
4	0.2452	0.2194	-0.129	0.6104	-6.218	1.348	1.4185	-5.954	1.9689	-0.0146	-1.356
5	-1.256	-5.075	4.3461	-3.793	-3.498	1.6737	-3.317	5.1555	-3.668	-1.85	-0.0355
6	1.1968	0.9939	-1.903	0.3297	2.1827	-3.403	5.0701	-4.061	1.727	1.4227	-1.1108
7	-0.749	-2.344	-0.356	-1.375	3.3366	-0.005	-1.592	3.7412	-1.566	-0.1358	-0.717
8	0.3522	1.3888	5.1627	0.8912	-0.982	-0.315	1.9615	-5.07	2.0683	-1.0633	-1.0107
9	-0.337	-0.493	-1.764	-0.253	0.7348	-1.286	-1.318	0.2298	-0.349	-0.8304	-1.9413

Table 10. Values of W2 for all networks

	Network 1	Network 2	Network 3	Network 4	Network 5
1	4.7438	−0.91436	0.58293	−2.6139	1.3252
2	−3.95	−9.189	3.1252	−7.7125	4.735
3	0.7001	−1.1951	−7.7107	9.9937	5.3579
4	0.41432	7.5362	2.5274	−2.0389	3.1819
5	3.1558	5.1853	−5.2972	−4.7375	−12.4253
6	8.6444	2.3507	−1.2873	−2.799	2.7128
7	−9.0507	0.41996	−11.5006	8.7345	−5.4653
8	−2.5667	5.9921	4.72	−1.7085	9.1684
9	9.1814	−9.8637	−2.1901	−2.6973	4.2928
10	0.8907	−8.8103	1.588	3.5318	−1.5109
11	1.115	3.0858	1.806	−0.62734	−1.3119

Extraction of Watermark Signal

Now we examine the extraction process in detail. We take the target content, Lena image, and process a frequency transform using DCT. We load the coordinates of selected feature subblocks and the network weights to build a neural network for extraction of the watermark signals. We simply feed forward the network with the input values, the DCT coefficients values that are induced from the selected feature subblocks. If the target content is the same image as the embedded image, with having proper input values and network weights, network will output the same watermark signals.

Figure 13. High pass filtered Lena image

Experiments and Future Works

Experiment 1. Extraction of Watermark signals from high pass Filtered Lena Image

In this experiment, we will examine if we can retrieve a watermark signal from a graphically changed image. Here, we chose high pass filter as the alteration method. The high pass filtered Lena image is shown in Figure 13.

First, we load the coordinates of the feature subblocks and the network weight of the trained network for the original Lena image. Then, we retrieve input values for each pattern from the high pass filtered Lena image. Input values are

Table 11. Input values of the high pass filtered Lena image

	value1	value2	value3	value4	value5	value6	value7	value8
pattern1	1.00888	−0.0139	0.004637	0.00496	0.00263	0.00595	−0.0001	−0.001
pattern2	1.14925	0.00056	0.001914	−0.0016	0.00125	−2E−06	−0.0009	−0.0015
pattern3	1.12463	−0.0015	0.001524	−0.0001	−0.0024	0.00246	−0.0008	−0.0018
pattern4	0.79388	0.04599	0.008206	0.0019	−0.0051	−0.0003	−0.0005	0.00089
pattern5	1.14588	−0.0045	0.000869	0.00026	0.00063	3.8E−05	−0.0004	0.0002
pattern6	1.14463	0.03505	−0.02606	0.04334	−0.0009	−0.0036	0.00381	0.0047
pattern7	1.13475	−7E−05	−0.00079	−0.0011	0.001	0.00055	0.00204	0.0006
pattern8	0.81063	−0.0077	−0.01581	−0.0041	−0.0014	−0.0055	−0.0064	0.00528
pattern9	0.98075	0.041	0.028526	0.00453	−0.0008	−0.0031	−0.0015	−0.0035
pattern10	1.07588	0.02589	0.019186	0.0032	−0.0036	−0.0031	−0.0004	−0.001
pattern11	1.20313	−0.0173	0.003244	0.00017	0.00213	0.00398	0.00201	0.00167
pattern12	1.16463	−0.002	0.00111	0.0012	0.00113	−0.0017	0.00164	3.8E−05
pattern13	0.91713	−0.054	0.000265	0.00905	−0.0036	−0.0021	−0.0003	−0.0045
pattern14	1.28488	−0.0311	−0.00076	0.00165	0.00688	0.00353	−0.002	0.00089
pattern15	1.17988	−0.0042	−0.00069	0.00124	−0.0029	−0.0003	0.00019	0.00268
pattern16	0.7115	0.14118	−0.01411	−0.0195	−0.0005	−0.0081	0.00711	−0.0026
pattern17	1.0425	−0.0109	−0.00099	−0.0023	0	−0.0023	0.00149	−0.0036
pattern18	1.18663	0.00531	0.016029	−0.0108	−0.0029	−0.0013	0.00772	0.00028
pattern19	0.628	0.0505	0.013859	−0.0004	−0.0005	−0.0024	0.00714	0.00182
pattern20	0.97938	−0.0045	0.008103	0.00279	0.00138	−0.0011	0.00015	−0.0002
pattern21	1.17125	0.01574	−0.03805	0.02973	−0.0063	0.00236	0.00155	−0.0013
pattern22	1.11525	0.00066	−0.00203	0.00333	−0.0018	0.00125	−0.001	−0.0017
pattern23	1.1555	−0.0054	0.003828	0.00184	−0.0005	−0.0006	−0.0018	0.00315
pattern24	1.01425	0.01084	−0.00426	0.00342	0.0035	0.00052	−0.0025	0.00122
pattern25	1.045	0.00216	−0.00332	−0.0014	−0.0018	3.4E−05	0.00057	−0.0003
pattern26	1.005	−0.0147	0.003732	−0.0089	0	2.4E−05	0.00727	0.0016
pattern27	0.985	−0.0104	−0.00329	−0.003	0.00025	−8E−05	−0.0005	0.00196
pattern28	0.9915	−0.0058	0.067984	−0.0315	0.011	−0.0004	0.00152	−0.0063
pattern29	1.2675	0.00346	−0.03987	−0.0523	−0.014	−0.0158	−0.0006	−0.0044
pattern30	1.18825	0.00271	−0.00378	0.00245	−0.0025	0.00106	0.00153	0.00328
pattern31	1.00875	−0.0034	0.00222	0.00269	0.00375	0.00291	0.00328	−0.0002
pattern32	1.25938	−0.0087	−0.00721	−0.0011	0.00238	0.00085	0.00146	−4E−05

induced using the coordinates of selected feature subblocks, and values are taken diagonally from DCT coefficients. Notice that compared with the input values of the selected feature blocks of original Lena image, the input values retrieved from high pass filtered Lena image are being quite changed, as shown in Table 11.

Feed forward propagation of these input values to the neural network with network weights of the trained network, we get output signals as shown in Figure 14, 15, 16, 17, and 18.

As you can see, the output signals for high pass filtered Lena image are slightly different compared to the output signals for the original image, but with the same output threshold of 0.5 being used as in the learning process, we were able to retrieve the same watermark signals for all 32 sets of input patterns from high pass filtered Lena image.

Figure 14. Output signals of network 1 (high pass filtered)

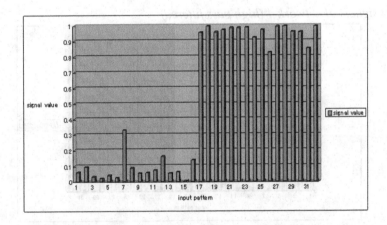

Figure 15. Output signals of network 2 (high pass filtered)

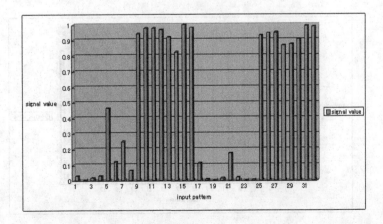

Figure 16. Output signals of network 3 (high pass filtered)

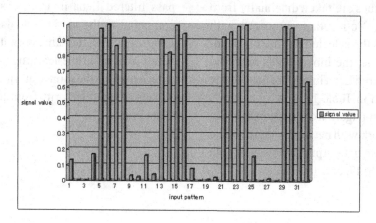

Figure 17. Output signals of network 4 (high pass filtered)

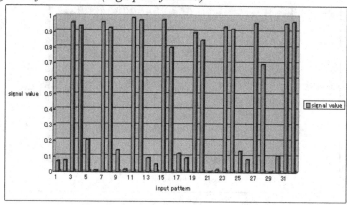

Figure 18. Output signals of network 5 (high pass filtered)

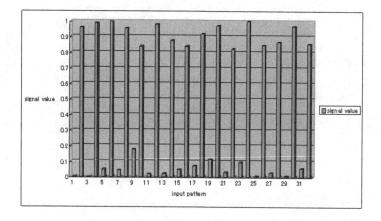

Experiment 2. Changing the Values of DCT Coefficients Directly

In this experiment, we will directly alter the DCT coefficients values of the pixels after the frequency transform is being processed. We change the value of DCT coefficients to 0 for the values lower than the boundary value that increase from 0 to 2 with the step of 0.1. In this experiment, we examined the percentage of proper signal values for the neural network with three different parameter settings as the boundary changes:

a. Number of hidden neurons = 10 and value of learning threshold = 0.05
b. Number of hidden neurons = 10 and value of learning threshold = 0.1
c. Number of hidden neurons = 20 and value of learning threshold = 0.1

There was not much notable difference in the result for (a), (b), and (c), so we can say that the learning threshold and the number of neurons in hidden layer does not affect vastly the output signals. However, the calculation cost and the

Figure 19. (a) Percentage of output units correctly outputting signals after the alteration of image data (when learning threshold is 0.05 and number of hidden neuron=10)

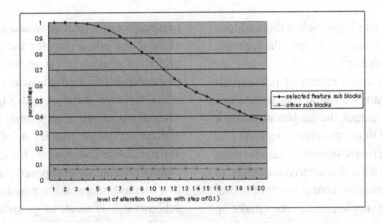

Figure 20. (b) Percentage of output units correctly outputting signals after the alteration of image data (when learning threshold is 0.1 and number of hidden neuron=10)

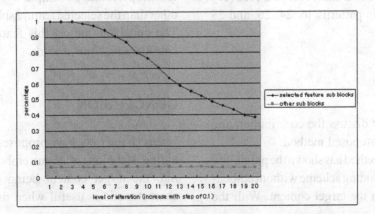

Figure 21. (c) Percentage of output units correctly outputting signals after the alteration of image data (when learning threshold is 0.1 and number of hidden neuron=20)

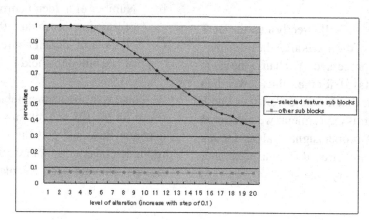

convergence time was higher when more hidden layer neurons were used and lower the learning threshold was predefined.

When we look at the results of this experiment more in detail, we found that once some patterns failed to output the proper watermark signals, some of those patterns succeeded to output proper watermark signals as the alteration process advanced. This characteristic implies, in some cases, that complex connectivity of neural network and other supplement neurons make up for the damaged input neuron to output the proper signals. In table 12, we show the transition of output signals values as boundary values increase by 0.2 for all 32 patterns. You can observe a recovery of output signals in patterns 16, 24, 26, and 28 in this experiment.

DISCUSSION

In this section, we discuss the contribution and limitations of the proposed method.

The proposed method has shown the possibility of an information-hiding scheme without embedding any data into the target content. With the

perspective of information security, this method showed the possibility for the applications for digital watermark and steganography. Using the proposed method for digital watermark, it has both characteristics of robust and fragile watermark. This characteristic is determined by the quality of preprocessing for retrieving of the input values and parameter adjustments for learning process. Meanwhile, because proposed watermark extraction method relies on the position of the feature subblocks, it is weak to geometric attacks like shrinking, expanding, and rotation of the image. This problem will be considered as future works of this proposed method. In experiment 2, notice that the percentage of output signals by subblocks other than the selected feature subblocks is stable. The understanding of this feature will be also considered as future work.

CONCLUSION

In this chapter, we have proposed an information hiding technique without embedding any data into the target content being employed. This characteristic is useful when the user does not

Table 12. Output values for all 32 patterns

	0.2	0.4	0.6	0.8	1.0	1.2	1.4	1.6	1.8	2.0
pattern1	1	1	1	1	1	1	1	1	1	1
pattern2	2	2	2	2	2	2	2	2	2	2
pattern3	3	3	3	3	11	11	11	11	11	11
pattern4	10	10	10	10	10	10	10	9	9	9
pattern5	5	5	5	5	9	9	13	13	13	26
pattern6	6	6	6	6	6	6	6	6	6	6
pattern7	7	7	7	7	7	7	7	7	7	7
pattern8	8	8	8	20	20	20	20	27	27	27
pattern9	9	9	9	9	9	9	9	9	5	5
pattern10	10	10	10	10	10	10	10	9	9	9
pattern11	11	11	11	11	11	11	3	3	3	3
pattern12	12	12	12	12	12	12	12	12	12	12
pattern13	13	13	13	13	13	13	13	13	13	14
pattern14	14	14	14	14	14	14	14	14	14	14
pattern15	15	15	15	15	15	15	15	15	15	11
pattern16	16	16	16	16	16	16	32	16	16	16
pattern17	17	17	17	17	17	17	17	17	17	17
pattern18	18	18	18	18	20	20	20	20	8	8
pattern19	19	19	19	19	19	19	27	27	27	27
pattern20	20	20	20	20	20	20	16	16	16	32
pattern21	21	21	21	21	21	21	21	21	21	21
pattern22	22	22	22	22	22	22	22	22	22	22
pattern23	23	23	23	23	23	7	7	16	16	16
pattern24	24	24	24	24	32	24	24	24	24	24
pattern25	25	25	25	25	25	25	25	25	25	25
pattern26	26	26	26	28	28	28	28	26	26	26
pattern27	27	27	27	27	27	27	27	27	27	27
pattern28	28	28	28	28	4	3	12	12	28	28
pattern29	29	29	29	29	29	29	29	29	29	29
pattern30	30	30	30	30	30	30	30	30	30	27
pattern31	31	31	31	31	31	31	31	31	31	27
pattern32	32	32	32	32	32	32	32	32	24	24

want to damage the content, but wishes to protect the intellectual property rights.

The proposed method uses multilayered perceptron neural network model for classifying the input patterns to the corresponding watermark signals. For input values, we used DCT coefficients, but proposed method does not limit the frequency transformation method to DCT alone. Other frequency transformations, such as DFT and DWT, can be used to employ the watermark scheme.

In the experiment, we showed the robustness of this scheme to a high pass filter alteration. Also, for the experiment with direct change of DCT coefficients, watermark signals were not completely lost, but as the degree of alteration becomes stronger, watermark signals have failed to output proper signals and some have recovered. This implies that this scheme has both robust and fragile characteristics, and can be conditioned with the parameter adjustments. The proposed method cultivated the damageless watermark scheme, and we hope more research will be accelerated in the areas of information hiding and information security.

REFERENCES

Aihara, K. (1990). Chaotic neural networks. In H. Kawakami (Ed.), Bifurcation phenomena in nonlinear system and theory of dynamical systems. *Advanced Series on Dynamical Systems, 8,* 143-161.

Ando, R., & Takefuji, Y. (2003). Location-driven watermark extraction using supervised learning on frequency domain. *WSEAS TRANSACTIONS ON COMPUTERS, 2*(1), 163-169.

Baumgarte, F., Ferekidis, C., & Fuchs, H. (1995). A nonlinear psychoacoustic model applied to the ISO MPEG Layer 3 Coder. Preprint 4087. *99th AES Convention.*

Bender, W., Gruhl, D., & Morimoto, H. (1995). Techniques for data hiding. *Proceedings of SPIE, 2020,* 2420-2440.

Boney, L., Tewfik, A. H., & Hamdy, K. N. (1996). Digital watermarks for audio signals. *IEEE*

Proceedings of the International Conference on Multimedia Computing and Systems, 473-480.

Brassil, J., Low, S., Maxemchuk, N. F., & O'Gorman, L. (1994). Electric marking and identification techniques to discourage document copying. *Proceedings of IEEE INFOCOM'94, 3,* 1278-1287.

Brassil, J., & O'Gorman, L. (1996). Watermarking document images with bounding box expansion. *Proceedings of the First International Information Hiding Workshop*, 1174, 227-235.

Broomhead, D., & Lowe, D. (1988). Multivariable functional interpolation and adaptive networks. *Complex Systems, 2,* 321-355.

Chang, C. Y., & Su, S. J. (2005). Apply the counterpropagation neural network to digital image copyright authentication. *2005 9th International Workshop on Cellular Neural Networks and Their Applications IEEE,* 110-113.

Cox, I. J., Kilian, J., Leightont, T., & Shamoon, T. (1997). Secure spread spectrum watermarking for images, audio and video. *IEEE Transactions on Image Processing, 6*(2), 1673-1687.

Cox, I. J., Miller, M. L., & Muttoo, S. K. (2002). *Digital watermarking.* Morgan Kaufmann Pub.

Davis, K. J., & Najarian, K. Maximizing strength of digital watermarks using neural networks. (2001). *IEEE Proceedings of International Joint Conference on Neural Neworks, 4,* 2893-2898.

Delaigle, J. F., De Vleeschouwer, C., & Macq, B. (1998). Watermarking algorithm based on a human visual model. *Signal Processing, 66,* 319-335.

Echizen, I., Yoshiura, H., Arai, T., Himura, H., & Takeuchi, T. (1999). General quality maintenance module for motion picture watermarking. *IEEE Transaction on Consumer Electronics, 45,* 1150-1158.

Eckhorn, R., Reitboeck, H. J., Arndt, M., & Dicke, P. (1990). Feature linking via synchronization among distributed assemblies: simulations of results from Cat Visual Cortex. *Neural Computing, 2,* 293-307.

Elman, J. (1994). Finding structure in time. *Cognitive Science, 14,* 179-211.

Gruhl, D., Lu, A., & Bender, W. (1996). Echo hiding. *Proceedings of the First International Information Hiding Workshop, 1174,* 295-316.

Hong, F., Shi, L., & Luo, T. (2004). A semi-fragile watermarking scheme based on neural network. *IEEE Proceedings of the Third International Conference on Machine Learning and Cybernetics, 6,* 3536-3541.

Hopfield, J. J., & Tank, D. W. (1985). Neural computation of decisions in optimization problems. *Biological Cybernetics, 52,* 141-152.

Johnson, J. L. (1994). Pulse-coupled neural nets: Translation, rotation, scale, distortion and intensity signal invariances for images. *Applied Optics, 33*(26), 6239-6253.

Kahn, D. (1996). The history of steganography. *Lecture Notes in Computer Science, 1174,* 1-5. Information Hiding, Springer-Verlag.

Katzenbeisser, S., & Petitcolas, F. A. P. (2000). Information hiding techniques for steganography and digital watermarking. Artech House.

Kim, Y. C., Byeong, C., & Choi, C. (2002). Two-step detection algorithm in a HVS-based blind watermarking on still images. *Revised Papers of Digital Watermarking First International Workshop IWDW 2002, 2613,* 235-248.

Kohonen, T. (1982). Self-organized formation of topologically correct feature maps. *Biological Cybernetics, 43,* 59-63.

Kohonen, T. (1995). *Self-organizing maps.* Springer-Verlag.

Liu, Q., & Jiang, X. (2005). Design and realization of a meaningful digital watermarking algorithm based on RBF neural network. *IEEE International Conference on Neural Networks and Brain, 1,* 214-218.

Lou, D. C., Liu, J. L., & Hu, M. C. (2003). Adaptive digital watermarking using neural network technique. *Proceedings of IEEE 37th Annual 2003 International Carnahan Conference on Security Technology,* 325-332.

Maxwell, T., Giles, C., Lee, T. C., & Chen, H. H. (1986). Nonlinear dynamics of artificial neural systems. *AIP Conference Proceedings, 151,* 299-304.

McCulloch, W. S., & Pitts, W. H. (1943). A logical calculus of the ideas immanent in nervous activity. *Bulletin of Mathematical Biophysics, 5,* 115-133.

Moody, J. E., & Darken, C. (1989). Fast learning in networks of locally-tuned processing units. *Neural Computation, 1,* 281-294.

ORuanaidh, J. J. K., & Pun, T. (1998). Rotation, scale and translation invariant spread spectrum digital image watermarking. *Signal Processing. 66,* 303-317.

Poggio, T., & Girosi, F. (1990). Regularization algorithms for learning that are equivalent to multilayer networks. *Science, 247*(4945), 978-982.

Pu, Y., Liao, K., Zhou, J., & Zhang, N. (2004). A public adaptive watermark algorithm for color images based on principal component analysis of generalized hebb. *IEEE Proceedings of International Conference on Information Acquisition,* 484-488.

Ramos, M. G., & Hemami, S. S. (1997). Psychovisually-based multiresolution image segmenta-tion. *Proceedings of International Conference on Image Processing, 3,* 66-69.

Reither, M. K., & Rubin, A. D. (1998). Crowds anonymity for Web transactions. *ACM Transaction On Information and System Security, 1*(1), 66-92.

Rosenblatt, F. (1985). The perceptron: Probabilistic model for information storage and organization in the brain. *Psychology Review, 65,* 386-408.

Rummelhart, D. E., McClelland, J. L., & the PDP Research Group. (1986). *Parallel Distributed Processing, 1.* The MIT Press.

Swanson, M. D., Zhu, B., & Tewfil, A. H. (1996). Transparent robust image watermarking. *Proceedings of International Conference on Image Processing, 3,* 211-214.

Takefuji, Y., Lee, K., & Aiso, H. (1992). An artificial maximum neural network: A winner-take-all neuron model forcing the state of the system in a solution domain. *Biological Cybernetics, 67,* 243-251.

Westen, S. J. P., Lagendijk, R. L., & Biemond, J. (1996). Optimization of JPEG color image coding using a human visual system model. *Proceedings of the SPIE, 2657,* 370-381.

Wolfe, P. J., & Godsill, S. J. (2000). Towards a perceptually optimal spectral amplitude estimator for audio signal enhancement. *Proceedings of the IEEE International Conference on Acoustics, Speech, and Signal Processing, 2,* 821-824.

Zhang, F., & Zhang, H. (2004). Applications of neural network to watermarking capacity. *IEEE International Symposium on Communications and Information Technology 2004, 1,* 340-343.

Zhang, J., Wang, N. C., & Xiong, F. (2002). Hiding a logo watermark into the multiwavelet domain using neural networks. *Proceedings of 14th IEEE*

International Conference on Tools with Artificial Intelligence, 477-482.

Zhang, X., & Zhang, F. (2005). A blind watermarking algorithm based on neural network. *ICNN&B '05 International Conference on Neural Networks and Brain IEEE, 2*, 1073-1076.

Zhang, Z. M., Li, R. Y., & Wang, L. (2003). Adaptive watermark scheme with RBF neural networks. *Proceedings of the 2003 International Conference on Neural Networks and Signal Processing IEEE, 2*, 1517-1520.

Chapter VI
Perceptual Data Hiding in Still Images

Mauro Barni
University of Siena, Italy

Franco Bartolini
University of Florence, Italy

Alessia De Rosa
University of Florence, Italy

ABSTRACT

The idea of embedding some information within a digital media, in such a way that the inserted data are intrinsically part of the media itself, has aroused a considerable interest in different fields. One of the more examined issues is the possibility of hiding the highest possible amount of information without affecting the visual quality of the host data. For such a purpose, the understanding of the mechanisms underlying human vision is a mandatory requirement. Hence, the main phenomena regulating the human Vvisual system will be firstly discussed and their exploitation in a data hiding system will be then considered.

INTRODUCTION

In the last 10 years, digital watermarking has received increasing attention, since it is seen as an effective tool for copyright protection of digital data (Petitcolas, Anderson, & Kuhn, 1999), one of the most crucial problems slowing down the diffusion of new multimedia services such as electronic commerce, open access to digital archives, distribution of documents in digital format and so on. According to the watermarking paradigm, the protection of copyrighted data is accomplished by injecting into the data an invisible signal, that is, the watermark, conveying information about data ownership, its provenance or any other information that can be useful to enforce copyright laws.

Recently, the idea of embedding some information within a digital document in such a way that the inserted data are intrinsically part of the document itself has been progressively applied to other purposes as well, including broadcast monitoring, data authentication, data indexing, content labelling, hidden annotation, and so on.

Regardless of the specific purpose, it is general agreed that one of the main requirements a data hiding scheme must satisfy regards invisibility; that is, the digital code must be embedded in an imperceptible way so that its presence does not affect the quality of the to-be-protected data.

As far as the embedding of a hidden signal within a host image is concerned, it is evident that the understanding of the mechanisms underlying human vision is a mandatory requirement (Cox & Miller, 1997; Tewfik & Swanson, 1997; Wolfgang, Podilchuk, & Delp, 1999). All the more that, in addition to the invisibility constraint, many applications require that the embedded information be resistant against the most common image manipulations. This, in turn, calls for the necessity of embedding a watermark whose strength is as high as possible, a task which clearly can take great advantage from the availability of an accurate model to describe the human visual system (HVS) behaviour. In other words, we can say that the goal of perceptual data hiding is twofold: to better hide the watermark, thus making it less perceivable to the eye, and to allow to the use of the highest possible watermark strength, thus influencing positively the performance of the data recovery step.

Many approaches have been proposed so far to model the characteristics of the HVS and to exploit such models to improve the effectiveness of existing watermarking systems (Podilchuk & Zeng, 1998; Wolfgang et al., 1999). Though all the proposed methods rely on some general

knowledge about the most important features of HVS, we can divide the approaches proposed so far into theoretical (Kundur & Hatzinakos, 1997; Podilchuk & Zeng, 1998; Swanson, Zhu, & Tewfik, 1998; Wolfgang et al., 1999) and heuristic (Bartolini, Barni, Cappellini & Piva, 1998; Delaigle, Vleeschouwer, & Macq, 1998; Van Schyndel, Tirkel, & Osborne, 1994) ones. Even if a theoretically grounded approach to the problem would be clearly preferable, heuristic algorithms sometimes provide better results due to some problems with HVS models currently in use (Bartolini, 1998; Delaigle, 1998).

In this chapter, we will first give a detailed description of the main phenomena regulating the HVS, and we will consider the exploitation of these concepts in a data hiding system. Then, some limits of classical HVS models will be highlighted and some possible solutions to get around these problems pointed out. Finally, we will describe a complete mask building procedure, as a possible exploitation of HVS characteristics for perceptual data hiding in still images.

BASICS OF HUMAN VISUAL SYSTEM MODELLING

Even if the human visual system is certainly one of the most complex biological devices far from being exactly described, each person has daily experience of the main phenomena that influence the ability of the HVS to perceive (or not to perceive) certain stimuli. In order to exemplify such phenomena, it may very instructive to consider two copies of the same image, one being a disturbed version of the other. For instance, we can consider the two images depicted in Figure 1, showing, on the left, a noiseless version of the *house* image, and, on the right, a noisy version of the same image. It is readily seen that: (1) noise is not visible in high activity regions, for example, on foliage; (2) noise is very visible in uniform

Figure 1. Noiseless (left) and noisy (right) versions of the House image

areas such as the sky or the street; (3) noise is less visible in correspondence of edges; (4) noise is less visible in dark and bright areas.

As it can be easily experienced, the above observations do not depend on the particular image depicted in the figure. On the contrary, they can be generalised, thus deriving some very general rules: (1) disturbances are less visible in highly textured regions than in uniform areas; (2) noise is more easily perceived around edges than in textured areas, but less easily than in flat regions; (3) the human eye is less sensitive to disturbances in dark and bright regions. In the last decades, several mathematical models have been developed to describe the above basic mechanisms. In the following, the main concepts underlying these models are presented.

Basically, a model describing the human visual perception is based on two main concepts: the *contrast sensitivity function* and the *contrast masking model*. The first concept is concerned with the sensitivity of the human eye to a sine grating stimulus; as the sensitivity of the eye depends strongly on display background luminance and spatial frequency of the stimulus, these two parameters have to be taken into account in the mathematical description of human sensitivity. The second concept considers the effect of one stimulus on the detectability of another, where the stimuli can be coincident (*iso-frequency masking*),

or non-coincident (*non iso-frequency masking*) in frequency and orientation.

Contrast Sensitivity

Contrast represents the dynamic range of luminance in a region of a picture. If we consider an image characterised by a uniform background luminance L and a small superimposed patch of uniform luminance $L+\Delta L$, the contrast can be expressed as:

$$C = \frac{\Delta L}{L}. \tag{1}$$

For understanding how a human observer is able to perceive this variation of luminance, we can refer to the experiments performed by Weber in the middle of 18th century. According to Weber's experimental set-up, ΔL is increased until the human eye can perceive the difference between the patch and the background. Weber observed that the ratio between the *just noticeable* value of the superimposed stimulus ΔL_{jn} and L is nearly constant to 0.02; the only exception is represented by very low and very high luminance values, a fact that is in complete agreement with the rules listed before, that is, disturbances are less visible in dark and bright areas. Such behaviour is justified by the fact that receptors are not able to perceive luminance changes above and below a given range (saturation effect).

However, a problem with the above experimental set-up is that the case of a uniform luminance stimuli superimposed to a uniform luminance background is not a realistic one: hence, a different definition of the contrast must be given. In particular, by letting $L(x, y)$ be the luminance of a pixel at position (x, y) and L_o the local mean background luminance, a local contrast definition can be written as:

$$C = \frac{L(x,y) - L_o}{L_o}. \qquad (2)$$

This formulation is still a simplification of real images, where more complex texture patterns are present. The easiest way to get closer to the case of real images consists in decomposing the disturbing signal into a sum of sinusoidal signals, and then investigating the HVS behaviour in the presence of a single sinusoidal stimulus, and then considering the combination of more stimuli. To this aim, let us consider an image obtained by summing a sinusoidal stimulus to a uniform background. The spatial luminance of the image is given by:

$$L(x, y) = L_o + \Delta L \cos(2\pi f(x \cos\theta + y \sin\theta)), \qquad (3)$$

where f, θ and ΔL are, respectively, the frequency, orientation and amplitude of the superimposed stimulus. Note that the frequency f, measured in *cycles/degree,* is a function of the frequency ν measured in *cycles/m* and the viewing distance D between the observer and the monitor expressed in meter:

$$f = (\pi D/180)\nu.$$

In order to evaluate the smallest sinusoid a human eye can distinguish from the background, ΔL is increased until the observer perceives it. We refer to such a threshold value of ΔL as the luminance value of the *just noticeable* sinusoidal

stimulus, and we will refer to it as ΔL_{jn}. Instead of ΔL_{jn}, it is usually preferred to consider the minimum contrast necessary to just detect a sine wave of a given frequency f and orientation θ superimposed to a background L_o, thus leading to the concept of *just noticeable contrast* (JNC) (Eckert & Bradley, 1998):

$$JNC = \frac{\Delta L_{jn}}{L_o}. \qquad (4)$$

The inverse of *JNC* is commonly referred to as the *contrast sensitivity function* (CSF) (Damera-Venkata, Kite, Geisler, Evans, & Bovik, 2000) and gives an indication of the capability of the human eye to notice a sinusoidal stimulus on a uniform background:

$$S_c = \frac{1}{JNC} = \frac{L_o}{\Delta L_{jn}}. \qquad (5)$$

By repeating the above experiment for different viewing conditions and different values of f and θ, it is found that the major factors *JNC* (or equivalently S_c) depends upon are: (1) the frequency of the stimulus f, (2) the orientation of the stimulus θ, (3) background luminance L_o, and (4) the viewing angle w, that is, the ratio between the square root of the area A of the monitor and the viewing distance D:

$$w = 180\sqrt{A} / \pi D.$$

Many analytical expressions of *CSF* can be found in the scientific literature. In this chapter, we only consider the one obtained by Barten (1990) by fitting data of psychophysical experiments. According to Barten's model, the factors influencing human vision are taken into account by the following expression:

$$S_c(f, \theta, w, L_o) = a(f, w, L_o) f \exp(-\Gamma(\theta) b(L_o) f) \cdot$$
$$\cdot \sqrt{1 + c \cdot \exp(b(L_o) f)}, \qquad (6)$$

with:

$$a(f,w,L_o) = \frac{540\,(1+0.7/L_o)^{-0.2}}{1+\dfrac{12}{w\cdot(1+f/3)^2}},$$

$$b(L_o) = 0.3\,(1+100/L_o)^{0.15},$$

$$c = 0.06,$$

$$\Gamma(\theta) = 1.08 - 0.08\cos(4\theta), \qquad (7)$$

where the frequency of the stimulus *f* is measured in *cycles/degree;* the orientation of the stimulus θ in *degrees;* the observer viewing angle *w* in *degrees,* and the mean local background luminance L_0 in *candelas/m²*. In particular, the term Γ(θ) takes into account that the eye sensitivity is not isotropic.

In fact, psychophysical experiments showed less sensitivity to ±45 degrees oriented stimuli than to vertically and horizontally oriented ones, an effect that is even more pronounced at high frequencies: about -3dB at six *cycles/degree* and -1dB at 1 *cycle/degree* (Comes & Macq, 1990).

In Figures 2, 3 and 4, the plot of S_c against luminance and frequency is shown. In particular, in Figure 2 the plots of *CSF* with respect to frequency

are reported for several values of background luminance; results refer to a horizontal stimulus (i.e., θ = 0) and to an observer viewing angle *w* = 180/, which is obtained when the monitor is viewed from a distance of four time its height. As it can be seen, all the curves exhibit the same trend for all values of background luminance: the maximum sensitivity is reached in the middle range of frequencies, while in the low and high part of the frequency range the HVS has a lower sensitivity.

In Figure 3 the just noticeable stimulus ΔL_{jn} is plotted against luminance L, for a frequency of 15 *cycles/degree*. This plot is consistent with the phenomenon that disturbances are less visible in dark and bright regions and shows the results achieved by following Weber's experiment. Finally, Figure 4 highlights how horizontal (or vertical) stimuli are more visible than those oriented at 45°.

Contrast Masking

The term *masking* is commonly used to refer to any destructive interaction and interference among stimuli that are closely coupled (Legge

Figure 2. Plots of Sc against frequency for values of background luminance of 0.01, 0.1, 1, 10, 100 cd/m2 (from bottom to top)

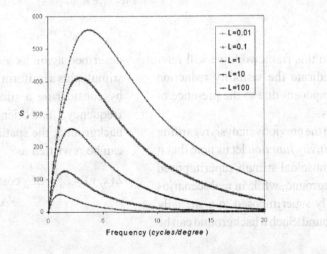

Figure 3.Plot of the just noticeable stimulus versus image background luminance, for a frequency of 15 cycles/degree

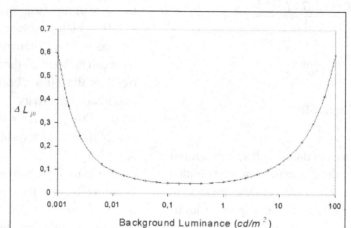

Figure 4. Plots of the Sc with respect to frequency for horizontal and diagonal stimuli and background luminance of 50 cd/m2

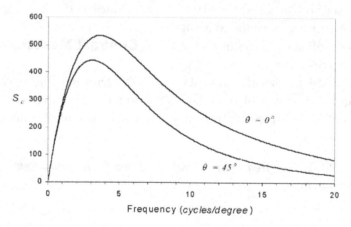

& Foley, 1980). In this framework we will refer to masking to indicate the visibility reduction of one image component due to the presence of other components.

By referring to the previous analysis regarding the *contrast sensitivity function* let us note that it only considers sinusoidal stimuli superimposed to a uniform background, while in real scenarios stimuli are usually superimposed to a spatially changing background. Such a background can be described again as a combination of sinusoidal stimuli plus a uniform luminance value L_o. Thus, by considering a stimulus of amplitude ΔL_m, frequency f_m and orientation θ_m for describing the background, the spatial luminance of the image can be rewritten as:

$$L(x,y) = L_o + \Delta L_m \cos(2\pi f_m(x\cos\theta_m + y\sin\theta_m)) + \\ + \Delta L \cos(2\pi f(x\cos\theta + y\sin\theta)).$$

$$(8)$$

In particular, the stimulus ΔL_m is called *masking stimulus* since its presence usually increases the *JNC* of another stimulus ΔL (e.g., a disturbance). The stimuli can be coincident in frequency and orientation (i.e., $f_m = f$ and $\theta_m = \theta$), leading to *iso-frequency masking*, or non-coincident (i.e. $f_m \neq f$ and $\theta_m \neq \theta$), leading to *non- iso-frequency masking*. In the first case, *JNC* elevation is maximal; in the latter, *JNC* elevation decreases regularly as the masking frequency departs from the stimulus frequency.

In the following both *iso* and *non-iso-frequency masking* will be considered and a *masked just noticeable contrast* function (*JNC_m*) detailed to model these masking effects.

Iso-Frequency Masking

By relying on the works by Watson (Watson, 1987, 1993), the *masked JNC* can be written as a function of the *non-masked JNC*:

$$JNC_m(f,\theta,w,L_o) = JNC(f,\theta,w,L_o)\cdot$$

$$\cdot F\left(\frac{C_m(f,\theta,w,L_o)}{JNC(f,\theta,w,L_o)}\right), \qquad (9)$$

where F is a non-linear function indicating how much *JNC* increments in presence of a masking signal, and C_m is the contrast of the masking image component, that is, $C_m = \Delta L_m/L_o$.

The function $F(\cdot)$ can be approximated by the following relation (Watson, 1987):

$$F(X) = \max\{1, |X|^{W}\}, \qquad (10)$$

where W is an exponent lying between 0.4 and 0.95.

Let us note that expression (10) does not take the so-called *pedestal effect* into account (Legge & Foley, 1980). In fact, it assumes that the presence of one stimulus can only decrease the detectability of another stimulus at the same frequency and orientation. Indeed, several studies have shown that a low value of the masking contrast C_m increases noise visibility (Foley & Legge, 1981); in particular, when the masking component is not perceptible, that is, $C_m < JNC$, then a more exact expression for F would also assume values below one. In Figure 5, the trends of the masking function $F(X)$ obtained by fitting experimental results (solid line) and by using

Figure 5. Plot of the masking function F(X) (solid line) and its approximation (dashed line) given by equation (10), where it is assumed W =0.6. The pedestal effect is highlighted

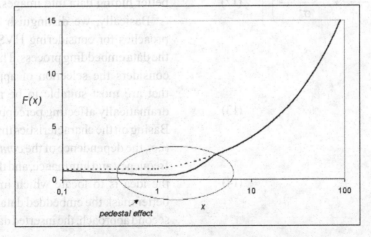

equation (10) (dashed line) are shown: the *pedestal effect* is also highlighted.

By inserting equation (10) in equation (9), we get:

$$JNC_m(f,\theta,w,L_o) = JNC(f,\theta,w,L_o) \cdot$$
$$\cdot \max\left(1, \left|\frac{C_m(f,\theta,w,L_o)}{JNC(f,\theta,w,L_o)}\right|^W\right). \quad (11)$$

It is important to note that masking only affects the AC components of the image. The effect of the DC coefficient on the threshold is expressed by equation (6), in which the influence of background mean luminance L_o on human vision is taken into account.

Non-Iso-Frequency Masking

When the masking frequency (f_m, θ_m) departs from signal frequency (f, θ) JNC_m increment decreases. A possibility to model *non-iso-frequency masking* consists in introducing in equation (11) a weighing function, which takes into account that each frequency component contributes differently to the masking, according to its frequency position. The weighing function can be modelled as Gaussian-like (Comes & Macq, 1990):

$$g(f_m/f, \theta_m - \theta)$$
$$= \exp\left[-\left(\frac{\log_2^2(f_m/f)}{\sigma_f^2} + \frac{(\theta_m - \theta)^2}{\sigma_\theta^2}\right)\right], \quad (12)$$

where,

$$\sigma_f = 1.2\log_2 B_f,$$
$$\sigma_\theta = 1.2 B_\theta, \quad (13)$$

$$B_f = \sqrt{2},$$
$$B_\theta = 27 - 3\log_2 f. \quad (14)$$

By inserting the weighing function (12) in the JNC_m expression, the value of the *masked just noticeable contrast* is obtained:

$$JNC_m(f,\theta,w,L_o) = JNC(f,\theta,w,L_o) \cdot$$
$$\cdot \max\left(1, \left|g(f_m/f, \theta_m - \theta)\frac{C_m(f_m,\theta_m,w,L_m)}{JNC(f_m,\theta_m,w,L_m)}\right|^W\right), \quad (15)$$

where the stimulus at spatial frequency (f, θ) is masked by the stimulus at spatial frequency (f_m, θ_m). Note that the mean luminance's L_o and L_m can be supposed to be identical when both the frequencies f and f_m belong to the same spatial region. Furthermore, when $(f_m, \theta_m) = (f, \theta)$ the weighing function assumes value 1, thus reducing to equation (11).

EXPLOITATION OF HVS CONCEPTS FOR DATA HIDING

It is widely known among watermarking researchers that HVS characteristics have to be carefully considered for developing a watermarking system that minimises the image visual degradation while maximising robustness (Cox & Miller, 1997; Tewfik & Swanson, 1997). Let us, thus, see how the concepts deriving from the analysis of the models of human perception can be exploited for better hiding data into images.

Basically, we distinguish two different approaches for considering HVS concepts during the data embedding process. The former approach considers the selection of appropriate features that are most suitable to be modified, without dramatically affecting perceptual image quality. Basing on the characteristics that control the HVS (i.e., the dependence of the *contrast sensitivity* on frequency and luminance, and the *masking effect*), the idea is to locate which image features can better mask the embedded data. By following the second approach, the inserted data, embedded into an image without a particular care for the selection of the most suitable features, are adapted to the local image content for better reducing their perceptibility. In other words, by referring to the just noticeable contrast, the maximum amount of data that can be introduced into an image is locally adapted.

Let us consider host feature selection first. By carefully observing the simple basic rules describing the mechanisms underlying the HVS we discussed above, it is readily seen that some of them are more naturally expressed in the spatial domain, whereas others are more easily modelled in the frequency domain. Let us consider, for example, the *CSF* and the masking models described in the previous section. The most suitable domain to describe them is, obviously, the frequency domain. This is not the case, however, when the lower sensitivity to disturbances in bright and dark regions has to be taken into account, a phenomenon that is clearly easier to describe in the spatial domain. Despite their simplicity, these examples point out the difficulty of fully exploiting the characteristics of the HVS by simply choosing the set of features the mark has to be inserted in. Of course, this does not mean that a proper selection of the host feature is of no help in watermark hiding. On the contrary, many systems have been proposed where embedding is performed in a feature domain that is known to be relatively more immune to disturbances. This is the case of frequency domain watermarking algorithms. Let us consider the curves reported in Figures 2 and 4. If we ignore very low frequencies (due to its very small extension the region of very low frequencies is usually not considered), we see how watermark hiding is more easily achieved avoiding marking the low frequency portion of the spectrum where disturbances are more easily perceived by the HSV. By relying on perceptibility considerations only, the frequency portion of the spectrum turns out to be a perfect place to hide information. When considering robustness to attacks, though, a high frequency watermark

turns out to be too vulnerable to attacks such as low-pass filtering and JPEG compression, for which a low-pass watermark would be preferable. The most adopted solution consists in trading off between the two requirements, thus embedding the watermark into the medium-high portion of the frequency spectrum.

Similar considerations are valid for hybrid techniques, that is, those techniques embedding the watermark in a domain retaining both spatial and frequency localisation, as it is the case, for example, of wavelet- or block-DCT-based systems. In particular, the situation for block-DCT methods is identical to the frequency domain case; high frequency coefficients are usually preferred for embedding, in order to reduce visibility. The same objective can be reached in the discrete wavelet transform (*DWT*) case by performing embedding in the finest sub-bands. By starting from these considerations, we can conclude that perceptual data hiding through feature selection is not very easy to be performed. In particular, if it is desired that watermark recovery has to be achieved also after image manipulations (attacks), which can make the selected features no longer available or identifiable, the sole possibility is to select the features on a fixed basis. This choice, nevertheless, implies that the embedded data are not always inserted into the most suitable image features.

The second possibility of exploiting the properties of the HVS to effectively hide a message into a host image consists in first designing the watermark in an arbitrary domain without taking HVS considerations into account, and then modifying the disturbance introduced by the watermark by locally adapting it to the image content. To be more specific the watermarked image is obtained by blending the original image, say S_o, and the to-be-inserted signal, here identified by a disturbance image S_d having the same cardinality of S_o, in such a way that the embedded signal is weighed by a function (*M*). *M,* which should be calculated by exploiting all the concepts regulating the HVS, gives a point-by-point measure of how insensitive to disturbances the cover image is. The perceptually adapted watermarked image (S'_w) can be thus obtained as follows:

$$S'_w = S_o + M \otimes S_d, \qquad (16)$$

where by $\otimes$ we have indicated the sample-by-sample product, between the masking function M and the watermark image S_d (see Figure 6).

The inserted watermark S_d can be obtained as the difference between the image S_w watermarked without taking care about perceptibility issues (e.g., uniformly) and the original image S_o:

$$S_d = S_w - S_o. \qquad (17)$$

Regardless of the domain where watermark embedding has been performed, and on the embedding rule, this difference always models the signal added to the original image for carrying the hidden information.

Whereas the general shape of M is easily found (e.g., lower values are expected in flat areas, whereas textured areas should be characterised by higher values of M), the exact definition of M is a complicated task, possibly involving a complex manual tuning phase. Let us suppose, for example, that M takes values in the [0,1] interval; that is, the effect of the blending mask is only to reduce the watermark strength in the most perceptually sensitive regions. In this case S_w should be tuned so that the hidden signal is just below the visibility threshold in very textured regions (where M is likely to take values close to 1) and well visible in all the other image areas. The mask, if properly designed, will reduce watermark strength on the other image regions in such a way to make it imperceptible everywhere. This procedure requires a manual tuning of the watermark strength during the embedding process to achieve S_w and this limits its efficacy when a large amount of images need to be watermarked.

A different possibility is that mask values indicate directly the maximum amount of the watermark strength that can be used for each region of the image at hand: in this case mask values are not normalised between [0,1], and the image can be watermarked to achieve S_w without tuning the watermark strength in advance.

In the following sections we will describe how this second approach can be implemented by relying on the HVS model introduced previously. Before going into the details of mask building, however, some limitations of classical HVS models will be pointed out and some innovative solutions outlined.

LIMITS OF CLASSICAL HVS MODELS

AND A New Approach

Having described (in the second section) the main phenomena regulating the HVS, we now consider how these factors can be modelled to be used during a data hiding process. Let us recall the two concepts that mainly influence the human perception: the *contrast sensitivity* and the *masking effect*. The strict dependence of these factors on both frequency and luminance of the considered stimuli imposes the need to achieve good models that simultaneously take into account the two parameters.

Several HVS models have been proposed so far; without going into a description of related literature, we will point out some important limits of classical approaches, and describe some possible solutions to cope with these problems. More specifically, we will detail a new approach for HVS modelling, which will be exploited in the next section for building a blending mask.

The first problem in the models proposed so far is the lack of simultaneous spatial and frequency localisation. Classical models usually work either in the spatial domain, thus achieving a good

Figure 6. A general scheme for exploiting a masking function in a data hiding system

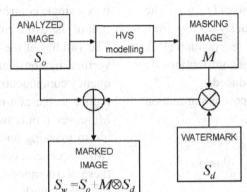

spatial localisation, or in the frequency domain, thus achieving a good frequency localisation, but a simultaneous spatial and frequency localisation is not satisfactorily obtained.

To consider frequency localisation, a possibility for theoretical models operating in the spatial domain is to apply a multiple channel filtering. Such an approach, however, presents the drawback of artificially introducing a partitioning of the frequency plane, which separates the effects of close frequencies (that actually influence each other) when they belong to different channels. On the other hand, the main problem with classical HVS masking models operating in the frequency domain is that sinusoidal stimuli (e.g., a watermark embedded in the frequency domain) are spread all over the image, and since images are usually non-stationary, the possible presence of a masking signal is a spatially varying property, and, as

such, is difficult to be handled in the frequency domain.

A possibility to trade off between spatial and frequency localisation consists in splitting the analysed $N \times N$ image into $n \times n$ blocks. Each block is, then, *DCT* transformed (see Figure 7). Block-based analysis permits considering the image properties localised spatially, by taking into account all the sinusoidal masking stimuli present only in the block itself.

A second problem comes out when the masking effect is considered. Most masking models only account for the presence of a single sinusoidal mask by considering the iso-frequency case. This is not the case in practical applications where the masking signal, namely the host image, is nothing but a sinusoid.

To take into account the non-sinusoidal nature of the masking signal (the host image), for each

Figure 7. Block-based DCT analysis of the image permits to trade off between spatial and frequency localisation

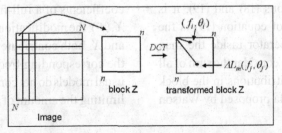

i-th position in each block Z, the contributions of all the surrounding frequencies (f_j, θ_j) of the same block must be considered. By starting from the *non- iso-frequency masking* (equation (15)), a sum of the weighed masking contributions on the whole block must be introduced.

Swanson et al. (1998) propose a summation rule of the form:

$$JNC_m(f_i, \theta_i, w, L_Z) = \left\{ \sum_{j \in Z} \left[JNC(f_i, \theta_i, w, L_Z) \cdot \right. \right.$$

$$\left. \left. \cdot \max \left\{ 1, \left| g(f_j / f_i, \theta_j - \theta_i) \frac{C_m(f_j, \theta_j, w, L_Z)}{JNC(f_j, \theta_j, w, L_Z)} \right|^W \right\} \right]^2 \right\}^{1/2} \cdot$$

$$(18)$$

Such a rule presents some limits, which will be evidenced in a while, thus calling for a different summation rule:

$$JNC_m(f_i, \theta_i, w, L_Z) = JNC(f_i, \theta_i, w, L_Z) \cdot$$

$$\cdot \max \left\{ 1, \left[\sum_{j \in Z} \left| g(f_j / f_i, \theta_j - \theta_i) \frac{C_m(f_j, \theta_j, w, L_Z)}{JNC(f_j, \theta_j, w, L_Z)} \right| \right]^W \right\}.$$

$$(19)$$

Let us note that the contrast of the masking component C_m is given by:

$$C_m(f_j, \theta_j, w, L_Z) = \frac{\Delta L_m(f_j, \theta_j, w)}{L_Z}, \qquad (20)$$

where $\Delta L_m(f_j, \theta_j)$ is the amplitude of the sinusoidal masking component at frequency (f_j, θ_j). Furthermore, for each block Z the mean luminance L_z is measured based on the value of the corresponding DC coefficient.

By comparing equations (18) and (19), it is evident that the novelty of equation (19) is the introduction of the Σ operator inside the max operator. In particular, we consider the sum of all the weighed masking contributions in the block and then apply the formula proposed by Watson

for the masked JNC to the sum, by considering it as a single contribution (this justifies the position of the exponent W outside the Σ operator). The validity of the proposed expression can be verified by considering that if all masking frequency components are null, equation (19) must reduce to the non-masked JNC (equation (11)). Moreover, if only two close frequencies contribute to masking and, as an extreme case, these two frequencies coincide, the masking effect of these two components must be added as a single sinusoidal mask.

Such conditions are not satisfied by equation (18). It can be observed, in fact, that if no masking frequency is present in Z, the masked JNC differs from the non-masked JNC by a factor $(N_z)^{1/2}$, where N_z indicates the number of frequency components contained in Z. In other words, contributions of masking components are always considered even when such components are null. From experimental results we evidenced that this situation occurs with a probability of around 50%. In addition, if equation (18) is adopted, when two coincident frequencies contribute to the masking, their masking effects cannot be added as a single sinusoidal mask.

As a third consideration it appears that all the techniques described so far produce masking functions that depend only on the image characteristics, that is, on the characteristics of the masking signal, but not on the characteristics of the disturbing signal. On the contrary, to estimate the maximum amount of disturbing signal that can be inserted into an image by preserving its perceptual quality, it should be considered how the modifications caused by watermark insertion influence each other. For example, we consider two contiguous coefficients of a full-frame transform $X_1(f_1)$ and $X_2(f_2)$: the modifications imposed separately to X_1 and X_2 both contribute to the disturbance of both the corresponding frequencies f_1 and f_2. Instead, usual models do not consider this effect, by simply limiting the amount of modification of each coefficient in dependence on the masking capability of its neighbourhood, but without considering the disturbance of neighbouring coefficients.

A different approach must then be valued: instead of considering the single disturbing components separately, we adopt a new formula for expressing the disturb contrast for each position of the image, which we call the *Equivalent Disturb Contrast* C_{deq}. Such a formula takes into account all the considerations expressed until now. In particular, to trade off between spatial and frequency localisation of noise, a *block-based DCT* decomposition is applied to the disturbing image. Furthermore, to take into account the non-sinusoidal characteristics of the noise signal, for each *i*-th position of block Z all the disturbing components belonging to the same block are added by using the weighing function g (equation (12)). The equivalent disturb contrast C_{deq} is then written as:

$$C_{d_{eq}}(f_i, \theta_i, w, L_Z) =$$

$$\sum_{j \in Z} \left| g(f_j / f_i, \theta_j - \theta_i) C_d(f_i, \theta_i, w, L_Z) \right| \quad (21)$$

where C_d is the contrast of the disturb component defined as:

$$C_d(f_j, \theta_j, w, L_Z) = \frac{\Delta L_d(f_j, \theta_j, w)}{L_Z}, \quad (22)$$

with $\Delta L_d (f_j, \theta_j, w)$ being the amplitude of the sinusoidal noise signal at frequency (f_j, θ_j).

In conclusion, in order to guarantee the invisibility of a disturbance (i.e., the watermark) in a given image, for each frequency of each block Z, the equivalent disturb contrast C_{deq} computed by equation (21) must be smaller than the value of the masked just noticeable contrast JNC_m obtained by equation (19), which is:

$$C_{d_{eq}}(f_i, \theta_i, w, L_Z) \leq JNC_m(f_i, \theta_i, w, L_Z) \quad \forall i \in Z, \forall Z$$

$$(23)$$

IMPROVED MASK BUILDING FOR DATA HIDING

The goal of this section is to present a method for building a mask that indicates, for each region of a given image, the maximum allowable energy of the watermark, under the constraint of image quality preservation. Such an approach will be based on the enhanced HVS model presented in the previous section, and it will provide a masking function for improving watermark invisibility and strength.

Before going on, it is worth noting that, so far, the behaviour of the HVS has been described in terms of luminance; however, digital images are usually stored as grey-level values, and a watermarking system will directly affect grey-level values. It is the goal of the next section to describe how grey-level values are related to the luminance perceived by the eye.

Luminance vs. Grey-Level Pixel Values

The luminance perceived by the eye does not depend solely on the grey level of the pixels forming the image. On the contrary, several other factors must be taken into account, including: the environment lighting conditions, the shape of the filter modelling the low pass behaviour of the eye, and of course the way the image is reproduced. In this framework we will concentrate on the case of pictures reproduced by a cathode ray tube (CRT), for which the dependence between grey-level values and luminance is better known and more easily modelled.

It is known that the relation between the grey level I of an image pixel and the luminance L of the light emitted by the corresponding CRT element is a non-linear one. More specifically, such a relation as is usually modelled by the expression (20):

$$L = L(I) = q + (mI)^\gamma, \quad (24)$$

with q defining luminance corresponding to a black image, m defines the contrast and γ accounts for the intrinsic non-linearity of the CRT emitting elements (the phosphors). While γ is a characteristic parameter of any given CRT, q and m depend on "brightness" and "contrast" regulations usually accessible to the user through the CRT electronics.

A first possibility to map HVS concepts from luminance to grey-level domain consists in mapping grey-level values through (24), thus obtaining a luminance image, operating on this image according to the proposed model, and finally going back to grey-level domain through the inverse of (24). Alternatively, we can try to directly write the just noticeable contrast as a function of grey-level values. In analogy to equation (8), this can be done by considering a generic grey-level image composed of a uniform background I_o, a masking sinusoidal signal of amplitude ΔI_m and a disturbing sinusoidal stimulus of amplitude ΔI:

$$I(x,y) = I_o + \Delta I_m \cos(2\pi f_m (x\cos\theta_m + y\sin\theta_m)) + \\ + \Delta I \cos(2\pi f(x\cos\theta + y\sin\theta)),$$

$$(25)$$

which is mapped to a luminance pattern through equation (24):

$$L(x,y) = L(I(x,y)) \approx L(I_o) + \\ L'(I_o)\Delta I_m \cos(2\pi f_m(x\cos\theta_m + y\sin\theta_m)) + \\ L'(I_o)\Delta I \cos(2\pi f(x\cos\theta + y\sin\theta)),$$

$$(26)$$

where $L'(I_o)$ is the derivative of the luminance mapping function given in (24) and where a linear approximation of $L(x,y)$ is adopted. By comparing (26) with (8) we have that, as a first approximation, $\Delta L_m = L'(I_o) \Delta I_m$ and $\Delta L = L'(I_o) \Delta I$. The just noticeable contrast in the grey-level domain can thus be expressed by the formula:

$$JNC_I(f_i,\theta_i,w,I_o) = \frac{\Delta I_{jn}(f_i,\theta_i,w)}{I_o} \approx \frac{\Delta L_{jn}(f_i,\theta_i,w)}{I_o L'(I_o)} = \\ = \frac{JNC(f_i,\theta_i,w,L_o)L_o}{I_o L'(I_o)} \approx \\ \approx \frac{L(I_o)}{I_o L'(I_o)} JNC(f_i,\theta_i,w,L(I_o)).$$

$$(27)$$

Once q, m, and γ are known, the above equations permit operating directly on grey-level

Figure 8. Plot of the just noticeable grey-level stimulus versus image background grey-level, for a frequency of 5 cycles/degree. The amplitude of the just noticeable disturb increases for low and high background grey-level values.

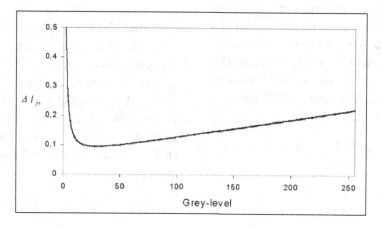

images. In Figure 8 the just noticeable grey-level visibility threshold ($\Delta I_{jn} = I \cdot JNC_I$) is reported with respect to grey-level values for an angular frequency of 5 cycles/degree: the values of the parameters describing the CRT response have been set to $q = 0.04$, $m = 0.03$ and $\gamma = 2.2$ and have been estimated on a Philips CRT monitor. It is evident how this plot is in agreement with the fact that more noise can be tolerated in the dark and bright regions of the image.

By using the previous relation for JNC_I, both the masked just noticeable contrast and the equivalent disturb contrast can be expressed directly in the grey-level domain. By referring to equation (19) and (21), we obtain:

$$JNC_{Im}(f_i, \theta_i, w, I_Z) \approx JNC_I(f_i, \theta_i, w, I_Z) \cdot$$

$$\cdot \max\left\{1, \left[\sum_{j \in Z}\left|g(f_j / f_i, \theta_j - \theta_i)\frac{C_{Im}(f_j, \theta_j, w, I_z)}{JNC_I(f_j, \theta_j, w, I_z)}\right|\right]^W\right\},$$

$$(28)$$

and:

$$C_{I_{deq}}(f_i, \theta_i, w, I_z)$$

$$= \sum_{j \in Z}\left|g(f_j / f_i, \theta_j - \theta_i)C_{I_d}(f_j, \theta_j, w, I_z)\right|$$

$$(29)$$

where the contrast values JNC_I, C_{Im}, C_{Id} are computed by referring to equation (27), whereby any contrast C_{Id} can be given the form:

$$C_I(f_i, \theta_i, w, I_0)$$

$$= \frac{\Delta I(f_i, \theta_i, w)}{I_0} \approx \frac{L(I_0)}{I_0 L'(I_0)}C(f_i, \theta_i, w, L(I_0))$$

$$(30)$$

By expressing equation (23) in the grey-level domain, we finally find the relation assuring the invisibility of the watermark, by processing directly grey-level images:

$$C_{I_{deq}}(f_i, \theta_i, w, I_Z) \leq JNC_{Im}(f_i, \theta_i, w, I_Z), \ \forall i \in Z, \forall Z.$$

$$(31)$$

By relying on this formula we will now present an approach for building an improved masking function.

Improved Mask Building

Let us consider an original signal (i.e., an image) S_o and its marked version S_w. The difference between S_w and S_o, that is, the inserted watermark S_d, represents the disturbing signal, while S_o represents the masking signal. Now, by applying the approach detailed in the previous section, it is possible to determine the maximum allowable energy of the watermark in order to preserve image quality. In particular, a *block-based DCT* analysis is applied to both S_o and S_d in order to obtain for each coefficient of each block the masked just noticeable contrast and the equivalent disturb contrast expressions.

The host image S_o is divided into blocks of size $n \times n$. Let us indicate them by $B_o{}^z(i, k)$. Then each block is *DCT*-transformed into $b_o{}^z(u, v)$. This transform allows us to decompose each image block as the sum of a set of sinusoidal stimuli. In particular, for each block Z the mean grey-level is given by $I_z = b'_o{}^z(0,0) = b_o{}^z(0,0)/2n$. Furthermore, each coefficient at frequency (u, v) gives birth to two sinusoidal stimuli, having the same amplitude, the same frequency f_{uv}, but opposite orientations $\pm\theta_{uv}$. The amplitude is generally given by $b'_o{}^z(u, v) = b_o{}^z(u, v)/2n$, except when $\theta_{uv} \in \{0, \pi\}$ then it results $b'_o{}^z(u, v) = b_o{}^z(u, v)/n$.

By relying on equation (28), for a *DCT* coefficient at spatial frequency (u, v) the contributions of all the surrounding frequencies of the same block Z are considered and the value of the masked just noticeable contrast is obtained through the following expression:

157

$$JNC_{I_m}(u,v,w,b_o^{'Z}(0,0)) = JNC_I(u,v,w,b_o^{'Z}(0,0)) \cdot$$

$$\cdot \max\left\{1, \left[\sum_{u'=0,v'=0}^{n-1,n-1}\left|g'(u,u',v,v')\frac{b_o^{'Z}(u',v')/b_o^{'Z}(0,0)}{JNC_I(u',v',w,b_o^{'Z}(0,0))}\right|\right]^W\right\},$$

$$(32)$$

where $JNC_I(u,v,w,b_o^{'Z}(0,0))$ is the non-masked just noticeable contrast for the coefficient at frequency (u,v), $b_o^{'Z}(u',v')/b_o^{'Z}(0,0)$ is the contrast of the masking coefficient, and $g'(u,u',v,v')$ is the weighing function that can be obtained by equation (12) as:

$$g'(u,u',v,v') = \exp\left[-\left(\frac{\log_2^2(f_{u'v'}/f_{uv})}{\sigma_f^2}\right)\right] \cdot$$

$$\cdot \exp\left[-\left(\frac{(\theta_{u'v'}-\theta_{uv})^2+(-\theta_{u'v'}-\theta_{uv})^2}{\sigma_\theta^2}\right)\right],$$

$$(33)$$

where the fact that each *DCT* coefficient accounts for two sinusoidal components with the same spatial frequencies but opposite orientations, and that the just noticeable contrast has the same value for stimuli having opposite orientations, has been considered.

In order to guarantee the invisibility of a sinusoidal disturbance in a given block, the contrast of the component of the disturbance at a given frequency (u,v) must be smaller than the value of the JNC_{I_m} obtained by equation (32). A *block based DCT* is also applied to the disturbing signal S_d, computed as the difference between the watermarked signal S_w and the original signal S_o. Each block Z of S_d (i.e., $B_d^Z(i,k)$) is decomposed as a sum of sinusoidal stimuli (i.e., $b_d^Z(u,v)$).

What we want to get is a threshold on the maximum allowable modification that each coefficient can sustain. We have to consider that nearby watermarking coefficients will reinforce each other; thus, by relying on equation (29), we can rewrite the equivalent disturb contrast at coefficient (u,v) in block Z as:

$$C_{I_{deq}}(u,v,w,b_o^{'Z}(0,0)) = \sum_{u'=0,v'=0}^{n-1,n-1}\left|g'(u,u',v,v')\cdot\right.$$

$$\left. \cdot \frac{c(u')c(v')}{n}\frac{b_d^{'Z}(u',v')}{b_o^{'Z}(0,0)}\right|,$$

$$(34)$$

where $b_d^{'Z}(u',v')/b_o^{'Z}(0,0)$ is the contrast of the disturbing signal, and where we have assumed that the same weighing function can be used for modelling the reinforcing effect of neighbouring disturbances. By relying on equation (31), the invisibility constraint results to be:

$$C_{I_{deq}}(u,v,w,b_o^{'Z}(0,0)) \le JNC_{I_m}(u,v,w,b_o^{'Z}(0,0)),$$

$$\forall(u,v)\in Z \qquad (35)$$

Based on this approach, it is possible to build a masking function for spatially shaping any kind of watermark. By referring to equation (16), let us suppose that the mask M is block-wise constant, and let us indicate with M_Z the value assumed by the mask in block Z. By exploiting the linearity property of the *DCT* transform, it is easy to verify that for satisfying the invisibility constraint we must have:

$$M_Z \cdot C_{I_{deq}}(u,v,w,b_o^{'Z}(0,0)) \le JNC_{I_m}(u,v,w,b_o^{'Z}(0,0)),$$

$$\forall(u,v)\in Z, \qquad (36)$$

thus boiling down to:

$$M_Z = \min_{(u,v)}\frac{JNC_{I_m}(u,v,w,b_o^{'Z}(0,0))}{C_{I_{deq}}(u,v,w,b_o^{'Z}(0,0))}, \quad \forall(u,v)\in Z.$$

$$(37)$$

In Figures 9 to12 the resulting masking functions are shown for some standard images, namely *Lena, harbor, boat* and *airplane*. These masks produce reliable results, especially on textured areas. This is mainly due to the fact that the disturbing signal frequency content is also considered for building the mask. Moreover, this method allows the maximum amount of watermarking energy that each image can tolerate to be automatically obtained, without resorting to manual tuning.

CONCLUSION

Two of the main requirements a data-hiding scheme must satisfy regard invisibility and robustness. The watermark must be invisible so that its presence does not affect the quality of the to-be-protected data; on the other hand, it must be resistant against the most common image manipulations, calling for the necessity of embedding a watermark with as high a strength as possible. The availability of accurate models describing the phenomena regulating human vision can give great advantage to satisfy the above requirements.

By starting from the analysis of the main important HVS concepts, we have explored how these factors can be exploited during the data-hiding process. Some important limits of the classical approaches have been pointed out, as well as possible solutions to cope with them. Finally, we have detailed a new possible approach for HVS modelling and its exploitation for building a sensitivity mask.

Due to the space constraints, we limited our analysis to mask building algorithms directly derived from the HVS model. For a couple of alternative (more heuristic) approaches to mask building, readers are referred to Bartolini et al. (1998) and Pereira, Voloshynovskiy and Pun (2001). We also ignored visual masking in domains other than the DFT and DCT ones. A detailed description of an HVS-based data-hiding system operating in the wavelet domain, may be found in Barni, Bartolini and Piva (2001). To further explore the importance and the role of perceptual considerations in a data hiding system, readers may also refer to Wolfgang et al. (1999) and Podilchuk and Zeng (1998).

We purposely limited our analysis to the case of grey-level images, since in many cases the watermark is inserted in the luminance component of the host image. It has to be said, though, that advantages in terms of both robustness and imperceptibility are likely to be got by considering the way the HVS handles colours.

REFERENCES

Ahumada, A.J., Jr., & Beard, B.L. (1996, February). Object detection in a noisy scene. *Proceedings of SPIE: Vol. 2657. Human Vision, Visual Processing, and Digital Display VII* (pp. 190-199). Bellingham, WA.

Barni, M., Bartolini, F., & Piva, A. (2001, May). Improved wavelet-based watermarking through pixel-wise masking. *IEEE Transactions on Image Processing, 10*(5), 783-791.

Barten, P.G. (1990, October). Evaluation of subjective image quality with the square-root integral method. *Journal of Optical Society of America, 7*(10), 2024-2031.

Bartolini, F., Barni, M., Cappellini, V., & Piva, A. (1998, October). Mask building for perceptually hiding frequency embedded watermarks. *Proceedings of IEEE International Conference of Image Processing '98,* (vol. 1, pp. 450-454). Chicago, IL.

Comes, S., & Macq, B. (1990, October). Human visual quality criterion. *Proceedings of SPIE: Vol. 1360. Visual Communications and Image Processing* (pp. 2-13). Lausanne, CH.

Cox, I., & Miller, M.L. (1997, February). A review of watermarking and the importance of perceptual modeling. *Proceedings of SPIE: Vol. 3016. Human Vision and Electronic Imaging II* (pp. 92-99). Bellingham, WA.

Damera-Venkata, N., Kite, T.D., Geisler, W.S., Evans, B.L., & Bovik, A.C. (2000, April). Image quality assessment based on a degradation model. *IEEE Transactions on Image Processing, 9*(4), 636-650.

Delaigle, J.F., De Vleeschouwer, C., & Macq, B. (1998, May). Watermarking algorithm based on a human visual model. *Signal Processing, 66*(3), 319-336.

Eckert, M.P., & Bradley, A.P. (1998). Perceptual quality metrics applied to still image compression. *Signal Processing, 70,* 177-200.

Foley, J.M., & Legge, G.E. (1981). Contrast detection and near-threshold discrimination. *Vision Research, 21,* 1041-1053.

Kundur, D., & Hatzinakos, D. (1997, October). A robust digital watermarking method using wavelet-based fusion. *Proceedings of IEEE International Conference of Image Processing '97: Vol. 1* (pp. 544-547). Santa Barbara, CA.

Legge, G.E., & Foley, J.M. (1980, December). Contrast masking in human vision. *Journal of Optical Society of America, 70*(12), 1458-1471.

Pereira, S., Voloshynovskiy, S., & Pun, T. (2001, June). Optimal transform domain watermark embedding via linear programming. *Signal Processing, 81*(6), 1251-1260.

Petitcolas, F.A., Anderson, R.J., & Kuhn, M.G. (1999, July). Information hiding: A survey. *Proceedings of IEEE, 87*(7), 1062-1078.

Podilchuk, C.I., & Zeng, W. (1998, May). Image-adaptive watermarking using visual models. *IEEE Journal on Selected Areas in Communications, 16*(4), 525-539.

Swanson, M.D., Zhu, B., & Tewfik, A.H. (1998, May). Multiresolution scene-based video watermarking using perceptual models. *IEEE Journal on Selected Areas in Communications, 16*(4), 540-550.

Tewfik, A.H., & Swanson, M. (1997, July). Data hiding for multimedia personalization, interaction, and protection. *IEEE Signal Processing Magazine, 14*(4), 41-44.

Van Schyndel, R.G., Tirkel, A.Z., & Osborne, C.F. (1994, November). A digital watermark. *Proceedings of IEEE International Conference of Image Processing '94: Vol. 2* (pp. 86-90). Austin, TX.

Voloshynovskiy, S., Pereira, S., Iquise, V., & Pun, T. (2001, June). Attack modelling: Towards a second generation watermarking benchmark. *Signal Processing, 81*(6), 1177-1214.

Watson, A.B. (1987, December). Efficiency of an image code based on human vision. *Journal of Optical Society of America, 4*(12), 2401-2417.

Watson, A.B. (1993, February). Dct quantization matrices visually optimized for individual images. *Proceedings of SPIE: Vol. 1913. Human Vision, Visual Processing and Digital Display IV* (pp. 202-216). Bellingham, WA.

Wolfgang, R.B., Podilchuk, C.I., & Delp, E.J. (1999, July). Perceptual watermarks for digital images and video. *Proceedings of IEEE, 87*(7), 1108-1126.

Section II
Solutions

Chapter VII
Online Personal Data Licensing:
Regulating Abuse of Personal
Data in Cyberspace

Yuh-Jzer Joung
National Taiwan University, Taiwan

Shi-Cho Cha
National Taiwan University of Science and Technology, Taiwan

ABSTRACT

We propose a new technical and legal approach, called online personal data licensing (OPDL), for responding to concerns about the privacy of personal data. Unlike traditional privacy-enhancing technologies that typically aim to hide personal data, OPDL enables individuals to concretize their consent to allow others to use their personal data as licenses. Service providers must obtain licenses before legally collecting, processing, or using a person's data. By allowing individuals to issue their own licenses and to determine the content of the licenses, OPDL brings the control of personal data back to their owner, and ensures that the use of the data is strictly under the owner's consent. In contrast, most Web-based service providers today use passive consent, which usually results in situations in which users have inadvertently given the providers the authorization to use their personal data. Besides, users generally do not have information on who still owns a copy of their data, and how their data have been, or will be, used.

INTRODUCTION

Personal data have been used for many different purposes in cyberspace. For example, in customer relationship management (CRM) and one-to-one marketing, service providers collect their customers' data and use them to understand the customers' wants, goals, and needs, so as to improve their quality of service and the customers' loyalty and lifetime value (Hanson, 1999).

An unfortunate problem, however, is that most people are not aware of who has collected their personal data, who has used that data, for what purposes, and who still holds a copy of the data. In fact, the advances in the Internet and information technologies, although allowing personal data to be efficiently collected and processed, have at the same time turned cyberspace into a hotbed for data abuse, for example, e-mail spamming (Cerf, 2005; Peeger & Bloom, 2005), and credit card fraud (Walia, 2006).

To face these new challenges, many countries have enacted laws to regulate abuse of personal data in cyberspace, for example, the Australian Privacy Act (Australian Government, 1988), the British Data Protection Act (British Government, 1998), the Personal Information Protection and Electronic Document Act of Canada (Canada Government, 2000), the German Federal Data Protection Act (German Government, 2001), and so forth. Moreover, the European Parliament and Council passed the European Union's Directive 95/46/EC, on the protection of individuals with regard to the processing of personal data and on the free movement of such data, in 1995 (European Union, 1995). It requires the member states of the EU to put their national legislation in line with the provisions of the directive. Transmission of personal data to non-EU countries that do not meet its standard for data protection is prohibited. Because of the stricture on cross-border flows of personal data in the Directive and the emergence of well-networked global policy communities, laws on personal data protection in different countries are progressively toward a convergence (Bennett, 1997). That is, although the words of personal data protection laws may be different in different countries, they usually follow some basic principles.

However, even though some basic principles have been established, the current Internet architecture does not easily allow abuse of personal data to be discovered and proved. This is because Internet service providers are usually required to obtain a user's consent when his/her data are to be collected and processed. For example, the EU Directive stipulates that personal data can be processed only if the owner (the *data subject*) has unambiguously given his/her consent (European Union, 1995). There are many types of consent, such as *oral/verbal, written, proxy, passive*, and so forth (University of Washington, 2006). Obviously, written consent can provide the strongest power of evidence, especially when disputes occur. Considering the dynamics of cyberspace and the flow of information, however, it is very inefficient and inconvenient for users and service providers to proceed with written consent. Therefore, passive consent is generally allowed and adopted in many countries. To obtain a passive consent, a Web site simply discloses its practices about personal data at its site. If one continually uses the site's services or even registers as a member of the site, then this will be considered as an indication that consent has been given to the site.

A problem with passive consent is that it is very hard for users to prove that the sites have used their personal data in accordance with their understandings. To see this, suppose that when a person registered as a member of an online shopping site, the privacy policies of the site did not express an intention to collect its users' transactional behaviors. Some days after, the site decided to do so for, say, one-to-one marketing. The site did not actively inform its users about this decision, but only modified (perhaps silently) its disclosed privacy policies. If the person later discovers that the site has collected his personal data without his consent and decides to make a complaint against the site, he needs to prove that the modified privacy policies are *not* the ones he saw when he registered at the site. Clearly, this complaint is hard to make a case, as the user may not have enough evidence to support him.

To make cyberspace more "regulable" (Lessig, 2000) without sacrificing efficiency, we propose *online personal data licensing* (OPDL) (Cha & Joung, 2002). Our goal is to build a privacy protection framework in cyberspace so that application and service providers that support OPDL can meet the requirement of personal data protection in most countries. Simply speaking, OPDL brings the control of personal data back to individuals themselves by requiring application and service providers to obtain a *license* from a person before collecting, processing, and using his/her personal data. As such, people can be made more aware of the authorization of the use of their personal data. They can also obtain more clear information about who has owned a copy of their personal data, the status of their licenses, and the content of the licenses. If needed, updates to a person's personal data can be sent or notified to the current licensees of the data. Such functionality is generally not possible in current Web applications. Moreover, the whole licensing process can be made either automatically or semiautomatically to catch the dynamics in cyberspace.

The rest of the chapter is organized as follows. Section 2 provides some background of the problem and the related work. Section 3 is an overview of the framework. Section 4 discusses the usage of data licenses. The detailed components of OPDL are presented in Section 5. Finally, conclusions and future work are offered in Section 6.

BACKGROUND

We review the background by starting with some principles that have been established for personal data protection in cyberspace. Then we discuss the general framework proposed by the World Wide Web Consortium (W3C)[1] for individuals to control the collection, use, and dissemination of their personal information, thereby protecting their privacy. Techniques for enhancing privacy will also be briefly reviewed. As our approach to protecting personal data is to actively authorize the *right* to legally use them, some similar concept in managing "digital right" will also be highlighted.

Basic Personal Data Protection Principles

With the advances of network and database technologies, large data banks of personal information can be easily collected and built over the Internet. Even though the use of the data banks may be regulated by laws by which they were created and managed, distribution of data across different regions and countries may encounter conflicts of laws. Therefore, communities were formed to codify some "global" policy about personal data. On the other hand, because of the fast advances of information technologies, policymakers always face the likelihood that their regulatory efforts will become useless by the time they are implemented. Therefore, a set of basic rules with sufficient breadth and adaptability are needed (Bennett, 1997).

In this context, the Organization for Economic Cooperation and Development (OECD) codified *Guidelines on the Protection and Privacy of Transborder Flows of Personal Data* (OECD, 1980). The guidelines, listed next, have great impact on later policy making about personal data protection:

- **Collection and limitation:** There should be limits to the collection of personal data. Moreover, data should be obtained by lawful and fair means with consent of data subjects.
- **Data quality:** Collected data should be kept up to date, accurate, and complete.
- **Purpose specification:** Purposes should be specified and disclosed while data are collected.
- **Use limitation:** The subsequent use of collected data should fulfill the purposes disclosed while data are collected.
- **Security safeguards:** Personal data should be protected by reasonable security safeguards.

- **Openness:** The developments, practices, and policies with respect to personal data should be open.
- **Individual participation:** Individuals should have the right to obtain data about themselves and the right to challenge the accuracy of such data.
- **Accountability:** A data controller should be accountable to the data subject in complying with these principles.

To achieve better enforcement of the principles, the European Parliament and Council passed the European Union's Directive 95/46/EC, on the protection of individuals with regard to the processing of personal data and on the free movement of such data, in 1995 (European Union, 1995). Besides requiring the member states of the EU to follow the directive, its Article 26 prohibits transmission of personal data to countries that do not adopt "adequate" protection policies to personal data. In other words, if a company in a country wishes to provide service, in which exchanges of personal data are necessary, to the EU countries, the country should have legislated appropriate laws to protect personal data. Therefore, the Directive also urges other countries to take similar steps.

On the other hand, because the First Amendment to the U.S. Constitution imposes limits on the government's ability to regulate the flow of information (including personal data) (Isenberg, 2002), the U.S. data protection laws are narrowly tailored to some specific domains (such as video renting, financial institutions, health care organizations, etc.). To reconcile the basic differences about personal data protection with European countries, the U.S. Department of Commerce reached an agreement with the European Commission on a "safe harbor" framework (U.S. Department of Commerce, 2000). Therefore, the following seven Safe Harbor principles can be treated as current international principles about personal data protection:

- **Notice:** An organization must clearly tell individuals about why it needs to collect and use their personal data, how to contact the organization for any inquiries or complaints, the types of third parties to which it discloses their personal data, and the choices and means that the organization offers for individuals to limit the use and disclosure of their data.
- **Choice:** Individuals must have options to decide whether or not to allow an organization to collect and use their data.
- **Onward transfer:** If an organization wishes to disclose its collected data to a third party, the organization must comply with the notice and choice principles.
- **Security:** Organizations must adopt reasonable security safeguards to protect collected personal data.
- **Data integrity:** The use of personal data of an organization should obey the purposes for which the data have been collected.
- **Access:** Individuals must have right to access their personal data that an organization holds, and to maintain correctness of the data.
- **Enforcement:** The organization must provide a dispute resolution mechanism for investigating and resolving its customers' complaints and disputes.

The design of OPDL is based on these seven principles. OPDL requires service providers to obtain licenses from individuals before collecting and using their data. By requiring service providers to make a proposal describing their purposes and related information, and by allowing individuals to determine whether or not to accept the proposal, OPDL clearly meets the notice and choice principles. The onward transfer principle can be satisfied as well by requiring service providers to specify whether or not they intend to share data with a third party. Similarly, the security principle can be satisfied by requiring service providers to state in their proposals their security policies, risk assessment, and controls against risks, so that individuals can know what security safeguards they have adopted to protect personal data. The data integrity principle can be satisfied in the following two ways: (1) Licenses can be checked while data are used, and (2) Service providers can be verified and audited by a third party certification organization. The certification organization can also provide dispute resolutions to meet the enforcement principle. Finally, to achieve the access principle, OPDL requires service providers to provide a standard interface for receiving update notifications so that individuals can maintain correctness of their data, and revoke their licenses if legally permitted.

Platform for Privacy Preferences (P3P)

Accompanied with the hope of industry and individuals, the first formal specifications of platform for privacy preferences (P3P) were proposed by the World Wide Web Consortium (W3C) in April 2002 (Cranor, Langheinrich, Marchiori, Presler-Marshall, & Reagle 2002) for privacy protection in the Web. The original concept can be described as follows: P3P defines a vocabulary and specification for a Web site to declare its privacy practices. The privacy practices are represented as machine readable "proposals" to describe what personal data will be collected by the site, for what purposes, other recipients of the data, and the destruction timetable. When a user requests a Web page (to which the user has not yet achieved a privacy agreement) from the site, a set of proposals is sent to the user. The user's agent can then choose one proposal that matches the user's preferences, and sends an agreement ID back to the site to express acceptance of the proposal. After receiving the agreement, the site will transfer the requested page to the user. If none of the proposals is accepted by the user, the

site can send another set of proposals for further negotiation.

In this process, the Web site may also request the user's data. This feature was originated from open profiling standard (OPS) (Hensley, Metral, Shardanand, Converse, & Meyers 1997). OPS was intended to provide privacy protection for personal profile information exchange over the Web, and was folded into the early P3P. If the user accepts a proposal, the requested data along with the agreement ID are transmitted to the site (in HTTP request header (Kristol, 2001)). The automatic transfer of personal data raises some controversies, however. So the P3P Specification Working Group later decided to remove this function (W3C, 1999). The negotiation module was also simplified due to the complexity of the original process. These two modifications have then established the prototype of current P3P.

Generally speaking, P3P provides a standard protocol for a Web site to express its privacy practices, and for a user's browsing agent (e.g., Internet Explorer) to determine whether or not the practices match the user's privacy preferences. P3P, however, lacks a mechanism for users or third-party organizations to verify if Web sites have faithfully executed the practices (EPIC & Junkbuster, 2000), and for applications to check if the use of personal data collected by the sites has indeed been authorized by individuals and are used in a way that is in accordance with what the individuals have agreed when releasing their personal data. OPDL, on the other hand, concretizes the agreements between individuals and Web sites into licenses that can then be used to legally resolve privacy disputes between them, and can also be used by applications to prevent abuse of personal information.

Moreover, P3P presumes no single privacy standard, such as the aforementioned OECD Privacy Guidelines or the Safe Harbor Privacy Principles. In fact, we can see that P3P meets only the notice and choice principles of the Safe

Harbor Privacy Principles. The fact that P3P does not provide a means for individuals to access and update their personal data at the service providers is one of the reasons that the European Union has explicitly rejected P3P as part of its privacy protection framework (European Commission, 1998). In contrast, OPDL is designed based on the privacy principles so as to provide a simple and uniformly agreed environment for online activities.

Privacy Enhancing Technologies

As described by Burkert (Burkert, 1997), privacy enhancing technologies (PETs), which refer to technical and organizational concepts that aim at protecting personal identity, can be classified into the following four types:

- The subject-oriented PETs seek to ensure the anonymity of an acting subject in transactions or in the relationship to existing data. For example, LPWA (Gabber, Gibbons, Kristol, Matias, & Mayer, 1999), and Crowds (Reiter & Rubin, 1998) prevent a user from being identified or tracked while surfing the Web by relaying messages among one or more proxies.
- The object-oriented PETs construct electronic equivalents to cash (e.g., the eCash system (Chaum, 1982)) or other barter objects so that the objects cannot be linked to a specific person who uses the objects.
- The transaction-oriented PETs destroy transaction records automatically after a preset time. For example, personal channel agent (PCA) (Hall, 1998) enables individuals to create many different e-mail addresses for different purposes, for example, giving different e-mail addresses to different service providers. Then, if a user finds that a spammer sends unsolicited commercial e-mails to him/her through one of his/her

e-mail address, he/she can invalidate the e-mail address easily.

- The system-oriented PETs create zones of interaction where the identities of activating subjects are hidden. For example, GNUnet (Bennett & Grothoff, 2003) provides a peer-to-peer file-sharing framework that allows both file providers and requesters to be anonymous under the disguise of other peer computers.

Both OPDL and PETs aim to protect personal data from being abused. However, OPDL and PETs achieve this goal from two very different approaches: PETs help a person to hide his/her personal information in cyberspace, while OPDL actively allows personal information to be used, but requires the use be accompanied by a license under the owner's consent.

Digital Rights Management

Digital rights management (DRM) technologies (Sonera Plaza, 2002) (e.g., Windows Media Rights Manager (WMRM) and IBM's Electronic Media Management System (EMMS)) have recently been developed as a protection against the illegal distribution of copyrighted online publications such as music, e-books, and videos. The technologies embed copyright information into online publications so that users must obtain licenses in order to read the publications. The publications may also be encrypted so that they can only be accessed based on the keys in the licenses. Obviously, licenses play an important role to allow a system to automatically check whether or not end users have permission to access the content of a publication. Several standards of licenses have also been designed for this purpose, for example, the extensive media commerce language (XMCL) (Ayars, 2002) (used by IBM's EMMS), and the extensive rights markup language (XrML) (ContentGuard Holdings, Inc., 2002) (used by Microsoft's WMRM).

Both DRM and OPDL aim to regulate the use of data. However, because their targets are different (DRM on digital media, while OPDL on personal data), there are differences between the two. In particular, the types of elements in personal data are far more complex than that of digital media. In fact, personal data may contain digital media (e.g., a person's portrait or his/her self-introduction voice), but not vice versa. Because of this, licenses in OPDL need to deal with more issues than licenses in DRM, especially on privacy. In contrast, a license in DRM is usually for a whole, nondecomposable digital publication.

Moreover, because of the complexity of personal data, several issues need to be taken into account when issuing a data license, including, for example, the purpose of using the data, security levels of the requesters, personal preferences, and update notifications. So a licensing proposal needs to be presented, verified, and possibly negotiated, before issuing a license. In contrast, DRM licenses are generally simpler, concerning primarily how long a digital publication is valid.

Finally, data licenses in OPDL are typically issued by individuals to service providers. DRM, on the other hand, are designed for individuals to acquire licenses from service providers.

Overview of the Framework

Generally speaking, OPDL acts as a delegate for data subjects (the owners of data) to generate licenses to use their personal data. As depicted in Figure 1, when a requester requests a person's data, the request is sent through the *data licensing interface*. Requests are more or less like a proposal, and so we refer to them as *licensing proposals*. The main components of a licensing proposal include the data that are requested, the purposes, and the retention timetable. Note that personal data may refer to dynamic click-streams a person generates while he/she is surfing a Web site.

The kernel of OPDL is *personal data licenser*. Its implementation is not compelled to any form;

for example, it can be implemented as a software agent in a person's computer, or as service offered by a service provider, or even on a peer-to-peer (P2P) network (Cha, Joung, & Lue, 2003). The main components of personal data licenser are also shown in Figure 1. The components include three databases: the person's data that the licenser manages, the preferences the person set on licensing, and the logs of licensing proposals (called *Access Log* in the figure). There are also six functional components. *Agreement Negotiator* deals with requests based on a person's licensing preferences. The *Notification Mechanism* deals with the following two situations:

- To some sensitive data, data subjects can specify more strict preference policies so that the Notification Mechanism will inform them to let them make the final decision.
- When people wish to modify the content of issued licenses (including the data content), the related Internet services will be notified through their *Update Notification Interface*.

After verifying that a licensing proposal does meet a data subject's preferences, the Agreement Negotiator generates a license for the use of requested data. To prevent the content of the license from being altered and to ensure that the license is indeed issued by the genuine data subject, the license will be digitally signed by the data subject. The signature is required to legally resolve possible disputes in between the licenser and licensee, for example, about the content of the license. The use of digital signature requires keys be issued by a trusted center, for example, Certification Authorities (CAs) or Key Generation Centers (Fiat & Shamir, 1986; Shamir, 1985). It also accompanies with the key management problem. As there is already rich literature on this subject (see, e.g., (CCITT, 1988; Chokhani, 1994; Kent, 1993; Menezes, van Oorschot, & Vanstone, 1997)), we omit details of this here.

Figure 1. Architecture of online personal data licensing

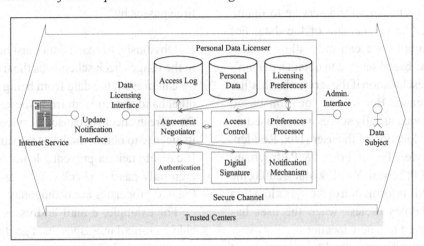

The license, which also contains the requested personal data, is then sent back to the requester. Licensing proposals and the issued licenses are recorded in Access Log to allow data subjects to trace them through *Administration Interface*. The Administration Interface also provides functions for data subjects to set or modify their personal data and preferences. The actual processing of the preferences is done by the *Preferences Processor*.

Security mechanisms must be employed to protect the data. The *Authentication mechanism* verifies users' identities. *Access Control* checks if requesters have the authorization to access the requested objects. Secure channels can be established to protect communications. For example, a requester can build secure sockets layer (SSL) (Freier, Karlton, & Kocher, 1996) communication channel with the Personal Data Licenser, and X.509 certificates (CCITT, 1988) can be exchanged for both parties to authenticate each other.

Usage of Licenses

This section shows how licenses can be used to ensure that a person's data are processed in the same way as specified in a data license. In general, the use of licenses can be classified as follows, depending on whether or not a license can be checked directly:

- **Direct check:** Licenses must be checked before data are used or collected. This case can further be divided into the following two subcases:
  - **Usage check:** Licenses must be shown when the data are used. For example, we can modify a person's e-mail server so that it only accepts an e-mail if a license to use the person's e-mail address is attached in the e-mail. So when a site wants to send advertisements to a person, it must first obtain an agreement from the person. Moreover, an online retailer can ask a valid license for using a credit card number to be shown during a transaction to prevent credit card fraud. Note that the license generated by the credit card holder may contain time information to ensure that it can be used only for this transaction so as to present security attacks such as replay and masquerade.

- **Refresh check:** Licenses must be used as permission for a service to obtain the "latest" version of the data. For example, we can only allow a location-based service to obtain a person's latest location if the service has his/her license. Because a location-based service usually serves a user based on the location of the user (Dix, Rodden, Davies, Trevor, Friday, & Palfreyman, 2000; Tewari, Youll, & Maes, 2003), the "old" information of the user's location becomes useless when the user has moved to a new location.

- **Passive (indirect) check:** Licenses must be shown when a trusted authority wishes to check whether or not a service provider has obtained its customers' consent to collect or use their data when, for example, the authority receives complaints about the possibility of personal data abuse. That is, licenses can be used in an auditing process to prevent data abuse. An automatic procedure can be developed to check the licenses of personal data stored at a service provider. The procedure can be integrated into an internal audit system to improve users' confidence. Like TRUSTe (Benassi, 1999), an organization or company can also be established to serve for external auditing to increase service providers' credibility.

Intuitively, direct check is preferred because of its immediate effect on data protection. However, not every type of personal data is suitable to the scheme. To see this, we first define the following properties:

Definition 1—(Preventable): A data is *preventable* if the use of the data must go through a trusted authority.

Definition 2—(Invalidatable): A data is *invalidatable* if the data can be invalidated by a person, or will become invalid automatically when the time passes by.

Obviously, licensed data must be preventable in the usage check scheme, as the trusted authority can prevent the data from being used. On the other hand, data are required to be invalidatable in the refresh check, because a service needs to use its license to obtain the latest version of the data. If data are neither preventable nor invalidatable, then only passive check can be used. Note that the two properties are orthogonal.

For example, e-mail addresses are preventable, as e-mail messages must go through e-mail servers. E-mail addresses are typically noninvalidatable, as invalidating an e-mail address will cause other people unable to communicate with the addressee via the e-mail address. However, e-mail addresses can also be made invalidatable by allowing a person to create a temporal e-mail address that is valid only in a specified period (e.g., Personal Channel Agent (Hall, 1998)). Credit card number is also preventable. By definition, data whose usage, for example, the opening of a file/document, does not need to go through a third party are nonpreventable. However, some technique can be devised to alter this. For example, by using digital rights management (DRM), protected (encrypted) digital media can only be opened/operated via a dedicated "player."

Location-based information in a mobile wireless service is an example of invalidatable data. In such a service, as a user will roam around different places, a user's location will be invalidated when he/she moves to another place. Depending on the application, some location information may or may not go through a third party, and thus it can be either preventable or nonpreventable. For example, if the information is used to log a person's traveling path, then it is nonpreventable. However, if the location information is used to push some advertisement to the user (say, for marketing) via some telecom company that operates the wireless service, then the location information becomes preventable. On the other hand, user ID and user's behavior log are typical examples of noninvalidatable data, as they remain valid once acquired by someone.

Main Component

This section describes main components of OPDL. We begin by presenting an example in Figure 2 that illustrates typical scenarios for using OPDL to access service providers:

- **Step 1:** A user clicks a "sign-in" button at the site "http://exampleshop."
- **Step 2:** Instead of sending a registration form back to the user, the site finds out the user's Personal Data Licenser and sends it a licensing proposal. If the proposal matches the user's preferences, a license (along with the requested data) will be transmitted to the site. Then, the site starts to provide services to the user. Otherwise, the following steps will proceed.

- **Step 3:** The notification mechanism generates a notification form to ask the user to decide whether or not to accept the proposal.
- **Step 4:** The user views the notification form and decides to accept this proposal.
- **Step 5:** After receiving the user's confirmation, the personal data licenser sends a license to the site. The site then starts to provide services to the user.
- **Step 6:** After the user has issued a license to the site, he/she can obtain the latest value of his/her personal data at the site and modify them through the update notification interface.

In the following sections, we will discuss licensing proposals, automatic processing of proposals, licenses, and update notifications in detail.

Licensing Proposals

Licensing proposals are based on P3P policies (Cranor, Langheinrich, Marchiori, Presler-Mar-

Figure 2. Integrating OPDL into Web-based service

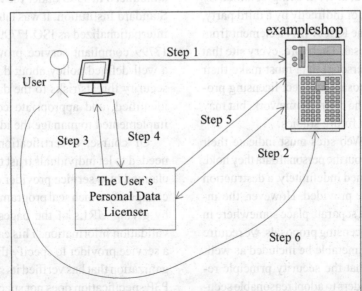

shall, & Reagle, 2002). P3P defines a vocabulary and specification for a Web site to express its privacy policies. The privacy statements are represented as machine readable "proposals" to describe what personal data will be collected by the site, for what purposes, other recipients of the data, and the destruction timetable. We made the following modifications to let them fit into our framework.

First, personal data in P3P are classified into 18 categories, including physical contact information, purchase information, demographic and socioeconomic data, and so forth. For example, a person's gender, blood type, and birthday belong to demographic and socioeconomic data. A site may only specify the categories of personal data it wishes to collect. In licensing proposals, however, we require specific items of personal data in the categories be explicitly specified.

Second, in P3P, requesters must specify the recipients of data. The recipients, however, may include an unrelated third party whose true identity is not known to the user. All recipients of the data are specified in the RECIPIENT element of the policy (where the site that proposes the policy is represented as <ours/> in value, and anonymous recipients are expressed as <other-recipient/>). To avoid personal data from being obtained by an anonymous site, or indirectly by a third party, we have removed the RECIPIENT element from our licensing proposal. Therefore, every site that wishes to obtain personal data must make their own licensing proposals. Indirect licensing proposals complicate the entire framework, but may be worth trying for future studies.

Third, in P3P, Web sites must indicate their retention policies about the personal data they hold. If data are not retained indefinitely, a destruction timetable should be provided. However, the information is put in a separate place somewhere in their Web sites. In licensing proposals, we require that a destruction timetable be included as well.

Finally, recall that the security principle requires service providers to adopt reasonable secu-rity safeguards to protect collected personal data. P3P, in general, does not support this principle, and so we need to make some modification in order to adopt it into our licensing proposals. For this, a security evaluation framework is needed for users to evaluate the degree of data security in a service provider. Several such frameworks have been proposed for this purpose, for example, the trusted computer system evaluation criteria (TCSEC) (U.S. Department of Defense, 1985). TCSEC is proposed by the U.S. Department of Defense (DoD) to provide a metric to evaluate the degree of trust it can place in computer systems for the secure processing of sensitive information. TCSEC, together with other similar standards like the German Green Book and the British CLEF, was later folded into a single worldwide standard called the Common Criteria in 1994 (Kaufman, Perlman, & Speciner, 2002).

These frameworks are designed to evaluate computer systems. A standard is also required to evaluate and verify the data security of an organization. Some recent emerging standards, such as BS 7799 and ISO 17799, enable a person to judge whether or not an organization has defined and put in place effective security processes (Calder & Watkins, 2002). (BS 7799 was first announced in 1995 under the auspices of British Standard Institution. It was later replaced by and internationalized as ISO 17799.) A BS 7799/ISO 17799 compliant service provider should have a well-defined policy about data security. Main security threats/risks to the data should also be identified, and appropriate controls should be implemented to manage the identified risk.

Of course, a certification organization is needed to let individuals trust the security policy claimed by a service provider. In P3P, Web sites can specify which seal programs they have passed by giving URLs of the pages that contain the validation information. This can also be used for a service provider to specify the certification organization that has verified its security. However, P3P specification does not specify any automatic verification procedure for a user agent to decide the truth of a seal. If a user himself needs to read the validation page for verification, then this would conflict with a design philosophy of P3P: to allow its user to automate decision making (Cranor, Langheinrich, Marchiori, Presler-Marshall, & Reagle, 2002). Therefore, we recommend that there should be a verification interface between certification organizations and user agents. The name of a service provider that needs to be verified can be sent to a certification organization (through, e.g., HTTP GET method). Then, the certification organization can transmit responses (in Web pages) with a well-defined structure to the requesting user agent directly.

To illustrate how these issues are taken into account in licensing proposals, Figure 3 shows an example of a P3P-based licensing proposal. In this proposal, an online shopping site (exampleshop) wishes to collect some personal data from its members and to use these data for some purposes. It has another version of human readable proposal disclosed in "http://exampleshop/humanreadableproposal.html." The proposal is signed by the site to avoid masquerade. In this example, the URLs of the site's security policy, risk assessments, and controls about the risks are offered in the SECURITY-POLICY element so that users can evaluate the data security of the site. In the DISPUTES element, the site states that the proposal is verified by "certification. example.org."

The security information disclosed by a proposal is generally very difficult for a user to understand. So some characterization about the degree of security safeguards a site uses should be attached in its licensing proposals. The characterization should also be machine-readable so that user agents can process it automatically. For the characterization, we borrow the concepts of divisions in TCSEC to provide individuals a simple yardstick for judging the degree of security safeguards. At this point, although TCSEC had folded into Common Criteria, Common Criteria is still

too complicated for a user to understand or even to set his/her preferences. For example, to describe the security safeguards of an information system, Common Criteria classifies the security function into 10 classes, where each class may have several components (with a total of 61 components). Each component may further be divided into several levels (Common Criteria, 1999). Obviously, it is almost a mission impossible to ask every user to understand and to deal with these hundreds of security function components.

In TCSEC, there are four divisions of security, A, B, C, and D, among which division A has the highest level of security. Division D is reserved for information systems that cannot meet the requirements of the higher-level divisions. The remaining three introduce three concepts about security policies: Division C shows the concept of "discretionary protection," where an information system must ensure that access to collected data is accountable, and data and users (the persons that are to use the data, not the owner of the data) are identifiable. Furthermore, audit information about what action is initiated and by whom is kept so that actions affecting security can be traced to the responsible party. Then, division B brings in the concept of "mandatory protection." That is, a division B-compliant information system must enforce a set of mandatory access control rules. Finally, division A is characterized by the use of formal security verification methods to assure that the security controls employed by the information systems can effectively protect personal data used by the information systems.

These features are used by OPDL and represented as tag elements of DISCRETIONARY, MANDATORY, FORMAL-VERIFIED, respectively. As shown in Figure 4, the tags can be considered as abstracts about the security policies disclosed by a requester, and are grouped based on different a data set (with POLICY-TAG elements).

The other information in the example in Figure 3 expresses the site's practices about personal data.

This is put in the STATEMENT elements. In the example, the site needs id/password to authenticate its members, and takes mandatory protection on the data. The information is retained until its members decide to opt-out (stop using the service). The site will trace its users' click-streams to secure and improve the site. The click-streams will also be used to determine their habits, interests, or other characteristics for the purpose of research, analysis, reporting, generating recommendations, and tailoring the site. These data will be destructed after 2 years. Similarly, some demographic data, such as birthday and gender, will also be used to provide tailored services. Finally, the site will use its members' address, telephone, and e-mail

address to contact them and to provide some recommendations and advertisements.

Automatic Proposal Processing

To automate proposal processing in OPDL, users can set their privacy preferences so that software agents can decide whether or not to accept a proposal based on the privacy preferences a user set. The privacy preferences are presented in rules based on APPEL (Cranor, Langheinrich, & Marchiori, 2002). This section describes preference rules, and discusses how the rules can be used by a Personal Data Licenser to process a proposal. For example, Figure 5 shows a person's privacy

Figure 3. An example of a licensing proposal based on P3P

```
<POLICY name="example proposal"
        discuri="http://exampleshop/humanreadableproposal.html" sigalgorithm="DSA"
        signature=" sbxJTQ/YWtQGf75ay/2E6ybTo51gYeInMC0CFQCHapEh+cL14zg5fYeyl580uj6="
        date="2003/3/6 12:34:23 GMT" ID="f1099c8f2f">
<SECURITY-POLICY discuri="http://exampleshop/securitypolicy.html"
        risks="http://exampleshop/mainrisks.html" controls="http://exampleshop/riskcontrol.html" />
<DISPUTES-GROUP>
<DISPUTES resolution-type="independent" service="http://www.certification.example.org"
        verification="http://www.certification.example.org/verify?entity=exampleshop&
        proposalid=f31e0e5fea" short-description="certification.example.org">
<REMEDIES><correct/></REMEDIES> </DISPUTES></DISPUTES-GROUP>
<STATEMENT> <CONSEQUENCE> ...... </CONSEQUENCE>
        <PURPOSE><individual-decision/></PURPOSE>
        <RETENTION><stated-purpose/></RETENTION>
        <POLICY-TAG><MANDATORY /></POLICY-TAG>
        <DATA-GROUP><DATA ref="#user.login.id"/><DATA ref="#user.login.password"/>
        </DATA-GROUP></STATEMENT>
<STATEMENT><CONSEQUENCE> ......</CONSEQUENCE>
        <RETENTION duration="2y"><stated-purpose/></RETENTION>
        <PURPOSE><admin/><develop/><tailoring/><individual-analysis/><individual-decision/>
        </PURPOSE>
        <POLICY-TAG><DISCRETIONARY /></POLICY-TAG>
        <DATA-GROUP><DATA ref="#user.dynamic.clickstream"/> </DATA-GROUP>
</STATEMENT>
<STATEMENT><CONSEQUENCE> ......</CONSEQUENCE>
        <PURPOSE><stated-purpose/><individual-analysis/><individual-decision/></PURPOSE>
        <RETENTION><indefinitely/></RETENTION>
        <POLICY-TAG><DISCRETIONARY /></POLICY-TAG>
        <DATA-GROUP><DATA ref="#user.bdate"/><DATA ref="#user.gender"/></DATA-GROUP>
</STATEMENT>
<STATEMENT> <CONSEQUENCE> ...... </CONSEQUENCE>
        <PURPOSE><contact/><telemarketing/></PURPOSE>
        <RETENTION><stated-purpose/></RETENTION>
        <POLICY-TAG><DISCRETIONARY /></POLICY-TAG>
        <DATA-GROUP> <DATA ref="#user.name"/> <DATA ref="#user.home-info.postal"/>
        <DATA ref="#user.home-info.telecom.telephone"/>
        <DATA ref="#user.home-info.online.email"/ih/DATA-GROUP>
</STATEMENT>
</POLICY>
```

Figure 4. Representation of security safeguards in a proposal

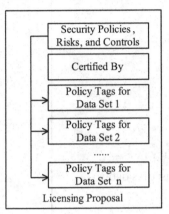

preferences setting. The example contains four preference rules: the first rule allows requesters to obtain the person's birth date, gender, and job title; the second rule says that a proposal will be rejected directly if the proposal is not verified by *trustcertorg* or the requested data are not to be protected under a discretionary security policy; the third rule allows "TrustOrganization" to collect the person's click-stream for administration purposes and the data will not be retained after the stated purpose is vanished; the fourth rule says that all other information requests should inform the person to allow him/her to make the final decision.

In general, the components of a preference rule can be categorized into two types: (1) the actions taken when a proposal matches the rule, and (2) one or more expressions. The actions of a rule are (a) reject or accept a proposal directly, and (b) inform the user to make the final decision. An expression can be viewed as a predicate asserting some subjects in an incoming licensing proposal.

The possible subjects include:

- Data targeted by the rule, such as a user's gender (with name #user.gender), birthday (with name #user.bdate), or job title (with name #user.jobtitle).
- The target data requester.
- The requirement on a certification organization.
- The security requirement.
- The constraint on request purposes.
- The constraint on retention policies.

An expression is evaluated to TRUE/FALSE depending on if the "predicate" asserted by the expression is true or not. For example, an expression <DATA ref = "#user.gender"/> is TRUE if a licensing proposal does request the user's gender. If a rule contains more than one expression, the evaluated values are logically combined based on the *connective* attribute of the rule. A proposal matches a rule if the evaluation of the rule is TRUE.

Figure 6 shows how a personal data licenser processes a proposal based on a user's preference rules. Basically, to ensure that personal data are licensed strictly under the owner's consent, our approach is somewhat conservative: if any one of the rules blocks the proposal, then the proposal is rejected. A notification form will be generated and sent to the user if the action of a matching rule is to notify the user (in the *prompt* attribute of the rule). Moreover, a notification form will also be generated if no preference rule has been set by the user. Figure 7 shows an example notification form based on the licensing proposal in Figure 3. The user can obtain detailed information about the requester and the licensing proposal by clicking the hyperlinks in the form. Some requested data are auto-filled by personal data licenser so that the user does not need to input them over again. The form also shows that the requester will collect some data, such as click-streams, in his/her proposal. If the licensing proposal is accepted, the user can click the "I Accept" button to inform his/her personal data licenser to issue a license.

Figure 5. A user's privacy preferences setting

```
<RULESET>
<RULE behavior = "request" prompt ="no">
<POLICY>
        <STATEMENT>
        <DATA-GROUP connective= "or">
        <DATA ref = "#user.bdate"/>
        <DATA ref = "#user.gender"/>
        <DATA ref = "#user.jobtitle"/>
        </DATA-GROUP>
        </STATEMENT>
</POLICY>
</RULE>
<RULE behavior = "block" prompt ="no">
<POLICY connective = "non-or">
        <POLICY-TAG><DISCRETIONARY /></POLICY-TAG>
        <DISPUTES-GROUP>
        <DISPUTES service="http://trustcertorg"/></DISPUTES-GROUP>
</POLICY>
</RULE>
<RULE behavior = "request" prompt ="no">
<POLICY>
        <ENTITY><DATA ref="#business.name">TrustOrganization</DATA>
        </ENTITY>
        <STATEMENT>
        <PURPOSE connective="or-exact"><admin/></PURPOSE>
        <RETENTION connective="or-exact"><stated-purpose/></RETENTION>
        </STATEMENT>
</POLICY>
</RULE>
<RULE behavior = "limited" prompt = "yes">
        <OTHERWISE/>
</RULE>
```

Figure 6. Proposals processing

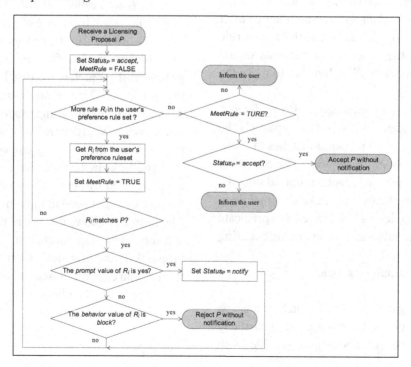

Figure 7. A notification form generated from the proposal in Figure 3

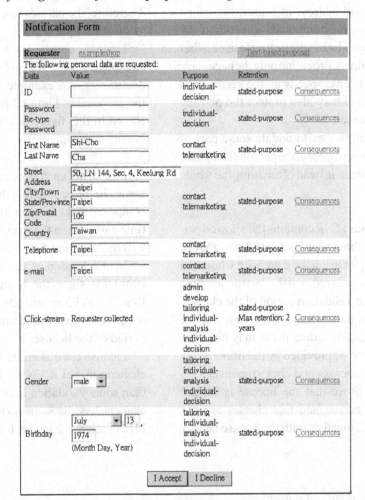

Licenses

This section discusses the design and implementation issues of licenses. Figure 8 shows the logical view of a license. Suppose that a license is issued from a person X (with private key SK_X) to a service provider Y. The main components of the license include a header H and a number of clauses $C_1,...,C_n$. The header contains the general information about the license, for example, the licenser, the licensee, the time the license is issued, and the security level claimed by the licensee. The clauses describe the licenser's allowed practices about personal data. Clauses are generally independent, meaning that one clause can be extracted from the license without affecting the integrity of another. The extracted clause can also be treated as a license (by appending an appropriate header). This decomposable feature has the following benefits:

- An audit or verification mechanism may only need part of the license, and so there is no need for a service provider to present the whole license. For example, when using e-mail address of a user, the user's mail server may only need to verify if the service provider has the license to use his/her e-mail address. Providing only the necessary part of a license speeds up the verification process, and may also protect the privacy of the licenser.

• If a person wishes to update some part of his/her issued license, the person can update related clauses instead of reissuing the whole license.

For each clause C_i, it contains the allowed privacy practices about a set D_i of data items; that is, the purposes P_i for using the data, with whom (S_i) the information is shared, and the destruction time T_i of the data (or validation period of the clause). In addition, the person may also assign a set of values V_i to D_i. (Some data items may not have an initial value to be provided by the licenser, for example, behavior logs and click streams).

Finally, to prove that the license is indeed issued by the person and that clauses are not altered, each C_i, together with the license header

H, is signed with the licenser's private key SK_X. Therefore, the clauses can be verified separately, as discussed previously.

Licenses can be implemented based on the vocabulary of P3P, and are stored as XML documents. An example of a license based on the proposal in Figure 3 is given in Figure 9. As shown in this figure, a license includes the following components:

First of all, each license has a unique ID as its name. To make sure that the name is unique, it is composed of the licenser's unique identity and the timestamp when the license is issued. The name will then be used for update notification.

In the header of the license, ISSUER and HOLDER show the licenser and the licensee. ISSUE_DATE records the time the license is issued. It can then be used to calculate the validation period of the license.

License clauses are represented as CLAUSE elements in the LICENSE_BODY. Basically, other than some validation information, the CLAUSE element has the same structure as the STATE-MENT element in the licensing proposal. The

Figure 8. Logical view of a license

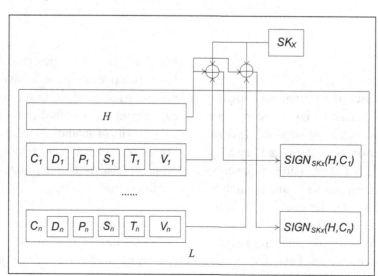

signature of each clause is encoded in BASE64 format and is attached as attributes in the clause for verification. Note that an XML document usually has multiple representation forms. For example, an empty element (e.g., <CONSEQUENCE />) can also be represented as a start-end tag pair (e.g., <CONSEQUENCE></>). Therefore, contents of licenses must be canonicalized (Boyer, 2001) while licenses are signed and verified. Finally, the default values of data items can be set as contents of the corresponding DATA elements in the license.

To meet the individual participation principle, individuals can inform licensees of the update to the contents of their licenses. To achieve this,

OPDL-compatible services should provide an Update Notification Interface so that individuals can send update notifications to them.

The detailed process of an update notification can be depicted in Figure 10. If a person X wishes to update his/her license issued to a service provider Y, he/she can send an update request U_X to the service provider through his/her personal data licenser. The request may belong to one of the following types:

- **addLicenseClause(L_{ID}, C_{new}, $SIGN_{SK_X}$(H, C_{new})):** To add a new clause C_{new} into a license with ID = L_{ID}. The content of the new clause C_{new} and its signature $SIGN_{SK_X}$(H, C_{new}) is also

Figure 9. A license based on the licensing proposal in Figure 3

```
<LICENSE ID="CSC f1099c5ea6"> <LICENSE HEADER>
<ISSUER><NAME>Shi-Cho Cha</NAME><CERT SERIAL>12345678</CERT SERIAL></ISSUER>
<ISSUE DATE>Fri Jul 14 16:16:58 GMT+8:00</ISSUE DATE>
<HOLDER><NAME>exampleshop</NAME><CERT SERIAL>87654321</CERT SERAL></HOLDER>
</LICENSE HEADER>
<LICENSE BODY>
<CLAUSE ID="f1099c8f2f" sigalgorithm="DSA" signature="MC0CFQCHapEh+cL14In5fYeyl580uj6
       tcwIUP/ZVsOFg64zw/1F7 waTo51gWFzg=">
<CONSEQUENCE> .....</CONSEQUENCE>
<PURPOSE><individual-decision/></PURPOSE>
<RETENTION><stated-purpose/></RETENTION>
<POLICY-TAG><MANDATORY /></POLICY-TAG>
<DATA-GROUP><DATA ref="#user.login.id"> shichoc </DATA>
<DATA ref="#user.login.password"/></DATA-GROUP>
</CLAUSE>
<CLAUSE ID="f10b83dbb9" sigalgorithm="DSA" signature="MC0CFQCWsmkv6kpEKCeKhVswPDb
       R9TN7GgIUP3k8rDZPlahL0QkCv0BizABFeil=">
<CONSEQUENCE> ......</CONSEQUENCE>
<RETENTION duration="2y"><stated-purpose/></RETENTION>
<PURPOSE><admin/><develop/><tailoring/><individual-analysis/><individual-decision/></PURPOSE>
<POLICY-TAG><DISCRETIONARY /></POLICY-TAG>
<DATA-GROUP><DATA ref="#user.dynamic.clickstream"/></DATA-GROUP></CLAUSE>
<CLAUSE ID="f11e0955e5" sigalgorithm="DSA" signature="MCwCFFKcscvKr5PJApq+zcuSGuqcc6
       Z4AhQWxV4hOxAMPKtfZAKhZPTd6qZbYQ==" >
<CONSEQUENCE> ...... </CONSEQUENCE>
<PURPOSE><stated-purpose/><individual-analysis/><individual-decision/></PURPOSE>
<RETENTION><indefinitely/></RETENTION>
<POLICY-TAG><DISCRETIONARY /></POLICY-TAG>
<DATA-GROUP><DATA ref="#user.bdate"/><DATA ref="#user.gender">Male </DATA>
</DATA-GROUP></CLAUSE>
<CLAUSE ID="f19068a0e6" sigalgorithm="DSA" signature="MCwCFHzXv5zI9wTqd5Dbg+wkr1tG7A
       opAhQVaaK88Wq8JJYGTAi6472MFc8SCw==">
<CONSEQUENCE> ...... </CONSEQUENCE>
<PURPOSE><contact/><telemarketing/></PURPOSE>
<RETENTION><stated-purpose/></RETENTION>
<POLICY-TAG><MANDATORY /></POLICY-TAG>
<DATA-GROUP> <DATA ref="#user.name"> Shi-Cho Cha </DATA>
<DATA ref="#user.home-info.postal"/><DATA ref="#user.home-info.telecom.telephone"/>
<DATA ref="#user.home-info.online.email">csc@mba.ntu.edu.tw</DATA>
</DATA-GROUP>
</CLAUSE></LICENSE BODY> </LICENSE>
```

transmitted. These data can be appended to the original license because clauses of a license are mutually independent.

- **deleteLicenseClause(L_{ID}, C_{ID}):** To invalidate a clause C_{ID} in a license.
- **updateClause(L_{ID}, C_{ID}, C_{new}, $SIGN_{SK_X}$(H, C_{new})):** To update the content of a clause in a license.
- **withdrawLicense(L_{ID}):** To withdraw a license.
- **queryLicensedData(L_{ID}, D):** To query the latest value of a data item D that is licensed in license L_{ID}.

The P3P vocabulary can be used in the same way as in licenses to express an update request, and so a detailed demonstration is skipped here.

After receiving an update request, the service provider signs its response R_{U_X} and the update request with its private key SK_Y. The response along with the signature $SIGN_{SK_Y}(R_{U_X}, U_X)$ are transmitted back to the person. As in data licenses, the signature can be used to solve disputes between the person and the service provider about the genuineness of the update request.

In some situations, updates to licenses must be guaranteed, for example, the revocation of a credit card. A malicious service provider may deny an update request by ignoring response to the request. A third-party notification complaint center is therefore required here to deal with the complaints from individuals, and to distinguish the situation in which the service provider's update notification interfaces is transiently unavailable, from the situation in which the service provider has ignored the update request on purpose. To do so, if a person does not receive the response to its update request from the service provider after a number of attempts, the person sends his/her complaint $COMP_{U_X}$ about the update request to the notification complaint center. The notification complaint center then takes the responsibility of confirming the truth of the complaint. Some remedies may be taken if the complaint has been confirmed.

One may wonder who will serve for the complaint service. We first observe that current seal programs also have similar functions. For example, TRUSTe's WatchDog Dispute Resolution Service[2] enables a person to file a complaint about a TRUSTe-approved Web site. If the complaint has been confirmed, TRUSTe may require the site to change its stated privacy policy, to remove the site from the TRUSTe program, or even to sue the

Figure 10. Update notifications

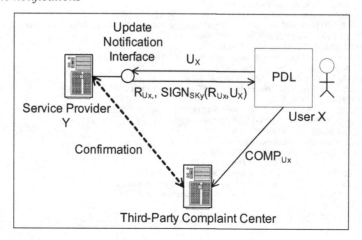

site for breach of its contract with TRUSTe. For OPDL, as described before, a third-party certification organization plays an important role in verifying the faithful execution of a site's proposal and its security policy. The organization can also serve for the complaint service.

Note that depending on whether or not licenses can be transferred (directly or indirectly), license revocation may become a complicated process. For example, suppose a service provider Y has a license L_y that is dependent on a license L_x hold by X. Then, a revocation of L_x at X may incur the revocation of L_y at Y. That is, a revocation may trigger a sequence of revocations at different sites. This type of chained revocations will be considered in the future.

A more fundamental question is whether or not we should allow a license to be modified or even withdrawn after it is issued. In fact, the answer may depend on the laws of a country, as well as on the content of the license. Here we discuss only the general concept of data licenses. Their applications to specific circumstances are left to the future work.

CONCLUSION AND FUTURE WORK

We have proposed a novel technical and legal approach, called *online personal data licensing*, to address concerns about the abuse of personal data in cyberspace. The objective is to require service providers to obtain licenses before legally collecting, processing, or using a person's personal data. By allowing people to issue their own licenses and to determine the content of the licenses, OPDL brings the control of personal data back to the owner, and ensures that the use of the data is strictly under the owner's consent. In contrast, most Web-based service providers today use passive consent, which usually results in situations in which users have inadvertently given the providers the authorization to use their personal data. Besides, users generally do not

have information on who still owns a copy of their data, and how their data have been, or will be, used.

Data licenses provide strong evidence to prove that personal data used by services providers are obtained under the owner's consent. Because they are issued automatically or semiautomatically through OPDL, they can be considered as a type of *proxy consent*. As more and more countries have electronic signature acts (e.g., the U.S. E-SIGN Act and the Taiwan Electronic Signatures Law), licenses can eventually provide the same power of evidence as a written consent in cyberspace. Moreover, because licenses are digitalized and have standard format, they can be checked and verified automatically. The use of data licenses can therefore reduce the increasing privacy disputes between users and service providers, and regulate the abuse of personal data without sacrificing too much efficiency.

We have also described how to implement OPDL based on P3P: The privacy policies of P3P for Web sites to disclose their privacy practices can be extended in OPDL for Web sites to express licensing proposals. The vocabulary used by P3P can also be used for expressing the content of a license. Finally, individuals' privacy preferences can be presented in APPEL rules so that licensing proposals can be processed automatically or semiautomatically.

Furthermore, OPDL also extends P3P to meet the security and individual principles of online privacy: By reading the security labels in a licensing proposal, a person can understand the security level a service provider adopts to protect his/her data. Moreover, a person may update his/her licenses through the interface provided by each OPDL-compatible site. Overall, OPDL can also be viewed as an extension of P3P, and this chapter hopefully can contribute to the improvement of P3P specifications.

Our future work includes the following directions. First, the success of OPDL relies on legislation: Giving the licenses the evidence power in law, and requiring nonowners of personal data to obtain licenses from their owners before collecting, processing, and using the data. How the laws should be made requires deliberate integration between information technologies and jurisprudence, and remains an important and interesting future work.

Second, we observe that OPDL focuses on the collection and process of personal data in the Internet. However, Internet is not the only source of personal data for enterprises to collect. For example, they may request their customers to fill in paper with their personal data for communication or other purposes. Other forms may also be used in the physical world. This brings up an integration problem about the exchange and use of licenses in different formats, which will be considered in the future.

Third, because OPDL adopts P3P for users to express their privacy preferences, it also takes the critique about the specification: too complex for users to manage their privacy preferences. Therefore, a friendly user interface or a set of default preference settings is needed to remove this concern.

Finally, the current prototype of OPDL we have designed provides only a simple request and reply architecture. More complex features can be added. For example, a negotiation mechanism can be designed for requesters and personal data licenser to reach an agreement both parties can accept. Some basic negotiation process for OPDL has been proposed in (Joung, Yen, Huang, & Huang, 2005), but a more complex negotiation mechanism involving assessment of personal data may be devised. Indeed, personal data may be treated as properties (Lessig, 2000), and so a pricing mechanism can be investigated for requesters to pay for the license fee (i.e., to lease personal data). For example, people may charge commercial e-mail senders for using their e-mail addresses to send advertisements. Pricing e-mails have been proven effective in coping with unsolicited e-mails (Loder, Alstyne, & Wash, 2004; Van Zandt, 2004), and OPDL provides a framework to concretize the licensing of using an e-mail address. Other types of personal data may be explored from the viewpoint of information economics to see their effectiveness.

REFERENCES

Australian Government. (1988). *Privacy Act.* Retrieved from http://www.privacy.gov.au/act/privacyact/

Ayars, J. (2002). *XMCL—The eXtensible Media Commerce Language.* W3C note, W3C. Retrieved December 18, 2006, from http://www.w3.org/TR/xmcl/

Benassi, P. (1999). TRUSTe: An online privacy seal program. *Communications of the ACM, 42*(2): 56-59.

Bennett, C. J. (1997). Convergence revisited: Toward a global policy for the protection of personal data? In P. E. Agre & M. Rotenberg (Eds.), *Technology and privacy: The new landscape* (pp. 99-124). Cambridge, MA: MIT Press.

Bennett, K., & Grothoff, C. (2003). GAP—Practical anonymous networking. In Proceedings of the Third International Workshop on Privacy Enhancing Technologies (PET 2003), Dresden, Germany, March 26-28. *Lecture Notes in Computer Science, 2760,* 141-160.

Boyer, J. (2001). *Canonical XML.* W3C Recommendation Version 1.0, W3C.

British Government. (1998). *Data Protection Law.* Retrieved December 18, 2006, from http://www.opsi.gov.uk/acts/acts1998/19980029.htm

Burkert, H. (1997). Privacy-enhancing technologies: Typology, critique, vision. In P. E. Agre & M. Rotenberg, (Eds.), *Technology and privacy: The new landscape* (pp. 125-142). Cambridge, MA: MIT Press.

Calder, A., & Watkins, S. (2002). *IT Governance: Data Security and BS 7799 / ISO 17799*. Kogan Page Ltd.

Canada Government. (2000). *Personal Information Protection and Electronic Documents Act*. Retrieved December 18, 2006, from http://laws.justice.gc.ca/en/P-8.6/text.html

CCITT. (1988). *Recommendation X:509: The Directory—Authentication Framework*.

Cerf, V. G. (2005). Spam, spim, and spit. *Communications of the ACM, 48*(4), 39-43.

Cha, S. -C., & Joung, Y. -J. (2002). Online personal data licensing. In *Proceedings of the Third International Conference on Law and Technology (LawTech 2002)* (pp. 28-33).

Cha, S. -C., Joung, Y. -J., & Lue, Y. -E. (2003). Building universal profile systems over a peer-to-peer network. In *Proceedings of the Third IEEE Workshop on Internet Applications (WIAPP 2003)* (pp.142-151).

Chaum, D. (1982). Blind signatures for untraceable payments. In *Proceedings of CRYPTO'82* (pp. 199-203). New York: Plenum Press.

Chokhani, S. (1994). Toward a national public key infrastructure. *IEEE Communications Magazine, 32*(9), 70-74.

Common Criteria. (1999). *Common Criteria for Information Technology Security* Evaluation. Common Criteria Project Sponsoring Organisations. Version 2.1, adopted by ISO/IEC as ISO/IEC International Standard (IS) 15408 1-3.

ContentGuard Holdings, Inc. (2002). *XrML 2.1 technical overview*. Retrieved December 18, 2006, from http://xml.coverpages.org/XrMLTechnicalOverview21-DRAFT.pdf

Cranor, L., Langheinrich, M., & Marchiori, M. (2002). *A P3P preference exchange language 1.0 (APPEL1.0)*. Working draft, World Wide Web Consortium.

Cranor, L., Langheinrich, M., Marchiori, M., Presler-Marshall, M., & Reagle, J. (2002). *The platform for privacy preferences 1.0 (P3P 1.0) specification*. Recommendations, World Wide Web Consortium. P3P 1.1. Retrieved from http://www.w3c.org/TR/P3P11/ in Nov. 2006

Dix, A., Rodden, T., Davies, N., Trevor, J., Friday, A., & Palfreyman, K. (2000). Exploiting space and location as a design framework for interactive mobile systems. *ACM Transactions on Computer-Human Interaction, 7*(3), 285-321.

EPIC & Junkbuster (2000). *Pretty poor privacy: An assessment of P3P and Internet privacy*. Retrieved December 18, 2006, from http://www.epic.org/reports/prettypoorprivacy.html

European Commission. (1998). *Draft opinion of the working party on the protection of individuals with regard to the processing of personal data*. Retrieved December 18, 2006, from http://www.epic.org/privacy/internet/ec-p3p.html

European Union. (1995). Directive 95/46/EC on the protection of individuals with regard to the processing of personal data and on the free movement of such data. *Official Journal of the European Communities*, p. 31.

Fiat, A., & Shamir, A. (1986). How to prove yourself: Practical solutions to identification and signature problems. In *Proceedings of CRYPTO'86* (pp. 186-194).

Freier, A. O., Karlton, P., & Kocher, P. C. (1996). *The SSL protocol version 3.0. Specification draft, Internet Engineering Task Force (IETF)*. Internet drafT.

Gabber, E., Gibbons, P. B., Kristol, D. M., Matias, Y., & Mayer, A. (1999). Consistent, yet anonymous, Web access with LPWA. *Communications of the ACM, 42*(2), 42-47.

German Government. (2001). *Federal Data Protection Act*. Retrieved December 18, 2006, from http://www.datenschutz-berlin.de/recht/de/bdsg/bdsg01_eng.htm

Hall, R. J. (1998). How to avoid unwanted email. *Communications of the ACM, 41*(3), 88-95.

Hanson, W. (1999). *Principles of Internet marketing*. South-Western College Publishing.

Hensley, P., Metral, M., Shardanand, U., Converse, D., & Meyers, M. (1997). *Proposal for an open profiling standard*. Retrieved December 18, 2006, from http://www.w3.org/TR/NOTE-OPS-FrameWork.html

Isenberg, D. (2002). *The GigaLaw—Guide to Internet law*. Random House Trade Paperbacks.

Joung, Y.-J., Yen, C., Huang, C.-T., & Huang, Y.-J. (2005). On personal data license design and negotiation. In *Proceedings of the 29th International Computer Software and Applications Conference (COMPSAC 2005)* (pp.281-286). IEEE Computer Society.

Kaufman, C., Perlman, R., & Speciner, M. (2002). *Network security: Private communication in a public world*. Prentice Hall.

Kent, S. (1993). RFC 1422: *Privacy enhancement for Internet electronic mail: Part II: Certificate-based key management*. Retrieved December 18, 2006, from http://www.ietf.org/rfc/rfc1422.txt

Kristol, D. M. (2001). HTTP cookies: Standards, privacy, and politics. *ACM Transactions on Internet Technology, 1*(2), 151-198.

Lessig, L. (2000). *Code and other laws of cyberspace*. Basic Books.

Loder, T., Alstyne, M. V., & Wash, R. (2004). An economic answer to unsolicited communication. In *Proceedings of the 5th ACM conference on Electronic commerce* (EC'04) (pp.40-50). New York: ACM Press.

Menezes, A. J., van Oorschot, P. C., & Vanstone, S. A. (1997). *Handbook of applied cryptography*. CRC Press.

OECD. (1980). *OECD guidelines on the protection of privacy and transborder flows of personal data*. Organization for Economic Cooperation and Development.

Peeger, S. L., & Bloom, G. (2005). Canning spam: Proposed solutions to unwanted email. *IEEE Security and Privacy, 3*(2), 40-47.

Reiter, M. K., & Rubin, A. D. (1998). Crowds: Anonymity for web transactions. *ACM Transactions on Information and System Security, 1*(1), 66-92.

Shamir, A. (1985). Identity-based cryptosystems and signature schemes. In Proceedings of CRYPTO'84. *Lecture Notes in Computer Science, 96,* 47-53.

Sonera Plaza. (2002). *Digital Rights Management* white paper. Technical report, Sonera Plaza Ltd. Retrieved December 18, 2006, from http://www.medialab.sonera.fi

Tewari, G., Youll, J., & Maes, P. (2003). Personalized location-based brokering using an agent-based intermediary architecture. *Decision Support Systems, 34*(2), 127-137.

University of Washington. (2006). *Human subjects manual*. Retrieved December 18, 2006, from http://www.washington.edu/research/hsd/hsd-man4.html

U.S. Department of Commerce. (2000). *Safe Harbor Privacy Principles*. Retrieved December 18, 2006, from http://www.export.gov/safeharbor/SHPRINCIPLESFINAL.htm

U.S. Department of Defense. (1985). *Trusted Computer System Evaluation Criteria*. Technical Report DoD 5200.28.

Van Zandt, T. (2004). Information overload in a network of targeted communication. *RAND Journal of Economics, 35*(3), 542-560.

W3C. (1999). *Removing data transfer from P3P*. Retrieved December 18, 2006, from http://www.w3c.org/P3P/data-transfer.html

Walia, S. (2006). Battling e-commerce credit card fraud. In *e-Commerce Times*. Retrieved May 25 2006, http://www.ecommercetimes.com/story/50558.html

ENDNOTES

1. http://www.w3.org/
2. TRUSTe: Make Privacy Your Choice, http://www.truste.org

Chapter VIII
Property Protection and User Authentication in IP Networks Through Challenge–Response Mechanisms:
Present, Past, and Future Trends

Giaime Ginesu
University of Cagliari, Italy

Mirko Luca Lobina
University of Cagliari, Italy

Daniele D. Giusto
University of Cagliari, Italy

ABSTRACT

Authentication is the way of identifying an individual. The techniques used to accomplish such practice strongly depend on the involved parties, their interconnection, and the required level of security. In all cases, authentication is used to enforce property protection, and may be specifically intended for the copyright protection of digital contents published on the Internet. This chapter introduces the basic concepts of authentication, explaining their relationship with property protection. The basic functionalities of challenge-response frameworks are presented, together with several applications and the future trends.

INTRODUCTION

Authentication (Greek: αυθεντικός, from "authentes" = "one acting on one's own authority") is the process of identifying an individual, merely ensuring that the individual is who he/she claims to be. Such practice is essential in networking and distributed systems, where a party has not always the opportunity of verifying ad personam the identity of the other/s involved. The parties may be users, hosts, or processes, and they are generally referred to as principals in the authentication literature. During the authentication phase, the principals exchange messages and use the received ones to make decisions on how to act. Obviously, to prevent malicious interferences, all the messages exchanged between principals are usually ciphered. The complete sequence of ciphered messages exchanged between principals is an authentication protocol (AP). The AP can perform a mutual authentication, that is, two-way authentication, when two principals are able to suitably authenticate each other, or a one-way authentication, when only one principal is authenticated. As an example, mutual authentication refers to a client authenticating itself to a server and that server authenticating itself to the client in such a way that both parties are assured of the others' identity. Typically, this is done for a client process and a server process without any physical interaction. Challenge-response (CR) is a common AP, where a principal is prompted (the challenge) to provide some private information (the response) in order to access a service. Basically, given two principals sharing private information, that is, a secret key, CR is a one-way authentication (client-to-server) system that ensures the private information will be never sent uncrypted. However, many evolutions have been brought to the original idea. Thus, CR is a black box, whose features strongly depend on what a principal is, has, and knows. Independently from prior considerations and specifically in IP networks, an AP is intended for property protection purposes, avoiding anything in the networked/distributed system from being considered public domain and taken without permission from the creator/owner of its copyright. The objectives of this chapter are:

1. To provide essential information and strategies of existing CR frameworks, including basic hashing/encrypting techniques.

2. To focus on one of the seemingly most prolific fields related to AP: biometry applied to authentication.

3. To present a general and high-level overview of mutual image-based authentication, that is, IBA applied to this *milieu*.

BACKGROUND

This section defines the role of authentication, referring to the differences with identification, its role in the AAA (authentication, authorization, and accounting) hierarchy, its main properties and protocols, and its relationship with intellectual property protection. Specifically, the protocols are described both with common hashing/encrypting approaches and biometric features to focus on the different branches of security functions developed in the last years.

Authentication and Identification

The processes of identification and authentication are not the same practice, referring to implementation, protocols, and performances, even though the user may perceive them mistakenly as synonyms. Identification is the procedure where a unique piece of information is associated with a particular identity. It is performed by acquiring an identifier, that is, a piece of information that defines or indicates an entity, or a group of entities. Then, the process of identification is a one-to-many match test. On the other hand, authentication is the process of validating that the owning entity is really using the owned identity during interaction. Authentication is a one-to-one comparison, and could be addressed as an identification subroutine (Figure 1). A user generally claims only his/her credentials to be identified. Without his/her identity, the system searches (one-to-many search) for the profile matching with the presented credentials among a determined group of profiles and optionally performs authentication, inquiring for any other required information, that is, the couple (identity, credentials). Usually, the identity is defined by the username, and the credentials are a set of values to prove the user is the one he/she pretends to be. Reasonably, the complete framework of identification and authentication is more secure than identification alone, thanks to the two factors process.

Authentication, Authorization and Accounting (AAA)

The security functions of a generic system are usually divided into authentication, authorization, and accounting (AAA). AAA constitutes a complete framework to control the access to resources and to audit the users' activities. As indicated in Figure 2, the three steps are consecutive. First, two principals must recognize each other (authentication) and subsequently establish a reciprocal relationship (authorization). Finally, they can monitor several parameters related to their communication (accounting). These are better described in the following. The authentication provides the techniques to identify a user by means of a unique set of criteria through his/her identity and credentials. After logging in, the user must be authorized to perform some classes of activities or services. Thus, the security system has to state what type of actions the trustfully authenticated user has the right to perform. Authorization is essentially an enforcing of the security system. After authentication and authorization, the security

system should monitor the resources employed by the user. This is the last step of accounting, whose main purpose is the protection from intrusion of atypical profiles within the system.

Authentication Features

Authentication can be categorized on the basis of the location of the involved parties, the typology of the communication session, and the type of interaction. In the following, these attributes are explained in detail.

Local and Remote

First of all we must explain the context in which the terms local and remote are defined in respect to authentication. Local authentication consists in authenticating a principal who tries to gain access to another principal's resources that reside on the same environment, such as the same server or the same trusted network. The authenticating principal is often considered to be reliable, since it is held under local control. Clearly, this situation is simpler than the classic remote authentication scheme, where the system cannot trust directly an alien authenticating principal. Remote authentication consists of authenticating a principal who tries to gain access to another principal's resources from a separate environment. It presents stronger security issues and still represents a great challenge for security experts. Any authentication protocol should be designed to avoid malicious external intrusion.

Figure 1. Authentication and identification

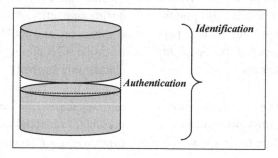

Figure 2. Authentication, authorization and accounting

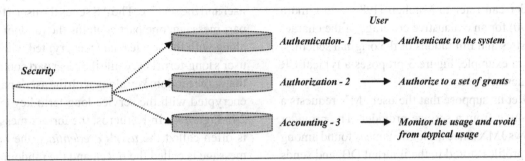

Static, Rigid, or Continuous

These features refer to the nature of the communication session, after the authentication phase. Static authentication describes the situation where the message exchange between principals takes place in clear, that is, without ciphering of the messages, once a party is authenticated to another. Inversely, rigid authentication implies a secure channel and is typically employed for the transmission of sensible data. Finally, continuous authentication entails an ad-hoc memoryless transmission channel. In this case, the two communicating principals have to perform reciprocal authentication at each step of conversation. That is, each process/host/party never trusts the other involved in the authentication phase without evidence of identification being previously provided. In this case, authentication takes place every time the parties want to trade a message.

Let us consider, for example, that a user wishes to trade stocks through an online brokerage house. If the brokerage perceives a business benefit to tracking the user's actions on the site, continuous mode may be useful. In continuous mode, the brokerage would authenticate the user at the first attempt to access the site and then track the user continuously during the length of time spent for the transactions.

Online and Off-Line

Online authentication implies interaction with a live party. In this case, the system is more robust against any kind of attacks that use old credentials. On the other hand, the authenticating party is exposed to a great variety of attacks that may be somewhat related to the use of an insecure channel, for example, sniffing. As an alternative or supplement to online authentication, various techniques have been employed to verify that the authenticating principal is trustful. For example, anticounterfeiting techniques involve the employ of unique or difficult characteristics of credentials that can be sensed to verify their authenticity. Private personal identification data has also been used along with coding techniques. When such techniques serve as the sole basis of certification (without online checking), the verification is generally called "off-line" authentication. Off-line authentication avoids the risks related to continuous message exchange, but is less realistic when considering hosts connected remotely via the Internet. It is generally adopted in case of personal ID-based authentication, such as smart card or printed documents.

Authentication Protocols

This section provides the reader with a specific overview of the cryptographic designs applied in

CR frameworks during the response phase. The reader can refer to Mitchell (1989) and Omura (1990) for an exhaustive coverage of the characteristics and limitations of the original schemes. As an example, Figure 3 proposes a typical CR framework.

Let us suppose that the user JMX requests a resource from a service provider. The provider knows JMX since the login name is found among the profiles stored in the internal DB, and sends him/her a challenge. The user replies with a response that depends on up to three factors: the challenge itself, a private information whose knowledge is shared by user and system, and the method that allows obtaining the correct response starting from challenge and private information, again shared by the two principals.

Kerberos, extensible authentication protocol (EAP), NTLM, and password authentication protocol (PAP) are typical examples of authentication protocols. Kerberos relies on the fundamental basis that the two principals (user and service) implicitly trust the Kerberos authentication server (AS), which serves as a mediator. In order for this to work, both the user and the service must have a shared secret key registered with the AS. Such keys are generally referred to as long-term keys, since they last for weeks or months. The main steps are as follows. First, the user sends a request (typically the service name) to the AS, asking it to authenticate him/her to the service (Step 1 in Figure 4). In the second step, the AS introduces the user and the service to each other; a new random

secret key is generated to be shared only by the user and the service. The AS sends the user a two-part message: one part contains the random key along with the service name, encrypted with the user's long-term key, while the other part contains that same random key along with the user's name, encrypted with the service long-term key (Step 2 in Figure 4). In Kerberos, the former message is often called the *user's credentials*, the latter message is called the *ticket*, and the random key is called the *session key*. Only the user knows the session key, thus he/she generates a new message (the authenticator) and encrypts it with the session key. he/she sends the authenticator, along with the ticket, to the service (Step 3 in Figure 4). The service decrypts the ticket with its long-term key and retrieves the session key. Since the service trusts the AS, it knows that only the legitimate user could have created such an authenticator. This completes the user authentication to the service (Step 4 in Figure 4).

EAP is a universal authentication framework frequently used in wireless/wired networks and point-to-point connections. It is defined as an Internet Standard by RFC 3748. EAP is not a specific authentication mechanism, but an authentication framework. In this sense, it provides some common functions and a negotiation of the desired authentication mechanism. Such mechanisms are called EAP methods. Currently, there are about 40 different methods, such as EAP-MD5. One of the most interesting applications is the generation of a pairwise master key (PMK) for authenticat-

Figure 3. Challenge-response scheme

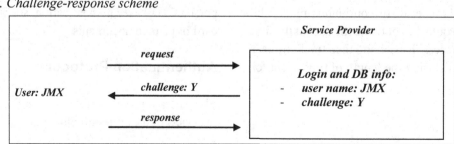

Figure 4. Kerberos scheme

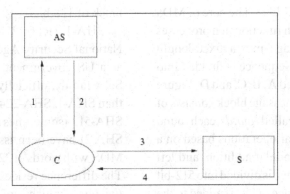

ing clients in a wireless environment. A detailed description of the framework is presented in the previously cited RFC.

NTLM is a suite of authentication and session security protocols used in various Microsoft network protocol implementations. It is probably best recognized as part of the "Integrated Windows Authentication" stack for HTTP authentication; however, it is also used in Microsoft implementations of SMTP, POP3, IMAP, Telnet, SIP, and possibly others. It consists of three sequential messages, commonly referred to as Type 1 (negotiation), Type 2 (challenge), and Type 3 (authentication). The client sends a Type 1 message to the server, which responds with a Type 2 message. This contains a challenge generated by the server. The client replies to the challenge with a Type 3 message. This holds several pieces of information about the client, including the client's domain and adopted username. The responses in the Type 3 message are the most critical piece of the overall authentication session, as they prove to the server that the client has knowledge of the account password.

Finally, the password authentication protocol (PAP) provides a simple method for the peer to establish its identity using a two-way handshake. PAP is not a strong authentication method. Passwords are sent over the circuit in text format,

and there is no protection against sniffing. An exhaustive description and discussion on the PAP flaws is presented in Ma et al. (Ma, McCrindle, & Cheng, 2006).

Cryptographic Techniques

Any information exchanged during authentication obviously constitutes a sensible data and its privacy is fundamental for the security of the overall authentication system. This is particularly true when considering the response phase, which implies the submission of passwords, authentication keys, or identity clues. Therefore, such information should not travel in clear. During the authentication phase, the CR framework uses common cryptographic schemes, such as hash or encryption, in order to prevent an eavesdropper from deducing the response by means of brute force attack, or dictionary attack (Schneier, 1995). The hash value is created by applying a hash function and a seed, consisting in a string obtained as the combination of the given password and usually other values, for example, pseudorandom data.

MD5 (Message-Digest algorithm 5) and SHA-1 (Secure Hash algorithm) are frequently used as cryptographic hash functions. MD5 was designed by Ronald Rivest in 1991 to replace an earlier hash function, MD4, and is defined as an Internet standard in RFC 1321. The core of MD5 works with a 128-bit hash function that processes a variable length message into a fixed-length output of 128 bits. This sequence is divided into four 32-bit words, denoted A, B, C, and D (Figure 5). The processing of a message block consists of four similar stages, also called *rounds*; each round is composed of 16 similar operations based on a nonlinear function F, modular addition, and left rotation. The input message is divided into 512-bit message blocks (a sequence of bits is added to the original message to make its length a multiple of 512: this operation is known as "padding") and

the 128-bit hash function is performed on every block of 128 bits.

SHA-1 (RFC 3174) was designed by the National Security Agency (NSA) and published as a US government standard. It is part of the SHA family, officially published in 1993. Other than SHA-1, SHA-224, SHA-256, SHA-384, and SHA-512 (sometimes collectively referred to as SHA-2) have been issued. SHA-1 works as the MD5, with words of 32 bits and blocks of 512 bits. The difference resides on the output size, that is, *the digest*, which is of 160 bits, and is the core of SHA-1 operating on a sequence of five different words (A, B, C, D, and E).

A different solution consists in the encryption of a public key. Let us focus on DES and RSA frameworks. DES (data encryption system) is an official Federal Information Processing Standard (FIPS) for the United States in 1976. At present, it is considered insecure for many applications, since its 56-bit keys have been broken in less than 24 hours. The detailed description of the DES strategy can be found in Burr (n.d.). The RSA was publicly described in 1977 (Rivest, Shamir, & Adleman 1998) by Ron Rivest, Adi Shamir and Len Adleman at MIT. RSA framework uses two keys: public and private. The public key is visible

Figure 5. MD5

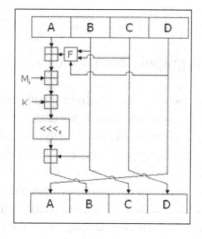

Figure 6. RSA algorithm

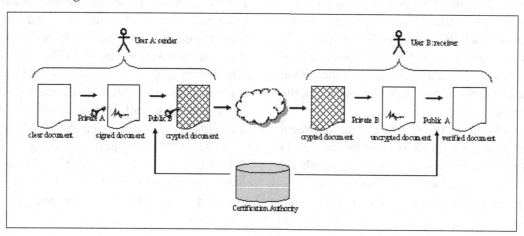

by anyone and is used to encrypt or verity the messages. On the other side, messages can only be signed or decrypted by means of the private key. In other words, anybody can encrypt a message, but only the holder of a private key can actually decrypt the message and read it. The complete sequence of steps for encryption/decryption and signature/verification is described in Figure 6.

When used in real systems, RSA must be combined with other strategies to avoid several problems. The first is the length/structure of the message to be encoded: this can lead definitely to a security reduction. The operative solution is the aforementioned padding of the message prior to RSA encryption. The PKCS (public key cryptography standards), described in RFC 3447, has been specifically designed for this aim. Early versions of the PKCS standard used ad-hoc schemes that were later found vulnerable to several kinds of attacks. Modern approaches use secure techniques such as optimal asymmetric encryption padding (OAEP) (Bellare & Rogaway, 1995) to protect messages from these attacks. Several standards among those previously cited have no practical use in modern communications due to their complexity, time-consumption, and problems related to the distribution of personal keys. Furthermore, wireless IP networking is generally limited by small computational capability, hardware incompatibilities and poor handiness of user terminals. In other words, the necessity of implementing very effective and simple solutions prevails on sophisticated techniques. From a commercial point of view, authentication in such context is mainly based on the WEP protocol (based on the RC4 stream cipher), traditionally used for WLAN protection (IEEE 802.11). This protocol can be attacked and broken relatively easily, allowing hackers to gain unauthorized access to digital data. The weakness of WEP has been partly solved by Wi-Fi protected access (WPA) and WAP2, both presented by the Wi-Fi Alliance in the IEEE 802.11i draft.

Authentication and Intellectual Property Protection

Intellectual property (IP) may be thought of as any intangible proprietary information. It can be anything from a particular manufacturing process to the plans for a product commercialization, a chemical formula, or an algorithm. The World Intellectual Property Organization formally defines it as the creations of the mind: inventions, literary and artistic works, symbols, names, images, and designs used in commerce. From a legal standpoint, there are four types of intellectual property: patents, trademarks, copyright, and trade secrets. IP protection is then an essential task for the proper exploitation of all results deriving from any creative process. Unfortunately, such practice is as well understood as hard to achieve, and reports estimate that intellectual property theft costs U.S. companies about $300 billion each year. The simplest approach to perform IP protection is to restrict the access to the contents only to granted subjects. The selective right to use digital contents, as offered by the basic CR frameworks, is one of the first attempts to achieve such a result in the digital era. Obviously, different access types can lead to different levels of authorization, for example, visualization only, local copy, modification, and so forth. In this sense, the subject of this chapter, CR frameworks, offers the first level of abstraction in order to solve the IP protection problem, presenting solutions of different complexity in case of different IP circumstances. Encryption, hashing, watermarking, and transaction tracking are just a few examples of techniques to be implemented in or used together with CR frameworks, in order to finalize a digital IP protection system.

Authentication Based on Biometric Features

Among the pieces of information that may be used for challenge-response authentication, biometric features (Jain, Bolle, & Pankanti, 1999; Kung, Mak, & Lin, 2004) have a relatively long history, ranging back to the theory of fingerprint identification in 1880. By definition, biometric authentication is the verification of a user's identity by means of a physical trait or behavioral characteristic that cannot be easily changed. Since the discovery of fingerprint identification, a multitude of different biometric features have been considered, and many processing systems and techniques have been developed accordingly. The basic idea behind biometric authentication is to recognize the user by something he/she is, instead of something he/she knows, for example, password, or has, for example, hardware key. As a result, such authentication systems are very straight, that is, the user must not remember any piece of information nor possess any physical key, and have been widely regarded as the most foolproof, provided the biometric feature is well-defined and unique. On the other hand, issues arise from their physical intrusiveness, the reliability of the considered feature, and the cost of the technology/system. Moreover, the collection of personal physical information might raise ethic and legal issues.

For the purpose of this work, we briefly illustrate two examples of biometric authentication. The first, fingerprint recognition (Maltoni, Maio, Jain, & Prabhakar, 2005; Uchida, 2005), is the most mature and acknowledged biometric feature for identification. On the other hand, the latter, facial identification (Chelappa, Wilson, & Sirohey, 1995; Phillips, Moon, Rauss, & Rizvi, 1997; Samal & Lyengar, 1992; Zhao, Chellappa, Rosenfeld, Phillips, 2003), has been receiving considerable interest and constitutes one of the most lively research areas in the field of biometrics.

Fingerprint-based identification may be achieved through two different approaches. The minutiae-based matching consists in analyzing the local ridge patterns, that is, minutiae, (Figure 7). A complete fingerprint consists of about 100 minutiae points on average, while a measured fingerprint area consists of about 30-60 minutiae points on average, depending on both the finger and the sensor. The minutiae points are represented by a dots distribution in a coordinate system. Such a method is robust to fingerprint rotation and translation, but the extraction of minutiae can be negatively affected by noise and low average quality of the acquired image. The correlation-based approach is based on global pattern matching. The reference and test images are first aligned and checked for correspondence. This method is less robust against image distortions, which are unavoidable since fingers are not rigid. Current

Figure 7. Minutiae-based fingerprint matching

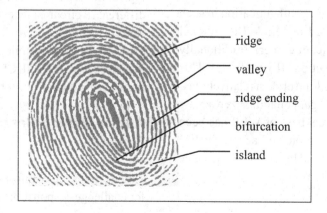

fingerprint identification systems may achieve a false accept rate (FAR) of 1/100,000, with a false reject rate (FRR) of 1%, and matching speed of a few hundreds of msec.

The face is one of the most natural biometric features for identity authentication, also thanks to the fact that a face image can be easily acquired using an off-the-shelf desktop camera. The environment surrounding a face recognition application plays a fundamental role in the complexity of the method. A controlled environment generally comprises the acquisition of frontal and/or profile photographs, with uniform background and identical poses among the participants (*mug shots*). Given the complexity of a general setting, such approach is generally preferred to the uncontrolled one. Consequently, an application system typically restricts one of many aspects, including the environment (fixed location, fixed lighting, uniform background, single face, etc.), the allowable face change (neutral expression, negligible aging, etc.), the number of individuals to be matched against, and the viewing condition (front view, no occlusion, etc.).

A wide variety of approaches to machine recognition of faces have been developed in the literature. Their categorization depends on different criteria. In terms of the sensing modality, a system can take 2D or 3D images, color or infrared images, or any combination. In terms of viewing angle, a system may be designed for frontal, profile, or general views, or any combination. In terms of temporal component, a system can take a static image or time-varying image sequences as input. In terms of computational tools, a system can use programmed knowledge rules, statistical decision rules, neural networks, genetic algorithms, or others.

Similar to fingerprint recognition, the approaches used to perform face recognition may be categorized into two groups: holistic or global approaches and feature-based approaches. Global approaches use a single feature vector that represents the whole face image as input to a classifier. Several classifiers have been proposed in the literature, for example, minimum distance classification in the eigenspace, Fisher's discriminant analysis, and neural networks. Global techniques work well for frontal face views, but they are not robust against pose and environment changes in general.

Feature-based approaches rely on the identification and matching of several representative features, such as interocular distance, distance

Figure 8. Examples of facial recognition methods: local features (left) and eigenfaces (right)

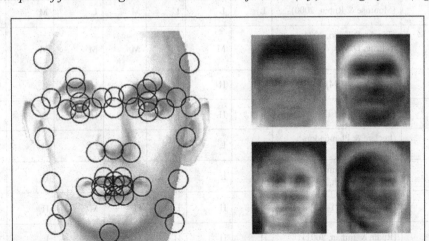

between the lips and the nose, distance between the nose tip and the eyes, distance between the lips and the line joining the two eyes, eccentricity of the face, ratio of the dimensions of the bounding box of the face, width of the lips, and so forth. Feature-based methods are robust against geometric transforms, but are critical in the identification of features (Figure 8).

In Table I (Yun, 2002) a comparison of several biometric methods is reported on the basis of the features used for identification. Universality describes how common a biometric is found in each individual. Uniqueness is how well the biometric separates two individuals. Permanence measures how well a biometric resists aging. Collectability explains how easy it is to acquire the biometric. Performance indicates the accuracy, speed, and robustness of the system capturing the biometric. Acceptability indicates the degree of approval of a technology by the public in everyday life. Finally, circumvention is how easy it is to fool the authentication system. Rankings range from low (L) to high (H). Unfortunately, reliability and acceptability are often inversely proportional. For instance, while signature recognition has a high collectability and acceptability but low reliability and accuracy performance, DNA-based authentication offers high reliability but is poor on acceptability.

Table 1. Biometric authentication

Method	Reference	Universality	Uniqueness	Permanence	Collectability	Performance	Acceptability	Circumvention
Face	(Zhao et al., 2003)	H	L	M	H	L	H	L
Fingerprint	(Driscoll, 1994)	M	H	H	M	H	M	H
Hand geometry	(Faundez-Zanuy, 2005; Hashemi,& Fatemizadeh 2005; Sanchez-Reillo, Sanchez-Avila, & Gonzalez-Marcos, 2000)	M	M	M	H	M	M	M
Keystroke dynamics	(Monrose & Rubin, 2000)	L	L	L	M	L	M	M
Hand vein	(Tanaka & Kubo, 2004; Yuhang, Dayan, & Kejun, 2005)	M	M	M	M	M	M	H
Iris	(Daugman, 1994)	H	H	H	M	H	L	H
Retina	(Simon & Goldstein, 1935)	H	H	M	L	H	L	H
Signature	(Leclerc & Plamondon, 1994)	L	L	L	H	L	H	L
Voice	(Atal, 1976; Campbell, 1997; Gish & Schmidt, 1994)	M	L	L	M	L	H	L
Facial Thermogram	(Proloski, 1997)	H	H	L	H	M	H	H
DNA	(Rudin & Inman, 2001)	H	H	H	L	H	L	L

Another good example of trade-off between reliability and intrusiveness are the cases of retina scan and facial recognition. A retina scan requires the user to stare firmly at an acquisition system for 15 seconds, which may result in annoying interaction. On the other hand, the reliability of facial recognition methods greatly depends on application, demographic aspects such as sex, age, and time-delay, environment conditions, such as lighting and orientation, and never exceeds 80% in the best case (Phillips, Grother, Micheals, Blackburn, Tabassi, & Bone, 2003).

A very promising area is represented by multiple features authentication. In this case, several biometric features are collected and analyzed simultaneously, for example, hand and fingerprint. The approaches that follow such architecture generally offer a high level of accuracy and security at the expense of simplicity and cost, and are therefore indicated in critical applications. It must be noticed that multiple features authentication may be achieved also by the combination of a biometric feature and a traditional one, such as iris scan plus ID card identification.

Biometric authentication represents a very lively sector for research and development. In fact, thanks to its wide adoption at all security levels, ranging from personal computer login apparatus to high-security military applications, the future trend points to a very fast and consistent evolution of such authentication mechanisms. While the current biometric market is dominated by fingerprint authentication (44%) (Biometrics Market and Industry Report, 2006-2010), other methods, such as face recognition or multiple features authentication, are promising. From the same report, the 2005 annual biometric revenue is estimated in 1,539 million US$ and is predicted to grow by 374% by 2010. Such figures well represent the great interest that biometric authentication is raising in the industry and consumer world.

FUTURE WORKS

Given the extension of the object of this chapter, a full-spectrum discussion of future trends would be either too generic or extended. Rather, we want to concentrate the attention on a few aspects of challenge-response mechanisms that present particular interest and are the object of current research and development. The first argument, strong password authentication, is principally about the evolution of common CR schemes used for message exchange, as described in the background section. The last argument, image-based authentication, is mostly related to the type of information used in the challenge-response exchange. The aspects related to mutual authentication through graphical passwords and the role of image scrambling and cryptography are discussed.

Strong Password Authentication

Strong password authentication embodies the challenge of CR frameworks against eavesdropping attacks, with particular interest for novel environments such as wireless networks. A strong password is characterized by extremely high entropy in a way it cannot be easily deduced. Many strong password strategies have been proposed in the last decade. In this subsection we provide the reader with a comprehensive description of the state of art, discussing the advantages and disadvantages of each strategy.

One of the first effective strategies against eavesdropping has been proposed by Haller (1994) and it is known as S/KEY. S/KEY is a one-time password authentication system: any given password may be used exactly one time only, after which it is no longer valid. The system requires that both principals share one secret key, *w*, that is never transmitted except during registration. Then, a secure hash function (a function that is easy to compute in forward direction, but computationally infeasible to reverse) is used for generating the one-time passwords by taking *w* as seed. Specifically, S/KEY uses the MD4 as hash function, taking 8 bytes of input and producing 8 bytes output, so that one-time passwords are 64 bits (8 bytes) long. The plural "passwords" has been used on purpose, since the output of the algorithm is a sequence of passwords to be used consecutively. Then, the core of the devised strategy is the transmission of the personal passwords, which are again used for verifying the user's authenticity at the server side. An eavesdropper, having monitored the authentication data exchange, would not be able to retrieve the personal key because of the use of an unknown hash function (far too complex to invert). Furthermore, the passwords are related in a way that would be computationally impractical to deduce any password from the preceding sequence.

The state of the art in strong password authentication starts back in 1990 with the SAS strategy, proposed by Sandirigama et al. (Sandirigama, Shimizu, & Noda, 2000). This algorithm has been found vulnerable to replay attacks (a form of network attack in which a valid data transmission is maliciously or fraudulently repeated or delayed, and carried out either by the originator or by an adversary who intercepts the data and retransmits it) and denial-of service attacks (an offensive action where the adversary could use some method upon the server so that the access requests issued by the legitimate user will be denied by the server) by Lin et al. (Lin, Sun, & Hwang, 2001) in 1991. Lin also proposed a solution with the OSPA (optimal strong-password authentication) protocol and its enhancement (Lin, Shen, & Hwang, 2003), which is robust against stolen-verifier (actually, in many schemes the verifiers of the passwords are stored by the server to enhance the passwords' security) and man-in-the-middle attacks (an attacker is able to

read, insert, and modify at will, messages between two parties without either party knowing that the link between them has been compromised.). Most recent strategies can be found in Chang and Chang (2004) and Goyal et al. (Goyal, Kumar, Singh, Abraham, Sanyal, 2005). Both seem to be robust against online replay, dictionary, and denial-of-service attacks.

Strong password authentication finds a key application field in wireless networks, whose diffusion and evolution is proceeding rapidly. In such environments, both authentication and data transfer are performed through the wireless link. Then, this scenario is particularly critical in terms of security. For this reason, new forms of hash functions and authentication methods are continuously proposed in the state–of-the-art literature. Usually, the process of producing novel frameworks is a trial-and-error procedure that continuously leads to finding and fixing new security issues. Most novel methods are aimed at strong mutual authentication in order to maintain a safe synchronous data communication between two principals during each authentication phase. Moreover, authentication in a wireless environment seems to be very sensitive, among all cited forms of attack, to the stolen-verifier attack, in which the attacker steals the user's verifier and impersonates the user. At present, several variants of the proposed techniques, in particular of the SAS strategy, try to solve this problem. The last desired feature for strong password authentication strategies will be lightness, to be implemented in low-spec machines, as mobile phones.

Image-Based Authentication

Image-based authentication (IBA) represents a relatively novel idea in the field of authentication systems. All systems based on the exchange or selection of some graphical information fall within such classification, while the justification for such systems resides in three main aspects:

user friendliness, ease of memorization, and the technical evolution of user terminals and connection capability (Suo, Zhu, & Owen, 2005).

The evolution of IBA methods may be chronologically arranged into two stages. An initial stage ranges from 1995 to 2000 with the works of Blonder (2005), who introduced the concept of graphical password. The project developed at Lucent Technologies' labs comprises a relatively simple password selection scheme, consisting in the identification of a number of image areas, tap regions, in a given order. Authorization takes place upon recognition of the correct details sequence. The system allows for a certain region tolerance, depending on the required security level. Other methods include the systems by Naor, Shamir, and Pinkas (Naor & Pinkas, 1997; Naor & Shamir, 1995), Jermyn et al. (Jermyn, May, Monrose, Riter, & Rubin, 1999), and Dhamija and Perrig (2000).

An evolution stage ranges from 2001 until the present. Some works are visual password (VisualPass), server authentication (Epshtein & Krawczyk, 2002), graphical password (Sobrado & Birget, 2002), ImagePassword (Wei, 2002), A wase-E (Takada & Koike, 2003), passfaces system (PassfacesTM), Viskey (Viskey), picture password (Jansen, Gavrila, Korolev, Ayers, & Swanstrom, 2003), passpic (PassfacesTM), PicturePIN (Pointsec), visual security for wireless handheld devices (Duncan, Akhtari, & Bradford, 2004), Associative memory scheme (Weinshall, 2004) and application-scalable image-based authentication framework with JPEG2000 (Ginesu,

Giusto, & Onali, 2005). All previous methods try to develop the idea of image-based authentication while optimizing the aspects related to security, ease of memorization, computational complexity, and user-friendliness. An optimal system has not yet been produced, and all solutions represent a compromise among the aforementioned requirements.

A typical image-based authentication method consists in the exchange of some graphical information between final user and authentication server. All systems are founded on the ground truth that "pictures speak louder than words" from several points of view. In this case, the memorization process is more effective with visual information rather than complex alphanumeric sequences (Pierce, 2003). In the example of Figure 9 (Onali & Ginesu, 2006), the user is first asked to recognize his/her pass-image, that is, the image that was selected during registration. The authentication process continues by iteratively identifying one portion of the selected image.

The main concerns related to these methods depend on three factors: ease of memorization/ recalling, data transfer, and security. While the first factor can be measured through extended subjective testing only, the other two strictly depend on the developed system and can be esteemed exactly. Data transfer performance is especially critical in mobile or portable applications, when the exchange of large volumes of data is either technically unfeasible or too expensive. Such an aspect can be optimized with the adoption of image compressing routines and the accurate design

Figure 9. Example of IBA method

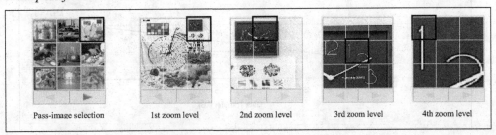

| Pass-image selection | 1st zoom level | 2nd zoom level | 3rd zoom level | 4th zoom level |

and minimization of the system information flow. Security depends on a multitude of factors, such as possible input combinations, security of the communication link, usage environment, and others. As an example, we show the performance estimation from (Ginesu, Giusto, & Onali, 2006) in Figure 10. The proposed method (MIBA) is compared with three other graphical authentication systems on the basis of data transfer and level of security for different numbers of authentication steps.

Other graphical authentication systems are based on slightly different approaches. DAS (Draw A Secret) (Jermyn, 1999), for instance, asks the user to draw his/her secret image on a reference grid (Figure 11 left). The password is constituted by both the shape and the way it was generated. Password recognition is then achieved by evaluating the similarity between drawn and stored image and the similarity between executed and stored path progress. In graphical password (Sobrado & Birget, 2002), the user must recognize a particular geometrical configuration given by several pass-objects among a pseudorandom objects distribution (Figure 11 right). Authentication is then based on the correct selection of a particular region, for example, the cross intersection in the given example.

Image watermarking, scrambling, and encryption (Furht & Kirovski, 2004; Lee & Jung, 2001; Rey & Dugelay, 2002), play an important role in visual authentication methods, providing for additional protection from the illegal manipulation and acquisition of visual data. Some visual login systems based on encryption algorithms have been proposed in the literature. An example of visual cryptography (Naor & Pinkas, 1997; Naor & Shamir, 1995) provides each user with a transparency, that is, a portion of visual information that reveals a secret when combined with

Figure 10. Security against data transfer performance from (Ginesu et al., 2006)

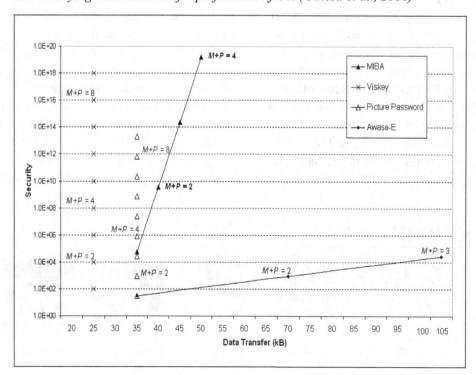

Figure 11. Other graphical authentication systems: DAS and Graphical Password

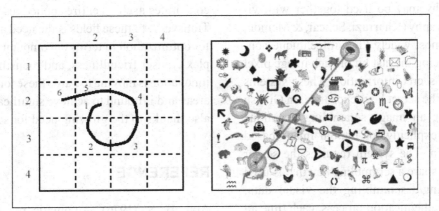

Figure 12. Message exchange scheme for the registration and authentication phases of Ginesu et al. (2006)

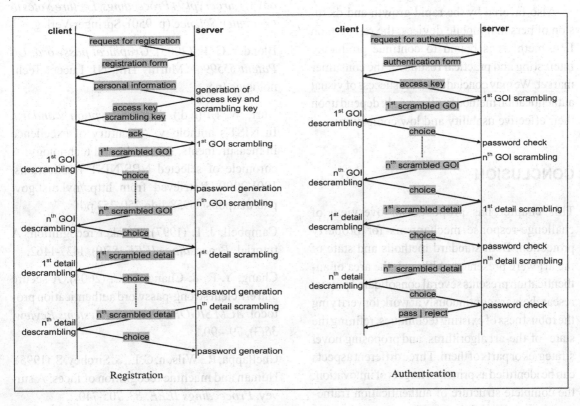

another sent by the server during authentication. Steganography may be used together with visual cryptography (Kharrazi, Sencar, & Memon, 2004). The most widely known technique consists in replacing the last bit of each image pixel with a bit of secret information. These systems rely only on the secret keys exchange. In Ginesu et al. (2006), an image scrambling technique is proposed explicitly for mutual image-based authentication. The system requires the server and client to share a scrambling key that is used for scrambling/descrambling the visual data. During the authentication process, each time an interaction requires a piece of visual information, its encrypted version with the scrambling key is provided. Then, the client must descramble the visual information in order to make its content understandable and usable, for example, selection of the graphical password (Figure 12).

Also favored by the rapid growth and diffusion of personal mobile devices, the research on IBA methods is bound to continue producing interesting and practical results for the consumer market. We may conclude that the success of visual authentication methods will strongly depend upon their effective usability and low complexity.

CONCLUSION

This chapter has proposed an overview of challenge-response mechanisms for property protection. Both standard methods and state of the art were presented. Although the area of authentication presents several consolidated points, researchers are continuously at work for verifying the robustness of existing techniques, refining the state–of-the-art algorithms, and proposing novel strategies or parts of them. Three different aspects can be identified as principal targets of innovation: the complete structure of authentication frameworks; the underlying algorithms for performing security function, such as ciphering, hashing, and so forth; and the typologies of information used

as personal identification. Each of these aspects constitutes itself an entire applied research field. Transverse to these fields is the need and request for optimization in terms of computational complexity, user friendliness, and robustness. Thus, innovation is moving towards these four research areas and is bound to achieve significant results, also thanks to the growing need for security.

REFERENCE

Atal, B. S. (1976). Automatic recognition of speakers from their voices. *Proceedings IEEE, 64,* 460-475.

Bellare, M., & Rogaway, P. (1995). Optimal asymmetric encryption—How to encrypt with RSA. *Extended abstract in Advances in Cryptology—Eurocrypt 94 Proceedings, Lecture Notes in Computer Scienc*e (p. 950). Springer-Verlag.

Blonder, G. E. (2005). *Graphical password, US Patent 5559961.* Murray Hill, NJ: Lucent Technologies Inc.

Burr, W. E. (n.d.). *Data encryption standard.* In NIST's anthology, A century of excellence in measurements, standards, and technology: A chronicle of selected NBS/NIST Publications, 1901-2000. Retrieved from http://nvl.nist.gov/pub/nistpubs/sp958-lide/250-253.pdf

Campbell, J. P. (1997). Speaker recognition: A tutorial. *Proceedings IEEE, 85*(9), 1437-1462.

Chang, Y.-F., & Chang, C.-C. (2004). A secure and efficient strong-password authentication protocol. *ACM SIGOPS Operating Systems Review, 38*(3), 79 - 90.

Chellappa, R., Wilson, C. L., & Sirohey, S. (1995). Human and machine recognition of faces: A survey. *Proceedings IEEE, 83,* 705-740.

Daugman, J. G. (1994). United States Patent No. 5,291,560. *Biometric Personal Identification*

System Based on Iris Analysis. Washington DC: U.S. Government Printing Office.

Dhamija, R. (2000). *Hash visualization in user authentication*. Computer Human Interaction Conference.

Dhamija, R., & Perrig, A. (2000). Déjà vu: A user study using images for authentication. In *Proceedings of the 9th Usenix Security Symposium*.

Driscoll, D. (1994). Fingerprint ID systems. *Advanced Imaging, 9*(20).

Duncan, M. V., Akhtari, M. S., & Bradford, P. G. (2004). Visual security for wireless handheld devices. *The Journal of Science & Health at the University of Alabama, 2*. Retrieved from http://www.bama.ua.edu/~joshua/archive/may04/Duncan%20et%20al.pdf

Epshtein, D., & Krawczyk, H. (2002). Image-based authentication of public keys and applications to SSH. Project report, Technion—Dept. of Electrical Engineering, Technion .

Faundez-Zanuy, M. (2005). Biometric verification of humans by means of hand geometry. In *Proceedings of the 39th International Carnahan Conference on Security Technology CCST 2005,* 61-67.

Furht, B., & Kirovski, F. (2004). *Multimedia security handbook*. CRC Press.

Ginesu, G., Giusto, D. D., & Onali, T. (2005). Application-scalable image-based authentication framework with JPEG2000. *IEEE International Workshop on Multimedia Signal Processing MMSP05*.

Ginesu, G., Giusto, D. D., & Onali, T. (2006). *Mutual image-based authentication framework with JPEG2000 in Wireless Environment*. EURASIP Journal on Wireless Communications and Networking.

Gish, H., & Schmidt, M. (1994). Text-independent speaker identification. *IEEE Signal Processing Magazine, 11*(4), 18-32.

Goyal, V., Kumar, V., Singh, M., Abraham, A., & Sanyal, S. (2005). CompChall: Addressing password guessing attacks. *ITCC05, 1,* 739-744.

Haller, N. M. (1994). The S/KEY (TM) one-time password system. In *Proceedings of Internet Society Symposium on Network and Distributed System Security,* 151-158.

Hashemi, J., & Fatemizadeh, E. (2005). Biometric identification through hand geometry. *International Conference on Computer as a Tool EUROCON 2005, 2,* 1011-1014.

International Biometric Group. (2006). *Biometrics market and industry report 2006-2010*. Retrieved from http://www.biometricgroup.com/reports/public/market_report.html

Jain, A. K., Bolle, R., & Pankanti, S. (1999). *BIOMETRICS: Personal identification in networked society*. Kluwer Academic Publishers.

Jansen, W., Gavrila, S., Korolev, V., Ayers, R., & Swanstrom, R. (2003). *Picture password: A visual login technique for mobile devices*. NIST IR 7030.

Jermyn, I., May, A., Monrose, F., Riter, M., & Rubin, A. (1999). The design and analysis of graphical passwords. In *Proceedings of 8th USENIX Security Symposium*.

Kharrazi, M., Sencar, H.T., & Memon, N. (2004). *Image steganography: Concepts and practice*. Lecture Note Series. Institute for Mathematical Sciences, National University of Singapore.

Kung, S. Y., Mak, M. W., & Lin, S. H. (2004). *Biometric authentication: A machine learning approach*. Prentice Hall.

Leclerc, F., & Plamondon, R. (1994). Automatic signature verification: The state of the art - 1989-

1993. *International Journal of Pattern Recognition and Artificial Intelligence, 8*(3), 643-660.

Lee, J., & Jung, S. (2001). A survey of watermarking techniques applied to multimedia. *Proceedings 2001 IEEE International Symposium on Industrial Electronics (ISIE2001), 1*, 272-277.

Lin, C. L., Sun, H. M., & Hwang, T. (2001). Attacks and solutions on strong-password authentication. *IEICE Transactions on Communications, E84-B*(9), 2622-2627.

Lin, C.-W., Shen J.-J., & Hwang M.-S. (2003). Security enhancement for optimal strong-password authentication protocol. *ACM Operating System Review, 37*(3), 12-16.

Ma, X., McCrindle, R., & Cheng, X. (2006). *Verifying and fixing password authentication protocol.* SNPD'06.

Maltoni, D., Maio, D., Jain, A. K., & Prabhakar, S. (2005). *Handbook of fingerprint recognition.* Springer.

Mitchell, C. (1989). Limitations of challenge-response entity authentication. *IEEE Electronic Letters, 25*(17), 1195-1196.

Monrose, F., & Rubin, A. D. (2000). Keystroke dynamics as a biometric for authentication. *Future Generation Computer Systems, 16*(4), 351-359.

Naor, M., & Pinkas, B. (1997). Visual authentication and identification. In B. Kaliski (Ed.), *Advances in Cryptology—Crypto '97, 1294*, 322-336.

Naor, M., & Shamir, A. (1995). Visual cryptography. In A. De Santis (Ed.), *Advances in Cryptology—EuroCrypt '94, 950*, 1–12.

Omura, J. K. (1990). Novel applications of cryptography in digital communications. *IEEE Communication Magazine, 28*(5), 21-29.

Onali, T., & Ginesu, G. (2006). *Transmission-efficient image-based authentication for mobile devices.* Lecture Notes in Computer Science, 3893.

PassfacesTM. Retrieved from http://www.realuser.com

PassPicc. Retrieved from http://www.authord.com/PassPic/

Perrig, A., & Song, D. (1999). *Hash visualization: A new technique to improve real-world security.* International Workshop on Cryptographic Techniques and E-Commerce CrypTEC '99.

Phillips, P. J., Grother, P., Micheals, R. J., Blackburn, D. M., Tabassi, E., & Bone, M. (2003). *Face Recognition Vendor Test 2002.*

Phillips, P. J., Moon, H., Rauss, P., & Rizvi, S. A. (1997). The FERET evaluation methodology for face-recognition algorithms. In *Proceedings IEEE Conference Computer Vision and Pattern Recognition CVPR 97*, 137-143.

Pierce, J. D., Warren, M. J., Mackay, D. R., & Wells, J. G. (2004). Graphical authentication: Justifications and objectives. In *Proceedings of the 2nd Australian Information Security Management Conference, Securing the Future (AISM 2004)* (pp. 49-63).

Pointsec Mobile Technologies. Retrieved from http://www.pointsec.com

Prokoski, F. J. (1997). *Security and non-diagnostic medical uses for thermal imaging.* American Academy of Thermology 1997 Annual Meeting, Pittsburgh.

Rey, C., & Dugelay, J. (2002). A survey of watermarking algorithms for image authentication. *EURASIP Journal on Applied Signal Processing, 6*, 613-621.

Rivest, R., Shamir, A., & Adleman, L., (1998). A method for obtaining digital signatures and public-key cryptosystems. *Communications of the ACM, 21*(2), 120-126. Previously released as an MIT "Technical Memo" in April 1977. Initial publication of the RSA scheme.

Rudin, N., & Inman, K. (2001). *An introduction to forensic DNA analysis* (2nd ed). CRC Press.

Samal, A., & Lyengar, P.A. (1992). Automatic recognition and analysis of human faces and facialexpressions: *A survey. Pattern Recognition, 25*, 65-77.

Sanchez-Reillo, R., Sanchez-Avila, C., & Gonzalez-Marcos, A. (2000). Biometric identification through hand geometry measurements. *IEEE Transactions on Pattern Analysis and Machine Intelligence, 22*(10), 1168-1171.

Sandirigama, M., Shimizu, A., & Noda, M. T. (2000). Simple and secure password authentication protocol (SAS). *IEICE Transactions on Communications, E83-B*(6), 1363-1365.

Schneier B. (1995) Applied cryptography (2nd ed.). Wiley.

Simon, C., & Goldstein, I. (1935). A new scientific method of identification. *New York State Journal of Medicine, 35*(18), 901-906.

Sobrado L., & Birget, J. C. (2002). Graphical passwords. *The Rutgers Scholar, 4.*

Suo, X., Zhu, Y., & Owen, G. S. (2005). Graphical passwords: *A survey. 21st Annual Computer Security Applications Conference (ACSAC 2005),* Tucson AZ.

Takada, T., & Koike, H. (2003). Awase-E: Image-based authentication for mobile phones using user's favorite images. In *Proceedings of 5th International Symposium* (pp. 347-351), Mobile HCI 2003. Springer.

Tanaka, T., & Kubo, N. (2004). Biometric authentication by hand vein patterns. *SICE 2004 Annual Conference,* 1, 249-253.

Uchida, K. (2005). Fingerprint identification. *NEC Journal of Advanced Technology, 2*(1).

Viskey. Retrieved from http://www.viskey.com

VisualPass. Retrieved from http://penguin.poly.edu/seminars/visualpass/visualpasswords.ppt

Wei, L. (2002). Retrieved from http://wlu-share.tripod.com/ImgPasswd.htm

Weinshall, D. (2004). *Secure authentication schemes suitable for an associative memory.* Leibniz Center for Research in Computer Science, Technical Report 2004-00.

Yuhang, D. Dayan, Z., & Kejun, W. (2005). A study of hand vein recognition method. *IEEE International Conference Mechatronics and Automation, 4,* 2106-2110.

Yun, Y. W. (2002). The "123" of Biometric Technology. *Synthesis Journal.*

Zhao, W., Chellappa, R., Rosenfeld, A., & Phillips, P. J. (2003). Face recognition: A literature survey. *ACM Computing Surveys,* 399-458.

Chapter IX
Q–R Code Combined with Designed Mark

Jun Sasaki
Iwate Prefectural University, Japan

Hiroaki Shimomukai
Gingatsushin Co. Ltd., Japan

Yutaka Funyu
Iwate Prefectural University, Japan

ABSTRACT

The mobile Internet has been used widely in Japan. If we use a cellular phone with the Quick Response (Q-R) code reader function (a two-dimensional code developed by Denso-Wave Corporation), we can very easily access a Web site. However, though the existence of Q-R code reader function in the cellular phone is well-known, not many people use the function. The reason is that the Q-R code is not intuitive because it was developed to be read by machines. Our idea to solve the problem is to combine the Q-R code with a designed particular picture or graphic. We propose a method to produce the designed Q-R code and we develop its production system. This chapter describes the proposed method, the production system, and evaluation results using some designed Q-R codes produced by the system.

INTRODUCTION

Internet users are in large number, and users using Web access by mobile phone have been increasing rapidly. Web accessibility is discussed widely, and the guidelines have appeared generally (Loiacono,

2003). Social mobile applications and search technology by mobile phone are described in some articles (Dailey Paulson, 2005; Smith, 2005). Ubiquitous society computing systems are used everywhere and by everyone; it will be important to develop a new technology for easy access to and

Copyright © 2008, IGI Global, distributing in print or electronic forms without written permission of IGI Global is prohibited.

understanding about Web sites for mobile phone (Hong , 2005).

In recent times, a 2D (two dimensional) code such as Quick Response (Q-R) (Q-R code, 2006), code developed by Denso-Wave Corporation, has been a popular way to access a Web site using a cellular phone. We proposed and developed a reliable and useful information distribution system named "Kuchicomi Network," which was reported in the 15th European-Japanese Conference on Information Modelling and Knowledge Bases (15th-EJC 2005) (Sasaki, Yoneda, & Funyu, 2005; Sasaki, et al., 2006). In this system, Q-R code, which includes the uniform resource locator (URL) of the Kuchikomi site, is used to access the site easily for a user.

Although about 90% of people know about 2D code in Japan (Mitsubishi Research Institute, Inc. Report, 2005), only about 40% are real users. As the two-dimensional code was developed to be read only by machines, there are no easily recognised characteristics for humans to see. With this in mind, we have developed a designed two-dimensional code that is more recognisable so that more people will be able to use it (Sasaki, at al., 2006).

The designed 2D code is produced by combining a 2D code with a particular picture or graphic of a character or mark. We propose its production method and a system to develop and to evaluate it. After experimental evaluation on the designed two-dimensional code produced by the system, we can obtain a good effect on the human feeling about the two-dimensional code.

BACKGROUND

When we use a credit card in a real shop or an Internet shop, our privacy information is transferred to the financial company by using the secure electronic transaction (SET) protocol to keep the information secure (Mastercard & Visa, 1997).

Much research has reported privacy technologies such as privacy enhancing technology (PET) for the Internet user (Goldberg, Wanger, &

Brewer, 1997; Rezgul & Bouguettaya, 2003). An advanced protocol named 3-D Secure™ , where a password is needed to input, has been used more than SET (Visa, 2002).

Recently, as Ubiquitous Society has been come, we can access everywhere using mobile devices. More enhanced technologies are required. Tamaru et al. (Tamaru, Nakazawa, Takashio, & Tokuda, 2003) proposed a privacy profile negotiation protocol (PPNP) for services in public spaces. The proposal is related with an access control technology to access private information according to a privacy policy. Furthermore, the World Wide Web Consortium (W3C) provides platform for privacy preferences (P3P) as a privacy policy of Web application service (W3C, 2006).

There are some kinds of certification technologies, for example, by password, by hardware token such as ID cards or USB key, or by Vaio Metrics, which is a certification method by using human characteristics such as fingerprint or iris. These technologies are compared and evaluated logically by many researchers (O'Gorman, 2003). Password is the most popular method to make a certification to access a Web site. But, disadvantages of password certification method are described, while a two-method combination by password and hardware token and Vaio Metrics are proposed in some papers (Kun, 2004). There is a different method than password. Rachna proposed that a user selects the before registered image picture in many given image pictures (Rachna & Dphamiji, 2000). Though this method would be more reliable than using password, it would be a little complicated because it is also using a human's memory.

On the other hand, secure communication is an important issue, as well as the certification function to realize a high-secure information system. There is a standard activity to make a secure communication by using security code such as secure socket layer (SSL)/transport layer security (TLS) (Housley, Polk, Ford, & Solo, 2002). Further, new problems occur such as phishing, which is a stealing method of user's password by using a fake Web site (Bellovin, 2004). Nielsen says that user education is not the answer to security problems. He says "Internet scams cannot be thwarted by placing the burden on users to defend themselves at all times. Beleaguered users need protection, and the technology must change to provide this" (Nielsen, 2004).

Wu, Miller, and Garfinkel, have proposed a secure Web authentication with mobile phones (Wu, et al., 2004). They introduce a solution to use a mobile phone as a hand-held authentication token and a security proxy that allows the system to be used with unmodified third-party Web services. Their goal is to create an authentication system that is both secure and highly usable. Their solution can be deployed as a good backup to password login. When a user forgets his/her password, he/she can still log in using a mobile phone instead.

Japanese cellar companies, such as NTT DoCoMo or KDDI, have each a certification center that sends certification information to a user's mobile phone through the mobile Internet (KDDI, 2006; NTT DoCoMo, 2006).

Tanaka and Teshigawara (2006) have proposed and have been developing secure user authentication with Nijigen code (SUAN). It is a new certification method using a mobile phone and the two-dimensional code. From the viewpoint of previously mentioned trends, two-dimensional code such as Q-R code would be more significant code. We can say that the designed Q-R code technology introduced in this chapter has big possibility and market to put authentication on the code as original and important code.

The "C-C code" developed by Code Com Corporation (C-C code, 2006) is a current technology that makes two-dimensional code more useful by printing a number under the code. The code can be accessed by typing the number into a cellular phone, even without a two-dimensional code reader available. Although this is the way to expand the accessibility of the code, it does not improve the

design characteristics. On the other hand, "Color code," developed by Color Zip Corporation (Color code, 2006) uses color cells to make the designed characteristics, but, there is a limitation in the color distribution rule in Color code that makes it unsuitable to combine a meaningful code with a free-designed mark.

Combination with the Q-R Code and a Designed Mark

In this chapter, we propose a method to combine Q-R code, which is the most familiar 2D code in Japan, with a designed picture.

When a two-dimensional code is read by a charge-coupled device (CCD) camera, for example, it is transmitted as two picture parts, shadow and highlight. Our idea is that if we could include a designed picture on the Q-R code without destroying the shadow and highlight condition, it would be advantageous. If we combined a Q-R code with a designed picture consisting of particular mark or character in the overlapped part of shadow in the Q-R code, we could transfer that part of the designed picture color into a dark color recognized as shadow by a Q-R code reader. In our proposal, the luminosity of the color in the overlapped part can be classified into five levels, as shown in Figure1. A color in level 1 is too dark to be recognized as a designed color because it cannot be distinguished from the black of the Q-R code. A color in level 2 can be available in the designed color, and can be recognized as shadow of the Q-R code. A color in level 3 is not suitable for the designed Q-R code because it is in the middle level where the recognition of shadow or highlight could change, depending on the reading environment conditions, such as lighting. A color in level 4 can be available in the designed color and can be recognized as highlight of the Q-R code. A color in level 5 is too bright to be recognized as a designed color because it cannot be distinguished from white of the Q-R code.

Figure 1. Five levels in luminosity of a color

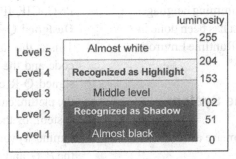

Equations for Color Transfer

The principal of color transfer is shown in Figure 2. When the original color, C_o, with elements of R (red), G (Green), and B (Blue), in an original designed mark, are set in R_o, G_o, and B_o, each color of highlight or shadow in the overlapped part of Q-R code and the original mark is transferred into following color of C_h with R_h, G_h, and B_h color elements, or C_s with R_s, G_s, and B_s color elements, respectively. Here, R_i, G_i, and B_i ($i = o$, h, s) is a luminosity value from 0 to 255 of each color element.

The equations for color transfer are as follows:

For the highlight part:

$$R_h = R_4(1 + R_o / 256), G_h = G_4(1 + G_o / 256), B_h = B_4(1 + B_o / 256) \qquad (1)$$

For the shadow part:

$$R_s = R_2(1 + R_o / 256), G_s = G_2(1 + G_o / 256), B_s = B_2(1 + B_o / 256). \qquad (2)$$

Here, R_2, G_2, and B_2 are the minimum luminosity values in the level 2, and R_4, G_4, and B_4 are those in the level 4 for the color of an original mark.

Designed Q-R Code Production System

To efficiently produce samples of the designed Q-R code based on our proposed method, and to do quantitative evaluations on them, we developed the designed Q-R code production system.

This system is available on computers with the Java Runtime Environment installed. The implementation environments are Apple Power Book 15

Figure 2. Principal of color transfer

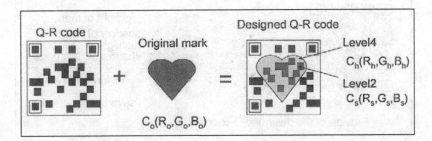

inch as the hardware, Apple Mac OSX 10.4.2 as the OS, and Java2SE 1.4.2 for programming language. Additionally, the operational test has been done in the environment with the Java2 Runtime Environment on the Windows XP OS.

Functions Offered by the System

Functions offered by the system are as follows:

- **Usual Q-R code formation function:** This is the function that forms the usual Q-R code after a user inputs necessary items for the application form. The input items are the contents of the Q-R code, such as URL, e-mail address, message text sentence, and so forth, version information, error correction ratio, mask type, margin, and the magnification ratio for display of the Q-R code.
- **Picture reading function:** This is the function that reads the picture selected from candidates of files to be combined with the Q-R code. In this system, the designed Q-R code is produced as soon as the picture is read.

The possible file formats able to be read are PNG, GIF, JPEG, and BMP.

- **Designed Q-R code production function:** This is the function that combines the Q-R code and the picture, and produces the designed Q-R code. The color conversion of the picture can be done automatically by the system, or the user can manually input the luminosity values as hexadecimal numbers for the *R*, *G*, and *B*. We can make many kinds of samples efficiently with any color for experiments using the system.
- **Designed Q-R code output function:** This is the function that prints out the designed Q-R code to a color printer, or as a picture file whose format is PNG or JPEG.

Display Example of the System

An example of the display screen is shown in Figure 3. We can specify all of the functions in the system by using only this display. There is an input window for contents at upper left of the layout. In the mid-

Figure 3. Display of the designed Q-R code production system

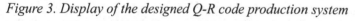
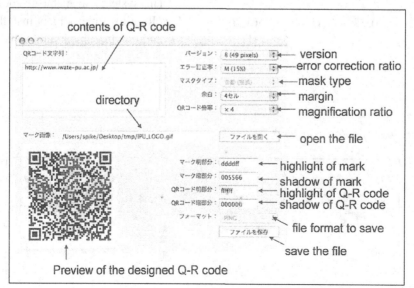

dle of the display, we can select the picture file to be combined with the Q-R code. At bottom left of the display is a preview of the designed Q-R code produced by the system. If we change the values of items shown in right of the display, the view of the designed Q-R code is changed in real time.

Outline of the Experiments

We evaluated the designed Q-R code by experiments using the developed system.

We produced two kinds of Q-R code using the production system; one is the designed Q-R code of our proposed method, and the other is usual Q-R code. All of the designed Q-R codes are confirmed to be read perfectly without error by the "QR checker" (QR checker, 2006), software for verification based on Japanese Standard of JIS X 0510 provided by Denso-wave Corporation.

Then we created a questionnaire for our students to assess their impressions of the designed Q-R codes. One hundred and five students were surveyed, comprising 79 males, 24 females, and 2 unknowns, all of whom were students in the Faculty of Software and Information Science of Iwate Prefectural University.

Main Results of Questionaire

The main results of the questionnaire are as follows:

1. Ratio of knowing usual Q-R code; 94%.
2. Ratio of having an experience of using usual Q-R code; 64%.
3. Ratio of students who want to read usual Q-R code than the designed Q-R code; 24%.
4. Ratio of students who want to read the designed Q-R code than usual Q-R code; 73%.
5. The possibility of prediction for the contents of the designed Q-R code; possible; 84%, impossible; 15%.
6. The number of students who had impressions of usual Q-R code; "cellular phone"; 83, "cannot understand the contents at glance";79, "not familiar"; 22.
7. The number of students who had impressions of the designed Q-R code; "can understand the contents at glance";67, "new"; 48, "familiar";39.
8. Free opinion on the designed Q-R code:
    *   Very good because we can predict the contents of Q-R code.

Figure 4. Selected color groups and classes in the experiment

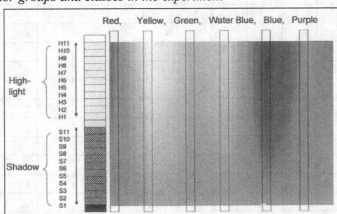

- It is simple, and could catch on.
- Good idea because the space for Q-R code can be reduced by overlapping Q-R code and the mark.
- Entering the mark, it becomes more familiar.
- Contents are easy to understand certainly, but it feels to be a little harsh.
- Unless explanation of the designed Q-R code, confusion may occur.
- Contents may be easy to understand usually, but there would be little afraid of misunderstanding.

Judging by the questionnaire results, the users were more interested in the proposed designed Q-R code than the usual Q-R code. We found it was possible to assume the contents of the code at a glance from the designed Q-R code. But we also confirmed that a few people had a bad impression of the designed Q-R code. In order to solve the problem, it is necessary to research the optimal overlap technique of the mark and code from the user's view point of user's impression.

Experimental Method

In order to clarify the color characteristics of the designed Q-R code, we carried out some additional experiments.

We selected six color groups, red, yellow, green, water blue, blue, and purple. Then, we divided each color group into 22 classes that consisted of 11 shadow classes and 11 high-light classes. The selected color groups and classes are shown in Figure 4.

According to the combination of the color groups and the classes, we made some designed Q-R code samples. For example, if a sample name is RH1S1, it means that the color group of the overlapped part of the sample is R (Red), the high-light class is $H1$, and the shadow class is $S1$. We tried to evaluate each sample from the viewpoint of both impressions by human and error characteristics by a Q-R code reader.

If we evaluate all combinations shown in Figure 4, the number of samples will be 121. As all combinations are so many that humans cannot evaluate them, we selected only 25 combinations as representative as follows:

Table 1. Selection of samples (X=25)

	S1	S2	S3	S4	S5	S6	S7	S8	S9	S10	S11
H1	X										X
H2		X				X				X	
H3			X						X		
H4				X				X			
H5					X		X				
H6		X				X				X	
H7				X			X				
H8				X				X			
H9		X							X		
H10		X				X				X	
H11	X										X

Figure 5. An example of a sample sheet (group Red)

$XH1S1$, $XH1S11$, $XH2S2$, $XH2S6$, $XH2S10$
$XH3S3$, $XH3S9$, $XH4S4$, $XH4S8$, $XH5S5$
$XH5S7$, $XH6S21$, $XH6S6$, $XH6S10$, $XH7S5$
$XH7S7$, $XH8S4$, $XH8S8$, $XH9S3$,
 $XH9S9$, $XH10S2$,
$XH10S6$, $XH10S10$, $XH11S1$, $XH11S11$

Here, X means the initial of color, namely, X = R (Red), Y(Yellow), G (Green), W(Water blue), B (Blue), or P (Purple).

We selected 25 samples for each color group as shown in Table 1 where samples are marked as X.

The evaluation method is as follows:

1. We make sample sheets by using designed Q-R code production system we developed. There, 25 samples are included in each color group. An example of the sample sheet is shown in Figure 5.We made six kinds of sample sheets, red, yellow, green, water blue, blue, and purple.
2. We measured error characteristics for each sample by QR checker of Denso Wave Corporation.
3. We showed every kind of the sample sheet to 19 people and gave a questionnaire. Impression score is calculated as sum of opinion scores, where good is +1, bad is -1, and others is 0 points.

Experimental Results

This section shows evaluation results of sample sheets, made by the method described before, for each color group.

Figure 6 shows the result for group Red, where each sample sheet is distributed by its impression score. There are 16 no-error designed Q-R code in 25 samples. Impression of each sample is comparatively good impression. Right side samples and left side samples are evaluated as good and bad impression, respectively.

Figure 7 shows the result for group Yellow. There are 15 no-error designed Q-R code. All samples are evaluated as comparatively bad impression.

Figure 8 shows the result for group Green. There are 10 no-error designed Q-R code. Good impression sample is only one.

Figure 9 shows the result for group Water blue. There are 11 no-error samples. All samples are evaluated as bad impression.

Figure 10 shows the result for group Blue. There are 11 no-error samples. Good impression samples are few. Figure 11 shows the result for group Purple. There are 16 no-error samples. Good impression samples are comparatively many.

Table 2 shows the summary of the experimental results on color characteristics of the de-

Figure 6. Evaluation result for group Red

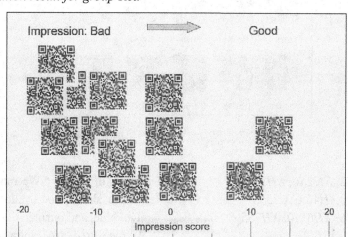

Figure 7. Evaluation result for group Yellow

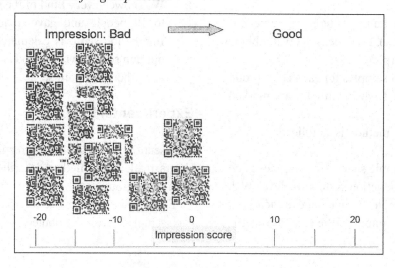

Figure 8. Evaluation result for group Green

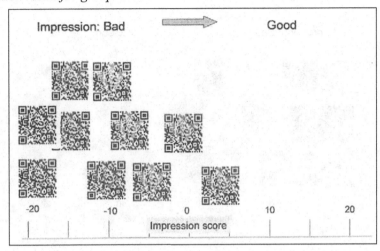

Figure 9. Evaluation result for group Water blue

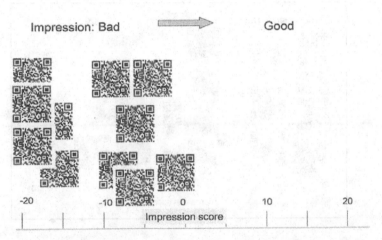

signed Q-R code. We find that the group Red and group Purple have comparatively many no-error samples, and they have good impression score. Other groups of Yellow, Green, Water blue, and Blue have comparatively few no-error samples and low impression score.

Effect of the Designed Q-R Code

We expect that the effect of the designed Q-R code will be very large. As people become more familiar with the designed code, they will become interested in using it. Additionally, the layout of advertisement space on a newspaper or a leaflet with Q-R code becomes more flexible because there is no problem of overlap of pictures and Q-R code. As a result, new businesses will be created; for example, sales of designed Q-R codes, and providing established businesses with tools to make Q-R codes, and Web sites for cellular phones and so forth. Further, we are looking forward to prevention of forgery or alteration of the Q-R code

Figure 10. Evaluation result for group Blue

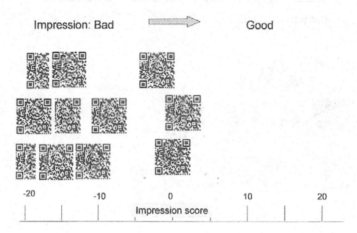

Figure 11. Evaluation result for group Purple

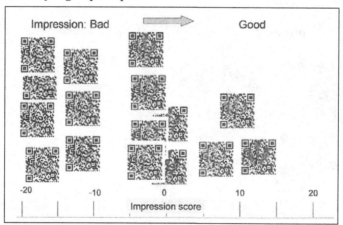

Table 2. Experimental results on color characteristics

		Group					
		Red	Yellow	Green	Water blue	Blue	Purple
Number of no-error samples in 25 samples		16	15	10	11	11	16
Impression Score	Ave.	-6.1	-12.5	-9.8	-11.4	-10.8	-5.1
	Max.	13	0	-1	-2	0	13
	Min.	-15	-19	-19	-19	-19	-19

because the copyright of the designed Q-R code can be registered as intellectual property.

CONCLUSION

In this chapter, we proposed the designed Q-R code, which is more recognisable for people than the usual Q-R code, and developed a method to produce it. In addition, we conducted a survey with various designed Q-R codes produced by the system that gave a good result, showing most people were interested in it and it was possible to assume the contents of the code at glance. Further study is needed to clarify the optimal overlap condition of a designed mark and Q-R code, because a few people have bad impression of it. Its effective utilization method should be also studied.

The designed Q-R code we proposed has already been transferred to the Gingatsushin Co. Ltd., and it is commercialized now.

ACKNOWLEDGMENT

We thank Mr. Takahiro Tabata, Mr. Ryuhachiro Suzuki, and Mr. Yoshinobu Sasaki of the Gingatsushin Co.Ltd., along with their useful advice related to this research.

REFERENCES

Bellovin, S. M. (2004). Spamming, phishing, authentication, and privacy. *Communication of the ACM, 47*(12), 144.

C-C code. (2006). Retrieved from http://www.codecom.jp/

Color code.(2006). Retrieved from http://www.colorzip.co.jp/ja/

Dailey Paulson, L. (2005). Search technology goes mobile. *IEEE Computer*, August.

Dphamiji, R., & Perring, A. (2000). *Déjà vu: A user study using image for authentication.* 9th Usenix Security Symposium.

Goldberg, I., Wanger, D., & Brewer, E. A. (1997). Privacy-enhancing technologies for the Internet. In *Proceeding of 42nd IEEE spring COMPCON*, San Jose, CA, Feb 1997.

Hong, J. I. (2005). Minimizing security risks in Ubicomp Systems. *IEEE Computer*, December.

Housley, R., Polk, W., Ford, W., & Solo, D. (2002). Internet X.509 public key infrastructure certificate and certificate revocation list (CRL) profile. *RFC 3280* (Proposed Standard).

KDDI. (2006). *Security pass*. Retrieved from http://www.kddi.com/business/service/mobile/security_pass/

Kun, M. S. (2004). *Password insecurity: Securing a system with multifactor authentication.* SANS2005.

Loiacono, E. T. (2003). Improving Web accessibility. *IEEE Computer,* January.

Mastercard & Visa. (1997). *SET secure electronic transaction specification, Book 1: Business description* ver1.0.

Mitsubishi Research Institute, Inc. (2005). In *Proceedings of the 14th portable telephone service user investigation.*

Nielsen, J. (2004). *User education is not the answer to security problems.* Retrieved from http://www.useit.com/alertbox/20041025.html

NTT DoCoMo. (2006). *First Pass.* Retrieved from http://www.docomo.biz/html/product/firstpass/

O'Gorman, L. (2003). Comparing passwords, tokens, and biometrics for user authentication. *Proceedings of the IEEE, 91*, 2021-2040.

Q-R code. (2006). Retrieved from http://www.qrcode.com/

QR checker. (2006). Retrieved from http://www.denso-wave.com/ja/adcd/product/qrchecker/index.html

Rezgul, A., & Bouguettaya, A. (2003). Privacy on Web: Facts, challenges, and solutions. *IEEE Security & Privacy*, 40-49.

Sasaki, J., Yoneda, T., & Funyu, Y. (2005). A reliable and useful information distribution system: Kuchikomi Network. In *Proceedings of the 15th European-Japanese Conference (EJC) on Information Modelling and Knowledge Base.*

Sasaki, J., Yoneda, T., & Funyu, Y. (2006). A reliable and useful information distribution system: The "Kuchikomi Network." *Information Modelling and Knowledge Bases XVII* (pp. 180-190).

Sasaki, J., Shimomukai, H., Yoneda, T., & Funyu, Y. (2006). Development of designed Q-R code. In *Proceedings of the 16th European-Japanese Conference (EJC) on Information Modelling and Knowledge Base.*

Smith, I. (2005). Social-mobile applications. *IEEE Computer,* April.

SUAN (Secure User Authentication with Nijigen code). Retrieved from http://suan.asg

Tamaru, S., Nakazawa, J., Takashio, K. & Tokuda, H. (2003). PPNP: A privacy profile negotiation protocol for services in public spaces. In *Proceeding of fifth international conference on Ubiquitous Computing (UbiComp2003)*, Seattle, WA., Oct. 2003.

Visa. (2002). *3-D Secure™ Introduction* version 1.0.2.

W3C. (2006). *Platform for privacy preferences project.* Retrieved from http://www.w3.org/P3P/

Wu, M., Miller, R., & Garfinkel, S.L. (2004). Secure Web authentication with mobile phones, *DIMACS symposium on usable privacy and security 2004.*

Chapter X
Visual Environment for DOM–Based Wrapping and Client–Side Linkage of Web Applications

Kimihito Ito
Hokkaido University Research Center for Zoonosis Control, Japan

Yuzura Tanaka
Meme Media Laboratory, Hokkaido University, Japan

ABSTRACT

Web applications, which are computer programs ported to the Web, allow end-users to use various remote services and tools through their Web browsers. There are an enormous number of Web applications on the Web, and they are becoming the basic infrastructure of everyday life. In spite of the remarkable development of Web-based infrastructure, it is still difficult for end-users to compose new integrated tools of both existing Web applications and legacy local applications, such as spreadsheets, chart tools, and database. In this chapter, the authors propose a new framework where end-users can wrap remote Web applications into visual components, called pads, and functionally combine them together through drag-and-drop operations. The authors use, as the basis, a meme media architecture IntelligentPad that was proposed by the second author. In the IntelligentPad architecture, each visual component, called a pad, has slots as data I/O ports. By pasting a pad onto another pad, users can integrate their functionalities. The framework presented in this chapter allows users to visually create a wrapper pad for any Web application by defining HTML nodes within the Web application to work as slots. Examples of such a node include input-forms and text strings on Web pages. Users can directly manipulate both wrapped Web applications and wrapped local legacy tools on their desktop screen to define application linkages among them. Since no programming expertise is required to wrap Web applications or to functionally combine them together, end-users can build new integrated tools of both wrapped Web applications and local legacy applications.

INTRODUCTION

During the last several years, the main portion of information resources on the World Wide Web (Berners-Lee, Cailliau, Luotonen, Henrik Nielsen, & Secret, 1994) has shifted from handmade HTML pages to server-generated HTML pages, such as those using Common Gateway Interface (CGI), Active Server Page (ASP), Java Servlets, Java Server Pages (JSP), and PHP: Hypertext Preprocessor (PHP). A Web application is an application program that has an HTML-based front end for users to utilize some services provided by a remote HTTP server. There are an enormous number of Web applications on the Web, and they are becoming the basic infrastructure of everyday life. Many companies and researchers provide Web applications, such as search engines, financial services, scientific analysis tools, and various other kinds of database services. Basically, Web applications allow every end-user to use various remote services and tools through their Web browsers.

We have now more than 10^9 pages on the Web, and most of those pages are crawled by major search engines. Although we have seen remarkable developments in information retrieval technologies, such as ranking and clustering of Web pages, it still takes a lot of time to get satisfactory information by trying to retrieve documents from the Web. The more pages we have on the Web, the more time it will take for users to get satisfactory results from the Web.

Our objective is to support users' intellectual activities using the Web. We assume target users to be specialists in a domain, such as finance or bioinformatics, but novices in computer programming. We call them end-users.

The end-users access Web applications through Web browsers. Thus, to combine two Web applications, users need to open these two Web pages, to input some data on the first page, to copy a part of the result, and to paste this copy into the input-form on the second page. Users need to repeat this process if they want to apply the same processing to other inputs. In UNIX, users can compose command sequences using pipes and redirections. UNIX users can perform a job that is not implemented as a single command. On the other hand, Internet users cannot combine existing Web applications into a single application.

From this point of view, we propose a new framework for the visual wrapping and linking of Web applications in order to dynamically and visually compose an integrated function. The framework allows users to rapidly wrap any Web application with a wrapper component through direct manipulation. The key idea of the framework is the use of the IntelligentPad architecture (Tanaka, 2003; Tanaka & Imataki, 1989), which allows users to combine these wrapped visual components, called pads, by pasting pads on another pad, to compose a composite pad. This composition defines application linkages among Web applications to integrate them into a single composite function. Users can also combine wrapped Web applications together with wrapped legacy local applications, such as spreadsheets, charts, and databases to integrate their functionalities.

The remarkable development of Web engineering makes the revision and approval cycles of Web applications shorter and shorter. Because the providers of Web applications need to increase the quality and competitiveness of their applications, they often revise the format of front-end HTML pages, and sometimes they change URLs.

Many researchers have worked on developing a robust wrapping method for Web applications (Kushmerick, 2000; Phelps & Wilensky, 2000). Some wrapping methods have robustness for format changes. From the viewpoint of computational learning theory, it is impossible to deal with every kind of format change. We do not focus on such robustness in this chapter. We focus on how, instantaneously, users can create wrappers for Web applications when the users need to reuse them in functional combinations with other applications.

In this chapter, we give an overview of a DOM-based technology for the Web application linkage using IntelligentPad architecture. In our previous works, we presented the framework of our wrapping method (Ito & Tanaka, 2002), gave basic strategies for the wrapping and functional linkage using IntelligentPad architecture (Ito & Tanaka, 2003b), and discussed its application to mobile computing (Ito & Tanaka, 2003a). In Ito and Tanaka (2003c), we focused on Web application wrapping through instruction by demonstration.

This chapter is organized as follows: The next section reviews related works on Web application wrapping and functional linkage among Web applications. In Section 3, we address some fundamental requirements concerning the end-users' reuse of existing Web applications. Details of the IntelligentPad architecture are presented in Section 4. Our methodology for the Web application wrapping through mouse operations is described in Section 5. Functional linkage among wrapped Web applications is described in Section 6. Copyright issue is discussed in Section 7, and we conclude Section 8 with our future research plans.

BACKGROUND

Web service technologies, such as simple object access protocol (SOAP), enable us to interoperate services published over the Web (World Wide Web Consortium, 2000). However, they assume that the application program interface (API) library to access such a service is a priori provided by its server side. Users need to write a program to interoperate between more than one Web service. Our technologies, on the other hand, provide only the client-side direct manipulation operations for users to reedit intellectual resources embedded in

Web pages, and to define a new combination of them together with their interoperation.

Open hypermedia systems (OHSs) (Anderson, Taylor, & Whitehead, 2000; Carr, Hall, & De Roure, 1999; Davis, Hall, Heath, Hill, & Wilkins, 1992; Davis, Knight, & Hall, 1994; Grønbæk, Bouvin, & Sloth, 1997; Will & Leggett, 1996;Wiil, Nürnberg, & Leggett, 1999) allow links and annotations to be added to documents outside the author's control, and are designed to be integrated with any number of applications to provide hypertext functionality to everything from spreadsheets to graphics editors. OHSs use a link service (Daivis et al., 1994) to resolve the source anchor of a link to all the possible destinations by querying a link database to identify relevant links. Links in OHS can be extended to application linkages among Web applications. Our framework plays similar roles, as such OHS technologies play, to define linkages among Web applications.

Many studies have been done on the visual wrapping of Web pages. However, there have been few research studies done on techniques that allow end-users to wrap Web applications and to define functional linkage in the same environment.

Bauer and Dengler (2000) have introduced a programming by demonstrations (PBD) method in which even naive users can configure their own Web-based information services, satisfying their individual information needs. They have implemented the method into InfoBeans (Bauer & Dengler, 1999). By accessing an InfoBox with an ordinary Web browser, users can wrap Web applications. By connecting channels among InfoBeans on the InfoBox, users can also integrate them functionally together. Because the system uses a specialized proxy server on the server side, InfoBeans does not allow users to combine wrapped Web applications and local legacy applications.

WebL (Kistler & Marais, 1998) is a script language for writing Web wrappers and defining functional linkages amongst them. While the language has strong expressive power to fetch Web pages and to extract texts from pages, users have to write program codes to functionally combine Web applications together.

W4F (Sahuguet & Azavant 2001), which is a semiautomatic wrapper generator, provides a GUI support tool to define an extraction. The system creates a wrapper class written in Java from a user's demonstration. To use this wrapper class, users need to write program codes. DEbyE (Golgher, Laender, da Silva, & Ribeiro-Neto, 2000) provides a more powerful GUI support tool for the wrapping of Web applications. DEbyE stores the extracted text portions in an XML repository. Users have to use another XML tool to combine the extracted data from Web applications. LExIKON (Grieser, Jantke, Lange, & Thomas, 2000) learns the underlying relationship among objects within a Web page from a user-specified ordered set of text strings. There is no GUI support tool for the joining of two extracted relations. WebView (Freire, Kumar, B., & Lieuwen, 2001) allows us to define customized views of Web contents. However, it seems difficult for end-users to create a new view that integrates different Web applications.

There are some research studies on recording and playing a macro operation on a Web browser. WebVCR (Anupam, Freire, Kumar, & Lieuwen, 2000) provides a VCR-style interface to record and replay users' actions. It replays a series of browsing steps in "smart bookmarks," that are shortcuts to Web contents that require multiple steps to be retrieved. However, it is difficult for end-users to combine more than one recorded navigation together.

Web Application Linkage

We define a *Web application* as an application program that has an HTML-based front end for the user to utilize some services provided by a remote HTTP server.

An Example Scenario

Consider the following example scenario: A Japanese investor wants to know stock quotes of some major US companies in Japanese yen. The investor knows that there is a Web application providing a real-time stock-price browsing

Figure 1. An outline of our approach to define functional linkage among Web applications (A video demonstration is available at   http://km.meme.hokudai.ac.jp/people/itok/CHIP/movies)

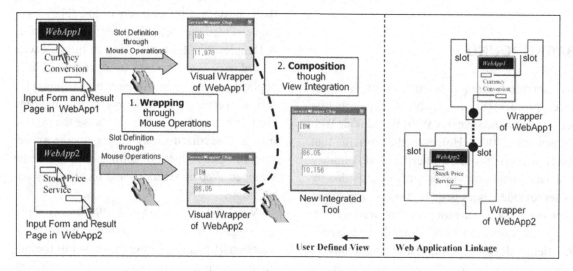

service of US companies, (e.g., Quote.com). In addition, the investor knows that there is a Web application providing a service that converts the US dollar into Japanese yen, based on the current exchange rate, (e.g., Yahoo Corporation, Currency Conversion).

The investor opens the stock-price page and the currency conversion page using two Web browsers. He or she inputs the word "IBM" into the input form on the stock-price page. As a result, the Web server returns an HTML page that contains a stock quote of IBM in US dollars. Using his or her mouse, the investor copies the quote, and pastes it into the input-form of the currency conversion page. Then, the server of the service provider converts the quote into Japanese yen. Suppose that the investor also wants to know the stock quotes of Microsoft and AT&T in the Euro; he or she needs to repeat similar operations.

What this investor wants to do is to combine these two services into a single application for browsing the US stock market in Japanese yen. What kind of software will help him? In this chapter, we will propose our solution to this question.

Requirements and our Approach

The end-users' creation of functional linkages among Web applications requires the following capabilities:

1. Easy specification of input and output portions of Web applications to reuse embedded functions in them.
2. Easy definition of functional linkages amongst Web applications to compose a new integrated application.
3. Easy decomposition and recomposition of composite functions in the user-defined integrated applications.

We will propose the use of IntelligentPad (Tanaka, 2003; Tanaka & Imataki, 1989) tech-

nologies to achieve these three capabilities. IntelligentPad architecture allows users to combine media component objects (called *pad*s), such as multimedia documents and application programs, through their view integration. Each pad has slots as data I/O ports. Through drag-and-drop operations, users can connect a pad to a slot of another pad. This operation simultaneously defines both a composite view and a functional linkage between two pads through a slot connection.

Here we will summarize our approach to Web application linkages as follows:

1. Create visual wrapper components of Web applications by specifying some portions on the Web pages through mouse operations to work as slots.
2. Visually combine wrapped Web applications together to compose a new integrated application that performs a composite function.
3. Decompose an integrated application visually to recompose another composite application visually.

Figure 1 shows an outline of our approach to define functional linkages among Web applications through users' mouse operations. Suppose *WebApp*1 and *WebApp*2 represent Web applications of a currency conversion service and a real-time stock quote service, respectively. Consider the example scenario of a Japanese investor, which we presented at the beginning of the section. he/she wants to know stock quotes of some major US companies in Japanese yen. What he/she first does is to create visual wrapper components of *WebApp*1 and *WebApp*2. The user specifies the input form for a US dollar amount, and the text string representing the converted Japanese yen amount, to work as slots in *WebApp*1. The operations produce the wrapper of *WebApp*1 that is, the currency conversion page. The user also specifies an input form for a company name, and the text string representing the retrieved stock quote, to work as slots in *WebApp*2. The operations produce the wrapper of *WebApp2* that is, the real-time stock quote page. Next, the user visually combines these wrapped Web applications together to compose a new integrated application that performs a composite function of *WebApp1* and *WebApp2*. The user connects the US dollar slot of *WebApp1* to the slot representing the current stock quote in *WebApp2* through drag-and-drop operations. The functions provided by *WebApp1* and *WebApp2* are combined to compose a single application. Users may also decompose the composition through drag-and-drop operations. Users require no programming expertise to wrap or combine Web applications, or to decompose composite ones.

IntelligentPad Architecture

IntelligentPad is a software architecture proposed by the second author in 1989 (Tanaka &

Imataki, 1989). In this section, we summarize its architecture. Further details of the IntelligentPad architecture are given in a book (Tanaka, 2003) by the same author.

IntelligentPad represents each component as a *pad*, (i.e., a sheet of paper on the screen). A pad can be pasted onto another pad to define both a physical containment relationship and a functional linkage between them. When pad P_1 is pasted onto pad P_2, the pad P_1 becomes a child of P_2, and P_2 becomes the parent of P_1 (Figure 2). No pad may have more than one parent pad. Pads can be pasted together to define various multimedia documents and application tools. Unless otherwise specified, composite pads are always decomposable and reeditable.

Each pad has both a standard user interface and a standard connection interface (Figure 2). The user interface of a pad has a card-like view on the screen and a standard set of operations

Table 1. *A summary of three standard messages*

Message	Summary
set *slotame value*	a child sets the specified value to its parent's slot
gimme *slotname*	a child requests its parent to return the value of its specified slot
update	a parent notifies its children that some slot value has been changed

Figure 2. *User interface and connection interface of pads. If a user pastes P_1 onto a slot of P_2, then the primary slot of P_1 is connected to the slot of P_2.*

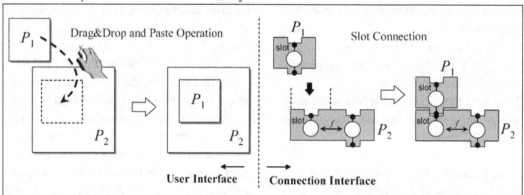

like "move," "resize," "copy," "paste," and "peel." Users can easily replicate any pad, paste a pad onto another, and peel a pad off a composite pad. Pads are decomposable persistent objects. You can easily decompose any composite pad by simply peeling off the primitive or composite pad from its parent pad. As its connection interface, each pad provides a list of slots that work as I/O ports and a single connection to a slot of its parent pad.

Each pad is pasted onto one parent, at most, with its connection to one of the parent pad slots. Connected pads form a tree structure. We do not restrict the maximum depth of the tree.

For application linkage between pads, IntelligentPad uses three standard messages, "set," "gimme," and "update." We show an outline of these three messages in Table 1.

A list of slots defines the application-linkage interface of each pad. Each slot can be accessed either by a set message: **set** *slotname value,* or by a gimme message: **gimme** *slotname.* Each of these two messages invokes the respective procedure attached to the slot. Each slot s_i may have two attached procedures, *set_proc_i* for the set message and *gimme_proc_i* for the gimme message. The default for *set_proc_i* stores the parameter value into the slot register, while the default for *gimme_proc_i* returns the slot register value; but more complex procedures can be created by programming, if wanted. The slots and attached procedures, set by the developer, define the internal mechanism of each pad. A pad that is a parent to one or more children can inform the children of changes to its own state by sending the **update** message (which has no arguments). The interpretation of the update message again depends on the implementation of the sender and the receiver pads. It is usually used to inform the child pads of a parent's state change.

Each pad has just one primary slot. When the value of the primary slot of a child is changed, the child sends a set message with the new slot value to its parents. Using this value, the parent changes its own slot values. Then, the parent notifies all of its children of its state change by sending an update message. Each child that has received an update message sends a gimme message to the parent pad, changes its own slot values using the return value of this gimme message, and then sends an update message to each of its children.

Figure 3. Three standard messages, 'set', 'gimme' and 'update', between pads

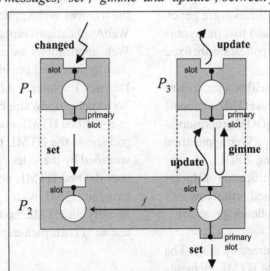

Figure 4. Wrapping of a Web application

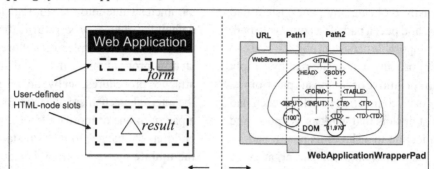

Using this mechanism, state changes are propagated from one pad to all the pads connected to it through slots (Figure 3).

Wrapping Web Applications

While researchers working on information extraction from the Web use the verb "to wrap" in the sense of extracting information from the target Web page, we use the same verb in the sense of defining data I/O ports to input and to output data to and from a Web application.

A Web application has an HTML-based front end for the user. We assume that HTML pages returned by the same Web application are generated by a common template, and that the syntax and the semantics in the Web application are fixed for some time interval.

Using the API of a legacy Web browser, such as Internet Explorer, we can access HTML elements in a document object model (DOM) representation of a Web page provided by a Web application (World Wide Web Consortium, 2003).

We adopt DOM-based identification of objects within HTML documents, as well as the browser's API to access them, for the following reasons:

1.   HTML DOM is standardized by W3C. The tag-specific interfaces of HTML elements interfaces are also standardized and legacy Web browsers implement the interface.

2.   The internal DOM representation of a Web page loaded by a Web browser corresponds to the view structure of the document rendered by the Web browser.

3.   A Web browser converts an ill-formed HTML into a well-formed HTML in an appropriate way when the browser constructs an internal DOM representation to render the Web page.

Figure 4 shows an abstract architecture of a general wrapper for Web applications. We call the wrapper WebApplicationWrapperPad. Using WebApplicationWrapperPads, users can wrap Web applications as a pad. Its rendering and parsing functions are implemented by wrapping Internet Explorer's API (Microsoft, 2006). A WebApplicationWrapperPad has the URL slot and user-defined HTML node slots. The view of this pad shows the HTML page at the URL address specified by the value of the URL slot. Through user-defined HTML node slots, other pads access the HTML nodes assigned to the slots. To identify an HTML node to assign to a slot, we use an HTML path expression.

HTML Paths

To identify an HTML node, we use an HTML path expression, which is a specialization of an XPath expression. We use the same notation for the locations steps as we use for the abbreviated form of XPath's location steps (World Wide Web Consortium, 1999).

An *HTML path* is a concatenation of node identifiers along a path from the root to the specified element. Each element identifier consists of a tag name and an index, *i*, where this node is the *i*th sibling that has the same tag name. We define the syntax of HTML paths as follows:

HTML-path ::=   *Step*
                        | *HTML-path* '/'*Step*
Step   ::=   *tagname*[*i*]
                        | @ *attribute-name*
                        | text(*regular-expression*)

The semantics of an HTML path is the same as the semantics of a location path in XPath expres-

sion. For example, TR[1] selects the TR element that is the first child of the context node, and TR[1]/TD[1] selects the first TD element of the first TR element of the context node. The general XPath expression syntax also includes predicate expression to handle the existence of children, and the values of attributes. For instance, the XPath expression, TD[./INPUT][5], selects the fifth TD element of the context node that has an INPUT element as its child, and the XPath expression, TD[@class="warning"][5], selects the fifth TD element of the context node that has a class attribute with the value "warning." The predicate expression is able to have any XPath expression within it. Therefore, for a given HTML element, *e*, there are infinitely many XPath expressions that select the element *e* (Figure 5). In order to generate an XPath expression that points to an HTML element, we have to choose an XPath expression from these infinitely many expressions. On the other hand, based on our definition of the HTML path expressions, there exists just one HTML path expression for a given HTML element *e*. There-

Figure 5. A set of XPath that point to a given HTML element

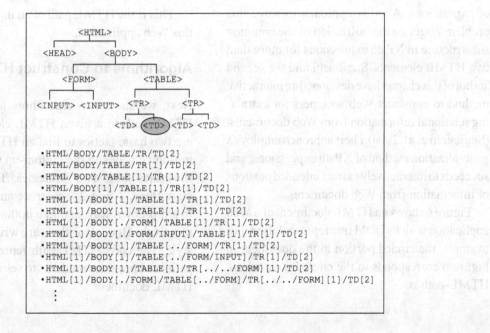

```
• HTML/BODY/TABLE/TR/TD[2]
• HTML/BODY/TABLE/TR[1]/TD[2]
• HTML/BODY/TABLE[1]/TR[1]/TD[2]
• HTML/BODY[1]/TABLE[1]/TR[1]/TD[2]
• HTML[1]/BODY[1]/TABLE[1]/TR[1]/TD[2]
• HTML[1]/BODY[1]/TABLE[1]/TR[1]/TD[2]
• HTML[1]/BODY[./FORM]/TABLE[1]/TR[1]/TD[2]
• HTML[1]/BODY[./FORM/INPUT]/TABLE[1]/TR[1]/TD[2]
• HTML[1]/BODY[1]/TABLE[../FORM]/TR[1]/TD[2]
• HTML[1]/BODY[1]/TABLE[../FORM/INPUT]/TR[1]/TD[2]
• HTML[1]/BODY[1]/TABLE[1]/TR[../../FORM][1]/TD[2]
• HTML[1]/BODY[./FORM]/TABLE[../FORM]/TR[../../FORM][1]/TD[2]
⋮
```

Figure 6. An HTML document with its DOM tree

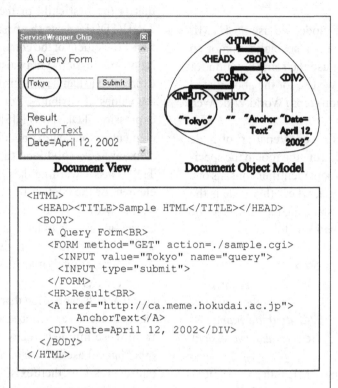

```
<HTML>
  <HEAD><TITLE>Sample HTML</TITLE></HEAD>
  <BODY>
    A Query Form<BR>
    <FORM method="GET" action=./sample.cgi>
      <INPUT value="Tokyo" name="query">
      <INPUT type="submit">
    </FORM>
    <HR>Result<BR>
    <A href="http://ca.meme.hokudai.ac.jp">
        AnchorText</A>
    <DIV>Date=April 12, 2002</DIV>
  </BODY>
</HTML>
```

fore, the restriction of the language to the HTML path gives a solution to the problem of choice of expressions. Another approach to solve this problem might be the utilization of the common substructure in XPath expressions for more than two HTML elements. Sugibuchi and the second author of this chapter have developed an interactive method to construct Web wrappers for extracting relational information from Web documents. (Sugibuchi et.al, 2004).Their approach employs a generalization method of XPath expressions, and succeeds to interactively extract intended portions of information from Web documents.

Figure 6 shows an HTML document of a Web application with its DOM tree representation. For example, the circled portion in the document in Figure 6 corresponds to the circled node whose HTML-path is:

HTML[1]/BODY[1]/FORM[1]/INPUT[1]

This is the HTML path of an input element of this Web application.

Algorithms to Construct HTML Paths

Next, we show two algorithms for finding an HTML path to a given HTML element. There are two basic tactics to find an HTML path, the top-down way and the bottom-up way. Figure 7 illustrates these two strategies. The following algorithms, 1 and 2, construct an HTML path in a top-down way, and in a bottom-up way, respectively. Both algorithms are written in the C# style. The class HTML path represents HTML paths and provides methods to select nodes in an HTML document.

In general, the bottom-up approach of algorithm 2 runs faster than the top-down approach of algorithm 1. However, due to the DOM implementation in the Internet Explorer 6.0, the bottom-up approach often constructs a wrong path. For this reason, we currently adopt the top-down approach in our implementation.

Evaluation of an HTML Path

The value identified by an HTML path:

HTML[1]/BODY[1]/A[1]/@href

is the string "http://ca.meme.hokudai.ac.jp".

```
Algorithm 1. Top-down Approach
public static HTMLPath TopDownSearch(IHTMLDOMNode from_node,
                                     IHTMLDOMNode target_node){
        HTMLPath path=null;
        Hashtable hash=new Hashtable();
        foreach(IHTMLDOMNode child in
                (IHTMLDOMChildrenCollection)from_node.childNodes){
                if(hash.ContainsKey(child.nodeName)){
                hash[child.nodeName]=((int)hash[child.nodeName])+1;
        }else{
                hash[child.nodeName]=1;
        }
        if(child==target_node){
                path=new HTMLPath();
                LocationStep step=
                new LocationStep("child",
                        child.nodeName,
                        (int)hash[child.nodeName]);
                path.Add(step);
                break;
        }else{
                if(child.nodeType==1){
                        path=TopDownSearch(child,target_node);
                        if(path!=null){
                                LocationStep step=
                                new LocationStep("child",
                                        child.nodeName,
                                        (int)hash[child.nodeName]);
                                path.Insert(0,step);
                                break;
                        }
                }
        }
}
        return path;
}
```

Figure 7. Top-down search and bottom-up search for the HTML-Path to a given element

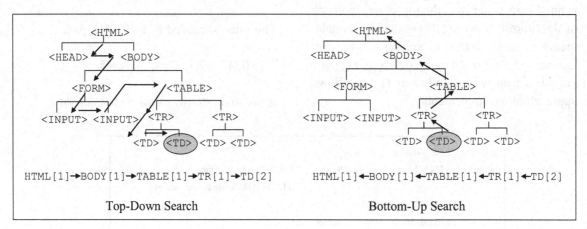

The step text (*regular-expression*) captures a substring of the inner text. This regular expression must contain just one pair of parentheses "(" and ")." This function allows us to extract and to edit the text within an HTML element flexibly.

We use this extension for the following reason: some Web applications use text-based legacy applications as their back ends. Objects within the Web pages returned by such Web applications may not be separated by HTML tags. They may use non-HTML delimiters, such as "=" or ":," to make objects separate. We found that many Web applications in bioinformatics use these kinds of delimiters.

Let e be an HTML element obtained by HTML path p. And let r_{left}, $r_{capture}$ and r_{right} be regular expressions. Then the text identified by the following expression: $p/\text{text}(r_{left} (r_{capture})r_{right})$,

```
Algorithm 2. Bottom-up Approach
public static HTMLPath BottomUpSearch(IHTMLDOMNode from_node,
                                IHTMLDOMNode target_node){
        HTMLPath path=null;
        if(from_node==target_node)
                return new HTMLPath();
        else{
                IHTMLDOMNode parent=ParentOf(target_node);
                int index=IndexOf(parent,target_node);
                path=BottomUpSearch(from_node,parent);
                if(path!=null){
                        LocationStep step=
                        new LocationStep("child", target_node.nodeName, index);
                        path.Add(step);
                }
        }
        return path;
}
```

is a substring s of the inner text of the element e, where s matches $r_{capture}$, s is followed by a string that matches $r_{left,}$ and the string that matches r_{right} is preceded by s. In Figure 6, for example, the text identified by "HTML[1]/BODY[1]/DIV[1]/text(Date=(.*),2002)" is the text "April 12."

Wrapping Web Applications

A Web application A is called a *single-page Web application*, if every result page returned by A contains an input-form for the next query for A. In other words, we can define slots for both input and output on a single page returned by a single-page Web application. Examples of single-page Web applications include Google Search Page, Quote. com & News, and Yahoo's Currency Exchange.

Using a WebApplicationWrapperPad, we may wrap a single-page Web application into a pad. Many Web applications return result pages that have exactly the same syntactic and semantic structure for different input queries. If this new page has the same structure as the previous page, we can evaluate a new query using the same HTML path.

A value change of a slot in a WebApplicationWrapperPad causes its view to update, and possibly changes the value of other slots. Set procedures of slots in a WebApplicationWrapperPad are defined as follows:

1. If the value of the URL slot is changed, then the WebApplicationWrapperPad downloads the page at the URL address and replaces the stored DOM representation with the new one.
2. If the user clicks an anchor or submits a form on the WebApplicationWrapperPad, then the wrapper pad downloads the target page and updates the stored DOM representation.
3. If the value of an HTML node slot is changed, then the WebApplicationWrapperPad changes the value of each node specified by the corresponding HTML path.

- If the HTML node slot is an input element contained in a form, the wrapper pad submits the form value to the appropriate Web server. The wrapper pad loads a new page obtained from the server and updates the stored DOM representation

4. Whenever the WebApplicationWrapperPad updates the stored DOM representation, it renders a new view according to the new DOM tree. The values of all the HTML node slots will be changed to the values of the corresponding nodes in the new DOM tree.

Many Web applications use more than one page to output and input data to and from users. For the wrapping of a Web application that uses more than one page for its input and output, we may extend an HTML path to a concatenation of a *navigation path* and an HTML path. A navigation path is a sequence of user operations. Examples of user operations include opening a page specified by a URL, clicking an anchor, and submitting some data to a form. Using a navigation path, we can represent how to access a Web page. Further details of wrapping multipage Web applications are given in Ito and Tanaka (2003b, 2003c).

User Interface for the Wrapping

To create a wrapped visual component of a Web application, users may just open the Web page they want to wrap using a WebApplicationWrapperPad, which is a kind of Web browser. The user can specify an HTML node or a text string to work as a slot on this pad.

To hide HTML paths from users, the system calculates HTML path expressions from users' operations. Users can directly specify any HTML node as a slot using a mouse.

There are two ways for users to specify an HTML node to work as a slot:

Figure 8. User interface for the slot

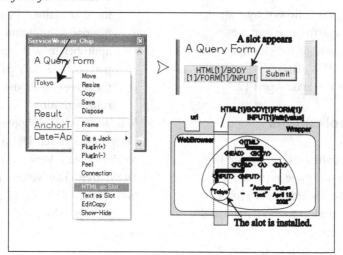

- Specify an HTML element to work as a slot.
- Specify a text portion to work as a slot.

If a user clicks the right mouse button at some region that he/she wants to specify to work as a slot, a pop-up menu will be shown (Figure 8).

Selecting "HTML as Slot" in the pop-up menu, the user can use the HTML element at this location as a slot. We use the following heuristics to find its HTML path.

Let p be the HTML path of the element.

1. If the element is a textinput element or textarea element in a form element, WebApplicationWrapperPad installs a slot named $p/@$value.
2. If the element is an anchor element, WebApplication-WrapperPad installs a slot named $p/@$href.
3. WebApplicationWrapperPad installs a slot named p, otherwise.

In Figure 8, the user selects a text input element to use as a text input slot. WebApplicationWrapperPad installs a slot named:

HTML[1]/BODY[1]/FORM[1]/INPUT[1]/@ value.

Selecting "Text as Slot" in the pop-up menu, the user can use the selected string as a slot. Let p be the HTML-path of the element e that contains the selected text portion. The WebApplicationWrapperPad installs a slot named with p/text(l (.*)r), where l and r are respectively a preceding substring and a following substring of the selected portion in e. A dialog box then appears to ask the user to confirm the two text strings l and r.

In Figure 9, a user creates a wrapper pad that wraps a currency conversion Web application. Firstly, the user may open the target page on a WebApplicationWrapperPad. Secondly, using his/her mouse, he/she may specify regions that he/she wants to work as slots. Then the slots will appear as sunken shaded regions on this page. The user may keep the background Web page visible, or make it invisible. Thirdly, the user may embed other pads, such as TextPads, into these slots. Finally, the user may arbitrarily relocate and resize the embedded pads to design their layout. If the user inputs some data to the TextPad embedded in the input-form slot, then the

WebApplicationWrapperPad will send this form value to the server. As a result, the text value of the TextPad embedded in the result text slot will get a new output text.

FUNCTIONAL LINKAGE AMONG WRAPPED WEB APPLICATIONS

Functional Linkage of Wrapped Web Applications Through view Integration

A pad that wraps a Web application provides slots for some of the original's input forms and output text strings. Since wrapped Web applications are pads, you may combine wrapped Web applications together through drag-and-drop operations.

Figure 10 shows a WebApplicationWrapperPad showing the Web page of a real-time stock-quote browsing service. We have wrapped this page, defining a slot for the current stock quote. Then we paste the wrapped currency conversion Web application with its dollar amount slot specified as its primary slot on this wrapped stock-price page. We connect the conversion pad to the newly

defined current stock-quote slot. The right-hand side in this figure shows a composite pad combining these two wrapped Web applications. For the input of different company names, we use the input form of the original Web page. Since this Web application uses the same page layout for different companies, the same path expression correctly identifies the current stock-quote information part for each different company. The current stock quote in US dollars is converted to Japanese yen by the wrapped currency conversion Web application.

Through data linkage between slots specified by a user, these wrapped Web applications cooperate with each other. Each wrapped Web application accesses its Web server to load Web pages (Figure 11). If a slot value of a wrapper changes into a new value, the new value is sent to its parent pad or children pads through the slot-connection mechanism of IntelligentPad architecture, which was shown in the previous section. Functional linkage between a wrapped Web application and wrapped non-Web legacy applications can be also easily defined through the same mechanism.

Figure 9. Defining a wrapper of a Web application through mouse operations

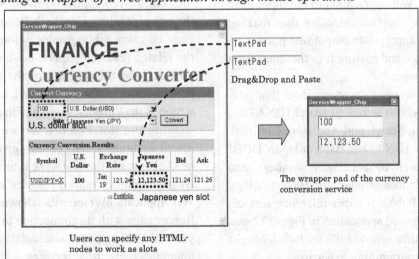

Figure 10. Dynamic linkage definition among visually wrapped Web applications

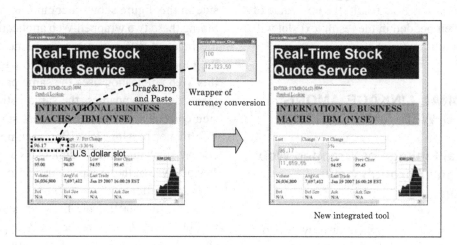

New integrated tool

A Practical Example

Our framework opens a new vista in the reuse of scientific knowledge. In bioinformatics, for example, there are already many different kinds of database services, analysis services, and related reference information services; some services may have been linked to each other using hyperlinks, but lots of related services have been left unlinked. They are hard to interoperate with each other. There is no way on the client side to connect the output of one Web application to the input form of another Web application, other than making a copy of the appropriate output text portion on the source page and pasting it in the input form of the target page.

Figure 12 shows a composite tool that integrates DDBJ's Blast homology search (DNA Data Bank of Japan, Search and Analysis), GenBank Report service (DNA Data Bank of Japan, DDBJ sequence search by accession number), and PubMed's (National Center for Biotechnology Information, PubMed) paper reference service. The new integrated application in Figure 12 was composed within several minutes by a biologist who has no programming expertise.

Blast service allows us to input a sample DNA sequence, and outputs genes with similar DNA sequences. The biologist has specified the input form and the accession number of the first candidate sequence to work as slots. The accession number works as an anchor linking to a GenBank Report Web page containing the detailed information about this gene. Its corresponding slot contains the URL to the target GenBank Report page. he/she has pasted a WebApplicationWrapperPad with its connection to this second slot. As a result, this child WebApplicationWrapperPad shows the corresponding GenBank Report page. This page contains bibliographic information about the related research papers. he/she has visually specified the title portion of the first research paper to work as a slot of this pad. he/she has also wrapped the PubMed service with its input form working as a slot. PubMed service returns a list of full documents that contains given keywords. he/she has made this slot work as the primary slot. By pasting this wrapped PubMed service on the WebApplicationWrapperPad showing a GenBank Report page with its connection to the title slot, you will obtain a composite tool that functionally integrates these three services.

Figure 11. Data linkage among different Web applications

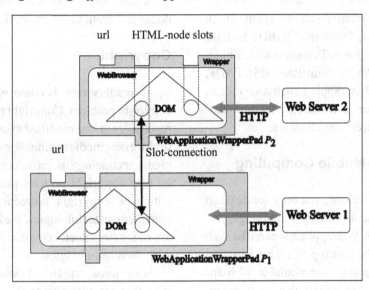

Figure 12. Dynamic gene annotation with visually wrapped Web applications. This was composed within several minutes by a biologist who has no programming expertise.

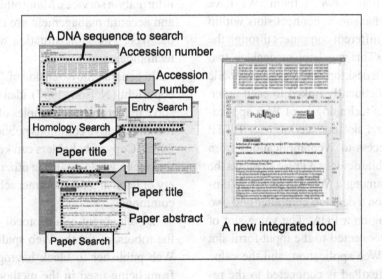

Data Format Conversion

There are Web applications that use different data formats or encodings for semantically equivalent data. Some readers may think that the difference in data format may cause a serious problem in our approach. However, a wrapped format-conversion service can be used as a filter, as long as such a Web application is provided by some provider. In the bioinformatics research area, such format conversion services are provided by many sites. For instance, READSEQ receives in formatted texts of amino-acid/nucleotide sequences and converts them into texts that have a different format. READSEQ has a WWW interface, and can handle more than a dozen sequence formats. These formats include IG, GenBank, NBRF, EMBL, GCG, DNAStrider, Fitch, Pearson/Fasta, Zuker, Olsen, Phylip3.2, Phylip, Plain/Raw, MSF, PAUP, PIR, and ASN.1. By wrapping such a service as a converter pad, users can combine Web applications that use different data formats.

Application to Mobile Computing

Our framework is suitable not only for desktop computing, but also for mobile computing.

Most of available Web applications on the Web are designed for the desktop PC. This situation causes difficulty in utilizing available Web applications on a mobile device with a small screen. The framework presented in this chapter allows users to wrap an existing Web application into a pad form. Once a Web application is wrapped as a pad, it can be combined with other pads through the slot connection between them. We have developed a mechanism to connect slots within pads running on different computers through the HTTP protocol. This mechanism enables two pads running on a desktop computer and mobile devices to be functionally linked to each other. A combination of technologies of Web application wrapping and slot connection over HTTP facilitates the access to Web applications from small-screen mobile devices. Figure 13 shows the slot connection among a WebApplicationWrapperPad running on a desktop computer and two TextPads running on a PDA. The value slot of one TextPad is connected to the input-form slot of the wrapped Web application, and the value slot of another TextPad is connected to the result-text slot of the WebApplicationWrapperPad defined by the user. If the user inputs some data to the TextPad running on the PDA, then the WebApplicationWrapperPad will send this form value to the server. As a result, the text value of the TextPad connected to the result-text slot will get a new output text according to the returned document from the Web application.

Copyright

Some readers may become worried about the copyright problem. Copyright policies have been reconsidered and modified every time people introduce new media technologies. Whenever a new media technology is introduced, the consensus on new copyright policies gradually coevolves with new copyright protection and/or license management technologies. We have been, and we are observing, such coevolution of new policies with Web technologies.

Some have established closed services on the Web that are exclusive to their members, while others have established a closed network, such as the I-mode cellular phone network in Japan by NTT DoCoMo, to implement a micropayment scheme for charging each access to the registered information services. Many other types of license and account management are currently tried on the Web. The same situation will occur for our technologies.

In general, the extension of T. Nelson's Transcopyright (Nelson, 1997) idea to the Web may solve this problem. Examples of such extensions include creative commons public license (Lessig, 2005). Copyright holders can keep their rights to the public while retaining others through a variety of licensing and contract schemes of creative commons.

Development of a protocol that is similar to the robots.txt for the Web spiders will enable a Web publisher to block having his/her service from being used in the method. The robots.txt protocol is a convention to prevent Web spiders from collecting the resources of Web sites. Implementation of such a protocol, and the statements indicating the disallowance of the reuse, will be able to avoid copyright violations.

Figure 13. Data linkage among Web applications and mobile devices

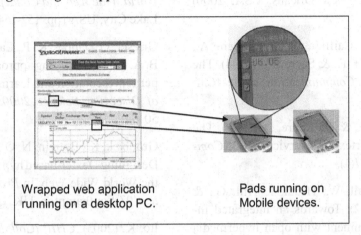

Wrapped web application running on a desktop PC.

Pads running on Mobile devices.

CONCLUSION

We have proposed a new framework for visually and dynamically defining functional linkages among Web applications to compose a single application tool. This framework is based on the IntelligentPad architecture. Users can visually and dynamically wrap Web applications into visual components, and visually combine them together to define functional linkages among them. Users can also visually define functional linkages among wrapped Web applications, and such local tools in pad forms as chart drawing tools and spreadsheet tools to compose a single integrated tool. We have focused on how instantaneously users can create wrappers of Web applications when the users need to reuse them with other applications. A prototype system can be downloaded from our Web site (Ito, 2003).

Our approach for wrapping and linking is also applicable to interactive applications that use standardized API. For example, we may wrap ActiveX components of Microsoft Windows as pads. An advantage of Web application wrapping is that most components that constitute a Web page are visible both to the user and to the system. A hypermedia system using open API can be also wrapped as pads with their hypertext functionalities.

For the support of users, we need to introduce checking and validation mechanisms to detect format-changes and exceptions in the Web application.

REFERENCES

Anderson, K. M., Taylor, R. N., & Whitehead, E. J. (2000). Chimera: Hypermedia for heterogeneous software development enviroments. *ACM Transactions on Information Systems,18*(3), 211-245.

Anupam, V., Freire, J., Kumar, B., & Lieuwen, D. F. (2000). Automating Web navigation with the WebVCR. In *Proceedings of WWW9, (Amsterdam, Netherlands, 2000), Computer Networks, 33*(1-6), 503-517.

Bauer, M., & Dengler, D. (1999). InfoBeans - Configuration of personalized information services. In *Proceedings of IUI'99*, (Los Angeles, USA, 1999) (pp.153-156).

Bauer, M., Dengler, D., & Paul, G. (2000). Instructible agents for Web mining. In *Proceed-*

ings of IUI2000, (New Orleans, USA, 2000) (pp. 21-28).

Berners-Lee, T., Cailliau, R., Luotonen, A., Henrik Nielsen, H. F., & Secret, A. (1994). The World-Wide Web. *Communications of the ACM, 37*(8), 76-82.

Carr, L., Hall, W., & De Roure, D. (1999). The evolution of hypertext link services. *ACM Computing Surveys, 31*(4).

Davis, H. C., Hall, W., Heath, I., Hill, G., & Wilkins, R. (1992). Towards an integrated information environment with open hypermedia systems. In *Proceedings of ECHT'92*, (Milan, Italy, 1992) (pp. 181-190).

Davis, H. C., Knight, S., & Hall, W. (1994). Light hypermedia link services: A study of third party application integration. In *Proceedings of ECHT'94*, (Edinburgh, UK, 1994) (pp. 41-50).

DNA Data Bank of Japan. *DDBJ sequence search by accession number.* Retrieved from http://getentry.ddbj.nig.ac.jp/getstart-e.html

DNA Data Bank of Japan. *Search and Analysis.* Retrieved from http://www.ddbj.nig.ac.jp/E-mail/homology.html

Freire, J., Kumar, B., & Lieuwen, D. (2001). Web-Views: Accessing personalized Web content and services. In *Proceedings of WWW2001*, (Hong Kong, China, 2001) (pp.576-586).

Fujima, J., Lunzer, A., Hornbæk, K., & Tanaka, Y. (2004). Clip, connect, clone: Combining application elements to build custom interfaces for information access. In *Proceedings of the 17ᵗʰ Annual ACM Symposium on User Interface Software and Technology*, Santa Fe, NM, October 24-27, 2004 (pp.175-184).

Golgher, P. B., Laender, A. H. F., da Silva, A. S., & Ribeiro-Neto, B. (2000). An example-based environment for wrapper generation. In *Proceedings of the 2ⁿᵈ International Workshop on The*

World Wide Web and Conceptual Modeling, Salt Lake City, USA (pp. 152-164).

Grieser, G., Jantke, K. P., Lange, S., & Thomas, B. A. (2000). Unifying approach to HTML wrapper representation and learning. In *Proceedings of Discovery Science 2000*, Kyoto, Japan (pp. 50-64).

Grønbæk, K., Bouvin, N. O., & Sloth, L. (1997). Designing Dexter-based hypermedia services for the World Wide Web. In *Proceedings of Hypertext'97*, Southampton, UK, (pp.146-156).

Ito, K. (2003). *CHIP (Collaborating Host-Independent Pads).* Retrieved from http://km.meme.hokudai.ac.jp/people/itok/CHIP

Ito, K., & Tanaka, Y. (2002). Visual wrapping and composition of Web applications for their interoperations. In *CDROM of WWW2002*, Honolulu, USA, Poster Tracks 64.

Ito, K., & Tanaka, Y. (2003a). Visual wrapping and functional linkage of Web applications. In *Proceedings of Workshop on Emerging Applications for Wireless and Mobile Access*, Budapest, Hungary.

Ito, K., & Tanaka, Y. (2003b). A visual environment for dynamic Web application composition. In *Proceedings of 14ᵗʰ ACM Conference on Hypertext and Hypermedia* (pp. 184-193).

Ito, K., & Tanaka, Y. (2003c). Web application wrapping by demonstration. In *Proceedings of the 13ᵗʰ European—Japanese Conference on Information Modelling and Knowledge Bases*, Kitakyushu, Japan.

Kistler, T., & Marais, H. (1998). WebL—A programming language for the Web. In Proceedings of WWW7, (Brisbane, Australia, 1998), *Computer Networks, 30*(1-7), 259-270.

Kushmerick, N. (2000). Wrapper induction: Efficiency and expressiveness. *Artificial Intelligence, 118*(1-2), 15-68.

Lessig, L. (2005). *Free culture: The nature and future of creativity.* Penguin.

Malcolm, K. C., Poltrock, S. E., & Schuler, D. (1991). Industrial strength hypermedia: Requirements for a large engineering enterprise. In *Proceedings of Hypertext'91*, San Antonio (pp. 13-24).

National Center for Biotechnology Information. *PubMed.* Retrieved from http://www.ncbi.nlm. nih.gov

Nelson, T. H. (1997). Transcopyright: A simple legal arrangement for sharing, re-use, and republication of copyrighted material on the net. In Proceedings of WWCA'97, (Tsukuba, Japan, 1997). *Lecture Notes in Computer Science, 1274,* 7-14.

Phelps, T. A., & Wilensky, R. (2000). Robust intradocument locations. In Proceedings of WWW9, (Amsterdam, Netherlands, 2000). *Computer Networks, 33*(1-6), 105-118.

Quote.com—Your source for financial markets quotes, charts, news and education. Retrieved from http://new.quote.com/

Sahuguet, A., & Azavant, F. (2001). Building intelligent Web applications using lightweight wrappers. *Data & Knowledge Engineering, 36*(3), 283-316.

Sugibuchi, T., Tanaka, Y. (2004). Integrated visualization framework for relational databases and Web resources. Intuitive Human Interfaces for Organizing and Accessing Intellectual Assets. *Lecture Notes in Computer Science, 3359,* 159-174

Tanaka, Y. (1996). Meme media and a World-wide meme pool. In *Proceedings of MM'96*, Boston, USA (pp. 175-186).

Tanaka, Y. (2003). *Meme media and meme market architectures: Knowledge media for editing,*

distributing, and managing intellectual resources. John Wiley & Sons.

Tanaka, Y., Fujima, J., & Sugibuchi, T. (2001). Meme media and meme pools for re-editing and redistributing intellectual assets. In *Proceedings of OHS-7/SC-3/AH-3,* Aarhus, Denmark. *Lecture Notes in Computer Science, 2266,* 28-46.

Tanaka, Y., & Imataki, T. (1989). IntelligentPad: A hypermedia system allowing functional compositions of active media objects through direct manipulations. In *Proceedings of IFIP'89*, San Francisco (pp. 541-546).

Tanaka Y, & Ito K. (2004b). Meme media architecture for the reediting and redistribution of Web resources. Flexible Query Answering Systems, FQAS 2004. *Lecture Notes in Computer Science, 3055,* 1-12

Tanaka Y, Ito K., & Kurosaki D. (2004a). Meme media architectures for re-editing and redistributing intellectual assets over the Web. *International Journal of Hum. Comput. Stud., 60*(4), 489-526.

Tanaka, Y., Nagasaki, A., Akaishi, M., & Noguchi, T. (1992). A synthetic media architecture for an object-oriented open platform. In *Proceedings of IFIP'92*, Madrid, Spain (pp. 104-110).

Wiil, U. K., & Leggett, J. J. (1996). The hyperdisco approach to open hypermedia systems. In *Proceedings of Hypertext'96*, Washington (pp.140-148).

Wiil, U. K., Nürnberg, P. J., & Leggett, J. J. (1999). Hypermedia research directions: An infrastructure perspective. *ACM Computing Surveys, 31*(4).

World Wide Web Consortium. (1999). *XML path language (XPath).* Retrieved from http://www. w3.org/TR/xpath

World Wide Web Consortium. (2000). *Simple object access protocol (SOAP)* 1.1. Retrieved from http://www.w3.org/TR/SOAP/

World Wide Web Consortium. (2003). *Document object model (DOM) level 2 HTML specification.* Retrieved from http://www.w3.org/DOM/

Yahoo Corporation. *Currency Conversion.* Retrieved from http://quote.yahoo.com/m3?u

Chapter XI
Symbolic Computation for DS–CDMA Code Acquisition Using First Order Logic

Ruo Ando
Keio University, Japan

Yoshiyasu Takefuji
Keio University, Japan

ABSTRACT

Code division multiple access (CDMA) is widely used because of its effectiveness to send multiple signal and confidentiality of career signal. We present a formulation of state-space problem of which solution is directed by redundant reasoning control method for semiheuristic and lightweight DS-CDMA code acquisition. The reasoning of the state-space problem provides us with the way to find a K bit synchronized sequence among K dephased sequences with less calculation cost, compared with serial search and matched filter. In this process, redundancy-restriction method, called weighting strategy, enhances the searching ability of FOL (first order logic) reasoning for the faster and lightweight code acquisition. The combination of weighting strategy and correlator enables us to achieve the peak-detection within K/3 times of calculating inner products and its measurement. Our system is evaluated by the reduced cost of proving state-space problem using weighting strategy and its robustness of using the proposal code acquisition framework. Experiment shows that the proposal method is robust if K/N sequences are grouped with N ranging from 3 to 5.

INTRODUCTION

Code division multiple access (CDMA) is widely used because of its effectiveness to send multiple

signals and confidentiality of career signal (Viterbi, 1979). Therefore, CDMA is an important technique for multimedia communication. Synchronization is an important task for telecommunication, especially for CDMA. In this chapter, we propose a symbolic computation for direct sequence CDMA code acquisition using FOL (first order logic) applying this puzzle:

"the billiard balls and balance scale puzzle"

There are N billiard balls, $N - 1$ of which are identical in weight. The remaining ball–the odd one–has a different weight. We are not informed whether it is heavier or lighter. We have a balance scale for weighting the balls. Can we find which ball is the odd ball in $N/4$ weightings, and also find out whether it is lighter or heavier than the others? In the proposal system, this puzzle is formulated as state-space problem, which is solved by automated reasoning with some resolution strategies.

Direct Sequence—Code Division Multiple Access (DS-CDMA)

Since 1990, as the usage of cellular phone has expanded, the market of wireless communication has been increased dramatically. Among many wireless communication systems, direct sequence code division multiple access is applied to represent low bandwidth wireless communication devices, such as cellular phones. In CDMA, all users send signals in the same bandwidth, simultaneously, with the unique code assigned to each terminal. Every user can coexist and transmit at the same time with smaller interface compared with TDMA and FDMA (Duel-Hallen, Holtzman, & Zvonar, 1995). This multiple-access system protects users from interference and jamming. These advantages are possible since the cross-correlations between the code of target user and one of the other users are small, while pseudonoise has a maximal value repeating itself every period. The receiver can decode information of each user when the code acquisition is completed, which means that we can detect the point where the correlation

between the received signal and unique code in each terminal has maximal value. The perfect synchronization is an important task in any sort of telecommunication. Particularly in CDMA, the unique sequence must be synchronized precisely to the received signal. Unless a maximal output from the correlator is not acquired, each user in CDMA system cannot get the information.

PN Sequence

As we discussed in the previous section, the pseudonoise plays an important role in the simultaneous usage of the same bandwidth. To achieve the immunity of interference, jamming, and radio multipath fading, the assigned code must have these properties:

- **Balance property:** Relative frequencies of 0 and 1 are each 1/2.
- **Run property:** Run lengths of zeros and ones are as expected in a Bernoulli sequence.
- **Shift property:** If the random sequence is shifted by any nonzero number of elements, the resulting sequence will have an equal number of agreements and disagreements with the original sequence. The m-sequence has the balance, run, and shift properties. The m sequences are almost ideal when viewed in terms of their autocorrelation function.

Proposed Method

In this chapter, we formulate the state-space problem for DS-CDMA code acquisition. Typical state space decides if a state is reachable from another state or finds the shortest path between two states. We begin with the initial state and apply a kind of transition axiom to pass from one solvable state to another. In our model, the solution of the problem provides the way of code acquisition of PN sequences, of which properties are the balance, run and shift property.

Figure 1. PN sequence

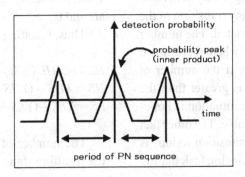

Formulation

In this chapter, we apply automated reasoning for the formulation of DS-CDMA code acquisition. From the beginning of the 1960s, automated reasoning has been improved with puzzles, mainly represented as state-space problem. The famous state-space problems that can be solved by automated reasoning method are "the checkerboard and dominoes puzzle," "the missionaries and cannibals puzzle," and "the billiard balls and balance scale puzzle." Among state-space problem, concerning DS-CDMA code acquisition, the billiard balls and balance scale puzzle is applied.

There are N billiard balls, N − 1, of which are identical in weight. The remaining bal   the odd on–has a different weight. We are not informed whether it is heavier or lighter. We have a balance scale for weighting the balls. Can we find which ball is the odd ball in N/4 weightings, and also find out whether it is lighter or heavier than the others?

The solution of this puzzle assumes that finding the odd ball, that is, detecting synchronized sequence, can be achieved in N/4 weightings.

Compared with serial search and matched filter (Mustapha & Ormondroyd, 1999), the proposal method based on this puzzle is lightweight. The key of formulation of the puzzle is that, from the properties of PN sequences discussed in section 1.2, the $N - 1$ sequences excluding the synchronized one could be represented as "the same weight." Owing to the shift property of *PN* sequences, the result of inner product calculation is not changed if we add some sequences that are not synchronized.

The notion of state is the point of this puzzle. The transition axioms to pass from one achievable state to the other one are used. According to this puzzle, the sequences are classified into "standard," "heavy or standard," "light or standard," or "heavy or light or standard." In the initial state, all N sequences are recognized as heavy or light or standard. And then, putting these conditions together, we can formulate the DS-CDMA code acquisition as follows:

There are N sequences, including synchronized sequence of which auto-correlation is −1 or 1. You are not told whether its correlation is 1 or −1. Can you find which sequence is the synchronized one in N/4 weightings, and also find out whether its class is "heavy or standard" or "light or standard"?

On the process of reasoning, many generated states are solvable, of which any transition of the state is not to lead goals, is deleted. The number of outcomes that can occur when there are n weightings remaining is 3^n. If the number of possibilities for the odd ball is greater than the number of outcomes, then the situation is hopeless; that is, the state is unsolvable. The other fact necessary for applying the transition axiom is there are three cases after balancing (calculating inner product).

Let the sequences in initial state that is heavy or light or standard be XHLS, the sequences picked up for multiplier YHLS, the sequences picked up for multiplicand ZHLS, and let the number of users be M.

Case 1: "scale balanced" with inner product around N/M. All the sequences calculated are standard weight (unsynchronized).

Thus, resulting state is:

$$HLS = XHLS - (YHLS + ZHLS)$$
$$HS = XHS - (YHS + ZHS)$$
$$LS = XLS - (YLS + ZLS)$$

The number of standard class sequences in the resulting state:

$$S = XS + YHLS + ZHLS*YHS + ZHS + YLS + ZLS$$

Case 2: "scale tips left" with inner product around $-N/M$. Thus, resulting state is:

$$HLS = XHLS = 0$$
$$HS = XHS - (YHS + ZHS)$$
$$LS = XLS - (YLS + ZLS)$$

The number of standard class sequences in the resulting state:

$$S = XS + ZLS + YHS + (XHLS - YHLS - ZHLS)$$
$$+ (XHS - YHS - ZHS) + (XLS - YLS - ZLS)$$

Case 3: "scale tips right" with inner product around 0.

Thus, resulting state is:

$$HLS = XHLS = 0$$
$$HS = XHS - (YHS + ZHS)$$
$$LS = XLS - (YLS + ZLS)$$

The number of standard class sequences in the resulting state:

$$S = XS + ZLS + YHS + (XHLS - YHLS - ZHLS)$$
$$+ (XHS - YHS - ZHS) + (XLS - YLS - ZLS)$$

We apply the inference rule of hyperresolution as the approach for the reasoning program to know that this problem has been solved. Also, we choose the set of support strategy discussed in the following section. The clauses placed in the set of support are the clauses that give the initial state and the one that denies that the initial state is solvable. The state with which the initial state is generated a proof by contradiction is found is three. In one, no weightings remain, $N - 1$ of billiard balls are known to be of standard weight, and one belongs to HS class. A second state is the counterpart to this one but with the Nth ball known to be in LS class. A final state is that all N sequences are known to be of standard weight, which means this puzzle is not solvable. In the process of resolution, the third process turns out be useful although in this state, the problem is incorrectly given.

ATP STRATEGY

On the usage of OTTER, the automated reasoning program, a strategy is available to prevent the reasoning program from wandering through the examination of various combinations of facts, the vast number of paths of inquiry. There exist some categories of strategies in OTTER, ordering strategy, restriction strategy, and pruning strategy. Without these directions, the program would seldom reach the solution generating too many resolutions and clauses, even for the simplest problems.

Set of Support Strategy

Set of support was introduced by Wos et al. (Wos, Robinson, & Carson, 1965). If the clause T is retrieved from S, SOS is possible with the satisfiability of $S - T$. Set of support strategy enables the researcher to select one clause characterizing the searching to be placed in the initializing list called SOS. For the searching to be feasible and more effective, the resolution of more than one clause not in SOS is inhibited in order to prevent the prover going into an abundant searching place. Figure 2 shows the resolution process in set of support strategy, where $S = \{P$ and Q and R, P and R, Q and R, $R\}$. The restriction imposes the reasoning so that the program does not apply an inference rule to a set of clauses that are not the complement of set of support.

Figure 2. Set of support

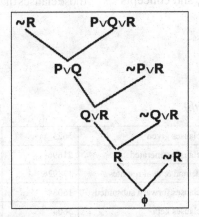

Hyperresolution

In *generating encoder*, we apply the inference rule called *hyperresolution*, which is a kind of resolution that can do resolutions at once compared with several steps in another rule. For hyperresolution (Wos, 1998), these must be the negative or mixed clause with the remaining clauses equal to the number of literals in the negative or mixed clause. Figure 3 shows the framework of hyperresolution. The positive clause is described as satellites, the negative clause nucleus. "Hyper" means that in this resolution more process has occurred than another resolution such as binary resolution.

In this chapter, we utilize the open source software organized techniques for theorem proving and effective research (OTTER). OTTER is a first order logic prover, of which statements written in prolog-style format with equality featuring the inference rules binary resolution, hyperresolution, and binary paramodulation. This prover has autonomous mode where the user inputs a set of clauses that OTTER does a syntactic analysis. OTTER 3.3 was released on August 2003, similar to

Figure 3. Hyperresolution

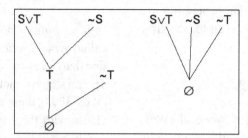

AURA and LMA/ITP theorem provers associated with Argonne National Laboratory. The problem in this chapter originated from "the billiard balls and balance scale puzzle" is solved on OTTER with formulation for CDMA code acquisition. In the next section, we discuss the statistics and CPU utilization of the process of proof.

Weighting Strategy

In contrast to the restriction strategies, which block reasoning path to apply inference rules to many kinds of subsets of clauses, a direction (ordering) strategy dictates what to set focus on next. Among these strategies, we apply weighting strategy. With this direction strategy, we can assign priorities to terms, clauses, and concepts

that make it possible to reflect the knowledge and intuition about how a reasoning program should proceed. Weighting strategy, opposite of the restriction strategy called set of support, can be used complementarily. In the situation where the set of support strategy is adopted, the remaining clauses can be processed to complete the application of various inference rules. After the clauses assigned to set of support have been the focus of attention, we can choose among the new clauses generated and retained for the following various kinds of inference application. With weighting, you can supply various criteria for defining interests and for defining complex information. After the input clauses have been the focus of attention, the choice is made from among the new clauses, those clauses that have been generated and retained

Table 1. 16 sequences (16 bit length)

clauses given	5625
clauses generated	21696
demod & eval rewrites	178926
clauses forward subsumed	16084
clauses kept	5604
empty clauses	16
user CPU time	109.23
system CPU time	.33

because they represent new information that is deemed acceptable.

NUMERIC RESULT

Evaluation of Weighting Strategy

The performance measurements were collected on a Linux kernel 2.4.8-13 host computer system using Pentium III 700 MHz with 512K RAM.

In contrast to the restriction strategies, which block a reasoning path to apply an inference rules to many kinds of subsets of clauses, a direction (ordering) strategy dictates what to set focus on next. Among these strategies, we apply weighting strategy. With this direction strategy, we can assign priorities to terms, clauses, and concepts that make it possible to reflect the knowledge and intuition about how a reasoning program should proceed. Weighting strategy, opposite to the restriction strategy called set of support, can be used complementarily. In the situation where the set of support strategy is adopted, the remaining clauses can be processed to complete the application of various inference rules. After the clauses assigned to set of support have been the focus of attention, we can choose among the new clauses generated and retained for the following various kinds of inference application. With weighting, you can supply various criteria for defining interests and for defining complex information. After the input clauses have been the focus of attention, the choice is made from among the new clauses,

Table 2. 32 sequences (32 bit length)

clauses given	1773
clauses generated	69478
demod & eval rewrites	573078
clauses forward subsumed	51692
clauses kept	17772
empty clauses	28
user CPU time	1709.7
system CPU time	1.75

Table 3. 12 sequences (12 bit length)

clauses given	153
clauses generated	444
demod & eval rewrites	3630
clauses forward subsumed	288
clauses kept	152
empty clauses	8
user CPU time	14.7
system CPU time	0.02

Table 4. 16 sequences (12-bit length) with weighting

clauses given	148
clauses generated	432
demod & eval rewrites	3531
clauses forward subsumed	280
clauses kept	147
empty clauses	8
user CPU time	14.36
system CPU time	0.02

Figure 4. 3 user CDMA model

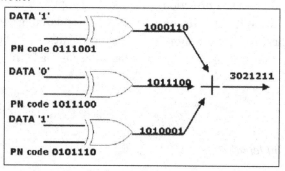

those clauses that have been generated and retained because they represent new information that is deemed acceptable.

Table 1 and 2 show the results of solving problems with each 16 and 32 sequences. It does not show liner increase, which means some kinds of resolution strategy is necessary according to the kind of PN sequences.

Table 3 and 4 shows the result of solving the problem with 12-bit sequences. In Table 4, weighting strategy is enabled. Experiments show that weighting is effective to reduce redundant clause generation, for faster problem solving.

Results of Inner Products Calculation

As we discussed before, the proposal system provides the cost reduction of DS-CDMA code acquisition. In our model, we can find the synchronized PN sequence among N sequences in N/K (K = 2, 3, 4) times of inner product calculation. In the experiment, we pick up 128-bit PN sequences and 3 user models shown in Figure 4. To make this technique more lightweight, we grouped 4 and 8 sequences. According to the properties of PN sequences discussed in previously, it is expected that detection probability is not changed if several 0/1 sequences are added to one.

Table 5 lists the inner product of each user. In this 3-user model, the value 40 is set as threshold. Experiments show that the proposal method is effective because the average of inner product is around 40. However, several values are over 40 in table 5 (8 sequences * 16 uses). Table 6 lists the result in 4 sequences*32 users. It is expected to be better that we group more than 32 groups by adding each 4 sequences.

Table 5. 16 groups of 8 users

	USER1	USER2	USER3
Synchronized (including peak)	-44	-52	-36
Another (average)	18.7	19.87	17.73

Table 6. 32 groups of 4 users

	USER1	USER2	USER3
Synchronized (including peak)	-78	-46	-70
Another (average)	9.29	7.8	11.8

To put all things together, the proposal method can acquire the code of N sequences in where T is times of calculating inner product; L is the number of groups.

CONCLUSION

We have presented the formulation of state-space problem of which solution is directed by redundant reasoning control method for the heuristic and lightweight DS-CDMA code acquisition. The reasoning of the state-space problem provides us with the way to find a K-bit synchronized sequence among K-dephased sequences with less calculation cost compared with serial search and matched filter. In this process, redundancy restriction method, called weighting strategy, enhances the searching ability of first order logic (FOL) reasoning for the faster and lightweight code acquisition. The combination of weighting strategy and correlator enables us to achieve the peak-detection within $K/3$ times of calculating inner products and its measurement. Our system is evaluated by the reduced cost of proving state-space problem using weighting strategy and its robustness of using the proposal code acquisition framework. Experiment shows that the proposal method is robust if K/N sequences are grouped with N ranging from 3 to 5.

REFERENCE

Duel-Hallen, A., Holtzman, J., & Zvonar, Z. (1995). Advantages of CDMA and spread spectrum techniques over FDMA and TDMA in cellular mobile radio applications. *IEEE Personal Communications Magazine*

Gilhousen, K., Jacobs, I., Padovani, R., Viterbi, A., Weaver, L., & Wheatley, C. (1995). On the capacity of a cellular CDMA system. *IEEE Trans. on Vehicular Technology Multiuser detection for CDMA systems.*

Jung, P., Baier, P., & Steil, A. (1992). *IEEE Trans. on Vehicular Technology.*

Keshavarzian, A., & Salehi, J. A. (2002). Optical orthogonal code acquisition in fiber-optic CDMA systems via the simple serial-search method. *IEEE Transaction on Communications, 50*(3).

Kohno, R., Meidan, R., & Milstein, L. (1995). Spread spectrum access methods for wireless communications. *IEEE Communication Magazine.*

Mustapha, M. M., & Ormondroyd, R. F. (1999). Performance of a serial-search synchronizer for fiber-based optical CDMA system in the presence of multi-user interference. *Proc.SPIE, 3899,* 297-306.

Mustapha, M. M., & Ormondroyd, R. F. (2000). Dual-threshold sequential detection code synchronization for an optical CDMA network in the presence if multi-user interference. *IEEE J.Lightwave Technol, 18,* 1742-1748.

Viterbi, A. J. (1979). Spread spectrum communications—myths and realities. *IEEE Communication Magazine.*

Wos, L. (1998). The problem of explaining the disparate performance of hyperresolution and paramodulation. *J. Autom. Reasoning, 4*(2), 215-219.

Wos, L., Robinson, G., & Carson, D. (1965). Efficiency and completeness of the set of support strategy in theorem proving. *J. ACM,* 536-541.

Chapter XII
Device Driver Based Computer in Broadband Age

Yoshiyasu Takefuji
Keio University, Japan

Koichiro Shoji
SciencePark Corporation, Japan

Takashi Nozaki
SciencePark Corporation, Japan

ABSTRACT

In this chapter, we present a device-driver-based computer that realizes the reduction of mode (domain or vertical) switching overheads between user and kernel mode with innovative attributes, including shared keyboards and mice, access-controlled files, and timed files. Experimented results show that old personal computers can revive again with the proposed Driverware technology. The proposed Driverware can improve the CPU resource utilization by three times.

BACKGROUND

On April 19, 1965, Moore predicted that the number of transistors per integrated circuit would double every 18 months (Moore, 2001). Ruley showed that the speed of CPU has been double every 18 months (Ruley, 2001). Although the recent progress of semiconductor technology has been providing us over 2 GHz (gigahertz) CPU

devices, you may not be able to obtain such dramatic improvements with your personal computer because you do not sense the high-speed CPU devices. In existing popular operating systems, including Microsoft Windows, Macintosh, Linux, and FreeBSD, your user software programs do not maximize the performance of such a high-speed CPU and other resources. In this chapter, a device driver-based computer is proposed, where the "Driverware" software program plays a key role. "Driverware" allows you to dramatically improve user software programs in your personal computer without replacing the current operating system. The technical aspects of the root of all evil that waste your CPU resources in user software programs are caused by device driver programs. A device driver is a software program to control a hardware component or peripheral device of a computer, such as a hard disk, a CD/DVD player, a network device, a mouse, keyboard, a video card, and so on. Driverware provides the current operating system a thin layer closest to the hardware layer, where communications and controls among device drivers can be established. Overheads involved in device drivers are significantly reduced by the driver-to-driver communications and controls. When playing a CD/DVD audio/video player or a network video stream on your GHz CPU-based personal computer in the broadband network, you may still face frame drop or abrupt audio skips if you do Web browsing simultaneously. Four device drivers, including a network device driver, a video device driver, audio device driver, and a display device driver, are involved in this network video stream processing. If the priority of network device driver is lower than that of the other drivers, you may face the frame drop. If four device drivers are properly balanced and their priorities are taken care of, then you will be satisfied with the current network video stream without using a special hardware such as a network video stream receiver. Driverware allows device drivers to communicate each other, and to efficiently control computer resources in order to reduce overheads involved in device drivers. Frame drops and abrupt audio skips are minimized by the proposed Driverware. Until the advent of Driverware, there has been no general-purpose device-driver-based computer. The key element of Driverware is based on distributed delegation of authority, while conventional user programs are based on the centralized control. In user programs, overheads are caused by unnecessary

thread* switching in a process, context (horizontal) switching between processes, and mode (domain or vertical) switching between kernel and user mode. The proposed Driverware contributes to reduce the mode-switching overheads. We have measured the mode-switching overheads involved in device drivers for the first time in the world. Based on the measured result, your old personal computers in the garage can revive again.

The framework for minimizing overheads of vertical and horizontal switching was proposed in 1994 (Inohara & Masuda, 1994). Horizontal switching problems in user mode were discussed in Borg (2001). Ousterhout has measured the mode and context-switching overheads in RISC/CISC machines under the Unix operating system in 1990 (Ousterhout, 1990). In 1996, Lai and his colleagues measured the mode and context-switching overheads in Intel x86-based machines under Linux/FreeBSD/Solaris operating systems, respectively (Lai & Baker, 1996). Based on the existing results, reducing the context-switching overheads plays a key role in overall system performance, where the context switching overhead is larger than the mode-switching overhead by 10 times. Ultimately optimized context-switching operating system, RT-Linux has been introduced (Ramamritham & Stankovic, 1994; Zhou & Petrov, 2006). Based on the context-switching overhead reduction, TUX Threaded Linux Web server (Bar, 2000)), and other Web servers have shown the high performance, respectively (Quynh & Takefuji, 2006).

In the real world, the majority of users use Microsoft operating systems for personal use (Sun, Lin, & Wu, 2006). Based on our study, the mode-switching overhead reduction is more important than the context-switching overhead reduction under Microsoft operating systems. Figure 1 shows the table of the mode-switching and context-switching overheads, where more than 2 months were used for switching overhead measurement. In Windows 2000 operating system (Microsoft, 2006), 7.4 microseconds are required per the mode-switching overhead with a Celeron 800MHz CPU. For mode-switching measurement, 10 million integer additive operations were experimented under Windows 2000, Linux, and FreeBSD respectively.

The relationship between waste resource rate vs. ftp-network transfer speed, as shown in Figure 2, indicates how much your CPU resources are not used for your applications. Figure 2 shows that,

Figure 1. Mode-switching and context-switching overheads

Switching Time:					unit: microsecond
	Mode Switching		Context Switching		
Windows 2000 (Professional)	7.4	Celeron 800MHz	7.10	*7 Pentium III 500MHz	
Linux (RedHat 7.2)	0.25	Celeron 800MHz	1.56	* Celeron 800MHz	
FreeBSD (4.5R)	0.48	Celeron 800MHz	2.40	* Celeron 800MHz	
			*7 John D. Regehr, * measured by lmbench 2.0		

Figure 2. Waste resource rate vs. transfer speed

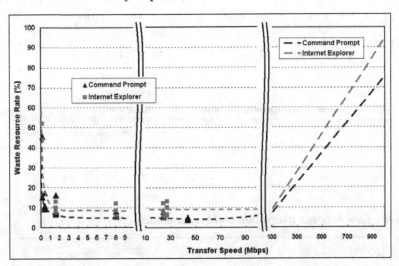

Figure 3. File transfer speed comparison

Load	Program	ftp processor time (%)	Transfer speed (MB/sec)	Estimated transfer speed with cpu full processing (MB/sec)
on	DriverWare	21.9	5.629	25.650
	ftp.exe	37.0	3.173	8.566
off	DriverWare	21.3	5.916	27.797
	ftp.exe	89.5	8.261	9.230

A thread is one part of a larger program that can be executed independent of the whole (ComputerUser, 2006).

from 0 Mbps to 1 Mbps, the waste resource rate increases along with less transfer speed. From 1 Mbps to 100 Mbps it is almost flat and from 100 Mbps to 1 Gbps it increases with transfer speed. For example, you will waste 92 % of CPU resources in 1 gigabit-per-second transfer speed using the Internet Explorer. In other words, only 8% can be used for your applications. We assume that 100% CPU resources are used only for ftp process in our measurement. Figure 3 shows file transfer speed comparison between the normal ftp program and the Driverware ftp program. It indicates that CPU utilization is improved by about three times. In this chapter, the mode-switching overhead reduction is detailed.

Figure 4. Processing time flow between user and kernel mode

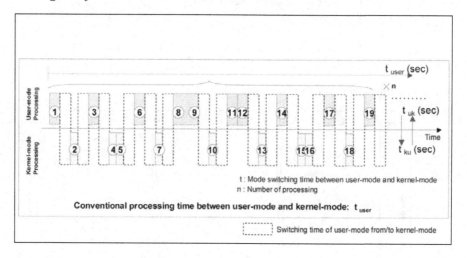

Figure 5. Sequence flow between user mode and kernel mode

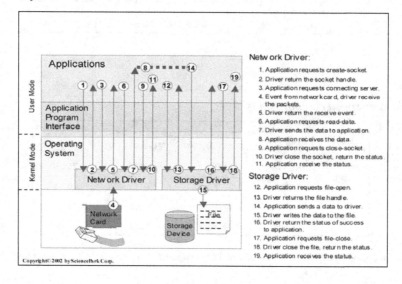

What is Going on in your Centralized Control User Programs?

In your personal computer, the system is composed of hardware (keyboard, mouse, hard disk, CPU board, network card, LCD display, and so on), operating system, and user application programs. Unless you buy a special hardware device, conventional user application programs based on the centralized control generate mode-switching overheads between user and kernel mode. For example, in the network device driver, when the user application program requests open socket, the mode switching from user to kernel mode is needed to complete the task. Centralized-control user programs inherently have a disadvantage of mode-switching overheads between user and kernel mode. All operations involved in network and storage device driver are shown in Figure 4 and Figure 5. Figure 4 shows that the total mode-switching overheads, surrounded by broken lines, are equivalent to the total waste of CPU resources. Eleven operations are involved in network device driver and eight operations in storage device driver. Fourteen operations (O1, O2, O3, O5, O6,

O7, O9, O10, O12, O13, O14, O16, O17, O18) out of nineteen operations must cross the user-kernel boundary, which causes fundamental mode (domain or vertical) switching overheads. When you do browsing over the Internet, you would like to download some files. The operation sequence flow is as follows:

When clicking the downloadable file using a Web browser (O1), the browser requests data acquisition to the network device driver after setting Web server address and port number (O1 and O2). Web server establishes the connection and sends the requested file. Network card returns the data-receive event to the network driver (O4). The network driver returns the receive event to the Web browser (O5). Web browser receives the data (O6, O7, and O8). Web browser displays the dialog window to specify the directory for saving the downloadable file and user must input the file name (O12 and O13). Download progress bar is displayed and the file downloading will be completed (O14-O19).

As shown in Figure 4 and Figure 5, a sequence flow is described where 14 operations must transit from user mode to kernel mode or vice versa. The

Figure 6. Driverware solution to operations as shown in Figure 5

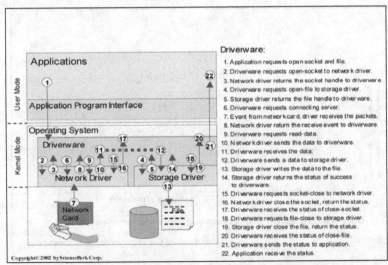

mode-switching time t_{uk} from user mode to kernel mode and t_{ku} from kernel mode to user mode are consumed as waste of CPU resources. The total computation time of the typical user application program user is composed of user processing time, kernel processing time, accumulated switching time from user mode to kernel mode, and accumulated switching time from kernel mode to user mode.

Device Driver-Based Computing

Device driver-based computing is based on Driverware where the operations of driver-driver communications and controls are achieved. Figure 6 shows the device-driver-based computing where most mode-switching overheads are reduced. Fourteen operations that cross the user-kernel boundary are reduced into two operations in Driverware. The overhead reduction is achieved by enabling driver-driver communications and controls in the kernel mode. Until now, there has been no general purpose distributed-control solution by reducing mode, vertical, or domain-switching

overheads between user and kernel mode. Vertical or mode-switching overheads can be reduced by the distributed delegation of authority.

Between several device drivers, security controls can be established within Driverware where several new attributes are generated as a by-product. A file in Driverware is called access-controlled file. For example, as soon as a user without access permission touches or reads the access controlled file, immediately the user's keyboard will be locked. Another new attributed file is called timed file in Driverware, like a tape in the "mission impossible" movie where it will disappear within a certain specified period of time without user's intention. Driverware allows every device driver to have a state sense operation and an action operation against any computing resources.

CONCLUSION

Device driver-based computer is proposed in this chapter, where mode (domain or vertical)

Figure 7. A processing time flow by Driverware solution

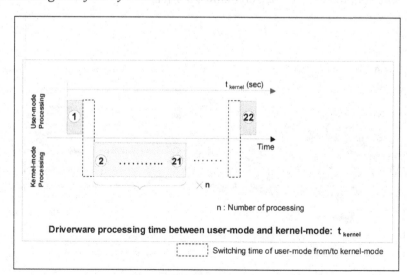

switching overheads between user and kernel mode are dramatically reduced, and every computer resource will have new attributes, including shared keyboards and mice, access controlled files, and timed files like mission impossible files tape. Experimented results show that old personal computers can revive again with the proposed Driverware technology. The proposed Driverware can improve the CPU resource utilization by three times.

ACKNOWLEDGMENT

We thank Tomoyuki Kawade, Hideaki Miura, and Jianping Wei for their many helpful comments and experiments of device driver benchmarking. Part of this research is supported by Department of the Air Force through a special contract (Takefuji, 2003; Takefuji, 2005).

REFERENCES

Bar, M. (2000). Kernel korner. *The Linux Process Model. Linux Journal, 71*(24).

Borg, A. (2001). *Avoiding blocking system calls in a user-level thread scheduler for shared memory multiprocessors*. Dissertation of Univ. Malta, June 2001.

ComputerUser. (2006). Thread. *ComputerUser high-tech dictionary*. Retrieved December 30, 2006, from http://www.computeruser.com/resources/dictionary/definition.html?lookup=8392

Inohara, S., & Masuda, T. (1994). A framework for minimizing thread management overhead based on asynchronous cooperation between user and kernel schedulers. *TR94-02, University of Tokyo*.

Lai, K., & Baker, M. (1996). A performance comparison of UNIX operating systems on the Pentium. *Proceedings of the USENIX 1996 Annual Technical Conference.*

Microsoft. (2006). Windows 2000. *Microsoft Windows 2000*. Retrieved December 30, 2006, from http://www.microsoft.com/windows2000/default.mspx

Moore, G. E. (2001). Cramming more components onto integrated circuits. *Electronics, 38*(8).

Ousterhout, J. K. (1990). Why aren't operation systems getting faster as fast as hardware? *USENIX Summer Conference, June 11-15, 1990.*

Ramamritham, K., & Stankovic, J. (1994). Scheduling algorithms and operating systems support for real-time systems. *Proceedings of IEEE, 8*(21), 55-67.

Regehr, J. D. (2001). *Using hierarchical scheduling to support soft real-time applications in general-purpose operating systems*. Dissertation of Univ. of Virginia, 2001.

Ruley, J. D. (2001). The future of Moore's law, Part 1. Retrieved June 25, 2001, from http://www.byte.com

Sun, H. M., Lin, Y. H., & Wu, M. F. (2006). API monitoring system for defeating worms and exploits in MS-Windows system. *Proceedings of Information Security and Privacy, Lecture Notes in Computer Science, 4058*, 159-170.

Takefuji, Y. (2003). Technical report of DRIVERWARE IMMUNE. *US Air Force Office of Scientific Research with Grant Number AOARD 03-4049*

Takefuji, Y. (2005). Nullification of unknown malicious code execution with buffer overflows. Driverware IMMUNE – Final Report. Technical report of DRIVERWARE IMMUNE, *US Air Force Office of Scientific Research with Grant Number AOARD 03-4049.*

Quynh, A. N., & Takefuji, Y. (2006). Towards an invisible honeypot monitoring system. *Proceed-*

ings of Information Security and Privacy, Lecture Notes in Computer Science, 4058, 111-122.

Zhou, X., & Petrov, P. (20 control applications. In *Proceedings of the 43rd annual conference on Design automation* (pp.352-257).

Section III
Surveys

Chapter XIII
Cultivating Communities Through the Knowledge Commons:
The Case of Open Content Licenses

Natalie Pang
Monash University, Australia

ABSTRACT

In recent years, impacts of information and communication technologies, market enclosures, and the struggle to retain public goods have had significant impacts on the nature of interactions of communities. This chapter examines communities in the context of the knowledge commons–a space by which "a particular type of freedom" (Benkler, 2004) can be practised. It is also an appropriate concept applied to the discussion of communities and the ways they work. As Castells (2003) noted, self-knowledge "is always a construction no matter how much it feels like a discovery," and this construction is enabled when people work, or associate themselves with each other. In particular, the chapter is concerned about the structure of open content licenses operating within such domains. The chapter first explores the concept of the knowledge commons to understand the types of intellectual property that are distinctive to communities (public, communal, and private). Thereafter, licenses, as a structure, are examined as they may apply within such contexts. A significant influence on the discussion is the contemporary media environment operating in today resulting in the breaking down of boundaries, the blurring of distinctions between an original and a copy, and shifting the nature of production in communities. These debates lead to a case for open content licenses as appropriate structural mechanisms for communities.

INTRODUCTION

A struggle is emerging in the world, as highlighted by Slater (2005). It is a struggle to produce and protect what is referred to as the knowledge commons, a space and vicinity of "common" goods produced by communities of people. The idea of a commons is not new; it has been around since the first human cooperation and collective action. Men hunting together for food, sharing and complementing their skills and produce for their villages; the commons is rooted in communities of social trust and cooperation (Bollier, 2004). Originating from the historical commons, the commons, as defined by Benkler (2003), generally are "institutional spaces, in which we can practice a particular type of freedom—freedom from the constraints we normally accept as necessary preconditions to functional markets." Moritz (2004) defines the knowledge commons as "zones of free and equitable use for data, information and knowledge," consisting of physical, logical, and content layers of resources (Bollier, 2004).

Almost at the same time, the knowledge commons can be thought of as a form of defiance against contemporary organisations of enclosures around knowledge and informational goods. It is certainly so, and before the issues of copyrights and open content licenses can be discussed, it is necessary to first understand the motivations of the communities who create, defend, and are sustained by the very same knowledge resources.

The Romans in the ancient ages identified three types of property (Diegeser, 2003): *res privatæ*, res *publicæ,* and *res communes*. Res privatæ identified property that is possessed by an individual, family, or a company. The second type of property is associated with things that are used by the state, and these are commonly seen today as public parks, roads, and buildings. The last type of property, *res communes*, recognized resources that are common to all, such as resources in the natural world (e.g., water and air).

The knowledge commons, as it exists and referred to in this chapter associates itself with the last type of property. Generally referred to as the public domain today, property that exists in this space is distinct from things in the private sphere, though this chapter asserts a further distinction between the public and the commons domains. Copyright, as it was first conceptualized, was intended to benefit creators, while at the same time

ensuring a healthy level of works to be available publicly. Copyright, as a system of checks and balances, maintains such protection and circulation. This chapter argues that technological changes and fundamental shifts in the media environment of today call for an alternative mechanism to copyright. Though the boundaries between the private, the public, and the commons (especially the last two domains) have disintegrated over the years, it is important for this discussion to shed light on these distinctions. They are also essential in order to understand the contemporary scenarios of today and their impacts, which will be discussed later in this chapter.

One of the most significant influences on the original concept of the commons is the enclosure movement. Very broadly, it refers to privatization, and in the contemporary context; such privatization is usually undertaken by corporations in the name of efficiency and quality. Yet privatization in terms of resources (e.g., financial and knowledge gained) is not the only thing that is happening. The enclosure movement, which originated in the 18th century amongst farmers in England, caused boundaries around intellectual property contained in resources to be formed. What once belonged to many later only belonged to a few. It is somewhat like the exclusive club, where if one becomes a member (insider), there is plenty to be gained and an array of privileges to be capitalized on, and the distance with the nonmember (outsider) widens intentionally. Therefore, if we were to visualize the original concept of the commons, where all common resources is represented on one axis, and compare that with the effect that enclosures have on them, it might resemble something like Figure 1.

In this figure, the commons is conceptualized on the vertical axis as a space where all common resources reside. Enclosures, on the other hand, are conceptualized on the horizontal axis. The circles representing collective communities that appear within this interaction are constantly evolving, expanding, and contracting, as shown

Figure 1. A visual imagination of the commons and enclosures

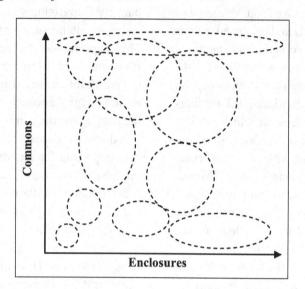

by the dotted lines around them. These groups form enclosures within themselves around the commons' space, and these enclosures grow larger as they traverse on the horizontal axis. This can be thought of as the exclusive club mentioned earlier, where a large yet private group of members enjoy equal and exclusive privileges. As a nonmember, access to those knowledge, resources, or privileges is almost impossible. Such groups are low in terms of their openness in the commons space ;yet within those boundaries, there is still a pool of resources brought together by a collective or through collective action. But because of this, there are very few overlaps between these communities: they remain in silos because of these enclosures.

On the other hand, as communities increase in their openness (see vertical axis) in the commons and members of one community frequently find themselves belonging to other communities on the same basis of interactions, overlaps often happen at this level as communities collaborate and share knowledge with one another. There are mechanisms in place for these communities to facilitate such collaboration, such as a free-to-all membership so long as there is sufficient interest aligned between the individual and the community, partnerships, and collaboration programs, and communication tools within and between these communities. And then there are communities that share their resources to all; yet one must be a member in order to contribute. The Cooperation Commons (http://www.cooperation-commons.com/) founded by Howard Rheingold (Rheingold, 2002) is based on this principle. As the site states: *You do not need a login to view the documents, the blog, or any section of this site. You do need a login to add an entry to the summary documents or to blog. If you are interested in summarizing or blogging, or in being a member of our Google Group discussion, contact....* Many research groups take on this form as well, where there is a limited membership but almost unlimited access to the resources created within the community. On the highest level, there is very little or no enclosures, and plenty of collaboration to create resources in the commons. Such communities often have almost invisible boundaries surrounding its memberships and ownerships; knowledge and other resources produced are co-owned, shared, and freely available for all to access. These communities do this on the principle that the more there is collaboration around knowledge and the creation of resources, the higher would be the value and credibility on such knowledge and resources. A contemporary example is Wikipedia.

Understanding the enclosures or the lack of them (in the commons) is critical to the discussion in this chapter; the relevance (or irrelevance) of copyright in the groups and resources created described, and the case for open content licenses, especially in the contemporary media environment. Still, Figure 1 is a somewhat simplistic presentation of the commons and the enclosures that have been formed, and it is only thus visualized for the purpose of this discussion. It must also be highlighted that even in these two paradigms, there are different forms and levels continuously evolving.

What are open content licenses and how different are they from the role of copyright and licenses? And how do they provide protection for intellectual property? Some initial background here aims to provide contextual understandings on scenarios in the contemporary media environment in which open content licenses are the most relevant. This is not to say that copyright is not useful or irrelevant. Copyright has been around for nearly 300 years, and has been used by all creators of literary works, artists, musicians, and so on. There are still scenarios where copyright is useful, but it is not within the scope of this chapter to discuss them at length.

Before proceeding with the discussion, it should be clarified that copyright usually consists of a bundle of rights (Liang, 2004, p. 25):

- **Reproduction rights:** The right to reproduce copies or the work (for example, making copies of a book from a manuscript).
- **Adaptation rights:** The right to produce derivative works based on the copyrighted work (for example, creating a film based on a book).
- **Distribution rights:** The right to distribute copies of the work (for example, circulating the book in bookshops).
- **Performance rights:** The right to perform the copyrighted work publicly, (for example, having a reading of the book or a dramatic performance of a play).
- **Display rights:** The right to display the copyrighted work publicly (for example, showing a film or work of art).

These rights are available to original works of authorship, but in the context of copyright law, originality "only refers to the fact that the work was not copied from another or to the point of origin" (Liang, 2004, p. 25). So long as a certain piece of work can demonstrate that it has not been copied from somewhere else or some effort was needed in creating a final outcome of a work, then the condition of originality would have been satisfied. As the discussion unfolds later, there are extreme difficulties in trying to maintain such distinctions, especially in the contemporary media environment.

The chapter now turns to the next discussion, significant in providing background knowledge to realizing the relevance and value of open content licenses, and applying them to appropriate scenarios. Thereafter, the commons-based model of production is discussed, along with several examples to illustrate its relevance in the contemporary media environment. This is then examined through the lens of open content licenses.

RES PRIVATÆ, RES PUBLICÆ, AND RES COMMUNES IN MODERN SOCIETY

As highlighted earlier, three main domains of production exist: res privatæ, res publicæ, and res communes. This section will talk about them but concentrate on the last two, and their common misunderstandings.

Res privatæ: Referring to the private domain, all works that are produced and not freely shared belong to the private domain. Profit-making organisations often work within this domain. Personal works such as literature, paintings, music scores, and compositions exist in this domain when they are first created, but can be later articulated to the different domains of private, public, or the community using licenses.

Res publicæ: Quite simply, this refers to all resources that exist in the public domain. Examples of institutions in the public domain are public libraries, museums, parks, and public broadcasting agencies. Works produced in the public domain are free and equal for all to use and provide a space of respite from the market forces. The ancient understanding of the Romans project that things that are owned or defined by the state government is also the equivalent of the commons domain (in the next discussion), but it should be maintained that this is not necessarily the case, even though they do contribute to the commons domain in many ways.

Res communes: This refers to the domain, where resources that are common to all are found. It is necessary to discuss the enclosures within this domain, where people form enclosures around the commons, and access is fragmented not by the market, but by the memberships, interests, or clubs of people. Although within many of such memberships and clubs, the resources are similar to those of the commons; they are collectively owned, collaborative, there is equal access, and is often free, but such features are contingent upon the maintenance of membership or interests. Property produced by such enclosed communities is not necessarily transferred to the commons domain; but it must be highlighted that many of such groups do contribute to the commons by

contributing free resources that are of quality (as they have been collectively produced) and to do this, they use certain structural mechanisms such as open content licenses. This domain must also not be confused with the earlier domain, referred to as the public domain. Quite often the commons domain is larger than what is state owned, and there are occasions where what is state owned may not be in public interest or access. But undeniably, both domains frequently visit and invigorate one another.

Having said that, it should also be mentioned that within this domain, many levels of *res communes* exist; some are more exclusive than others, and some are active in the commons by their contributions, and members frequently move from one group to another because of this. It is, however, not within the scope of this chapter to talk about these levels of differentiations. But it must be recognized that this domain of resources has grown significantly, especially in recent times, and because of certain groups, this domain has become one of the main ways by which the commons and the public domain is nurtured and maintained.

By now, it should be clear that the three domains of res privatæ, res publicæ, and res communes, as originally conceptualized by the Romans are now significantly different in the modern society. While it remains that res privatæ still refers to individual and market forces, the other two domains are frequently misunderstood. At the same time, these domains of property become less dichotomous in nature, with actions of the market, the state, and the larger human and civil community moving across the various domains.

When copyright began, there were clear distinctions between the three domains of resources: the private, the public, and the community domain; copyright was effectively used to regulate resources in these three domains. More so, in recent times, the use of copyright licenses has moved towards a heightened regulation of resources in the private sphere instead; the alternative, the open content licenses, is seen as the way and counteract against that; in their goal to nurture and ensure a healthy level of contributions to the public and commons domains (Lessig, 2004).

Copy: Right and Left Licenses

The concept of copyright is multifaceted according to its use and application to various contexts such as the types of collections, organisation, and creators. Liang (2004, p. 13) stated, quite simply and importantly, that copyright "in a broad historical and cultural view...is a recent and by no means universal concept."

The Renaissance period, which saw Europe emerge out of darkness towards a revival of learning, also saw the appearance of great scientists, inventors, artists, and other geniuses such as Leonardo Da Vinci, Donatello, and Michelangelo. It is important to note that it was also marked with institutional revelations, such as the establishment of the Vatican Library in Italy in the 1400s, and the formation of the Laurentian Library by the famous Florentine family. Universities began and also grew, and accompanying this growth were the developments of university libraries (Johnson, 1970). Bookmaking was revolutionalised by Gutenberg, replacing handwritten books with printed ones. Large volumes of printed books were then placed on open shelves in bookshops and libraries, making the written word accessible to the masses (Krasner-Khait, 2001). This period marked a golden age of literacy, where the absorption and the creation of knowledge in various disciplines such as the arts, literature, science, architecture, and technology were equally matched by their dissemination. Also marking this period was the rise of commerce and exploration, and the knowledge amassed by people and institutions of this period translated into rich and diverse collections found in personal, private institutional, public libraries, and also in commercial institutions in the market, such as bookshops.

Such was the world that needed copyright. At the beginning of the period, printers were freely reprinting popular books without getting permissions or paying royalties, and copyright was an effective way by which this industry could be regulated. It was a system that wanted to function as a system of checks, benefiting original authors and allowing noncommercial institutions (such as the public library) or groups to "exist as an alternative, noncommercial" distribution channel for the storage and use of knowledge works, and more importantly, to facilitate learning and further inspirations based on such learning and exchanges over these works.

In many ways, copyright is still doing what it was set out to do. But with the rapid establishments of market forces, copyright, as a system to benefit original creators, has been displaced, and sometimes fallen into the hands of media corporations, such as recording labels and publishing houses instead. Many examples of how copyright is used today demonstrate a common deviation from its original purpose, of regulating the publishing industry, to regulating consumers, content creators, and audiences of these works. Consider the following:

- Many works that are created are rewritten interpretations or adaptations of an original work, such as the many adaptations of *Faustus*, by Christopher Marlowe, Fernando Peddoa, Alfred Jarry, Thomas Mann, and Michel Butor (Liang, 2004).

- Numerous works are inspired by real stories, events, narratives contained in personal journals, diaries, and letters. Confucius stated once "I have finished my greatest work and I am proud to say that not a single idea in it is mine" (Liang, 2004, p. 13).

- Many works exist publicly and are common to all, such as folktales, and spread by storytellers across generations. These works exist through a concerted and collective effort, and no one could claim authority over any version as the "original." The *Tales of the 1001 Nights* is one such example.

- Again, for the same works, copyright cannot stop commercial corporations from appropriating these works and turn them into proprietary and copyrighted products of the corporation. Walt Disney Corporation established its wealth on fairy tales such as Snow White and Sinbad (Liang, 2004).
- Copyright originally had little or no application to music composition. Most musical themes "were freely adapted and copied from one composer to another. Bach's *Concerto in D Major BWV 972* for example is simply a re-orchestration of the ninth movement of Vivaldi's *L'Estro Armonica*" (Liang, 2004, p. 15). Copyright only began for music, and its use, distribution, and composition, with the growth of the recording industry in 20th century.

It must be realized that copyright accounts for much of the enclosures that exist against the global knowledge commons. Take an example of a public park in China that has been built collectively by generations of people in a village, and has existed for many decades. Trees, grass, benches, and stories are freely available in the park and are in the commons; there is no claim of ownership over them because these resources are jointly held by people in the village. It is a powerful collective endeavour, demonstrated by the size, facilities, infrastructure, stories, and recreation found in the park (see Figure 2). Yet it is also highly possible that because there are no claims, a corporation intending to turn this park into a theme park can come along to appropriate the things that are of value, and start charging for entries, or the use of facilities in them. Copyright cannot stop such actions. Such practices are already rampant on the Internet and in digital media; and even though the distinction between the original and the copy is blurred, copyright tries to artificially maintain them (Liang, 2004). The fact that distinctions are blurring is significant to the discussion of intellectual property protection; and this will be discussed in greater detail later. Such examples of copyright use only demonstrate how copyright is in the hands of large corporations and not in the best interests of the community or creators. The sometimes ignored and neglected outcome is the shrinking and fragmentation of the commons, and the public domain.

It is essential at this point to recognize a recent movement that is quickly becoming very popular and commonly augmented as alternatives to copyright. Broadly referred to as the "copyleft"

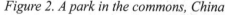

Figure 2. A park in the commons, China

movement, it serves as a discourse to restrictions imposed by copyright. The copyleft movement is rooted in the principles of open source, free, or shared software – incorporating the ideologies of "free distribution, usage and collaborative development" (Liang, 2004, p. 18). Yet it is far from being a model that abandons what copyright was intended to do. Within the existing legal framework, this model allows one to stipulate a certain degree of freedom to the way resources that are created are used, and distributed. It is a model that seeks to intervene with what has become an inherent "tyranny" in copyright (Boynton, 2004). In 1790, copyright protection lasted for 14 years and was renewable only once before a certain work or resource entered the public domain. From 1831-1909, the term was increased from 28 to 56 years. The tenure seems to grow worse, because as of today, copyright protection for individual lasts for 70 years after the death of the creator, and for corporations, 95 years after publication. Because of such shifts in favour of the private domain, the amount and flow of resources in the public and commons domains have been sluggish (Boynton, 2004). This provides a strong motivation for an alternative to copyright. In general, it is copyleft, as most people know it. More specifically, we refer to a category of open content licenses that is based on the same principles and has seen significant developments in recent years.

The Contemporary Media Environment

This is more of a fact than a statement: the Internet has significantly changed the way the world works. The use and impact of technology on everyday lives has often been heard and researched on. There are profound shifts in the way communities interact because of the changing nature of mediating technologies. But the contemporary media environment we now reside in is not limited to simply changing the way people interact;

they have changed the nature of organisations, groups, production, and soon to be revealed in later discussions, the continuum of the private and public boundaries that are so important to the knowledge commons. Most of these are nothing new to us, but it is our intention to examine the ways the contemporary media environment has changed the relevance (irrelevance) of copyright, and the three domains of resources: private, public, and the commons. Highlighting these changes is also crucial to driving the case for open content licenses. Through a number of examples, this section aims to demonstrate pragmatic scenarios challenging the assumptions of traditional copyright and licenses.

Boundaries in the Contemporary Media Environment

Before the realization of the Internet and distributed networks, there were boundaries. These were boundaries that existed to distinguish the private from the public, and all forms of common property. These boundaries were necessary for a number of reasons. Property and information inherent in them was distributed. Such distribution separates action from the private and the community and the public, and it is in such order that collective action can be seen (Olson, 1965). The second reason differentiates an action from participating in the commons or the public domain; this reason is found in the traditional collective action theory as originally conceptualized by Olson (1965) and others (Oliver & Marwell, 1988; Olson & Zeckhauser, 1966); that in order to participate or contribute, there must be a conscious, coordinated, and known intention amongst people in a community, and no one member or individual may be able to contribute to the public or communal good for the benefit of others; only widespread contributions can.

Perhaps in some cases these boundaries still exist, but with contemporary information and communication technologies, such boundaries are breaking down both on micro and structural levels. Participation can now happen without knowledge of others in a community, or the conscious intention of contributing to property with communal or public good properties. Bimber, Flanagin, and Stohl (2005) refer to this as the second-order communality, and there are many examples of such actions in our everyday lives: as unconscious as the sharing of a bookmark with others, and as conscious as adding value through the posting of a review on a Web page or community blog. Value is derived from the communal or public good through such sharing and retrieval of useful information that has also been value-added by the contributions of others. Contemporary technologies and the media environment, along with its communities of people, provide such functionalities, and make it possible for knowledge to increase in value the more it is used and shared.

Another implication that comes with the breaking down of boundaries is that information and property continually move back and forth between the private, the public, and the commons realms. While copyright has been an effective framework to regulate property with distinctive boundaries, it may no longer be effective to maintain them just so that copyright can be applied. It must be realized that we are operating in a world that has significantly changed its nature of production, and there must be at least parallel efforts in aligning changes to the policies that regulate such modes of production.

The Nature of Production in Communities

It was once heard, "isolation is deadly" (Pang, Denison, Johanson, Schauder, & Williamson, 2006). The use and growth of the number of linked pages on the Internet has certainly proved how this revelation is already inherent in people. When copyright began, it was a time when the expressions of ideas, and the sharing of them, were limited to people with political, social, or economic causes. With the Internet and usable communication technologies, and simply because it is now so easy to share, the world is seeing an exponential growth of what Lessig (2004) refers to as noncommercial publishing. It is more than a mere platform of expression, but one that reflects a paradigm shift in the way people create knowledge, communicate, collaborate, interact, and distribute their works. Benkler (c.f. Boynton, 2004) once said, "No one writes from nothing…we all take the world as it is and use it, remix it." And very much so, as we see even in times of old, that one story inspires another, and one's knowledge is the amassed wisdom of a few others. The well-known impressionist movement in painting was largely influenced by earlier artistic movements, such as Classicism and Realism. Pioneers of the movement-Auguste Renoir, Claude Monet, Alfred Sisley, and Frederic Bazille-knew each other from common and conventional painting classes and shared the common goal to defy the conventional definitions of art in that era. Thereafter this group grew, and through working together and influencing one another, knowledge of similar approaches and techniques were shared, and the movement was born lasting from 1867 to 1886 (Pioch, 2006)

Amassed and collective wisdom works pretty much the same way. Useful contributions emerge from an interactive process where one sees participation in groups, forums, discussion lists, and the integrated reflection of one's thoughts, such as writing (in today's context, blogging; but even though blogging can be a solitary pursuit, it is often mediated and networked by track backs and thoughts from interested people). Rather than the explicit pursuit of a goal or purpose, knowledge is produced collectively with other people, and interactively through participation.

The networked environment is a platform permitting individuals and communities to come together for collective action using "decentralized cooperation strategies" (Benkler, 2006, p. 63). Before this environment came about, collective action was thought to be extremely difficult unless there was a centralized coordinating body ensuring the congruent pursuit of explicit goals and minimizing the problem of free riding by individuals (Olson, 1965).

The possible misunderstanding about the Internet is that it is a trend, representative of new technologies, interactions, and communication. And as with all fads, the things we are seeing, using, and changing will fade away over time. Not so: the commons, and the collaborative model of knowledge production has been around since the first human cooperation, and the Internet and other information and communication technologies have only made the social networks integrated in this model faster, and much more transparent. Social networks, once amplified by information and communication technologies, enable broader, faster, and lower cost of coordination of activities (Schauder & Pang, 2006).

Take, for example, projects in the open source movement. The successful case of the Linux operating system, and efforts such as the "open source unionism" (Freeman & Rogers, 2002) demonstrate new types of "cooperative endeavours and organizing structures" (Bimber et al., 2005, p. 375). Far exceeding these structural changes is a model that inherently accepts that intelligence in communities cannot help but be distributed, creating unique advantages out of such distributed intelligence.

But the open source story is not just another case in point. It is a social network that has been enabled and structurally changed with distributed networks made efficiently possible by information and communication technologies. Such is the nature of production increasingly witnessed in the contemporary media environment. And this model is efficient for a number of reasons. Knowledge and the production of property appreciates in its worth because of the additional value and dialogues contributed by other participants in a community, and increases in significance through higher global usage. At the same time, inefficiencies imposed by copyright and the intellectual property regime can be addressed through this model (Kogut & Metiu, 2001) with the decentralization of innovation, from mega content owners to creators.

What is in a Copy?

Satirically speaking, there is a new disorder on the Internet; a disorder that is altogether welcoming and hostile, depending on whose side you are on. Fondly known as the copy, it refers to duplicates of a file (property) that could be distributed on the Internet. The difference that the Internet makes should be realized. In the past, when the world is without it, copies were made by teachers for use in the classroom, by singers creating samples of their works, and by art galleries creating portfolios of artists for showcasing purposes, just to name a few examples. It was an act that was somewhat acceptable simply because copies were simply inferior to the original, and replicates were akin to clones, like the original but not quite authentic, and not quite the same. Let us first say that the Internet was not originally conceptualized to encourage the disorder we speak of ; the original vs. the copy. When the World Wide Web was conceptualized, and the Internet was born, it was assumed that links (to an original) were favoured over having a copy that was probably inferior to the original. On top of this, digital storage was expensive and cumbersome. The Internet was born to facilitate networks, and through links and references one's knowledge and property could be referred to another, and the sharing of resources could be encouraged.

Yet an almost parallel transformation of technologies was taking place alongside developments of the Internet, with media storage, file types, and formats that were also adapted for use on the Internet. Media storage has now become relatively inexpensive, playing back copies of a file is easy, and file formats and types are becoming interoperable, as vendors understand benefits in collaboration. There is little (or rather, almost none) loss of quality in a copy to speak of, and it has become much easier to include a copy of a property instead of a link to an original.

As a result, a copy is inconsistently referenced to an original, or returned to an original server, rendering the distinction between an original and a copy of intellectual property almost nonexistent on the Internet. The copyright framework tries to artificially maintain these distinctions (Liang, 2004), but it must be realized that there is a need to reexamine ways by which the goals of copyright can be better achieved with alternatives. In addition, the costs of making copies in the contemporary media environment has also become relatively insignificant compared to the time when copyright was effective for physical copies of books, cassettes, videos, and photographs. In the media environment of today, the marginal costs of reproduction or distribution has lost its meaning (Schlachter, 1997).

As presented earlier, while there is nothing in the copyright framework to stop corporations from appropriating resources in the public and commons domain for commercial purposes, copyright, as it functions on the Internet, is perhaps even worse, with the ability to remain anonymous. The copying and pirating of works is now easily achievable without the disclosure of identity, or bearing any risks or losses (Schlachter, 1997).

The Case for Open Content Licenses

The chapter has so far presented a number of arguments towards the need for open content licenses, and they are quickly recaptured as stated:

- The nature of knowledge production is one that requires dialogues and sharing of knowledge, which in turn encourages innovation and sustain communities.

- Friendly structures are needed to ensure a healthy level of resources and knowledge in the commons and public domains.
- Changes in the media environment result in paradigm shifts in the way people interact; how they create, retrieve, share, and use knowledge.
- The changed media environment results in empowering communities to optimize shared knowledge in a powerful and dynamic manner, thus enabling greater levels of creation of intellectual property.
- Breaking down of boundaries defining private, public, and community resources reflect the need for a new structure regulating the creation, use, and dissemination of resources in these domains.

Beyond these reasons, there lies a social perspective to the need for open content licenses. In order to avoid the balkanization of content and communities, license structures that are friendly to open content are desirable to promote creation, innovation, and encourage communities to grow by leveraging on a healthy knowledge commons. Contrary to popular belief, the knowledge commons is not necessarily unsympathetic to market forces (Bollier, 2004), as both are needed to encourage and inspire each other. Most open content licenses allow people to add proprietary works to the knowledge commons so long as they are used in ways as specified by the creators. This permits businesses and professionals to contribute to the public and community domains without necessarily giving away all of their work.

At the same time, most successful projects based on the open content license and collaborative production model reflect a hybrid of networks: between the large, disconnected and distributed groups, and the smaller, cohesive, and occasionally hierarchically organized groups. Whatever their structures, they are based on a peer-to-peer sharing model and the more cohesive they are, the likelier they are to generate their own norms and ways of production. These are seen as strong and weak ties in social network theory and are both necessary (Granovetter, 1983) in order to provide individuals and communities with, respectively, bonding and bridging links to knowledge, resources, and one another for assistance and support (Schauder & Pang, 2006). Healthy social networks are essential to a healthy public sphere (Boeder, 2005).

This also explains how, in the context of online participation, individuals can participate as a passive looker sometimes and an active contributor at other times, even with only partial knowledge of the network. In the case of communities, open content licenses act as structures by which collective action is possible within a media environment that is highly decentralized and emergent (Benkler, 2006; Bimber et al., 2005). The growth and adoption of open content licenses by businesses, cultural communities, and governments worldwide, plainly illustrate their case, and the adaptability of them in various settings. Though not intended to be an exhaustive list, some examples are discussed here.

In July 2006, the Croatian government "adopted an open software policy and issued guidelines for developing and using open source software in government institutions" (Vervloesem, 2006). Said Domagoj Juricic, Deputy State Secretary of the Central State Administrative Office for e-Croatia, "...the Croatian government has recognized the importance of market alternatives considering the platforms, tools, and other solutions that could help us build a qualitative e-society...the policy is not about replacing something, it is about treating things equally" (Vervloesem, 2006). Croatia is not the only country that has adopted the open source movement and, as part of that movement, embraced the use of open content licenses in its public policies. Indonesia has also adopted an open source policy towards the use of software and content creation, and considers it as a strategic move to counter piracy problems (Antara, 2006). Similar benefits have also been found for using

open content licenses in publishing, especially in developing countries (Papin-Ramcharan & Dawe, 2006).

Many collaborative software developments, such as those found at the Fresh Meat Community (http://www.freshmeat.net), and even commercial content management systems such as Plone and Drupal have also widely adopted open content licenses. One of the most popular forms of open content license is the GNU General Public License, widely used in open source software developments. Significantly different from the usual copyright model, this license relies on the user community to also be coproducers of software. Derivative works that are produced must also be licensed with the GNU General Public License; preventing proprietary works from being produced based on the collective contributions of others. Unlike copyright, this license would also ensure that software codes, once contributed, would stay in the knowledge commons for others to use.

The charm of open content licenses is spreading to individual home computer users. Other than avoiding exorbitant fees that come with proprietary software (Yaqoob, 2006), many users have also found motivation in using software that is not only legal and affordable, but also allows them to take ownership of the growth and development of the very same software they were using (Ali, 2006).

But the model is not limited to software and policies. The open content licensing model is also used widely in the creation of content, such as the very popular Wikipedia. The license being used by Wikipedia is the GNU Free Documentation License, to fulfill Wikipedia's goal of "... Wikipedia content can be copied, modified, and redistributed so long as the new version grants the same freedoms to others and acknowledges the authors of the Wikipedia article used (a direct link back to the article satisfies our author credit requirement). Wikipedia articles therefore will remain free forever and can be used by anybody subject to certain restrictions, most of which serve to ensure that freedom…" (Wikipedia, 2006). As one would observe, this license is used to grant the same type of freedom one would find in the earlier software example.

A Brief Guide to Open Content Licenses

Recalling in earlier discussion the rights that are contained in the copyright framework, the open content license model differs fundamentally in that it seeks to grant to the user a certain number of freedoms. Some uses of open content licenses have been already mentioned in earlier text, and it must be warranted that there are several other examples, applicable to various content and media domains. One of the most well-known initiatives is the Creative Commons licenses, which are also localized for different jurisdictions such as India, China, Japan, Korea, Australia, Italy, Taiwan, Brazil, Netherlands, France, Austria, Spain, United Kingdom, Croatia, and so on. It is not within the scope of this chapter to speak about the different types of open content licenses; there are already several excellent works written, such as Liang (2004) and Laurent (2004), and this chapter refers to those works for that purpose.

The following lists the common characteristics of open content licenses (Liang, 2004, p. 43). Most of them are already explained in detail by Liang (2004); however, it is the intention of this section to discuss them as they relate to the knowledge commons and the nature of production in communities:

- **Basis/validity of the license:** Although open content licenses allow certain freedom to be granted to users, they also assert the copyright of the author, ensuring that derivative works that are produced are not restrictive or proprietary.

  This allows trust to be developed and sustained in a network; therefore avoiding problems of selfish appropriations of col-

lectively produced work. Hardin's infamous article symbolized this idea, where he puts forward that when a scarce resource is used as a common by individuals, the environment and resources would be degraded over time. In a nutshell, Hardin (1968) concluded that having the commons also implied setting oneself up for a tragedy: "Therein is the tragedy. Each man is locked into a system that compels him to increase his herd without limit—in a world that is limited. Ruin is the destination toward which all men rush, each pursuing his own best interest in a society that believes in the freedom of the commons" (Hardin, 1968). Already with the media environment there is already a degree of fragmentation of resources and open content licenses as a structure could help to better address such potential problems of appropriations.

- **Rights granted:** Unlike most copyright licenses, in open content licenses, users are granted freedom by granting certain rights, such as the right to copy and distribute the work, and in some cases, the right to modify, create, and distribute derivative works.

  Recalling the discussion around enclosures, these rights, granted through the open content licenses, effectively break down the enclosures and boundaries surrounding resources, communities, and the production of knowledge. This also explains why we often find that members of one community grounded in the principles of the knowledge commons are often members of multiple communities. Rights granted under the open content licenses allow them to actively bring their knowledge to a vast diversity of communities and, in turn, enable them to apply what they learn from others in these communities to their own areas.

- **Derivative works:** Refer to any work that is produced based on an original work. In open content licenses, any derivative work that is allowed to produce must also carry with it the same open content license that the original work was tagged with. The right to create derivate work usually includes the right to create it in all media.

The way open content licenses deal with derivative work is significantly different from copyright licenses. Quite plainly, the structure ensures that works that have been produced for the public and commons domain cannot be easily taken out of for commercial purposes. In doing so, a healthy level of resources in the public and commons domain is nurtured; this in turn cultivates the communities that thrive on using such knowledge.

- **Commercial/noncommercial usage:** The common assumption is that by using open content licenses, all works are granted for free. Not necessarily so; the creator does have the option to indicate whether or not a certain work is to be used for both commercial and noncommercial purposes, or only for noncommercial purposes.

  As mentioned in an earlier discussion, although the commons is distinct from the market, there must be a healthy level of both the market and the commons in order to invigorate one another (Bollier, 2004). This aspect of open content licenses allows the nurturing of both market and social communities in one single structure.

- **Procedural requirements imposed:** Most open content licenses also impose procedural requirements when a user wants to distribute an original or derivate work. This requires that the distribution is accompanied by a copy of the license, or the inclusion of any other sign, symbol, or information about the nature of the license, and indication of where this license may be obtained.

- **Appropriate credits:** Open content licenses are very strict in making sure that appropriate credits are given to the creator of a

work, when the work is distributed to a third party, and when modifications are made or derivative works are created.

By these characteristics, all rights and obligations imposed under the license, and the appropriate credits, would also be passed onto third parties acquiring a certain piece of work. In social network theory, this further strengthens strong or bonding ties that are already formed in a community. At the same time, weak ties between a closely knit community and those outside the community (third parties) can be effectively bridged (Granovetter, 1983; Schauder & Pang, 2006). Like before, these aspects of open content licenses will not only allow trust to be nurtured and a community to be cultivated; they will also ensure that proper acknowledgements be accorded to creators.

- **They do not affect fair use rights:** Unlike copyright licenses, open content licenses ensure a certain degree of fair use of a work, even if there is disagreement with the terms and conditions imposed by the license.

  This ensures that members in a community are empowered to still remain in participation, even if they do not agree, or only have partial knowledge of the community network. This is especially effective in the contemporary media environment, where a certain level of participation exists in the form of usage.

- **Absence of warranty:** Most open content licenses state that there is no warranty for the work, and it is provided on an "as is" basis, though there are options for warranties to be arranged between the licensee and the third party.

  While many might regard this as a possible drawback of open content licenses, it reflects an important character of the knowledge commons in the way the user is conceptualized. The term "user" is in fact inadequate: within the knowledge commons most users are also seen as coproducers of a work, even if they do not directly modify or create derivative works; their feedback in using the work is used to further improve the work itself. Works are seen as continuously evolving, with time and the collective knowledge of others.

Other standard legal clauses, such as severability, limitation on liability, and termination, are commonly applied in open content licenses (Liang, 2004). The section has discussed characteristics of open content licenses in a way that demonstrates their implications for communities, and in the context of this chapter, the knowledge commons. While demonstrating that there are more than enough reasons to examine open content licenses as they apply to communities, the discussion has also attempted to show how they are essential to function as a type of structure for communities to operate under.

FUTURE TRENDS

As modern information and communication technologies become more pervasive and ubiquitous, communities, whether it is communities of practice or those that make up civil society (Pang & Schauder, 2006), work increasingly within such environments. Open content licenses will increase in their usage and popularity because of their applications in the contemporary media environment. Since the first conceptualization of open content licenses, there has been a significant increase in its use, and growth in the community that supports them. Open content licenses are also increasing in their desirability for governments seeking to cultivate growth and healthy public and community domains within cultural institutions, businesses, and social communities.

Yet the well-known tension remains, between the commons and the market, and in this case between advocates of open content models and proprietary market forces. This tension is already well manifested in the conflicts between creators of software (Antara, 2006), and as more and more cultural institutions, governments, and community organisations adopt open content licenses, one can also expect opposing market forces to rise against such movements. Nevertheless, with more communities realizing that only with an appropriate structure can constructive collective action be possible, the growth of open content licenses is inevitable, as they provide such a structure for communities.

It is therefore not surprising that large corporations are already turning around and attempting to adopt certain aspects of open content licenses, though the reasons for doing so are many: recognition of its benefits, and sometimes a change directed by the demands of customers (Mears, 2006; Ricciuti, 2002). There is also a rise of smaller market entities that begin their businesses using the open content licensing model (Mears, 2006). Being small entities, such companies depend on the collective knowledge they can gain outside of their corporative network to grow, and they realize that such benefits can be gained through the open content licensing model. But this is changing, as many larger companies are also jumping on this wagon in recognition of the benefits that open content models and its licenses can give (Ricciuti, 2002). Amazon.com and Air New Zealand are some of such examples (Ricciuti, 2002).

Such organisational trends could also very well be anticipated in community networks. The creation and dissemination of knowledge resources in community networks is increasingly a reflexive state of affairs: comprising of reflections and actions, the thinking and the doing between people in a community network. The protection of intellectual property in such contexts is no longer a prescriptive process and has to be carefully considered. As more community networks realize their benefits, it is expected that there will be proliferation of open content models and its licensing structures in community networks, and the larger civil society.

With the intensification of these trends over time, and the creation and distribution of intellectual property by communities becoming increasingly robust in the contemporary media environment, the reality of copyright to function in such contexts may decrease in its application and importance (Schlachter, 1997).

CONCLUSION

Changes in the media environment have made it difficult for copyright to be enforced in communities. Other than the threats imposed by the media environment for the copyright framework, the dynamics of collective action and production in communities have also presented the need for alternative licensing mechanisms. These make up the scenarios presented in this chapter arguing for the case of using open content licenses as structural mechanisms for communities. Because they function to ensure rights to be granted to users, they become powerful and effective empowerment for communities that needed dialogues, collaboration, and innovation.

Beyond the knowledge commons lies the unforgettable community: it is a concept of collaboration, coproduction, and one that allows communities to thrive on the using and sharing of collective wisdom; open content licenses function as a paradigm by which intellectual property in such constructs can be managed. Theorists often wonder why open source projects have become so popular in recent years. The chapter has also demonstrated that users of open content licenses do not deprive themselves of their rights to creation, or disregard intellectual property in any way. Whether or not open content licenses are to be used remains a choice that one must make; but as this chapter has discussed, although the popularity and growth of open content licenses

may not have been well anticipated ahead of its time, it is perhaps clear in hindsight.

REFERENCES

Ali, N. D. (2006). The open and closed case. *SPIDER, September 2006*, 7-9.

Antara. (2006). *IBM, Microsoft protest Indonesia's open source policy*. Retrieved October 1, 2006, from http://www.antara.co.id/en/seenws/?id=16383

Benkler, Y. (2003). The political economy of commons. *UPGRADE: European Journal for the Informatics Professional, 4*(3), 6-9.

Benkler, Y. (2006). *The wealth of networks: How social production transforms markets and freedom*. London: Yale University Press.

Bimber, B., Flanagin, A. J., & Stohl, C. (2005). Reconceptualizing collective action in the contemporary media environment. *Communication Theory, 15*(4), 365-388.

Boeder, P. (2005). Habermas' heritage: The future of the public sphere in the network society. *First Monday, 10*(9). Retrieved October 13, 2006, from http://firstmonday.org/issues/issue10_9/boeder/index.html

Bollier, D. (2004). Why we must talk about the information commons. *Law Library Journal, 96*(2), 267-282.

Boynton, R. S. (2004). The tyranny of copyright? *The New York Times, January 24, 2004*. Retrieved October 8, 2006, from http://www.nytimes.com/2004/01/25/magazine/25COPYRIGHT.html?ei=5007&en=9eb265b1f26e8b14&ex=1390366800&partner=USERLAND&pagewanted=all&position=

Castells, M. (2003). *The power of identity*. Malden, MA: Blackwell Publishing.

Digeser, E. D. (2003). Citizenship and the roman res publica: Cicero and a Christian corollary. *Critical Review of International Social and Political Philosophy, 6*(1), 5-21.

Freeman, R. B., & Rogers, J. (2002). Open source unionism: Beyond exclusive collective bargaining. *Working USA: Journal of Labor and Society, 5*, 3-4.

Granovetter, M. (1983). The strength of weak ties: A network theory revisited. *Sociological Theory, 1*, 201-233.

Hardin, G. (1968). The tragedy of the commons. *Science, 62*, 1243-1248.

Johnson, E. D. (1970). *History of libraries in the western world*. Metuchen, NJ: Scarecrow Press Inc.

Kogut, B., & Metiu, A. (2001). Open-source software development and distributed innovation. *Oxford Review of Economic Policy, 17*, 248-264.

Krasner-Khait, B. (2001). Survivor: The history of the library. *History Magazine, (October/November)*. Retrieved July 11, 2006, from http://www.history-magazine.com/libraries.html

Laurent, A. M. S. (2004). *Understanding open source and free software licensing*. Cambridge: O'Reilly.

Lessig, L. (2004). *Free culture: The nature and future of creativity*. New York: Penguin Books.

Liang, L. (2004). *A guide to open content licenses*. The Netherlands: Piet Zwart Institute.

Mears, J. (2006). Open source unlocks options for many small-to-medium sized businesses. *Network World*. Retrieved October 11, 2006, from http://www.linuxworld.com/cgi-bin/mailto/x_linux.cgi

Moritz, T. D. (2004). Conservation partnerships in the commons? Sharing data and information, experience and knowledge, as the essence of partnerships. *Museum International, 56*(4), 24-31.

Oliver, P., & Marwell, G. (1988). The paradox of group size in collective action: A theory of the critical mass, II. *American Sociological Review, 53*, 1-8.

Olson, M. (1965). *The logic of collective action*. Cambridge: Harvard University Press.

Olson, M., & Zeckhauser, R. (1966). An economic theory of alliances. *Review of Economics and Statistics, 48*, 266-279.

Pang, N., Denison, T., Johanson, G., Schauder, D., & Williamson, K. (2006, October). *Empowering communities through memories: The role of public libraries*. Paper presented at the 3rd Prato International Community Informatics Conference, Prato, Italy.

Pang, N., & Schauder, D. (2006). User-centred design and the culture of knowledge creating communities: A theoretical reassessment. In F. V. Burstein & H. Linger (Eds.), *The local and global in knowledge management—Why culture matters* (pp. 151-166). Kew, VIC, Australia: Australian Scholarly Publishing.

Papin-Ramcharan, J. I., & Dawe, R. A. (2006). Open access publishing: A developing country view. *First Monday, 11* (6). Retrieved October 1, 2006, from http://firstmonday.org/issues/issue11_6/papin/index.html

Pioch, N. (2006). *Impressionism*. Retrieved October 1, 2006, from http://www.ibiblio.org/wm/paint/glo/impressionism/

Rheingold, H. (2002). *Smart mobs: The next social revolution*. Cambridge: Perseus Books Group.

Ricciuti, M. (2002). Open source: Rebels at the gate. *Business Tech: CNet News*. Retrieved October 12, 2006, from http://news.com.com/2009-1001-961354.html

Schauder, D., & Pang, N. (2006). *Keynote presentation: Digital storytelling.* Paper presented at the Museums Australia 2006 seminar: Storytelling through emerging technologies. Victoria, Australia.

Schlachter, E. (1997). The intellectual property renaissance in cyberspace: Why copyright law could be unimportant on the Internet. *Berkeley Technology Law Journal, 12*(1). Retrieved October 12, 2006, from http://btlj.boalt.org/data/articles/12-1_spring_1997_symp_2-schlachter.pdf

Slater, J. B. (2005). When America sneezes. *Mute, 2*(1), 5.

Vervloesem, K. (2006). Croatian government adopts open source software policy. *News Forge.* Retrieved October 16, 2006, from http://www.newsforge.com/article.pl?sid=06/08/11/1855229

Wikipedia. (2006). *Wikipedia: Copyrights.* Retrieved October 13, 2006, from http://en.wikipedia.org/wiki/Wikipedia:Copyrights

Yaqoob, N. (2006). My Ubuntu experience. *SPIDER, September 2006*, 10-12.

Chapter XIV
E-Commerce and Digital Libraries

Suliman Al-Hawamdeh
Nanyang Technological University, Singapore

Schubert Foo
Nanyang Technological University, Singapore

ABSTRACT

Until recently, digital libraries have provided free access to either limited resources owned by an organization or information available in the public domain. For digital libraries to provide access to copyrighted material, an access control and charging mechanism needs to be put in place. Electronic commerce provides digital libraries with the mechanism to provide access to copyrighted material in a way that will protect the interest of both the copyright owner and the digital library. In fact, many organizations, such as the Association for Computing Machinery (ACM) and the Institute of Electrical and Electronics Engineers (IEEE), have already started to make their collections available online. The subscription model seems to be the favourable option at this point of time. However, for many ad hoc users, the subscription model can be expensive and not an option. In order to cater to a wider range of users, digital libraries need to go beyond the subscription models and explore other possibilities, such as the use of micro payments, that appear to be an alternative logical solution. But, even before that can happen, digital libraries will need to foremost address a number of outstanding issues, among which including access control, content management, information organization, and so on. This chapter discusses these issues and challenges confronting digital libraries in their adoption of e-commerce, including e-commerce charging models.

INTRODUCTION

Digital Library Research Initiatives in the United States and the increased interested in digital libraries by computer science researchers has provided the impetus for the growing proliferation of digital libraries around the world. Most existing digital libraries have mainly focused on digitizing individual collections and making them available on the Web for users to search, access, and use. They are providing a new means of fast and effective access to information in different forms and formats. Nonetheless, the development of digital libraries also translates into significant financial requirements, which, in the past, has been borne largely by government funding agencies, academic institutions, and other non-profit organizations.

By virtue of the basic principles of economics and business, digital libraries are looking for alternative forms of revenue generation in order to meet the ever-increasing needs of users through the provision of new value-added services and products. In this respect, e-commerce can provide digital libraries with the means to support their operation and provide them with a sustainable source of funding. This is a natural evolution in the use of digital libraries, as content management and electronic publishing are gaining momentum and popularity.

However, before digital libraries can engage in e-commerce activities, many issues need to be addressed. Some of these issues include intellectual property, access control, backup and archiving, and micro payments. In this chapter, we will look at these issues and highlight problems and opportunities related to digital libraries as a viable e-commerce business model.

Characteristics of Digital Libraries

The "digital library" is a term that implies the use of digital technologies by libraries and information resource centers to acquire, store, conserve, and provide access to information. But with the increased interest in other areas such as electronic commerce and knowledge management, the concept of digital library has gone beyond the digitization of library collections. It has been expanded to encompass the whole impact of digital and networking technologies on libraries and the wider information field. Researchers from many

fields including computer science, engineering, library and information science are investigating not only the digitization of catalogues and collections or the effective use of networked resources but also the meaning of these developments for both information providers and users alike. Beside the technical issues that engineers are dealing with, there are a number of issues such as acquisition, content management, charging, and intellectual property that require the help of business and legal experts.

As digital libraries are being embraced by many communities, the definitions and characteristics of digital libraries vary rom one community to another. To the engineering and computer science community, digital library is a metaphor for the new kinds of distributed database services that manage unstructured multimedia. It is a digital working environment that integrates various resources and makes them available to the users. From the business community perspective, digital library presents a new opportunity and a new marketplace for the world's information resources and services. From the library and information science perspective, it has been seen as "the logical extensions and augmentations of physical libraries in the electronic information society. Extensions amplify existing resources and services and augmentations enable new kinds of human solving and expression" (Marchionini, 1999).

According to the Digital Library Federation (DLF), digital libraries are "organizations that provide the resources, including the specialized staff, to select, structure, offer intellectual access to, interpret, distribute, preserve the integrity of, and ensure the persistence over time of collections of digital works so that they are readily and economically available for use by a defined community or set of communities" (Digital Library Federation, 2001). From the above, it is clear that the stakeholders of digital libraries are many and wide-ranging. They include publishers, individual authors and creators, librarians, commercial information providers, federal, state and local governments, schools, colleges, universities and research centers, corporate technology providers, and major information user organizations in both the public and private sectors. With this, it is not surprising to find a myriad of different definitions and interpretations of a digital library. It could be a service, an architecture, information resources, databases, text, numbers, graphics, sound, video or a set of tools and capabilities to locate, retrieve, and utilize the available information resources. It is a coordinated collection of services, which is based on collections of materials, some of which may not be directly under the control of the organization providing a service in which they play a role. However, this should not be confused with virtual libraries or resource gateways that merely provide a link to external resources without any extra effort to manage those resources. As those resources are normally not under the control of the organization, maintaining content and keeping the links up to date is extremely difficult.

But while the definition of the digital library is still evolving, it might be easier to look at the characteristic and functionality provided by the digital library. Garrett (1993) outlined some of these characteristics that are worth noting :

- **Ubiquity:** At lease some set of services must be accessible at any time from any physical location.
- **Transparency:** The internal functioning of infrastructure components and interactions must be invisible to users. Users must be able to access services using their user interface of choice.
- **Robustness and scalability:** The infrastructure must be powerful enough to withstand a wide range of potential risks and continue to function without disruption to users and service providers.
- **Security and confidentiality:** The infrastructure must include mechanisms which ensure that parties to any transaction can reliably be identified to each other, that con-

fidentiality of the parties and the transaction can be assured where appropriate, and that the system cannot be easily compromised.
- **Billing, payment, and contracting:** The infrastructure must support both financial transactions in payment for goods and services and the delivery and utilization of electronically generated and managed tokens (e.g., digital cash).
- **Searching and discovery:** The infrastructure must provide for a wide range of resource identification strategies, from highly specific searches to generic browsing.

Clearly, the above characteristics involve access to information, content management, search and retrieval of information, payments, security and confidentiality, technology and infrastructure. While some of these issues sound manageable, other issues such as payments and intellectual property still pose significant challenges and are still candidates for further research and development. The following sections address some of these issues confronting digital library development, and, in particular, those affecting the electronic commerce aspect of the digital library.

ISSUES CONFRONTING DIGITAL LIBRARIES

Content Management

Content management is an important and critical activity in digital libraries. It involves the creation, storage, and subsequent retrieval and dissemination of information or metadata. In this respect, content management can be closely linked to online search services. While most of the collections in digital libraries are still text-based, this is expected to change in future as more and more material will be made available in multimedia format. As the content is expected to come from various sources, it will also come in different formats, such as word processor files, spreadsheet files, PDF files, CAD/CAM files, and so on. However, Rowley (1998) pointed out that despite the growing importance of multimedia approaches, most of the collections are still text based. The volume of text-based information is increasing at an alarming rate, and its diversity of form—from the relatively unstructured memos, letters or journal articles, to the more formally structured reports, directories or books—is continually broadening. The management of content will also involve capturing and validating information. Nonetheless, issues related to ownership and intellectual property will continue to hamper the development of digital libraries. Most of the digital libraries that exist today either own the content or just provide a link to the information resource. Access control and intellectual property are therefore fundamental issues in the operation of large digital libraries.

Issues Facing the Content Organization in Digital Format

Information organization is an area that is still evolving and will continue to do so for some time. Statistical-based information storage retrieval models have failed to provide an effective approach to the organization of large amounts of digital information. On the other hand, more effective tools, which have been used manually by the librarians to organize information in the traditional libraries, are considered slow, tedious, and very expensive. Given the vast amount of information available today, it is important to organize it in a way that allows for modification in the retrieval system. This is highlighted by Arms, Banchi, and Overly (1997) where flexible organization of information is one of the key design challenges in any digital library. The purpose of the information architecture is to represent the richness and variety of library information, using them as building blocks of the digital library system. With the different types of material in a digital library, information

can be organized using a hybrid approach that combines the statistical-based techniques with manual organization tools. Many companies are developing tools that will enable libraries to create taxonomies and organize information in a more meaningful and useful way.

The growth in size and heterogeneity represents one set of challenges for designers of search and retrieval tools. The ability of these tools to cope with the exponential increase of information will impact directly on the content management of the digital systems. Another challenge pertains to searcher behaviour. Recent studies have shown that users have difficulty in finding the resources they are seeking. Using log file analysis, Catledge and Pitkow (1995) found that users typically did not know the location of the documents they sought and used various heuristic techniques to navigate the Internet, with the use of hyperlinks being the most popular method. They also found that users rarely cross more than two layers in a hypertext structure before returning to their entry point. This shows the importance of information organization and content management in digital libraries.

The organization of information is still an issue in content management that needs to be addressed. Some outstanding issues include the following:

• The nature of digital materials and the relationship between different components. A digitized document may consist of pages, folders, index, graphics, or illustration in the form of multimedia information. A computer program, for example, is assembled from many files, both source and binary, with complex rules of inclusion. Materials belonging to collections can be a collections in the traditional, custodial sense or may be a compound document with components maintained and physically located in different places, although it appears to the user as one entity, in reality it can be put together as a collection of links or an executable component.

- Digital collections can be stored in several formats that require different tools to interpret and display. Sometimes, these formats are standard and it is possible to convert from one format to another. At other times, the different formats contain proprietary information that requires special tools for display and conversion, thereby creating content management and maintenance problems.

- Since digital information is easy to manipulate, different versions can be created at any time. Versions can differ by one single bit resulting in duplicate information. Also digital information can exist in different levels of resolution. For example, a scanned photograph may have a high-resolution archival version, a medium-quality version, and a thumbnail. In many cases, this is required if we want to address the retrieval and display issues on one hand, and printing quality issues on the other hand.

- Each element of digital information may have different access rights associated with it. This is essential if digital libraries are used in an environment were information needs to be filtered according to confidentiality or is sold at different prices.

- The manner in which the user wishes to access material may depend upon the characteristics of the computer systems and networks, and the size of the material. For example, a user connected to the digital library over a high-speed network may have a different pattern of work than the same user when using a dial-up line. Thus, taking into account the response time and the speed by which information can be delivered to the users becomes another factor of consideration.

It is clear from the above that the organization of information should take into consideration

many issues. Borgman (1997) noted that the issues of interoperability, portability, and data exchange related to multi-lingual character sets have received little attention except in Europe. Supporting searching and display in multiple languages is an increasingly important issue for all digital libraries accessible on the Internet. Even if a digital library contains materials in only one language, the content needs to be searchable and displayable on computers in countries speaking other languages. Data needs to be exchanged between digital libraries, whether in a single language or in multiple languages. Data exchanges may be large batch updates or interactive hyperlinks. In any of these cases, character sets must be represented in a consistent manner if exchanges are to succeed.

Information retrieval in a multimedia environment is normally more complex. Most of the information systems available today (including digital libraries) still rely on keywords and database attributes for the retrieval of images and sound. No matter how good the image descriptions used for indexing is a lot of information in the image will still not be accessible. Croft (1995) noted that general solutions to multimedia indexing are very difficult, and those that do exist tend to be of limited utility. The most progress is being made in well-defined applications in a single medium, such as searching for music or for photographs of faces.

Copyright and Intellectual Property

Digital libraries as any other Web applications are still not protected from copying, downloading, and reuse. Digital technology makes reproduction of electronic documents easy and inexpensive. A copy of an original electronic document is also original, making it difficult to preserve the original document or treat it different from the other copies. In a central depository system where the original document is normally stored, the digital library system will have to make copies of this document for viewing or editing purposes whenever users access the document. In the Web environment, a copy is normally downloaded to the users machines and sometimes cached into the temporary directory for subsequent access.

The ease in which copies can be made and distributed prompted many to predict that electronic publishing will not prevail, as there might not be many people willing to put their works on the Web due to lack of protection. As legislators grapple with the issues of copyright, electronic document delivery is already taking place both within and outside the restrictions of copyright. The sentiments expressed by Oppenheim (1992) reflect those of many with regard to copyright in that:

the information world is essentially a global one ... and the legal framework in which the industry operates is in places very confused, and in some cases, such as data protection, it is unwittingly swept up by legislation not aimed at it all. In other areas such as liability and confidentiality of searches, it will face increasing pressures from its consumers in the coming years.

Although the copyright issues in many areas have not been fully addressed, attempts have been made recently to introduce greater restrictions upon copyright and intellectual property. One such notable effort is by the Clinton Administration's Intellectual Property Working Group, which issued its Copyright Amendment recommendation code named "Green Paper." The Green Paper recommends amending the copyright law to guard against unauthorized digital transmission of copyrighted materials (Mohideen, 1996). The four main principal implications of the law include:

- Copyright should proscribe the authorized copying of these works.
- Copyright should in no way inhibit the rightful use of these works.

- Copyright should not block the development of dissemination of these works.
- Copyright should not grant anyone more economic power than is necessary to achieve the incentives to create.

Based on these principles, the U.S. Copyright Commission concluded that making some changes to the Copyright Act of 1976 could develop protection of computer programs. Congress has accepted the recommendations.

The question of *Intellectual Property* versus the *Freedom of Information* has been widely debated. There are two opposing views to this issue. One is that creators of information should be amply rewarded for their works. On the other hand, there is the notion that nobody really owns information, and society would be better off if knowledge is available for all. In the old system, copyrights always protected the physical entities by prohibiting the reproduction of the work without permission from the author. This also includes photocopying with the exception of fair use for educational purpose. In the Internet environment, downloading and printing is not much different from photocopying, although controlling this activity is extremely difficult.

In the past, copyright and patent laws were developed to compensate the *Inventors* for their creations. The systems of both law and practice were based on physical expression. In the absence of successful new models for non-physical transaction, how can we create reliable payment for mental works? In cyberspace, with no clear national and local boundaries to contain the scene of a crime and determine the method of prosecution, there are no clear cultural agreements on what a crime might be (Barlow, 1995).

Intellectual Property Management

For digital libraries to succeed, an intellectual property system needs to be developed to manage copyrighted material and ensure that the rights of authors and creators are protected. Garett (1993) proposed having an intellectual property management system to manage intellectual property in a distributed networked environment. This system should assure copyright owners that users would not be allowed to create derivative works without permission or to disseminate the information beyond what is permitted. Besides controlling the copying of information, owners and users also would like to ensure that information has not been intercepted or altered in anyway. To be able to achieve this, Garett suggested that the intellectual property management system must be capable of the following:

- Provide for confidential, automated rights and royalty exchange.
- Ensure owners and users that information is protected from unauthorized, accidental or intentional misattribution, alteration, or misuse.
- Ensure rapid, seamless, efficient linking of requests to authorizations.
- Include efficient and secure billing and accounting mechanisms.

Another method of protecting intellectual property and copyright as proposed by Marchionini (1999) is through using technical solutions. The solutions are in the form of encryption algorithms and digital watermarking. So far, techniques have been developed whereby visible or hidden watermarks on digital objects have been incorporated into commercial products. According to Marchionini, these techniques insure the veracity of an object and may discourage the copying and distribution in the open market place. Examples of such systems currently being tested include Cybercash, Digicash, and Netbill. Cybercash use a third party intermediary to effect transfer of property and payment while Digicash issues money in the form of bit stream tokens that are exchanged for intellectual property. Netbill uses prefunded accounts to enable intellectual property transfer.

Cataloguing and Indexing

The exponential growth of the Web has made available vast amount of information on a huge range of topics. But the technology and the methods of accessing this information have not advanced sufficiently to deal with the influx of information. There is a growing awareness and consensus that the information on the Web is very poorly organized and of variable quality and stability, so that it is difficult to conceptualize, browse, search, filter, or reference (Levy, 1995). Traditionally, librarians have made use of established information organization tools such as the Anglo-American Cataloging Rules (AACR2) to organize, index, and catalog library resources. This works fine with the printed material by providing access to the bibliographic information only. When it comes to content indexing on the Web, these tools are inadequate and expensive to use due to the large amount of information available on the Web. The other major problem with the traditional approach is the fact that it is a largely intellectual manual process and that the costs can be prohibitive in the Web environment. This is further exacerbated that information on the Web is prone to sudden and instant updates and changes. An automated indexing process is therefore more useful and suitable. The success of automatic indexing should therefore lead to fast access and lower costs. The other major difference between traditional libraries and digital libraries is the content and format of the information stored. Digital libraries contain multimedia information, images, graphics, and other objects where traditional cataloging rules do not deal with.

Currently, indexing and retrieval of images is carried out using textual description or database attributes assigned to the image at the time of indexing. Indexing and retrieval based on image content is still very much in the research stage. In the Web environment, metadata is used to provide a description of an object for indexing purposes. Metadata is data about data, which is highly structured like its MARC (MAchine Readable Catalogue) counterpart in order for retrieval software to understand exactly how to treat each descriptive element in order to limit a search to a particular field.

Some of the digital libraries, such as the State Library of Victoria Multimedia Catalogue, attempted to use the MARC format to catalog digital objects only to find that it did not work adequately. In some cases, it becomes very complex requiring highly trained staff and specialized input systems. Digital librarians have identified three categories of metadata information about digital resources: descriptive (or intellectual), structural, and administrative. Of these categories, MARC only works well with intellectual metadata. Descriptive metadata includes the creator of the resource, its title, and appropriate subject headings. Structural metadata describes how the item is structured. In a book, pages follow one another, but as a digital object, if each page is scanned as an image, metadata must "bind" hundreds of separate image files together into a logical whole and provide ways to navigate the digital document. Administrative metadata could include information on how the digital file was produced and its ownership. Unlike MARC, which is a standard specified by AACR2, metadata standards are still evolving and there is still no consensus on a particular standard to follow (Tennant, 1997).

The other main concern with cataloging and indexing is the hefty cost involved. Basically, the cost to assign values to index attributes depends on the amount of work that is needed to determine what information to post. If the index is prepared before scanning, such as filling out a form, then adding index records to the database is strictly a data entry effort. However, if the information is derived from a reading or the document or an analysis of photographs, it will be very costly indeed. According to a report prepared for the Washington State Library Council (1999), a 15-element index record with 500 characters of entry may take between 30 seconds and a few minutes to complete. For thousands or hundred of thousands of items, this translates into very high costs.

Access Control

Access to most digital libraries was initially free to promote the site and attract users. Materials available on these sites are limited due to the lack of an appropriate and good access control system. When digital libraries deal with copyrighted material or private information, they are faced with the necessary task of developing access control facilities. A good example is the course reserve system developed by many universities to manage courseware. Most course reserve systems provide different levels of access control depending on the type of material and the enrollment of the students. Another reason for having a flexible and good access control system is the need for cross-organizational access management for Web-based resources. This is another area of great interest to information consuming institutions and information-resource providers. These organizations would like to enable access to a particular networked resource or to a particular member of an institutional consumer community. While access to users should be easy and flexible, it should also protect the privacy of the user and should not depend entirely on the user's location or network address but rather on the user's membership in appropriate communities. It should also provide the necessary management and demographic information to institutional consumer administrators and to resource providers.

A flexible and good access management system should do more than provide the technical infrastructure. It should also address a number of other difficult issues such as access policies and deployment of technology. Two important technical infrastructure components are required for an institutional access management system. First is the ability of a user to obtain an identity on the network, known as authentication, and the second is the ability to correlate a user's identity with rights and permissions to use various services, called authorization.

Given the problem surrounding the development of a good access control in digital libraries, there are a number of issues that need to be taken into consideration when developing and deploying an access control infrastructure:

- The system must address real-world situations. It should take into consideration the technology being used to verify users' as well as the level of user expertise. In the Internet and e-commerce environment, verification of users is rather difficult and a Public Key Infrastructure (PKI) might be needed to address the security and trust problems.
- The system should protect users' privacy and protect users' information from illegal or inappropriate use.
- It should provide different level of access to information depending on the type and nature of that information. Some services might be made accessible to the public while others can be restricted to paid users, managers, or heads of divisions.
- Access to information should not be hampered by technology and made difficult as a result of security or access right measures. It should remain efficient and simple.
- It should be easy to control and manage. Web-based user registration and verification reduces the time and cost involved in administering the system. It should be as painless to manage and to scale as current technology permits.

For libraries to engage in e-commerce activities, they need to deploy an access control system, not only to protect information resources but to also enable them to charge and collect money. Thus, access control in digital libraries will need to be integrated with payment and intellectual property management.

E-Commerce in Libraries

Libraries have so far been very slow to embrace electronic commerce. This is largely due to that fact that most libraries are originally institutionalized as non-profit organizations. Furthermore, the cost of setting up an e-commerce infrastructure is a barrier as libraries are generally not cash-rich organizations. However, electronic commerce and Internet have played a significant role in the way libraries operate and the way library services have developed. Many libraries have made their presence felt on the Web by making their collections searchable and their services accessible. The web sites of the New York Public Library (NYPL), the British Library, and Singapore National Library Board (NLB) are good examples of libraries using current technology to enhance and extend their services to current and future clientele.

Whether in a digital or traditional environment, libraries were set to provide various mechanisms for knowledge archiving, preservation, and maintenance of culture, knowledge sharing, information retrieval, education and social interaction. Barker (1994) states that as an educational knowledge transfer system, a library fulfils a number of important requirements, these being:

- The library is a meeting place—a place where people can interact and exchange ideas.
- The library provides a range of resources to which access is otherwise difficult.
- The library provides an effective mechanism for information acquisition and dissemination.
- The library provides access to experts in different fields and helps users to locate relevant information.
- The library is an educational institution and plays an important educational role in the fulfillment of lifelong learning.

In keeping up with the changes and advances in technology and the need to create self-sustain-ing entities, some libraries are changing their practices and adapting to the new environment by starting to charge their users for certain classes of value-added services, such as document delivery, reference services, and information research. The Canadian Institute for Scientific and Technical Information (CISTI) is an example of such a library or resource center that charges the public for value-added services (Song, 1999). In Singapore, the Library 2000 Report recommended that basic library services remain free, however value-added services such as translating, analyzing, and repackaging information will be chargeable (Fong, 1997). Currently, the National Library Board (NLB) of Singapore has adopted and implemented cashless payments through the use of the cash-cards. The use of cash-cards at NLB branches for all transactions was introduced in 1998 in an effort to automate payment processing. Although the introduction of cash-card systems at NLB branches initially drew some negative responses, the majority of library users soon grew accustomed to this mode of payment.

The cash-card system developed by Network for Electronic Transfers (S) Pte Ltd (NETS) and Kent Ridge Digital Laboratories (KRDL) of Singapore enabled the cash-card to be conveniently used at NLB branches. C-ONE, Singapore's first attempt at developing an electronic commerce system to enable cash card payments over the Internet, was introduced at some NLB libraries in 1999. The cash-card, which is basically a stored-value card, is useful for micro-payments. The value of the card can be topped at machines through the use of bankcards. However, the main drawback of the cash card and NETS is that they are only usable in Singapore.

As another example, the Library of Virginia introduced electronic commerce by enabling its patrons to adopt a book or shop online from its gift shop via its Web site that is credit card enabled (Harris, 2000). In more noticeable emerging trends, some libraries have begun to develop partnerships with vendors such as booksellers.

The Tacoma Public Library is one such library where it allows its patrons to order books from the online bookseller, Amazon.com, via its online public access catalogue (OPAC) system. For each transaction, it earns 15% commission on the sale (Fialkoff, 1998).

Digital libraries are being developed for the preservation and access of heritage material through digitization efforts. At the same time, the digitized documents are potential revenue generators for these digital libraries. In addition, the digital library is an avenue through which electronic publications and value-added services can be accessed. With the presence of NetLibrary, many options are available to libraries (physical and digital) to offer electronic books for access to their members. NetLibrary goes through the process of acquiring the distribution rights to books from publishers and has made approximately 14,000 books available for access. Some of these books can be accessed for free while others require payment (Breeding, 2000). Electronic commerce and digital libraries are complementary in that "a digital library may require the transactional aspects of EC to manage the purchasing and distribution of its content, while a digital library can be used as a resource in electronic commerce to manage products, services and consumers" (Adam & Yesha, 1996).

The platform for libraries to innovate within their designated roles is reaching new heights with the aid of technology and electronic commerce. Traditional methods of doing things can be performed more effectively through an electronic exposure. The World Wide Web has created new avenues of delivering traditional services and created an environment of creative business development within the realms of the library world.

Charging Models for Digital Libraries

Since the definition of a digital library is till evolving, there is no prevailing e-commerce model for digital libraries. However, most of the goods sold on digital libraries are content such as electronic journals and databases. But there is no reason that digital libraries cannot sell physical goods such as postcards, books, T-shirts, mugs and other forms of goods. Given that, digital libraries might have to adopt different charging models. These charging models need to be integrated into a seamless and convenient interface. Some of the charging models that can be used for digital libraries include the prepaid subscription model, pay later subscription model, and pay now or as you use model.

Prepaid Subscription Model

In this model, the buyer maintains a virtual account with the seller that has been debited with a certain amount that is normally the annual or monthly subscription value. Depending on the terms and conditions of the subscription arrangement, the account can then be used for subsequent payments during payment transaction. This provides a very convenient form of payment where a user need not submit payment details each time to effect a transaction.

Pay Later Subscription Model

This is similar to the prepaid subscription model with the exception of "use first and pay later." This model also requires users (buyers) to register with the service provided. A virtual account is created and maintained. At the end of the subscription period, a bill is sent to the user for payment. Payment methods using credit cards fall in this category. In the case of e-commerce, credit card is a very common and convenient payment type and will be expected to be available in the digital library by many users. Most of the e-commerce Web sites operating under this model require the user credit card number upon registration. The credit card will be charged at the end of the subscription period.

Pay Now or As You Use Model

This model requires the user to pay immediately after completing the transaction. For example, if the payment method selected by the buyer is the cash card, then the amount of the transaction will be immediately deducted from the cash card and deposited into the electronic wallet of the seller. In the context of digital libraries, this type of payment mode is appropriate where payment must be collected before a user can access a service, such as downloading of documents, articles, software, etc. The problem with this model is that some of the payment techniques used, such as cash cards and NETS, are not standard and users cannot use them from abroad. Since credit card payments are not suitable for micro-payments and small amounts, there is a need for a standardized charging mechanism, such as cybercash or digital cash. Currently none of these charging techniques are accepted as a standard.

In fact, the issue of micro-payment is not restricted to libraries but to many sprouting new businesses on the Web.

According to the micro-payment model of Amazon.com, a micro-payment constitutes an amount of US$2 or less. It was cited that these payments are difficult for many sites to collect because the cost of processing such small transactions is higher than the fee itself (Regan, 2001). This issue greatly impacts the libraries, as they are generally non-profit, so that they are effectively incurring more costs to provide such a service to allow users to make micro-payments online.

Given that, how can consumers pay for such micro-payments at their convenience that does not incur a high overhead for the online merchant? In respect to this, many various commercial suppliers (such as CyberCoin of CyberCash.com, MicroPayment by IBM and Millicent by Compaq) have developed products in response to addressing the need for micro-payment transaction and processing.

These suppliers attempt to connect buyers and sellers on the Internet to a worldwide microcommerce environment. For the example of MilliCent (Compaq Computer Corporation, 2001), buyers will first need to open an account with them or through authorised brokers, and fund it in one of three ways, namely, through an online credit card or debit card transaction, by direct billing their monthly Internet Service Provider (ISP) statement or telephone bill, or through pre-paid cards purchased anonymously through convenience stores. Funds are held in the account in any currency until needed and then spent at vendor Web sites with the simple click of a mouse. The system takes care of the actual payment, handles currency conversion if required, resolves content delivery problems, and automatically processes refund requests. On the part of the seller, they open vendor accounts by first selecting a licensed payment hosting provider from the MilliCent Web site. This might be their ISP, a preferred Commerce Hosting Provider (CSP), or MilliCent itself. Once the account is opened, the vendor is "live" as part of the network. Using their browser, vendors assign prices to individual objects to be sold or to groups of objects. As a final step, vendors generally update their Web site HTML pages to visually reflect pricing to Web site visitors. Alternatively, vendors are allowed to integrate the software directly into their Web sites. By directly controlling their own payment processing, advanced vendors can increase their Web site responsiveness for end-users, better integrate MilliCent into their day-to-day operations, and eliminate any fees charged by MilliCent payment hosting providers.

Micro-payment is also an issue facing digital libraries as a direct result of intellectual property management. Digital libraries will not be able to provide services for copyrighted material unless a charging mechanism that takes intellectual property into account is put in place. Monash University implemented a course reserve system as well as a formula to calculate charges for copyright materials in an electronic course reserve system (Hawamdeh, 1999). The formula takes into account the number of pages scanned, viewed or printed, the retail price of the printed material or monographs, and the number of users enrolled in the course. This could form a basis for licensing and use of copyrighted material in universities and large corporations. Implementing such a formula can help the library to provide copyright clearance and manage charges when necessary.

XML MIGHT HOLD THE KEY

Digital libraries have started recently to take advantage of XML to better organize and manage digital resources. XML or extensible markup language came about as a result of combining standard generalized markup language (SGML) and the Web. Due to the limitations inherited in hypertext markup language (HTML), there is a need to extend HTML capabilities to better display and manipulate Web pages. SGML, on the other hand, is powerful but too complicated. XML achieves much of the power of SGML but without the complexity associated with the use and implementation of SGML.

XML promises to solve many of the problems associated with diverse data types by allowing for user-defined markup rather than browser-defined markup. It provides markup that describes the content similar to that of SGML and goes beyond merely describing the format. This description of content has implications for extracting and reusing the content in ways that allows micro-payments and charge-per-use mechanisms. For example, a book marked in XML can then be displayed and manipulated in various ways. It can be displayed chapter-by-chapter, in sections or even paragraphs. XML-encoded material can be viewed both on the Web and personal devices such as e-book readers and personal digital assistants. The Open eBook Forum is working on a standard method of encoding e-books in XML specifically to provide an easy method for interchanging books across reading devices (www.openebook.org).

The efforts to provide an open XML-based infrastructure enabling the global use of electronic business information in an interoperable and secure environment are underway. ebXML, sponsored by UN/CEFACT and OASIS, is a modular suite of specifications that enables enterprises of any size and in any geographical location to conduct business over the Internet (http://www. ebxml.org/geninfo.htm). By taking advantage of these efforts, digital libraries will be in a better position to implement electronic commerce and micro-payment systems.

CONCLUSION

In this chapter we addressed some of the issues and challenges facing digital libraries in their adoption of e-commerce. Some of these issues can be resolved using technology such as access control, cataloging, and indexing. Others, such as content management, quality of information, copyright and intellectual property, go beyond technical issues and extend to policies and regulation. To make e-commerce a viable option for digital libraries, the issue of to micro-payments and charging must first be resolved. Such an issue is not restricted to digital libraries but also to many businesses on the Web that deal with content such as music and gaming. It is obviously infeasible to collect small amounts when the cost of processing such small transactions is higher than the fee to be collected itself. As technology advances, digital libraries will continue to look for new ways in which content and other services can be delivered and a fee correspondingly collected. This could be achieved through new charging mechanisms, such as CyberCash and across-country NETS mechanism.

REFERENCES

Adam, N., & Yesha, Y., (1996). Electronic commerce and digital libraries: Towards a digital agora. *ACM Computing Surveys.*

Al-Hawamdeh, S. (1999). Integrating electronic course reserve into the digital library framework. *Singapore Journal of Library and Information Management, 28,* 64-72.

Arms, W.Y., Banchi, C., & Overly, E.A. (1997). An architecture for information in digital libraries. *D-Lib Magazine,* February, [Online] http://www. dlib.org/dlib/february97/cnri/02arms1.html.

Barker, P. (1994). Electronic libraries—Visions of the future. *The Electronic Library, 12*(4), 221-230.

Barlow, J.P. (1995). Selling wine without bottles. *Proceedings of Digital Libraries Conference: Moving forward into the information era,* Singapore.

Breeding, M. (2000). NetLibrary, Innovative interfaces to add to e-books to library collections. *Information Today, 17*(3), 1-3.

Borgman, C.L. (1997). Multi media, multi cultural and multi lingual digital libraries. *D-Lib Magazine,* June [Online] http://www.dlib.org/ dlib/june97/06borgman.html.

Catledge, L.D., & Pitkow, J.E., (1995). Characterizing browsing strategies in the World-Wide Web. *Proceedings of the 3rd International World Wide Web Conference, Volume 28 of Computer Networks and ISDN Systems,* April 10-14, Darmstadt, Germany. [Online] http://www.igd.fhg. de/archive/1995_www95/proceedings/papers/80/ userpatterns/UserPatterns.Paper4.formatted. html.

Compaq Computer Corporation, (2001). *The MilliCent microcommerce network* [Online] http://www.millicent.com/home.html.

Croft, W.B. (1995). What do people want from information retrieval? (The top 10 research issues for companies that use and sell IR systems). *D-Lib Magazine,* November. [Online] http://www.dlib.org/dlib/november95/11croft.html

Digital Library Federation (2001). [Online] http://www.clir.org/diglib/dlfhomepage.htm

Fialkoff, F. (1998). Linking to online booksellers. *Library Journal, 123*(11), 68.

Fong, W.W.,(1997). Library information and technology in *Southeast Asia. Information Technology and Libraries, 16*(1), 20-27.

Garrett, J. (1993). Digital libraries: The grand challenges. [Online] http://www.ifla.org/documents/libraries/net/garrett.txt

Harris, L.E. (2000). Libraries and e-commerce: Improving information services and beyond. *Information Outlook, 4*(3), 24-30.

Levy, D.M. (1995). Cataloging in the digital order. [Online] http://csdl.tamu.edu/DL95/papers/levy/levy.html

Marchionini, G. (1999). Research development in digital libraries [Online]. http://www.glue.umd.edu/~march/digital_library_R_and_D.html

Mohideen, H. (1996). Dealing with copyright issues in digital libraries. Libraries in national development, *Proceedings of Tenth Congress of Southeast Asian Librarians.* Kuala Lumpur.

Oppenheim, C. (1992). *The legal and regulatory environment for electronic information.* Calne, Wilts., Calne, UK: Infonortics Ltd.

Regan, K. (2001) Amazon testing micropayments via music downloads. [Online] http://www.ecommercetimes.com/perl/story/7822.html

Rowley, J. (1998). *The electronic library.* London: Library Association Publishing.

Song, S. (1999). *Electronic commerce and its impacts to library and information profession.* [Online] http://www.slis.ualberta.ca/538-99/ssong/termproj.htm

Tennant, R. (1997). Digital potential and pitfalls. *Library Journal, 122*(19), 21-22. Also available in Library Journal Digital, InfoTech News: Digital Libraries, November 15. [Online] http://www.libraryjournal.com/articles/infotech/digitallibraries/19971115_2014.asp

Washington State Library Council (1999). *Issues in Digitization: A report prepared for the Washington State Library Council,* Jan 5.

Chapter XV
Intellectual Property Protection and Standardization

Knut Blind
Fraunhofer Institute for Systems and Innovation Research, Germany

Nikolaus Thumm
Swiss Federal Institute of Intellectual Property, Switzerland

ABSTRACT

This chapter presents the first attempt at analyzing the relationship between strategies to protect intellectual property rights and their impact on the likelihood of joining formal standardization processes, based on a small sample of European companies. On the one hand, theory suggests that the stronger the protection of one's own technological know-how, the higher the likelihood to join formal standardization processes in order to leverage the value of the technological portfolio. On the other hand, companies at the leading edge are often in such a strong position that they do not need the support of standards to market their products successfully. The results of the statistical analysis show that the higher the patent intensities of companies, the lower their tendency to join standardization processes, supporting the latter theoretical hypothesis.

INTRODUCTION

Over the last decade both the number of patent applications submitted to national and international patent offices and the number of standards claimed at standardization bodies have risen tremendously. In patenting, a 'pro-patent era' began in the mid-1980s. At the European level, it accompanied the establishment of a coherent legal European framework, introducing new national and European legislation for different technological fields. Standardization processes, measured by their output (i.e., the number of formal standards) also increased, especially in Europe (Blind, 2002a). One indication of this trend was the creation of new standardization bodies such as the ETSI, the

European Telecommunication Standards Institute. Both phenomena have already been the subject of scientific analysis.[1]

The ambivalence of intellectual property rights and *de facto* industry standards, or *de jure* standards for technological development, is triggered by two different economic mechanisms. Intellectual property rights (IPRs) provide knowledge producers with the temporary right of exclusive exploitation of the benefits deriving from the new knowledge. In this way, IPR provides knowledge producers with the publicly desirable incentive to invest in R&D. They provide holders with a temporary monopoly position, but IPR limits the free diffusion of technological knowledge. Potential users can either not get access to required knowledge or have to pay for it (licensing). Some IPRs, like patents, include at least a positive element of diffusion by the publication of the protected specifications.

In contrast to intellectual property rights, standards released by standards development organizations are decisive for the diffusion of new technologies. They make information about new technologies available to everyone for a small fee and come near to being a classical public good. Innovation researchers until now have concentrated primarily on the analysis of mechanisms that foster the generation of new technological knowledge. However, only the broad diffusion of technology triggered by standards and technical rules can foster economic growth.

Intellectual property rights and standardisation are important social institutions that play active roles in technical innovation. They share certain similarities as institutions: for example, both patenting and standardisation essentially serve to codify technical information into non-dubious, replicable language. At the same time, their roles are essentially different. A patent describes the parameters of a technology (product or process) over which the patentee owns limited rights, while standard specifications are elaborated by diverse interest groups in order to provide common ground for the future development of new technologies. This common ground consists of not only standards to reduce the variety of possible technological trajectories to a minimum, but also of compatibility standards that allow the exploitation of network externalities and of quality standards for increasing consumer acceptance.[2]

The traditional point of conflict between IPR and standardisation occurs when the implementation of a standard, by its essence, necessitates the application of proprietary technology. Both processes bring together two (p. 11) seemingly contradictory processes: the creation of variety and its successive reduction through selection. Effective long-term adaptation requires that these two processes be kept in balance (p. 11) (Carlsson & Stankiewicz, 1994).

Since involvement in standardisation processes is accompanied by the danger that the other participants could use the disclosed and unprotected technological knowledge for their own purposes, R&D-intensive companies whose knowledge is either insufficiently protected by IPR or extremely valuable may be reluctant to join standardisation processes. Although a variety of protection instruments exists, it is difficult to measure their effectiveness. One formal means of legal protection is patenting. Since applying for a patent entails significant costs (such as fees and costs for legal advice), the expected economic value must be higher than the actual expenses. Thus, a patent application will be made only if the value of the technological know-how reaches a certain level. In addition, the know-how to be protected must also be of value to competitors and not only the company itself. In other words, the number of patent applications indicates not only the intensity with which knowledge protection instruments are used, but also the dimensions of the expected economic value of the company's technological knowledge base. Since IPR tends to concentrate in the areas of greater technical complexity, it becomes virtually impossible to adopt a standard without incorporating proprietary material.

The interaction of standardisation and intellectual property rights has not yet been the subject of in-depth analysis. The only research to date is a study, "Interaction of Standardisation and Intellectual Property Rights," funded by the Directorate General Research of the European Commission (EC Contract No G6MA-CT-2000-01001) (see Blind et al., 2002). The study was carried out by the Fraunhofer Institute for Systems and Innovation Research (FhG-ISI) and the Institute for Prospective Technological Studies (IPTS) on a small sample of 149 European companies, more than half of which were from the United Kingdom, Germany, and France, covering a wide range of industries; however, with a focus on research and development and manufacturing of chemicals. Except for a few individual case studies, this survey connected the IPR strategies of companies with their standardisation activities for the first time. We have used the survey data derived from this study as the basis for the empirical results presented in this article.

Based on the previously outlined differences between the strategy of participating in standardisation and that of using intellectual property rights, we propose several hypotheses that are investigated in the following analysis:

- The mode of IPR protection has an influence on the likelihood of joining standardisation processes: The more formal/informal the protection instruments, the lower/higher the likelihood of unintended spillovers in standardisation processes and the higher/lower the probability of joining standardisation processes.
- The higher the patent intensity, the higher the likelihood of joining standardisation processes because of a lower danger of spillovers.

- Or: the higher the patent intensity, the stronger the technological advantage of a company for success on the market without relying on standardisation.
- Patenting is mainly driven by strategic goals. The more patenting is used as a strategic instrument, the higher the likelihood of joining standardisation bodies in order to raise licensing revenues or improve market position.

The remainder of this chapter is structured as follows: Firstly, IPR strategies are analyzed, different means of IP protection discussed, and the individual intellectual property strategies of the companies in our sample described. The descriptive statistics of the use of different protection strategies, patent motives, and standardisation engagement and motives are outlined. With the help of a simple statistical analysis, we will both look at the importance of different factors determining the decision to participate in the standardisation process. Finally, a summary of the results concerning the interface between IPR strategies and standardisation concludes the analysis.

USE OF PROTECTION STRATEGIES AND MOTIVES FOR PATENTING

Intellectual property rights are supposed to be an important incentive for research and development, and they are held to be a necessary precondition for science and technology to progress. A patent on an invention grants certain rights to the applicant for the use of that invention. There is a trade-off between the disclosure of detailed information by the inventor against the guarantee of a limited monopoly awarded by the state.[3] The patent system is designed as an incentive mechanism for the creation of new, economically valuable knowledge and as a knowledge-dissemination mechanism to spread this information. In economic literature,

Figure 1. Importance of protection strategies (very low = 1 to very high = 5)

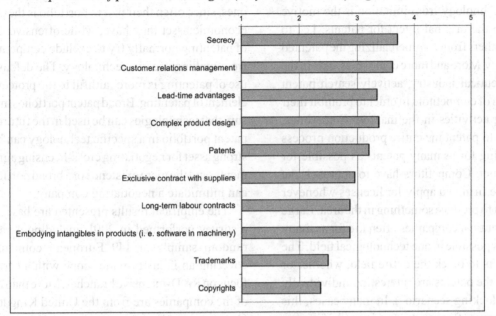

IPRs are predominantly understood in terms of their contribution to the 'incentive structure' and less for their role in distributing information about innovation throughout the economy.[4] However, in some instances the information from patent applications has been used for imitation of technology. Consequently, the applicants changed their behavior by trying to disclose as little information as possible in their patent applications. Finally, there are much more effective and efficient instruments to observe the emerging of innovations, like screening trade magazines or visiting trade exhibitions.

The economic argument for IPR is that there is a market failure in the case of technological knowledge. Technological knowledge is a public good. The non-excludability characteristic of technological knowledge, together with the non-rivalry characteristic, led under free-market conditions to a reduced incentive for investment in innovation (R&D investments) and to inefficient diffusion by following secrecy strategies. This is

the usual argument for why government intervention, in the form of an intellectual property rights system, is required. "Patents are designed to create a market for knowledge by assigning propriety property rights to innovators which enable them to overcome the problem of non-excludability while, at the same time, encouraging the maximum diffusion of knowledge by making it public."[5] Consequently, IPRs are only a second-best solution, which is the price to be paid for innovative activity (Deardorff, 1992, p. 38).

Although it is clear that patents are an important incentive for research and development, it is also clear that, in addition to their initial purpose to protect, they are used in many other ways.[6] The original concept of patents, with the intention of protecting and fostering the distribution of inventions, is becoming less important as many secondary uses increase in importance. Not all economically useful inventions are patented or even patentable, and often secrecy is considered a more appropriate tool for protection, especially where product life cycles are relatively short.[7] To protect technology from imitation is the motive closest to the original intent for patents, i.e., to prohibit others from commercializing the patented technology. More and more companies, e.g., in the pharmaceutical industry, actively search patent portfolios of competitors in order to prohibit their patenting activities in the market.[8] Sometimes, firms try to patent the entire production process by applying for as many patents as possible for one product. Competitors have to approach the respective firm and apply for licenses whenever they want to produce something in the area. Large pharmaceutical companies often file for as many patents as possible in one technological field. The intention is to block the entire field, whether or not all of the patents are interesting individually (i.e., a "blocking scenario"). In many cases, this strategy comes from an economic need: If it is not done by the inventor, then some other competitor can take the initiative and place a patent in the technological niche. Firms can respond to patent blocking by either trying to invalidate patents, invent around them, or simply ignore them and risk an infringement suit (Grandstrand, 1999, p. 219). More cooperatively, companies can try to obtain foreign technology through acquisitioning, establishing a joint venture, or licensing the necessary technology. Patents can also be used as a basis for alliances that aim at moving the patent holder into a better negotiating position against competitors (i.e., swap patents) (Thumm, 2001).

Many of the patenting motives mentioned can be used in a defensive way as well as in an offensive way, aiming more at hindering competitors than protecting one's own inventions. This depends very much on the coherency of the patenting strategy.[9] Strategic use of patenting is useful to, but not limited to small and medium-sized biotechnology businesses, as well as large firms. Restrained by their economic resources, such companies use strategic patenting to achieve a competitive advantage without expending too many of their own resources.[10] In a way, small

companies depend more on patenting than larger ones, since often their patent portfolio is the only economic asset they have, while offensive uses of patenting normally try to exclude competitors from making use of a technology. The defensive use of patenting is more faithful to the protective element of patenting. Broad patent portfolios make sure that technologies can be used in the future. A patent portfolio in a specific technology can be a strong asset for negotiating cross-licensing agreements, and the mere existence of a broad portfolio can intimidate a negotiating company.

The empirical results presented are based on a survey performed in 2001, including a small random sample of 149 European companies covering an industry-wide scope with a certain focus on R&D-intensive branches. More than half of the companies are from the United Kingdom, Germany, and France, covering a wide range of industries with a focus on research and development and manufacturing of chemicals. Half of the companies have less than 250 employees, while one-third have more than 1,000.

These companies answered a question about the relative importance of various measures to protect inventions or innovations developed in their enterprise during the period 1998-2000. Figure 1 presents the ranking of the importance of the various protection strategies. Secrecy and other more informal measures such as customer relations management, lead-time advantages, and complex product design turned out to be the most important protection strategies. This finding is consistent with the results of other investigations which showed that secrecy is generally valued higher for firms, independent of their size (Arundel, 2001, p. 614). In contrast to other surveys, like the Community Innovation Survey, where patents have a low level of importance in comparison with other means of protection, patents reach an above-average score in our sample.[11] Other formal protection measures such as trademarks and copyrights are less important.

Figure 2. Importance of patenting motives (very low = 1 to very high = 5)

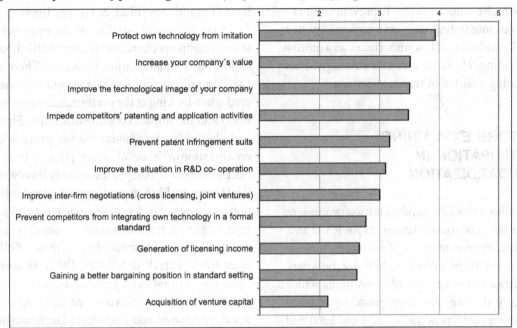

The importance of patenting and complex product design increases with firm size, but so does the importance of secrecy. Lead-time advantage as a protection tool is more relevant in Germany, the UK, Austria, and Switzerland, whereas exclusive contracts are by comparison more common in the three Mediterranean countries (France, Italy, and Spain). Other surveys showed secrecy to be an effective alternative to patenting.[12] Our sample, however, shows a positive correlation between patenting and secrecy at the same time (Rammer, 2002). Surprisingly, secrecy, as a protection tool, is more important for patenting-intensive companies and/or for R&D-intensive companies.

The companies in the sample were asked about their preferences among a number of motives why they make use of patenting. Firms indicated that protecting technology from imitation has the highest importance as a motive for patenting (compare Figure 2), and that this is particularly true for those companies using the patenting system intensively. This corresponds with the

classical (defensive) use of patents, but also with the economic reasoning behind patenting, the so-called 'innovation effect' of patents (Mazzoleni & Nelson, 1998). Competitors are excluded from commercializing the patented technology. The results of the survey also show that the value of the company and improving the technology image of the company are also important patenting motives. More aggressive uses of patenting are considered to be of lower importance than defensive ones. Impeding competitors' patenting and application activities scored very highly. The relevance of this motive to patent is positively correlated with the firm size. Aggressive patenting is obviously more an issue with bigger companies that have the relevant capacities. The business-related aspects of patenting, such as the generation of licensing income and the acquisition of venture capital, are of relatively low importance. This is astonishing since, classically, industry uses patents as an instrument to make money by licensing and to achieve highest economic returns, even though only a rather small fraction of patents turns out to have high economic value. To prevent competitors from integrating their own technology in a formal standard is of low importance as a motive for patenting. The same is true for gaining a better bargaining position in standard-setting.

FACTORS EXPLAINING PARTICIPATION IN STANDARDIZATION

The decision to join a standardisation process, as well as the allocation of resources for R&D and, therefore, the commitment of resources, is made on the firm level (see Wakelin, 1998, for the latter). In contrast to the benefits of innovations which primarily the firm can appropriate by reduced production costs, penetrating new markets, and exploiting monopoly rents, new standards published and distributed by standard development organizations are, at first glance, a public good.[14] In reality, however, the general possibility is for everybody to buy a standard at a reasonable price; only the core of companies that have the relevant technological know-how can use the new technical specification effectively and efficiently.[15] Therefore, the participants in the standardisation process may have advantages compared to outsiders, due to their early involvement in the development of the standard and the accompanying process of knowledge exchange and creation. Salop and Scheffman (1983, 1987) underline this argument, in that the establishment of product standards may be a strategy by which firms could disadvantage rivals by raising their costs. In addition, only the companies that are in the same branch or are using the same technology may benefit in general from a new standard. Therefore, the single company is also an appropriate unit of analysis, especially when considering the relationships between innovation, standardisation, and export behavior, despite the explicit technological spillovers of standards, which justify an analysis at a branch

(see Blind, 2002b) or even at a macroeconomic level (Jungmittag, Blind, & Grupp, 1999).

In the following, we discuss the influence of several company characteristics on the likelihood of joining standardisation activities. There are two contradictory trends that should be considered when looking at the performance of firms in R&D and the impact on standardisation. Firstly, and obviously, the standardisation process is a continuation of the development phase of internal R&D. Therefore, companies actively involved in R&D are more likely to participate in standardisation processes in order to continue their previous activities and to reach marketable products or process technologies compatible with those of other companies (Farrell & Saloner, 1985). However, involvement in a standardisation process is accompanied by the danger that other participants could use the disclosed and unprotected technological knowledge for their own purposes. Therefore, R&D-intensive companies may be more reluctant to join standardisation processes and, instead, try to market their products alone without relying on standardized input technologies, common interfaces to complementary products of other competitors, or even uniform product designs. On the other hand, companies with minimal R&D can compensate by entering standardisation clubs of R&D-intensive firms to benefit from the technology transfer, especially since the specifications of standards can be integrated without any significant R&D capacity. An analysis by Love and Roper (1999) of the substitute relationship between one's own R&D and technology transfer supports this view. In general, company R&D intensity is an ambivalent indicator for the likelihood of joining standardisation processes.

When discussing the role of the export activities, a two-way causality has to be considered. Due to the institutional paradigms of most national standardisation development bodies, the participation in standardisation processes at a national level also influences the standardisation at the European or international levels. Therefore, exporting companies that try to influence supranational standards in order to secure market shares in foreign markets are more likely to participate in standardisation at the national and international levels. However, the influence of a single company on the standardisation processes decreases as the territorial responsibility of the standards committee becomes broader. This fact reduces the motivation of exporters to join standardisation at the supranational level. Nevertheless, companies actively involved in standardisation should be more successful in exporting their goods and services due to their influence on the product specification of supranational standards.

Standardisation is certainly a strategy to shape foreign markets according to the specifications of one's own products or technologies, and the advantage to be had is shared by all other participants, including—although with a certain time lag—the companies implementing the standards. Standardisation constrains competition for a very short time by giving the participants a leading position, which is only temporary, since the codification of the technical specifications allows the other competitors to catch up, at least by the time the standard is officially published. Companies wanting a market lead ahead of the competitors, which results in a monopolistic position with high market shares worldwide (indicated by very high export shares), will be reluctant to join standardisation processes.

The participation in standardisation processes incurs significant costs, for example for highly qualified employees, travel expenses, etc. Since these costs have a fixed-cost effect, small and medium-sized companies are less likely to join standardisation processes and behave more as free-riders. In addition, larger companies are more able to internalize some of the generated positive externalities of standards compared to smaller companies. Therefore, standardisation is less favorable for smaller companies, not only because of costs, but also benefits.

With respect to patents and their involvement in the standardisation process, the following hypotheses can be derived. The higher the patent intensity, the higher the likelihood, especially for R&D-intensive companies, to join standardisation processes because their know-how (which may be disclosed during the standardisation process) is sufficiently protected. On the other hand, it may be argued that a high patent intensity represents a very valuable stock of knowledge possessed by the company. In addition, patent protection may not be sufficient[16] since, besides the disclosure of the company's knowledge in the patent document, during the discussions among the participants of the standardisation process additional information may leak out to the potential competitors. Therefore, a high patent intensity may also lead to a lower likelihood of joining standardisation processes. Very often, large companies possessing large market shares will try to establish proprietary *de facto* industry standards based on broad and sophisticated patent portfolios which allow them to defend their leading position for a longer period and to reappropriate the investments spent for establishing the standard. Such a strategy automatically excludes the support of a formal standardisation process.[17] Therefore, the counter-hypothesis assumes a negative relationship between the patent intensity of a company and its likelihood to join standardisation processes. In general, it can be said that a company's R&D and patenting intensity may have a total negative impact on the likelihood of the company joining standardisation processes.

The definitions of the main company-specific, quantitative variables in the data set are the following (where X stands for exports in €, TT for total turnover in €, R&D for expenditure in €. The subscript i is for the firm and j for the sector.)

Size: $Size_{ij} = logEmployees_{ij}$;
Export intensity: $Exp_{ij} = X_{ij}/TT_{ij}$;
R&D intensity: $R\&D_{ij} = 100*R\&D_{ij}/TT_{ij}$;
Patent intensity: $Pat_{ij} = 100*Patents_{ij}/Employees_{ij}$

Some descriptive statistics for the variables are presented in Figure 3 for the two separate groups of standardizers and non-standardizers. In general, the export intensity and the R&D intensity of both sub-groups are very high. Furthermore, there are several obvious differences between the two classes. The lower export intensity of standardizers was not expected due to the theoretical considerations. The explanation for this sample feature can probably be found in the explanation above, which postulates that companies seeking incontestable competitive advantage avoid formal standardisation processes in order to obtain significant market shares abroad based on the uniqueness of their products.

The explanation for the lower R&D intensity of companies joining the standardisation process supports the substitutive relationship between one's own R&D effort, and the participation in standardisation processes and the reluctance of R&D-intensive companies to disclose their knowledge in standardisation processes. Finally,

the patent intensity of the companies joining the standardisation process is just half of the value of the non-standardisers. This clearly shows that companies with a strong patent portfolio are nevertheless reluctant to join standardisation processes and probably try to be successful in the market without using standardized components or designs of final products. This finding is remarkable in so far as theoretical considerations would point in different directions. IPR is an essential asset in the standardisation war between companies. Firms with a strong copyright and patent portfolio possess an explicit advantage over their competitors (Shapiro & Varian, 1999, p. 295).

Summarizing the findings of our statistical analyses, we have to find an explanation for the much higher negative ratio in the case of patent intensity in comparison to the slightly negative ratio of the R&D. Regarding this aspect, one has to consider that most standard development organizations require that patent holders are willing to license their rights at reasonable and

Figure 3. Main charactersitics of standardisers and non-standardisers

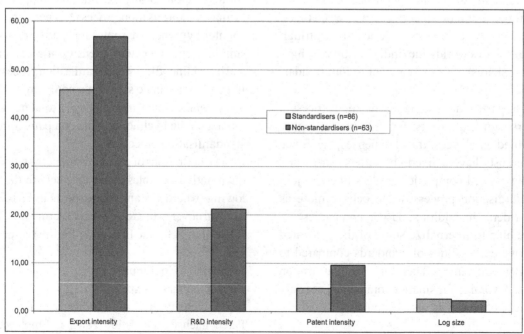

non-discriminatory conditions. Consequently, some companies with broad and valuable patent portfolios are more reluctant to join formal standardisation processes, whereas for the R&D intensity itself, the insignificance can be explained by the ambivalence of the complementary and substitutive relationship. One further dimension has to be mentioned. Besides formal standardisation processes, companies can also choose to join informal standardisation processes, which are more flexible regarding patent rights of the involved parties. Consequently, companies with strong patent portfolios have alternatives with lower opportunity costs to promote the diffusion and marketing of their technologies.

CONCLUSION

This chapter presents the first attempt at analyzing the relationship between strategies to protect intellectual property rights and their impact on the likelihood of joining formal standardisation processes, based on a small sample of European companies. On the one hand, theory suggests that the stronger the protection of the company's own technological know-how, the higher the likelihood to join formal standardisation processes in order to leverage the value of its own technological portfolio. Behind this hypothesis is the assumption that companies should try to achieve both a combination and strong link of standards and IPR. This would provide them with an even stronger market position. A strong IPR portfolio is an essential weapon within a standards war, when companies try to achieve a de facto standard position in the market (Shapiro & Varian, 1999, p. 295). On the other hand, companies at the leading edge are often in such a strong position that they do not need the support of standards to market their products successfully. The statistical results to explain the likelihood to join standardisation processes support the latter theoretical hypothesis, because the higher the R&D and patent intensi-

ties of companies, the lower the tendency to join standardisation processes.

The final question that has to be addressed is: What follows from this result for policy makers? If companies with a strong technological base stay away from standardisation processes, the quality of the standards released may fall behind the technological leading edge and their broad diffusion may be inhibited because of this. Consequently, the positive economic impacts of standards will not be full exploited. In order to solve this shortcoming, solutions have to be found that create additional incentives for technologically strong companies to join standardisation processes, and reduce simultaneously the threat that they suffer from unintentional spillovers of technological know-how to other participants of the standardisation processes.

ACKNOWLEDGMENT

The authors thank three anonymous reviewers and the participants of the SIIT2003 in Delft and the EURAS 2003 workshop in Aachen for their comments. Furthermore, we are grateful for the financial support of DG Research of the European Commission for financial support (EC Contract No G6MA-CT-2000-02001).

REFERENCES

Antonelli, C. (1994). Localized technological change and the evolution of standards as economic institutions. *Information Economics and Policy, 6,* 195-216.

Arundel, A. (2001). The relative effectiveness of patents and secrecy for appropriation. *Research Policy, 30,* 611-624.

Arundel, A., van de Paal, G., & Soete, L. (1995). *Innovation strategies of Europe's largest industrial firms: Results of the PACE survey for information sources, public research, protection of innovations and government programmes.* Directorate General XIII, European Commission, EIMS Publication.

Bekkers, R., Duysters, G., & Verspagen, B. (2002). Intellectual property rights, strategic technology agreements and market structure; the case of GSM. *Research Policy, 31*(7), 1141-1161.

Blind, K. (2001). Standardisation, R&D and export activities: Empirical evidence at firm level. *Proceedings of the Third Interdisciplinary Workshop on Standardization Research* (pp. 165-186), University of the German Federal Armed Forces, Hamburg: University der Bundeswehr.

Blind, K. (2002a). *Normen als Indikatoren für die Diffusion neuer Technologien, Endbericht für das Bundesministerium für Bildung und Forschung im Rahmen der Untersuchung "zur Technologischen Leistungsfähigkeit Deutschlands" zum Schwerpunkt "methodische Erweiterungen des Indikatorensystems."* Karlsruhe: ISI.

Blind, K. (2002b). Driving forces for standardisation at standardisation development organisations. *Applied Economics, 34*(16), 1985-1998.

Blind, K. (2004). *The economics of standards: Theory, evidence, policy.* Cheltenham: Edward Elgar.

Blind, K., Bierhals, R., Iversen, E., Hossain, K., Rixius, B., Thumm, N., & van Reekum, R. (2002). *Study on the interaction between standardisation and intellectual property rights.* Final Report for DG Research of the European Commission (EC Contract No G6MA-CT-2000-02001). Karlsruhe: ISI.

Blind, K., & Thumm, N. (2003). Interdependencies between intellectual property protection and standardisation strategies. *Proceedings of EURAS 2002* (pp. 88-106), Aachener Beiträge zur Informatik, Band 33, Wissenschaftsverlag Mainz, Aachen.

Drahos, P. (1996). *A philosophy of intellectual property.* Brookfield; Singapore; Sydney: Aldershot.

Farrell, J., & Saloner, G. (1985). Standardization, compatibility, and innovation. *RAND Journal of Economics, 16,* 70-83.

Geroski, P. (1995). Markets for technology: Knowledge, innovation and appropriability. In P. Stoneman (Ed.), *Handbook of the economics of innovation and technological change.* Blackwell.

Grandstrand, O. (1999). *The economics and management of intellectual property.* Cheltenham: Edward Elgar.

Hall, B.H., & Ziedonis, R.H. (2001). The patent paradox revisited: An empirical analysis of patenting in the U.S. semiconductor industry, 1979-1995. *Rand Journal of Economics, 32,* 101-128.

Harabi, N. (1995). Appropriability of technical innovations: An empirical analysis. *Research Policy, 24,* 981-992.

Heller, M., & Eisenberg, R. (1998). Can patents deter innovation? The anticommons in biomedical research. *Science, 280,* 698-701.

Jungmittag, A., Blind, K., & Grupp, H. (1999). Innovation, standardization and the long-term production function: A co-integration approach for Germany, 1960-1996. *Zeitschrift für Wirtschafts und Sozialwissenschaften, 119,* 205-222.

Kortum, S., & Lerner, J. (1999). What is behind the recent surge in patenting? *Research Policy, 28*(1), 1-22.

Lemley, M.A. (2002). *Intellectual property rights and standard setting organizations.* Contribution to the public hearing on competition and intellectual property law and policy in the knowledge-based economy in 2001 and 2002. Available online at: http://www.ftc.gov/opp/intellect/index.htm

Mazzoleni, R., & Nelson, R. (1998). The benefits and costs of strong patent protection: A contribution to the current debate. *Research Policy, 27*(3), 273-84.

Meeus, M.T.H., Faber, J., & Oerlemans, L.A.G. (2002). *Why do firms participate in standardization? An empirical exploration of the relation between isomorphism and institutional dynamics in standardization.* Working Paper, Department of Innovation Studies, University of Utrecht.

Merges, R.P. (1999). *Institutions for intellectual property transactions: The case of patent pools.* Working Paper, Revision 1999, University of California at Berkeley.

Ordover, J.A. (1991). A patent system for both diffusion and exclusion. *Journal of Economic Perspectives, 5*(1), 43-60.

Rammer, C. (2002). *Patente und Marken als Schutzmechanismen für Innovationen.* Studien zum deutschen Innovationssystem Nr. 11-2003, Zentrum für Europäische Wirtschaftsforschung (ZEW), Mannheim.

Rapp, R.T., & Stiroh, L.J. (2002). *Standard setting and market power.* Contribution to the Public Hearing on Competition and Intellectual Property Law and Policy in the Knowledge-Based Economy in 2001 and 2002. Available online at http://www.ftc.gov/opp/intellect/index.htm.

Salop, S.C., & Scheffman, D.T. (1983). Raising rivals' costs. *American Economic Review, 73*(2), 267-271.

Salop, S.C., & Scheffman, D.T. (1987). Cost-raising strategies. *Journal of Industrial Economics, 36*(1), 19-34.

Scherer, F.M., & Ross, D. (Eds.). (1990). *Industrial market structure and economic performance.* Dallas, Geneva: 3.A.

Shapiro, C. (2001). Navigating the patent thicket: Cross licenses, patent pools, and standard setting.

In A. Jaffe, J, Lerner, & S. Stern (Ed.), *Innovation policy and the economy* (vol. 1, pp. 119-150). Boston: MIT Press.

Shapiro, C., & Varian, H. (1999). *Information rules. A strategic guide to the network economy.* Boston: Harvard Business School Press.

Swann, P. (2000). *The economics of standardization.* Final Report for Standards and Technical Regulations, Directorate Department of Trade and Industry, University of Manchester.

Thumm, N. (2001). Management of intellectual property rights in European biotechnology firms. *Technological Forecasting and Social Change, 67*(July), 259-272.

Thumm, N. (2002). Europe's construction of a patent system for biotechnological inventions: An assessment of industry views. *Technological Forecasting and Social Change, 69*(December), 917-928.

Wakelin, K. (1998). Innovation and export behaviour at the firm level. *Research Policy, 26,* 829-841.

ENDNOTES

[1] Especially patents: For a comprehensive analysis of the recent surge in patenting in the U.S. (see Kortun and Lerner, 1999).

[2] See Swann (2000) for a recent overview of the different effects of standards.

[3] Compare Scherer (1990, p. 623).

[4] This is empirically underlined by the very low usage of patents as a source for innovation; cf. Eurostat (2000, p. 30).

[5] Geroski, P. (1995, p. 97). Analogously, Ordover (1991) prefers a strong patent regime, which facilitates a broad diffusion of knowledge, in coordination with an efficient licensing system.

⁶ A number of motives for the biotechnology industry are explained in Thumm (2001).

⁷ Various surveys demonstrate that manufacturing firms estimate secrecy higher than appropriation methods (Arundel, van de Paal, & Soete, 1995; Arundel, 2001; Harabi, 1995).

⁸ So-called patent portfolio races, see, e.g., Hall and Ziedonis (2001) for the semiconductor industry and Heller and Eisenberg (1998) for the biotechnology industry.

⁹ For a systematic overview on various patenting strategies, see Grandstrand (1999, p. 232).

¹⁰ In addition, these companies depend even more than big firms on the regulatory framework (see Thumm, 2002).

¹¹ In the survey among U.S. companies, Cohen et al. (2000) find that patents are very important in the chemical sector, whereas in the manufacturing industry, in electrical machinery, and in medical instruments, secrecy is the most important protection measure.

¹² Cf. Arundel (2001, p. 622). Secrecy in general is more important for process innovation, where its level of importance turns out to be independent from the firm size. Larger companies tend to be more familiar with formal appropriation methodologies, and consequently, for product innovations the importance of secrecy decreases with the firm size.

¹³ A previous and extended version can be found in Blind and Thumm (2003). The applied regression approach is developed in Blind (2004).

¹⁴ In the case of privately owned de facto standards caused by network externalities, the R&D decision will change towards a socially ineffective speed up of R&D. Cf. Kristiansen (1998).

¹⁵ Therefore, Antonelli (1994) goes even further and characterizes standards as non-pure private goods.

¹⁶ See above, since secrecy is the most important protection strategy, whereas patenting is only of secondary importance.

¹⁷ However, there are examples where companies tried to influence the formal standardisation process into specification which seemed to be very good in the technological sense or not very promising concerning market acceptance in order to increase the market shares of their technologies or products.

This work was previously published in International Journal of IT Standards and Standardization Research, Vol. 2, No. 2, edited by K. Blind and N. Thumm, pp. 60-75, copyright 2004 by IGI Publishing, formerly known as Idea Group Publishing (an imprint of IGI Global).

Chapter XVI
The Performance of Standard Setting Organizations:
Using Patent Data for Evaluation

Marc Rysman
Boston Univeristy, USA

Tim Simcoe
University of Toronto, Canada

ABSTRACT

This chapter uses citations to patents disclosed in the standard setting process to measure the technological significance of voluntary standard setting organizations (SSOs). We find that SSO patents are outliers in several dimensions and importantly, are cited far more frequently than a set of control patents. More surprisingly, we find that SSO patents receive citations for a much longer period of time. Furthermore, we find a significant correlation between citation and the disclosure of a patent to an SSO, which may imply a marginal impact of disclosure. These results provide the first empirical look at patents disclosed to SSO's, and show that these organizations both select important technologies and play a role in establishing their significance.

INTRODUCTION

Voluntary standard setting organizations (SSOs) provide a venue for market participants to develop compatible standards on which to develop new products. These organizations provide an opportunity for markets to reach compatibility without relying on possibly costly and inefficient government regulation and market-based standards wars. Given their potentially important role in high-technology markets, SSO's have been the subject of substantial amount of research using social science methods, with *JITSR* being an example. However, this research has primarily focused on determining the incentives of market players to participate and implement standard setting, and on the optimal internal organization of SSOs. Our knowledge of the economic and technological impact of these institutions remains quite limited. Evaluating the role of SSOs is difficult because they operate in diverse markets and their effect on outcome variables such as price and quantity are often uncertain.[1]

This chapter attempts to evaluate the contribution of SSOs to the innovative process. We exploit patents disclosed in the standardization process as a metric for measurement. The treatment of intellectual property is an ubiquitous problem for SSOs and participants regularly must disclose relevant patents to SSOs in the process of negotiating a standard. In this chapter, we use these patents as a window into the role of SSOs in technological innovation. Patents are easily compared across time and industries, and many properties are well-known as a result of a large amount of research in economics and related fields.

Following the literature on patents, we use patent citations as a measure of economic and technological importance (Jaffe & Trajtenberg, 2002). Citations are well-known to be correlated with economic measures of the importance of a patent, such stock market valuation and the likelihood of renewal. We use patents identified in the intellectual property disclosure records of four SSOs: the European Telecommunications Standards Institute (ETSI), the Institute for Electrical and Electronic Engineers (IEEE), the Internet Engineering Task Force (IETF), and the International Telecommunications Union (ITU). We construct control samples based on technological class and application year of the patents.

We show that patents associated with standard settings differ from control patents in several important dimensions. They are more likely to be part of international families, more likely to be continuation applications, and much more likely to be litigated. Importantly, we find that SSO patents receive far more citations than an average patent, around 3.5 times higher. More surprisingly, SSO patents receive citations over a much longer time period. We show that the average age at which a citation is received is higher for SSO than control patents and that the difference is economically and statistically significant. Interestingly, this difference is greater when we compare SSO patents to a group of highly cited control patents. One explanation for this long-lived citation pattern may be that innovations associated with standards are subject to lock-in and network effects, leading them to be important for a longer period than the average patent.

Two reasons that SSO patents differ from other patents are that the SSO *selects* patents that represent important technologies and that the SSO actually *causes* technologies to have the citation profile we observe. That is, we may wonder whether SSO patents would have had similar citation patterns if they had never been associated with an SSO. The selection effect is natural given that SSOs explicitly attempt to identify the best technology to serve a given need. Finding that the selection effect is important suggests that SSOs are successful in identifying important technologies. The causal effect may arise because an SSO embeds a technology in a standard that then exhibits long-lasting economic importance because of network effects and lock-in. Another source for a causal effect may be that because an SSO disclosure represents a public announcement, it attracts attention to a patent. Finding a causal effect for SSOs suggests that over and above the stated goals of SSOs in facilitating interconnection between complementary markets, SSOs have a further role in determining the path of technological innovation into the future.

In this chapter, we exploit the timing of disclosures to separate between the selection and causation effects. That is, the extent to which the citation pattern changes after a patent is disclosed to an SSO gives a measure of the causal effect of the SSO. We are cautious in this interpretation as the timing of disclosure depends on the economic environment. In subsequent paragraphs, we discuss why the endogeneity of disclosure could lead us to over or under-estimate the causation effect. However, given the lack of a truly exogenous determination of disclosure, we find this approach a logical starting place.

Our regression approach compares disclosed to undisclosed SSO patents and compares patents before and after disclosure. We find an economically and statistically significant correlation of citations with disclosure. To the extent that we measure the causal effect of an SSO, it appears that the causal effect represents between 25% and 40% of the difference in citations between SSO and non-SSO patents.

This chapter contributes to a growing empirical literature that examines the impact of particular institutions on the process of technological change. Examples of this research include Furman and Stern's (2004) study of biological resource centers and studies of the university-industry interface, including Mowery et al (1999) and Markiewicz (2004). In the next section, we describe the four SSOs that are examined in this chapter and how they treat intellectual property. The Data section describes the data set, while the Citation Patterns section takes an initial look at the difference in citation patterns between the SSO and control samples. The Selection vs. Causation section examines the postdisclosure increase in citation rates. The Conclusion section offers some conclusions.

SSOs AND INTELLECTUAL PROPERTY

Before using patent data to study the role of SSO's in the innovation process, it is important to understand the role of patents and intellectual property in the standard setting process. This section describes the four organizations studied and describes how each of them deals with intellectual property.

We use data collected from four major SSOs. These groups are the European Telecommunication Standards Institute (ETSI), the Institute of Electrical and Electronics Engineers (IEEE), the Internet Engineering Task Force (IETF), and the International Telecommunications Union-Telecommunication Standardization Sector (ITU-T, or often, ITU). Both ETSI and the ITU are international institutions that focus primarily on telecommunications standards. While international in scope, the IEEE and IETF draw the majority of their participants from North America, and are usually associated with the computer hardware and software industries although some of their most significant standards are communications protocols.

Of the four SSOs that we examine, the ITU is the oldest, with origins dating back to around 1865. Its original mission was to promote international coordination among the various rapidly expanding domestic telephone networks. The ITU is based in Switzerland and is associated with the United Nations. Its membership consists of delegates from member nations along with representatives of the larger firms or network operators in each of these countries. The organization's standard setting activities continue to emphasize the protocols used to operate the international telephone network, with work areas that include numbering and addressing, network services, physical interconnection, monitoring and accounting, traffic management, and quality of service.

The IEEE is only slightly younger than the ITU. It was founded in 1884 by several pioneers in the field of electrical engineering. Although the IEEE is a professional society whose members are individual engineers, it is possible to become a corporate member when participating in its standard setting activities. The IEEE's standard setting efforts cover a wide range of subjects, from electrical safety, to cryptography, to standards for semiconductor testing equipment. In recent years, the IEEE's most commercially significant standards

Figure 1. Intellectual property disclosures

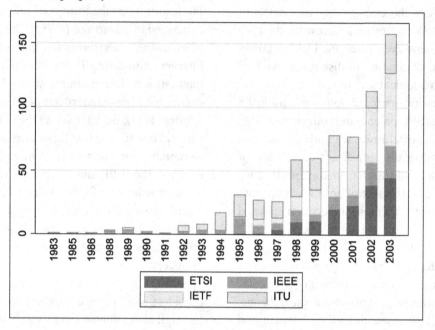

work has revolved around the 802.11 specifications for wireless computer networking.

ETSI was formed in 1988 to provide a less formal and more industry-driven forum than the ITU for European telecom standardization. The organization is located in southern France and participants are typically firms—as opposed to the member-state representatives of the ITU. ETSI has played a prominent role in creating several generations of mobile telephony standards that are in use throughout Europe and much of the rest of the world. In particular, it is the forum where a variety of network operators, electronics suppliers, and cellular handset manufacturers reached key agreements on the GSM and 3G wireless protocols.

Finally, the IETF is the least formal of the four SSOs studied in this chapter. This organization grew out the ARPANET engineering community that emerged during the 1970s, and did not resemble a formal SSO until the late 1980s or early 1990s (Mowery & Simcoe, 2002). The IETF cre-

ates a host of protocols used to run the Internet. Prominent examples include the Internet's core transport protocols (TCP/IP and Ethernet), standards used to allocate network addresses (DHCP), and specifications used by popular applications such as e-mail or file transfer. From its inception, membership in the IETF and its various working groups has been open to any interested individual. Much of the IETF's work takes place in online forums sponsored by individual committees and is visible to the general public.

Because all four of the SSO's examined in this chapter are more or less "open," each of them must deal with the increasing tension between open standards and intellectual property protection. The goal of most SSOs is to promote widespread implementation and adoption of the specifications they produce. However, these goals often conflict with those of individual participants who may hold intellectual property rights in a proposed standard. Patent owners frequently seek royalty payments for the use of their technology—even (or, perhaps, especially) when it is essential to the implementation of an industry standard. Moreover, many firms realize that owning intellectual property rights in an industry standard can result in substantial licensing revenues. This creates strong incentives to push for one's own technology within the SSO, and may lead to long-delays or breakdowns in the standard setting process (Simcoe, 2004).

While most SSOs would like to avoid the distributional conflicts and obstacles to implementation that patents can produce, they often have no choice other than to evaluate a variety of proposals that are subject to some type of intellectual property protection. In part, this is because of the well-documented surge in patenting that began in the mid-1980s. This increase reflects a growing awareness of patents' strategic significance, as well as the actions of courts, policy-makers, and patent offices. Awareness of the tension between SSOs and their patent-holding members has also increased because of a number of high-profile legal conflicts.[2]

Given the increasing importance of the intellectual property issue, many SSOs have been debating their own policies for dealing with patents. Lemley (2002) presents a survey of the various policies that SSOs have adopted. All four of the SSOs examined in this chapter use variations on the relatively common policy of "reasonable and non-discriminatory licensing" (RAND). Under this policy, SSO members agree to disclose any known property rights as soon as they become aware of them. (They are not, however, obliged to carry out a search.) When a patent or other piece of intellectual property is discovered, the SSO seeks assurances from the owner that they will license the technology to any interested standards implementor on reasonable and nondiscriminatory terms.[3] While SSOs and their individual committees are generally inclined to search for technologies that are unprotected or available on a royalty-free basis, their job is to evaluate the potential tradeoff between technical quality and openness.[4]

Table 1 illustrates the growth in intellectual property disclosures at the four SSOs that we study. (We define a disclosure is an announcement by a single firm on a given date that it potentially owns one or more pieces of intellectual property.) While the number of intellectual property disclosures was initially quite small, it began to grow during the early 1990s. By the late 1990s, all four SSOs were experiencing significant growth.

For our purposes, the rise in intellectual property disclosures means that we have access to a publicly available list of patents associated with standard setting. Many features of patents, such as the number of citations they receive, are easily compared across different industries and time periods. We utilize the information contained in intellectual property disclosures to identify standards-related patents whose citation rates may provide a window onto the potential impact of SSOs.

Our study builds on the large literature in economics utilizing patent data. Jaffe and Trajtenberg (2002) describe patents and their citations as a "paper trail" following the innovative process, allowing researchers to track the flow of ideas over time and space. Because citations legally delimit the scope of the citing patent, citations should have an economic implication. A number of papers have established the relationship between the number of citations a patent receives and its economic importance. For instance, Pakes (1986) uses patent renewal decisions and Hall, Jaffe, and Trajtenberg (2005) use stock market valuations of patent holders. In this chapter, we do not take a strong stand on the meaning of a patent citation, on optimal IPR policies or even on whether patenting encourages innovation or not. Rather, we exploit existing framework for patenting and IPR disclosures to obtain a method for systematically evaluating the role of SSOs in the innovative process. Naturally, this approach does not give us a representative sample of all standards that an SSO generates, and we have a restricted set of SSOs to begin with. However, we

Table 1. Intellectual property disclosures

	Disclosures		Claims per Disclosure			Patents	
	Earliest	Total	Mean	Median	Max	All Patents	US Patents
ETSI	1990	262	36.5	4	1582	847	672
IEEE	1988	125	3.4	1	37	313	252
IETF	1995	314	1.5	1	27	193	97
ITU	1983	821	1.0	1	2	339	188

hope that even conditioning on the data we have, we are able to provide important insights into the impact of SSOs.

A note of caution: patents may be disclosed for proposals that never become standards, and proposals may become standards but not require licensing of every patent that was disclosed in relation to the proposal. We observe only intellectual property disclosures, not whether they were included in the final standard, whether the proposal became a standard or often even what proposal they were disclosed in relation to. Making these distinctions might be useful for a number of questions but such data are not available to us at this time.

DATA

This section describes the sample of SSO patents that we use to study the standard setting process. All of these data were collected from the publicly available records of ETSI, the IEEE, IETF, and ITU. We begin by describing the complete sample of intellectual property disclosures. We then examine the 1,113 U.S. patents contained in one or more of these disclosures. After discussing some of the issues associated with these patents, we conclude by describing the creation of our initial control sample.

Although the four SSOs in this study have similar intellectual property policies, the scope and specificity of individual disclosures varies dramatically across organizations. These differences reflect variation in the participants, policies, and objectives of the four institutions. In order to provide some intuition for the type of disclosure information provided by these SSOs, we group the data using a particular definition of "disclosure." We define a disclosure as an announcement by a single firm on a given date that it owns (or may own) one or more pieces of intellectual property related to a single standard setting initiative. When a firm claims that a single patent covers two or more standards, each one counts as a separate disclosure. When a single announcement lists more than one patent or patent application, we will refer to each piece of intellectual property in the disclosure as a claim. Since we do not work with the claims data from individual patents, this should not lead to much confusion.

Table 1 illustrates some of the variation in how intellectual property is disclosed across the four SSOs in this study. First, the data for each organization begin at a different point in time. While the ITU disclosures begin in 1983, intellectual property did not become an issue at the IETF until 1995. Second, there are substantial differences in the number of claims per disclosure. While the ITU has the largest number of disclosures, almost all of them contain a single claim. At ETSI, on the other hand, the median disclosure makes four claims, and one contains more than 1500. Finally, individual claims vary in their level of specificity. For example, it was a common practice at the IETF for several years to "disclose" the existence of an unpublished patent application without providing any information that could be used to verify its existence. This variation in claim-specificity can be seen by comparing the number of patents disclosed to the total number of claims at an SSO.

The final column in Table 1 shows the number of U.S. patents contained in the data set. This figure is smaller than the number of patents claimed at each SSO for two reasons. First, many disclosures list non-U.S. patents. This is particularly true at ETSI, where the large number of claims per disclosure often reflects the disclosure of patent families which cover the same invention in several legal jurisdictions. Second, there are several patents that get disclosed more than once (both within and between SSOs). For example, there are a number of cryptography patents that seem to be disclosed on a regular basis when SSOs deal with issues of computer security.

After removing all of the foreign patents, patent applications, and duplicate observations, the intellectual property disclosures made at ETSI,

the IEEE, IETF, and ITU yield a sample of 1,113 unique U.S. patents. We do not claim that these patents are broadly representative of the technology evaluated by these four SSOs. More likely, they are concentrated within several of the most commercially significant standard setting efforts. Nevertheless, these patents provide a unique opportunity to study the role of SSOs in the innovation process.

We obtained citation data for these patents by linking the SSO sample to the NBER US patent data file (Hall, Jaffe, & Trajtenberg, 2002).[5] These data also contain several important patent characteristics, such as application and grant dates, and the name of assignees. Figure 2 shows the distribution of grant dates for the patents in the SSO sample.

It is clear from Figure 2 that the majority of patents listed in SSO disclosures were not granted by the USPTO until the mid-1990s. This is not surprising, given the surge in patenting and the timing of the disclosures in Table 1. However, because these are relatively new patents, it is important to consider the issue of sample truncation. In particular, many of the SSO patents were

Figure 2. Grant dates of SSO patents

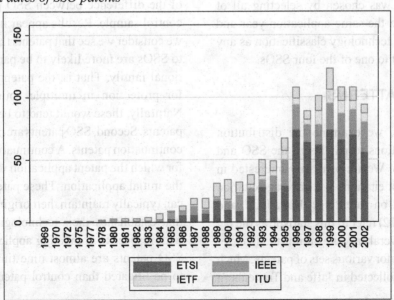

Table 2. Comparison of SSO and control patents

	SSO Patents	Control Patents
International Family	57.8%	31.4%
Continuation Applications	36.3%	25.4%
Litigated	5.51%	0.64%

Table 3. Average number of citations per patent

	IETF	IEEE	ITU	ETSI
SSO	37.03	28.8	27.77	31.44
Control	8.55	8.24	7.97	8.53

granted near the end of our sample (our citation data extend to 2004). While we would like to study the long run impacts of SSO affiliation, the data are not sufficient to consider what happens to SSO patents after about 15 years. This issue becomes even more severe when we focus on comparing the pre and post disclosure periods which in many cases may only last one or two years.

Throughout the analysis, we will be comparing the SSO patents to a control sample. The baseline control sample was chosen by selecting all of the patents with the same application year and primary 3-digit technology classification as any patent disclosed to one of the four SSOs.

CITATION PATTERNS

In this section, we examine the distribution of forward-citations to patents in the SSO and control samples. We are primarily interested in the age profile of citations—the average citation rate conditional on patent age. Hall, Jaffe, and Trajtenberg (2002) refer to this statistic as the lag distribution. Several papers examine the shape of this distribution for various sets of patents. Much of this work is collected in Jaffe and Trajtenberg

(2002). See Hall and Trajtenberg (2002). We begin with a direct comparison of the average citation rates for SSO and control patents. We then turn to an econometric model with application-year and citing-year fixed effects to account for time trends in citing propensity and differences in the "fertility" of inventions across vintage years.

Before presenting data about citations, we begin a few simple measures of the importance of SSO patents. We provide three comparisons of the difference between SSO patents and the control sample. Results appear in Table x. First, we consider we see that patents that are disclosed to SSOs are more likely to be part of an international family. That is, the patent holder applied for protection in multiple countries at once. Naturally, these would tend to be more valuable patents. Second, SSO patents are more likely to be continuation patents. A continuation patent is one for which the patent application was altered after the initial application. These patent applications can typically maintain their original priority date that establishes their technological precedence with respect to competing applications. Finally, SSO patents are almost nine times more likely to be litigated than control patents.[6] Obviously, litigation is a sign of the economic importance of a patent.

First, we compare the number of citations that each group of patent receives. Table 3 shows the average number of citations per patent at each SSO and at their associated control group. SSO patents receive substantially more citations than patents from similar technology classes, ranging from 3.5 to more than 4 times greater. This result is not surprising as we know that most patents receive very few citations and we expect that patents that would be important enough to be disclosed would also represent important technologies.

More surprising is that SSO patents receive citations over a longer period of time. Hall, Jaffe, and Trajtenberg (2001) establish that most patents exhibit a peaked citation pattern, with a distinct peak occurring in age 4 or 5. We show that SSO patents exhibit a much smaller peak with substantial number of citations coming relatively late in the patents life. To see this, we compute the

average number of citations received at each age for SSO and control patents separately. Figure 3 graphs these results with the lines normalized to integrate to 1. That is, we can interpret these graphs as probability distribution functions over the age at which a patent receives a citation. In each case, control patents exhibit the highly peaked pattern common to groups of patents that have been studied in the past (e.g., Hall, Jaffe, & Trajtenberg, 2001). In contrast, SSO patents have much lower peaks and instead have a much greater probability of receiving citations later in the age process.

One of the most striking facts about Figure 3 is the particularly long citation life exhibited at the IETF. A quick search reveals that there are several notable patents appearing in the tail of the age profile for the IETF, as well as the IEEE. These patents include numbers 4,405,829 and 4,200,770, which cover the basics of public-key cryptography, as well as 4,063,220 which describes the Ethernet

Figure 3. Distribution of citations over age for SSO and control patents

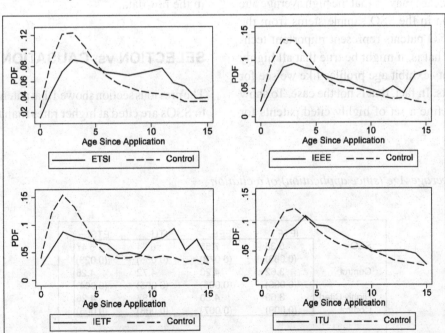

networking.[7] These are exceptional patents in many respects—including the fact that they are disclosed on separate occasions in more than one SSO. So, while these patents are excellent examples of the potential impact of an SSO on the innovation process, it is hard to believe that the *average* patent from among the 400 disclosed at these SSO's in 2003 will turn out to have a similar citation trajectory. Nevertheless, it is interesting to consider whether the importance of the inventions embodied in these early patents could have enhanced the future influence of their respective SSOs.

It is straightforward to use our data to compute the average age at which an SSO receives a citation. Doing so provides simple summary of the graphs in Figure 3 and makes it straightforward to compute whether the differences between SSO and control patents are statistically significant. Table 4 presents the average age (since application) at which a patent receives a citations. Strikingly, SSO patents have a higher age in each case, by 1 to 3 years. The small standard errors associated with these estimates indicate that these differences are statistically significant.

One concern may be that the high average age of a citation in the SSO sample stems from the fact that SSO patents represent important technologies. That is, it might be true that all highly cited patents exhibit age profiles like we see for SSO patents. In fact, that is not the case. To show this, we define a set of highly cited patents for each control group. Highly cited patents are in the top decile of citations received for their application year. In this way, highly cited control patents have an average citation rate as least slightly greater than SSO patents for each SSO. Table 4 presents results for highly cited patents in the third row. Strikingly, the average age for highly cited patents may be slightly higher than the entire control sample, but is still well below that of SSO patents.

One should exercise caution in drawing conclusions based on the unconditional age profile. These computations do not make any adjustment for differences in the application-year or citing-year, which Hall, Jaffe, and Trajtenberg (2001) establish as potentially important. Furthermore, they do not address potential truncation bias inherent in observing citations only up until 2004. Addressing these concerns requires a regression framework and brings up potentially difficult questions of how to separately identify age effects from citation-year and application-year effects (Hall, Mairresse, & Turner, 2005). We take up these issues in Rysman and Simcoe (2006) and remarkably, confirm the results established above in the raw data.

SELECTION vs. CAUSATION

The previous section showed that patents disclosed to SSOs are cited at higher rates than the average

Table 4. Average Age (since application) of a citation

	IETF	IEEE	ITU	ETSI
SSO	5.38	7.55	6.34	5.47
	(0.063)	(0.073)	(0.055)	(0.023)
Control	3.62	4.20	4.72	4.26
	(0.006)	(0.005)	(0.005)	(0.004)
Highly Cited Control	3.69	4.30	4.87	4.26
	(0.009)	(0.007)	(0.008)	(0.006)

patent. We interpret this as evidence that these patents embody significant inventions. However, this evidence is insufficient to distinguish whether SSO's select technologies that would have been important regardless or whether SSOs actually influence on the importance of these technologies. In this section, we use the timing of intellectual property disclosures to distinguish these affects. Our goal is to use the disclosure event to estimate the marginal impact of the standard setting organization on patent citation rates.

To be clear, this interpretation depends on the date of disclosure being an exogenous event. This condition is unlikely to be met in practice and the sign of the associated bias is difficult to predict. Suppose the selection effect dominates and patent holders tend to disclose important patents to SSOs, but they do not realize the importance of patents for some number of years. Then, they may choose to disclose patents at the time they can predict that citations will increase. In that case, we will observe an increase in citations around the date of disclosure but presumably, the patent would have experienced the increase without disclosure and the correlation between citations and disclosure would overestimate the marginal impact. Conversely, suppose there is a large causal effect of disclosure but market participants can predict which patents will be disclosed some period in advance. In that case, patents may begin to receive citations before disclosure, which would cause the correlation between disclosure and citations to understate the impact of SSO disclosure on citations. With these concerns in mind, we interpret the correlation between disclosure and citations with caution. But as we lack truly exogenous events pushing patents into SSO negotiations, this approach seems to be the appropriate starting place for distinguishing between the selection and causation effects.

We estimate the impact of disclosure in two ways. In the first approach, we are interested in comparing the size of the SSO effect to the size of the disclosure effect. That is, we want to measure the extra effect on an SSO patent of being disclosed. We use the following regression framework:

$$C_{it} = f(\alpha_y, \alpha_t, \alpha_a, \alpha_c, \alpha_i^{SSO}, \alpha_{it}^{DISC}, \varepsilon_{it})$$

In this equation, the dependent variable is the number of citations to patent i in year t. The variables of primary interest are α_i^{SSO} which is a dummy variable for SSO patents and α_{it}^{DISC}, which is a dummy variable for patent i having been disclosed by period t. That is, the variable is "on" for all periods after disclosure. The control variables are a series of dummy variables for the application year, α_y, the year in which cites are received (the application year of patents that cite patent i), α_t, the age of the patent, α_a, and the 3-digit technology class from the NBER patent database, α_c. Note that age is defined to be $a = t-y$, which implies that the age variables are a linear function of the year and cohort variables and hence, not separately identified. To address this issue, we assume that a single age coefficient applied to all ages greater than 11, by which time most patents receive very few citations.[8] The term ε_i captures unobservable terms. In practice, we estimate with a Poisson regression, which predicts count data like what we observe. We construct robust standard errors that allow for errors that are clustered around each patent.

In this regression, the disclosure dummy coefficient is estimated entirely from within-SSO variation. For instance, if all SSO patents were disclosed in the same year or at the same age, α_{it}^{DISC} would not be identified. Implicit in this approach is the assumption that the age process is the same for SSO and control patents, even though Figure 3 suggests that the age profiles are different for SSO patents. In fact, it we could include a set of age dummy variables for SSOs only and interpret them as the *difference* in the age profile for SSO patents and control patents. However, capturing the SSO effect in a single dummy variable makes the size of the SSO effect easily comparable to

Table 5. Results for importance of disclosure

	IETF	IEEE	ITU	ETSI
SSO	1.225	0.818	0.868	1.058
	(0.086)	(0.082)	(0.094)	(0.065)
Disclosure	0.114	0.412	0.291	0.285
	(0.198)	(0.169)	(0.112)	(0.063)
% Disclosure	24.8%	40.0%	36.0%	31.6%
observations	197,851	458,734	519,865	301,050
SSO obs.	922	2,482	2,405	6,329

Notes: A Poisson regression of citations on control dummies and dummies for SSO patents and for the periods in or after disclosure to the SSO

the size of the disclosure effect. Results for the disclosure dummy are very similar if we allow for a set of SSO age dummies.

Table 5 presents results. We present only the coefficients of primary interest. Not surprisingly, the SSO dummy is positive and precisely estimated for all four SSOs. In addition, the disclosure dummy is positive and significant as well for all but the IETF. If we interpret the dummy on disclosure as representing the marginal impact of the SSO on the citation count, we can say that between 25% and 40% of the high citations counts for SSO patents are due to being disclosed to an SSO, and the rest is a selection effect. We computed these numbers based on the percentage increase in the number of citations from making a patent an SSO patent and then disclosing it.[9] This result strikes us as very reasonable, although we do not have strong priors over this statistic.

These results suggest an economically significant disclosure effect. In addition, we find similar results if we define disclosure to occur one year after the reported disclosure year in order to account for some sort of lag. However, it would be interesting to do more complex analysis. For instance, we might be interested in how citations vary in the years just before and after disclosure, or how age profiles change when we control for disclosure. We are limited in our ability to

answer these questions because of the scarcity of data when using only within-SSO variation. For these purposes, we are currently exploring the use a control sample comparison. While the process of matching patents to a control sample brings up well known problems with unobserved heterogeneity, the larger sample size allows us to pose new and interesting questions.

CONCLUSION

While the importance of SSOs has been widely remarked by academics and practitioners, there have been few attempts to systematically measure their role in economic performance or technological change. Moreover, since much of the evidence for SSOs' importance is based on specific examples of technologies they have endorsed, there continues to be some debate over whether they actually influence the process of cumulative development or merely choose to select and evaluate important technologies. This is the first chapter to address these issues using patent citations as a measure of SSO performance.

Using data from the patents disclosed in the standard setting process at ETSI, IEEE, IETF, and the ITU, we showed show that the SSO patents collect many more citations, typically around three times as many. Furthermore, they have a different age profile of citations, receiving them over a longer time span. Finally, we exploited the timing of SSO patent disclosures to show that there is a correlation between citations and the act of disclosure, representing more than 20% of the total difference between SSO and non-SSO patents.

Subject to concerns about the exogeneity of the disclosure event, the large selection effect suggests that SSOs are successful in identifying important technologies. Furthermore, the significant causal effect suggests that current SSO decisions impact the path of future technological innovation. This may occur because SSOs embed technologies in standards that are difficult to switch away from because of network effects. Alternatively, it may be simply the attention attracted to a technology by a disclosure, possibly due to the disclosure's indication that a patent-holder is willing to license its technology.

The treatment of intellectual property at SSOs is a subject of interest to many in the technology policy-making community, and a number of recent events have increased the prominence of this issue. These events include the Rambus case, the surge in intellectual property disclosures at SSOs, the W3C's (an SSO that sets Web-based standards) decision to adopt a royalty-free licensing policy, and the Standards Development Organization Act of 2004, which extended certain antitrust protections originally contained in the National Cooperative R&D Act to American SSOs. While this chapter emphasizes the positive question of SSOs' role in technological change, the finding that these institutions not only select important technologies but also may influence their future significance suggests that the policy interest in these issues are justified. While we hope to address a number of these questions in future research, we should acknowledge that it is hard to draw any clear welfare implications from the current results. In particular, the impact of having patents in an industry standard will depend on the rules of the SSO, participants' willingness to license any essential intellectual property, and whether they do so on "reasonable and non-discriminatory" terms. Nevertheless, this chapter provides some of the first large-sample statistical evidence related to the patents disclosed in the standard setting process, and should be an important starting point for future research.

REFERENCES

Blind, K. (2004). *Economics of standards.* Northampton: Elgar.

Chiao, B., Lerner, J., & Tirole, J. (2005). *The rules of standard-setting organizations: An empirical analysis.* Unpublished Manuscript, Harvard Business School.

Furman, J., & Stern, S. (2004). *Climbing atop the shoulders of giants: The impact of institutions on cumulative research.* Unpublished Manuscript, Northwestern University.

Gandal, N., Gantman, N., & Genesove, D. (2005). Intellectual property and standardization committee participation in the U.S. modem industry. In S. Greenstein & V. Stango (Eds.), *Standards and public policy.* Cambridge: Cambridge University Press.

Greenstein, S., & Stango, V. (Eds.). (2005). *Standards and public policy.* Cambridge: Cambridge Press.

Hall, B., Jaffe, A., & Trajtenberg, M. (2002). The NBER patent citations data file: Lessons, insights, and methodological tools. In A. Jaffe, & M. Trajtenberg (Eds.), *Patents, citations and innovations: A window on the knowledge economy.* Cambridge: MIT Press.

Hall, B., Jaffe, A., & Trajtenberg, M. (2005) Market value and patent citations. *RAND Journal of Economics, 36*(1), 26-38.

Hall, B., Jaffe, A., & Trajtenberg, M. (2002). The NBER Patent Citations Data File: Lessons, Insights, and Methodological Tools. In A. Jaffe & M. Trajtenberg (Eds.), *Patents, citations and innovations: A window on the knowledge economy.* Cambridge: MIT Press, 2002.

Hall, B., Mairesse, J., & Turner, L. (2005). *Identifying age, cohort and period effects in scientific research productivity.* Unpublished Manuscript, University of California at Berkeley.

Jaffe, A., & Trajtenberg, M. (2002). *Patents, citations and innovations: A window on the knowledge economy.* Cambridge: MIT Press.

Lemley, M. (2002). Intellectual property rights and standard setting organizations. *California Law Review, 90,* 1889-1981.

Markiewicz, K. (2004). *University patenting and the rate of knowledge exploitation.* Unpublished Manuscript, University of California at Berkeley.

Mehta, A., Rysman, M., & Simcoe, T. (2005). *Identifying age profiles of patent citations.* Unpublished Manuscript, Boston University.

Mowery, D.C., & Simcoe, T. (2002). Is the Internet a US invention? An economic and technological history of computer networking. *Research Policy, 31*(8-9), 1369-1387.

Pakes, A. (1986). Patents as option: Some estimates of the value of holding European patent stocks. *Econometrica, 54*(4), 755-784.

Rysman, M., & Simcoe, T. (2006). *Patents and the performance of voluntary standard setting organizations.* Unpublished Manuscript, Boston University.

Simcoe, T. (2004). *Design by committee? The organization of technical standards development.* Dissertation, University of California at Berkeley.

Toivanen, O. (2005). *Choosing standards.* Unpublished Manuscript, University of Helsinki.

ENDNOTES

[1] Although the authors have backgrounds in Economics, we know of only a few empirical studies of standard setting organization in the economics literature, all very recent. See Chiao, Lerner and Tirole (2005), Gandal, Gantman and Genesove (2005), Toivanen (2004) and Blind (2005). However, interest seems to be growing in this area For example, see Greenstein and Stango, 2005.

[2] The most well-known is the Rambus case. The documents for the case can be found at the FTC web site http://www.ftc.gov/os/adjpro/d9302/

[3] In practice, the "reasonable and non-discriminatory" requirement in a RAND licensing policy seems to imply very few obligations on the part of prospective licensors. The reasonableness requirement is rarely taken to mean that the technology must be offered at a uniform price. When the intellectual-property holder has not made an ex ante commitment to some set of licensing terms, each potential implementor of the standards will negotiate their own terms. While licensors are expected to negotiate in good faith with any potential developer, the individual terms offered may vary widely. SSOs have been very hesitant to get further involved in the negotiating process. In part this reflects their own concerns about the antitrust implications associated with any type of collective pricing agreement. At the same time, it also likely reflects their fear of alienating particular members.

[4] Each of the SSOs considered below uses some variation on a RAND IPR policy. All of them have produced specifications that

contain proprietary technology at some point. The IETF's policy is the least centralized, in that it leaves most of the decision-making to the discretion of its individual working groups. IEEE follows the guidelines established by ANSI. ETSI's policy is the most explicit of the four. In particular, it specifies a set of rules for dealing with a situation where some intellectual property is determined to be essential to a standards development effort.

[5] These data have been updated through 2002 and are available on Bronwyn Hall's web site http://emlab.berkeley.edu/users/bhhall/bhdata.html

[6] We thank Stuart Graham of the Georgia Institute of Technology for providing us with a list of litigated patents.

[7] The inventors on the first patent are Ronald Rivest, Adi Shamir and Leonard Adelman, whose initials are the basis for RSA crypotography. The second patent's inventors include Martin Hellman and Bailey Diffie. The third patent's inventor was Robert Metcalfe, who created Ethernet while working at Xerox PARC.

[8] Mehta, Rysman and Simcoe (2005) show that there are important age effects that begin with the grant year rather than the application year. Age defined as $a = t-g$, where g is the grant year, generates an age profile that can be separately identified from cohort (y) and time (t) effects. This issue is further explored with respect to SSOs in Rysman and Simcoe (2006).

[9] In a Poission regression, this "marginal effect" of the independent variable is computed by taking the exponent of the coefficient.

This work was previously published in International Journal of IT Standards and Standardization Research edited by K. Jakobs, pp. 25-40, copyright 2007 by IGI Publishing, formerly known as Idea Group Publishing (an imprint of IGI Global).

Chapter XVII
Patents and Standards in the ICT Sector:
Are Submarine Patents a Substantive Problem or a Red Herring?

Aura Soininen
Lappeenranta University of Technology and Attorneys-at-Law Borenius & Kemppinen, Ltd, Finland

ABSTRACT

Multiple cases have been reported in which patents have posed dilemmas in the context of cooperative standard setting. Problems have come to the fore with regard to GSM, WCDMA, and CDMA standards, for example. Furthermore, JPEG and HTML standards, as well as VL-bus and SDRAM technologies, have faced patent-related difficulties. Nevertheless, it could be argued that complications have arisen in only a small fraction of standardization efforts, and that patents do not therefore constitute a real quandary. This article assesses the extent and the causes of the patent dilemma in the ICT sector through a brief analysis of how ICT companies' patent strategies and technology-licensing practices relate to standard setting and by exemplifying and quantifying the problem on the basis of relevant articles, academic research papers, court cases and on-line discussions. Particular attention is paid to so-called submarine patents, which bear most significance with respect to the prevailing policy concern regarding the efficacy of the patent system.

INTRODUCTION

Background

Our society is filled with various types of standards, commonly agreed ways of doing things.

Standards may be sociocultural, political, economic, or technical. Language is a standard, the metric system is a standard, and so is our social etiquette (Cunningham, 2005). Technical standards could be defined as any set of technical specifications that either provide or are intended to provide a common design for a product or a process. They range from a loose set of product characterizations to detailed and exact specifications for technical interfaces. Some of them control product interoperability, some ensure quality or safety, and some are so-called measurement standards (Grindley, 2002).

Particularly interoperability/compatibility standards are paramount in industries such as information and communications technology (ICT) that are dependent on interconnectivity. In fact, the telecommunications industry has relied on them throughout its history. These standards define the format for the interface, allowing different core products, often from different manufacturers, to use the same complementary goods and services, or to be connected together as networks (Grindley, 2002; Teece, 2000). Thus, interoperability standards enable gadgets to work together and thereby they further the goal of increased communicative potential. This follows that their use may also lead to financial benefits due to so-called network externalities (Cunningham, 2005; Shurmer & Lea, 1995). These strong network effects are present when a product or a service becomes more valuable to users as more people use it. Examples of products that benefit from network effects include e-mail, Internet access, fax machines, and modems (Shapiro & Varian, 1999).

A further economic effect of interoperability standards is that they reduce the switching costs from one supplier to another by preventing producers and consumers from being locked into a proprietary system. Standards, however, do not totally eliminate switching costs. When producers and users become committed to a particular system or standard, and the longer they stay with it, the more expensive and difficult it is for them to switch to another that is comparable (Blind, 2004). Consequently, due to these strong economic effects, control of the outcome of standard setting may yield significant economic advantage on the sale of both core and related products (Hjelm,

2000). Patents that provide their holders with a defined right to prevent others from making, using and selling an invention can be used to gain that leverage or to control the adoption of a standard. Therefore, potential conflicts between patent rights and the need for standardization affect the ICT industry and the consumers at large, and these economic effects need to be bared in mind when examining the deficiencies of prevailing standard-setting procedures and the legal framework.

This article studies the patent-related dilemmas that may arise both in the course of standard setting and after the standard has been established. Potential conflicts and their causes are identified and exemplified on specific case studies, and the study of Blind, Bierhals, Thumm, Hossain, Sillwood, Iverser, et al. (2002) is used to quantify the problems further. The aim is to find out whether the problem with patents, particularly with so-called submarine patents, is substantial, or whether it is only a minor concern that has attracted undeserved attention. Term "submarine patent" is used here for patent applications and patents that may yield significant economic power because they "read on" a standard and come to the fore after it has been established.

Standardization and Patents in General

Standards can be established in many ways: the markets determine *de facto* standards, and organized standards bodies agree upon *de jure* standards. These bodies could be said to include government legislators, official standards organizations, various industry committees, and consortia. Unlike de facto standards, de jure standards are usually established in advance and are later implemented by multiple vendors (Grindley, 2002; Messerschmitt & Szyperski, 2003; Mueller 2001).

Standards emerge from all the sources in the ICT sector listed previously. The Internet Society

(ISOC), the Organization for the Advancement of Structured Information Standards (OASIS), the World Wide Web Consortium (W3C), and the Internet Engineering Task Force (IETF) could be mentioned as examples of bodies active in the field of software and the Internet. Then again, the European Telecommunications Standardization Institute (ETSI), the American National Standardization Institute (ANSI), the International Telecommunications Union (ITU), and the International Organization for Standardization (ISO) could be mentioned as organizations operating in the telecommunications industry (Rahnasto, 2003).

A further distinction is that between open and proprietary standards. The purpose of open standards is to provide an industry with well-documented open specifications that could be implemented without prior business and legal arrangements (Caplan, 2003; Messerschmitt & Szyperski, 2003). Furthermore, with open standards, unlike proprietary standards, development of the specification is open to participants without restrictions. The openness may not always be absolute, however, and as a consequence the term "open standards" has various interpretations in practice (Caplan, 2003; Messerchmitt & Szyperski, 2003). In fact, although patent-free standards have traditionally been preferred in the interests of ensuring their success and promoting their use, it has become more difficult to design standards that do not contain any patentable inventions. This holds true particularly when the aim is to choose pre-eminent technology for a standard (Frank, 2002; Soininen, 2005). Therefore, it is not rare to call a standard open even if it includes patented technology providing that licenses are accessible to all. This definition has been adopted in this article as well.

As to the connection between de facto and de jure standards and open and proprietary standards, privately set de facto standards are typically proprietary in nature (Lemley, 2002) meaning that the patent holder controls their utilization. Then

again, official standards organizations typically promote open standards, and those originating from various industry groups and consortia may fall in either category or somewhere in between depending on whether everyone has been able to participate in the selection of the technical specification, or whether the standard has been agreed upon by a handful of companies having the technical knowledge in the area and who then have it adopted throughout the industry (Rahnasto, 2003). The focus of this article is on open, commonly agreed de jure standards.

As said earlier, although open standards are in principle available for anyone to use proprietary technology may be involved in their implementation, and using the specification may require a license (Rahnasto, 2003). Consequently, many official standards organizations and also some consortia have policies that permit their members to contribute proprietary technology under certain conditions: disclosure of the contributor's essential patents may be required, and before the technology is elected, patent holders are asked whether they are willing to offer a license at least on a non-discriminatory basis and on fair and reasonable terms (Frank, 2002). The purpose is to protect the patent holder's interests while fostering standards that incorporate the best technology and have the capacity for worldwide promulgation (Berman, 2005; Soininen, 2005). These organizations are called together as "standards bodies" or "standards organizations" from now on.

From the companies' perspective the dilemma between patents and open standards arises from the need to ensure returns on R&D investments through the exclusion of others while interoperability requires the inclusion of other parties. In fact, patent holders are free to refuse licensing altogether or they may choose the licensees and the licensing terms freely as long as the practice complies with relevant legislation, such as competition regulation/ antrust regulation. Thus, companies appear not to be very willing to license their patented technologies to everyone, particularly not to their competitors, on a royalty-free basis or for low returns. It seems, however, that in the context of common standards a limited exception can often be made for business reasons (Interview data U.S., 2004). Indeed, the use of common protocols and interfaces may expand the markets for networks of products that implement them, and producers then compete by innovating on top of the standardized functions (Peterson, 2002a). Nonetheless, even if a company decided to take part in standard setting, the interests of firms, individual contributors and users participating diverge and patents may be utilized strategically to achieve patent holder's objectives. Consequently, the standardization process may turn out to be burdensome as the mere existence of vested interests, for example, intellectual property rights (IPRs), complicates matters (Farrell, 1996; Shurmer & Lea, 1995; Soininen, 2005). Identifying relevant patents and agreeing on their beforehand cause complications and delays to the standardization process.

The relationship between ICT companies' patent strategies and technology licensing practices discussed earlier in general and in respect to open standards is one of the main questions that need to be addressed further in order to find an explanation to why it is that patents may raise such thorny issues in respect to standards. Moreover, attention has to be paid to the standards organizations' practices and bylaws aimed at reducing that tension in practice.

Standardization and Submarine Patents

As mentioned earlier, different types of standards bodies play an important role in establishing standards in the ICT sector, and many of them allow patented or patentable technology to be submitted, but specifically require disclosure of the patents and occasionally even of pending patent applications during the standardization process, as well as their licensing. This is to clarify relevant rights during the process of standard develop-

ment and reduce the risks of submarine patents so that patent holders cannot claim infringements afterwards, and thereby prevent others from using a standard, or to extract overly high licensing fees. If all essential, relevant rights are clarified during the process, a well-informed decision can be made (Kipnis, 2000). It might also be possible to design around the identified patents and patent applications, or to choose another technology for a standard. In fact, since patent-free standards are often the first choice, disclosure may have a negative effect on what technology is chosen (Soininen, 2005). For instance, when selecting the GSM standard another viable option was apparently rejected because it was considered too proprietary (Bekkers, Verspagen, & Smits, 2002).

Since proprietary technology may easily be discriminated, companies may even have an incentive to manipulate the standardization process and hide the fact that they have relevant patents. Standardization namely gives patents market power they did not have before (Rahnasto, 2003), which in turn improves the holder's negotiation position following the election and adoption of a standard. Furthermore, the disclosure requirement has its shortcomings and therefore companies may not even need to break the rules to capture an industry standard. The disclosure requirement is not necessarily extended beyond the personal knowledge of the individual participant, it may not be practically possible for a company to clarify all the patents and patent applications, and the obligation does not always cover pending patent applications, especially unpublished ones (Lemley, 2002). Consequently, a large share of the rights is not necessarily considered during the standardization process. Moreover, since standard setting may take a long time, many years in some cases, undertakings usually continue their R&D projects and file more and amend their existing patent applications during that period. Therefore, if the obligation to disclose does not hold throughout the standard setting, it is even more likely that patents will surface after it has been established (Soininen, 2005).

The optimal scope of the disclosure requirement, what happens if the guidelines are breached, and what course of action should be taken if there was no contractual duty or even a recommendation to disclose patents or pending applications and a patent surfaces after the adoption of the standard, remain matters for debate both outside and inside the courts. The submarine patent risk stemming partially from non-disclosure also involves third-party patents. Indeed, as Lemelson's submarine patent tactic has demonstrated, it is ideal from the patent holder's perspective to have a patent claiming technology that becomes widely adopted within an industry (Soininen, 2005). In fact, the submarine patent scenario could be said to have become more probable in recent years as numerous cases have been reported in which, despite efforts to identify relevant patents, claims have surfaced after the standard has been agreed upon (Blind et al., 2002). Furthermore, the importance of patents in business has increased in many respects and the legal framework constituting of patent laws and competition/antitrust regulation that may pose limits to the utilization of patents could also be described as pro-patent even though the system has been severely criticized (FTC, 2003; OECD, 2004). This has resulted not only in a higher number of applied-for and granted patents, but also in more aggressive enforcement and increases in technology licensing, bare patent licensing and cross-licensing, which in turn has the potential of generating more conflicts (Peterson, 2002). In fact, it appears that there is an increase in all types of patent claims and charges that relate to standards, and particularly in telecommunications, negotiations over such matters cause delays in the development of standards worldwide (Krechmer, 2005). Therefore it is essential to study the patent landscape in the ICT sector further, take a closer look at realized disputes and examine the loopholes of the system. Only by understanding how it is failing, it is possible to implement better practices.

Standardization and Licensing

There is another quandary involving patents and standards in addition to the submarine patent dilemma described earlier, and that has to do with licensing. This dilemma relates mainly to the mainstream obligation to license one's essential patents on fair, reasonable and non-discriminatory terms (RAND). The problem is that this problem may be limited in firms' patent statements in various ways, resulting in unexpected hold-ups. Companies may, for example, agree to license only patents that are essential for using that portion of the standard they have suggested, or they may impose limits by stating that licenses are available to any qualified applicants (Frank, 2002; Rahnasto, 2003; Soininen, 2005). One typical qualification is that licenses are offered only to companies that offer reciprocal treatment or promise not to threaten patent litigation against the licensing company (Berman, 2005). Moreover, specific licensing terms are not typically agreed upon during the standardization process so that the standards organization would play a role in it (Kipnis, 2000). Each company negotiates terms separately, which allows it to apply its own interpretations of what is considered fair, reasonable and nondiscriminatory (Frank, 2002; Rahnasto, 2003). In fact, it is for this reason that manufacturers participating in standards committees may even be forced to delay the standards development in order to negotiate acceptable terms before the final vote. The worst-case scenario is that the sum of license fees exceeds the total profit available to a product manufacturer, and that the standard never becomes adopted (Krechmer, 2005). Ultimately, consideration of the fairness, reasonableness and nondiscriminatory nature of the terms is left to the courts (Soininen, 2005). So far, however, the courts have not provided proper guidelines on how to determine what is fair, reasonable and nondiscriminatory (Rahnasto, 2003).

Thus, the problems related to the adoption of standardized technology may have to do with disagreement over the content of a company's licensing statement, even in the absence of submarine patents. One might even wonder, considering the large number of patents that are being reported as essential in the course of standardization, whether the disclosure obligation bears any significance in practice. Therefore, it is not enough to concentrate merely on the submarine patent problem and its causes when there is a possibility that limiting that particular risk might have only minimal effect.

RESEARCH OBJECTIVE AND METHODOLOGY

Standard setting is the cornerstone of today's economy, and it is essential particularly in the ICT sector. The most important feature of open standards is that they have the potential to become widely promulgated and used without undue restriction: this is essential to their success and to the very idea of something being or becoming a standard. Patents may, however, be used exclusively and therefore they may jeopardize the purpose for which standards have been created. Indeed, submarine patents as well as perplexity regarding proper licensing terms may result in increased costs in the form of excessive licensing fees, or they may force the industry to abandon the standard altogether meaning that the societal benefits may be lost. Since patents help companies to gain leverage over the standard-setting procedure and the adoption of the standard, potential dilemmas addressed in this article are also a policy concern. One may ask particularly in the context of so-called submarine patents whether the patent system fulfils its goal. These patents have factually been hidden and thus they have not contributed to technological development

of that specific industry, as is the purpose of the patent system.

This article examines the patent-related dilemmas and analyses their causes by exemplifying and quantifying them on the basis of newspaper stories, online articles, research papers, and trial documents. Further data was collected from interviews with eleven Finnish ICT companies and eight U.S. ICT companies in order to illustrate the relationship between patent strategies and licensing practices in general and in the context of standard setting. The interviews with the Finnish companies focused on patent strategies and were conducted by the author in 2003. Those with U.S. companies based in the Bay Area, CA, were more general and related to their innovation models, appropriability strategies and licensing practices. They were conducted by the author in cooperation with Pia Hurmelinna-Laukkanen and were completed in 2004. The interviewed firms included different types of ICT companies operating in the fields of information technology (software, hardware and related services for different purposes), chip interface technology, audio technologies, and digital entertainment products designed for computers and the Internet, and telecommunications. It should be noted that most of the U.S. case companies were larger than the Finnish companies, their revenues spanning from $60 million to $19,000 million. Furthermore, the size of their patent portfolios was substantially larger and varied mostly between 300 and 2,000 issued patents (one of the companies did not have patents at all). Only one Finnish company had a substantial portfolio of over 5,000 issued patent families, two of them had a medium-sized portfolio of approximately 60 issued patent families and close to 200 pending applications, and the rest had less than 10 issued patents/pending patent applications. The U.S. companies were also more actively involved in standard setting than the Finnish companies.

Obviously, it is difficult to make generalizations on the basis of such limited data. Thus, the data are used to complement other studies and views presented in the literature. In some cases, however, there were common features applicable to all of the firms, or several of them were found to have certain common denominators. Then again, some of the results are presented as examples of corporate operational models. One reason for this is that the interviews were in-depth in nature, meaning that the discussion was sometimes focused more on certain areas, and it would not therefore be possible to say whether the expressed views were common to all of the companies or not. Furthermore, in some situations less than 8 (U.S.) or 11 (Finnish) companies yielded relevant data: only a few companies in the Finnish sample were involved in setting standards. In the following, I refer to the interview data as interview data U.S. (2004) and interview data Finland (2003).

I will start by re-examining the submarine patent concept because the original meaning of submarine patents has largely disappeared as a result of legislative amendments. Nevertheless, certain aspects of the current patent law still contribute to their existence. I will then study ICT companies' patent strategies and technology licensing practices in order to demonstrate the general developments in the area and tensions between proprietary and open operation models and their implications on standardization. After that I will review the disclosure and licensing challenges that have been reported in the context of standardization and patents, and examine the likelihood of such conflicts. I conclude the article by considering the extent of the problems and whether the submarine patent problem really exists and can be limited, or whether it is merely a red herring that needs no further attention. It should however be noted that the sufficiency and flexibility of the prevailing legal framework applicable to solving potential conflicts is not particularly examined in this article even though it is clear that applicable legal tools influence companies' negotiation power, and thereby their behavior

during and after standard setting. These legal tools could also prove helpful in minimizing the harmful societal effects of submarine patents. This type of in-depth analysis would be the next phase following the recognition of the prevailing problem, its magnitude and main causes.

THE ORIGINS OF SUBMARINE PATENTS

The term submarine patent has been traditionally used to refer to (U.S.) patents that are issued after a long, intentionally delayed pendency at the patent office. The purpose of prolonging the application period by filing continuation applications, for example, has been to keep the invention secret as long as necessary for the industry to mature on the basis of the technology. When the industry is faced with the challenge of changing the technology, the patent is allowed to be issued, and the patent holder is in a position to prevent others from utilizing the invention and to demand royalties from those who began to use the technology while the application was pending (Heinze, 2002). Indeed, in the U.S. it is possible to file continuation applications and to preserve the priority date of the parent application as long as the parent application and the following continuation application disclose the same invention. There are no limitations on how many times a parent application can be continued (Graham & Mowery, 2002). The application period may thus last over a decade, and all this may happen even if the patent has not made any contribution to the development of the technology it covers: if it has been secretly pending for a long time, no-one has had the opportunity to find out about the invention, design alternative technologies, or develop the patented technology further. Thus, the trade-off between the inventor (the right to exclude others) and society (detailed information about the invention), the keystone of the patent system, is not in

Figure 1. Continuation patents as a proportion of issued patents: software patents compared with all other pat-ents, 1987-1999 (Graham & Mowery, 2002)

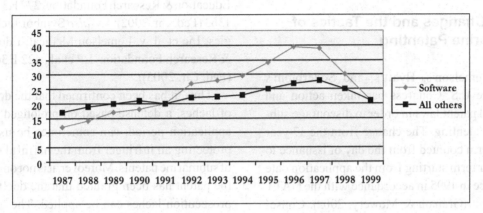

balance (Soininen, 2005). Figure 1 illustrates the popularity of continuations in relation to software and other patents in the U.S.

It is clear from the statistics in Figure 1 that continuations are filed frequently. Nevertheless, submarine patents as defined earlier are rare. In many cases it is inefficiency in the patent office that causes long delays rather than intentional postponement on the patentee's part (Ferguson, 1999). Nonetheless, Jerome Lemelson's patents in particular, issued after decades of pendency at the patent office, have attracted a lot of public attention (Stroyd, 2000; Vanchaver, 2001). Lemelson, who was above all a visionary who anticipated where technology was heading, applied for patents for inventions that he did not himself implement, and amended his applications when necessary to prevent them from being issued. Some of his applications were continued half a dozen times, potentially adding years to the process each time (Varchaver, 2001). He claimed a total of more than 500 patents on basic technologies used nowadays in industrial robots and automated warehouses, as well as in fax machines, VCRs, bar-code scanners, camcorders, and the Sony Walkman. His "machine vision" patent No. 5,283,641 was issued after 42 years of pendency (Stroyd, 2000; Ferguson, 1999; The Lemelson Foundation, n.d.; Soininen, 2005).

Lemelson was active in enforcing his rights. Once someone had developed a product that had some relation to one of his patents, the potential violator was confronted and reasonable compensation was demanded. Aggressive enforcement continues even today, after the death of Lemelson himself. Although quite a few of his patents have been challenged in court, over 750 companies paid royalties for them in 2001 (Soininen, 2005; Stroyd, 2000; Varchaver, 2001). Lemelson is not the only one to have used submarine patenting tactics, however. Another famous example is Gilbert Hyatt, whose patent for a single-chip microcontroller was issued in 1990 after 20 years of pendency. It was successfully challenged by Texas Instruments, but by that time Hyatt had already been able to collect approximately $70 million in royalties. Submarine patentees also include Olof Soderblom, whose patent for token-ring technology was pending in secrecy in the USPTO for 13 years until it was granted in 1981 (Heinze, 2002). While the application was pending, other companies developed token-ring technologies independently. This development took place in connection with a public-standard-setting process carried out by the Institute of Electrical and Electronic Engineers (IEEE). Since Soderblom's patent surfaced companies have been forced to pay him more than 100 million dollars in royalties (IPO, n.d; Soininen, 2005).

Legal Changes and the Tactics of Submarine Patenting

Since Lemelson's, Hyatt's, and Soderblom's times the U.S. Congress has taken action and amended patent laws in order to discourage submarine patenting. The change from the 17-year patent term counted from the day of issuance to a 20-year term starting from the application date took place in 1995 in accordance with the GATT agreement (Graham & Mowery, 2002). Consequently, a prolonged application period reduces the life of an issued patent. Another amendment made in 1999 was related to the publication of patent applications within 18 months from filing. Although there are exceptions to this rule, the change has reduced the prospect of surprising an industry before 1999 all patent applications filed in the U.S. remained secret until the patent was issued (Graham & Mowery, 2002; Heinze, 2002; Soininen, 2005). A further modification to the Patents Act that would obligate disclosure of all patent applications within 18 months has also been proposed recently before Congress. The introduced bill, H.R. 2795: Patent reform Act of 2005, is currently in the committee hearing phase (GovTrack.us, n.d.).

Furthermore, the U.S. Court of Appeal for the Federal Circuit held some years ago in the Symbol Technologies et al. v. Lemelson case that the equitable doctrine of prosecution laches, which is one of the defenses that can be used in patent infringement cases in order to demonstrate that even though there was a patent infringement, the patent should be held unenforceable, can be applied when the patent is issued following an unreasonable and unexplained delay by the applicant during the patent prosecution. Here, it does not matter whether the patentee's practice of keeping the application pending for many years has been accomplished strictly in accordance with the rules or not (Calderone & Custer, 2005; Soininen, 2005; Symbol Technologies Inc. v. Lemelson Medical, Education & Research Foundation, 277 F.3d 1361, 1363 (Fed. Cir. 2002); *See also* Symbol Technologies, Inc et al. v. Lemelson Medical, Education & Research Foundation, LP et al., 422 F.3d 1378 (Fed. Cir. 2005)).

Thus, it has been confirmed that the doctrine of laches, a defense based on prolonged patent application period, can sometimes be used for protecting an infringer from the harmful effects of submarine patents. Moreover, it is not only after the patent has been granted that the doctrine of prosecution laches can be applied. The Federal Circuit made it clear in the In re Bogese case that it is possible for the USPTO to address the issue before the patent is granted, and to reject it on this basis (In re Bogese II, 303 F.3d 1362, 1367 (Fed. Cir. 2002)). As far as Europe is concerned, patent applications have traditionally been automatically published within 18 months from filing, and the 20-year patent term has begun from the filing date. Moreover, although it is possible to file divisional applications, continuations are not allowed (Graham & Mowery, 2002; Soininen, 2005).

Submarine Patents Today

If submarine patents are defined narrowly as meaning patents issued after a long, intentionally delayed, secret pendency at the patent office, they do not seem to exist. Nonetheless, despite the legal amendments, circumstances in which patent applications are concealed long enough for the industry to start using a technology without knowing about the lurking patent arise particularly in fields characterized by fast technological development. In some parts of the ICT industry, for example, 18 months of secrecy may already be too long, and prolonging the application phase intentionally is not required for achieving the intended result (Soininen, 2005). Furthermore, patent applicants filing only in the U.S. may currently opt out of the 18-month publication rule and file continuations in order to detect industry developments and to postpone the grant of the patent for five years or so. Since the U.S. is a large and relatively lucrative market, particularly in the computer and software sector (Mueller, 2001), many companies do not even seek international patent protection. Also, provided that the numbers of filed ICT patent applications and granted patents continue their upward trend (OECD, 2005; OECD, 2004), it is getting more and more difficult to be aware of all relevant patents and applications. Especially if inventions are systemic, and innovation is fast and cumulative, multiple patented or patentable inventions may be incorporated into one innovation (Bessen, 2003; FTC, 2003), and therefore infringement is not merely a coincidence that can be avoided but is likely no matter how well the patents and pending patent applications are screened (Interview data U.S., 2004; Watts & Baigent, 2002). For this reason, published patent applications and granted patents may, in reality, be hidden (Soininen, 2005).

Another issue that has to be taken into account is that the scope of a patent typically changes during prosecution. Patent examiners often come up with patentability bars during examination, and require that the scope is limited in some way. Furthermore, as mentioned, the applicant may be able to add and amend patent claims during prosecution so that the scope will better reflect developments in the industry. Here the original application sets the limits for such changes, as its claims must support the new claim and no new matter can be included (EPC, Art 123; Mueller, 2001). As a consequence, although patent application might have been deemed non-essential at the time it was first published, the situation may change before it is granted. Certainly, one element of surprise relates to claim interpretation. Although a patent is a relatively well-defined right, the boundaries are never exact. The scope is not clear until it has been tested in court.

The concept of the submarine patent is understood in this article as broadly referring to patent applications and patents that surface after the standard has been established and take the industry by surprise. Here it does not matter, whether the patent application has been secretly pending or not, even though this possibility certainly contributes to the problem.

Tensions between patents and standards are examined in the following, and the problem of submarine patents and its causes are identified and exemplified further. ICT companies patent strategies and technology-licensing practices are analyzed briefly at first in order to place the dilemmas between patents and standards into a broader context and to find those practical elements that may contribute to them.

PATENT STRATEGIES AND TECHNOLOGY LICENSING PRACTICES IN THE ICT SECTOR

General Developments

With the shift from an industrial economy toward an information economy, the importance of intellectual property rights (IPRs) has increased. Today, a large proportion of companies' assets constitute intangibles, and IPRs are used to protect and profit from certain of these. Patents, for instance, provide their holders with the right to forbid others from utilizing patented inventions. Holders may thus gain competitive advantage due to their ability to stand out from the competition, or they may use their position to choose their licensees, which is one of their core rights due to the exhaustion doctrine (Kipnis, 2000). Then again, if the patent holder issues a license, as a rule he is entitled to secure any monetary or other compensation he is able to extract from the licensee (Shurmer & Lea, 1995) as long as the licensing terms are coherent with relevant regulation. The objective of licensing is to generate more revenue for the undertaking than it would be able to produce if it manufactured the patented products or utilized patented methods only by itself. Indeed, a well-reasoned licensing program helps a company to position itself favorably in the market place (Megantz, 2002; Soininen, 2005).

Obviously, there are differences between industries with respect to licensing tendencies, but generally speaking, the markets for technology licensing the component of which patents have grown. In fact, in a survey conducted by the OECD/BIAC, 60% of the responding companies reported increased inward and outward licensing, and 40% reported increased cross-licensing. Other types of knowledge sharing have become more common too, and collaboration takes place in the form of sponsored and collaborative research, strategic alliances, as well as in mergers and acquisitions. This has been said to stem from the growing technological complexity, increased technological opportunities, rapid technological change, intense competition, and the higher costs and risks of innovation. As a consequence, companies have namely become more focused on certain areas while they acquire complementary technologies increasingly from other undertakings and universities (OECD, 2004).

The features mentioned previously apply also to the ICT sector, and companies lean heavily on cooperation and networks. Contemporary academic literature refers to this type of innovation as the open innovation model, in contrast to the closed model that used to dominate. Companies applying the closed model seek ultimate control and do everything themselves, while those adopting open innovation realize that valuable ideas do not only originate within their firms, and that it does not have to be the company itself that releases these ideas in the market. Whereas making innovation proprietary and exclusive is a central feature of the closed innovation model, open innovation is characterized by the exploitation of intellectual property in order to create value. The boundary between the company and its environment is said to have become more permeable, enabling ideas

and knowledge to flow more freely (Chesbrough, 2003).

One further characteristic of the competitive environment of the ICT sector is so-called coopetition that was pointed out by one of the U.S. interviewees. Coopetition basically means that companies may very well be business partners in some fields and compete aggressively in others (Interview data U.S., 2004). Naturally, all the elements mentioned before signaling the importance of networks, openness in innovation, and coopetition are reflected in ICT firms' patenting practices, the use of patents in their business, enforcement and infringement avoidance. Furthermore they affect the technology licensing tendencies and licensing terms. Similarly it is possible to detect their implications on standardization and also on settling of disputes as some of the example cases discussed later on demonstrate.

The U.S. Patent Landscape

The patent landscape of the U.S. ICT sector could be described as a thicket to the birth of which strong patent system, technological complexity and fast technological development have contributed. Thus, although a reading of the patent laws gives the impression that there is a correspondence between a product and a patent, this is not necessarily the case: patents may overlap, and the manufacture of one product may require access to hundreds or thousands of patents, or one patent may "read on" many types of products, not just one (FTC, 2003). Therefore, in order to avoid the resulting hold-up problem, many U.S. ICT companies employ defensive patent strategies, and if they have the resources to do so they build large patent portfolios in order to guarantee that others cannot prohibit them from innovating. This in turn increases the number of relevant patents in the industry. Naturally, in addition to the better negotiation position and increased ability to agree on the licensing and cross-licensing they facilitate, patents also provide the means to prevent outright imitation in these cases (FTC, 2003; Interview data U.S., 2004; Soininen, 2005).

In general, the significance of patents as protection mechanisms used to exclude others and thus to generate competitive advantage appears not to be very high in the ICT field, and it is rather competition that spurs innovation in this sector (FTC, 2003). This was reflected in the patent-enforcement activities of the U.S. companies that were interviewed, and which operated on the basis of a defensive patent strategy. Unlike the company that employed an offensive patent strategy and attempted to generate its revenues from technology and patent licensing, defensively operating firms focused more on their core businesses of making and selling products rather than devoting resources to detecting infringements (Interview data U.S., 2004). Similarly, Messerschmitt and Szyperski (2003) have observed that the exclusionary use of patents is less common in the software industry than in some other industries such as biotechnology and pharmaceuticals. In their opinion this is in part because patents tend to be less fundamental and they can be circumvented easily. Furthermore, according to a quantitative study of U.S. manufacturing firms conducted by Cohen, Nelson, and Walsh (2000), compared to other appropriability mechanisms such as secrecy, other legal tools, lead time, complementary sales, services and manufacturing, patents ranked rather low in effectiveness in fields such as the manufacture of electrical equipment and electronic components, semiconductors and communications equipment, all of which are connected to the ICT sector. Moreover, there were substantial variations between industries: patents appeared to be most important in the chemical industry. This does not mean that they are not acquired for other purposes, such as those indicated earlier, and naturally all of their functions are based on the patent holder's ability to prevent others from utilizing the invention.

Since many ICT companies are dependent on one another as indicated earlier and patents are not vital for protection, they generally have no reason to complicate their business relationships by claiming patent infringement. However, while particularly large U.S. ICT firms seem to be aggressive in building patent portfolios mainly for defensive purposes, offensive patent strategies tend to predominate for individuals and small software companies (Messerschmitt & Szyperski, 2003). Indeed, various sources have reported an increase in companies that derive their revenue purely from patents. These companies, also called patent trolls, do not typically have any R&D of their own, nor do they manufacture any products themselves: unlike most ICT companies therefore, they are not dependent on other firms. Their business is to force companies involved in manufacturing to license their patents by claiming patent infringement (FTC, 2003; Interview data U.S., 2004; Peterson, 2002b; Surowiecki, 2006). Patent trolls seek for direct licensing revenues and do not usually benefit from a cross-license. Therefore a defensive patent strategy that might otherwise help certain ICT companies to maintain their freedom-to-operate, and that has proven successful also in the context of standards as will be illustrated later has only minimal influence on them.

It is not only patent trolls that seek to make better use of their patent portfolios, however. The prevailing trend in the U.S. has been to found patent-licensing programs, sometimes by forming a separate patent-licensing unit, for the purpose of generating extra revenues mainly from inventions that are not considered core to the company's main operations (Rivette & Kline, 2000). This trend is likely to have an effect also on standardization as standards are becoming more and more vital for the ICT industry and thus they also carry a lot of economic significance. Consequently, having a patent that claims a broadly adopted standard may be a dream come true for a company seeking licensing revenues and not operating in that particular technology area.

Basically, patents are viewed as core elements of corporate business strategies in the U.S. ICT sector. They are employed for multiple purposes in different contexts. They may be used as protection measures and as components in joint ventures, in patent pools, and technology licensing arrangements. A license may also be a pure patent license or a broad cross-license providing a company with not-to-sue coverage. Furthermore, patents may be used to attract other types of resources to the company. They serve as indicators of innovativeness, and can be helpful in attracting financing: they can be used as collateral and are seen as a positive indication in the eyes of venture-capital investors and potential buyers. In fact, one trend that is detectable in the U.S. is the increased tendency of selling and buying patent portfolios and individual patents (FTC, 2003; Interview data U.S., 2004). This may happen in conjunction with the acquisition of an entire company, or patents may be bought from bankrupt firms. This follows that it is not easy to avoid patent infringement as patents may easily find their way to unknown parties meaning that a notification of potential patent infringement may practically come from anyone.

There is one further feature about the U.S. patent landscape that should be noted. It has been claimed that a substantive number of patents are being granted particularly in new areas such as software and the Internet that do not actually fulfill the patentability requirements. These so-called bad patents have contributed to various patent-related difficulties and they have been deemed to be one of the main reasons why the U.S. patent system is not in balance (FTC, 2003).

The European Patent Landscape

So far Europe has not faced patent trolling on a large scale, which could be explained by the fact that the consequences of litigation and infringe-

ment are less severe: while the average cost of patent litigation in the U.S. amounts to more than $2 million per side (Vermont, 2002), in Finland the figure for hearing an infringement the case in the district court is closer to EUR 150 000 per side. Of course the total amount of litigation costs may be fundamentally higher if the case involves various phases such as a precautionary measure claim, and both infringement and annulment actions. Moreover, the damages issued are substantial in the U.S. For instance, in 1990 the Federal District Court awarded $910 million in damages to Polaroid in its patent-infringement litigation against Kodak, Alpex Computers was awarded $260 million for patent infringement (litigation against Nintendo) in 1994, and in 2003 Microsoft was forced to pay Eolas $521 million for infringement of an Internet browser patent (PwC Advisory, 2006). By way of comparison, the largest amount of damages ever awarded in Finland was EUR 252,282 (Labsystems Oy v. Biohit Oy, HO S 94/1922, Court of Appeal).

Furthermore, the patent web in the ICT sector appears to be less complex in Europe than in the U.S., although there are certainly variations between different technology areas. For instance, the European mobile-phone industry and the electronics field are areas in which large patent portfolios are common (OECD, 2004; Watts & Baigent, 2002). However, with the exception of the large telecommunications and electronics companies, patents seem to be regarded not so much as strategic assets, but rather as legal tools applied and used for protecting the results of the company's own R&D efforts, and occasionally for licensing (DLA, 2004; Interview data Finland, 2003).

It was evident, for instance, from the interviews with the Finnish companies that were not involved in the mobile-phone area as manufacturers, and had less than 70 issued patent families, that small-scale portfolio building was the preferred strategy for avoiding otherwise weak patent protection. There were no cross-licenses, however, and the companies appeared to be able to operate freely without paying much attention to the patents of others (Interview data Finland, 2003). In general, the patent application part of the patent strategy was well thought out, although it should be noted that the process was technology-oriented and lacked the type of business acumen that was present in the U.S. (Interview data Finland, 2003). In fact, this is a conclusion that has been shared also by others. For instance Kratzman (2005) pointed out in his research:

Finnish patents tend to be academic and not written to generate revenue. They are not commercial nor do they cover multiple applications, an essential element in generating licensing interest. (p. 14)

With respect to the utilization of the patents in the company's business transactions and the infringement surveillance, they could be described as incidental, perhaps because patents were not regarded as important contributors to the company's revenue stream, and most Finnish companies had so few of them. Lead time, constant innovation and, in the area of software, copyright protection, were considered more important (Interview data Finland, 2003). Furthermore, attitudes towards patents appear to be largely negative, even indifferent, in the software industry in particular (Interview data Finland, 2003), which, based on Blind et al. (2001), applies not only to Finland but also to the rest of the Europe as far as independent software developers are concerned. It should be noted, though, that even small and medium-sized companies are beginning to realize the importance of strategic patent management, perhaps partially as a response to the attention paid to patents by investors. Generally speaking, there is a steady increase in the propensity of filing patents in the European ICT sector (OECD, 2005), which in turn will probably increase the likelihood of patent-based conflicts, and make it more difficult to design around the patents when selecting a standard, for instance. Currently,

however, European companies appear not to be employing their patents as aggressively as U.S. undertakings and therefore there is a chance that even though European companies had patents that could be characterized as submarines, this would not create substantial hindrances to the industry. On the other hand, markets for technology are international and as the case with GSM standard that will be discussed in the licensing section of this article illustrates, also patent strategies of U.S. companies tend to influence European standardization efforts.

Licensing Practices in the ICT Sector

As regards to companies licensing practices, some companies tend to be more open in their operations than others. Usually it is rather easy to outsource the manufacturing of products, their distribution and marketing, but it is the development that R&D-intensive companies prefer to keep to themselves. This could be detected in the technology-licensing practices of the U.S. ICT companies, which, given the reported increase of 4000% in licensing revenues from 1980 to 1990 (Vermont, 2002) and the recent fascination surrounding the success of open-source software licensing, were surprisingly closed, particularly in terms of licensing in external technologies.

One of the interviewees explained the situation by saying that it was difficult to find useful technologies, and counting on outside technologies was usually considered risky due to potential problems with third-party rights and quality issues, for example. In-house R&D was simply trusted more. When companies did rely on external technologies, they rather acquired the entire company than licensed-in the technology. If they did license-in it was largely limited to non-core elements and design tools. As for licensing-in open-source software, the companies were very careful, and typically had tools in place to make sure that they audited what came in (Interview data U.S., 2004).

When it comes to licensing out their technologies interviewed companies tended to be more open, and there was one company whose business model was based mainly on this. Furthermore, licensing out was used in order to integrate in-house technologies into other companies' products and to make them compatible so that the market for that technology would expand. The licensing models adopted in the interviewed software companies were basically very broad for distribution purposes, and they licensed software to their customers as a package and to other companies to be used as embedded in their products. However, with the exception of commonly established standards, other types of technology licensing that did not involve a complete product were limited (Interview data U.S., 2004).

The licensing terms companies follow naturally vary depending on the subject matter, the business model adopted for the particular product or technology, and the parties involved. Nevertheless, there are certain typical configurations that reflect the extent of control the licensor or the licensee has. The scope of the license is paramount: the licensor retains more control over the technology if he or she grants only non-exclusive rights, which appears to be the most common form in the ICT sector. The possibility to define the degree of exclusivity, for example, in terms of geographic areas or certain uses, and the ability to assign and sublicense the rights are other key elements in determining the scope of a license (Poltorak & Lerner, 2004). Incorporating technical assistance also gives the licensor control over the licensed technology. In the case of trademarks in particular, the licensor has good reason to control the quality of the licensed products, and to put in place certain procedures for testing them and inspecting the licensee's production facilities (Megatz, 2002). It is also advisable to include a termination clause to enable either party to get out of the contractual relationship if necessary. One of the most intriguing termination clauses that reflects the atmosphere in the ICT industry

relates to patent peace: such clauses are frequently used in open-source licenses, for instance, and in their broadest form they provide the licensor with the right to terminate the license in the face of claims by the licensee regarding infringement on any of its patents. Representations, warranties, and indemnification clauses related to risk allocation, as well as royalty rates, also affect the balance of the contractual relationship.

Most importantly, however, attention needs to focus on terms relating to modifications, improvements, and therefore also grant-backs. From the licensor's perspective, it is often advantageous to obtain the rights to any improvements developed by the licensee, preferably including the right to sublicense the improvements to other licensees. This would prevent the licensee from using a fundamental improvement or an extensive new development to gain control over the licensor's core technology. Then again, access to improvements developed by the licensor is important for the licensee in ensuring the continued viability of the licensed product or technology (Megantz, 2002).

Some of the companies interviewed had adopted a very restrictive approach to modifications, allowing them only rarely and even then often requiring grant-back terms. Control was maintained through the heavy involvement of the licensor's engineers in the implementation phase, and through quality control. The licensor also typically maintained the right to modify the license terms. Then again, in the context of software licenses, the licensees had very few rights, the source code was seldom provided, and reverse engineering was typically prohibited. Obviously, this depended on whether it was an end-user license, an OEM agreement or a VAP bundle agreement. On the other hand, some companies had adopted a more open approach and operated on a more flexible and market-driven basis. Interfaces were opened up, for instance, and one of the companies even licensed out its software under various open-source agreements (Interview data U.S., 2004).

It could be concluded from previous discussion that R&D intensive ICT companies have rather control-seeking licensing models, but they may be flexible too if it suits the company's business model. Thus, since standards are of crucial importance in this industry, exceptions are often made for the essential purpose of securing product compatibility, interoperability and interconnection (Interview data U.S., 2004). In fact, since many companies may be developing equipment or software for the same systems and platforms, for example, and there are inevitably huge numbers of relevant patents involved (Watts & Baigent, 2002), standardization may prove effective in providing access to essential patents held by various firms. On the other hand, it must be remembered that companies' prevailing licensing practices tend to show also in the standard-setting context, and although the patent policies of standards organizations typically give specified options to the patent holder, different licensing terms can be used to maintain control over the technology as indicated already in the background section of this article. Furthermore, it is only the essential patents need to be licensed when a company participates in setting a standard. As one of the interviewees pointed out, this constitutes a fairly thin layer. Only patents that are technically or commercially necessary to ensure compliance with the standard must be licensed, and only to the extent that it is necessary. Therefore, if the patent holder has waived its rights, for instance, patents cannot be asserted for complying with the standard, but they can be asserted if something extra is being done (Interview data U.S., 2004). Then again those companies that do not benefit from a common standard or are after royalties have generally no interest in taking part in standard setting because doing so could require the licensing of their rights under royalty-free or RAND terms.

The licensing quandaries will be discussed later on, and I will now turn to a more detailed analysis of the submarine patent risk stemming from deficient identification of essential patents to which some of the factors presented in this and the earlier section clearly contribute. Generally speaking the highlighted importance of intellectual property rights and their substantial role as part of companies' business strategies has made it more difficult to avoid conflicts of interests.

STANDARDIZATION AND SUBMARINE PATENTS

Both patents providing their holders with exclusive rights, and open standards expected to be widely promulgated without exclusive control are important to the ICT sector. As they both want different things resolution is not always easy (Cunningham, 2005). From the perspective of this article the core element contributing to the tension between patents and standards, is that it is not always known in advance whether undertakings have patents or pending patent applications that might cover the standards technology. This complicates matters, since patents that surface after the adoption of the standard may, in the worst case, result in no other choice than abandoning it. Although both licensing and patent identification quandaries that were introduced briefly already in the background section may lead to significant economic losses, it is more difficult to anticipate the consequences and to avoid problems in the latter case. Therefore, submarine patents that surface after a standard has been elected and adopted are not only a practical dilemma but also a policy concern. Submarine patents may face the industry with unpredictable predicaments, and ultimately harm consumers. Cases in which unidentified patents of standard setters have caused concern and resulted in legal disputes include Dell and Rambus litigations. Third-party submarines contain the patents of Forgent Networks, Inc and Eolas Technologies, Inc among others.

The most effective way to reduce the possibility of hidden patents that have the potential to cause complications with respect to the adoption of a standard is to conduct a proper patent due diligence periodically and to agree upon the contravening issues beforehand. This is where the patent policies of standards organizations that are aimed at creating shared expectations among standardization participants with respect to licensing and disclosure rules come to the fore (Interview data U.S., 2004; Ohana, 2005). Indeed, if companies participate in setting a standard they usually do their best to follow the standardization organization's patent policies, and consider any deviation unethical (Interview data U.S., 2004; Ohana, 2005). Sometimes the rules are simply not very transparent, and since different standardization organizations have different types of policies it may be burdensome to be aware of and to comply with them all, particularly if the company is involved in many standards organizations. In fact, about 40% of companies in Blind et al. (2002) sample group reported that they had problems due to the unclear IPR structure, resulting, for instance, in the late identification of the patent holders. There is a need for rules that hold as few surprises as possible (Interview data U.S., 2004; Ohana, 2005).

The standards organization's patent policies and their shortcomings with respect to the disclosure obligation are examined in subsequent paragraphs. Since companies adopting the standard ultimately bear the responsibility for patent infringement, there is then a brief glimpse into that part of companies' patent strategies that is aimed at reducing that risk. Combined with what has been said earlier about the patent system and the patent landscape in the ICT sector, these sections constitute the analysis of the causes contributing to the likelihood of infringing others' essential patents in the ICT sector and the challenges companies face in settling these disputes particularly due to the emergence of so-called patent trolls. Case studies illustrate the situation further and give examples of actualized disagreements. The fact that many disputes have been handled in court demonstrates that it has not been possible to settle the issues amicably and that there are significant economic interests involved.

Patent Policies

Many, although not all, standards bodies that are responsible or involved in coordinating the development of standards have implemented explicit IPR or patent policies for handling issues to do with standardization and patents. These policies aim at discouraging the manipulation of the process in order to gain market power, and at easing the tension between the open nature of standards and the proprietary nature of IPRs (Feldman & Rees, 2000; Kipnis, 2000; Soininen, 2005). The policies guide the participant's behavior, and from the legal point of view their nature and content affect the determination of whether a company participating in standard setting and failing to disclose its relevant rights has breached a contract, defrauded, competed unfairly or deceptively or abused its dominant position, for example. Therefore, if the patent policy is deficient, it is difficult to challenge the patent holder's right to prevent all others from using his invention, discriminate among licensees or to condition the license however he wants to as long as this is done in accordance with relevant laws. In the following attention is paid to the nature, extent, scope and timeframe of the prevailing disclosure obligations of different organizations such as ITU, ANSI, ETSI, W3C, OASIS, and IETF and their ability to reduce the risk of submarine patents is assessed.

Nature of the Policy

It has been argued that without legally binding policies standards could easily become the subject of "hold-up" because once a standard has been established, all the patents necessary to comply with it become truly essential. The more widely the standard is adopted, the more power the patent holders gain (Shapiro, 2001). Nonetheless, not all standards organizations aspire to control their participants through imposing on them explicit contractual obligations, and many use their policies more as a "code of practice" (e.g., ITU-T Patent Policy, n.d.). ANSI, for example, has taken the position that it does not mandate disclosure or impose licensing obligations on patent holders because this would overburden the process. It relies more on its participants to voluntarily act in accordance with the policy. Nevertheless, according to Marasco (2003) it has not so far faced abuse of the process. Actually, even though the guideline-nature of the disclosure requirement may narrow down the possibilities to enforce it in court and to claim damages in case of an infringement, non-obligatory rules may also bear significance when it is determined whether a certain participant has operated in good faith under some other principle of law, such as Federal Trade Commission Act, Section 5 that prohibits unfair and deceptive business practices. The case studies of Dell and Rambus examined later will demonstrate this issue further.

The Duty to Disclose

The patent policies of standardization organizations differ in their approach to disclosure in terms of duty to disclose, the scope of the disclosure and its timing. For the most part, they tend to rely on their participants (submitters or members [Perens, n.d.]) to voluntarily disclose all patents that could influence the standard. This is by no means a simple task, and failing to disclose patents that are essential for using the standard may happen by accident. Searching the portfolio is time-consuming and expensive, and therefore companies may not want to make the expense of searching them. Also, it is not always easy to recognize all essential patents and patent applications. This follows that particularly in big companies with

large portfolios a company's representative in a standard-setting process may not know whether a proposed standard incorporates a patent within his company's portfolio (Kipnis, 2000; Peterson, 2002b; Soininen, 2005).

It is probably for this reason that standards organizations generally take no responsibility for finding all relevant IPRs, or for verifying the information disclosed by the contributors (e.g., ANSI, 2003b; IETF, 2005; OASIS, 2005), and they are not keen on imposing such obligations on their participants. Thus, many of them do not require disclosure that goes beyond the personal knowledge of the discloser (e.g., IETF, 2005; OASIS, 2005), nor do they require their participants to carry out patent searches (e.g., ANSI, 2005a; ETSI, 2005; ITU-T, 2005; OASIS, 2005; W3C, 2004), which in turn increases the probability that relevant patents remain undisclosed (Soininen, 2005).

Scope of the Disclosure Requirement

Another contributing factor to the submarine patent risk is that it is not necessarily required for companies to disclose their pending, particularly unpublished, patent applications (e.g., ANSI, 2003b: ANSI, 2003a; Kipnis, 2000; Lemley, 2002). The W3C disclosure requirement is an exception, however. It also extends to the unpublished patent claims that were developed based on information from a W3C Working Group or W3C document (W3C, 2004). The OASIS policy also requires the disclosure of all patents and/or patent applications known to the technical committee member (OASIS, 2005). The problem with announcing pending patents is that, although the protection provided by a patent is always unclear until confirmed in court, the scope is even more ambiguous until the patent is issued, and it is therefore not possible to assess whether it will be essential in order to use the technology. It is also possible that it will never be granted. The problem is, however, that if there is no obligation to disclose pending patent applications, waiting until the standard has been agreed upon before allowing the patent to be issued does not constitute a policy breach. In fact, given the need to make informative decisions about standard "characteristics," there has been discussion on whether participants should also be obliged to disclose their potential patenting activity. The U.S. patent system includes a so-called grace period, which allows the inventor to file for a patent up to one year after disclosing it in a printed publication. Thus, it is possible for a company that has submitted a technical proposal to the standards body to then file for a patent covering it after the standard has been elected.

Opinions on the scope of the disclosure obligation are divided. Some people feel that, although companies were required to state their possible interest in patenting their technology, it is never certain that they will apply these patents in reality, or that they will be granted or even essential. On the one hand, if companies had to announce their potential pending patents, other committee members could take them into account when decisions about standardized technology were made (Kipnis, 2000). At the same time, there might be a risk of "sham" announcements in these cases (Soininen, 2005).

Timing of the Disclosure

The timeframe of the disclosure requirement also bears significance in respect to the causes of the submarine patent problem. Since standardization may be valid for years and companies' R&D development is definitely not frozen during that time, it is likely that pending patent applications will be modified and new applications filed during the process. Therefore, although a company may have no pending patent applications or granted patents at the beginning, it might have them when the standard is finally set. For this reason, some standards bodies, such as W3C, have patent

policies that incorporate an obligation to disclose essential patents throughout the entire process (W3C, 2004). The ETSI IPR Policy also requires each member to make reasonable efforts to inform the ETSI in good time about any essential patents, both its own and third-party, of which it becomes aware at any stage (ETSI, 2005). Then again, the IETF policy encourages contributors to update their disclosures if the claims are modified, or if a patent is granted or abandoned (IETF, 2005).

Third-Party Patents

Standards organizations patent policies can never bind third parties and even though some patent policies do encourage also other interested parties as well as contributors to bring attention to potential third-party patents (e.g., IETF, 2005; ITU-T, n.d.; ITU-T, 2005; OASIS, 2005), this is not enough to record all of them. One option to increase the awareness of third-party rights would be to conduct a patent search. Standards bodies are not typically involved in such an activity, however (e.g., IETF, 2005; OASIS, 2005). On the other hand, ETSI is now considering an ex ante approach to declaring relevant patents with respect to the Long-term Evolution (LTE) standard (Informamedia.com, 2006). This would at least diminish the likelihood that new essential patents emerge after the standard has been elected and it remains to be seen whether this approach will be adopted on a broader scale.

It could be concluded that patent policies are helpful in reducing particularly the risk of standard setters' submarine patents and even though they could be strengthened in many ways to narrow down the possibility of manipulating the process in order to gain market power, some of the difficulties are mainly practical. Therefore it might not be possible to avoid them even if companies were posed an obligation to disclose their potential patenting activity, for instance. The only effect of doing so could be that companies are discouraged from participating which in turn would increase the risk that patents remain undisclosed and generate problems at a later stage.

Patent Strategies to Avoid Infringement

There may be a room for improvement in standards bodies patent policies but it is not only loopholes in them but also deficiencies in companies' own patent strategies that contribute to the fact that relevant rights may remain unnoticed and standard adopters may face predicaments due to them. Obviously, it is the company incorporating a standard into its products and services that ultimately bears the risk of infringing others' patents, and therefore identifying relevant rights is not by any means only the responsibility of standards organizations. Indeed, in addition to enhancing a company's own patenting, licensing and enforcement activities, a proficient patent strategy also helps in avoiding patent infringements.

A major goal in managing corporate patent liability is to avoid being sued and paying substantial royalties to other patent holders. What is even more important is to avoid being prevented from using a particular technology, which could force the company out of a lucrative market (Miele, 2000). Furthermore, the costs of patent litigation, particularly in the U.S., could be substantial and a drain on financial and human resources (Knight, 2001). Thus, if it is necessary to prevent significant liability, the company should consider refraining from using technology that infringes others' rights. In some cases this is not possible, and the company has to employ such technology that has been patented by others in order to operate in a particular market. Keeping both situations in mind, there are certain steps that could be taken in order to reduce the liability, the likelihood that patent holders will assert their rights against the company, and the amount of royalties that should be paid in cases in which patent liability cannot be avoided (Miele, 2000). One of these steps includes identifying patent problems early in the product

cycles. For instance, a freedom-to-operate search conducted on the basis of patent classification numbers and certain keywords might be useful for identifying close references, which could then be examined in more detail (Knight, 2001) before the product is released onto the market. Another step is to monitor the patent activities of the company's closest and biggest competitors because companies are often particularly sensitive to infringing activities that originate from their competitors (Miele, 2000).

In practice avoiding infringements is not that easy and companies' patent strategies are not flawless. No patent search is or can be 100% thorough (Knight, 2001), and as many Finnish interviewees mentioned, it may be difficult to identify relevant rights and to make sense of the scope of patent rights (Interview data Finland, 2003). Sometimes, a company may not even have any specialized infringement surveillance. Indeed, in Finnish companies infringement checkpoints were rarely incorporated into R&D projects. This does not indicate, however, that there was no knowledge whatsoever about the patent landscape: information regarding other companies' patent position can be obtained as a side product when the company is considering patenting its own inventions and conducts prior art searches for that purpose (Interview data Finland, 2003). As far as the U.S. companies were concerned, the extent of due diligence with regard to others patents varied depending on the situation: some technology areas were more important, and some were known to be more heavily patented than others, thus requiring more thorough clarification. Nevertheless, these companies typically did not have any systematic patent clearance (Interview data U.S., 2004).

A further risk-reducing alternative to freedom-to-operate analysis and other types of patent surveillance is to use the porcupine approach discussed earlier in the section on patent strategy in the ICT sector. This means that a company builds a defensive patent portfolio aimed at reducing potential infringement allocations and making settlement easier. It may also have broad cross-licenses in place, thereby removing a huge block of patents from its surveillance list (Interview data Finland, 2003; Interview data U.S., 2004). This is a strategy that has been favored by large U.S. and multinational Finnish ICT companies, but unfortunately it does not work well against individual patent holders or so-called patent trolling companies. The fact that patents are being assigned more than before, further increases the risk that they find their way to such parties that do not come up in competitor surveillance and remain unnoticed for that reason.

In sum, companies may take certain precautions to prevent patent liability, but even if they do, the risk of patent infringement remains particularly high in areas in which it is simply not possible to keep track of new filed applications and issued patents. As one of the U.S. interviewees stated, there is always a risk that others' patents will read on your product. You can do all the clearance work and look at all the patents that are out there, but the next week a new patent may be granted (Interview data U.S., 2004). Nevertheless, there are many improvements that could be made in order to strengthen the infringement surveillance, and instead of fighting only their own battles during the standard-adoption phase, companies could pool their expertise and resources and help to limit the submarine patent risk already before the standard is established.

Case Studies of Standard-Setters' Submarine Patents

Standards organizations' IPR policies related to disclosure do not cover every situation, which is understandable, since weight must also be given to the flexibility of the process. Also the means ICT companies have currently implemented in order to avoid infringement of other companies' patents do not help much in identifying relevant rights. The unfortunate consequences are that despite the efforts there still is a high risk that patents surface after the establishment of the standard, and these (essential) patents are much more valuable then than they would have been previously: it gets more difficult to change the specification as time passes and the technology becomes adopted. Therefore, particularly if they are not breaching IPR policy, some patent holders may seize the opportunity and seek to hide the fact that they have essential patents, or pending applications—otherwise the standard could be modified so that it no longer covers them.

The problem with standard-setters' submarine patents is not only theoretical, because the risk has actualized also in reality. Cases that have involved undisclosed patenting activities and have resulted in legal disputes include Dell, Rambus and Unocal from which Dell and Rambus cases are discussed in the following. These examples demonstrate further the importance and role of a proficient patent policy since it does not merely help to reduce the submarine patent risk beforehand but it also influences the possibilities to solve the problem later on. The previously-mentioned example cases indicate, for instance, that competition authorities do not take misbehavior during standard setting lightly and are keen on examining doubtful situations even though the merits of the case may not be sufficient in order to find fault from the defendant's side. In the end the result is dependent on the wording of the policy and proof of misbehavior. In a way legal tools that are available provide the last means to solve actualized conflicts. Luckily, litigation is not always needed. For instance IBM's behavior in relation to ebXML standard implies that consequences of the failure to disclose are not always detrimental. Since many ICT companies are largely dependent on one another it may be possible to reach an amicable solution rather easily in some situations.

Federal Trade Commission vs. Dell Computer Corp. (1995)

In the Dell (1995) case the Federal Trade Commission (FTC) accused Dell Computer Corporation, on the basis of Section 5 of the FTC Act which prohibits unfair or deceptive business practices, of intentionally concealing its patent during the Video Electronics Standards Association (VESA) VL-bus technology standardization process. Although VESA's IPR policy required that its members disclose any potentially conflicting patents, Dell certified that it did not have such patents. After the standard had been widely adopted in the marketplace, Dell sought to enforce its patent against VESA members. The Commission found that even if Dell's actions were not strictly speaking intentional, the company had failed to act in good faith. It also stated that had Dell disclosed its patents properly, VESA would have incorporated different technology into the standard. Dell's misrepresentation therefore caused restraints on competition resulting in the hindrance of industry acceptance and increased costs in terms of implementing the bus design (Federal Trade Commission v. Dell Computer Corp., FTC File No. 931 0097 (2 November 1995)) (Soininen, 2005).

In the end, a consent decree was agreed upon and Dell promised not to assert its patents against computer manufacturers that complied with the standard (Balto & Wolman, 2003; Hemphill, 2005; Lemley, 2002). It should be noted, however, that even though a satisfactory result was reached through a settlement the case was not decided in court leaving the industry with ambivalence about the proper interpretation. In fact, the Rambus litigation discussed later indicates that the conclusion could have been different if the case had been litigated further.

Rambus, Inc vs. Infineon Technologies AG (Fed. Cir. 2003) and Federal Trade Commission vs. Rambus, Inc

Rambus has faced two litigations due to its actions in the Joint Electronics Devices Engineering Council (JEDEC). The first one, Rambus, Inc v. Infineon Technologies AG (2003), arose when Rambus sued Infineon for synchronous dynamic random access memory (SDRAM) patent infringement. Infineon counter-claimed that Rambus had defrauded it when it failed to disclose patents and pending patent applications during its membership of JEDEC and while JEDEC was developing the industry standard for SDRAM. More specifically, Rambus had filed for a patent '898 for Rambus DRAM technology in 1990, it cooperated in forming the standard from 1992 until 1996 when it resigned from the standards body just before the final vote, and both during and after its participation it had filed continuation and multiple divisional applications based on the original 898 application, and by doing so it amended its patent protection to cover the SDRAM technology. Later, it allowed these patents to be issued, and began to defend its own patents aggressively, requiring companies to pay royalties. Nonetheless, the Federal Circuit came to the conclusion that Rambus had not fraudulently failed to disclose its patent applications, but held that its duty to disclose as a JEDEC participant applied only to those containing claims that could reasonably be considered necessary in order to practice the proposed standard, and that this obligation arose only when the work had formally begun. The court held further that the duty to disclose did not cover the participant's future plans or intentions, that is, filing or amending patent applications, and criticized JEDEC's patent policy for its staggering lack of defining details. It thereby left its members with vaguely defined expectations as to what they believed the policy required. (Rambus, Inc v. Infineon Technologies AG, No. 01-1449 [Fed. Cir. 2003]; Soininen, 2005).

The second litigation, FTC v. Rambus, Inc was based on Section 5 of the FTC Act, and it is still pending. The FTC has accused Rambus of a series of anti-competitive acts and practices, claiming that through deliberate and intentional means it has illegally monopolized, attempted to monopolize, or otherwise engaged in unfair methods of competition in certain markets related to the technological features necessary for the design and manufacture of a common form of digital computer memory. It further claims that Rambus's anti-competitive behavior has, among other things, increased the royalties associated with the manufacture, sale, or use of synchronous DRAM technology, and has reduced the incentive to produce memory using it and to participate in JEDEC or other industry standard-setting organizations or activities (Administrative Complaint, 2002; Soininen, 2005).

The difference between FTC v. Rambus and the Dell case is that in the former the FTC is attempting to demonstrate that Rambus gained market power through its misbehavior, and thus that the industry is locked into the JEDEC's SDRAM standard. According to the FTC, "It is not economically feasible for the industry to attempt to alter or work around the JEDEC standards in order to avoid payment of royalties to Rambus" (Administrative Complaint, 2002). In its initial decision released on 24 February 2004, Judge MacGuire stated that the FTC "failed to sustain their burden of establishing liability for the violations alleged," and dismissed the complaint. In her opinion there was no evidence, for example, that Rambus had violated JEDEC patent policy, or that the challenged conduct had had anti-competitive effects (Initial Decision, 2004; Soininen, 2005). To conclude, even though a standard setter has operated unethically and the other participants disapprove his conduct, it may

be difficult to challenge it in court particularly if proper guidelines are lacking.

IBM and the ebXML Standard

Even though Dell and Rambus attempted to enforce their rights against those who had adopted the standard, patent holders do not always seek royalties although a patent emerges after the standard has been established. One reason for a submarine patent holder to comply with the standards organization's policy is the bad publicity, which may result in the loss of credibility as a fair standardization participant (Sarvas & Soininen, 2002). For example, IBM claimed in April 2002 that it had one patent and one patent application that were relevant for implementing the open, royalty-free ebXML standard developed by OASIS in cooperation with the United Nations, and that it was willing to license them on RAND terms. IBM's announcement caused strong reactions in the public and in the industry, particularly because IBM had participated in the design of the standard. Furthermore, IBM had previously announced that it was willing to contribute to the standard without any restrictions, but had nevertheless made comments regarding the licensing terms and conditions of the two patents. However, soon after the news reached the public, IBM agreed to license the patents royalty-free (Berlind, 2002a; Berlind, 200b; Wong, 2002).

Case Studies of Third-Party Submarines

Those companies that do not benefit from a specific standard simply do not participate in setting it and therefore it may happen that third parties who are not covered by patent policies have patents that "read on" the standard, and do not appear before its adoption. If the patent holder then decides to enforce his rights, the benefits of the standard may be lost. In fact, many businesses that received patents during the technology boom were either purchased by other companies or landed in holding companies. Thus, in some cases a standards organization may adopt a standard believing it is royalty-free, and then find out that the new owner, which did not participate in the standard-setting process, is aggressively trying to enforce its IPRs (Clark, 2002). For instance, the director of intellectual property at Jupiter Networks Inc has observed a sudden surge in these types of third-party patent-infringement assertions, some of which are valid and some are not. This surge is understandable in his opinion, because patent holders hope to profit from the wide deployment of products that must implement Internet standards. He described a typical patent-assertion scenario in which a patent holder dusts off issued patents directed to old but related technologies or modifies claims in pending patent applications to read on published standards, and then targets standards-compliant networking-equipment manufacturers (Lo, 2002). The case studies presented in subsequent paragraphs illustrate the type of legal disputes that may arise if a third-party patent holder attempts to enforce his rights. Basically, the accused infringer can defend itself by claiming non-infringement or unenforceability, or by attempting to invalidate the patent. These are the strategies followed also in the case studies presented.

Forgent Networks and the JPEG Standard

A third-party claim arose in 2002 when Forgent Networks Inc searched its portfolio of 40 patents and found that it had a patent (US Patent 4,698,672) related to the implementation of a baseline version of the ISO/IEC 1098-1 standard, that is, the JPEG image standard that is one of the most popular formats for compressing and sharing files on the Internet, and is also used in various industries in products such as digital cameras, personal digital

assistants, cellular phones, printers and scanners. In its desperate search for profits, Forgent estimated the solidness of its infringement claim and entered into a multi-million-dollar licensing agreement with the Japanese companies Sony and Sanyo before making a public announcement in July 2002 of potential JPEG patent infringement and starting to pursue licensing fees from a range of companies. Forgent had, in fact, obtained the patent in question through the acquisition of Compression Albs Inc. in 1997. Since the inventors who originally filed for the patent in 1986 had not participated in the JPEG standardization process that was going on around that time, according to Forgent, no abuse of the standardization process had taken place (Clark, 2002; Lemos, 2002; Markoff, 2002; Reingold, 2006).

As a result of Forgent's aggressive patent enforcement, many U.S., European, and Asian companies agreed to license the '672 patent, and by April 2004 it had generated approximately $90 million in licensing fees. Those who did not agree to license willingly were sued for patent infringement. Indeed, on 22 April 2004 Forgent's subsidiary Compression Labs, Inc sued 31 major hardware and software vendors, including Dell and Apple Computers, for patent infringement, and on 6 August 2004 it initiated litigation against 11 companies (Asaravala, 2004; Forgent Networks, 2006).

Professionals in the field of compression technology and representatives of the JPEG committee doubted the validity of the patent and stated that there could be prior art available that would render it invalid. These doubts have been manifested in legal actions, such as those taken by 24 companies that filed a counter-complaint against Forgent and its subsidiary in the Delaware District Court seeking declaratory relief as to non-infringement, invalidity, and unenforceability of the patent. Even Microsoft, which had not been sued by Forgent at that time, filed a complaint against it on 15 April

2005, claiming that the patent had been obtained fraudulently. Furthermore, the non-profit Public Patent Foundation has filed a request for re-examination of the '627 patent in November 2005. In late January 2006 the U.S. Patent and Trademark Office (USPTO) made a decision to review the patent, which will in any case expire in October 2006 (Forgent Networks, 2006; Lemos, 2002; Reingold, 2006; Red Herring, 2006).

EOLAS and HTML Specification

Another third-party submarine example is the EOLAS case. Here, the dispute arose when Eolas Technologies Inc, which had licensed a patent from the University of California, sued Microsoft for the use of the patented invention, that is, the widely used feature of HTML, the format that describes the format of Web pages. After a long stream of litigation the Federal Circuit (2005) also found the patent valid and infringed (Eolas Technologies Incorporated and the Regents of the University of California v. Microsoft Corporation, Case Nr. 04-1234 (Fed.Cir, 2005)), and the Supreme Court refused to hear the case (Malone, 2005). At the request of W3C the Eolas patent was also re-examined by the USPTO, which released two preliminary findings claiming that it was invalid. Ultimately, the patent office kept the patent in force, however (Perens, n.d.).

Although a patent holder has a very strong negotiating position if the patent accidentally "surfaces" after the adoption of the standard and those who are accused of patent infringement can mainly defend themselves by trying to invalidate the patent, third-party patents do not always create problems. In many cases reasonable licensing terms can be agreed upon. As with the cases in which the patent holder had participated in the standard setting, business relationships and bad publicity may also be reasons why third-party patent holders comply with a standardization

organization's policy and license the patents royalty-free, for instance, although they may have no obligation to do so.

The Risk of Patent Problems and How to Reduce It?

It could be concluded from previous discussion that it is important to implement proficient patent policies that are clear, concise and transparent and hold as few surprises as possible. These policies should be drafted with an intention of influencing companies' behavior both during and after standard setting so that misconduct could be diminished and potential problems solved. The nature, extent, scope and the timeframe of the disclosure requirements are examples of such disclosure terms that could be clarified in order to reduce the submarine patent problem, which taking into account the recent litigations and the fact that 40% of companies in Blind and Thumm's sample group reported problems regarding unclear IPR structure (Blind et al., 2002) is not only theoretical. Furthermore, one way of reducing the problems that may result when not all patents are known prior to the establishment of a standard could be to require that essential patents granted in the future will be identified and potentially licensed under the same terms as the disclosed patents. In fact, it is a common requirement in patent pools for essential future patents to be subject to grant-back and thus to contribute to the pool. This requirement may occasionally have anticompetitive effects, however, Balto and Wolman (2003) and patent holders would probably consider this type of requirement too restrictive.

As regards to third-party patents that are becoming a more and more relevant concern there is a lot that could be done in order to reduce the risk they may pose to the adoption of a standard. First of all, the standard-setting participants could be encouraged to conduct more thorough patent searches already during the standardization procedure, and to let the standards organizations know about potential third-party claims. Secondly, third parties could be reserved an opportunity to make a patent statement early on, and thirdly, standards organizations could take a more active role in finding relevant patents themselves. Otherwise, if dealing with the increasing number of third-party patents was only left to companies implementing the standard, they would be in different positions and the openness of the standard could be endangered: only those companies that already have cross-licensing agreements in place, have enough leverage in order to negotiate a good deal with the patent holder, or have the resources to fight the patent in court might be able to adopt the standard.

A further way to limit the risk of submarine patent-related troubles arising from both standard-setters and third parties, and to help companies to solve the conflicts better and therefore to reduce the harmful consequences of such patents would be to renovate the legal framework. The possibilities and the need to do so have not been estimated in this article, however. Obviously, when considering the actions needed, the advantages and disadvantages should be estimated and balanced carefully. Therefore, it is in place to examine also the other patent and standard related quandary that has to do with licensing. These problems are similar to those experienced with submarine patents, and in fact, the GSM example presented later is in essence a submarine patent case. What basically differentiates submarine patent cases and those in which a patent has been properly disclosed is, however, the possibility to make informative decisions about the adoption of a standard, and to design around it or agree upon licensing terms in advance, and thus avoid great societal losses that would occur had the standard been already broadly adopted and if the parties were not able to solve the conflicts.

LICENSING OF PATENTS AND STANDARDIZATION

In case a patent holder has disclosed that it may have patents or pending patent applications that are essential for using a standard, standards bodies typically pose certain licensing alternatives for that company. The patent holder's options are usually the following: (1) the patent holder may state that it is willing to license its essential patents on royalty-free terms, (2) the patent holder may refuse from licensing altogether, (3) the patent holder may promise to license, but negotiate the terms separately, or (4) the patent folder may make a statement of licensing on fair, reasonable and nondiscriminatory terms (RAND). These alternatives are discussed further in subsequent paragraphs, and case studies are used to illustrate the licensing perplexities. The necessity and effects of addressing the submarine patent problem are estimated on this basis.

Royalty-Free Licensing

Royalty-free standards often have more chances of being broadly accepted and widely used than standards requiring licensing payments. For instance, the Internet has been said to require freely available standards in order to work effectively. Patent-based standards requiring royalty payments inhibit its development because they slow down or discourage the adoption of new technologies. As a consequence, companies frequently agree to make their patented technology available on a royalty-free basis, and hope to generate more profits by selling products that use their standardized technology (Clark, 2002; Interview data U.S., 2004).

As mentioned, given the benefits, standardization participants are often willing to license their patents on a royalty-free basis for the specific purpose of using the standard. This holds true particularly if they are able to make sure that the patents could nevertheless be utilized for defensive purposes if the need arose (Interview data U.S., 2004). Naturally, participation and agreement to license to everyone require that such conduct is in accordance with the firm's commercial interests: having its superior technology chosen for a standard may provide it with a head start in incorporating that technology into its products, for example. Then again, companies seeking licensing revenues through incorporating their proprietary inventions into a standard do not typically have a business motivation to participate in designing royalty-free standards (Soininen, 2005).

Refusal to License

If a royalty-free licensing scheme cannot be negotiated, and the patented technology cannot be designed around, it may nevertheless be in the interests of the public to get the patent holder to agree to license it at least on RAND terms. If the patent holder refuses to license on these vague terms, the standardization process is halted and other solutions are sought (Hjelm, 2000). Refusing to license at all is rare, however, although it is the most influential form of leveraging one's patent rights (Rahnasto, 2003). As the following case study demonstrates it has nevertheless played a major role in making the ETSI Wideband Code Division Multiple Access (WCDMA) standard backward compatible with the IS-95 standard favored by Qualcomm Inc, for instance (Soininen, 2005).

What happened in the WCDMA dispute was that Qualcomm accused ETSI of intentionally excluding Qualcomm's technology from its standards, thereby creating an unfavorable position for Qualcomm in the European third-generation telecommunications market. In order to make its voice better heard, the company claimed that the key technologies needed for WCDMA infringed its patents, and refused to license this technology unless the WCDMA was made backward compatible with the IS-95 standard. It seems that Qualcomm expected that a harmonized

standard would increase its licensing revenues fundamentally (Hjelm, 2000; Westman, 1999; Soininen, 2005).

Ericsson, who was another key patent holder in the technology involved, was of the opinion that Qualcomm's patents were not infringed, and to gain a better negotiation position it also sued Qualcomm for the infringement of Ericsson's CDMA patents (one of the U.S. standards) Qualcomm was employing. Finally, consensus was reached as a result of cooperation between Qualcomm and Ericsson. The companies entered into a series of definitive agreements that resolved all disputes relating to CDMA technology, and as a part of the settlement Ericsson acquired Qualcomm's terrestrial CDMA wireless infrastructure business, including its R&D facilities. Furthermore, the companies gave a promise to license essential WCDMA patents (Hjelm, 2000; Westman, 1999). The standardization process was practically frozen during this period, which lasted roughly a year (Sarvas & Soininen, 2002).

Indeed, as the previous example demonstrates companies operating in the ICT sector are dependent on each other and therefore conflicts in one area may result in complex legal battles in another. Nevertheless refusing to license may be a feasible strategy for a company that opposes a certain standard. A firm may also wish to delay the acceptance of a standard to give it more time to develop products that incorporate it.

Blank Promise to License

Firms typically agree to license their patents royalty-free, or on RAND or other terms, or they may merely agree to license but make no statement of the the terms and conditions. Particularly if the last-mentioned option is available and chosen, there is likely to be a fight over the proper licensing conditions. One example of a disagreement over proper licensing terms was the one that arose during the formation of the European GSM standard in the 1980s, which was first coordinated by

CEPT (Conference Europeenne des Administrations des Postes et des Telecommunications) and later by ETSI. In fact, this particular licensing dilemma, which involved Motorola, contributed to the change in patent culture that took place in the European telecommunications sector in which patenting had until that time been regarded as a secondary issue—specifically among the national telecommunications service providers whose markets had previously been monopolized but were now deregulated (Bekkers, Verspagen, & Smits, 2002; Granstrand, 1999).

What basically has been presented in literature to have happened in the context of the GSM standard was that a U.S. company, Motorola, for which patenting was a natural and integral part of doing business, entered the European scene and employed the aggressive patent strategy it was used to. While other standard setters operated in accordance with a "gentleman's agreement", shared their ideas and specifications during the standardization process in an open atmosphere, and refrained from patenting once the basic technical decisions had been made, Motorola pursued patent protection in the course of the process (Granstarand, 1999). Furthermore, Bekkers, Verpagen & Smits (2002) have argued that while most other companies agreed on licensing their essential rights on fair, reasonable and nondiscriminatory terms, Motorola refused to make general declarations. It declined monetary compensation and was only willing to cross-license its patents to certain companies. Although Siemens, Alcatel, Nokia and Ericsson were able to negotiate cross-licenses, Motorola's licensing strategy effectively prevented various other companies from entering the market. When a number of non-European companies finally managed to obtain all the necessary licenses to built GSM terminals in the late 1990s, the cross-licensees had already built up a strong market position. Moreover, since the cumulative licensing fee paid for a GSM handset was very high as confirmed by studies of Bekkers, et al., the price made it

difficult to compete if the company was not part of a cross-licensing agreement. In fact it has been argued that the licensing fees have totaled as much as 29% of the costs of the GSM handset (Bekkers et al. 2002)

RAND-Licensing

Even under the RAND system, specific licensing terms are typically not agreed upon during the standard setting. Revealing the terms after adoption can generate conflicts and hamper the parties' ability to compete in the affected market. Peterson (2002b) lists the following situations that could arise in this context: (1) the patent holder seeks a broad grant-back that appears non-discriminatory but has different effects on different parties; (2) the patentee requires a minimum annual royalty based on "administrative costs", which may have the effect of excluding smaller rivals and new entrants; (3) the patentee seeks royalties from downstream providers such as manufacturers of finished goods, and refuses to license to suppliers of upstream inputs such as IC vendors, and thus to increase its income, which however may increase competitors' costs and time to market; (4) the patent holder acquires admissions of infringement and validity, and/or retains the right to immediately terminate a license if the licensor challenges infringement or validity; (5) the patentee requires acceptance of venue, which might constitute a major problem for small companies or foreign competitors; and (6) the patent holder seeks a royalty that it considers "fair" but that exceeds the average profit margin of all the parties who need licenses. For instance, one of the U.S. interviewees mentioned that his company had been approached with a royalty requirement as high as 10% (Interview data U.S., 2004).

Furthermore, even though the company may have made it clear in its licensing statement that the license was only available under certain conditions it considered as fair, reasonable and nondiscriminatory, these terms may come as a surprise to some and cause disputes. For instance, the Townshend v. Rockwell International Corp. and Conexant Systems (N.D.Cal.2000) litigation arose when Townshend, whose patents "read on" the V.90 standard for 56K chipset modems and who had promised to license them on certain terms, filed a patent-infringement suit against Rockwell and its successor Conexant. In response Rockwell and Conexant asserted two antitrust counterclaims based on the Sherman Act Sections 1 (conspiracy) and 2 (monopolization and its attempt) among others, and claimed that Townshend and 3Com had conspired to restrain trade by deceiving the ITU into incorporating Townshend's patent into the industry standard, denying competitors access to the technology, and filing a patent-infringement lawsuit to prevent Conexant from using Townshend's technology. Furthermore, Townshend and 3Com were accused of having attempted to monopolize the market for 56K modem chipset products (Kirsch, 2000; Townshend v. Rockwell International Corp. and Conexant Systems, Inc., 55 U.S.P.Q.2d 1011 (N.D.Cal.2000)).

I am not going to go into the legal specialties of the case here, but the Court found all Rockwell's and Conexant's counterclaims unfounded. With regard to the antitrust-based claims it noted, among other things, that there had been no collusion, and since 3Com—to which Townshend had non-exclusively licensed its essential patent prior to the setting of the ITU V.90 standard—had declared during the standardization procedure that Townshend had relevant patents pending, ITU had not been deceived. Since 3Com had also made a proposition prior to the acceptance of the standard to license those patents for a per-unit royalty fee, or to cross-license them in return for technologies that were specified in the standard, or related to it and were otherwise practically necessary or desirable for technical or economic reasons in order to make a commercially viable product compliant with the standard, and further that it had not been shown that Rockwell and Conexant could not have obtained a license under those terms, Townshend's

actions could not be held anticompetitive (Kirsch, 2000; Townshend v. Rockwell International Corp. and Conexant Systems, Inc., 55 U.S.P.Q.2d 1011 (N.D.Cal.2000)).

The previous case illustrates that it is particularly difficult to defend oneself against such patent holders that have disclosed their patents properly and declared their licensing terms during the standard-setting procedure. Indeed, due to the flexibility in the interpretation of RAND, having patents in standardized technology could also become a valuable source of royalties or other resources. For instance, Qualcomm relies on a royalty stream resulting from others utilizing its patented technology incorporated into various standards. In fact, the pricing of Qualcomm's licenses has led to huge disagreement between Qualcomm and six other companies involved in the WCDMA 3G standard. Basically, Broadcom, Ericsson, NEX, Nokia, Panasonic Mobile Communications and Texas Instruments have all claimed that Qualcomm, who promised to license its essential WCDMA patents on RAND terms, is charging excessive and disproportionate royalties for them. Qualcomm has been claimed to charge the same royalty rate on the WCDMA 3G standard as it does for the CDMA2000 standard adopted in the U.S., although it has fewer essential patents in it. Furthermore, it offers lower royalty rates to handset customers who buy chipsets exclusively from Qualcomm than to manufacturers of chipsets for mobile phones, making entry into the market more difficult for chip makers (Nokia, 2005a; Outlaw.com, 2005; Nokia, 2005b).

As a result of this disagreement, all six of the previously-mentioned companies filed complaints to the European Commission in October 2005 requesting it to investigate and to put an end to Qualcomm's anticompetitive conduct (Nokia, 2005a, 2005b; Out-law.com, 2005). Qualcomm has responded to the allocations stating that they are legally without merit, and appear to be nothing more than an attempt by these licensees to renegotiate their license agreements. In a separate move, Qualcomm then filed a patent-infringement action against Nokia claiming that Nokia was infringing 12 of its patents that related to GSM, GPRS, and EDGE standards (Jacobs, 2005; Nokia, 2005c; Wireless Watch, 2005b).

This is not the end of Qualcomm's legal disputes, however. Previously, in July and again in October, the company had filed infringement suits based on the previously-mentioned patents against Broadcom. These actions were a follow-up of Broadcom's claims that included a patent-infringement action filed against Qualcomm in May 2005, a complaint with the U.S. International Trade Commission (ITC) suggesting that Qualcomm was unfairly importing products that infringed Broadcom's patents and requesting that the ITC investigate Qualcomm's imports, and a separate antitrust suit raised in July. This U.S. antitrust claim was based on similar grounds as the complaint made to the European Commission. In its antitrust complaint Broadcom charged Qualcomm with abuse of the wireless technology standards-setting process, failure to meet its commitments to license technology for cellular wireless standards on RAND terms, and various anticompetitive activities in the sales and marketing of chipsets based on CDMA technology (Gohring, 2005a, b; Regan, 2005).

As can be seen from the volume of suits and counter-suits discussed earlier, Qualcomm's strategy of using its essential patents as revenue generators is challenging and particularly litigation-sensitive, and it is not considered viable by all technology/patent-licensing firms even though their business model would support such activity. One of the U.S. interviewees stated, for example, that taking into consideration the current legal situation and the IPR policies adopted by many standards bodies, it was not beneficial for it to take any part in the standardization. Its business was based on technology and patent licensing, not on manufacturing products, and there was simply not enough monetary compensation involved in standards (Interview data U.S., 2004).

Cross-Licensing

As mentioned earlier, agreeing upon exact licensing terms is not part of the standard-setting procedure, and negotiations are held between the companies interested in using the standard. This follows that another reason beyond the technological benefits for promoting the selection of patented technology for a standard is the possibility to cross-license patents with those of other participants that also "read on" the standard. The more patents companies have, the less they have to pay others for using the standard. Cumulative royalties might otherwise reach the point of unprofitable manufacture (Alkio, 2003; Soininen, 2005). For this reason, companies have an incentive to obtain patents that are essential for using the standardized technology. They may therefore amend their pending patent applications and file for new ones during the standardization process in order to make sure that if a certain technology is chosen for a standard, their patents cover some of its elements. For example, with regard to the CDMA2000 standard, Qualcomm held 28%, Nokia 16%, NTT DoCoMo 13%, Ericsson 8%, Motorola 7% and Hitachi 5% of the essential patents involved. Then again, Ericsson has 30%, Nokia 21%, Qualcomm 20% and Motorola 14% of the essential patents included in the WCDMA standard (Alkio, 2003). In fact, it has been estimated that some of these major patent holders will end up with a total royalty of 7% of costs or less, while a nonpatent holder could pay 25% of the wholesale price in GSM and WCDMA royalties (Wireless Watch, 2005a).

In order to diminish the problem with too high royalties, some manufacturing firms and operators have declared that they would prefer to agree upon cumulative royalty caps beforehand (Wireless Watch, 2005a). For instance, Nokia was behind such a proposal in respect of 3G patents (Naraine, 2002a). Nevertheless, there are different views on whether agreeing on licensing terms is the job of the standards organization at all, and

Qualcomm, in particular, has opposed the royalty-cap proposition actively (Naraine, 2002b). Also one of the U.S. interviewees pointed out during the interview, that in the end, the markets determined whether a product was feasible at a certain price or not. This was not the licensor's responsibility. He further noted that the game in the industry seems to have turned into a price competition rather than the building up of value to customers and communicating that value to them (Interview data U.S., 2004). However, as far as the next version of the 3GPP-based radio standard, Long Term Evolution (LTE), is concerned, ETSI is considering getting all relevant patent holders to sign up to a pre-agreed cumulative cap of approximately 5% for royalties on the cost of LTE equipment (Informamedia.com, 2006).

Licensing and Submarine Patents

As explained earlier, standardization participants have diverging business interests that, combined with control over certain aspects of technology, complicate the standardization process and the adoption of standards particularly if monetary or other licensing compensation is pending. In fact, quantitative research conducted by Blind et al., (2002) has indicated that the dilemma is not rare at all: over 30% of European companies reported that they had faced dilemmas involving the high licensing fees demanded by the IPR/patent holders, and approximately 25% had had problems with cross-licensing (Blind et al., 2002; Soininen, 2005). However, if there were no compensation, fewer patent holders might be inclined to allow anyone to utilize their patented inventions, and technologically inferior technology might be chosen for the standard. In fact, it has been suggested that incentives offered to patent holders are not sufficient given the positive effects of standardization. Another quantitative study also conducted by Blind and Thumm (2002) demonstrated that the tendency to join standardization processes is lower if an undertaking has intense

patent activity than if it does not. It is suggested that this could be an indicator that the use of IPRs, reflecting the success of the company's own R&D activities, and participation in standardization are, to certain extent, alternative innovation strategies (Blind et al., 2002, Soininen, 2005). Unfortunately this finding also indicates that a large chunk of patents may fall into the category of third-party patents that have a high likelihood to remain unnoticed.

What basically differentiates submarine patent cases and those in which a patent has been properly disclosed is the possibility to make informative decisions about the adoption of a standard, design around it or to agree upon licensing terms in advance. However, standards organization's patent policies only require a general promise to license on RF or RAND terms. Exact licensing conditions are negotiated separately between the parties and this is often done after the standard has been elected. Therefore, with an exception of the fact that a licensing statement has been given and therefore there are more changes of challenging the company's licensing terms, these situations bear a lot of similarities to submarine patent cases. Obviously, if licensing terms were specified better and RAND terms were determined in accordance with the situation that has prevailed prior to the establishment of the standard, there would be less room for interpretation, and the patent holder would not be in such a good negotiation position. This follows that, even though it was possible to diminish the dilemma with submarine patents discussed earlier, licensing perplexities would probably continue to prevail. On the other hand early disclosure could at least diminish those significant economic losses that would occur if the submarine patent surfaced after the standard had been used broadly and various complementary products and services had been based on it. It should be pointed out, however, that the advantages of clearing all relevant patents beforehand also depends on whether the standard is such that it is constantly evolving as new features are incorporated into the system after the original standard has been set, or whether it remains unchanged after its establishment. In the former situations it would be important to be able to gain information also on those rights, which are essential for the purposes of implementing the standard in its amended form, while those rights that were initially essential may no longer be relevant at this phase.

DISCUSSION

In the previous sections I have identified multiple situations in which patents have caused concern during and after cooperative standard setting. These situations could basically be divided into those in which the holder of the disputed patent has participated in setting the standard and those in which the patent holder is a third party. Furthermore, a distinction could be made between patents that have been properly disclosed to the other participants, and the rights that come as a surprise either because the patent policy has not required their disclosure and no attention has been drawn to them, the patent holder has intentionally concealed them despite the patent policy, or the rights holder has accidentally neglected to disclose them.

The number-one reason for the disputes that have arisen in the previously-mentioned situations is that patent holders use their position of being able to prevent others from using an invention that is essential for operating the standard to require licensing fees or other terms that are unacceptable to companies operating in the industry. When talking about properly disclosed patents, the patent holder may have made a declaration prior to the publication of the standard specification to the effect that it was willing to license its essential patents royalty-free, or that it was willing to license them on fair, reasonable and non-discriminatory terms. Here, the patent holder may have posed certain limitations, or the patent

holder may have made only a blank promise of RF or RAND licensing, and a dispute may arise afterwards over what the correct interpretation of such a promise is. Sometimes, there may not be any kind of a promise.

The consequences of the patent holder refusing to license at all, or on terms accepted by most companies, depend on when the dilemma comes to light. The longer it takes for the dispute to arise the worse are the consequences from a societal perspective. Before the standard is set it may well be possible to design around the patents or to choose other technologies over heavily patented ones, and even after the standard specifications have been published, the abandoning of the standard altogether, or its modification, may not be detrimental as companies may have alternative standards to choose from. Of course, the time and the money invested in setting a standard would be lost. On the other hand, if the standard has already been broadly adopted it may be difficult and very costly to change the specifications without losing the network benefits. Ultimately, doing so would harm consumers who are already using a system in which various products are interchangeable and interoperable. Obviously, from the patent holder's perspective, the situation is reversed: the later his patent comes to the surface, the more leverage he gains.

I posed the question in the title of this article whether especially the submarine patent problem truly existed or whether it was a red herring. Although the evidence is largely anecdotal and further quantitative research is needed, I have to conclude that problems to do with unidentified patents do come to the surface after the standard has been established. Obviously, even though there is a high likelihood that plenty of relevant patents remain unnoticed, it is only a minor aspect of the variety of conflicts that patents give rise to during or after standardization, and plenty of standards can be adopted without actually having to face troubles with submarine patents. Particularly those situations in which it can be proven that a standard-setting participant breached the patent policy and purposefully concealed the existence of relevant patents or patent applications and thus misled the industry and manipulated the process in order to gain market power, appear to be rare. Companies typically try to do their best to comply with the patent policy.

Avoiding problems with submarine patents seems to be getting more challenging all the time, however. This is because ICT patents, some of which are valid and some of which are not, are increasing in number making it more difficult to avoid infringement. Furthermore, patents are being assigned more often than before and therefore they may end up in companies that did not participate in setting the standard. Patents are also utilized more aggressively in the field, and the more patent-holding companies are seeking to extract as high royalties as they can get from those implementing a standard the less likely it is that an amicable solution can be reached. As a consequence, particularly the U.S. red herring population seems to be growing quickly in number, even though certain legal provisions such as the U.S. Sherman Act, sections 1 and 2, which prohibit conspiracy and monopolization or its attempt, and the FTC Act, section 5, which prohibits the use of unfair and deceptive business practices, have been and could be used in an attempt to wipe out the most colorful individuals. Other legal tools include fraud, equitable estoppel that prevents a party that has not operated fairly from enforcing his rights, the doctrine of prosecution laches applicable to patents that have been issued following an unreasonable and unexplained delay during patent prosecution phase, and the implied-license and patent-misuse doctrines (Lemley, 2002; Mueller, 2001). Furthermore, non-infringement clarification and patent invalidation either in court or as an opposition (EPO) or re-examination (USPTO) procedure in the patent office could be attempted. In Europe the EC treaty, Art 81 (prohibits agreements and concerted practices that prevent, distort or restrict competition) and 82 (prohibits the abuse

of dominant position) could offer limited help as well. Unfortunately, the legal means have not appeared to be very effective so far. The fact that legal disputes have arisen demonstrates that the dilemmas are serious and that they bear significant economic weight, however.

What makes particularly the submarine patent problem interesting from the societal and patent policy perspective is that in this case companies implementing the standard have not, for some reason or other, been able to identify the relevant rights or to plan their operations so as to avoid infringement. Moreover, the consequences of not being able to continue to use a specific standard may have far-reaching effects not only on the competition in a certain field but also on consumers. Therefore, the purpose of the patent system—to promote innovation and facilitate technology transfer through granting the inventor an exclusive right in return for publishing his invention—may not merely restrain trade in the traditional sense, that is, legal monopoly versus free competition, but may also contravene the public interest in a way that is no longer reasonable given the role of patents in enhancing innovation. This, incidentally, has been seriously questioned in areas such as software and semiconductors. In fact, patents and standards are a policy concern linked to a more general concern regarding IPR protection and the possibility of using it in order to control product interoperability.

This article suggests that further attention should be paid to analyze the efficacy of the legal framework and the need for legislative amendments particularly in the context of standards and so-called submarine patents that come to surface after the standard has been established and adopted. As a practical matter for diminishing potential conflicts, clarifying patent policies in respect to disclosure and licensing obligations, conducting more thorough patent due diligence, and developing guidelines on how to determine RAND terms are recommended. It is further noted that limiting only the risk of submarine patents will not get us far in reducing the conflicts between patents and standards.

REFERENCES

Administrative Complaint (2002), Docket No 9302, 18 June 2002.

Alkio, M. (2003, March 9). Kovaa peliä patenteilla. *Helsingin Sanomat*, p. E3.

ANSI. (2003a). *Guidelines for implementation of the ANSI Patent Policy.*

ANSI. (2003b). *Patent policy.*

Asaravala, A. (2004, April 24). Forgent sues over JPEG patent. *Wired News*. Retrieved August 29, 2006, from http://www.wired.com/news/business/0,1367,63200,00.html

Balto, D.A., & Wolman, A.M. (2003). Intellectual property and antitrust: General principles. *IDEA The Journal of Law and Technology, 43*(3), 396-474.

Bekkers, R., Duysters, G., & Verspagen, B. (2002). Intellectual property rights, strategic technology agreements and market structure. The case of GSM. *Research Policy, 31*, 1141-1161.

Bekkers, R., Verspagen, B., & Smits, J. (2002). Intellectual property rights and standardization: The case of GSM. *Telecommunications Policy, 26*(3-4), 171-188.

Berlind, D. (2002a, April 16). IBM drops Internet patent bombshell. *Tech Update.*

Berlind, D. (2002b, April 25). The hidden toll of patents on standards. *Tech News on ZDNet*. Retrieved August 29, 2006, from http://news.zdnet.com/2100-9595_22-891852.html

Berman, V. (2005, January-February). Is it time to reexamine patent policy for standards? *IEEE Design & Test of Computers,* 71-73.

Bessen, J. (2003). *Strategic patenting of complex technologies* (Working Paper). Research on Innovation.

Blind, K. (2004). *The economics of standards.* Edward Elgar.

Blind, K., Bierhals, R., Thumm, N., Hossain, K., Sillwood, J., Iverser, E., et al. (2002). *Study on the interaction between standardisation and intellectual property rights* (EC Contract No G6MA-CT-2000-02001, 2002).

Blind, K., Edler, J., Nack, R., & Strauß, J. (2001). *Micro- and macroeconomic implications of the patentability of software innovations. Intellectual property rights in information technologies between competition and innovation* (Study on Behalf of German Federal Ministry of Economics and Technology).

In re Bogese II, 303 F.3d 1362, 1367, Federal Circuit (2002).

Initial Decision (2004). Docket No 9302, 23 February 2004.

Calderone, L.L., & Custer, T.L. (2005, November). *Prosecution laches as a defense in patent cases.* Flaster Greenberg Attorneys at Law. Retrieved August 29, 2006, from http://www.flastergreenberg.com/pdf/PatentArtic_prf3.pdf

Caplan, P. (2003). *Patents and open standards* (White paper prepared for the National Information Standards Organization).

Chesbrough, H. (2003). *Open innovation.* Harvard Business School Press.

Clark, D. (2002, October). Do Web standards and patents mix? *Computer*, pp. 19-22.

Clark, R. (2002, July 19). *Concerning recent patent claims*. Retrieved August 29, 2006, from http://www.jpeg.org/newsrel1.html

Cohen, W.M., Nelson, R.R., & Walsh, J.P. (2000, February). *Protecting their intellectual assets:*

Appropriability conditions and why U.S. manufacturing firms patent (or not) (NBER Working Paper Series).

Cunningham, A. (2005). Telecommunications, intellectual property, and standards. In I. Walden, & J. Angel (Eds.), *Telecommunications law and regulation*. Oxford.

DLA. (2004). *European intellectual property survey*.

Eolas Technologies Incorporated and the Regents of the University of California v. Microsoft Corporation, Case Nr. 04-1234, Federal Circuit, 2 March 2005.

ETSI. (2005). *IPR policy*.

Farrell, J. (1996). *Choosing the rules for formal standardization*. UC Berkeley.

Federal Trade Commission v. Dell Computer Corp., FTC File No. 931 0097, 2 November 1995.

Feldman, R.P., & Rees, M.R. (2000, July). The effect of industry standard setting on patent licensing and enforcement. *IEEE Communications Magazine*, pp. 112-116.

Ferguson, K. (1999). *20/20 foresight*. Retrieved August 29, 2006, from http://www.forbes.com/1999/04/19/feat.html

Forgent Networks. (2006). *Intellectual property, '672 patent cases*. Retrieved August 29, 2006, from http://www.forgent.com/ip/672cases.shtml

Frank, S.J. (2002, March). Can you patent an industry standard? *IEEE Spectrum*.

FTC. (2003). *To promote innovation: The proper balance of competition and patent law and policy*.

Graham, S.J.H., & Mowery, D.C. (2002, June 6-8). *Submarines in software? Continuations in U.S. software patenting in the 1980s and 1990s*. Paper presented at the DRUID Summer Conference on Industrial Dynamics of the New and Old Economy—Who is Embracing Whom?, Copenhagen/Elsinore.

Granstrand, O. (1999). *The economics and management of intellectual property*. Edward Elgar Publishing.

Grindley, P. (2002). *Standards, strategy and policy*. Oxford.

Gohring, N. (2005a). Qualcomm files a second suit against Broadcom. *InfoWorld*. Retrieved August 29, 2006, from http://www.infoworld.com/article/05/10/21/HNqualcommsecondsuit_1.html

Gohring, N. (2005b). Qualcomm files patent infringement suit against Nokia. *InfoWorld*. Retrieved August 29, 2006, from http://www.infoworld.com/article/05/11/07/hnqualcommsuit_1.html

GovTrack.us. 109th Congress, H.R. 2795: Patent Act of 2005. Retrieved August 29, 2006, from http://www.govtrack.us/congress/bill.xpd?bill=h109-2795

Hahn, R.W. (2001, March). Competition policy and the new economy. *Milken Institute Review*, 34-41.

Heinze, W.F. (2002, May). Dead patents walking. *IEEE Spectrum*, 52-54.

Hemphill, T.A. (2005, January). Technology standards development, patent ambush, and US antitrust policy. *Technology in Society, 27*(1), 55-67.

Hjelm, B. (2000). Standards and intellectual property rights in the age of global communication: A review of the international standardization of third-generation mobile system.

IETF. (2005). Intellectual property rights in IETF technology.

Informamedia.com. (2006, March 1). ETSI acts on unfair, unreasonable and discriminatory IPRs. *Informamedia.com.*

IPO. (n.d.). *21ˢᵗ Century Patent Coalition: "Submarine patents" ARE a significant problem.* Retrieved August 29, 2006, from http://www.ipo.org/contentmanagement/contentdisplay.cfm?contentid=7334

ITU-T (n.d.). *Patent policy.*

ITU-T (2005). *Patent policy implementation guidelines.*

Jacobs, P. (2005, December). Qualcomm defends patent licensing programme. *wirelessweb.* Retrieved August 29, 2006, from http://wireless.iop.org/articles/news/6/12/6/1

Kipnis, J. (2000, July). Beating the system: Abuses of the standards adoption process. *IEEE Communications Magazine,* pp. 102-105.

Kirsch, E.D. (2000). International standards participation: Lessons from Townshend & Dell. *International Lawyers Network. The bullet"iln",* *1*(2). Retrieved August 29, 2006, from http://www.ag-internet.com/push_news_one_two/internationalstandards.htm

Knight, H.J. (2001). *Patent strategy for researchers and research managers.* John Wiley & Sons.

Kratzman, V.A. (2005). *Technology transfer mid-term report next step recommendations.* FINPRO.

Krechmer, K. (2005, January). *Communications standards and patent rights: Conflict or coordination?* Paper presented at the Economics of the Software and Internet Industries Conference, Tolouse, France.

Labsystems Oy v. Biohit Oy. HO S 94/1922. Finnish Court of Appeal.

The Lemelson Foundation. (n.d.). Jerome H. Lemelson. Retrieved August 29, 2006, from http://www.lemelson.org/about/bio_jerry.php

Lemley, M.A. (2002). *Intellectual property rights and standard setting organizations* (UC Berkeley Public Law and Legal Theory Research Paper Series, Research Paper No. 84).

Lemos, R. (2002, July 23). Finding patent truth in JPEG claims. *CNET News.com.* Retrieved August 29, 2006, from http://news.com.com/Finding+patent+truth+in+JPEG+claim/2100-1001_3-945686.html

Lo, A.M. (Jupiter Networks, Inc) (2002). *A need for intervention: Keeping competition alive in the networking industry in the face of increasing patent assertions against standards.* FTC/DOJ Hearings on Competition and Intellectual Property Law and Policy In the Knowledge-Based Economy—Standard Setting and Intellectual Property, 18 April 2002.

Malone, S. (2005, November 1). *Microsoft loses Eolas Supreme Court appeal.* PC Pro. Retrieved August 29, 2006, from http://www.pcpro.co.uk/news/news/79431

Marasco, A. (ANSI). (2003, October 30). *IPR and standards.* Presentation at AIPLA.

Markoff, J. (2002, July 29). Patent claim strikes an electronics nerve. *The New York Times.*

Megantz, R.C. (2002). *Technology management. Developing and implementing effective licensing programs.* John Wiley & Sons.

Messerschmitt, D.G., & Szyperski, C. (2003). *Software ecosystem.* The MIT Press.

Miele, A.L. (2000). *Patent strategy: The manger's guide to profiting from patent portfolios.* John Wiley & Sons.

Mueller, J.M. (2001). Patenting industry standards. *John Marshall Law Review, 34*(897).

Naraine, R. (2002a, May 8). Nokia calls for 5% cap on 3G patent royalties. *internetnews.com*. Retrieved August 29, 2006, from http://internet-news.com/wireless/article.php/1041561

Naraine, R. (2002b, May 10). Qualcomm rejects Nokia patent cap proposal. *internetnews.com*. Retrieved August 29, 2006, from http://www.interetnews.com/wireless/article.php/1116381

Nokia. (2005a, October 28). *Leading mobile wireless technology companies call on European Commission to investigate Qualcomm's anticompetitive conduct*. Retrieved August 29, 2006, from http://press.nokia.com/PR/200510/1018639_5.html

Nokia. (2005b, October 28). *Leading mobile wireless technology companies call on European Commission to investigate Qualcomm's anti-competitive conduct*. Retrieved August 29, 2006, from http://europe.nokia.com/BaseProject/Sites/NokiaCom_CAMPAIGNS_57710/CDA/Categories/PressEvents/_Content/_Static_Files/transcript.pdf

Nokia. (2005c, November 7). *Nokia responds to reports of Qualcomm GSM patent infringement suit*. Retrieved August 29, 2006, from http://press.nokia.com/PR/200511/1019958_5.html

OASIS. (2005). *IPR policy*.

OECD. (2004). *Patents and innovation: Trends and policy challenges*. Retrieved August 29, 2006, from http://www.oecd.org/dataoecd/48/12/24508541.pdf

OECD. (2005). *Compendium of patent statistics*. Retrieved August 29, 2006, from http://www.oecd.org/dataoecd/60/24/8208325.pdf

Ohana, G. (Cisco Systems, Inc). (2005. October 6). Intellectual property rights: Policies in standard-setting: Areas of debate. In *Proceedings of From A to Veeck: Standardization and the Law, 2005 ANSI Annual Conference*. Retrieved August 29, 2006, from http://public.ansi.org/ansion-line/Documents/Meetings%20and%20Events/2005%20Annual%20Conference/Legal%20Conference/Ohana-Panel%20I.pdf

Out-law.com. (2005, November 31). Mobile-makers say 3G patent licensing breaks antitrust laws. Retrieved August 29, 2006, from http://www.out-law.com/page-6280

Peterson, S.K. (Hewlett-Packard Company). (2002a). *Consideration of patents during the setting of standards*. For FTC and DOJ Roundtable, Standard Setting Organizations: Evaluating the Anticompetitive Risks of Negotiating IP Licensing Terms and Conditions Before A Standard Is Set, 6 November 2002.

Peterson, S.K. (Hewlett-Packard Company). (2002b). *Patents and standard-setting processes*. FTC/DOJ Hearings on Competition and Intellectual Property Law and Policy in the Knowledge-Based Economy, 18 April 2002.

Perens, B. (n.d.). *The problem of software patents in standards*. Retrieved August 29, 2006, from http://perens.com/Articles/PatentFarming.html

Poltorak, A.I., & Lerner, P.J. (2004). *Essentials of licensing intellectual property*. John Wiley & Sons.

PwC Advisory. (2006). *2006 patent and trademark damages study*.

Rahnasto, I. (2003). *Intellectual property rights, external effects, and anti-trust law*. Oxford University Press.

Rambus, Inc v. Infineon Technologies AG. No. 01-1449. Federal Circuit, 29 January 2003.

Red Herring. (2006, February 3). JPEG patent reexamined. Retrieved August 29, 2006, from http://www.redherring.com/Article.aspx?a=15582&hed=JPEG+Patent+Reexamined&sector=Industries&subsector=Computing

Regan, K. (2005, July 5). Broadcom suit accuses Qualcomm of antitrust tactics. *E-Commerce*

Times. Retrieved August 29, 2006, from http://www.ecommercetimes.com/story/44395.html

Reingold, J. (2006, January). *Patently aggressive.* 102. Retrieved August 29, 2006, from http://www.fastcompany.com/magazine/102/patents.html

Rivette, K., & Kline, D. (2000). *Rembrandts in the attic.* Harvard Business School Press.

Sarvas, R., & Soininen, A. (2002, October). *Differences in European and U.S. patent regulation affecting wireless standardization.* Paper presented at the International Workshop on Wireless Strategy in the Enterprise, Berkeley, California.

Shapiro, C. (2001). *Navigating the patent thicket: Cross licenses, patent pools and standard setting.*

Shapiro, C., & Varian, H.R. (1999). *Information rules.* Harvard Business School Press.

Shurmer, M., & Lea, G. (1995, June). Telecommunications standardization and intellectual property rights: A fundamental dilemma? *Standardview, 3*(2).

Soininen, A. H. (2005).Open Standards and the Problem with Submarine Patents. Proceedings SIIT 2005 pp. 231-244 4th International conference on standardization and innovation in information technology.

Stroyd, A.H. (2000). *Lemelson bar coding patents: Attempting to sink the submariner.* Retrieved August 29, 2006, from http://www.mhia.org/PSC/pdf/Lemelson.PDF

Surowiecki, J. (2006, December 26/January 2). Blackberry picking. *The New Yorker*, Financial Page.

Symbol Technologies Inc. v. Lemelson Medical, Education & Research Foundation. 277 F.3d 1361, 1363. Federal Circuit, 2002.

Symbol Technologies, Inc et al. v. Lemelson Medical, Education & Research Foundation. LP et al., 422 F.3d 1378. Federal Circuit, 2005.

Teece, D.J. (2000). *Managing intellectual capital.* Oxford University Press.

Townshend v. Rockwell International Corp. and Conexant Systems, Inc., 55 U.S.P.Q.2d 1011. Northern District of California, 2000.

Varchaver, N. (2001, May 3). *Jerome Lemelson the patent king.* Retrieved August 29, 2006, from http://www.engin.brown.edu/courses/en90/fall/2003/Lemelson%20Fortune%20may%2014%202001%20article.pdf

Vermont, S. (2002). The economics of patent litigation. In B. Berman (Ed.), *From ideas to assets. Investing wisely in intellectual property.* John Wiley & Sons.

Watts, J.J.S., & Baigent, D.R. (2002). Intellectual property, standards and competition law: Navigating a minefield. *IEEE*, 837-842.

Westman, R. (1999, October). The battle of standards—And the road to peace. *On—The New World of Communication*, pp. 26-30.

Wireless Watch. (2005a, November 29). Mobile patents war shifts to email. *The Register.* Retrieved August 29, 2006, from http://www.theregister.co.uk/2005/11/29/mobile_email_patents_war/

Wireless Watch. (2005b, November 15). *The Register.* Qualcomm IP battle hots up. Retrieved August 29, 2006, from http://www.theregister.co.uk/2005/11/15/qualcomm_ip_battle/

Wong, W. (2002, April 18). IBM ebMXL patent plan royalty-free. *Tech Update.*

W3C (2004). *Patent policy.*

This work was previously published in International Journal of IT Standards and Standardization Research, Vol. 5, Issue 1, edited by K. Jakobs, pp. 41-83, copyright 2007 by IGI Publishing, formerly known as Idea Group Publishing (an imprint of IGI Global).

Chapter XVIII
Legal Protection of the Web Page as a Database

Davide Mula
LUISS Guido Carli, Italy

Mirko Luca Lobina
University of Cagliari, Italy

ABSTRACT

Nowadays the Web page is one of the most common medium used by people, institutions, and companies to promote themselves, to share knowledge, and to get through to every body in every part of the world. In spite of that, the Web page does not entitle one to a specific legal protection and because of this, every investment of time and money that stays off-stage is not protected by an unlawfully used. Seeing that no country in the world has a specific legislation on this issue in this chapter, we develop a theory that wants to give legal protection to Web pages using laws and treatment that are just present. In particular, we have developed a theory that considers Web pages as a database, so extends a database's legal protection to Web pages. We start to analyze each component of a database and to find them in a Web page so that we can compare those juridical goods. After that, we analyze present legislation concerning databases and in particular, World Intellectual Property Organization Copyright Treatments and European Directive 96/92/CE, which we consider as the better legislation in this field. In the end, we line future trends that seem to appreciate and apply our theory.

INTRODUCTION

Nowadays, thousands of Web pages offer a heterogeneous variety of digital information (i.e., text,

audio, video, and images). Such content can be available in a public way: an anonymous user could download, manipulate, and use them maliciously and, thus, establishing their ownership could be a serious problem in many circumstances.

The tendency is to face this problem at the same time, using technical and judicial approaches. On one hand, we can consider strategies oriented to the protection of the intellectual property, such as insertion of watermarks or, directly, limitations in the possibility of fruition of the contents published in the Web page (Braudaway & Mintzer, 2000). Secondly, we can refer to the judicial disciplines created expressly for the protection of the copyrights on digital information. In the specific, in this chapter, we explain our theory, which tries to give legal protection to a Web page considering it as a database, judicial good that has a specific legislation.

The chapter is organized as follows. At first we look at a judicial generalization of the conception of database, analyzing its every component and, after we compare Web page and database, introducing the guardianship of the Web page as a database. In the last part, we refer to the future trends and propose our conclusions on this topic.

BACKGROUND

The first institution that issued a database protection is the European Community by the directive 96/9/CE. The course to give protection to a database was started on April 15th, 1992, when the European Commission issued a formal proposal for a Directive on the legal protection of databases, which was later amended by the Commission on October 4th, 1993. After four years of discussions and proposals in 1996, the last version was approved, and directive 96/9/CE issued.

The EU Database Directive was created to harmonize the intellectual property laws regarding databases of the 18 countries of the European Union, by supplementing copyright to protect databases produced by *sweat of the brow* (Boyle, 2001). The Directive creates a new kind of intellectual property protection: a *sui generis* right. *Sui generis* is a Latin expression that means that

something is linked to a specific requisite for admission; in other words, this particular protection is given only to the database that meets all the requirements (Autelitano, 1999). It is important to observe that the term of protection is 15 years, but each time the database is updated significantly, the entire database, and not just the updated parts, receives another 15 years of protection. Consequently, active databases can be protected in perpetuity.

The Database Directive has created a two-tiered approach to the database's protection. On one hand, databases that, by originality of selection and arrangement qualify for copyright protection under national laws, will enjoy the same rights as other copyrighted works and, on the other hand, databases that do not meet such requirements will, nonetheless, be protected against unfair extraction under the terms of the Directive.

The top tier provided copyright protection for original selection and arrangement of facts in the database. In other words, the authorship is given when the Web page has the requirement of originality of selection and arrangement, and is important to observe that to have this legal protection, the author does not need to demonstrate his investments in term of money or time.

A second tier provided *sui generis* protection, prohibiting the unfair extraction of a substantial part of a database reflecting significant investment. A database could simultaneously receive both types of protection: copyright protection for the expression, in other words the selection and arrangement of the data; and *sui generis* protection against the extraction of a qualitatively substantial part of the data itself. In other words, the ownership, or *sui generis* protection, is given only when the author of the Web page could prove his investments, which must be considerable. About the concept of investment, the European Court of Justice, in the case C-444 02, established that *The expression 'investment in ...the obtaining ...of the contents' of a database in Article 7(1) of Directive 96/9 must be understood to refer to the resources used to seek out existing independent materials and collect them in the database. It does not cover the resources used for the creation of materials which make up the contents of a database.* Moreover, we can observe that "The right provided for by the Directive allows the maker of a database to prevent the use of the data it contains under certain circumstances. It is intended to protect databases or their contents without protecting the information they contain as such. It thus indirectly protects the investment involved in the making of the database" (Court of Justice of the European Communites, 2004, p. 3).

The Directive provides that databases be protected by copyright under national legislation to the extent that their selection and arrangement are sufficiently original to constitute the author's own intellectual creation. Thus, to prevent that in case a member nation did not provide similar protection under its laws, it would be forced to amend them to comply with the terms of the Directive (Marino, 2006).

If the European Community has issued the first law that give a protection to databases in USA, even today there is not a specific law to protect a database's owners, and a soft form of protection is given only by WIPO Copyright Treatment (Braun, 2003). We think that it is important to remember that the World Intellectual Property Organisation (WIPO) is a special organ of the UN that guarantees the interests and rights of inventors and those who hold the right of intellectual protection. Besides having eased the conclusion of multilateral accords for the protection of International patents, brands, design and copyrights, the WIPO is active in the field of technical cooperation, and it backs member states in creating structures that allow the effective protection of immaterial goods. In spite of everything, the course to issue a database's law is begun in 1978, but nowadays is not concluded. In 1978, the National Commission on New Technological Uses of Copyrighted Works submitted a report that states that computer databases fall within the protection of copyright as compilations.

The House Report concluded that the term *literary work* includes computer databases, but did not give to interpreters any clarification about the way to protect tangible databases.

In 1991, the Supreme Court addressed this question in *Feist Publications v. Rural Telephone Co.* Feist copied Rural's collection of white page listing in order to compile its own (Ghidini & Falce, 2001; Gorman, 1992). The District Court granted summary judgment to Rural, relying on the *sweat of the brow* doctrine, which justified protection because of the work involved in selection and arrangement of the client's data. The Supreme Court rejected the District Court's sentence and the *sweat of the brow* doctrine because, with the Copyright Act of 1976, Congress made it clear that originality was a requirement for copyright protection, and in this particular case, Rural's database does not have the originality requirement (Askanazi, Caplan, Descoteaux, Donohue, Glasser, Johnson, & Mena, 2002; Hayden, 1991). This sentence demonstrates that what the House Report said in 1978 was unclear, and shows how specific database protection is necessary.

To explain the doctrine known as *sweat of the brow,* we must consider that over the course of the nineteenth century, two rationales developed for protecting compilations under copyright. The earliest cases identified the constructor's effort, consider as his own expense, or skill, or labor, or money, as the critical contribution justifying protection [37]. The *sweat of the brow* aims to protect the value of this effort, extending copyright protection in a compilation beyond selection and arrangement to the facts themselves or, in other words, to the effort [29].

Before this Supreme Court sentence, several US District Courts had granted copyright protection to a collection of facts, such as a database, if the author of the database required a lot of effort to collect the facts or the data in general. Thus, District Courts have applied the *sweat of the brow* theory, which gives protection to a database, as what we have said previously. Under such protection, it was not even allowed to extract individual facts from the collection [10].

Under US law, the eligibility for copyright protection of electronic databases depends on the interaction of two contrasting, but well-established principles: the noncopyrightability of facts and the copyrightbility of factual compilations.

At the end, we can observe that in Europe, database protection is effective and complete, but in the USA, there is not a specific protection for a database and, for this reason, the only way to protect a database is to apply the Copyright Act and the WIPO Copyright Treatment. While under both the European Union and the US approaches, databases are eligible for copyright protection only if their selection and arrangement is sufficiently original; the *sui generis* protection offered by the directive 96/9/CE to noncopyrightable electronic databases has no counterpart under US law (Mc-Curdy, 2003).

Up until here we have seen database legislation in Europe and in the USA, but nothing about a Web page's protection. The reason is that no country in the world has issued a Web page's law and, for this reason, we are trying to develop a theory that starts from database legislation and arrives to give specific protection to a Web page. We further our thesis because we think that it is very important to give a specific protection to Web pages, but at the same time, we must consider which actions are permitted by present legislation.

Definition of Database and Web Page

The object of our research is to think about legal protection to Web pages considered as a whole. Indeed, currentyl we have legal protection for music, movie, photographs, and software, but there is no law or treatment that protects a Web page as a complete work, in spite of the money that many companies invest in this work.

We consider the Web page as a judicial good that can be protected via an analogical interpreta-

tion of directive 96/9/CE and WIPO Copyright Treaty, adopted in Geneva on December 20, 1996, which is related to the judicial protection of databases (Butler, 2000). Both of them consider databases as a collection of information, be they rough or elaborate. They are generally about determined topics or they contain material that has been organized in order to allow the user to research and get information. Directive 96/9/CE defines a database as *a collection of independent works, data or other materials arranged in a systematic or methodical way and individually accessible by electronic or other means,* and WIPO Copyright Treatment defines a database as *a compilations of data or other material, in any form, which by reason of the selection or arrangement of their contents constitute intellectual creations, are protected as such.*

We can observe that directive 96/9CE and WIPO Copyright Treatment give a similar definition of databases and, more or less, the same rights to the owner of a database (Brock, 1996). This point is very important because our research observes how we can compare a Web page and a database to extend judicial protection from the second to the first. Because the information can be about private subjects or companies, the risk that databases can affect the rights of various categories of subjects is real. The latter are protected by many countries; we analyze how they are protected in the European Union and in the USA (Davidson, 2003).

In foreseeing the specific forms of protection for databanks , WIPO and UE tried to shield the tiring activity of data collection, selection, and verification of questions. This type of protection intends to allow the creator of databanks to ban other subjects from putting their hands on full or partial information available in the databank.

With the birth of digital technology, databases have acquired a major potential of stocking and collecting information without leaving out the crucial economic factor. The European Union and WIPO's Member State considers databases as an efficient and precious instrument for the growth of commerce and thus, each one has decided to extend a uniform and specific protection. The directive 96/9/CE has, on one hand, left protection via single orders untouched, adding, on another hand, a form of *sui generis* protection allows the protection of investments made by attributing to the constructor an exclusive right on the information container in the database (Hayes, 2000). Also, the WIPO Copyright Treatment gives a particular protection to a database's constructor mentioning explicitly *without prejudice to any copyright subsisting in the data or material contained in the compilation.*

Now that the reasons and interests in creating a specific protection of databases has been discussed, the judicial nature of this feat needs to be clarified, in order to then analyse the adaptability of this form of protection to the Web pages.

The Database

The term "database" refers to all types of data collection, be they rough or elaborate, as long as they deal with specific topics, and is organized in order to allow the user to research and obtain the said information.

It is too obvious that, explained in this manner, the definition of a database could include various entities, different because of content and the complexity (Hicks, 1987). An encyclopaedia, dictionary, jurisprudence material, and even telephone directories could be included in these definitions; the common element between these entities is that they are instruments of collection and used for obtaining information, and thus, needing a specific protection against copy, especially in the digital format. It is obvious that digital technology offers greater possibilities than paper, be it in the proliferation of databases and even in their creation, allowing the insertion of texts, but even images, films, and sounds (Grutzmacher, 1999).

A legal definition of "database" is given by the community legislator via the directive 96/9/CE that, in art. 1 comma 2, declares that *for the purposes of this Directive, 'database' shall mean a collection of independent works, data or other materials arranged in a systematic or methodical way and individually accessible by electronic or other means.* In follow up to this, we can assert that this definition could be considered good also from the WIPO Copyright Treatment point of view. Indeed a WIPO Treatment definition does not add anything and, in general, we can consider it less accurate than the directive's definition.

Later on, the legislator decided to add onto article 3 that *1. In accordance with this Directive, databases which, by reason of the selection or arrangement of their contents, constitute the author's own intellectual creation shall be protected as such by copyright. No other criteria shall be applied to determine their eligibility for that protection. 2. The copyright protection of databases provided for by this Directive shall not extend to their contents and shall be without prejudice to any rights subsisting in those contents themselves.*

The protection of databases in linkage with copyright had already been granted by art. 10 number 2 of the TRIPs on the 15th of April 1994. The following analysis is indispensable because, if the community directive grants protection to the databases which, by reason of the selection or arrangement of their contents, constitute the author's own intellectual creation, art. 10 number 2 of the TRIP accord grants similar protection to all compiled data or material, that can be read from a machine or other form without, however, providing a specific definition of databases (Douglas, 1996). As we have done previously with WIPO, we think that it is important to remember that the TRIPS is an organ of the WTO that aims to enforce the intellectual property accords, monitoring the operations included in the accord, and by promoting the transparency of the politics of the accord members. Moreover, it can be consulted by members, in case of violation of the terms of the treaty.

About the European legal reality, we can observe that the definition provided in the directive responds to the needs of the community legislator in setting limits to the field of application of the directive and consequently, the obligations of harmonization imposed on the community members (Band & Gowdy, 1997). The limit imposed by the directive has the job of limiting the special sui generis protection that this grants to the databases. The precise definition is needed in order to define the reason for the protection, but also in order to establish the requisites needed for the protection. On the contrary, no innovation has come about concerning the already present protection given by the copyright, not even in the sense of limiting its area of application.

From all the elements described, it can be seen that the dispositions included in the decree are not in contrast with the details of the TRIPS accord and the WIPO treaty, because databases that are not included in the community law will be protected anyway by the copyright. In particular, in this research, we analyze European directive because it is more specific and because a database protected by WIPO Treatment could not be included under the directive's protection, but not vice versa.

The elements that, in particular, characterize the legal notions of a database are (Auteri, 2003):

1. **Collection of independent works, data or other materials:** The collection must be viewed in the sense of a reunion and together with the latter, a presentation of the selected elements, but always distinct in order to allow recognition individually or in reunion. In order to answer this need/requirement, not only will the fixation be necessary, but also the contextual reproduction of the elements,

an easy task due to the information technology available today. Thus, the nature of the elements inserted is apparently relevant, because it is not just about words, but also numbers, images, and sounds. It may be useful to state the definition of the International Standards Organization: *a representation of facts, concepts or instructions in a formalized manner suitable for communication, interpretation or processing by human beings or by automatic means* (Dommering & Hugenholtz, 1991).

The works are taken in consideration as the content of a database, both when they are destined to provide facts on which they intend to give information, and even as real and proper facts.

Other materials: These being sounds, images, films, they can have an integrative role with respect to the information provided or more simply, they can be primary sources of information.

2. **Individually accessible by electronic or other means:** This requisite is functional based on the accessibility of single units of information, possible as long as they remain distinct and do not mix with other elements that make up the work. The independence is request not only for other *elements* but also for pieces, work, and data. The independence is thus seen as the faculty to find, learn, and eventually extract information *by electronic or other means*. This requisite demands that the information must be presented according to some order, or through a system that allows the recovery and individuation of specific information (Di Cocco, 2005).

Such a requisite is not usually interpreted rigidly, unless there is not the need for displaying single infos in a sequence, leaving to other elements, like indices and hypertext links, the job of giving the piece its sense of union (Musso, 1998; Spada, 1997).

The elasticity of interpretation of this element leads to the major or minor attribution of the specific *sui generis* protection.

3. **Arranged in a systematic or methodical way:** This is a requisite that arises with the same concept of filling in, which implies not only research, the choice, or the unison of elements, but also a type of presentation of the information collected that allows the user to perceive the whole info and the independence of the data collected.

Both the definition of the database in the directive and the one in the WIPO Copyright Treatment recognise the author's creative support in the setting and placement of the material. The placing according to systematic criteria of the data collected is a basic notion of databases, but that does not mean that information has to be always displayed using the original method.

The term "Disposition" has in it the conception of coordination, intended as integration of data via a network of connections and the concept of organization, as the manifestation of a sequence, order of data placement.

On the one hand, in the analogical databases, the disposition of the material is done using a topographical placement of information helping the user with indices and notes; the other side is the electronic database where disposition is via computer based on technical needs that do not stick to the user's needs. On the other hand, it is important that the disposition of the material reveals only elements that can be perceived and used by the user.

The peculiarity of the electronic databases compared to the peculiarities of the analogical ones is that they do not reveal, with the aim of defining the database, as is the result by considering 21 of the EU Database Directive that states, it: *is not necessary for those materials to have been physically stored in an organized manner.*

Article 1 at comma 3 of the directive, however, excludes that protection given to the databases be extended to *computer programs used in the making or operation of databases accessible by electronic means.* However, the same directive, when considering 20, adds that *protection under this Directive may also apply to the materials necessary for the operation or consultation of certain databases such as thesaurus and indexation systems.* By excluding software (used for constructing or the functioning of the database) from the protection, the directive excludes that the foreseen requisites for databases can be found in those same programmes.

This is relevant for the attribution of the copyright protection, as the norm under examination seems to exclude from this protection the databanks whose creative character lies only in the disposition of the material thanks to the software used. The community legislator has distinguished between the necessary elements for the functioning and the elements necessary for the consultation of databases, declaring that the protection should be extended even to such elements, even though he indicated as example the TESAURO and index systems. The question needs to be solved on a technical level, but in case this is not possible, an eventual extension of the protection should not, according to the majority of the doctrine, create particular problems. After all, the protection would be extended to these programmes only in the measure in which they are necessary for the functioning of a specific database (Linn, 2000).

4. **Accessible by electronic or other means:** This requisite is intended in the sense of attributing to any user the faculty of accessing the single pieces of information available in the database, of learning about them and, in the final case, extracting them. The minority

doctrine does not seem to follow this, according to it, it is enough if the technician has access to the information.

Related to the databases, it is the same definition given by the norm that needs the availability of software specific for locating and for picking up single pieces of information, but it seems right to retain that for nondigital databases, the requisites should be more elastic.

The directive under examination recognises as the author of the database the physical or judicial person who creates the piece, and gives him/her, in virtue of this classification, the original economic rights over it (Lipton, 2003). All member states have not absorbed the directive in its totality; for example, the Italian legislator has excluded the chance that a judicial person be considered as author of the database, admitting, however, that the subject can assume the position and have economic rights as a derived right (Beutler, 1996; Jarach, 1979). We must observe that WIPO Copyright Treatment moves from a contrary point of view because it does not distinguish between a physical or judicial person. Thus, the WIPO treaty does not give any moral right to a database's constitutor, only an economic right.

The moral rights of the piece and the exclusive rights of making economical use are given to the author of the database. Concerning rights of every worker that collaborated to create a database, that is, content creator, database designers, or system developers, we have to observe that the European Directive and the WIPO Treatment do not recognise moral and economic rights to each one of the coworkers (Collie, 1994). Indeed, we have to remember that a database's legal protection is given only to the creation consider as a whole; at the same, consideration has to be extended to the Web page. Coworker have recognized moral and economic rights, but only for the specific job and, as often as not, these economic rights are automatically transferred from the coworker to the owner by the employment contract's regulations

(Lai, 1999). In other words, on one side, we have a specific right that recognizes each collaborator and, on the other side, we have a general right that recognizes the creation considered as whole.

The exclusive rights reserved for the database's author from article 5 of the directive 96/9/CE are:

a. Temporary or permanent reproduction by any means and in any form, in whole or in part, does not detect, as per the norm, the eventual private use of the copy made, which will be still equally subject to authorisation.

b. Translation, adaptation, arrangement, and any other alteration, translations, and individual pieces that are autonomously protected in their economic rights are not subject to the database's author's authorization.

c. Any form of distribution to the public of the database or of copies thereof. The first sale in the Community of a copy of the database by the right holder or with his consent shall exhaust the right to control resale of that copy within the Community.

d. Any communication, display or performance to the public.

e. Any reproduction, distribution, communication, display or performance to the public of the results of the acts referred to in *b*.

Referring to point c, it is important to underline that free delivery of examples for promotional reasons, teaching, or scientific research, are not to be considered as exercising the right of distribution. In the WIPO treaty, there is not any explicit limitation of the economical right, but article 10 declares *Contracting Parties may, in their national legislation, provide for limitations of or exceptions to the rights granted to authors of literary and artistic works under this Treaty in certain special cases that do not conflict with a normal exploitation of the work and do not unreasonably prejudice the legitimate interests of the author* and later *Contracting Parties shall, when applying the Berne Convention, confine any limitations of or exceptions to rights provided for therein to certain special cases that do not conflict with a normal exploitation of the work and do not unreasonably prejudice the legitimate interests of the author.* From all the elements described, it can be seen that there is not so much difference between European directive and WIPO Copyright Treatment.

Distribution is to be understood only as sale or transfer of property that can be done only with alienation or with the passing on of support material that incorporates the original or its copy. With regard to the "passing on," it is important to distinguish between material and immaterial support, as exhaustion of the right of distribution exists only in the first case; it seems correct to believe that the simple placing of a database online for the public does not lead to any type of exhaustion of the right.

The right to distribute has two particular exceptions, clearly underlined at the second comma of article 5 of the present directive:

a. In the case of reproduction for private purposes of a non-electronic database.
b. Where there is use for the sole purpose of illustration for teaching or scientific research, as long as the source is indicated and to the extent justified by the non-commercial purpose to be achieved.
c. Where there is use for the purposes of public security of for the purposes of an administrative or judicial procedure.
d. Where other exceptions to copyright which are traditionally authorized under national law are involved, without prejudice to points a., b. and c.

A part of the doctrine already held that, given the importance of databases as sources of information, and their increasing relevance for some major social and economic activities, it was seen as necessary that the temperament of the exclusive rights via licences foresaw such restrictions in specific cases, and with equal conditions for the author and the user (Giannantonio, 1997).

The maker of databases is completely another point. The community legislator has provided, for the latter, a specific point in art. 7, first comma, of the directive; this states: Member States shall provide for a right for the maker of a database which shows that there has been qualitatively and/or quantitatively a substantial investment in either the obtaining, verification or presentation of the contents to prevent extraction and/or re-utilization of the whole or of a substantial part, evaluated qualitatively and/or quantitatively, of the contents of that database. The community legislator has, in this instance, wanted to protect the investment of the maker, not only from a quantitative view, in other words based on the money invested, but also based on the qualitative point of view, considering, for example, the amount of time devoted (Winn, 2000). In this sense, the qualification of constructor could be of a Judicial person participating in the entrepreneurial activity, equally of a physical person, even if not an entrepreneur. Essential requisite in both cases is that the constructor must come from one of the European countries.

The protection given to the investments is completely unlinked from that guaranteed by copyright; in fact, if the copyright protects the structure of the database, the right of the maker aims at protecting the investments made by the parasite-like competition. This difference of ends, even in the most minimal duration of this sui generis protection, is reduced to 15 years from the date of completing of database.

In particular, the maker can ban the extraction and the reuse of substantial parts. Article 7 comma 2 alphabet a of the directive defines the extraction as the permanent or temporary transfer of all or a substantial part of the contents of a database to another medium by any means or in any form.

The same article continues to define the concept of reuse as any form of making available to the public all or a substantial part of the contents of a database by the distribution of copies, by renting, by on-line or other forms of transmission. The first sale of a copy of a database within the Community by the rightholder or with his consent shall exhaust the right to control resale of that copy within the Community; Public lending is not an act of extraction or re-utilization. In this definition, there are references to the concept of substantial part: the doctrine (Chimenti, 2001) shows that these words have to be interpreted with relation to single events and the problems caused to the legal owner. Besides banning extraction and the reuse of substantial parts of the compilation, the chance of ceding the activity is foreseen;, even though a precise contractual form does not exist for it, the community legislator allows free space here for each member.

In the judgment C-203/02, BHB Case, November 9 2004, the Court of Justice of CE defined substantial part as contents of [a] database' refers to the scale of the investment in the obtaining, verification or presentation of the contents of the subject of the act of extraction and/or re-utilisation, regardless of whether that subject represents a quantitatively substantial part of the general contents of the protected database. Any part which does not fulfil the definition of a substantial part, evaluated both quantitatively and qualitatively, falls within the definition of an insubstantial part of the contents of a database (Gledhill, 2001).

The Court made clear that the Copyright Clause does not protect a group of facts merely based on the amount of resources one invests in creating the database or compilation (Chalton, 1997). This is consistent with the notion that factual information is something that should be left in the public domain. Proponents of database legislation argue that business models emerging in the information age need *sweat of the brow* protection. Collections of information, especially those readily accessible via the Internet, related to news, stock market activity, travel, health, Internet usage patterns, and customer lists, have become valuable commodities. While companies invest substantial resources in gathering and maintaining such databases, Internet allows the cost of copying and disseminating such information to decrease rapidly. As the amount of free riders increases, incentive to invest resources in such databases will decrease if creators do not reap enough market return through increased competitors and less licenses or subscriber fees.

If what the Court said about a database is important to a database's constructor, we think that is more important to a Web page's creator, not only for the investment, but also for the moral right that creation of Web page should give to the constructor.

The Protection of Web Pages as a Database

After having focused on the basic characteristics of databases, it is now easier to discover the differences between typical elements of a Web page and those of a database.

It can be stated without much difficulty that a general similarity between the elements of a single Web site and those delineated in the definition of databases. The first requisite predicted for a database in the directive is the *collection of independent works, data or other materials*. The meaning of this expression used by the legislator has been clarified, and thus it is not too ring to say that all elements that are generally found in a Web page are included fully in the definition given to the content of a database.

An analysis of a similar result can be done also for the second requisite of databases: *individually accessible by electronic or other means*. The independence of single data in a Web page is highlighted by various elements; in particular, the division of information in single files, and their connection using hypertext links denotes the independence and, at the same time, the interconnection of the elements. It must be added that when all elements are in a single file, it is always possible to distinguish the single elements by making them independent, not only from a technical point of view, but also in content. Indeed, elaborator and software, every browser in particular, are able to distinguish the data in every single element, even though they are presented in the same way and the user can, using simple operations, manage to separate the single parts, and eventually get the files that the user is interested in.

The third requisite for databases imposes that *data be arranged in a systematic or methodical way.* When comparing a Web page with a database, we cannot forget what has already been mentioned about this requisite for this type of database. In fact, for this characteristic, it must be said that system and method must be felt when the user uses the site, not in the physical disposition of the information, which must answer the creator and the software's needs. It might be useful, based on what has been said until now, to confirm and remind again what article 21 of the directive 96/9/CE states *whereas it is not necessary for those materials to have been physically stored in an organized manner.*

The last requisite states that it be *accessible by electronic or other means* is a characteristic that can be checked by the simple presence of research instruments by the pieces of information available on the site, or furnished by browsers used for surfing the Web. Thus, it seems right to state that all the requisites needed for the definition of databases can be used directly for the Web page.

About requisites contained in WIPO Copyright Treatment, we can observe that only one of them is not explicitly included in directive 96/9/CE and is the requisite for a database *to by reason of the selection or arrangement of their contents constitute intellectual creations.* Any way we think, this requisite must be found in every Web page; also, if it is created on a software's model, because each page must be different in the content and the elements used. If we find two similar pages,

we can sustain that it is a copy or a plagiarized work and, in this case, the first creator could use this theory to protect what he/she has done (Unsworth, 1997).

At this point, we think it would be useful to summarize similarities and differences between a Web page and a database. A Web page is composed of different kinds of components as text, image, music, film clip, software (i.e., games on line), and each element has a specific legal protection of itself. Those elements are the same components that we can find in a database; in fact, a databank can contain text, image, music, film clips, and software. Going over, we can observe that every one can research each Web page's elements and access to them individually, as the European Directive requires for database. Withal, we can observe that database's requisites of *data arranged in a systematic or methodical way* and of *accessible by electronic or other means* are attended in a Web page's nature; indeed, Web page's prolog requires to respect a specific grammar or, in other words, to use a systematic or methodical way. At the end, we can sustain that database and Web page have the same structure and compositions; in fact, Web page could be considered as a database and database could be consider as a Web page. The only difference that we can point out is that a paper database does not lose its inner nature, that is, a telephone book; on the contrary, paper a Web page and it loses the Web page's inner nature. At the end of this short summary, we can sustain that in general, we can extend a database's legal protection to Web page.

The directive and the modality with which single member states have accepted the situation, offer a kind of inelastic protection, and it is not very adaptable to new events.

In fact, the derogations that create a restricted space for free utilisation are not applied to extraction, not even for private use of data from an electronic database. From what has been said, it can be deduced that even where a database is diffused free of charge, no private user could, based on the literal interpretation of the norm, consult it, or even less download files on their hard disks or auxiliary memory units. About the faculty of consulting, we have to observe that the ban arises even for simple consultation of data on the network as it is necessary that this be stored in the user's RAM and cache memory. In fact, all this process is part of the idea of extraction. We should not forget that for the connections, it is wrong to talk about hypertext connections, as the link only provides the server's address where the file can be found; it does not connect the two datas. In the World Wide Web, as in other hyper-textual systems, link is a sign of interconnection from a source to a destination. A link on a text, on a photo, or on other multimedia object permits one to open another file or page.

Interpreted in the way as explained, it will be extremely difficult for the *sui generis* protection to be applied to search engines; the access here is generally free, and only in rare cases is there a work behind the scenes, work related to the gaining of data, based on connections and other sites (Tyson & Sherry, 1997).

This type of discipline could be applicable for information groupings that are accessed via passwords, but we must consider that in these sites, a password is indispensable in order to access the various services. While the ban of reuse can be included in the contract for adhesion, while a rigid application on the network could result as an excessive restriction, potentially, it could mine the intrinsic nature of internet (Stazi, 2004; Tai, 2003). In fact, if it were attributed to selected information that is diffused with the protection, impeding the reproduction, as the info is part of a database, the whole physiognomy of the Internet would be radically changed from a virtual area where information is diffused so that it be freely available and usable. What needs to be protected is not the generality of information present on Internet, but the particular realities that need the investment of time and money and that, for their economic relevancy, require particular attention.

Moreover, we must observe that in the recent past, many legal theories have been developed to give a legal protection to software when there was not any treatment (Derclaye, 2000), and the same thing has been done about games and other judicial goods that, in the past, did not have specific protection. Indeed technology's develop faster than any legislator's work or law's evolution. In other words, frequently, when something new appears on the world scene and these things have a considerable economic value, lawyers begin to think about a legal protection to guarantee investments that stay off-stage and, in this way, also the development of new technology (Cohen, 1991; Colston, 2002).

In particular, we want to underline that this theory tries to protect not only the economic investment made by a big company, but also, and above all, the time investment of a single person or small associations (Crews, 1998). To demonstrate better what we have just said, we can remember what is written in the WIPO site's home page: *The World Intellectual Property Organization (WIPO) is a specialized agency of the United Nations. It is dedicated to developing a balanced and accessible international intellectual property (IP) system, which rewards creativity, stimulates innovation and contributes to economic development while safeguarding the public interest.*

For all that has been mentioned up to this point, it seems legitimate to believe that directive 96/9/CE for databases and WIPO Copyright Treatment can be extended to Web pages. However, it seems right that inside this theory, there be a distinction between Web page with restricted access, for which a protection seems necessary and rightful, and Web pages with free access, for which a protection seems necessary and rightful (Mansani, 1996) for the one that has to do with copyright, and for the Web page considered as a whole. In fact, if the Web page, with restricted access, needs protection, not only from the point of view of copyright, but also about the investment that has been done, a Web page with free access needs only a copyright protection.

FUTURE TRENDS

Future trends seem to follow our theory and in fact, we want to bring to your attention what the University of Leicester's Web site tells about protection of itself: *The University of Leicester World Wide Web site, as a database, is eligible for protection under copyright and Database Right. These rights are owned by the University of Leicester.* In simple language, the University of Leicester agrees with our thesis and for the first time, pays attention to the copyright of a Web page.

Analyzing what the University of Leicester's Web site tells about protection of itself, we found that the University attributes to itself every moral and economic right not only related to the content of each page, but also related to *all original content (including text, code, page design, graphics and sound)*[…].

University of Leicester links the protection of its Web site to the Copyright and Rights in Database Regulations 1997, the UK law that has acknowledged the European directive 96/9/CE. This link permits the writer to sustain all the more what was said previously.

We did not find any theory against our thesis, and we think that in the future, the doctrine and the jurisprudence will follow this road, considering in particular that a lot of Web sites are starting to adopt the same policy as the University of Leicester's Web site.

CONCLUSION

From what has been said, it can be deduced that even where a database is diffused free of charge, no private user could, based on the literal interpretation of the norm, consult it, or even less download files on their hard disks or auxiliary memory units (Mulholland, 2005). We should not forget that for the connections, it is wrong to talk about hypertext connections, as the link only

Figure 1.

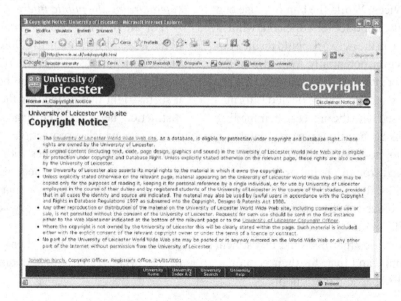

370

provides the server's address where the file can be found; it does not connect the two data.

Interpreted in the way explained previously, it will be extremely difficult for the *sui generis* protection to be applied to search engines. The access here is generally free, and only in rare cases is there work behind the scenes, work related to the gaining of data, based on connections and other sites. This type of discipline could be applicable for information groupings that are accessed via passwords, while a rigid application on the network could result as an excessive restriction; potentially, it could mine the intrinsic nature of Internet. In fact, if it were attributed to selected information that is diffused with the protection, impeding the reproduction as the info is part of a database, the whole physiognomy of the Internet would be radically changed from a virtual area where information is diffused so that it be freely available and usable. What needs to be protected is not the generality of information present on Internet, but the particular realities that need the investment of time and money and that, for their economic relevancy, require particular attention.

Waiting for an ad-hoc protection that will contemplate all specifics that could arise regarding the Web sites, this interpretative solution could be taken up and used not only by big company to protect their Web site, but also by each private constitutor that spends a lot of time to create their private Web site.

We think that this thesis does not damage Internet's philosophy of free information and free circulation of them (Correa, 2002), but that permit every Web page's creator to have a recognition of his/her work, and moral and economic rights related to it.

REFERENCES

Askanazi, J., Caplan, G., Descoteaux, D., Donohue, K., Glasser, D., Johnson, A., & Mena, E. (2002). *The future of database protection in U.S.* Copyright Law. Retrieved November 27, 2006, from http://www.law.duke.edu/journals/dltr/articles/2001dltr0017.html

Autelitano, F. (1999). Banche dati. La rilevanza delle banche dati nel sistema del "cyberlaw", *I Contratti, 10*, 925-935.

Auteri, P. (2003). Attuazione della direttiva 96/9/CE relativa alla tutela giuridica delle banche dati—[Artt. 1, 2], *Le nuove leggi civili commentate, 4-5*, 1175-1230.

Band, J., & Gowdy, J. S. (1997). Sui generis database protection—Has Its Time Come?, *D-Lib Magazine.* Retrieved September 25, 2006, from http://www.dlib.org/dlib/june97/06band.html

Beutler, S. (1996). The protection of multimedia products through the EC's directive. *Entertainment Law Review, 7*, 317.

Boyle, J. (2001). Comment & analysis: Whigs and hackers in cyberspace: Copyright regulations before the European Parliament should be treated as skeptically as they were by the Victorians. *Financial Times*, pp. 21.

Braudaway, G., & Mintzer, F. (2000). Automatic recovery of invisible image watermarks from geometrically distorted images. *Journal of Electronic Imaging, 9*(4), 477.

Braun, N. (2003). The interface between the protection of technological measures and the exercise of exceptions to copyright and related rights: comparing the situation in the United States and in the European community. *EIPR, 25*(11), 496.

Brock, F. (1996). Diritti d'autore. Opera collettiva. Autorizzazione alla riproduzione di articolo di rivista. Potere del direttore della rivista di rappresentare l'editore. *Rivista di diritto industriale, 3*, 227.

Butler, K. (2000). Databases are latest battleground in the intellectual property debate. *Investor's Business Daily*, pp. 28.

Chalton, S. (1997). The effect of the E.C. database directive on United Kingdom copyright law in relation to databases: A comparison of features. *EIPR*, *6*, 278.

Chimenti, L. (2001). I data bases nella direttiva 9/96 e nel d.lgs. 6 maggio 1999, n. 169, *Il diritto dell'informazione e dell'informatica, 1*, 199-211.

Cohen, J. H. (1991). Hybrids on the borderline between copyright and industrial property law. *Intellectual Property Journal*, *2*(4), 190.

Collie, I. (1994). Multimedia and moral rights. *Arts and Entertainment Law Review*, *6*, 194.

Colston, C. (2002). Challenges to information retrieval—A global solution? *International Journal of Law and Information Technology*, *10*(3), 294.

Correa, C. M. (2002). Fair use in the digital era, *IIC*, *4*, 535.

Court of Justice of the European Communites. (2004). *Press Release n° 46/04/EN*, p. 3.

Crews, K. D. (1998). Harmonization and the goals of copyright: Property rights or cultural progress? *Indiana Journal of Global Legal Studies, 6*, 117.

Davidson, M. J. (2003). *The legal protection of database*. UK: Cambridge.

Derclaye, E. (2000). Software copyright protection: Can Europe learn from American case law. *EIPR*, *22*(1), 7.

Di Cocco, C. (2005). *L'opera multimediale*. Italy: Giappichelli.

Dommering, J., & Hugenholtz, A. (1991). *An introduction to information law. Work of fact at the crossroads of freedom and protection, in copyright, freedom of expression and information law*. Boston: The Hague.

Douglas, J. (1996). The challenge of multimedia: Reform the Copyright Act? *Computers and Law*, *31*, 47.

Ghidini, G., & Falce, V. (2001). Intellectual property on communications standards: Balancing innovation and competition through the essential facilities doctrine, *Diritto d'Autore*, *3*, 315.

Giannantonio, E. (1997). *Manuale di diritto dell'informatica*. Italy: Giuffré.

Gledhill, D. (2001). William Hill t/akes racing database fight to OFT. *The Independent*, pp. 10.

Gorman, R. A. (1992). The Feist case: Reflection on a path breaking copyright decision. *Rutgers Computer & Technology Law Journal*, *18*, 731.

Grutzmacher, M. (1999). *Urheber, leistungs-und sui-generis-shutz von datenbanken*. Germany: Baden-Baden.

Hayden, J. F. (1991). Copyright protection of computer databases after Feist. *Harward Journal of Law & Technology*, *5*, 215.

Hayes, B. S. (2000). Integrating moral rights into U.S. law and the problem of the Works for Hire doctrine. *Ohio State Law Journal, 61*, 1013.

Hicks, W. B. (1987). Copyright and computer database: Is traditional compilation law adequate? *Texas Law Review*, *65*, 993.

Jarach, G. (1979). Considerazioni sui rapporti tra autori e utilizzatori delle opere dell'ingegno, *Il diritto di autore*, *2*(3), 587-598.

Lai, S. (1999). Digital copyright and watermarking, *EIPR*, *21*(4), 171.

Linn, A. (2000). *History of database protection: Legal issues of concern to the scientific community*. Retrieved September 25, 2006, from http://www.codata.org/data_access/linn.html

Lipton, J. (2003). Databases as intellectual property: New legal approaches. *EIPR, 25*(3), 139.

Mansani, L. (1996). La protezione dei database in Internet, *AIDA*, pp. 149.

Marino, F. (2006). *Database protection in the European Union*. Retrieved September 15, 2006, from www.jus.unitn.it/cardozo/Review/Students/Marino1.html

McCurdy, G. V. S. (2003). Intellectual property and competition: Does the essential facilities doctrine shed any new light? *EIPR, 20*(10), 473.

Mulholland, H. (2005). *U-turn on child protection database*. Retrieved September 6, 2006, from http://www.societyguardian.co.uk

Musso, A. (1998). Ipertesti e thesauri nella disciplina del diritto d'autore, *AIDA*, pp. 10.

Spada, P. (1997). Banche dati e diritto d'autore, *AIDA*, pp. 5.

Stazi, A. (2004). *La pubblicità commerciale on line*. Italy: Giuffrè.

Tai, E. T. T. (2003). Exhaustion and online delivery of digital works. *EIPR, 25-5*, 207.

Tyson, L., & Sherry, E. (1997). *Statutory protection for databases: Economic and public policy issues*. Retrieved August 25, 2006, from http://www.infoindustry.org/ppgrc/doclib/grdoc016.htm

Unsworth, J. (1997). *New copyright and database regulations: USPTO, WIPO, and You*. London: University of London & Oxford University.

Winn, E. (2000). Who owns the customer? The emerging law of commercial transactions in electronic customer data. *Business Law, 56*, 213.

Chapter XIX
Steganography and Steganalysis

Merrill Warkentin
Mississippi State University, USA

Mark B. Schmidt
St. Cloud State University, USA

Ernest Bekkering
Northeastern State University, USA

ABSTRACT

In the digital environment, steganography has increasingly received attention over the last decade. Steganography, which literally means "covered writing," includes any process that conceals data or information within other data or conceals the fact that a message is being sent. Though the focus on use of steganography for criminal and terrorist purposes detracts from the potential use for legitimate purposes, the focus in this chapter is on its role as a security threat. The history of stenography as a tool for covert purposes is addressed. Recent technical innovations in computerized steganography are presented, and selected widely available steganography tools are presented. Finally, a brief discussion of the role of steganalysis is presented.

INTRODUCTION

In the digital environment, steganography has received increasing attention over the last decade. The steganography process conceals the fact that a message is being sent, thereby preventing an observer from knowing that anything unusual is taking place. Neil F. Johnson of the Center for Secure Information Systems at George Mason University defines steganography as "the art of concealing the existence of information within seemingly innocuous carriers" (Johnson, 2003,

p. 2). Much of this attention has focused on the use of steganography for illegitimate purposes by terrorists and criminals, culminating in news stories about Al Qaeda's use of the technique in its communications. The extent of actual use by terrorists remains to be seen and, so far, has never been (publicly) proven. Yet, it has been suggested by government officials in the US and elsewhere that Al Qaeda and other organizations are hiding maps and photographs of terrorist targets and are also posting instructions for terrorist activities on sports chat rooms, pornographic bulletin boards, and other Web sites.

The preoccupation with stenography as a tool for covert purposes can be explained by reviewing its history. Though the term itself is based on the Greek word for "covered writing," the term was first used in the 14th century by the German mathematician Johannes Trithemius (1606) as the title for his book *Steganographia*. On the surface, the book presents a system of angel magic, but it actually describes a highly sophisticated system of cryptography. The actual hiding of information is much older. In ancient Greece, messages might be tattooed on slaves' shaved heads and then their hair would be allowed to grow back before they were sent out as messengers. A more benign form of information hiding was inscribing messages on the wooden base of wax tablets, rather than on the surface of the wax itself (Jupitermedia Corporation, 2003). More recent forms of hiding messages were used in World War II when spies and resistance fighters used milk, fruit juice, or even urine to write invisible coded messages. Heating the source document would reveal the writing, which had turned invisible to the naked eye after the unusual form of ink had dried up. Thus, the history of steganography has long been associated with an air of secrecy, far removed from peaceful and productive purposes.

Steganography Today

More technical forms of steganography have been in existence for several years. International workshops on information hiding and steganography have been held regularly since 1996 (Moulin & O'Sullivan, 2003). However, the majority of the development and use of computerized steganography has occurred since 2000 (Cole, 2003). Modern technology and connectivity have put steganographic capabilities within the reach of the average person with a computer and an Internet connection (Bartlett, 2002). Steganography does not necessarily encrypt a message, as is the case with cryptography. Instead, the goal is to conceal the fact that a message even exists in the first place (Anderson & Petitcolas, 1998). In today's fast-paced, high-tech society, people who want to send hidden messages have very efficient methods of getting a message to its destination with the use of computerized tools that encode a message in a graphic, sound, or other type of file.

New Practices for an Ancient Technique

With the onset of the digital age, many new and innovative mechanisms became available for information hiding. Steganographic techniques and software focused on hiding information and messages in audiovisual files such as graphics files, sound files, and video files. Insignificant and unused parts of these files were replaced with the digital data for the hidden information. The information itself could be protected even further by use of cryptography, where the information was converted into a form incomprehensible without knowledge of the specific cryptographic technique and key. This highlights an important difference between steganography and cryptography. The ultimate goal of cryptography is hiding and protecting the content of information, whereas steganography hides the presence of information itself. Another difference is the mode of transmission. Cryptographic messages can be transported by themselves. In steganography, to hide information, the secret content has to be hidden in a cover message. Whereas physical covers were used to hide information in the past, both the cover and hidden content can now be in digital form. Audiovisual files are ideal covers for several reasons. First, these types of files tend to be quite large in comparison to other file types, providing more opportunity for hiding information successfully. By keeping the ratio of hidden digital data to cover data low, the probability of discovery decreases. Furthermore, audiovisual files require special software to detect the presence of hidden information. ASCII-based data can be detected with simple string comparisons, whereas detection of hidden data in pixels and waves depends on detection of statistical anomalies. In other words, an unencrypted message could be detected in a text-based message by a relatively unsophisticated search engine or spybot, requiring less processing power than for detection in the audiovisual covers.

From a technical perspective, data can easily be hidden in an image file. One such technique to hide data is called *least significant bit* (LSB) insertion (Kessler, 2001). The LSB approach allows the last bit in a byte to be altered. While one might think that this would significantly alter the colors in an image file, it does not. In fact, the change is indiscernible to the human eye. As an example, consider three adjacent pixels (nine bytes) with the following RGB encoding:

$$10010101 \quad 00001101 \quad 11001001$$
$$10010110 \quad 00001111 \quad 11001010$$
$$10011111 \quad 00010000 \quad 11001011$$

An LSB algorithm could be used to hide the following nine bits 101101101. The last, or least significant, bit in each byte may be adjusted. The underlined bits indicate a change (notice that it is not necessary to change some of the bits).

$$10010101 \quad 0000110\underline{0} \quad 11001001$$
$$1001011\underline{1} \quad 0000111\underline{0} \quad 1100101\underline{1}$$
$$10011111 \quad 00010000 \quad 11001011$$

The above example demonstrates that to hide nine bits of information, the algorithm only needed to change four of the nine least significant bits in these nine bytes. Because changing the last bit causes an extremely small change in the color of a pixel (speck of color), the change in the graphic is imperceptible to the human eye. For a more detailed description of this process, please visit http://www.garykessler.net/library/steganography.html.

A special case of steganography can be the use of watermarking, which can have beneficial applications as well. Some watermarks are prominently displayed in an attempt to discourage or prevent unauthorized copying or use, while other watermarks are hidden intentionally. When the message, identification, or graphic is an attribute of the file itself and hidden from regular users, the technique can be termed digital watermarking. In pure steganography, the content of the information added to the file has its own significance. Furthermore, steganographic content is intended to be easily separated from the cover file with the proper software tools by the intended audience. Hidden watermarks can be considered to fall within the bounds of steganography. In our discussion, we will use this expanded definition use of the term steganography, and include the use of hidden watermarks. Good watermarks should be impossible to be separated from the file in which they have been inserted. Finally, steganographic message content can lose its significance when the information becomes outdated or stale. Ideally speaking, the protection afforded by hidden watermarking would last indefinitely.

Relationship to Cryptography

Cryptography is concerned with creating electronic artifacts (typically data files) that are encoded and cannot be interpreted by an intercepting party. As such, an encrypted message often appears to be random or unintelligible. However, the goal of sending steganographically hidden messages is to appear normal — the artifact might appear to be "normal." However, steganography is often used in conjunction with cryptography to create an especially tough challenge to those responsible for enterprise security. The two technologies are completely independent, and the use of one in no way dictates the use of the other. But we ask the reader to remember that wherever steganography is used, the security of the content will be enhanced by the use of cryptography.

Steganography Tools

Steganography tools are readily available and their simplicity has made it relatively easy for terrorists and other criminals to hide data in files (Schmidt, Bekkering, & Warkentin, 2004). There are several steganography tools that are publicly available, many of which are available over the Web at no cost. The interested reader is directed to http://www.jjtc.com/Steganography/toolmatrix.htm. This site, maintained by Neil

F. Johnson, currently lists and describes more than 140 examples of steganographic software publicly available.

An easy-to-use but effective steganography tool is SpamMimic. SpamMimic can be used by anyone with access to the Web without even downloading any software. To disguise a message, one can visit http://spammimic.com/ and type a message. The website will then create a message that looks like spam, but actually contains the covert message. The primary advantage for the communicating parties is that spam is typically ignored by many authorities and their systems such as Echelon and Carnivore (Clark, 2001). The recipient of the "spam" can then visit spammimic.com to decode the message. Since the message is unique and no digital signatures are generated, signature-based spam filters will not block these messages beyond the level of the normal false-positive messages blocked by filters. On inspection, the encoded SpamMimic messages also appear very innocuous and lack "red flag" words such as Viagra, porn, prescriptions, cheap, and so forth. This makes classification of encoded messages based on keywords equally unlikely.

Another user-friendly steganography tool is called S-Tools, which is also publicly available at no cost. BMP, GIF, and WAV files can be used as "host" files for steganographically embedded (hidden) messages. The *graphical user interface*

Table 1. Examples of steganography tools

TOOL	FILE TYPES	COST	ADDRESS
Camouflage	Several	Free	http://www.downseek.com/download/5746.asp
Invisible Secrets v4.0	JPEG, PNG, BMP, HTML, and WAV	$39.95	http://www.stegoarchive.com/
SecurEngine 2.0	BMP, JPG, and TXT	Free	http://www.freewareseek.com
Camera/Shy	GIF, and Web pages	Free	http://sourceforge.net/projects/camerashy/
Stegdetect (XSteg)	Detects the presence of steganography in JPEG	Free	http://packages.debian.org/cgi-bin/download.pl
MP3Stego	MP3	Free	http://www.petitcolas.net/fabien/software/index.html

(GUI) of S-Tools makes it intuitive to hide files simply by dragging them over the host image window. For an added level of protection, S-Tools can also encrypt its hidden file prior to creating the new image.

Steganalysis: The Process of Detecting Hidden Messages

How can an intercepted artifact (data file, message, video stream, etc.) be evaluated to determine if an embedded hidden message is present? Detection of steganographic content is the counterpart of hiding information through steganography. Just as cryptographers are involved in both sides of the coin—developing more secure codes and cracking adversaries' codes—and just as virus authors and antivirus software vendors are engaged in a continuous struggle for dominance, so is the field of steganography characterized by two faces. Steganography is used by those hiding messages and also by those detecting hidden messages. Research in steganography focuses on developing new steganographic techniques, but it is also focused on detection and deciphering of stenographic content.

This process is termed steganalysis and is often explained in the terms of the "Prisoner's Dilemma." In this analogy, two prisoners, Alfred and Bob, attempt to send each other secret messages. Each secret message is hidden in an innocuous message carried and inspected by the warden. Different scenarios lead to different results. One scenario is the assumption that there has been the possibility of data exchange between the prisoners before imprisonment. If Alfred and Bob can communicate and exchange a key before imprisonment, the key can be used to hide the existence of the message, and separating the hidden message from the cover is only possible if the key is known to an interceptor. Of course, the presence of hidden information can still be suspected or detected, even if the actual message cannot be obtained.

An alternative scenario relates to the role of the warden. The warden may have a passive role where he only checks the cover message for hidden content, but does not actively change the cover message. The warden will deliver the message as long as he does not notice anything unusual about the cover message and/or discovers the presence of hidden content. In this case, the safety of the hidden message relies solely on its ability to remain hidden from detection. On the other hand, if the warden actively alters the cover message, even if only slightly, then he may potentially destroy the hidden message. In this case, the safety of the hidden message relies not only on its ability to remain hidden, but also in resistance to changes in the cover. For example, writing messages in invisible ink might escape the attention of the warden, but would not survive photocopying.

The Computer Security Student gets the Bad Guy

Brokerage houses, including the fictitious Bull Run Investments, are privy to a great deal of sensitive financial information before it is publicly reported. It is illegal for employees to use "insider information" to achieve financial gain for themselves. Further, it is illegal for brokerage employees to supply such information to family, friends, or others before that information is released to the public. Any such illegal release of information would constitute a major security threat to Bull Run Investments, and could jeopardize its future.

Shady Profit was a brokerage employee with a questionable past. The U.S. *Securities and Exchange Commission* (SEC) has been on the trail of Mr. Profit for quite some time. It seemed that nearly every time there was a corporate merger where Bull Run Investments was involved, Mr. Profit's girlfriend, Imma Rich, would purchase large quantities of the acquired company prior to the announcement, thereby profiting on the sale after the price increased.

An interesting pattern emerged where Ms. Rich would purchase the stock the morning that Mr. Profit got word of the merger. The SEC knew that Mr. Profit was not telling Ms. Rich the news in person because she worked across town and she was not allowed in the Bull Run Investments office. Furthermore, the SEC had a tap on Mr. Profit's phone and no insider information was given over the phone, so it started investigating Mr. Profit's e-mail. The messages sent to Ms. Rich appeared to be innocuous. There were standard joke e-mails, several personal messages planning lunch, and a few links to Web sites. Everything seemed legitimate—the jokes were just jokes, the personal messages didn't contain any merger information, and the links were to photographs of restaurants on Mr. Profit's Web site. It was not until Kari Catchum, the fresh college graduate at the SEC who had taken a class in computer security, investigated the photographs that the SEC was able to build a case against Mr. Profit.

As it turns out, as soon as Mr. Profit received word of a merger, he edited his Web site with Microsoft FrontPage. He modified an image file of a certain restaurant by adding a ciphertext message to it using S-Tools (a program used for steganography). He would then send an e-mail to Ms. Rich asking her to join him for lunch at a restaurant and include a link to the photograph of the restaurant on his Web site. Ms. Rich would then follow the link, find the photograph, use S-Tools to obtain the ciphertext hidden in the picture, and finally decode the ciphertext to plaintext using their agreed-upon algorithm. Armed with the decoded company name, Ms. Rich would then purchase the stock before the public had access to the news. It was a brilliant scheme until Ms. Catchum investigated the photographs using steganalysis methods.

CONCLUSION

Stenography can be used in business environments, well beyond the prevailing image of steganography as a tool for spies, criminals, and terrorists. Though steganography offers potential for legitimate and illegitimate purposes, the focus of *chief security officers* (CSOs) and other managers of IT security is naturally on the illicit uses who may threaten organizational resources. If disloyal employees might pass trade secrets to competitors via standard e-mail protocols, without any apparent wrongdoing, the enterprise's security is threatened. If international terrorists might embed a secret message within a legitimate video broadcast or Web site display, national security is endangered. Constant vigilance must be exercised in order to ensure that the enterprise perimeter is not violated through steganographic methods. The cat-and-mouse game is likely to continue, so highly-secure environments (military, competitive industries, etc.) are advised to ensure that their staffs includes individuals with training and responsibility for such analysis.

REFERENCES

Anderson, R. J., & Petitcolas, F. A. P. (1998). On the limits of steganography. *IEEE Journal on Selected Areas in Communications, 16*(4), 474-481.

Bartlett, J. (2002, March 17). The ease of steganography and camouflage. *SANS Information Security Reading Room*. Retrieved October 29, 2003, from http://www.sans.org/rr/paper.php?id=762

Clark, E. (2001). A reason to love spam. *Network Magazine, 16*(20), 1.

Cole, E. (2003). *Hiding in plain sight: Steganography and the art of covert communication*. Indianapolis, IN: Wiley Publishing, Inc.

Johnson, N. F. (2003). *Steganography.* Retrieved December 15, 2004, from http://www.jjtc.com/stegdoc/steg1995.html

Jupitermedia Corporation. (2003). *Steganography.* Retrieved Aug. 31, 2003, from http://www.webopedia.com/TERM/S/steganography.html

Kessler, G. C. (2001). Steganography: Hiding data within data. Retrieved July 21, 2005, from http://www.garykessler.net/library/steganography.html

Moulin, P., & O'Sullivan, J. A. (2003). Information-theoretic analysis of information hiding. *IEEE Transactions on Information Theory, 49*(3), 563-593.

Schmidt, M. B., Bekkering, E., & Warkentin, M. (2004, April 14-16). On the illicit use of steganography and its detection, In *Proceedings of the 2004 ISOneWorld International Conference,* Las Vegas, NV (pp. 1-10).

Trithemius, J. (1606). *Steganographia.* Retrieved November 17, 2005, from http://www.esotericarchives.com/tritheim/stegano.htm

Chapter XX
Intellectual Property Protection in Multimedia Grids

Irene Kafeza
Attorney at Law, Greece

Eleanna Kafeza
Athens University of Economics and Business, Greece

ABSTRACT

The Grid environment is rapidly emerging as the dominant paradigm for wide-area-distributed application systems. The multimedia applications demand intense problem-solving capabilities, and Grid-computing makes it possible to share computing resources on an unprecedented scale among geographically distributed participants. In a Grid environment, virtual organisations are formulated and managed from a computing resource point of view. The Grid provider allows for the dynamic discovery of computing resources, the immediate allocation and provision of the resources, and the management and provision of secure access. Although the security problem in Grid environment is being addressed from the technological point of view, there is no work to identify the legal issues that are arising in Grid multimedia transactions.

INTRODUCTION

The new generation of advanced Grid technologies enabled the use of pervasively networked and interoperable computing resources as a technological infrastructure for easier access to processing, reproduction, and transmission of data. The shared access to widely distributed computing resources promises to greatly lower the time and costs of accessing and using multimedia data for a number of purposes. The placement of such powerful dynamically shaped technology into the mainstream comes with some complications. The danger this development brings with it is that, what is gained in efficiency may be lost because of copyright infringement; thus, new ways of dealing with security are necessary. Although the Grid's unsuitability to regulation seems a fact, the structure of intellectual property rights could force technological gatekeepers to block unauthorised uses of unauthorised data and allow only authorized data flows.

Graphics, visualization, computer games, streaming media, broadcasting, and e-health are only some examples of applications where high volumes of multimedia data need to be efficiently stored, accessed, transferred, and processed. Nowadays, with digital television archives, cameras, and sensors collecting real-time data ubiquitously, multimedia archives need petabytes of storage, while high computation power is necessary for content analysis. The Grid computing environment is a collection of heterogeneous computing resources that are physically diverse but interconnected, and shared by many individuals and organizations. Grid technology is designed to solve problems inherent to multimedia data-intensive applications that relate to storage and processing of remote data.

There are several issues to be addressed when access is granted to Grid resources. Grid resources are shared within a virtual organisation (Foster, Kesselman, & Tuecke, 2001). Different organisations pool resources together and collaborate in order to achieve a common goal. However, when composing the Grid, security is of major concern. A secure Grid platform will enable safe and stable collaboration of various resource owners and service users. This requirement is twofold: on one hand, a secure technical infrastructure has to be in place, and on the other hand, a legal framework has to be introduced to increase confidentiality and enable predictability of transactions on the Grid. Figure 1 is an example on how organisations can contribute their resources and create virtual organisations.

The most well-known Grid solution is the Globus Toolkit, an open source software tool kit used for building Grids. In Globus, the Grid security infrastructure (GSI) uses PKI and X.509 certificates. The system identifies every user/service on the Grid by a standard X.509 certificate that contains information about the user/service signed by a third party CA to certify it. GSI uses the secure socket layers/transport layer security (SSL/TSL) authentication (Kanaskar, Topaloglu,

Figure 1. Virtual organisations (VOs). Virtual organisation A is created by resources contributed by different organisations in order to solve life insurance problems. Similarly, organisations share computing cycles and data storage, creating virtual organisation B in order to deal with financial modelling problems.

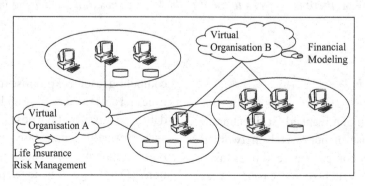

& Bayrak, 2005). The two parties exchange their certificates, and when each verifies that a trusted CA signed the other/s certificate, they establish an authenticated session (Foster, Kesselman, Tsudik, & Tuecke, 1998). However, from the legal point of view, several issues have to be addressed, in order to create a trusted Grid environment that will allow its use and sharing of multimedia data (Kesler, 2005).

Applying the arguments about the generative Internet (Zittrain, 2006) to the Grid environment, the Grid technology expands the boundaries of leverage, adaptability, and accessibility for information technology. Hundreds and thousands of machines can be connected, convey and change information, deploy programmes, in seconds, thus exposed to instantaneous change. In such an environment, publishers are vulnerable to latest tools of IP infringement, and information is available for installation within moments. Grid participants might have concerns about a computer virus that can exploit their ignorance, and be sceptical when allowing code to run on their machine. Cyber law has to deal effectively with these vulnerabilities without, at the same time, compromising the "generativity" property of the Grid.

A legal framework is necessary that will allow safe transactions among the organisations and/or individuals that dynamically form the Grid. Creating and managing contracts in the Grid environment is of paramount importance for planning and implementing Grids. In most cases, Grids operate in a globalized environment, and the parties have to establish contractual relationships. A master agreement is formed among the parties for the sharing of the resources. At run time, the Grid broker acts as an agent of the Grid provider, and dynamically discovers the appropriate resources that can execute the job. It can also allocate new nodes and negotiate the contract with them. Intellectual property requirements are magnified in the globalized Grid environment due to the distributed nature of the data and the

computing resources. The Grid provider transfers large volumes of multimedia data from the user to the Grid resources. In some cases, multimedia data is divided or it is cached and in other cases, duplication of data is necessary in order to achieve better performance and minimize transfer times. During this process, the data is copied; hence, potentially exposed to unauthorised use. The Grid provider should be aware of potential risks, and data access and policies have to be in place to offer protection from copyright infringement.

Although both international treaties and national legislation attempt to promote distributing computing development by providing basic rules regarding the protection of copyright in the digital environment, many unresolved questions remain regarding the specific application of these technologies. While there is no universal legal definition, there is a consensus that the combination of sound, text, and images in a digital format that is made accessible in a computer program, embodies an original expression of authorship sufficient to justify the protection of multimedia production under the copyright law. However, Grid technology is large-scale dissemination of information, together with the ability to process the data in a dynamic way, and thus introduces issues never discussed before. The adoption of Grid computing technologies that enables simultaneous commercialization of multimedia technologies is expected to aggravate the already existing exploitation of multimedia products by distributed environments. In addition, a number of important recent developments in new technologies in the field of multimedia caused unpredicted implications for the industry and legislation. As broadband networks become available in personal computing, and thus to Grid users, the sharing of digital content is being boosted. A Grid environment with embedded broadband connections facilitates the transfer of large multimedia files in a ubiquitous and pervasive way. Software applications, like MP3 players, DVD burners, video editors, voice processing, and technology that allow the mixing of audio and video samples, allows for efficient processing of multimedia data. Already steps are in place to bring the concept of Grid computing to commercial Grid applications (Niccolai, 2004)

BACKGROUND—LEGISLATION IN MULTIMEDIA GRIDS

New digital technologies, and especially the new ways of sharing and disseminating data through the Web, have posed significant challenges to safeguarding the intellectual property rights. In response to these challenges, the WIPO Internet Treaties (Figure 2), WIPO Copyright Treaty (WCT), and the WIPO Performances and Phonograms Treaty (WPPT) were adopted, incorporating certain provisions of TRIPs agreement, in order to update and supplement the Berne Convention and the Rome Convention and in particular, to address issues related to the dissemination of protected material over global networks.

Although multimedia productions are not explicitly listed in the list of copyrighted works, they are associated with the notion of creation in the literary, scientific, and artistic domain. Rights holders are granted the rights of reproduction, distribution, rental, rights of public performance and communication to the public, rights of translation, and adaptation under most of national and international treaties.

The author's reproduction right (Figure 3, no1) is probably at the core of multimedia Grid since any transmission of a work (Figure3, no2) presupposes the uploading into the computer memory its further distribution in Grid environment. The reproduction right is fully applicable to Grid environment and the storage of a protected work in a digital form in a Grid node constitutes a reproduction (Figure3, no3). In particular, when Grid brokers distribute and redistribute the tasks over Grid platform, multiple copies are made in various PCs, and it is necessary to determine whether the reproduction right applies to all copies, and whether the consent of the right holder is needed for each in order to avoid infringement.

Figure 2. WIPO-historical background

The need for international protection of intellectual property was addressed both in Berne and Paris Convention, each of which provided for the establishment of international secretariats, one for copyright and one for industrial property, both of which were located in Berne, Switzerland. In 1893, the two secretariats were merged to one intergovernmental organization called United International Bureau for the Protection of Intellectual Property (BIRPI), which was the predecessor of the World Intellectual Property Organization. The establishment of intergovernmental organizations was a necessity after the Second World War in order to handle independently specific subjects in international level.

BIRPI, in 1967, relocated in Geneva. The diplomatic conference in Stockholm, in 1967, revised it and after the entry into force of the Convention that establishes World Intellectual Property Organization, BIRPI became WIPO. This Convention, that established the World Intellectual Property Organization (WIPO), concluded in Stockholm on July 14, 1967, and entered into force in 1970. After the establishment of United Nations, all the previous intergovernmental organizations were turned to specialized agencies status. Under the UN system, the specialized agencies have independent status, has its own constitution, structure, governing bodies, and so forth. The World Intellectual Property Organization was established as one of the United Nation's system of organizations in 1974. WIPO's policy is to cooperate with governmental and intergovernmental bodies, and under its establishment agreement, its mission is to promote, through international cooperation, all aspects of creative intellectual property for the development of cultural and social progress; hence, in 1996 entered into a cooperation agreement with World Trade Organization (WTO)

WIPO's approach regarding technological development is to identify issues associated with these technologies, their difference to traditional frameworks, and provide with legal and administrative solutions. In this context two treaties, namely, the WIPO Copyright Treaty (WCT) on the protection of authors and the WIPO Phonograms and Performances Treaty (WPPT) on the protection of performers and phonogram producers, were adopted by WIPO in December 1996.

Figure 3. Legislation

1. The reproduction right is the right of the copyright owner to prevent others from making copies of his/her works without his/her authorization,. Art. 9(1)of Berne convention states that Authors of literary and artistic works protected by this Convention shall have the exclusive right of authorizing the reproduction of these works, in any manner or form.
2. Art10 of Rome Convention states that producers of phonograms shall enjoy the right to authorize or prohibit the direct or indirect reproduction of their phonograms. For copyright protection, literary and artistic work includes every original work of authorship. Art. 2 of Berne Convention defines the scope of protected works.
3. WIPO copyright Treaty, Agreed statements concerning Article 1(4): The reproduction right, as set out in Article 9 of the Berne Convention, and the exceptions permitted thereunder, fully apply in the digital environment, in particular to the use of works in digital form. It is understood that the storage of a protected work in digital form in an electronic medium constitutes a reproduction within the meaning of Article 9 of the Berne Convention.

In addition, when multimedia material are distributed through a wide range of PCs, we could probably argue that a public performance, the scope of which is defined in article 11 of Berne Convention, takes place, since it is viewed by different individuals at different times. It is also arguable whether the right of the communication to the public exists when a multimedia work is available to participating PCs/nodes if and when they would like to see it. As Grid technology offers unprecedented means for Grid users to manipulate copyright works and create derivative works, this could possible lead, also, to infringement of the author's right of integrity (Figure 4, no1).

The traditional copyright protection system has achieved a balance between copyright owner's exclusive right to control use of copies of their work, but with reasonable limits (Figure 4, no2) and with fair (Figure 4, no3) exceptions. This balance is under question in multimedia Grid environment where works, performances, phonograms, and other protected material are mixed and distributed in an innovative way that challenges the terms of licensed uses. At the same time, the development of a secure and clear legal framework on how to transfer the ownership in Grid computing, either by assignment or licenses, will result to a beneficiary situation, since right

holders will feel secure to exploit this environment fully, and make more valuable works available through this platform. Nevertheless, there is an increasing trend to employ contracts instead of copyright protection in order to preserve right holders rights.

There is not specific legislation to address the multimedia intellectual property protection issues in the Grid environment. The multimedia protection, per se is a combination of the existing regimes of protection for other similar intellectual property works (Stamatoudi, 2002). Nevertheless, the most appropriate law is copyright law for both multimedia developers and publishers (Brinson & Radcliffe, 1996). The WIPO Internet Treaties have been implemented in a number of countries, including the EU and the USA. In the United States, the Digital Millennium Copyright Act prevents unauthorized distribution of copy-protected works by criminalizing any technology intentionally designed to copy such files. The United States Copyright Act of 1976 (Figure 5, no1) provides copyright protection for original works of authorship fixed in any tangible medium of expression from which they can be perceived, reproduced, or otherwise communicated, either directly or with the aid of machine or device. In an attempt to deal with new technological develop-

Figure 4. WIPO Internet treaties

1. WIPO Performances and Phonograms Treaty states in art 5(1) that independently of a performer's economic rights, and even after the transfer of those rights, the performer shall, as regards his/her live aural performances or performances fixed in phonograms, have the right to claim to be identified as the performer of his/her performances, except where omission is dictated by the manner of the use of the performance, and to object to any distortion, mutilation or other modification of his/her performances that would be prejudicial to his/her reputation.

2. WIPO Internet Treaties provide flexibility to countries to develop appropriate limitations. Under the three-step set, as set out in Berne Convention and TRIPs agreement, exceptions are permitted in certain special cases where they do not conflict with normal exploitation of the work and do not unreasonably prejudice the legitimate interests of the right holder, Berne Convention,art.9(2), TRIPS agreement, art.13.

3. There are two categories of limitations concerning particular acts of exploitation normally requiring the authorization of rights owner. The first limitation is the exclusion of certain categories of works, such as those not fixed in a tangible medium. The second limitation concerns free use of the work and nonvoluntary licenses. Free use is also recognized as fair use and includes personal noncommercial use as news reporting or teaching purposes. Nonvoluntary licences are applied in the circumstances where new technologies have emerged, and rights owners would be reluctant to authorize the use of their work. Thus, these licences allow the use of works without the author's authorization, but require that compensation has to be paid. (Understanding copyright and related rights, http://www.wipo.int/about-ip/en/)

Figure 5. U.S. legislation

1. Under the U.S. Copyright Act of 1967, works of authorship include: literary works, musical works, including any accompanying words, dramatic words, including any accompanying music, pantomimes and choreographic works, pictorial, graphic, and sculptural works, motion pictures and other audiovisual works, sound recordings and architectural works (17 U.S.C. 102,2000). The Copyright Act of 1967 has expanded the scope of copyrightable subject matter from the previous copyright legislation, and grants authors the exclusive right to reproduce the copyrighted work in copies or phonorecords, to prepare derivative works based upon the copyrighted work, to distribute copies or phonorecords of the copyrighted works, pantomimes, and pictorial, graphic, or sculptural works, including the individual images of a motion picture or other audio visual work, to display the copyrighted work publicly, and in the case of sound recordings, to perform the copyrighted work publicly by means of a digital audio transmission (17 U.S.C. 106,2000).

2. Congress attempted to amend copyright law in order to deal efficiently with peer-to-peer service providers, introducing several Bills, like the Berkman Bill, that permitted copyright owners to disrupt infringing user's Internet connections, H.R. 5211, 107th Cong. 1 (a) (2002). However, this Bill did not make it to pass. Another attempt to regulate Internet copyright infringement was the Inducing Infringement of Copyrights Act, INDUCE Bill, S.2560, 108 Cong. (2004), which did not pass either. Under INDUCE Bill, a CD manufacturer or a DVD recorder manufacturer may be liable for contributory infringement, although these manufacturers do not rely on infringing public dissemination for its commercial viability. The Bill also could permit peer-to-peer software providers to be treated as primary infringers, S. 2560, 108th Cong. 2(g)(2)(2004).

3. Family Entertainment and Copyright Act of 2005, (FECA) PL 109-9, 109th Congress.

ments, the United States enacted further specific legislation (Figure 5, no 2) to deal with particular issues arising from digital multimedia technologies such as the Family Movie Act. The Family Movie Act (Figure 5, no 3) was enacted in order to protect the interests of consumers who find specific parts of movies offensive. FMA exempts, from copyright infringement, the technology that allows a consumer to intervene in existing multimedia products and skip or mute offensive material. One important issue is whether record companies or other right holders, whose creations have been used or mixed in multimedia products, are entitled to sue Grid broker for copyright infringement. There is not specific legislation regarding Grid providers, but it seems that ISPS legislation addresses similar issues:

European Union develops a coherent regulatory environment for intellectual property in order to encourage the development of the Information Society. The European community and its member states have signed both the WIPO Copyright Treaty and the WIPO Performances and Phonograms Treaty. Moreover, the European Parliament and the Council of European Union adopted the 2001/29/EC Directive (Figure 6, no 1) on the harmonization of certain aspects of copyright and related rights in the information society to address issues like the application of reproduction rights in the digital environment; the right to make available applicable to interactive transmissions on networks, limitations, and exceptions of rights; technological measures for protection. In order to create a harmonised legal framework, the 2001/29/EC and Databases Directive complement each other, deal with all aspects of copyright law, and apply the obligations that arise from the two Internet treaties of WIPO. The 2001/29/EC directive stimulates creativity by facilitating the developments in the field of new and multimedia products and services, and by attempting to reduce differences in copyright law legislation, thus reducing barriers in trade. The directive also stipulates that member states shall provide legal protection against the circumvention of technological measures (Figure 6, no 2).

Directive 96/9/EC , Databases directive, sets out harmonized rules regarding the copyright protection to original databases, defines the database, and introduces a *sui generis* protection for databases that require a substantial investment. Directive 96/9/EC (Figure 6, no 3), on the legal protection of the databases, seems the more appropriate legislation for multimedia products. In multimedia technology, the information is structured and may have hypertext links. Hypermedia is the multimedia version of hypertext. Burk (1998) states that in networked environment, copies of copyrighted material are routinely distributed as a necessary part of the networks operation; therefore, when analyzing theories of copyright infringement from hypertext linking, all the exclusive rights of the authors must be considered. Although it is straightforward to define the subject matters of copyright protection in literary and musical works, it is more complex to define audiovisual works, multimedia works under databases protection (Derclaye, 2002).

Database is a collection of independent works, data, or other materials arranged in a systematic or methodical way and are individually accessible by electronic or other means (Figure 6, no 4). The mixed work is subject to database protection, as well as its specific content material, such as illustrations, movies, video clips, documentaries, music, and software. Nevertheless, it might be difficult for a multimedia product to qualify for database protection if the mixed pieces such as video, text, music, could not be individually accessible. According to FECA (2005), individually accessible shall mean that the exclusive purpose of the database is to inform the user; the database must allow the possibility to search the database to find a particular item; that access to the items of the databases must be allowed. Nevertheless, it might be difficult for a multimedia product to qualify for database protection if the mixed pieces, such as video, text, music, could not be individu-

Figure 6. European Union legislation

1. Directive 2001/29/EC of the European Parliament and of the Council of 22 May 2001 on the harmonisation of certain aspects of copyright and related rights in the information society, Official Journal L 167 , 22/06/2001 P. 0010 - 0019
2. Art. 6 of Directive 2001/29/EC of the European Parliament and of the Council of 22 of May 2001 on the harmonization, refers to obligations that member states need to adopt as to technological measures.
3. Directive 96/9/EC of the European Parliament and the Council of 11 March 1006 on the legal protection of the databases, OJ L 077, 27/03/1996, p.0020-0028.
4. Dir. 96/9/EC on the legal protection of the databases, art.1 (2): For the purposes of this Directive, "database" shall mean a collection of independent works, data or other materials arranged in a systematic or methodical way and individually accessible by electronic or other means
5. Dir. 96/9/EC on the legal protection of the databases Art.4: Database authorship: 1. The author of a database shall be the natural person or group of natural persons who created the base or, where the legislation of the Member States so permits, the legal person designated as the right holder by that legislation.2. Where collective works are recognized by the legislation of a Member State, the economic rights shall be owned by the person holding the copyright. 3. In respect of a database created by a group of natural persons jointly, the exclusive rights shall be owned jointly.

ally accessible. That depends upon each case. The person or company that created the multimedia product is the right holder (Figure 6, no 5) of the final product, and he/she is granted the exclusive rights of the ownership.

DATA GRIDS AND GRID SERVICE PROVIDERS

Grid service providers are online intermediaries that facilitate the access to Grid environment. Data Grid (Chervenak, Foster, Kesselman, Salisbury, & Tueck, 2001) is a special case of Grid environments that provide the necessary infrastructure to access, transfer, and process massive datasets stored in a distributed manner, and to allow transfers of data stored in storage systems. Users are able to access and manipulate the data, as well as manage copies of these datasets; they can execute data intensive applications using the Grid resources, and can collaborate by sharing information. Grid environments have the following unique characteristics (Venugopal, Buyya, & Ramamohanarao., 2006):

- Massive datasets, where datasets are usually multimedia files, mages, video, and so forth, at the size of gigabytes and beyond.
- Shared data collections, where users are using the same resources for downloading and storing their data.
- Unified namespace, where each data element has a unique logical name, but may have several physical copies across the data Grid.
- Access restrictions, authentication and authorisation policies should be in place to enable data access.

Peer-to-peer networks are a related paradigm. Peer-to-peer networks, when used in content and file sharing, facilitate the process of locating the requested file to the user who posses the copies, and then directly allows it to be downloaded by the user who searched for it. In this process, data are replicated by multiple peers and are located by peers without the use of a central index. The distributed network architecture that shares computer resources and services between their nodes made easier copyright infringement, while it is difficult and expensive to identify the source of infringing materials and to actually locate the infringers. Moreover, it seems that the absence of central index as an intermediary requires the copyrights owners to focus their enforcement efforts against users.

The first generation peer-to-peer networks provided the infrastructure for audio files exchange, while current infrastructure allows sharing of any type of content file sharing including video, music, text, software real-time data, and mixed applications. The first system was Napster, which utilized a semicentralized architecture. Napster maintained servers that held lists of files located on individual host computers. Users, when connecting to Napster, selected a file from the list and directly connected to the host computer containing that file. Napster server did not contain copies of user files, but it served as a broker between host computers. After Napster shut down, a second generation of P2P networks developed with no centralized architecture, like Aimster. The Aimster user, after registering on the site, can communicate and swap files with other users, but the Aimster server, which collects the information obtained by users, does not make copies of the swapped files. Aimster users list the files they want to share, then they search for a requested file, and when Aimster server finds the requested file, transmits the file to the recipient via the Internet to download onto his/her computer. The Aimster system is proprietary software in which all communications are encrypted, and offers tutorials to users on how to use the system.

The liability of Grid service providers regarding injurious content stored by the Grid users in the Grid resources is highly controversial. In the past, distribution infrastructures became widespread, and the existing copyright enforcement mechanisms proved inadequate to deal with these new environments. At first, copyright owners sued the manufactures of the devices that could crack the encryption of copyrighted materials, in order to enforce their copyrights. That resulted in the enactment of legislation that provides anticircumvention protection that makes illegal the manufacture and distribution of the technologies that permit circumvention. After the development of new technologies, copyright owners filed lawsuits against developers and distributors of devices that enable copying and distribution of material, such as Mp3 players. At a later stage, right holders turned against ISPs, due to their role as gatekeepers to dissemination of information, because of their ability to use pricing mechanisms and apply technical standards. Copyright owners tried to transform ISPS as a medium for the enforcement mechanism due to their intermediate and monitoring position. At first, the courts held ISPs liable for the distribution materials under the strict liability rule. The courts replaced the strict liability rule with the secondary liability standard. In Religious Technology Centre vs. Netcom On-line Communication Services, Inc, the court accepted the standard of knowledge under the contributory liability doctrine, and held that an ISP is liable if it acquired sufficient knowledge regarding the infringing activity. Another strategy copyright owners employed was to sue individuals identified by the ISPS according to subpoenas issued under the relevant provisions of DMCA. The DMCA, 17 U.S.C. s.512, (h) (2000) gives the right to copyright owners to serve a subpoena on an ISP in order to point an infringer. Nevertheless, in RIAA vs. Verizon Internet services, Inc, the court held that ISPS can disclose information about an alleged infringer only if the user is storing infringing materials on the ISP''s servers, and not when the provider acts as a conduit for P2P file sharing

Courts have decided that when a service provider offers infringing and noninfringing uses, we need to estimate the uses in order to find whether there is a contributory infringement. Even if there is infringing uses, the provider can avoid liability if he/she shows that removing or reducing it substantially, is costly for the ISP (Schulman, 2005). In Aimster's case, it was clearly stated that we could not come to a conclusion regarding infringing activities unless we balance all these parameters. Aimster is a centralized P2P file-sharing system that permitted users to transfer files to others on the user's friends list. The AIM in Aimster stands for AOL instant messaging service. There is also "club Aimster," a paid service in which users can download the most popular music files more easily than in the free service. After a user registers with Aimster system, he/she can name any other user as friend and communicate online with him/her attaching the files he/she would like to share with him/her. If he/she has not designated other users as buddies, then the all the Aimster users become his/her friends. In Aimster C. Lit., 334 F.3d 643, 646 (7th Cir. 2003), the Aimster court held that "if a service facilitates both infringing and noninfringing uses, as in the case of AOL's instant-messaging service, and the detection and prevention of the infringing uses would be highly burdensome, the rule for which the recording industry is contending could result in the shutting down of the service or its annexation by the copyright owners, because the provider might find it impossible to estimate its potential damages liability to the copyright holders, and would anyway face the risk of being enjoined." P2P litigation tried to shape the way users behave and present a regulatory compliance model, which did not succeed its purpose since the users had already formed social norms regarding their online behaviour.

The Recording Industry Association of America, (RIAA) did not succeed in controlling technology to avoid copyright infringement; therefore, it focused on influencing end-user behaviour by both suing individual users and by launching a massive public-relations campaign presenting copying as immoral behaviour. Nevertheless, users developed an attitude towards distributed networks rather than a preference at a specific application. After Napster shut down, end users migrated to other networks, since file shares were not simply enamoured with Napster application; instead, they had internalized sharing norms that

transcended any particular application or network (Opderberck, 2005).

Thus, record companies, seeking to enforce their rights, attacked the legality of P2P networks and tried to condemn file sharing as immoral activity. However, the market developed new norms and technologies to elude liability and P2P networks were developed with no central server, like BitTorrent. The BitTorrent protocol is an open source file-sharing protocol that is particularly efficient with large files, such as digital movies and music. The followed procedure is that files are broken into small packets and BitTorrent protocol creates a "torent" file that contains data about the underlying files. The tracker servers consist of tracked files that specify the location of the related torrent files and coordinate their downloading. Upon completion of downloading, the torrent file is updated to indicate that the file is now available on another computer. Nevertheless, the efficient use of the system requires that the user should know the location of a torrent file. The latest generation of P2P clients are fully distributed. EDonkey is such an example that has agreed to pay $30 million to settle a copyright infringement case brought by six music labels. The EDonkey architecture is fully distributed without either central server or super nodes. Any computer in the network can be used as an indexing server.

Grid computing offers a distributed model that incorporates P2P connectivity on a much larger scale, and extends its uses. Currently, peer-to-peer content-sharing networks do not provide an integrated platform for both data distribution and integrated computation, and they have one application objective, the sharing of files. Data replication is one major activity in data Grid where the provider creates and maintains copies of the data at a different network location in order to increase performance. Users in the Grid environment have an integrated view of the data, where data format complexities are seamless to the user. It is questionable whether existing liability standards can apply to Grid providers. One possible solution could be (Grossman, 2005) the development of standard of joint liability of all the participants in the infringement procedure instead of copyright owners seeking to recover the harm caused by copyright infringement as efficiently as possible. Nevertheless (Pope, 2005), the necessity of regulating the distributed environments must not be too great so as to sustain their existence as sharing platforms of innovation and new ideas.

MOVIE-EDITING SOFTWARE: AN EXAMPLE MULTIMEDIA GRID APPLICATION

Grid environment is expected to be heavily used for image and video processing. Broadcasting networks (Harmer, Donachy, Perrott, Chambers, Craig, Mallon, & Wrigh, 2003) are using the Grid environment to efficiently store and process broadcast material. A typical 1-hour television program requires 25 gigabytes of storage, and its production could be 100 to 200 gigabytes. High-resolution digital video formats, as well as the interactive editing process that needs previewing, imposes new demands on the computation power to capture, store, and edit the video. Media broadcasting, the integration of storage media files with data streams from live events, timely distribution of broadcasts, video file rendering, video on demand, voice processing, are some typical applications that are now being implemented using the Grid infrastructure. The Grid infrastructure facilitates multimedia application by providing Grid software that can use peer-to-peer technology to find other PCs on the LAN that are running, for example, the video-editing software, then automatically divide computing jobs, and distribute the work. Moreover, in the Grid environment, special purpose software, like advanced video editing, that resides in specific

nodes on the gri,d is becoming available to the Grid user from his/her desktop PC.

According to webopedia, "video editing is the process of manipulating video images. Once the province of expensive machines called *video editors,* video-editing software is now available for personal computers and workstations. Video editing includes cutting segments (*trimming*), re-sequencing clips, and adding transitions and other special effects." The video-editing technology allows muting or skipping material according to the timings of the original DVD, and allows the user to have an altered version of the movie that does not exist in any physical form. The original DVD does not include the altered version and is not affected by its use with the technology. This industry has become known as "E-Rated" industry (Mitakis, 2004), and consists of two types of DVD alteration methods in order to edit the film. In the first method (Nokes, 2004), a master copy is made and repeatedly copied into either videocassettes containing either the original version or recordable DVDs. The second method provides software that the original copy of the movie remains the same, while the viewer watches a modified version. This software edits movies the time you watch them by skipping material or words according to the movies timings.

Grid providers offering video editing and similar multimedia applications should be aware that under existing copyright law, the copyright owners have the exclusive right to all adaptations to their original works. Nevertheless, the Family Entertainment and Copyright Act, entitled the Family Movie Act, provides an amendment to copyright principles, and exempts from infringement the use of movie-editing software that otherwise constitutes an infringement of the derivative right of the copyrighted work. Thus, the Family Movie Act permits the use, for private home viewing, of altered, unfixed works capable of repetition without infringing the copyright holder's derivative right. In order copyright law embeds technological developments that produce novel forms of expression, and existing forms of expression that can be used in a combined way under new technological infrastructures, expanded the scope of copyrightable subject matter (Figure 7, no 1). Thus, the derivative right protection has also been expanded (Figure 7, no 2), and although its infringement use should incorporate the copyrighted work in some form, it is not clear whether that form need to be physical. However, the Family Movie Act excepts only the digital movie editing technology from infringement; therefore, the movie editing outside the digital environment still constitutes an infringement act.

Through Grid computing it is possible to have efficient online sharing of large volume of broadcast media data, online sharing of computational power as well as access and use of nodes hosting specialised software. This environment is increasing the possibility of unauthorized copying and altering/processing of multimedia files.

MULTIMEDIA GRID LICENSING

The copyright system allows the exploitation of creator's work by giving the creators exclusive right to their works and prohibiting third parties to use their works without permission. Copyright owners can allow others to use their work in exchange of a compensation, which is

referred to as royalty. The transfer of copyright may take the form of an assignment or a licence. The assignment is a transfer of ownership; it is a property right and is governed by law, whereas in licensing, the owner of copyright retains ownership, but authorizes a third party to carry out certain acts covered by his/her economic right, generally for a specific period of time and for a specific purpose. Licensing requires a bargain between the right holder and the third party, and is concluded either in the form of a one-to-one basis or the collective management of rights basis. Right holders can also abandon the exercise of his/her rights by allowing other parties to use his/her creations free. Some projects have been organized under this model where right holders abandon their rights as described in the projects licensing terms such as general public license (CPL). The open source movement project builds their business models on existing copyright protection, but under specific terms.

CONTRACTING A NODE TO THE GRID

Grid technology separates applications and information from the infrastructure they run, thus, adjusting infrastructure to business demands. Any resources available within an organisation can participate in solving a Grid problem includ-

Figure 7. United States Constitution Intellectual Property Clause and United States Copyright Act

1. Under the United States Constitution there is an Intellectual Property Clause that grants to the Congress the power to promote the Progress of Science and useful Arts, by securing for limited times to Authors and inventors the exclusive right to their respective Writings and Discoveries (U.S. Const, art I, Section 8). The development of new technologies has led to an ever-expanding understanding of the word "writings" and consequently to an expanding in the scope of copyrightable subject matter.
2. The Copyright Act of 1870 introduced, for the first time, the derivative right, by providing that the authors reserve the right to dramatize or to translate their own works. Furthermore, the Copyright Act of 1909, in an effort to codify law as construed by the courts, broadened the derivative's right scope by granting to the copyright owner the exclusive right to translate his/her work into other languages or make any other version thereof. Under the 1967 Act, the Congress granted the author the exclusive right to prepare derivative works based upon the copyrighted work.

ing computing power, data, hardware, software, applications, networking services. At run time, the Grid broker acts as an agent of the Grid provider, and dynamically discovers the appropriate resources owned by an organisation that can execute the job. A master agreement has to be formed among the parties for the sharing of the resources, and there are several issues concerning the resource allocation.

The Grid environment challenges basic assumptions of ownership, access, usage, and assets. The existing metaphor that assumes an Internet location as a place, and the PC connected to the Internet as property of one owner, seems inadequate in the Grid environment. The master agreement between the Grid broker and the resource owner concerns CPU cycles, deployment of software, temporal constraints, ownership, access rights to the data that is stored on user resource, access and ownership of the programs running on the resource. Contracts are not property rights, but creations of exchanges (Nimmer, 2005) made in a marketplace, and they should be enforced independent of issues about the proper scope of property rights.

Having in mind that the Grid provider is also subject to service level agreements with his/her client, quality of service for multimedia Grid applications has to be guaranteed. In this sense, the contract between the broker and the resource owner should guarantee a certain degree of security regarding the availability of the resource, and adequate pricing techniques should be in place. At the same time, the resource owner is at risk when accepting third-party software to use the resource because of viruses and other malicious code. The software might fail to work, acquire control of the host system without user authorisation, and perform malicious actions, use memory that otherwise would be used by the owners programs, thus slowing down their operation.

In more dynamic Grid environments, intelligent agents are employed by the Grid to dynamically discover resources and negotiate the contract

of their participation in the Grid automatically (using Web services technology). In these case issues that pertain to intelligent agent, contracting should be carefully examined (Kafeza, Kafeza, & Chiu, 2005). Therefore, contracts between Grid providers and resource owners should clearly define who should bear the risk. This may vary depending on the nature of the relationship, and sometimes should be considered on a case-by-case basis.

Licensing in the Grid

A central issue in Grid computing is whether it is considered to be a lease agreement by the client or a service agreement by the Grid provider. Several issues can arise based on the adopted view. For example in the leasing case, the owner of the results of the Grid processing is the client, while in the service case, the service provider gives a license to the client to use the results. In a Grid environment, the Grid provider is entering into a contract agreement (e.g., click wrap) with all participating virtual organisations and independent Grid node providers. Before entering into the agreement, the Grid provider has to verify that the virtual organisation has the right to provide the resource to the Grid environment. It also has to specify service level agreements that will restrict the organisation. Due to the dynamic nature of the Grid environment, it is very important that the participating nodes remain consistent to their commitment of availability of the resource. This will enable the Grid broker to make an efficient scheduling of the resources and finish the data processing in time.

Copyright Law protection has proved to be ineffective in protecting the vendor software in Grid environment; therefore, software license agreements are utilizing contractual provisions that are more restrictive than copyright law, to protect software usage. There are two major issues that concern the Grid community regarding Grid licensing. The first issue stems from the fact that most of the software modules that implement Grid computing are open source, and the second issue is that Grid software provided by vendors executes in several nodes, and traditional licensing schemes are ineffective.

Most Grid software and middleware is developed by academic projects, and is released under open source licenses. Globus Toolkit is an open source project, and the most common component incorporated into a large number of Grid packages; therefore, vendors that implement Grid software based on Globus are concerned about licensing.

One of the most commonly used free software licenses is GPL. Software licensed under GPL is provided at no cost, or at very low cost, to cover the expenses of the transfer. GPL requires that any distributed modification must be licensed under the GPL. In GPL the licensees are restricted (Carver, 2005) from using GPL-covered code in proprietary derivatives in order to preserve access to the software for all users. In this sense, Grid software licensed under GPL discourages its commercialization because it is difficult for vendors to produce propriety software. Liability issues arise in enterprises when open source software is mixed with nonopen source software in the production environment.

According to Ian Foster (2005), Globus is using BSD licenses that allow individuals or organizations to make modifications or enhancements to the code without contributing that code back to the open source community. He argues that such licenses encourage a vibrant commercial support industry. It seems that licensing for open source Grid software and middleware is using an open-source licensing model, but other licensing issues are arising in commercial Grid products.

The vendors that develop Grid software and middleware utilize private contracts to control liability and separate the rights granted with the transfer of software from the rights excluded. The current software licenses work per processor, per device, or per user. The essence of Grid computing is to provide efficient resource on demand and it is differentiated from conventional distributed computing by permitting large-scale resource sharing. Grid accounting and Grid economics is a problem of major concern, and unless it is efficiently addressed, it is likely to damage the Grid market. Grid technology has started to move into mainstream enterprise, but software vendors cannot license their software to satisfy the needs of an on-demand computation model. Currently many companies sell Grid software "per processor" that makes Grid solutions not affordable, since Grid computing is based on a dynamic resource allocation. A problem can be solved in four machines for 30 days, or use partially up to 2,000 machines in 1 day; in the latter case, the enterprise should buy beforehand software licenses for 2,000 machines. The issues arise because the Grid user is paying full price for software that is not fully exploiting the machine that is shared in a virtual environment.

Users need dynamic pricing that will reflect their actual Grid usage, which might be a fraction of the maximum computing cycles they consume at peak times. Finding the pricing unit for the Grid is a problem to be solved. Issues like network cost, on-demand availability, CPU time, disk space, are to be considered. These issues should be addressed by new licensing schemes. There are some thorny issues to be addressed when considering new licensing schemes and their enforceability. According to [N-05], all agreed restrictions or conditions of use should be enforceable unless contradicting contract law doctrines. In the Grid environment, it is better for the market to tailor licensing in Grid transactions to fit actual needs rather than to use legislative or regulatory groups to impose the rules of copyright law.

Another issue that needs to be clarified (Madison, 2003) when dealing with the enforceability of licenses is whether there exist proper offer and acceptance. The Internet as a place metaphor seems to fail in the case of Grid environment. Wrongful access to a computer does not have a clear boundary since it might concern the information stored on the client PC, the use of the processor, the use of storage, the computation cycles, and the consumed bandwidth. As new pricing and accounting models are being developed in the Grid community, and while most of them are results of academic research and not widely adopted in the market, it is essential for every new licensing mechanism to be well understood and accepted by both parties.

Other Issues

In Grid environment, the Grid broker distributes software and data that allow Grid nodes to execute the specific jobs assigned to them. Although the Grid network objective is to share digital files and programs in a collaborative environment, the capabilities and connectivity that exists in the Grid environments allow recipients to easily distribute copyrighted material without authorization. As part of their services, Grid providers transfer data and software files that may be accessed and, by necessity, copied in the Grid nodes. Issues arise when the Grid nodes abuse the privilege and copy and/or post material that violates copyright law.

The software application provider (ASP) provides the software to be deployed to the Grid nodes for the data processing. The software application provider can be the client or another organisation or several other organisations or an intermediary. Several issues arise regarding this software:

1. The Grid provider usually has direct access to this software. This software is transmitted through the Grid network, giving to third parties an opportunity to copy and/or modify it. Therefore, the Grid provider is responsible to provide a Grid infrastructure that guarantees secure transfer of information. The Grid computing data exchange must be protected using secure communication channels (SSL/TLS) in combination with secure message exchange mechanisms (WS security, GSI).

2. In cases where the client requests from the Grid provider, the use of processing software of a third party without a valid licence or outside the scope of the licence, the Grid provider and the software provider may be found liable for intellectual property infringement.

3. If the Grid provider modifies the software or the results of the software for their own purposes, then the client is entitled to copyright protection.

Software licences used in a Grid environment should constrain the Grid provider and the Grid nodes to only make authorised use of the software. The software provider (which might be the client, the Grid broker, a member of the Grid virtual organisation or an intermediary) should be liable if it fails to obtain appropriate rights. The contract should restrict software modifications. At the same time, it should also clarify that the necessary exchange of data within the Grid environment for efficient computing is not misuse of data under applicable data protection laws.

Another approach is that because the Grid environment is an open, large scale, globally shared environment, when infringement occurs, it may be difficult to enforce rights in the protected work effectively against the direct infringers. Therefore, it seems that the only practical alternative might be to go after the Grid provider.

Other issues that have to be addressed in the Grid environment have to do with privacy. Data and data processing are protected by data-protection laws, thus, exposing the Grid provider and the Grid participants to liability issues. At the same time, the use of data in heterogeneously distributed and dynamic environments (like the Grid) increases concern of the clients regarding the misuse of their information. According to data protection principles, data held for any purpose or purposes shall not be used or disclosed in any manner incompatible with that purpose or those purposes. Statistical disclosure is a major risk in

Grid environments. When data are given to the Grid provider through the client or an intermediary, the provider partitions and replicates data in the Grid infrastructure. This replication offers fault tolerance and improved performance. Can the client claim that the data is not used for the purpose collected? How can the provider guarantee that each participating node will use the data only for the specified purposes?

In the Grid environment there is a need to balance competing interests of privacy. The user (the Grid client) is entitled to access his/her data held by the Grid broker and where appropriate, to have such data corrected or erased. A controversial point concerning the Grid broker's operation is that, while the user can request and obtain access to his/her data from the Grid broker, it is not clear whether this access includes revealing information regarding where the data reside, and other information regarding the Grid nodes that store and process the data. The advanced ability of the Grid agents to collect information could be considered as an invasion in individual's privacy and personal space. In service Grids, resource owners might provide their resources, but be unwilling to expose information regarding the characteristics of their resources, and even the fact that they participate in the Grid.

In the case of the Grid environment, the data circulation is dynamic. The transfer of data is based on the availability of nodes that can execute the task at the specific point in time, and the replication optimizing the performance of the Grid at the specific point in time. These are real-time decisions that cannot be predefined. Moreover, the rules that govern such decisions are part of the logic of the software of the Grid broker, and many times not publicly available. In discussing invasions of privacy, courts use the concept of reasonable expectation of privacy in the sense that data protection legislation protects information as to which the individual has exhibited a subjective expectation of privacy as long as the expectation

is one that society recognizes as reasonable. The Grid user reasonably expects, in good faith, that the Grid provider will make sure that the circulation of data is done for their efficient processing and for no other reason than that.

Multimedia Grids are part of an evolving approach that could eventually alter the communications landscape in a global scale. The characteristics of intellectual property protection in multimedia Grids are just beginning to become clear, and the legal framework that currently governs these activities must be clearly drawn and reevaluated. As multimedia Grids evolve and as their use becomes more popular, new problems will arise. From a legal point of view, researchers and legislators should cooperate in order to employ a uniform solution that will govern all intellectual property transactions in multimedia Grids. Since intellectual property protection seems to prove inadequate to deal with these issues, contractual protection seems to provide the solution.

The Grid provider and the resource owner should enter into contracts that facilitate the lawful and fair circulation of data within the Grid environment, and specify the obligations of the Grid provider and the Grid node. In data Grids, users usually (Giburd, Schuster, & Wolff, 2004) do not object to have the Grid provider collect and publish cumulative statistics, provided that the data cannot be manipulated to obtain information about a specific record or a specific data source. In cases where data mining algorithms are allowed to execute in the data, they should guarantee that the algorithm produces statistics that guarantee privacy.

We believe that appropriate software should be provided (by the Grid provider to the user) to allow the user to view and update the application data, as well as his/her personal data. The software should be able to inform the user regarding the number of nodes that execute his/her application, the number of partitions made of the application data, and the number of replicas of the data at the moment of request. Therefore, we believe that a combination of legal and technical solutions would best serve the multimedia Grid community.

CONCLUSION

It is clear that several legal issues arise in Grid environments, and several steps need to be taken in order to regulate the smooth execution of Grid transactions. In this work, we identified issues we are expecting to arise in court cases in the near future. Although well-drafted contracts may reduce the risks, they do not always provide a solution, and clients should be aware that not all risks can be contracted away. In addition, we believe that middleware should be developed that will allow for the efficient monitoring of the Grid procedures by the Grid broker. As the Grid technology is being commercialised, a legal framework is necessary that will deal with the described issues. As a first step, it is necessary for the legal and the industrial community to identify the problems and look for efficient solutions.

In our future work, we are looking into the problem of designing Grid middleware that will provide adequate accounting and monitoring mechanisms. We are also looking into the legal problems that are arising in a Grid-pervasive computing environment.

REFERENCES

Berne Convention for the Protection of Literary and Artistic Works. (1979). Retrieved from http://www.wipo.int/treaties/en/ip/berne/trtdocs_wo001.html

Brinson, D., & Radcliffe, F. M. (1996). *Multimedia: Law and business handbook: A practical guide for developers and publishers*. Ladera Press.

Burk, D. L. (1998). Proprietary rights in hypertext linkages. *Journal of Information Law and Technology*, (2).

Carver B. (2005). Share and share alike: Understanding and enforcing open source and free software licenses.*20 Berkley Technology Law Journal, 443*.

Chervenak, A., Foster, I., Kesselman, C., Salisbury C., & Tueck, S. (2001). The data Grid: Towards an architecture for the distributed management and analysis of large scientific datasets, *Journal of Network and Computer Applications, 23*, 187-200.

Derclaye E. (2002). What is a database? A critical analysis of the definition of a database in the European Database Directive and suggestions for an international definition. *The Journal of World Intellectual Property, 5*(6), 981-1011.

Foster, I. (2005). License to Grid. *The Globus Consortium Journal*.

Foster, I., Kesselman, C., Tsudik, G., & Tuecke, S. (1998). A security architecture for computational Grids. In *Proceedings of the 5th ACM Conference on Computer and Communications Security Conference* (pp. 83-92).

Foster, I., Kesselman, C., & Tuecke, S. (2001). The anatomy of the Grid: Enabling scalable virtual organizations. *International Journal on Supercomputer Applications, 15*(3).

Giburd, B, Schuster, A., & Wolff, R. (2004). *K-TTP: A new privacy model for large scale distributed environments*. Knowledge Discovery and Data Mining, KDD 2004, ACM, Seattle, USA.

Globus Toolkit Homepage. Retrieved from http://www.globus.org/toolkit/

Grossman, G. A. (2005). From Sony to Grokster, The failure of the copyright doctrines of contributory infringement and vicarious liability to resolve the war between content and destructive technologies. *Buffalo Law Review, 141.*

Harmer, T. J., Donachy, P., Perrott, R. H., Chambers, C., Craig, S., Mallon, B., & Wrigh, C. (2003). GridCast—Using the Grid in Broadcast Infrastructures. In *Proceedings of UK e-Science All Hands Meeting* (AHM03).

Kafeza, I., Kafeza, E., & Chiu, D. K. (2005). *Legal aspects of security in e-contracting with electronic agents.* In H. Sachar, P. Pohlmann, & N. Reimer (Eds.), *ISSE Securing Electronic Business Processes: Highlights of the Information Security Solutions Europe 2005 Conference,* GWV-Vieweg.

Kanaskar, N, Topaloglu, U., & Bayrak, C, (2005). Globus security model for Grid environment. *ACM SIGSOFT Software Engineering Notes, 30,* 6.

Kesler, J. C. (2005). Contractual and regulatory compliance challenges in Grid computing environments. In *Proceedings of the 2005 IEEE International Conference on Services Computing* (pp. 61-68).

Madison, M. (2003). Rights and the shape of the Internet. *44 Boston College Law Review, 433.*

Marrakesh agreement establishing the World Trade Organization, Morrocco. Retrieved from http://www.wto.org/english/docs_e/legal_e/27-trips_01_e.htm

McCarthy, C. (2006). File-sharing site eDonkey kicks it. *CNET news.* Retrieved from http://www.news.com.com

Mitakis, C. (2004). The e-rated industry: Fair use sheep or infringing goat? *Vanderbilt Journal of Entertainment Law and Practice, 291.*

Niccolai, J. (2004). Grid computing distributes the load across a network to speed processing. *PCWorld.*

Nimmer, R.. (2005). Introduction: Issues in licensing an introduction. *Houston Law Review, 42,* 941.

Nokes, S. W. (2004). E-rated movies: Coming soon to a home theater near you. *Georgetown Law Journal, 92,* 611.

Opderberck D. W. (2005). Peer to peer networks, Technological evolution, and intellectual property reverse private attorney general litigation. *Berkeley Technology Law Journal, 20,* 1685

Pope, C. (2005). Unfinished business: Are today's P2P networks liable for copyright infringement? *Duke Law & Technology Review, 22.*

Rome Convention for the Protection of Performers, Producers of Phonograms and Broadcasting Organizations. (1961). Retrieved from http://www.wipo.int/treaties/en/ip/rome

Schulman, J. (2005). Liability of Internet service providers for infringing activities of their customers: Will the INDUCE Act solve the problem? *Baltimore Intellectual Property Law Journal, 13.*

Stamatoudi, I. (2002). *Copyright and multimedia products. A comparative analysis.* Cambridge University Press.

Trade Related Aspects of Intellectual property rights (TRIPS) Agreement. (1994). Annex 1C

Venugopal, S., Buyya, R., & Ramamohanarao, K. (2006) A taxonomy of data Grids for distributed data sharing, management, and processing. *ACM Computing Surveys, 38*(1), 3.

WIPO Copyright Treaty. (1996). Geneva December 20, from http://www.wipo.int/treaties/en/ip/wct/trtdocs_wo033.html

WIPO Performances and Phonograms Treaty. (1996). Geneva December 20. Retrieved from http://www.wipo.int/treaties/en/ip/wppt/trtdocs_wo034.html

Zittrain, J. (2006).The generative Internet. *The Harvard Law Review Association, 119,* Harv. L. Rev. 1974.

Chapter XXI
Secure Image Archiving Using Novel Digital Watermarking Techniques

Ruo Ando
Keio University, Japan

Yoshiyasu Takefuji
Keio University, Japan

ABSTRACT

With the rapid advance in digital network, digital libraries, and particularly WWW (World Wide Web) services, we can retrieve many kinds of images on personal and mobile computer anytime and anywhere. At the same time, secure image archiving is becoming a major research area because the serious concern is raised about copyright protection and authority identification in digital media. A more sophisticated technique is required for future multimedia copyright protection. In this chapter we propose a secure image archiving using novel digital-watermarking techniques. Firstly, a nonlinear adaptive system (neural network) is applied for frequency-based digital watermarking. Secondly, we discuss application-oriented watermarking method for GIS image archiving. This chapter is divided into two parts. First section is about the way to apply nonlinear adaptive system for frequency-based image watermarking. We propose a new asymmetric technique employing nonlinear adaptive system trained on frequency domain. Our system uses two public keys to prevent removal attack and archive more fragile watermarking. In embedding, location information of frequency domain, where adaptive system is trained, is binalized, expressed in hexadecimal number, and encrypted in asymmetric cryptosystem. Encrypted location information is embedded in several parts of digital host contents. In generating key, supervised neural networks learn to assign the array of coefficients to teacher signal corresponding to the message to insert. This is one kind of transform-based method to generate public key from private key. In extracting, we use key matrix created by one-way signal processing of adaptive system. Proposal method is tested in still image, and we have empirically obtained the results that the proposal model is functional in implementing more secure and fragile watermarking compared with previous techniques, such as correlation and transform-based asymmetric watermarking. Several experiments are reported to validate the effectiveness of our watermarking method. Second section is about the application of GIS image archiving using digital watermarking technique. Recently, the utilization of GIS (geographical information system) is becoming rapidly pervasive. Consequently, new methodology of archiving and managing images is a pressing problem for GIS users. It is also expected that as the utilization of GIS becomes widely spread, protecting copyright and confidential images will be more important. In this chapter, we propose a three-layer image data format that makes it possible to synthesize two kinds of related images and analysis information in one image data size. To achieve the confidentiality of one hidden image, we apply the private watermarking scheme, where the algorithm is closed to the public. In the proposal model, encoder netlist embedded in the third layer is generated by FOL prover to achieve more secure and less information to decode it, compared with one operation of another block cipher such as RSA. Proposal system users can process two images without the cost of maintaining key and decoding operation.

INTRODUCTION

With the rapid advance in digital network, digital libraries, and particularly WWW (World Wide Web) services, digital watermarking is becoming a major research area because the serious concern is raised about copyright protection and authority identification in digital media. A more sophisticated technique is required for future multimedia copyright protection. Digital multimedia contents on the Internet are easily distributed, reproduced, and manipulated, compared with conventional analog data. In general, a digital watermark is a concealed code embedded into digital multimedia contents irremovably and imperceptibly in order to protect intellectual propriety rights. This chapter presents a new model of processing coefficients using supervised neural network. In our model, neural network is trained to assign coefficients to predefined secret code. Classification method of neural network can deal with predefined data, so it can detect weaker signal and figure out accurate recognition.

Geographical information systems (GIS) is a technological field under rapid progress that combines graphical features and tabular data according to the positions of the earth's surface. The prototype of GIS, which made it possible to program maps and store them on a computer for future modification if necessary, began around 1960. Currently, GIS are represented by several layers for manipulating, analyzing, and displaying for effective planning. The concept of overlaying different mapped features caused the situation that GIS is utilized for handling several maps. Consequently, in the process of GIS, overlaying and derivation are operated. As analysis of geographical images is becoming elaborate and complicated with the improvement of GIS, these bottlenecks are considered for further effective analysis and planning

Problem 1: Cost in managing image data. GIS image is analyzed and processed for a variety of purposes to generate the clipped or derived images. Also, the image is composed from many kinds of layer images for a particular valid analysis. Thumbnail images generated on the process of its use are rapidly increasing. As a result, the effective management of GIS image data is becoming apressing requirement. Usually header information and database are constructed separately, which costs to maintain and update these optional data.

Problem 2: Accessibility on the process of analysis. For GIS users, there are many situations that people have to discuss a particular area by considering several GIS images. In this case, maintaining the log of processing images and results of analysis is very important for effective research.

RELATED WORK

Digital watermarks can be divided into the following two points. At first, it could be categorized according to whether it uses an original image or not. Private (nonblind) watermarking needs the original data. This technique depends on the prewatermarked images to detect hidden code. Public (blind) watermarking requires performance without original image and watermark. Blind watermarking tends to be less robust and the most challenging method. Secondly, in embedding the hidden message, we should select the domain to process, that is, spatial domain and frequency domain. In spatial watermarking, the secret code is added to the spatial domain. Spatial watermark is easy to implement in the sense that it is embedded directly into an image's pixel data. On the other hand, frequency watermarking is based on some transform method such as FFT, DCT, and DWT (Craver & Katzenbeisser, 2001). Techniques in frequency domain are robust because they rely on the perceptual model of human vision. Recently, statistical models for coefficients in frequency domain have been proposed, such as Gaussian, Laplacian, and generalized Gaussian.

The research in GIS is classified into several fields, such as database modeling, simulation, image processing, and software engineering. GIS database is divided into modeling, which deals with effective data structure (Eggers, Su, & Girod, 2000), and recognition and retrieval system and analysis. The feature extraction from image is applying frequency transform such as DCT and DWT (Hachez & Quisquater, 2002). Recently, image processing of multispectrum sensing data is one of the major topics in GIS analysis (Cox, Kilian, Leighton, & Shamoon, 1997). Along with the popularization of Internet, recently, Web-based GIS management systems are expected to be more effective tools for data sharing and collection (Lin & Chang, 2000). As utilization of GIS is widely spread, some security problems such as protection of the copyright and confidential datas are more focused. Besides the security purpose, the digital watermarking is used in image classification (Kundur & Hatzinakos, 1997).

Asymmetric Watermarking

Digital watermarking is classified into two categories, according to the information disclosed for detectors: symmetric and asymmetric watermarking. In simple meaning, asymmetric watermarking is the technique using different types of keys. Traditional watermarking employs a symmetric scheme that requires the same key in embedding and detecting. The keys we need for message hiding and extraction are identical. So these conventional systems require the key for embedding watermark is disclosed completely in the verification process. This causes a security problem once attackers have signals similar to the embedding keys. They can easily remove the watermarks from the marked works by subtraction attack. In an asymmetric key cryptosystem, it must be almost impossible, even with current high performance computation, to deduce the private key from the public key. Therefore, an advantage of asymmetric watermarking is that the information about decoding key is not enough to remove watermark and that estimation of the secret message is not sufficient to eliminate watermark. As long as the some relation properties of embedded signal are satisfied, different watermarks can be used for many kinds of content. Consequently, the scheme is particularly secure to averaging attack.

Furthermore, asymmetric watermark is classified into two methods, watermark–characteristics-based method and transform-based method. Transform-based method is generating a detection key from previously defined key by some proper transform. Recently, many algorithms to render asymmetry were suggested; for example, eigenvector network, periodic watermark, neural network system, and so forth. Furon and Duhamel concluded from comparisons to public key cryptosystems that a one-way signal processing function is needed to build an asymmetric watermarking scheme. An asymmetric watermarking scheme has been defined as one for which the encryption key is different to the decoding key. Hence, the knowledge of the decoding key is not sufficient to remove the watermark. The security of the scheme presented here depends on the permutation, which is identical in both the embedder and detector. The scheme does not satisfy the requirements of a truly asymmetric scheme in that knowledge of the permutation key will allow attackers to destroy the watermark. Nevertheless, this scheme does not exhibit some of the important characteristics of asymmetric watermarking schemes. In particular, the detector is not dependent on any particular watermark signal, provided the correlation properties of the watermark are satisfied. In the current state of the art, a truly asymmetric public-key watermarking scheme remains to be found, and no scheme can afford to make all its detection parameters public. The extra security provided by our scheme therefore makes it an attractive option, provided that the private key can be kept secret. An advantage of this scheme is that estimation of the watermark by collusion attack is rendered impossible, so that the overall system is more secure. Knowledge of the public key does not enable an attacker to remove a watermark. More specifically, the public key must not reveal the location of the watermark in the cover. It must be computationally infeasible to deduce the private key from the public key.

Fragile Watermarking

Digital watermarking is classified into two categories according to the purpose: robust and fragile watermarking. In copyright protection, the robust watermark is applied to prove the origin even after some manipulation or alteration. Robust digital watermarks are used to provide a mechanism for copyright protection of digital contents by embedding authors and customer information. Robust watermark is also called copyright or fingerprint watermark. This watermark is for the contents that could be transferred, filtered, and compressed, owing to the user's purposes. Robust watermarks must be robust to many kinds of attacks, such as resizing, cropping, and filtering. To survive these attacks, current watermark schemes usually employ a spread spectrum approach.

In authentication applications of multimedia contents, the main purpose is to find the modification of data. The fragile watermark is designed for the objectives for authentication and integrity for host contents. This is an authentication technique to insert a signature designed to be undetectable after even slight manipulation of the content. So, fragile watermark is best used for protection and verification of original documents. As we discussed, in this chapter, the authentication of images is focused. Cryptography is probably the most common method used to authenticate the integrity of digital data. Cryptography is a traditional authentication method to conceal the message to an unauthorized person. In cryptography, digital signature preserves confidentiality and integrity. The signature is added to the encrypted message.

Fragile watermark is surely similar to cryptography, but can protect content by placing hidden information in the parts of content where it is not eliminated in normal usage. Fragile watermarking method takes advantages in inserting secret messages directly with no additional information to authenticate, while digital signature needs extra data transportation.

HVS Watermarking

A good watermark is supposed to be undetectable by human sense, and can only be perceived by computing the correlation or periodicity. A recent watermarking method applies human visual system (HVS) features to insert signatures into host images. The actual human visual system is very complicated, and can process vast information. Roughly speaking, it is composed of a receiver with a preprocessing stage, the eye and the retina, a transmission channel, the optic nerve, and a processing engine, the visual cortex. But in frequency domain, HVS are less sensitive in textured, edge, and rapid-changing regions. This characteristic makes these zones appropriate for embedding watermark. Psychophysical experiments have shown that the response of visual cortex is turned to the band-limited portion of the frequency domain. It gives evidence that the brain decomposes the spectra into perceptual channels that are bands in spatial frequency. Now HVS is a reasonable standard in measuring whether the media contents are tampered with or not, since our eyes are sensitive to modifications beyond perception.

As we discussed before, a good watermark is supposed to be invisible for human eyes and undetectable without information to detect. Also, it should remain in spite of spatial/temporal modification. To satisfy these requirements, a watermark using human visual system (HVS) has been proposed (Podilchuk & Zeng, 1998). According to HVS, human eyes are less accurate in the regions where the change is rapid, which make preferable zones to watermark. On the other hand, human visual system is sensitive in the regions where the value is changed smoothly, which in turn is not proper to embed the secret message.

Compared with previous watermarking techniques using global information, the adaptive watermarking based on HVS selects the appropriate parts of frequency domain, where the message will be imperceptible and robust for some changes (Kwon, Kwon, Nam, & Tewfik, 2002).

This content-adaptive watermarking has been researched mainly using a stochastic model based on frequency transform. They utilize the local properties of contents to select the optimal embedding blocks with following subband quantization and perceptual model. (Kundur & Hatzinakos, 1997).

Proposal Watermarking Scheme

In proposal method, we embed and detect location value. Location value is processed as input signal with nonlinear adaptive system, such as back propagation network. In inserting watermark, a key is generated. Compared with conventional model where signature is equivalent to the message to hide, we embed location code and train nonlinear adaptive system, such as neural networks, with teacher signal corresponding to secret message. In detecting secret message, output signal is converted to bit code, according to threshold (about more than 0.95). We can extract the secret message by processing input signal of the blocks where location value is indicating.

Our model is asymmetric in two meanings. First, location code is encrypted with private key and decrypted with public key. Second, the key to extract hidden bit code is transformed by one-way signal processing of neural network. To achieve more secure watermarking, location value is encrypted. In symmetric watermarks, attackers can remove watermarking. We apply asymmetric watermarking and encrypt location code with private key. In detection, we can decrypt location code with public key. Consequently, we have two keys to extract watermarks.

Compared with using ASCII code, location value embedding renders shorter code to insert. And all characters are assigned to 3 bit constantly. The code to insert is encrypted with private key, and we obtain more secure processing of asymmetric watermarking. In proposal method, the range of location value is from 0 to 7, because we use discrete cosign transform with blocks 8*8. Location value is expressed in hexadecimal number. In hexadecimal number, one bit change may cause bigger changes in decimal number.

The schematic diagram of embedding process is depicted in figure.

Watermark embedding process is divided into two steps: (1) embedding and (2) key generation. As we mentioned before, transform-based method to make a detection key from a given embedding key by proper transform is applied. In encryption

Figure 1. Embedding watermark

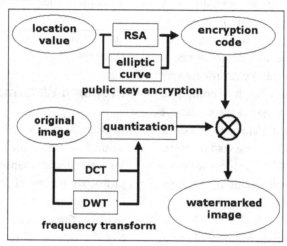

Figure 2 Detecting watermark

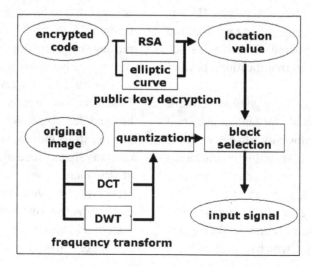

of location value, we use private key of RSA. But in generating key, we generate the key from location value by training nonlinear adaptive system. Consequently, we use two keys to extract hidden information. The schematic diagram of extraction process is illustrated in Figure 2.

In proposal model, extraction process is feed-forward, computing with input signal of the coefficients of the DCT/DWT blocks. We applied recognition process on frequency domain, and convert analog output signal to bit code. Extraction process is divided into two processes. First, we decrypt the location value with public key. Second, we set the input signal as the coefficients of the DCT block the decrypted value indicated. We use asymmetric cryptosystem because complete information disclosure of location value causes the possibility of removal attacks such as averaging attack. The details of each step are described in the following section.

Location Code Encryption

The proposal model aims for asymmetric and fragile watermarking. This step is concerned with asymmetric watermarking. To avoid removal attack, we use asymmetric cryptography for location value. In this chapter we applied RSA algorithms discussed in Section 3.1 to encrypt location value.

ADAPTIVE WATERMARKING AND KEY GENERATION USING NEURAL NETWORK

The adaptive watermarking based on HVS select the appropriate parts of frequency domain, where the message will be imperceptible and robust for some changes.

Watermark should be undetectable without key. In this case, the key is equivalent to connection weight matrix of back propagation. As shown in the figure, the supervised learning system process DCT coefficient as input signal. And in training, the hidden inserted is binalized as fixed output to neural net. Once the location value is embedded, the connection weight matrix is utilized as key to extract hidden code. In other words, learning process of neural network is transform process to generate key; connection weight matrix should be saved as key.

- **Step 1:** Calculate the DCT coefficients for each 8*8 block.
- **Step 2:** Quantize the DCT coefficients by standard JPEG quantization table.

Figure 3. Key generation. Asymmetric rendering

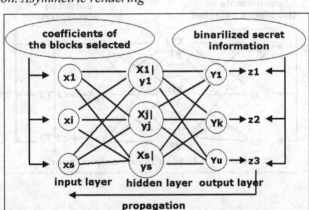

- **Step 3:** Select the DCT block.
- **Step 4:** Embed the encrypted value in selected block.
- **Step 5:** Train the supervised neural network with the teacher signal corresponding to secret bit code. Input signals are the coefficients of DCT block.

In processing on frequency domain, neural network takes advantages in calculating mainly in two aspects. (1) Neural network is a nonlinear system that is able to process the nonlinear behavior well. (2) Neural network has fault tolerance, that is, the network can continue to perform acceptably in spite of the failure of some elements in the network.

Location Code Decryption

Extraction step is divided into two steps: location code decryption and nonlinear signal processing. In this step, location value is decrypted with public key. In embedding, location value is expressed in hexadecimal code. So, if some manipulation is operated on host images, decrypted location value is changed.

Watermark Extraction

In extraction of watermarks, we need:

1. Information about the location of blocks where the neural network was trained.
2. Public key.
3. Connection weight matrix as key. Steps to detect watermark is as follows:
   - **Step 1:** Calculate the DCT coefficients for each 8*8 block.
   - **Step 2:** Quantize the DCT coefficients by standard JPEG qauntization table.
   - **Step 3:** Process input signal. Input signals are the coefficients of the block selected.

In this phase, recognition is processed by forward phase in backpropagation computing. In forwarding computation, the input signal is propagated from layer to layer in network, with the parameters fixed. This recognition phase is finished when each signal of the output layer is figured out.

1. Compared with using ASCII code, location value embedding renders shorter code to insert.

Figure 4. Watermark extraction

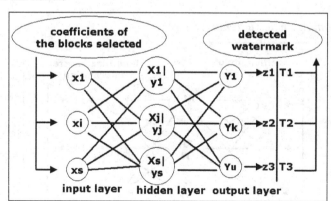

2. The code to insert is encrypted with private key, and we obtain security of asymmetric watermarking.

3. In proposal method, the range of location value is from 0 to 7 because we use DCT. Location value is expressed in hexadecimal number. In hexadecimal number, one-bit changes may be big changes compared with decimal number.

4. In proposal method, the range of location value is from 0 to 7 because we use DCT. Location value is expressed in hexadecimal number. In hexadecimal number, one-bit changes may be big changes compared with decimal number. 3.1 RSA

RSA is a public-key cryptosystem implemented for both encryption and authentication on Internet. It was invented in 1977 by Ron Rivest, Adi Shamir, and Leonard Adleman.

The steps of RSA are as follows:

1. The process begins to select P and Q, two large prime numbers (hundreds of digits).

2. Choose E such that E and $(P-1)(Q-1)$ are relatively prime, which means they have no prime factors in common. E does not have to be prime, but it must be odd. $(P-1)(Q-1)$ cannot be prime because it is an even number.

3. Find out D, its inverse, and mod $(P-1)(Q-1)$ so that $(DE-1)$ is divisible by $(P-1)(Q-1)$.
This could be written as:
$DE = 1 \bmod (P-1)(Q-1)$, and D is called as the multiplicative inverse of E.

4. Once these steps are done, message can be encrypted in blocks, and manipulated on the following:
where T is the plaintext (a positive number)

5. Similarly, C is decrypted through the following equation.
where C is the cipher text (a positive number)

It is impossible to deduce the private key from the public key. The cipher text can be decrypted only by corresponding private key. The public key is the pair (PQ, E). The primitive number D computed in Step 3 must not be revealed to anyone. The product PQ is called the modulus. E selected in Step 2 is the public exponent. We also call D as the decryption or secret exponent.

BACK PROPAGATION NETWORK

Backpropagation is the supervised learning algorithm of feed-forward neural network. This algorithm is processed in four steps: initialization, presentations of training examples, forward

Figure 5. Backpropagation network

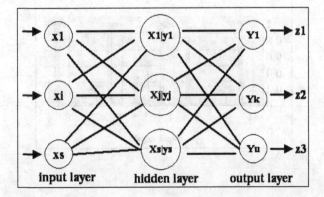

computation, and backward computation. In backward computation, we use the delta rule to modify connection weight of each neuron.

THREE LAYER IMAGE DATA STRUCTURE

Three layer image data structure is watermark-based technology that embeds two images and one archiving information header into a single image. In the figure, biotope map and header information is watermarked into the aerial image. This method relies on human visual system (HVS) watermarking, which is supposed to be invisible for human eyes and undetectable without information to detect. Aerial image and biotope map are usually analyzed by human experts. Consequently, it is possible to synthesize two images and its archiving header into one image without loss of effectiveness of analysis. As shown in the figure, three layer images are decomposed into eight layer as follows:

- **Layer [0]-[3]:** Assigned for aerial image data.
- **Layer [4]:** Header (archiving information and processing log).

- **Layer [5]-[7]:** Assigned for biotope map data.

Based on HVS watermarking techniques, users can analyze these two images while maintaining reasonable quality for analysis. Besides, it is possible to retrieve logs to process and archive without database and searching.

Experimental Results

To test this algorithm, we implemented a system for embedding and restoring 8 bits in images of size 256*256. We computed the DCT coefficients for each 8*8 block, and quantized those values by standard JPEG quantization table. In embedding the location value and training network, we set 8 perceptrons of input and output layer. In training network, we set the teacher signal (1,0,1,1,0,1,0,1).

Figure 6 shows the result of processing coefficients of the block selected correctly. The output of processing coefficients in irrelevant block is shown in Figure 7. Extraction failed when we selected the arrays of coefficients that were not processed as input signal in supervised learning.

Figure 6. Output signal by processing in the selected block

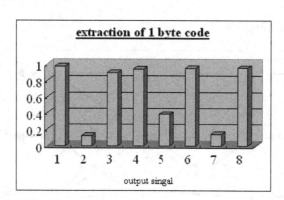

ecure Image Archiving Using Novel Digital Watermarking Techniques

In learning process, we prepare several insignificant patterns that all coefficients are extremely high or low, and train the network in order to assign these patterns to teacher signal such as (0,0,0,0,0,0,0,0) or (1,1,1,1,1,1,1,1). Experimental results show that our method is functional in recognizing the block that is not selected as a meaningless array, and in avoiding unexpected extraction from the incorrect blocks.

As we know, in proposal model, the location value is encrypted and embedded. Figure 8. shows the bit loss rate. The coefficients of high-frequency domain are modified to binary number 0/1. After filters listed in Figure 8, almost

Figure 7. Output signal by processing in the block where the network was not trained

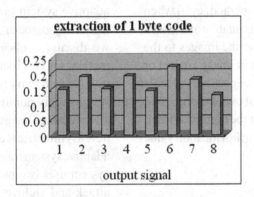

Figure 8. Bit loss rate after filters/attacks. Location value cannot be restored

filter / attack	bit loss rate
median filter 2*2	0.92
median filter 3*3	0.65
median filter 4*4	0.69
FMLR	0.44
sharpening 0*1	0.84
sharpening 0*5	0.87
sharpening 1*0	0.83
sharpening 5*0	0.86
sharpening 5*5	0.88
Gaussian	100
Geomtric transform1	0.88
Geomtric transform2	0.89
Geomtric transform2	0.86

all location information expressed by binarized and hexadecimal number has become unable to be restored. We have obtained the results that compared with correlation-based extraction, our method is more fragile in the sense that location information breaks down, for nonlinear adaptive systems output, the signals near (0,0,0,0,0,0,0,0), as shown in Figure 7.

To eliminate the watermark, filtering images may be attempted. For filtering attacks, our watermarking is robust because one location value is concealed in several pixels, as we discussed in Section 3. In the proposal method, even when an attacker still intends to eliminate watermarks without the key, he must filter the images to the extent that the many features of image are lost or broken. This means that the image is not valuable for attackers also. Figure 6. shows experimental evaluation of robustness after the high-pass filter. In our experiment, less than 30% of location value is changed after this filter.

CONCLUSION

Based on HVS watermarking techniques, users can analyze these two images while maintaining reasonable quality for analysis. Besides, it is possible to retrieve logs to process and archive without database and searching. With the rapid advance in digital network, digital libraries, and particularly WWW (World Wide Web) services, we can retrieve many kinds of images on personal and mobile computer anytime and anywhere. At the same time, secure image archiving is becoming a major research area because the serious concern is raised about copyright protection and authority identification in digital media. In this chapter, we propose a secure image archiving using novel digital watermarking techniques. Firstly, nonlinear adaptive system (neural network) is applied for frequency-based digital watermarking. Secondly, we discuss application-oriented watermarking method for GIS image archiving. This chapter is divided into two parts. First section is about the way to apply nonlinear adaptive system for frequency-based image watermarking. We propose a new asymmetric technique employing nonlinear adaptive system trained on frequency domain. Our system uses two public keys to prevent removal attack and archive more fragile watermarking. In embedding, location information of frequency domain, where adaptive system is trained, is binarized, expressed in hexadecimal number, and encrypted in asymmetric cryptosystem. And encrypted location information is embedded in

Figure 9. Host images of experiment

several parts of digital host contents. In generating key, supervised neural networks learn to assign the array of coefficients to teacher signal corresponding to the message to insert. This is one kind of transform-based method to generate public key from private key. In extracting, we use key matrix created by one-way signal processing of adaptive system. Proposal method is tested in still image. And we have empirically obtained the results that the proposal model is functional in implementing more secure and fragile watermarking compared with previous techniques, such as correlation and transform-based asymmetric watermarking. Several experiments are reported to validate the effectiveness of our watermarking method. Second section is about the application of GIS image archiving using digital watermarking technique. Recently, the utilization of GIS (geographical information gystem) is becoming rapidly pervasive. Consequently, new methodology of archiving and managing images is a pressing problem for GIS users. It is also expected that as the utilization of GIS becomes wide spread, protecting copyright and confidential images will be more important. In this chapter, we propose a three-layer image data format that makes it possible to synthesize two kinds of related images and analysis information in one image data size. To achieve the confidentiality of one hidden image, we apply the private watermarking scheme, where algorithm is closed to the public. In the proposal model, encoder netlist embedded in the third layer is generated by FOL prover to achieve more secure and less information to decode it, compared with one operation of another block cipher such as RSA. Proposal system users can process two images without the cost of maintaining key and decoding operation.

REFERENCES

Abdi, H., Valentin, D., & Edelman, B. (1999). *Neural networks.* Thousand Oaks, CA: Sage.

Anderson, J. A. (1995). *An introduction to neural networks.*

Bertsekas, D.P. (1999). *Nonlinear programming.* Athena Scientific.

Cox, I. J., Kilian, J., Leighton, T., & Shamoon, T. (1997). Secure spread spectrum watermarking for multimedia. *IEEE Trans. on Image Processing,* 1673-1687.

Craver, S., & Katzenbeisser, S. (2001). Copyright protection protocols based on asymmetric watermarking: The ticket concept. *Communications and Multimedia Security Issues of the New Century.* Kluwer Academic Publishers.

Eggers, J. J., Su, J. K., & Girod, B. (2000). Asymmetric watermarking schemes. *Tagungsband des GI Workshops Sicherheit in Mediendaten, Berlin, Germany.*

Fausett L. (1994). *Fundamentals of neural networks.* Arichtectures, algorithms, and applications. Englewood Cliffs, NJ: Prentice-Hall.

Fukushima, K. (1975). "Cognitron: A self-organizing multilayered neural network. *Biological Cybernetics, 20,* 121-136.

Hachez, G., & Quisquater, J. J. (2002). Which directions for asymmetric watermarking? In *Proceedings of the XI European Signal Processing Conference, EUSIPCO 2002.*

Hu, J., Huang, J., Huang, D., & Shi, Y. Q. (2002). A DWT-based fragile watermarking tolerant of JPEG compression. *IWDW 2002* (pp. 179-188).

Hurley, N. J., & Silvestre, G.. C. M. (2002). Nth order audio watermarking. In E. J. Delp III, P. W. Wong (Eds.), *Security and Watermarking of Multimedia Contents IV Proceedings of SPIE, 4675,* 102-110.

Kim, T. Y., Kim, T., & Choi, H. (2003). Correlation-based asymmetric watermark detector.

International Conference on Information Technology: Coding and Computing (ITCC 2003. (pp. 564-568).

Kundur, D., & Hatzinakos, D. (1997). A robust digital image watermarking method using wavelet-based fusion. In *Proceedings of the ICIP-97, 1,* 544-547.

Kwon, K. R., Kwon, S. G., Nam, J. H, & Tewfik, A. H. (2002). Content adaptive watermark embedding in the multiwavelet transform using as tochastic image model. *IWDW200* (pp.249-263).

Lewis-Beck, M. S., Bryman, A. E., & Liao, F. (2003). *The SAGE encyclopedia of social science research methods.* Sage Publications.

Lin, C. Y., & Chang, S. F. (2000). Semi-fragile watermarking for authenticating JPEG visual content. *SPIE Security and Watermarking of Multimedia Content II, EI'00* (pp. 140-151).

Marvel, L. M., Hartwig, G. W. Jr., & Boncelet, C. B. Jr. (2000). Compression-compatible fragile and semi-fragile tamper detection. *Proceedings of SPIE 3971,* (pp. 131-139).

Podilchuk, C. J., & Zeng, W. (1998). Image-adaptive watermarking using visual models. *IEEE Journal on Selected Areas in Communications, 16*(4), 525-539.

Compilation of References

"Free Mickey Mouse." (2002). *The Economist,* (October 12), 67.

"Patents and the Poor" (2001). *The Economist,* June 23, 21-23.

A&M Records, Inc. v. Abdallah, (1996). 948 F. Supp 1449 [C.D. Cal.].

A&M Records, Inc. v. Napster, (2001). 239 F. 3d 1004 [9th Cir].

Abdi, H., Valentin, D., & Edelman, B. (1999). *Neural networks.* Thousand Oaks, CA: Sage.

Adam, N. & Yesha, Y., (1996). Electronic commerce and digital libraries: Towards a digital agora. *ACM Computing Surveys.*

Administrative Complaint (2002), Docket No 9302, 18 June 2002.

Agi, I., & Gong, L. (1996). An empirical study of MPEG video transmissions. In *Proceedings of the Internet Society Symposium on Network and Distributed System Security* (pp. 137-144), San Diego, CA, Feb.

Aharonian, G. (1999). Does the Patent Office respect the software community? *IEEE Software, 16*(4), 87-89.

Ahn, J., Shim, H., Jeon, B., & Choi, I. (2004). Digital video scrambling method using intra prediction mode. PCM2004. *Springer LNCS, 3333,* 386-393.

Ahumada, A.J., Jr., & Beard, B.L. (1996, February). Object detection in a noisy scene. *Proceedings of SPIE: Vol. 2657. Human Vision, Visual Processing, and Digital Display VII* (pp. 190-199). Bellingham, WA.

Aihara, K. (1990). Chaotic neural networks. In H. Kawakami (Ed.), Bifurcation phenomena in nonlinear system and theory of dynamical systems. *Advanced Series on Dynamical Systems, 8,* 143-161.

Al-Hawamdeh, S., (1999). Integrating electronic course reserve into the digital library framework. *Singapore Journal of Library and Information Management, 28,* 64-72.

Ali, N. D. (2006). The open and closed case. *SPIDER, September 2006,* 7-9.

Alkio, M. (2003, March 9). Kovaa peliä patenteilla. *Helsingin Sanomat,* p. E3.

Amazon.com v. BarnesandNoble.com. (2001). 239 F. 3d 1343 [Fed. Cir.].

Amici Curiae Brief. (2003). *Metro-Goldwyn-Mayer Studios, Inc. v. Grokster, Ltd.* 259 F. Supp. 2d [C.D. Cal], on appeal.

Amsterdam Appellate Court (2002). BUMA & STEMRA v. KaZaA, March 28.

Anderson, J. A. (1995). *An introduction to neural networks.*

Anderson, K. M., Taylor, R. N., & Whitehead, E. J. (2000). Chimera: Hypermedia for heterogeneous software development enviroments. *ACM Transactions on Information Systems, 18*(3), 211-245.

Anderson, R. J., & Petitcolas, F. A. P. (1998). On the limits of steganography. *IEEE Journal on Selected Areas in Communications, 16*(4), 474-481.

Anderson, R., & Manifavas, C. (1997). Chameleon—A new kind of stream cipher. In *Lecture Notes in Computer Science, Fast Software Encryption* (pp. 107-113) Springer-Verlag.

Ando, R., & Takefuji, Y. (2003). Location-driven watermark extraction using supervised learning on frequency domain. *WSEAS TRANSACTIONS ON COMPUTERS, 2*(1), 163-169.

ANSI. (2003a). *Guidelines for implementation of the ANSI Patent Policy.*

ANSI. (2003b). *Patent policy.*

Antara. (2006). *IBM, Microsoft protest Indonesia's open source policy.* Retrieved October 1, 2006, from http://www.antara.co.id/en/seenws/?id=16383

Antonelli, C. (1994). Localized technological change and the evolution of standards as economic institutions. *Information Economics and Policy, 6,* 195-216.

Anupam, V., Freire, J., Kumar, B., & Lieuwen, D. F. (2000). Automating Web navigation with the WebVCR. In *Proceedings of WWW9, (Amsterdam, Netherlands, 2000), Computer Networks, 33*(1-6), 503-517.

Appellant's Opening Brief. (1998). *United States of America v. Microsoft Corporation* 253 F 3rd [D.C. Cir.].

Arms, W.Y., Banchi, C., & Overly, E.A., (1997). An architecture for information in digital libraries. *D-Lib Magazine,* February, [Online] http://www.dlib.org/dlib/february97/cnri/02arms1.html.

Arnold, M. (2000). Audio watermarking: Features, applications and algorithms. *IEEE International Conf. Multimedia and Expo, 2,* 1013-1016.

Arnold, M., & Schiltz, K. (2002). Quality evaluation of watermarked audio tracks. *SPIE Electronic Imaging, 4675,* 91-101.

Arundel, A. (2001). The relative effectiveness of patents and secrecy for appropriation. *Research Policy, 30,* 611-624.

Arundel, A., van de Paal, G., & Soete, L. (1995). *Innovation strategies of Europe's largest industrial firms: Results of the PACE survey for information sources, public research, protection of innovations and government programmes.*

Directorate General XIII, European Commission, EIMS Publication.

Asaravala, A. (2004, April 24). Forgent sues over JPEG patent. *Wired News.* Retrieved August 29, 2006, from http://www.wired.com/news/business/0,1367,63200,00.html

Askanazi, J., Caplan, G., Descoteaux, D., Donohue, K., Glasser, D., Johnson, A., & Mena, E. (2002). *The future of database protection in U.S.* Copyright Law. Retrieved November 27, 2006, from http://www.law.duke.edu/journals/dltr/articles/2001dltr0017.html

Atal, B. S., (1976). Automatic recognition of speakers from their voices. *Proceedings IEEE, 64,* 460-475.

Australian Government. (1988). *Privacy Act.* Retrieved from http://www.privacy.gov.au/act/privacyact/

Autelitano, F. (1999). Banche dati. La rilevanza delle banche dati nel sistema del "cyberlaw", *I Contratti, 10,* 925-935.

Auteri, P. (2003). Attuazione della direttiva 96/9/CE relativa alla tutela giuridica delle banche dati – [Artt. 1, 2], *Le nuove leggi civili commentate, 4-5,* 1175-1230.

Ayars, J. (2002). *XMCL—The eXtensible Media Commerce Language.* W3C note, W3C. Retrieved December 18, 2006, from http://www.w3.org/TR/xmcl/

Bach, J. R., Fuller, C., Gupta, A., Hampapur, A., Horowitz, B., Jain, R., & Shu, C. F. (1996). The Virage image search engine: An open framework for image management. In *Proceedings of SPIE Storage and Retrieval for Still Image and Video Databases IV* (pp. 76-87).

Balto, D.A., & Wolman, A.M. (2003). Intellectual property and antitrust: General principles. *IDEA The Journal of Law and Technology, 43*(3), 396-474.

Band, J., & Gowdy, J. S. (1997). Sui generis database protection—Has Its Time Come?, *D-Lib Magazine.* Retrieved September 25, 2006, from http://www.dlib.org/dlib/june97/06band.html

Bar, M. (2000). Kernel korner. *The Linux Process Model. Linux Journal, 71,*(24).

Barker, P., (1994). Electronic libraries—Visions of the future. *The Electronic Library, 12*(4), 221-230.

Barlow, J.P., (1995). Selling wine without bottles. *Proceedings of Digital Libraries Conference: Moving forward into the information era,* Singapore.

Barni, M., Bartolini, F., & Piva, A. (2001, May). Improved wavelet-based watermarking through pixel-wise masking. *IEEE Transactions on Image Processing, 10*(5), 783-791.

Barten, P.G. (1990, October). Evaluation of subjective image quality with the square-root integral method. *Journal of Optical Society of America, 7*(10), 2024-2031.

Bartlett, J. (2002, March 17). The ease of steganography and camouflage. *SANS Information Security Reading Room.* Retrieved October 29, 2003, from http://www.sans.org/rr/paper.php?id=762

Bartolini, F., Barni, M., Cappellini, V., & Piva, A. (1998, October). Mask building for perceptually hiding frequency embedded watermarks. *Proceedings of IEEE International Conference of Image Processing '98,* (vol. 1, pp. 450-454). Chicago, IL.

Bassia, Pitas, I., & Nicholaidis, N. (2001). Robust audio watermarking in the time domain. *IEEE Transaction on Multimedia, 3,* 232-241.

Bauer, M., & Dengler, D. (1999). InfoBeans - Configuration of personalized information services. In *Proceedings of IUI'99,* (Los Angeles, USA, 1999) (pp.153-156).

Bauer, M., Dengler, D., & Paul, G. (2000). Instructible agents for Web mining. In *Proceedings of IUI2000,* (New Orleans, USA, 2000) (pp. 21-28).

Baumgarte, F., Ferekidis, C., & Fuchs, H. (1995). A nonlinear psychoacoustic model applied to the ISO MPEG Layer 3 Coder. Preprint 4087. *99th AES Convention.*

Becker, L. (1977). *Property rights.* London: Routledge and Kegan Paul.

Bekkers, R., Duysters, G., & Verspagen, B. (2002). Intellectual property rights, strategic technology agreements and market structure; the case of GSM. *Research Policy, 31*(7), 1141-1161.

Bekkers, R., Duysters, G., & Verspagen, B. (2002). Intellectual property rights, strategic technology agreements and market structure. The case of GSM. *Research Policy, 31,* 1141-1161.

Bekkers, R., Verspagen, B., & Smits, J. (2002). Intellectual property rights and standardization: The case of GSM. *Telecommunications Policy, 26*(3-4), 171-188.

Bellare, M., & Rogaway, P. (1995). Optimal asymmetric encryption—How to encrypt with RSA. *Extended abstract in Advances in Cryptology—Eurocrypt 94 Proceedings, Lecture Notes in Computer Science* (p. 950). Springer-Verlag.

Bellovin, S. M. (2004). Spamming, phishing, authentication, and privacy. *Communication of the ACM, 47*(12), 144.

Benassi, P. (1999). TRUSTe: An online privacy seal program. *Communications of the ACM, 42*(2): 56-59.

Bender, W., Gruhl, D., & Morimoto, H. (1995). Techniques for data hiding. *Proceedings of SPIE, 2020,* 2420-2440.

Bender, W., Gruhl, D., Morimoto, N., & Lu, A. (1996). Techniques for data hiding. *IBM SYSTEMS JOURNAL, 35*(3-4).

Benkler, Y. (2003). The political economy of commons. *UPGRADE: European Journal for the Informatics Professional, 4*(3), 6-9.

Benkler, Y. (2006). *The wealth of networks: How social production transforms markets and freedom.* London: Yale University Press.

Bennett, C. J. (1997). Convergence revisited: Toward a global policy for the protection of personal data? In P. E. Agre & M. Rotenberg (Eds.), *Technology and privacy: The new landscape* (pp. 99-124). Cambridge, MA: MIT Press.

Bennett, K., & Grothoff, C. (2003). GAP—Practical anonymous networking. In Proceedings of the Third International Workshop on Privacy Enhancing Technologies (PET 2003), Dresden, Germany, March 26-28. *Lecture Notes in Computer Science, 2760* 141-160.

Bergstrom, T. C. (1975). Maximal elements of acyclic relations on compact sets. *Journal of Economic Theory, 10,* 403-404.

Berlind, D. (2002a, April 16). IBM drops Internet patent bombshell. *Tech Update.*

Berlind, D. (2002b, April 25). The hidden toll of patents on standards. *Tech News on ZDNet.* Retrieved August 29, 2006, from http://news.zdnet.com/2100-9595_22-891852.html

Berman, V. (2005, January-February). Is it time to reexamine patent policy for standards? *IEEE Design & Test of Computers,* 71-73.

Berne Convention for the Protection of Literary and Artistic Works. (1979). Retrieved from http://www.wipo.int/treaties/en/ip/berne/trtdocs_wo001.html

Berners-Lee, T., Cailliau, R., Luotonen, A., Henrik Nielsen, H. F., & Secret, A. (1994). The World-Wide Web. *Communications of the ACM, 37*(8), 76-82.

Bertsekas, D.P. (1999). *Nonlinear programming.* Athena Scientific.

Bessen, J. (2003). *Strategic patenting of complex technologies* (Working Paper). Research on Innovation.

Beutler, S. (1996). The protection of multimedia products through the EC's directive. *Entertainment Law Review, 7,* 317.

Bimber, B., Flanagin, A. J. & Stohl, C. (2005). Reconceptualizing collective action in the contemporary media environment. *Communication Theory, 15*(4), 365-388.

Blakley, G. R. (1979). Safeguarding cryptographic keys. In *Proceedings of the National Computer Conference, 48,* 313–317.

Blind, K. (2001). Standardisation, R&D and export activities: Empirical evidence at firm level. *Proceedings of the Third Interdisciplinary Workshop on Standardization Research* (pp. 165-186), University of the German Federal Armed Forces, Hamburg: University der Bundeswehr.

Blind, K. (2002a). *Normen als Indikatoren für die Diffusion neuer Technologien, Endbericht für das Bundesministerium für Bildung und Forschung im Rahmen der Untersuchung "zur Technologischen Leistungsfähigkeit Deutschlands"* zum Schwerpunkt *"methodische Erweiterungen des Indikatorensystems."* Karlsruhe: ISI.

Blind, K. (2002b). Driving forces for standardisation at standardisation development organisations. *Applied Economics, 34*(16), 1985-1998.

Blind, K. (2004). *The economics of standards: Theory, evidence, policy.* Cheltenham: Edward Elgar.

Blind, K., & Thumm, N. (2003). Interdependencies between intellectual property protection and standardisation strategies. *Proceedings of EURAS 2002* (pp. 88-106), Aachener Beiträge zur Informatik, Band 33, Wissenschaftsverlag Mainz, Aachen.

Blind, K., Bierhals, R., Iversen, E., Hossain, K., Rixius, B., Thumm, N., & van Reekum, R. (2002). *Study on the interaction between standardisation and intellectual property rights.* Final Report for DG Research of the European Commission (EC Contract No G6MA-CT-2000-02001). Karlsruhe: ISI.

Blind, K., Bierhals, R., Thumm, N., Hossain, K., Sillwood, J., Iverser, E., et al. (2002). *Study on the interaction between standardisation and intellectual property rights* (EC Contract No G6MA-CT-2000-02001, 2002).

Blind, K., Edler, J., Nack, R., & Strauß, J. (2001). *Micro- and macroeconomic implications of the patentability of software innovations. Intellectual property rights in information technologies between competition and innovation* (Study on Behalf of German Federal Ministry of Economics and Technology).

Blonder, G. E. (2005). *Graphical password, US Patent 5559961.* Murray Hill, NJ: Lucent Technologies Inc.

Boeder, P. (2005). Habermas' heritage: The future of the public sphere in the network society. *First Monday, 10*(9). Retrieved October 13, 2006, from http://firstmonday.org/issues/issue10_9/boeder/index.html

Bollier, D. (2004). Why we must talk about the information commons. *Law Library Journal, 96*(2), 267-282.

Boney, L., Tewfik, A. H., & Hamdy, K. N. (1996). Digital watermarks for audio signals. *IEEE Proceedings of the*

International Conference on Multimedia Computing and Systems, 473-480.

Borg, A. (2001). *Avoiding blocking system calls in a user-level thread scheduler for shared memory multiprocessors.* Dissertation of Univ. Malta, June 2001.

Borgman, C.L., (1997). Multimedia, multi cultural and multi lingual digital libraries. *D-Lib Magazine*, June [Online] http://www.dlib.org/dlib/june97/06borgman.html.

Boyer, J. (2001). *Canonical XML.* W3C Recommendation Version 1.0, W3C.

Boyle, J. (2001). Comment & analysis: Whigs and hackers in cyberspace: Copyright regulations before the European Parliament should be treated as skeptically as they were by the Victorians. *Financial Times*, pp. 21.

Boyle, J. (2004). A politics of intellectual property: Environmentalism for the Net. In R.A. Spinello & H.T. Tavani (Eds.), *Readings in CyberEthics (2nd ed.)*, pp. 273-293. Sudbury, MA: Jones and Bartlett Publishers.

Boynton, R. S. (2004). The tyranny of copyright? *The New York Times, January 24, 2004.* Retrieved October 8, 2006, from http://www.nytimes.com/2004/01/25/magazine/25COPYRIGHT.html?ei=5007&en=9eb265b1f26e8b14&ex=1390366800&partner=USERLAND&pagewanted=all&position=

Brandenburg, K., & Stoll, G. (1992). *The ISO/MPEG-audio codec: A generic standard for coding of high quality digital audio.* 92nd AES-Convention, preprint 3336.

Brassil, J., & O'Gorman, L. (1996). Watermarking document images with bounding box expansion. *Proceedings of the First International Information Hiding Workshop*, 1174, 227-235.

Brassil, J., Low, S., Maxemchuk, N. F., & O'Gorman, L. (1994). Electric marking and identification techniques to discourage document copying. *Proceedings of IEEE INFOCOM'94, 3,* 1278-1287.

Braudaway, G., & Mintzer, F. (2000). Automatic recovery of invisible image watermarks from geometrically distorted images. *Journal of Electronic Imaging, 9*(4), 477.

Braun, N. (2003). The interface between the protection of technological measures and the exercise of exceptions to copyright and related rights: comparing the situation in the United States and in the European community. *EIPR, 25*(11), 496.

Breeding, M., (2000). NetLibrary, Innovative interfaces to add to e-books to library collections. *Information Today, 17*(3), 1-3.

Brin, S., & Page, L. (1998). The anatomy of large-scale hypertextual Web search engine. In *Proceedings of the Seventh International World Wide Web Conference* (pp. 107-117).

Brinson, D., & Radcliffe, F. M. (1996). *Multimedia: Law and business handbook: A practical guide for developers and publishers.* Ladera Press.

British Government. (1998). *Data Protection Law.* Retrieved December 18, 2006, from http://www.opsi.gov.uk/acts/acts1998/19980029.htm

Brock, F. (1996). Diritti d'autore. Opera collettiva. Autorizzazione alla riproduzione di articolo di rivista. Potere del direttore della rivista di rappresentare l'editore. *Rivista di diritto industriale, 3,* 227.

Broomhead, D., & Lowe, D. (1988). Multivariable functional interpolation and adaptive networks. *Complex Systems, 2,* 321-355.

Burk, D. L. (1998). Proprietary rights in hypertext linkages. *Journal of Information Law and Technology*, (2).

Burkert, H. (1997). Privacy-enhancing technologies: Typology, critique, vision. In P. E. Agre & M. Rotenberg, (Eds.), *Technology and privacy: The new landscape* (pp. 125-142). Cambridge, MA: MIT Press.

Burr, W. E. (n.d.). *Data encryption standard.* In NIST's anthology, A century of excellence in measurements, standards, and technology: A chronicle of selected NBS/NIST Publications, 1901-2000. Retrieved from http://nvl.nist.gov/pub/nistpubs/sp958-lide/250-253.pdf.

Butler, K. (2000). Databases are latest battleground in the intellectual property debate. *Investor's Business Daily,* pp. 28.

Calder, A., & Watkins, S. (2002). *IT Governance: Data Security and BS 7799 / ISO 17799*. Kogan Page Ltd.

Calderone, L.L., & Custer, T.L. (2005, November). *Prosecution laches as a defense in patent cases*. Flaster Greenberg Attorneys at Law. Retrieved August 29, 2006, from http://www.flastergreenberg.com/pdf/PatentArtic_prf3.pdf

Campbell, F. W., & Kulikowski, J. J. (1966). Orientation selectivity of the human visual system. *Journal of Physiology, 187*, 437- 445.

Campbell, J. P. (1997). Speaker recognition: A tutorial. *Proceedings IEEE, 85*(9), 1437-1462.

Canada Government. (2000). *Personal Information Protection and Electronic Documents Act*. Retrieved December 18, 2006, from http://laws.justice.gc.ca/en/P-8.6/text.html

Caplan, P. (2003). *Patents and open standards* (White paper prepared for the National Information Standards Organization).

Carr, L., Hall, W., & De Roure, D. (1999). The evolution of hypertext link services. *ACM Computing Surveys, 31*(4).

Carver B. (2005). Share and share alike: Understanding and enforcing open source and free software licenses.*20 Berkley Technology Law Journal, 443*.

Castells, M. (2003). *The power of identity*. Malden, MA: Blackwell Publishing.

Catledge, L.D. & Pitkow, J.E., (1995). Characterizing browsing strategies in the World-Wide Web. *Proceedings of the 3rd International World Wide Web Conference, Volume 28 of Computer Networks and ISDN Systems,* April 10-14, Darmstadt, Germany. [Online] http://www.igd.fhg.de/archive/1995_www95/proceedings/papers/80/userpatterns/UserPatterns.Paper4.formatted.html.

C-C code. (2006). Retrieved from http://www.codecom.jp/

CCITT. (1988). *Recommendation X:509: The Directory—Authentication Framework*.

Cerf, V. G. (2005). Spam, spim, and spit. *Communications of the ACM, 48*(4), 39-43.

Cha, S. -C., & Joung, Y. -J. (2002). Online personal data licensing. In *Proceedings of the Third International Conference on Law and Technology (LawTech 2002)* (pp. 28-33).

Cha, S. -C., Joung, Y. -J., & Lue, Y. -E. (2003). Building universal profile systems over a peer-to-peer network. In *Proceedings of the Third IEEE Workshop on Internet Applications (WIAPP 2003)* (pp.142-151).

Chalton, S. (1997). The effect of the E.C. database directive on United Kingdom copyright law in relation to databases: A comparison of features. *EIPR, 6*, 278.

Chang, C. Y., & Su, S. J. (2005). Apply the counterpropagation neural network to digital image copyright authentication. *2005 9th International Workshop on Cellular Neural Networks and Their Applications IEEE,* 110-113.

Chang, Y.-F., & Chang, C.-C. (2004). A secure and efficient strong-password authentication protocol. *ACM SIGOPS Operating Systems Review, 38*(3), 79 - 90.

Chaum, D. (1982). Blind signatures for untraceable payments. In R. L., Rivest, A., Sherman, & Chaum, D. (Eds.), *Proceedings of CRYPTO'82* (pp. 199-203). New York: Plenum Press.

Chellappa, R., Wilson, C. L., & Sirohey, S. (1995). Human and machine recognition of faces: A survey. *Proceedings IEEE, 83*, 705-740.

Chen, B., & Wornell, G. W. (1999). Dither modulation: A new approach to digital watermarking and information embedding. *Proceedings of the SPIE – Security and watermarking of multimedia contents, 3657*, 342-353.

Cheng, H., & Li, X. (2000). Partial encryption of compressed images and videos. *IEEE Transactions on Signal Processing, 48*, 2439-2451.

Chervenak, A., Foster, I., Kesselman, C., Salisbury C., & Tueck, S.(2001). The data Grid: Towards an architecture for the distributed management and analysis of large scientific datasets, *Journal of Network and Computer Applications, 23*, 187-200.

Chesbrough, H. (2003). *Open innovation*. Harvard Business School Press.

Chiao, B., Lerner, J., & Tirole, J. (2005). *The rules of standard-setting organizations: An empirical analysis.* Unpublished Manuscript, Harvard Business School.

Chimenti, L. (2001). I data bases nella direttiva 9/96 e nel d.lgs. 6 maggio 1999, n. 169, *Il diritto dell'informazione e dell'informatica, 1*, 199-211.

Chokhani, S. (1994). Toward a national public key infrastructure. *IEEE Communications Magazine, 32*(9), 70-74.

Chu, W. W., Hsu, C. C., C'ardenas, A. F., & Taira, R. K. (1998). A knowledge-based image retrieval with spatial and temporal constructs. *IEEE Transactions on Knowledge and Data Engineering, 10*(6), 872-888.

Clark, D. (2002, October). Do Web standards and patents mix? *Computer*, pp. 19-22.

Clark, E. (2001). A reason to love spam. *Network Magazine, 16*(20), 1.

Clark, R. (2002, July 19). *Concerning recent patent claims.* Retrieved August 29, 2006, from http://www.jpeg.org/newsrel1.html

Cohen, J. H. (1991). Hybrids on the borderline between copyright and industrial property law. *Intellectual Property Journal, 2*(4), 190.

Cohen, W.M., Nelson, R.R., & Walsh, J.P. (2000, February). *Protecting their intellectual assets: Appropriability conditions and why U.S. manufacturing firms patent (or not)* (NBER Working Paper Series).

Cole, E. (2003). *Hiding in plain sight: Steganography and the art of covert communication.* Indianapolis, IN: Wiley Publishing, Inc.

Collie, I. (1994). Multimedia and moral rights. *Arts and Entertainment Law Review, 6*, 194.

Color code.(2006). Retrieved from http://www.colorzip.co.jp/ja/

Colston, C. (2002). Challenges to information retrieval—A global solution? *Internationl Journal of Law and Information Technology, 10*(3), 294.

Comes, S., & Macq, B. (1990, October). Human visual quality criterion. *Proceedings of SPIE: Vol. 1360. Visual Communications and Image Processing* (pp. 2-13). Lausanne, CH.

Common Criteria. (1999). *Common Criteria for Information Technology Security* Evaluation. Common Criteria Project Sponsoring Organisations. Version 2.1, adopted by ISO/IEC as ISO/IEC International Standard (IS) 15408 1-3.

Compaq Computer Corporation, (2001). *The MilliCent microcommerce network* [Online] http://www.millicent.com/home.html.

ComputerUser. (2006). Thread. *ComputerUser high-tech dictionary.* Retrieved December 30, 2006, from http://www.computeruser.com/resources/dictionary/definition.html?lookup=8392

ContentGuard Holdings, Inc. (2002). *XrML 2.1 technical overview.* Retrieved December 18, 2006, from http://xml.coverpages.org/XrMLTechnicalOverview21-DRAFT.pdf

Correa, C. M. (2002). Fair use in the digital era, *IIC, 4*, 535.

Court of Justice of the European Communites. (2004). *Press Release n° 46/04/EN*, p. 3.

Cox, I. J., Kilian, J., Leightont, T., & Shamoon, T. (1997). Secure spread spectrum watermarking for images, audio and video. *IEEE Transactions on Image Processing*, 6(2), 1673-1687.

Cox, I. J., Miller, M. L., & Muttoo, S. K. (2002). Digital watermarking. Morgan Kaufmann Pub.

Cox, I., & Miller, M.L. (1997, February). A review of watermarking and the importance of perceptual modeling. *Proceedings of SPIE: Vol. 3016. Human Vision and Electronic Imaging II* (pp. 92-99). Bellingham, WA.

Cranor, L., Langheinrich, M., & Marchiori, M. (2002a). *A P3P preference exchange language 1.0 (APPEL1.0).* Working draft, World Wide Web Consortium.

Cranor, L., Langheinrich, M., Marchiori, M., Presler-Marshall, M., & Reagle, J. (2002b). *The platform for privacy preferences 1.0 (P3P 1.0) specification.* Recommendations, World Wide Web Consortium. P3P 1.1. Retrieved from http://www.w3c.org/TR/P3P11/ in Nov. 2006

Craver, S., & Katzenbeisser, S. (2001). Copyright protection protocols based on asymmetric watermarking: The ticket concept. *Communications and Multimedia Security Issues of the New Century.* Kluwer Academic Publishers.

Craver, S., Memon, N., Yeo, B.-L., & Yeung, M. (1996). Can invisible watermarks resolve rightful ownerships? *IBM Research Technical Report RC 20509 IBM CyberJournal.*

Craver, S., Memon, N., Yeo, B.-L., & Yeung, M. (1997). Resolving rightful ownerships with invisible watermarking techniques: Limitations, attacks and implications. *IBM Research Technical Report RC 20755 IBM CyberJournal.*

Crews, K. D. (1998). Harmonization and the goals of copyright: Property rights or cultural progress? *Indiana Journal of Global Legal Studies, 6*, 117.

Croft, W.B. (1995). What do people want from information retrieval? (The top 10 research issues for companies that use and sell IR systems). *D-Lib Magazine,* November. [Online] http://www.dlib.org/dlib/november95/11croft.html.

Cunningham, A. (2005). Telecommunications, intellectual property, and standards. In I. Walden, & J. Angel (Eds.), *Telecommunications law and regulation.* Oxford.

Cvejic, N., Keskinarkaus, A., & Seppanen, T., (2001). Audio watermarking using m-sequences and temporal masking. *IEEE Workshops on Applications of Signal Processing to Audio and Acoustics,* 227-230.

Dachselt, F., & Wolfgang, S. (2001). Chaos and cryptography. *IEEE Trans. Circuits Syst. I, 48*(12), 1498-1509.

Dailey Paulson, L. (2005). Search technology goes mobile. *IEEE Computer,* August.

Damera-Venkata, N., Kite, T.D., Geisler, W.S., Evans, B.L., & Bovik, A.C. (2000, April). Image quality assessment based on a degradation model. *IEEE Transactions on Image Processing, 9*(4), 636-650.

Daugman, J. G. (1994). United States Patent No. 5,291,560. *Biometric Personal Identification System Based on Iris Analysis.* Washington DC: U.S. Government Printing Office.

Davidson, M. J. (2003). *The legal protection of database.* UK: Cambridge.

Davis, H. C., Hall, W., Heath, I., Hill, G.., & Wilkins, R. (1992). Towards an integrated information environment with open hypermedia systems. In *Proceedings of ECHT'92,* (Milan, Italy, 1992) (pp. 181-190).

Davis, H. C., Knight, S., & Hall, W. (1994). Light hypermedia link services: A study of third party application integration. In *Proceedings of ECHT'94,* (Edinburgh, UK, 1994) (pp. 41-50).

Davis, K. J., & Najarian, K. Maximizing strength of digital watermarks using neural networks. (2001). *IEEE Proceedings of International Joint Conference on Neural Neworks, 4,* 2893-2898.

Delaigle, J. F., De Vleeschouwer, C., & Macq, B. (1998). Watermarking algorithm based on a human visual model. *Signal Processing, 66,* 319-335.

Delaigle, J. F., Devleeschouwer, C., Macq, B., & Langendijk, L. (2002). Human visual system features enabling watermarking. *Proceedings of Multimedia and Expo,* ICME02, 489-492.

Delaigle, J.F., De Vleeschouwer, C., & Macq, B. (1998, May). Watermarking algorithm based on a human visual model. *Signal Processing, 66*(3), 319-336.

Delaney, K. (2003). KaZaA founder peddles software to speed file sharing. *The Wall Street Journal,* (September 8), B1.

Derclaye E. (2002). What is a database? A critical analysis of the definition of a database in the European Database Directive and suggestions for an international definition. *The Journal of World Intellectual Property, 5*(6), 981-1011.

Derclaye, E. (2000). Software copyright protection: Can Europe learn from American case law. *EIPR, 22*(1), 7.

Derrida, J. (1981). *Positions.* Trans. A. Bass. Chicago, IL: University of Chicago Press.

Dhamija, R. (2000). *Hash visualization in user authentication.* Computer Human Interaction Conference.

Dhamija, R., & Perrig, A. (2000). Déjà vu: A user study using images for authentication. In *Proceedings of the 9th Usenix Security Symposium.*

Di Cocco, C. (2005). *L'opera multimediale.* Italy: Giappichelli.

Diamond v. Diehr (1981). 450 U.S. 175.

Digeser, E. D. (2003). Citizenship and the roman res publica: Cicero and a Christian corollary. *Critical Review of International Social and Political Philosophy, 6* (1), 5-21.

Digital Library Federation (2001). [Online] http://www.clir.org/diglib/dlfhomepage.htm.

Digital Millennium Copyright Act (DMCA), (1998) U.S.C., § 103, Title 17, § 1201.

Dix, A., Rodden, T., Davies, N., Trevor, J., Friday, A., & Palfreyman, K. (2000). Exploiting space and location as a design framework for interactive mobile systems. *ACM Transactions on Computer-Human Interaction, 7*(3), 285-321.

DLA. (2004). *European intellectual property survey.*

DNA Data Bank of Japan. *DDBJ sequence search by accession number.* Retrieved from http://getentry.ddbj.nig.ac.jp/getstart-e.html

DNA Data Bank of Japan. *Search and Analysis.* Retrieved from http://www.ddbj.nig.ac.jp/E-mail/homology.html

Dogan, S. (2001). Is Napster a VCR? The implications of Sony for Napster and other Internet technologies. *Hastings Law Journal,* 52, 939.

Dommering, J., & Hugenholtz, A. (1991). *An introduction to information law. Work of fact at the crossroads of freedom and protection, in copyright, freedom of expression and information law.* Boston, MA: The Hague.

Douglas, J. (1996). The challenge of multimedia: Reform the Copyright Act? *Computers and Law, 31,* 47.

Dphamiji, R., & Perring, A. (2000). *Déjà vu: A user study using image for authentication.* 9th Usenix Security Symposium.

Drahos, P. (1996). *A philosophy of intellectual property.* Aldershot, UK: Dartmouth Publishing.

Driscoll, D. (1994). Fingerprint ID systems. *Advanced Imaging, 9*(20).

Duel-Hallen, A., Holtzman, J., & Zvonar, Z. (1995). Advantages of CDMA and spread spectrum techniques over FDMA and TDMA in cellular mobile radio applications. *IEEE Personal Communications Magazine*

Duncan, M. V., Akhtari, M. S. , & Bradford, P. G. (2004). Visual security for wireless handheld devices. *The Journal of Science & Health at the University of Alabama, 2.* Retrieved from http://www.bama.ua.edu/~joshua/archive/may04/Duncan%20et%20al.pdf

Dy, J. G., Brodley, C. E., Kak, A., Shyu, C.-R., & Broderick, L. S. (1999). The customized queries approach to CBIR. In *Proceedings of SPIE Storage and Retrieval for Image and Video Databases VII* 3656 (pp. 22-32).

Easterbrook, F. (1990). Intellectual property is still property. *Harvard Journal of Law and Public Policy,* 3, 110.

Echizen, I., Yoshiura, H., Arai, T., Himura, H., & Takeuchi, T. (1999). General quality maintenance module for motion picture watermarking. *IEEE Transaction on Consumer Electronics, 45,* 1150-1158.

Eckert, M.P., & Bradley, A.P. (1998). Perceptual quality metrics applied to still image compression. *Signal Processing, 70,* 177-200.

Eckhorn, R., Reitboeck, H. J., Arndt, M., & Dicke, P. (1990). Feature linking via synchronization among distributed assemblies: simulations of results from Cat Visual Cortex. *Neural Computing, 2,* 293-307.

Eggers, J. J. Su, J. K., & Girod, B. (2000). A blind watermarking scheme based on structured codebooks. *Secure Images and Image Authentication-IEE Colloquium,* 4/1-4/6.

Eggers, J. J., Su, J. K. & Girod, B. (2000). Asymmetric watermarking schemes. *Tagungsband des GI Workshops Sicherheit in Mediendaten, Berlin, Germany.*

Eldred v. Ashcroft (2003). 123 U.S. 769.

Elman, J. (1994). Finding structure in time. *Cognitive Science, 14,* 179-211.

Eolas Technologies Incorporated and the Regents of the University of California v. Microsoft Corporation, Case Nr. 04-1234, Federal Circuit, 2 March 2005.

EPIC & Junkbuster (2000). *Pretty poor privacy: An assessment of P3P and Internet privacy.* Retrieved December 18, 2006, from http://www.epic.org/reports/prettypoorprivacy.html

Epshtein, D. & Krawczyk, H. (2002). Image-based authentication of public keys and applications to SSH. Project report, Technion – Dept. of Electrical Engineering, Technion .

ETSI. (2005). *IPR policy.*

European Commission. (1998). *Draft opinion of the working party on the protection of individuals with regard to the processing of personal data.* Retrieved December 18, 2006, from http://www.epic.org/privacy/internet/ec-p3p.html

European Patent Office. (2001). *Guidelines for examination in the European Patent Office.*

European Union. (1995). Directive 95/46/EC on the protection of individuals with regard to the processing of personal data and on the free movement of such data. *Official Journal of the European Communities,* p. 31.

Farrell, J. (1996). *Choosing the rules for formal standardization.* UC Berkeley.

Farrell, J., & Saloner, G. (1985). Standardization, compatibility, and innovation. *RAND Journal of Economics, 16,* 70-83.

Faundez-Zanuy, M. (2005). Biometric verification of humans by means of hand geometry. In *Proceedings of the 39th International Carnahan Conference on Security Technology CCST 2005,* 61-67.

Fausett L. (1994). *Fundamentals of neural networks.* Arichtectures, algorithms, and applications. Englewood Cliffs, NJ: Prentice-Hall.

Federal Trade Commission v. Dell Computer Corp., FTC File No. 931 0097, 2 November 1995.

Feldman, R.P., & Rees, M.R. (2000, July). The effect of industry standard setting on patent licensing and enforcement. *IEEE Communications Magazine,* pp. 112-116.

Ferguson, K. (1999). 20/20 foresight. Retrieved August 29, 2006, from http://www.forbes.com/1999/04/19/feat.html

Ferwerda, J. A., Pattanaik, S. N., Shirley, P. & Greenberg, D. P. (1997). *Computer Graphics, 31,* 143-152.

Fialkoff, F., (1998). Linking to online booksellers. *Library Journal, 123*(11), 68.

Fiat, A., & Shamir, A. (1986). How to prove yourself: Practical solutions to identification and signature problems. In *Proceedings of CRYPTO'86* (pp. 186-194).

Fisher, W. (1998). *Theories of intellectual property.* Available at: http://cyber.law.harvard.edu/ipcoop/98fish.html.

Flickner, M., Sawhney, H., Niblack, W., Ashley, J., Huang, Q., Dom, B., Gorkani, M., Hafner, J., Lee, D., Petkovic, D., Steele, D., & Yanker, P. (1995). Query by image and video content: The QBIC system. *IEEE Computer, 28*(9), 23-32.

Foley, J.M., & Legge, G.E. (1981). Contrast detection and near-threshold discrimination. *Vision Research, 21,* 1041-1053.

Fong, W.W., (1997). Library information and technology in *Southeast Asia. Information Technology and Libraries, 16*(1), 20-27.

Forgent Networks. (2006). *Intellectual property, '672 patent cases.* Retrieved August 29, 2006, from http://www.forgent.com/ip/672cases.shtml

Foster, I. (2005). License to Grid. *The Globus Consortium Journal.*

Foster, I., Kesselman, C., & Tuecke, S. (2001). The anatomy of the Grid: Enabling scalable virtual organizations. *International Journal on Supercomputer Applications, 15*(3).

Foster, I., Kesselman, C., Tsudik, G., & Tuecke, S. (1998). A security architecture for computational Grids. In *Proceedings of the 5th ACM Conference on Computer and Communications Security Conference* (pp. 83-92).

Foucualt, M. (1969). Qu'est-ce qu'un Autuer? In *Textual Strategies*. Trans. J.V. Harari. Ithaca, NY: Cornell University Press.

Fox, B. & LaMacchia, B.A. (2003). Encouraging recognition of fair uses in DRM systems. *Communications of the ACM, 46*(4), 61-63.

Frank, S.J. (2002, March). Can you patent an industry standard? *IEEE Spectrum*.

Freeman, R. B., & Rogers, J. (2002). Open source unionism: Beyond exclusive collective bargaining. *Working USA: Journal of Labor and Society, 5*, 3-4.

Freier, A. O., Karlton, P., & Kocher, P. C. (1996). *The SSL protocol version 3.0. Specification draft, Internet Engineering Task Force (IETF)*. Internet draft draft-freier-ssl-version3-02.txt.

Freire, J., Kumar, B., & Lieuwen, D. (2001). WebViews: Accessing personalized Web content and services. In *Proceedings of WWW2001*, (Hong Kong, China, 2001) (pp.576-586).

Fridrich, J. (1997). *Secure image ciphering based on chaos* (final Technical Report RL-TR-97-155). Rome, NY: Rome Laboratory.

FTC. (2003). *To promote innovation: The proper balance of competition and patent law and policy*.

Fu, M. S., & Au, A. C. (2004). Joint visual cryptography and watermarking. In *Proceedings of the International Conference on Multimedia and Expro (ICME2004)*, (pp. 975-978).

Fujima, J., Lunzer, A., Hornbæk, K., & Tanaka, Y. (2004). Clip, connect, clone: Combining application elements to build custom interfaces for information access. In *Proceedings of the 17th Annual ACM Symposium on User Interface Software and Technology*, (Santa Fe, NM, USA, October 24-27, 2004) (pp.175-184).

Fukuhara, T., Ando, K., Watanabe, O., & Kiya, H. (2002). *Partial-scrambling of JPEG2000 images for security applications*. ISO/IEC JTC 1/SC29/WG1, N2430.

Fukushima, K. (1975). "Cognitron: A self-organizing multilayered neural network. *Biological Cybernetics, 20*, 121–136.

Furht, B. (1999). *Handbook of Internet and multimedia systems and applications*. CRC Press.

Furht, B., & Kirovski, F. (2004). *Multimedia security handbook*. CRC Press.

Furman, J., & Stern, S. (2004). *Climbing atop the shoulders of giants: The impact of institutions on cumulative research*. Unpublished Manuscript, Northwestern University.

Gabber, E., Gibbons, P. B., Kristol, D. M., Matias, Y., & Mayer, A. (1999). Consistent, yet anonymous, Web access with LPWA. *Communications of the ACM, 42*(2), 42-47.

Gandal, N., Gantman, N., & Genesove, D. (2005). Intellectual property and standardization committee participation in the U.S. modem industry. In S. Greenstein, & V. Stango (Eds.), *Standards and public policy*. Cambridge: Cambridge University Press.

Gang, L., Akansu, A. N., Ramkumar, M., & Xie, X. (2001). Online music protection and MP3 compression. In *Proceedings of International Symposium on Intelligent Multimedia, Video and Speech Processing*, Hong Kong, China, May, 13-16.

Garrett, J., (1993). Digital libraries: The grand challenges. [Online] http://www.ifla.org/documents/libraries/net/garrett.txt.

German Government. (2001). *Federal Data Protection Act*. Retrieved December 18, 2006, from http://www.datenschutz-berlin.de/recht/de/bdsg/bdsg01_eng.htm

Geroski, P. (1995). Markets for technology: Knowledge, innovation and appropriability. In P. Stoneman (Ed.), *Handbook of the economics of innovation and technological change*. Blackwell.

Gershwin v. Columbia Artists Management (1971). 443 F. 2d 1150 [2d Cir.].

Ghidini, G., & Falce, V. (2001). Intellectual property on communications standards: Balancing innovation and competition through the essential facilities doctrine, *Diritto d'Autore, 3*, 315.

Giannantonio, E. (1997). *Manuale di diritto dell'informatica.* Italy: Giuffré.

Giburd, B, Schuster, A., & Wolff, R. (2004). *K-TTP: A new privacy model for large scale distributed environments.* Knowledge Discovery and Data Mining, KDD 2004, ACM, Seattle, USA.

Gilhousen, K., Jacobs, I., Padovani, R., Viterbi, A., Weaver, L., & Wheatley, C. (1995). On the capacity of a cellular CDMA system. *IEEE Trans. on Vehicular Technology Multiuser detection for CDMA systems.*

Ginesu, G., Giusto, D. D., & Onali, T. (2005). Application-scalable image-based authentication framework with JPEG2000. *IEEE International Workshop on Multimedia Signal Processing MMSP05.*

Ginesu, G., Giusto, D. D., & Onali, T. (2006). *Mutual image-based authentication framework with JPEG2000 in Wireless Environment.* EURASIP Journal on Wireless Communications and Networking.

Gish, H., & Schmidt, M. (1994). Text-independent speaker identification. *IEEE Signal Processing Magazine, 11*(4), 18-32.

Gledhill, D. (2001). William Hill t/akes racing database fight to OFT. *The Independent,* pp. 10.

Gleick, J. (2000). Patently absurd. *New York Times Magazine,* (March 12), 44.

Globus Toolkit Homepage. Retrieved from http://www.globus.org/toolkit/

Gohring, N. (2005a). Qualcomm files a second suit against Broadcom. *InfoWorld.* Retrieved August 29, 2006, from http://www.infoworld.com/article/05/10/21/HNqualcommsecondsuit_1.html

Gohring, N. (2005b). Qualcomm files patent infringement suit against Nokia. *InfoWorld.* Retrieved August 29, 2006, from http://www.infoworld.com/article/05/11/07/hnqualcommsuit_1.html

Goldberg, I., Wanger, D., & Brewer, E. A. (1997). Privacy-enhancing technologies for the Internet. In *Proceeding of 42nd IEEE spring COMPCON,* San Jose, CA, Feb 1997.

Golgher, P. B., Laender, A. H. F., da Silva, A. S., & Ribeiro-Neto, B. (2000). An example-based environment for wrapper generation. In *Proceedings of the 2nd International Workshop on The World Wide Web and Conceptual Modeling,* (Salt Lake City, USA, 2000) (pp. 152-164).

Gordon, W.J. (1992). Asymmetric market failure and prisoner's dilemma in intellectual property. *University of Dayton Law Review,* 17, 853.

Gordon, W.J. (1993). A property right in self-expression: Equality and individualism in the natural law of intellectual property. *Yale Law Journal,* 102, 1533.

Gordy, J. D., & Bruton, L. T. (2000). Performance evaluation of digital audio watermarking algorithms. In *Proceedings of the 43rd Midwest Symposium on Circuits and Systems.*

Gorman, R. A. (1992). The Feist case: Reflection on a path breaking copyright decision. *Rutgers Computer & Technology Law Journal,* 18, 731.

Gorman, R. A., & Ginsburg, J. C. (1993). *Copyright for the nineties: Cases and materials (4th ed.).* Contemporary Legal Education Series. Charlottesville, NC: The Michie Company.

Gottschalk v. Benson (1972). 409 U.S. 63.

GovTrack.us. 109th Congress, H.R. 2795: Patent Act of 2005. Retrieved August 29, 2006, from http://www.govtrack.us/congress/bill.xpd?bill=h109-2795

Goyal, V., Kumar, V., Singh, M., Abraham, A., & Sanyal, S. (2005). CompChall: Addressing password guessing attacks. *ITCC05, 1,* 739-744.

Graham, S.J.H., & Mowery, D.C. (2002, June 6-8). *Submarines in software? Continuations in U.S. software patenting in the 1980s and 1990s.* Paper presented at the DRUID Summer Conference on Industrial Dynamics of the New and Old Economy—Who is Embracing Whom?, Copenhagen/Elsinore.

Grandstrand, O. (1999). *The economics and management of intellectual property.* Cheltenham: Edward Elgar.

Granovetter, M. (1983). The strength of weak ties: A network theory revisited. *Sociological Theory, 1,* 201-233.

Granstrand, O. (1999). *The economics and management of intellectual property.* Edward Elgar Publishing.

Greenstein, S., & Stango, V. (Eds.). (2005). *Standards and public policy.* Cambridge: Cambridge Press.

Grieser, G., Jantke, K. P., Lange, S., & Thomas, B. A. (2000). Unifying approach to HTML wrapper representation and learning. In *Proceedings of Discovery Science 2000,* (Kyoto, Japan, 2000) (pp. 50-64).

Grindley, P. (2002). *Standards, strategy and policy.* Oxford.

Grønbæk, K., Bouvin, N. O., & Sloth, L. (1997). Designing Dexter-based hypermedia services for the World Wide Web. In *Proceedings of Hypertext '97* (Southampton, UK, 1997) (pp.146-156).

Grosbois, R., Gerbelot, P., & Ebrahimi, T. (2001). Authentication and access control in the JPEG 2000 compressed domain. In *Proceedings of SPIE 46th Annual Meeting, Applications of Digital Image Processing XXIV, 4472,* 95-104. San Diego, July 29th-August 3rd, 2001.

Grossman, G. A. (2005). From Sony to Grokster, The failure of the copyright doctrines of contributory infringement and vicarious liability to resolve the war between content and destructive technologies. *Buffalo Law Review, 141.*

Grosso, A. (2000). The promise and the problems of the No Electronic Theft Act. *Communications of the ACM, 43*(2), 23-26.

Gruhl, D., Lu, A., & Bender, W. (1996). Echo hiding. *Proceedings of the First International Information Hiding Workshop, 1174,* 295-316.

Grutzmacher, M. (1999). *Urheber, leistungs-und sui-generis-shutz von datenbanken.* Germany: Baden-Baden.

Hachez, G. ,& Quisquater, J. J. (2002). Which directions for asymmetric watermarking? In *Proceedings of the XI European Signal Processing Conference, EUSIPCO 2002.*

Hahn, R.W. (2001, March). Competition policy and the new economy. *Milken Institute Review,* 34-41.

Halbert, D. (1999). *Intellectual property in the information age.* Westport, CT: Quorum Books.

Hall, B., Jaffe, A. & Trajtenberg, M. (2002). The NBER Patent Citations Data File: Lessons, Insights, and Methodological Tools. In A. Jaffe & M. Trajtenberg (Eds.), *Patents, citations and innovations: A window on the knowledge economy.* Cambridge: MIT Press, 2002.

Hall, B., Jaffe, A., & Trajtenberg, M. (2002). The NBER patent citations data file: Lessons, insights, and methodological tools. In A. Jaffe, & M. Trajtenberg (Eds.), *Patents, citations and innovations: A window on the knowledge economy.* Cambridge: MIT Press.

Hall, B., Jaffe, A., & Trajtenberg, M. (2005) Market value and patent citations. *RAND Journal of Economics, 36*(1), 26-38.

Hall, B., Mairesse, J., & Turner, L. (2005). *Identifying age, cohort and period effects in scientific research productivity.* Unpublished Manuscript, University of California at Berkeley.

Hall, B.H., & Ziedonis, R.H. (2001). The patent paradox revisited: An empirical analysis of patenting in the U.S. semiconductor industry, 1979-1995. *Rand Journal of Economics, 32,* 101-128.

Hall, R. J. (1998). How to avoid unwanted email. *Communications of the ACM, 41*(3), 88-95.

Haller, N. M. (1994). The S/KEY (TM) one-time password system. In *Proceedings of Internet Society Symposium on Network and Distributed System Security,* 151-158.

Hand, L. (1930). Opinion in *Nichols v. Universal Pictures* 45 F. 2d 119, [2nd Cir.].

Hand, L. (1936). Opinion in *Sheldon v. Metro-Goldwyn Pictures Corp.* 81 F. 2d 49, [2nd Cir.].

Hanson, W. (1999). *Principles of Internet marketing.* South-Western College Publishing.

Harabi, N. (1995). Appropriability of technical innovations: An empirical analysis. *Research Policy, 24,* 981-992.

Hardin, G. (1968). The tragedy of the commons. *Science, 62,* 1243-1248.

Harmer, T. J., Donachy, P., Perrott, R. H., Chambers, C., Craig, S., Mallon, B., & Wrigh, C. (2003). GridCast—Using the Grid in Broadcast Infrastructures. In *Proceedings of UK e-Science All Hands Meeting* (AHM03).

Harper & Row Publishers, Inc. v. Nation Enterprises. (1985). 471 U.S. 539, 85 L. Ed. 2d 588.

Harris, L.E., (2000). Libraries and e-commerce: Improving information services and beyond. *Information Outlook, 4*(3), 24-30.

Hashemi, J., & Fatemizadeh, E. (2005). Biometric identification through hand geometry. *International Conference on Computer as a Tool EUROCON 2005, 2*, 1011-1014.

Hayden, J. F. (1991). Copyright protection of computer databases after Feist. *Harward Journal of Law & Technology, 5*, 215.

Hayes, B. S. (2000). Integrating moral rights into U.S. law and the problem of the Works for Hire doctrine. *Ohio State Law Journal, 61*, 1013.

Hegel, G.W. F. (1944). *The phenomenology of mind.* Trans. J. Baille. New York: MacMillan & Co. (Original work published 1806).

Hegel, G.W.F. (1948). *Early theological writings.* Trans. T. Knox. Chicago, IL: University of Chicago Press. (Original work published 1800).

Hegel, G.W.F. (1952). *Philosophy of right.* Trans. T. Knox. London: Oxford University Press. (Original work published 1821).

Heinze, W.F. (2002, May). Dead patents walking. *IEEE Spectrum*, 52-54.

Heller, M., & Eisenberg, R. (1998). Can patents deter innovation? The anticommons in biomedical research. *Science, 280*, 698-701.

Hemphill, T.A. (2005, January). Technology standards development, patent ambush, and US antitrust policy. *Technology in Society, 27*(1), 55-67.

Hensley, P., Metral, M., Shardanand, U., Converse, D., & Meyers, M. (1997). *Proposal for an open profiling standard.* Retrieved December 18, 2006, from http://www.w3.org/TR/NOTE-OPS-FrameWork.html

Herkiloglu, K., Sener, S., & Gunsel, B. (2004). Robust audio watermarking by adaptive psychoacoustic masking. In *Proceedings of 12th IEEE Conference on Signal Processing and Communications Applications*, 29-32.

Hettinger, E.C. (1989). Justifying intellectual property. *Philosophy and Public Affairs, 18*, 31-52.

Hicks, W. B. (1987). Copyright and computer database: Is traditional compilation law adequate? *Texas Law Review, 65*, 993.

Hjelm, B. (2000). Standards and intellectual property rights in the age of global communication: A review of the international standardization of third-generation mobile system.

Ho, C., & Hsu, W. (2005). *Image protection system and method* (US Patent: US2005114669).

Hong, F., Shi, L., & Luo, T. (2004). A semi-fragile watermarking scheme based on neural network. *IEEE Proceedings of the Third International Conference on Machine Learning and Cybernetics, 6*, 3536-3541.

Hong, J. I. (2005). Minimizing security risks in Ubicomp Systems. *IEEE Computer*, December.

Hopfield, J. J., & Tank, D. W. (1985). Neural computation of decisions in optimization problems. *Biological Cybernetics, 52*, 141-152.

Housley, R., Polk, W., Ford, W., & Solo, D.(2002). Internet X.509 public key infrastructure certificate and certificate revocation list (CRL) profile. *RFC 3280* (Proposed Standard).

Hu, J., Huang, J., Huang, D., & Shi, Y. Q. (2002). A DWT-based fragile watermarking tolerant of JPEG compression. *IWDW 2002* (pp.179-188).

Huang, J., & Shi, Y. Q. (2002). Adaptive image watermarking scheme based on visual masking. *Electronic Letters, 34*(8), 748-750.

Hughes, J. (1997). The philosophy of intellectual property. In A. Moore (Ed.), *Intellectual property*, (pp. 107-177). Lanham, MD: Rowman & Littlefield.

Hurley, N. J., & Silvestre, G.. C. M. (2002). Nth order audio watermarking. In E. J. Delp III, P. W. Wong (Eds.), *Security and Watermarking of Multimedia Contents IV Proceedings of SPIE, 4675*, 102-110.

IETF. (2005). Intellectual property rights in IETF technology.

In re Aimster Copyright Litigation, (2002). 252 F. Supp 2d 634 [N.D. Ill], aff'd No 01 C 8133 [7th Cir, 2003].

In re Bogese II, 303 F.3d 1362, 1367, Federal Circuit (2002).

In re Independent Service Organization's Antitrust Liability. (2000). 203 F. 3d 1322 [Fed. Cir.].

Informamedia.com. (2006, March 1). ETSI acts on unfair, unreasonable and discriminatory IPRs. *Informamedia. com.*

Initial Decision (2004). Docket No 9302, 23 February 2004.

Inohara, S., & Masuda, T. (1994). A framework for minimizing thread management overhead based on asynchronous cooperation between user and kernel schedulers. *TR94-02, University of Tokyo.*

International Biometric Group. (2006). *Biometrics market and industry report 2006-2010.* Retrieved from http://www.biometricgroup.com/reports/public/market_report.html

IPO. (n.d.). *21st Century Patent Coalition: "Submarine patents" ARE a significant problem.* Retrieved August 29, 2006, from http://www.ipo.org/contentmanagement/contentdisplay.cfm?contentid=7334

Isenberg, D. (2002). *The GigaLaw—Guide to Internet law.* Random House Trade Paperbacks.

ISO/IEC Joint Technical Committee 1 Subcommittee 29 Working Group 11. (1993). *Information technology-coding of moving pictures and associated audio for digital storage media at up to about 1.5 Mbit/s, Part 3:Audio.* ISO/IEC 11172-3.

Ito, K. (2003). *CHIP (Collaborating Host-Independent Pads).* Retrieved from http://km.meme.hokudai.ac.jp/people/itok/CHIP

Ito, K., & Tanaka, Y. (2002). Visual wrapping and composition of Web applications for their interoperations. In *CDROM of WWW2002*, (Honolulu, USA, 2002), Poster Tracks 64.

Ito, K., & Tanaka, Y. (2003a). Visual wrapping and functional linkage of Web applications. In *Proceedings of Workshop on Emerging Applications for Wireless and Mobile Access*, (Budapest, Hungary, 2003).

Ito, K., & Tanaka, Y. (2003b). A visual environment for dynamic Web application composition. In *Proceedings of 14th ACM Conference on Hypertext and Hypermedia* (pp. 184-193).

Ito, K., & Tanaka, Y. (2003c). Web application wrapping by demonstration. In *Proceedings of the 13th European—Japanese Conference on Information Modelling and Knowledge Bases*, (Kitakyushu, Japan, 2003).

Jacobs, P. (2005, December). Qualcomm defends patent licensing programme. *wirelessweb.* Retrieved August 29, 2006, from http://wireless.iop.org/articles/news/6/12/6/1

Jaffe, A., & Trajtenberg, M. (2002). *Patents, citations and innovations: A window on the knowledge economy.* Cambridge: MIT Press.

Jain, A. K., Bolle, R., & Pankanti, S. (1999). *BIOMETRICS: Personal identification in networked society.* Kluwer Academic Publishers.

Jansen, W., Gavrila, S., Korolev, V., Ayers, R., & Swanstrom, R. (2003). *Picture password: A visual login technique for mobile devices.* NIST IR 7030.

Jarach, G. (1979). Considerazioni sui rapporti tra autori e utilizzatori delle opere dell'ingegno, *Il diritto di autore, 2*(3), 587-598.

Jermyn, I., May, A., Monrose, F., Riter, M., & Rubin, A. (1999). The design and analysis of graphical passwords. In *Proceedings of 8th USENIX Security Symposium.*

Johnson, E. D. (1970). *History of libraries in the western world.* Metuchen, NJ: Scarecrow Press Inc.

Johnson, J. L. (1994). Pulse-coupled neural nets: Translation, rotation, scale, distortion and intensity signal invariances for images. *Applied Optics, 33*(26), 6239-6253.

Johnson, N. F. (2003). *Steganography*. Retrieved December 15, 2004, from http://www.jjtc.com/stegdoc/steg1995.html

Joung, Y.-J., Yen, C., Huang, C.-T., & Huang, Y.-J. (2005). On personal data license design and negotiation. In *Proceedings of the 29th International Computer Software and Applications Conference (COMPSAC 2005)* (pp.281-286). IEEE Computer Society.

Jung, P., Baier, P., & Steil, A. (1992). *IEEE Trans. on Vehicular Technology.*

Jungmittag, A., Blind, K., & Grupp, H. (1999). Innovation, standardization and the long-term production function: A co-integration approach for Germany, 1960-1996. *Zeitschrift für Wirtschafts und Sozialwissenschaften, 119*, 205-222.

Jupitermedia Corporation. (2003). *Steganography*. Retrieved Aug. 31, 2003, from http://www.webopedia.com/TERM/S/steganography.html

Kafeza, I., Kafeza, E., & Chiu, D. K. (2005). *Legal aspects of security in e-contracting with electronic agents*. In H. Sachar, P. Pohlmann, & N. Reimer, *ISSE Securing Electronic Business Processes: Highlights of the Information Security Solutions Europe 2005 Conference*, GWV-Vieweg.

Kahn, D. (1996). The history of steganography. *Lecture Notes in Computer Science, 1174*, 1-5. Information Hiding, Springer-Verlag.

Kanaskar, N, Topaloglu, & U., Bayrak, C, (2005). Globus security model for Grid environment. *ACM SIGSOFT Software Engineering Notes, 30*, 6.

Katzenbeisser, S, & Petitcolas, F. A. P. (2000). Information hiding techniques for steganography and digital watermarking. Artech House.

Kaufman, C., Perlman, R., & Speciner, M. (2002). *Network security: Private communication in a public world*. Prentice Hall.

Kazakeviciute, G., Januskevicius, E., Rosenbaum, R., & Schumann, H. (2005). Tamper-proof image watermarking, based on existing public key infrastructure. *INFORMATICA, 16*(1).

KDDI. (2006). *Security pass*. Retrieved from http://www.kddi.com/business/service/mobile/security_pass/

Kent, S. (1993). RFC 1422: *Privacy enhancement for Internet electronic mail: Part II: Certificate-based key management*. Retrieved December 18, 2006, from http://www.ietf.org/rfc/rfc1422.txt

Keshavarzian, A. & Salehi, J. A. (2002). Optical orthogonal code acquisition in fiber-optic CDMA systems via the simple serial-search method. *IEEE Transaction on Communications, 50*(3).

Kesler, J. C. (2005). Contractual and regulatory compliance challenges in Grid computing environments. In *Proceedings of the 2005 IEEE International Conference on Services Computing* (pp. 61-68).

Kessler, G. C. (2001). Steganography: Hiding data within data. Retrieved July 21, 2005, from http://www.garykessler.net/library/steganography.html

Kharrazi, M., Sencar, H.T., & Memon, N. (2004). *Image steganography: Concepts and practice*. Lecture Note Series. Institute for Mathematical Sciences, National University of Singapore.

Kieff, F.S. (2000). Property rights and property rules for commercializing inventions. *Minnesota Law Review, 85*, 697.

Kim, H. (2000). Stochastic model based audio watermark and whitening filter for improved detection. *IEEE International Conference on Acoustics, Speech, and Signal Processing, 4*, 1971-1974.

Kim, H. J. (2003). *Audio watermarking techniques*. Pacific Rim workshop on Digital Steganography.

Kim, H. J., & Yeo, I. (2003). Modified patchwork algorithm: A novel audio watermarking scheme. *Transactions on Speech and Audio Processing, 11*(4), 381-386.

Kim, H. O., Lee, B. K., & Lee, N. Y. (2001). *Wavelet-based audio watermarking techniques: Robustness and fast synchronization*. Research Report 01-11, Division of Applied Mathematics-Kaist.

Kim, T. Y., Kim, T., & Choi, H. (2003). Correlation-based asymmetric watermark detector. *International Conference on Information Technology: Coding and Computing (ITCC 2003.* (pp.564-568).

Kim, Y. C., Byeong, C., & Choi, C. (2002). Two-step detection algorithm in a HVS-based blind watermarking on still images. *Revised Papers of Digital Watermarking First International Workshop IWDW 2002, 2613,* 235-248.

Kipnis, J. (2000, July). Beating the system: Abuses of the standards adoption process. *IEEE Communications Magazine,* pp. 102-105.

Kirsch, E.D. (2000). International standards participation: Lessons from Townshend & Dell. *International Lawyers Network. The bullet"iln", 1*(2). Retrieved August 29, 2006, from http://www.ag-internet.com/push_news_one_two/internationalstandards.htm

Kistler, T., & Marais, H. (1998). WebL—A programming language for the Web. In Proceedings of WWW7, (Brisbane, Australia, 1998), *Computer Networks, 30*(1-7), 259-270.

Knight, H.J. (2001). *Patent strategy for researchers and research managers.* John Wiley & Sons.

Kogut, B., & Metiu, A. (2001). Open-source software development and distributed innovation. *Oxford Review of Economic Policy, 17,* 248-264.

Kohno, R., Meidan, R., & Milstein, L. (1995). Spread spectrum access methods for wireless communications. *IEEE Communication Magazine.*

Kohonen, T. (1982). Self-organized formation of topologically correct feature maps. *Biological Cybernetics,43,* 59-63.

Kohonen, T. (1995). *Self-organizing maps.* Springer-Verlag.

Korn, P., Sidiropoulos, N., Faloutsos, C., Siegel, E., & Protopapas, Z. (1998). Fast and effective retrieval of medical tumor shapes. *IEEE Transactions on Knowledge and Data Engineering, 10*(6), 889–904.

Kortum, S., & Lerner, J. (1999). What is behind the recent surge in patenting? *Research Policy, 28*(1), 1-22.

Krasner-Khait, B. (2001). Survivor: The history of the library. *History Magazine, (October/November).* Retrieved July 11, 2006, from http://www.history-magazine.com/libraries.html

Kratzman, V.A. (2005). *Technology transfer mid-term report next step recommendations.* FINPRO.

Krechmer, K. (2005, January). *Communications standards and patent rights: Conflict or coordination?* Paper presented at the Economics of the Software and Internet Industries Conference, Tolouse, France.

Kristol, D. M. (2001). HTTP cookies: Standards, privacy, and politics. *ACM Transactions on Internet Technology, 1*(2), 151-198.

Kun, M. S. (2004). *Password insecurity: Securing a system with multifactor authentication.* SANS2005.

Kundur, D., & Hatzinakos, D. (1997). A robust digital image watermarking method using wavelet-based fusion. In *Proceedings of the ICIP-97, 1,* 544-547.

Kundur, D., & Karthik, K. (2004). Video fingerprinting and encryption principles for digital rights management. *Proceedings of the IEEE, 92*(6), 918-932.

Kung, S. Y., Mak, M. W., & Lin, S. H. (2004). *Biometric authentication: A machine learning approach.* Prentice Hall.

Kunkelmann, T., & Reineman, R. (1997). A scalable security architecture for multimedia communication standards. In *Proceedings of the 4th IEEE International Conference on Multimedia Computing and Systems* (pp. 660-663). Thomas Kunkelmann. Darinstadt Univ. of Technology. IT0. D-64283 Darmstadt, Germany.

Kushmerick, N. (2000). Wrapper induction: Efficiency and expressiveness. *Artificial Intelligence, 118*(1-2), 15-68.

Kwon, K. R., Kwon, S. G., Nam, J. H, & Tewfik, A. H. (2002). Content adaptive watermark embedding in the multiwavelet transform using as tochastic image model. *IWDW200,* (pp.249-263).

Labsystems Oy v. Biohit Oy. HO S 94/1922. Finnish Court of Appeal.

Lai, K., & Baker, M. (1996). A performance comparison of UNIX operating systems on the Pentium. *Proceedings of the USENIX 1996 Annual Technical Conference.*

Lai, S. (1999). Digital copyright and watermarking, *EIPR, 21*(4), 171.

Lambrecht, C., & Verscheure, O. (1996). Perceptual quality measure using a spatio-temporal model of the human visual system. *Proceedings of the SPIE, 2668,* 450-461.

Laurent, A. M. S. (2004). *Understanding open source and free software licensing.* Cambridge: O'Reilly.

Leclerc, F., & Plamondon, R. (1994). Automatic signature verification: The state of the art - 1989-1993. *International Journal of Pattern Recognition and Artificial Intelligence, 8*(3), 643-660.

Lee, J., & Jung, S. (2001). A survey of watermarking techniques applied to multimedia. *Proceedings 2001 IEEE International Symposium on Industrial Electronics (ISIE2001), 1,* 272-277.

Legge, G. E. & Foley, J. M. (1980). Contrast masking in human vision. *Journal Optical Society, 70,* 1458-1470.

Legge, G.E., & Foley, J.M. (1980, December). Contrast masking in human vision. *Journal of Optical Society of America, 70*(12), 1458-1471.

Lemley, M. (1997). Romantic authorship and the rhetoric of property. *Texas Law Review, 75,* 873.

Lemley, M. (2002). Intellectual property rights and standard setting organizations. *California Law Review, 90,* 1889 -1981.

Lemley, M.A. (2002). *Intellectual property rights and standard setting organizations.* Contribution to the public hearing on competition and intellectual property law and policy in the knowledge-based economy in 2001 and 2002. Available online at: http://www.ftc.gov/opp/intellect/index.htm.

Lemley, M.A. (2002). *Intellectual property rights and standard setting organizations* (UC Berkeley Public Law and Legal Theory Research Paper Series, Research Paper No. 84).

Lemos, R. (2002, July 23). Finding patent truth in JPEG claims. *CNET News.com.* Retrieved August 29, 2006, from http://news.com.com/Finding+patent+truth+in+JPEG+claim/2100-1001_3-945686.html

Lessig, L. (1999). *Code and other laws of cyberspace.* New York: Basic Books.

Lessig, L. (2001). *The future of ideas.* New York: Random House.

Lessig, L. (2004). *Free culture: The nature and future of creativity.* New York: Penguin Books.

Levy, D.M., (1995). Cataloging in the digital order. [Online] http://csdl.tamu.edu/DL95/papers/levy/levy.html.

Lewis-Beck, M. S., Bryman, A. E., & Liao, F. (2003). *The SAGE encyclopedia of social science research methods.* Sage Publications.

Li, S., Li, C., Chen, G., & Bourbakis, N.G. (2004). A general cryptanalysis of permutation-only multimedia encryption algorithms. *IACR's Cryptology ePrint Archive*: Report 2004/374.

Lian, S., Liu, Z., Ren, Z., & Wang, H. (2006a). Secure advanced video coding based on selective encryption algorithms. *IEEE Transactions on Consumer Electronics, 52*(2), 621-629.

Lian, S., Liu, Z., Ren, Z., & Wang, H. (2006b). Secure distribution scheme for compressed data streams. Accepted by *2006 IEEE Conference on Image Processing (ICIP 2006).*

Lian, S., Liu, Z., Ren, Z., & Wang, H. (2006c). Commutative watermarking and encryption for media data. *International Journal of Optical Engineering, 45*(8), 101-103.

Lian, S., Liu, Z., Ren, Z., & Wang, Z. (2005). Selective video encryption based on advanced video coding. In Proceedings of 2005 Pacific-Rim Conference on Multimedia (PCM2005), Part II. *Springer LNCS, 3768,* 281-290.

Lian, S., Sun, J., & Wang, Z. (2004b). Perceptual cryptography on SPIHT compressed images or videos. In *Proceedings of IEEE International Conference on Multimedia and*

Expro (I) (ICME 2004) (pp. 2195-2198), Taiwan, China, June 2004.

Lian, S., Sun, J., & Wang, Z. (2004d). A novel image encryption scheme based on JPEG encoding. In *Proceedings of the Eighth International Conference on Information Visualization* (IV04) (pp. 217-220), London: UK.

Lian, S., Sun, J., & Wang, Z. (2004e). Perceptual cryptography on JPEG2000 encoded images or videos. In *Proceedings of International Conference on Computer and Information Technology*, (pp. 78-83).

Lian, S., Sun, J., Zhang, D., & Wang, Z. (2004a). A selective image encryption scheme based on JPEG2000 codec. 2004 Pacific-Rim Conference on Multimedia (PCM2004). *Springer LNCS, 3332*, 65-72.

Lian, S., Wang, Z., & Sun, J. (2004c). A fast video encryption scheme suitable for network applications. In *Proceedings of International Conference on Communications, Circuits and Systems* (pp. 566-570), Chengdu, China.

Liang, L. (2004). *A guide to open content licenses*. The Netherlands: Piet Zwart Institute.

Lin, C. L., Sun, H. M., & Hwang, T. (2001). Attacks and solutions on strong-password authentication. *IEICE Transactions on Communications, E84-B*(9), 2622-2627.

Lin, C. Y., & Chang, S. F. (2000). Semi-fragile watermarking for authenticating JPEG visual content. *SPIE Security and Watermarking of Multimedia Content II, EI'00* (pp.140-151).

Lin, C.-W., Shen J.-J. & Hwang M.-S. (2003). Security enhancement for optimal strong-password authentication protocol. *ACM Operating System Review, 37*(3), 12-16.

Linn, A. (2000). *History of database protection: Legal issues of concern to the scientific community*. Retrieved September 25, 2006, from http://www.codata.org/data_access/linn.html

Lipton, J. (2003). Databases as intellectual property: New legal approaches. *EIPR, 25*(3), 139.

Liu, Q., & Jiang, X. (2005). Design and realization of a meaningful digital watermarking algorithm based on RBF

neural network. *IEEE International Conference on Neural Networks and Brain*, 1, 214-218.

Liu, Y., Dellaert, F. D., & Rothfus, W. E. (1998). Classification driven semantic based medical image indexing and retrieval. *Technical Report*. Pittsburgh, PA: The Robotics Institute, Carnegie Mellon University.

Lo, A.M. (Jupiter Networks, Inc). (2002). *A need for intervention: Keeping competition alive in the networking industry in the face of increasing patent assertions against standards*. FTC/DOJ Hearings on Competition and Intellectual Property Law and Policy In the Knowledge-Based Economy—Standard Setting and Intellectual Property, 18 April 2002.

Locke, J. (1952). *The second treatise of government*. Indianapolis, IN: Bobbs-Merrill. (Original work published 1690).

Loder, T., Alstyne, M. V., & Wash, R. (2004). An economic answer to unsolicited communication. In *Proceedings of the 5th ACM conference on Electronic commerce* (EC'04) (pp.40-50). New York: ACM Press.

Loiacono, E. T. (2003). Improving Web accessibility. *IEEE Computer*, January.

Lou, D. C., Liu, J. L., & Hu, M. C. (2003). Adaptive digital watermarking using neural network technique. *Proceedings of IEEE 37th Annual 2003 International Carnahan Conference on Security Technology*, 325-332.

Lubin, J. (1993). The use of psychophysical data and models in the analysis of display system performance. In A. B. Watson, *Digital images and human vision* (pp. 163-178).

Ma, X., McCrindle, R., & Cheng, X. (2006). *Verifying and fixing password authentication protocol*. SNPD'06.

MacIntyre, A. (1990). *Three rival versions of moral enquiry*. Notre Dame, IN: University of Notre Dame Press.

Macq, B. M., & Quisquater, J. J. (1995). Cryptology for digital TV broadcasting. In *Proceedings of the IEEE*, 83(6), 944-957.

Macq, B., & Quisquater, J. (1995). Cryptology for digital TV broadcasting. *Proceedings of the IEEE, 83*, 944-957.

Madison, M. (2003). Rights and the shape of the Internet. *44 Boston College Law Review, 433.*

Malcolm, K. C., Poltrock, S. E., & Schuler, D. (1991). Industrial strength hypermedia: Requirements for a large engineering enterprise. In *Proceedings of Hypertext '91,* (San Antonio, USA, 1991) (pp. 13-24).

Malone, S. (2005, November 1). *Microsoft loses Eolas Supreme Court appeal.* PC Pro. Retrieved August 29, 2006, from http://www.pcpro.co.uk/news/news/79431

Maltoni, D., Maio, D., Jain, A. K., & Prabhakar, S. (2005). *Handbook of fingerprint recognition.* Springer.

Mansani, L. (1996). La protezione dei database in Internet, *AIDA,* pp. 149.

Mansfield, E. (1986). Patents and innovation: An empirical study. *Management Science,* 32, 783.

Mansour, M. F., & Tewfik, A. H. (2001). Audio watermarking by time-scale modification. *International Conference on Acoustics, Speech, and Signal Processing,* 3, 1353-1356.

Mao, Y. B., Chen, G. R., & Lian, S. G. (2004). A novel fast image encryption scheme based on the 3D chaotic Baker map. *International Journal of Bifurcation and Chaos,* 14(10), 3613-3624.

Marasco, A. (ANSI). (2003, October 30). *IPR and standards.* Presentation at AIPLA.

Marchionini, G., (1999). Research development in digital libraries [Online]. http://www.glue.umd.edu/~march/digital_library_R_and_D.html.

Marino, F. (2006). *Database protection in the European Union.* Retrieved September 15, 2006, from www.jus.unitn.it/cardozo/Review/Students/Marino1.html

Markiewicz, K. (2004). *University patenting and the rate of knowledge exploitation.* Unpublished Manuscript, University of California at Berkeley.

Markoff, J. (2002, July 29). Patent claim strikes an electronics nerve. *The New York Times.*

Marr, D. (1982). *Vision: A computational investigation into the human representation and processing of visual information.* San Francisco: W. H. Freeman.

Marrakesh agreement establishing the World Trade Organization, Morrocco. Retrieved from http://www.wto.org/english/docs_e/legal_e/27-trips_01_e.htm

Martin, B. (1995). Against intellectual property. *Philosophy and Social Action,* 21(3), 7-22.

Marvel, L. M., Hartwig, G. W. Jr., & Boncelet, C. B. Jr. (2000). Compression-compatible fragile and semi-fragile tamper detection. *Proceedings of SPIE 3971,* (pp.131-139).

Mastercard & Visa. (1997). *SET secure electronic transaction specification, Book 1: Business description* ver1.0.

Matias, Y., & Shamir, A. (1987). A video scrambling technique based on space filling curves. In Proceedings of Advances in Cryptology-CRYPTO'87, *Springer LNCS, 293,* 398-417.

Maxwell, T., Giles, C., Lee, T. C., & Chen, H. H. (1986). Nonlinear dynamics of artificial neural systems. *AIP Conference Proceedings, 151,* 299-304.

Mazzoleni, R., & Nelson, R. (1998). The benefits and costs of strong patent protection: A contribution to the current debate. *Research Policy, 27*(3), 273-84.

McCarthy, C. (2006). File-sharing site eDonkey kicks it. *CNET news.* Retrieved from http://www.news.com.com

McCulloch, W. S., & Pitts, W. H. (1943). A logical calculus of the ideas immanent in nervous activity. *Bulletin of Mathematical Biophysics,*5, 115-133.

McCurdy, G. V. S. (2003). Intellectual property and competition: Does the essential facilities doctrine shed any new light? *EIPR, 20*(10), 473.

McSwain, W. (1999). The law of cyberspace. *Harvard Law Review,* 112, 1574.

Mears, J. (2006). Open source unlocks options for many small-to-medium sized businesses. *Network World.* Retrieved October 11, 2006, from http://www.linuxworld.com/cgi-bin/mailto/x_linux.cgi

Meeus, M.T.H., Faber, J., & Oerlemans, L.A.G. (2002). *Why do firms participate in standardization? An empirical exploration of the relation between isomorphism and institutional dynamics in standardization.* Working Paper, Department of Innovation Studies, University of Utrecht.

Megantz, R.C. (2002). *Technology management. Developing and implementing effective licensing programs.* John Wiley & Sons.

Mehta, A., Rysman, M., & Simcoe, T. (2005). *Identifying age profiles of patent citations.* Unpublished Manuscript, Boston University.

Menezes, A. J., van Oorschot, P. C., & Vanstone, S. A. (1997). *Handbook of applied cryptography.* CRC Press.

Merges, R. P. (1992). Uncertainty and the standard of patentability. *High Technology Law Journal, 7*(1), 10-12.

Merges, R. P. (1997). *Patent law and policy: Cases and materials* (2nd ed.). Contemporary Legal Education Series. Charlottesville, NC: The Michie Company.

Merges, R. P., Mennell, P., & Lemley, M. (2000). *Intellectual property in the new technological age.* New York: Aspen Law.

Merges, R.P. (1999). *Institutions for intellectual property transactions: The case of patent pools.* Working Paper, Revision 1999, University of California at Berkeley.

Messerschmitt, D.G., & Szyperski, C. (2003). *Software ecosystem.* The MIT Press.

Metro-Goldwyn-Mayer Studios, Inc. v. Grokster, Ltd. (2003). 259 F. Supp. 2d [C.D. Cal].

Microsoft. (2006). Windows 2000. *Microsoft Windows 2000.* Retrieved December 30, 2006, from http://www.microsoft.com/windows2000/default.mspx

Miele, A.L. (2000). *Patent strategy: The manger's guide to profiting from patent portfolios.* John Wiley & Sons.

Mitakis, C. (2004). The e-rated industry: Fair use sheep or infringing goat? *Vanderbilt Journal of Entertainment Law and Practice, 291.*

Mitchell, C. (1989). Limitations of challenge-response entity authentication. *IEEE Electronic Letters, 25*(17), 1195-1196.

Mitchell, D. S., Bin, Z., Tewfik, A. H., & Boney, L. (1998). Robust audio watermarking using perceptual masking, *IEEE Signal Processing, 66*(3), 337-355.

Mitsubishi Research Institute, Inc. (2005). In *Proceedings of the 14th portable telephone service user investigation.*

Mohideen, H., (1996). Dealing with copyright issues in digital libraries. Libraries in national development, *Proceedings of Tenth Congress of Southeast Asian Librarians.* Kuala Lumpur.

Mollin, R. A. (2006). *An introduction to cryptography.* CRC Press.

Monrose, F., & Rubin, A. D. (2000). Keystroke dynamics as a biometric for authentication. *Future Generation Computer Systems, 16*(4), 351-359.

Moody, J. E., & Darken, C. (1989). Fast learning in networks of locally-tuned processing units. *Neural Computation,1,* 281-294.

Moore, A. (2001). *Intellectual property and information control.* New Brunswick, NJ: Transaction Publishers.

Moore, G. E. (2001). Cramming more components onto integrated circuits. *Electronics, 38*(8).

Moritz, T. D. (2004). Conservation partnerships in the commons? Sharing data and information, experience and knowledge, as the essence of partnerships. *Museum International, 56*(4), 24-31.

Moulin, P., & O'Sullivan, J. A. (2003). Information-theoretic analysis of information hiding. *IEEE Transactions on Information Theory, 49*(3), 563-593.

Mowery, D.C., & Simcoe, T. (2002). Is the Internet a US invention? An economic and technological history of computer networking. *Research Policy, 31*(8-9), 1369-1387.

Mueller, J.M. (2001). Patenting industry standards. *John Marshall Law Review, 34*(897).

Mulholland, H. (2005). *U-turn on child protection database.* Retrieved September 6, 2006, from http://www.societyguardian.co.uk

Muntean, T., Grivel, E., Nafornita, I., & Najim, M. (2002). Audio digital watermarking for copyright protection. *International Workshop on Trends and Achievements in Information Technology.*

Musso, A. (1998). Ipertesti e thesauri nella disciplina del diritto d'autore, *AIDA*, pp. 10.

Mustapha, M. M., & Ormondroyd, R. F. (1999). Performance of a serial-search synchronizer for fiber-based optical CDMA system in the presence of multi-user interference. *Proc. SPIE, 3899,* 297-306.

Mustapha, M. M., & Ormondroyd, R. F. (2000). Dual-threshold sequential detection code synchronization for an optical CDMA network in the presence if multi-user interference. *IEEE J.Lightwave Technol, 18,* 1742-1748.

Nakajima, N., & Yamaguchi, Y. (2004). Enhancing registration tolerance of extended visual cryptography for natural images. *Journal of Electronics Imaging, 13*(3), 654-662.

Naor, M., & Pinkas, B. (1997). Visual authentication and identification. In B. Kaliski (Ed.), *Advances in Cryptology—Crypto '97, 1294,* 322-336.

Naor, M., & Shamir, A. (1994). Visual cryptography. In A. De Santis (Ed.), *Advances in Cryptology-Eurocrypt '94,. Lecture Notes in Computer Science, 950,* 1-12. Berlin: Springer-Verlag

Naor, M., & Shamir, A. (1995). Visual cryptography. In A. De Santis (Ed.), *Advances in Cryptology—EuroCrypt '94, 950,* 1–12.

Naraine, R. (2002a, May 8). Nokia calls for 5% cap on 3G patent royalties. *internetnews.com.* Retrieved August 29, 2006, from http://internetnews.com/wireless/article.php/1041561

Naraine, R. (2002b, May 10). Qualcomm rejects Nokia patent cap proposal. *internetnews.com.* Retrieved August 29, 2006, from http://www.interetnews.com/wireless/article.php/1116381

National Center for Biotechnology Information. *PubMed.* Retrieved from http://www.ncbi.nlm.nih.gov

Negroponte, N. (1995). *Being digital.* New York: Alfred A. Knopf.

Nelson, T. H. (1997). Transcopyright: A simple legal arrangement for sharing, re-use, and republication of copyrighted material on the net. In Proceedings of WWCA'97, (Tsukuba, Japan, 1997). *Lecture Notes in Computer Science, 1274,.7-14.*

Niccolai, J. (2004). Grid computing distributes the load across a network to speed processing. *PCWorld.*

Nielsen, J. (2004). *User education is not the answer to security problems.* Retrieved from http://www.useit.com/alertbox/20041025.html.

Nietzsche, F. (1962). *Also Sprach Zarathustra.* Stuttgart: Philipp Reclam. (Original work published 1892).

Nimmer, D. (2001). *Nimmer on copyright.* New York: Matthew Bender.

Nimmer, M., Marcus, P., Myers, D., & Nimmer, D. (1991). *Cases and materials on copyright (4th ed.).* St. Paul , MN: West Publishing.

Nimmer, R.. (2005). Introduction: Issues in licensing an introduction. *Houston Law Review, 42,* 941.

Nokes, S. W. (2004). E-rated movies: Coming soon to a home theater near you. *Georgetown Law Journal, 92,* 611.

Nokia. (2005a, October 28). *Leading mobile wireless technology companies call on European Commission to investigate Qualcomm's anti-competitive conduct.* Retrieved August 29, 2006, from http://press.nokia.com/PR/200510/1018639_5.html

Nokia. (2005b, October 28). *Leading mobile wireless technology companies call on European Commission to investigate Qualcomm's anti-competitive conduct.* Retrieved August 29, 2006, from http://europe.nokia.com/BaseProject/Sites/NokiaCom_CAMPAIGNS_57710/CDA/Categories/PressEvents/_Content/_Static_Files/transcript.pdf

Nokia. (2005c, November 7). *Nokia responds to reports of Qualcomm GSM patent infringement suit.* Retrieved August 29, 2006, from http://press.nokia.com/PR/200511/1019958_5.html

Norcen, R., & Uhl, A. (2003). Selective encryption of the JPEG2000 bitstream. IFIP International Federation for Information Processing, *Springer LNCS, 2828*, 194-204.

Nordhaus, W.D. (1969). *Invention, growth and welfare: A theoretical treatment of technological change.* Cambridge, MA: MIT Press.

NTT DoCoMo. (2006). *First Pass.* Retrieved from http://www.docomo.biz/html/product/firstpass/

O'Gorman, L. (2003). Comparing passwords, tokens, and biometrics for user authentication. *Proceedings of the IEEE, 91*, 2021-2040.

OASIS. (2005). *IPR policy.*

OECD. (1980). *OECD guidelines on the protection of privacy and transborder flows of personal data.* Organization for Economic Cooperation and Development.

OECD. (2004). *Patents and innovation: Trends and policy challenges.* Retrieved August 29, 2006, from http://www.oecd.org/dataoecd/48/12/24508541.pdf

OECD. (2005). *Compendium of patent statistics.* Retrieved August 29, 2006, from http://www.oecd.org/dataoecd/60/24/8208325.pdf

Ohana, G. (Cisco Systems, Inc). (2005. October 6). Intellectual property rights: Policies in standard-setting: Areas of debate. In *Proceedings of From A to Veeck: Standardization and the Law, 2005 ANSI Annual Conference.* Retrieved August 29, 2006, from http://public.ansi.org/ansionline/Documents/Meetings%20and%20Events/2005%20Annual%20Conference/Legal%20Conference/Ohana-Panel%20I.pdf

Olivecrona, K. (1974). Appropriation in the state of nature: Locke on the origin of property. *Journal of the History of Ideas, 35*, 211-235.

Oliver, P., & Marwell, G. (1988). The paradox of group size in collective action: A theory of the critical mass, II. *American Sociological Review, 53*, 1-8.

Olson, M. (1965). *The logic of collective action.* Cambridge: Harvard University Press.

Olson, M., & Zeckhauser, R. (1966). An economic theory of alliances. *Review of Economics and Statistics, 48*, 266-279.

Omura, J. K. (1990). Novel applications of cryptography in digital communications. *IEEE Communication Magazine, 28*(5), 21-29.

Onali, T., & Ginesu, G. (2006). *Transmission-efficient image-based authentication for mobile devices.* Lecture Notes in Computer Science, 3893.

Opderberck D. W. (2005). Peer to peer networks, Technological evolution, and intellectual property reverse private attorney general litigation. *Berkeley Technology Law Journal, 20,* 1685

Oppenheim, C., (1992). *The legal and regulatory environment for electronic information.* Calne, Wilts., Calne, UK: Infonortics Ltd.

Ordover, J.A. (1991). A patent system for both diffusion and exclusion. *Journal of Economic Perspectives, 5*(1), 43-60.

ORuanaidh, J. J. K., & Pun, T. (1998). Rotation, scale and translation invariant spread spectrum digital image watermarking. *Signal Processing.* 66, 303-317.

Ousterhout, J. K. (1990). Why aren't operation systems getting faster as fast as hardware? *USENIX Summer Conference, June 11-15, 1990.*

Out-law.com. (2005, November 31). Mobile-makers say 3G patent licensing breaks antitrust laws. Retrieved August 29, 2006, from http://www.out-law.com/page-6280

Oxman, J. (1999). *The FCC and the unregulation of the internet,* OPP Working Paper, No. 31. Available at: http://www.fcc.gov/Bureaus/Opp/working_papers/oppwp31.txt.

Pakes, A. (1986). Patents as option: Some estimates of the value of holding European patent stocks. *Econometrica, 54*(4), 755-784.

Palmer, T. (1997). Intellectual property: A non-Posnerian law and economics approach. In A.E. Moore (Ed.), *Intellectual property: Moral, legal, and international dilemmas,* (pp. 179-224). Lanham, MD: Rowman and Littlefield.

Pan, D. (1995). A tutorial on MPEG/audio compression. *IEEE MultiMedia, 2*(2), 60-74.

Pang, N., & Schauder, D. (2006). User-centred design and the culture of knowledge creating communities: A theoretical reassessment. In F. V. Burstein & H. Linger (Eds.), *The local and global in knowledge management—Why culture matters* (pp. 151-166). Kew, VIC, Australia: Australian Scholarly Publishing.

Pang, N., Denison, T., Johanson, G., Schauder, D., & Williamson, K. (2006, October). *Empowering communities through memories: The role of public libraries.* Paper presented at the 3rd Prato International Community Informatics Conference, Prato, Italy.

Pantle, A., & Sekuler, R. W. (1969). Contrast response of human visual mechanisms sensitive to orientation and direction of motion. *Vision Res., 9,* 397-406.

Papin-Ramcharan, J. I., & Dawe, R. A. (2006). Open access publishing: A developing country view. *First Monday, 11* (6). Retrieved October 1, 2006, from http://firstmonday.org/issues/issue11_6/papin/index.html

Parnes, R., & Parviainen, R. (2001). Large scale distributed watermarking of multicast media through encryption. In *Proc. IFIP Int. Conf. Communications and Multimedia Security* (pp. 21-22), Issues of the New Century, Darmstadt, Germany,.

PassfacesTM. Retrieved from http://www.realuser.com

PassPicc. Retrieved from http://www.authord.com/PassPic/

Peeger, S. L., & Bloom, G. (2005). Canning spam: Proposed solutions to unwanted email. *IEEE Security and Privacy, 3*(2), 40-47.

Pennebaker, W. B., & Mitchell, J. L. (1993). *JPEG still image compression standard.* New York: Van Nostrand Reinhold.

Pennebaker, W. B., & Mitchell, J. L. (1993). *JPEG: Still image data compression standard.* Van Nostrand Reinhold.

Pereira, S., Voloshynovskiy, S., & Pun, T. (2001, June). Optimal transform domain watermark embedding via linear programming. *Signal Processing, 81*(6), 1251-1260.

Perens, B. (n.d.). *The problem of software patents in standards.* Retrieved August 29, 2006, from http://perens.com/Articles/PatentFarming.html

Perrig, A., & Song, D. (1999). *Hash visualization: A new technique to improve real-world security.* International Workshop on Cryptographic Techniques and E-Commerce CrypTEC '99.

Peterson, S.K. (Hewlett-Packard Company). (2002a). *Consideration of patents during the setting of standards.* For FTC and DOJ Roundtable, Standard Setting Organizations: Evaluating the Anticompetitive Risks of Negotiating IP Licensing Terms and Conditions Before A Standard Is Set, 6 November 2002.

Peterson, S.K. (Hewlett-Packard Company). (2002b). *Patents and standard-setting processes.* FTC/DOJ Hearings on Competition and Intellectual Property Law and Policy in the Knowledge-Based Economy, 18 April 2002.

Petitcolas, F. A. P., Anderson, R. J. & Kuhn, M. G. (1999). Information hiding—A survey. *Proceedings of the IEEE—special issue on protection of multimedia content, 87*(7), 1062-1078.

Petitcolas, F.A., Anderson, R.J., & Kuhn, M.G. (1999, July). Information hiding: A survey. *Proceedings of IEEE, 87*(7), 1062-1078.

Pfarrhofer, R., & Uhl, A. (2005). Selective image encryption using JBIG. *Communications and Multimedia Security 2005,* 98-107.

Phelps, T. A., & Wilensky, R. (2000). Robust intra-document locations. In Proceedings of WWW9, (Amsterdam, Netherlands, 2000). *Computer Networks, 33*(1-6), 105-118.

Phillips, P. J., Grother, P., Micheals, R. J., Blackburn, D. M., Tabassi, E., & Bone, M. (2003). *Face Recognition Vendor Test 2002.*

Phillips, P. J., Moon, H., Rauss, P., & Rizvi, S. A. (1997). The FERET evaluation methodology for face-recognition algorithms. In *Proceedings IEEE Conference Computer Vision and Pattern Recognition CVPR 97,* 137-143.

Pichler, F., & Scharinger, J. (1996). Finite dimensional generalized Baker dynamical systems for cryptographic applications. *Lect. Notes in Comput. Sci., 1030*, 465-476.

Pierce, J. D., Warren, M. J., Mackay, D. R., & Wells, J. G. (2004). Graphical authentication: Justifications and objectives. In P*roceedings of the 2nd Australian Information Security Management Conference, Securing the Future (AISM 2004)* (pp. 49-63).

Pioch, N. (2006). *Impressionism.* Retrieved October 1, 2006, from http://www.ibiblio.org/wm/paint/glo/impressionism/

Plaintiffs' Joint Excerpts of Record (2003). *Metro-Goldwyn-Mayer Studios, Inc. v. Grokster*, Ltd. 259 F. Supp. 2d [C.D. Cal].

Podesser, M., Schmidt, H. P., & Uhl, A. (2002). Selective bitplane encryption for secure transmission of image data in mobile environments. In *Proceedings of the 5th IEEE Nordic Signal Processing Symposium (NORSIG 2002)* (CD-ROM) Tromso-Trondheim, Norway, October.

Podilchuk, C. J., & Zeng, W. (1998). Image-adaptive watermarking using visual models. *IEEE Journal on Selected Areas in Communications, 16*(4), 525-539.

Podilchuk, C.I., & Zeng, W. (1998, May). Image-adaptive watermarking using visual models. *IEEE Journal on Selected Areas in Communications, 16*(4), 525-539.

Poggio, T., & Girosi, F. (1990). Regularization algorithms for learning that are equivalent to multilayer networks. *Science,247*(4945), 978-982.

Pointsec Mobile Technologies. Retrieved from http://www.pointsec.com

Poirson, A., & Wandell, B. (1993). Appearance of colored patterns. *Journal of the Optical Society of America, 10*(12), 2458-2470.

Poltorak, A.I., & Lerner, P.J. (2004). *Essentials of licensing intellectual property.* John Wiley & Sons.

Pope, C. (2005). Unfinished business: Are today's P2P networks liable for copyright infringement? *Duke Law & Technology Review, 22.*

Priest, G. (1986). What economists can tell lawyers. *Research in Law and Economics, 8*, 19.

Probst, R., Lonsbury-Martin, B. L., & Martin, G. K. (1991). A review of otoacoustic emissions. *Journal of Acoustic Society, 89*, 2027-2067.

Prokoski, F. J. (1997). *Security and non-diagnostic medical uses for thermal imaging.* American Academy of Thermology 1997 Annual Meeting, Pittsburgh.

Pu, Y., Liao, K., Zhou, J., & Zhang, N. (2004). A public adaptive watermark algorithm for color images based on principal component analysis of generalized hebb. *IEEE Proceedings of International Conference on Information Acquisition*, 484-488.

PwC Advisory. (2006). *2006 patent and trademark damages study.*

Qi, D., Zou, J., & Han, X. (2000). A new class of scrambling transformation and its application in the image information covering. *Science in China—Series E (English Edition), 43*(3), 304-312.

Qiao, L., & Nahrstedt, K. (1997). A new algorithm for MPEG video encryption. In *Proceeding of the First International Conference on Imaging Science, Systems and Technology (CISST'97)* (pp. 21-29). Las Vegas, NV, July.

Qiao, L., & Nahrstedt, K. (2000). Comparison of MPEG encryption algorithm. *International Journal on Computers and Graphics, 22*(4), 437-448.

QR checker. (2006). Retrieved from http://www.denso-wave.com/ja/adcd/product/qrchecker/index.html

Q-R code. (2006). Retrieved from http://www.qrcode.com/

Quan, X., & Zhang, H. (2004). Audio watermarking for copyright protection based on psychoacoustic model and adaptive wavelet packet decomposition. *Proceedings of 2004 International Symposium on Intelligent Multimedia, Video and Speech Processing*, 282-285.

Quote.com—Your source for financial markets quotes, charts, news and education. Retrieved from http://new.quote.com/

Quynh, A. N., & Takefuji, Y. (2006). Towards an invisible honeypot monitoring system. *Proceedings of Information Security and Privacy, Lecture Notes in Computer Science, 4058,* 111-122.

Rahnasto, I. (2003). *Intellectual property rights, external effects, and anti-trust law.* Oxford University Press.

Ramamritham, K., & Stankovic, J. (1994). Scheduling algorithms and operating systems support for real-time systems. *Proceedings of IEEE, 8*(21), 55-67.

Rambus, Inc v. Infineon Technologies AG. No. 01-1449. Federal Circuit, 29 January 2003.

Rammer, C. (2002). *Patente und Marken als Schutzmechanismen für Innovationen.* Studien zum deutschen Innovationssystem Nr. 11-2003, Zentrum für Europäische Wirtschaftsforschung (ZEW), Mannheim.

Ramos, M. G.., & Hemami, S. S. (1997). Psychovisually-based multiresolution image segmentation. *Proceedings of International Conference on Image Processing, 3,* 66-69.

Rapp, R.T., & Stiroh, L.J. (2002). *Standard setting and market power.* Contribution to the Public Hearing on Competition and Intellectual Property Law and Policy in the Knowledge-Based Economy in 2001 and 2002. Available online at: http://www.ftc.gov/opp/intellect/index.htm.

Recommendation ITU-R BS.1387-1, 11/01.

Red Herring. (2006, February 3). JPEG patent reexamined. Retrieved August 29, 2006, from http://www.redherring.com/Article.aspx?a=15582&hed=JPEG+Patent+Reexamined&sector=Industries&subsector=Computing

Regan, K. (2005, July 5). Broadcom suit accuses Qualcomm of antitrust tactics. *E-Commerce Times.* Retrieved August 29, 2006, from http://www.ecommercetimes.com/story/44395.html

Regan, K., (2001) Amazon testing micropayments via music downloads. [Online] http://www.ecommercetimes.com/perl/story/7822.html.

Regehr, J. D. (2001). *Using hierarchical scheduling to support soft real-time applications in general-purpose operating systems.* Dissertation of Univ. of Virginia, 2001.

Reinbothe, J. (1999). The legal protection of non-creative databases. In *WIPO/EC/CONF/99/SPK/22-A* WIPO, Geneva, Switzerland. Presented Chapter to Protection of Database Workshop at International Conference of Electronic Commerce and Intellectual Property. Retrieved from http://ecommerce.wipo.int/meetings/1999/chapters/pdf/reinboth.pdf

Reingold, J. (2006, January). *Patently aggressive.* 102. Retrieved August 29, 2006, from http://www.fastcompany.com/magazine/102/patents.html

Reiter, M. K., & Rubin, A. D. (1998). Crowds: Anonymity for web transactions. *ACM Transactions on Information and System Security, 1*(1), 66-92.

Rey, C., & Dugelay, J. (2002). *A survey of watermarking algorithms for image authentication.* EURASIP Journal on Applied Signal Processing, 6, 613-621.

Rezgul, A. & Bouguettaya, A. (2003). Privacy on Web: Facts, challenges, and solutions. *IEEE Security & Privacy,* 40-49.

Rheingold, H. (2002). *Smart mobs: The next social revolution.* Cambridge: Perseus Books Group.

Ricciuti, M. (2002). Open source: Rebels at the gate. *Business Tech: CNet News.* Retrieved October 12, 2006, from http://news.com.com/2009-1001-961354.html

Rivest, R., Shamir, A., & Adleman, L., (1998). A method for obtaining digital signatures and public-key cryptosystems. *Communications of the ACM, 21*(2), 120–126. Previously released as an MIT "Technical Memo" in April 1977. Initial publication of the RSA scheme.

Rivette, K., & Kline, D. (2000). *Rembrandts in the attic.* Harvard Business School Press.

Robert, A., & Picard, J. (2005). On the use of masking models for image and audio watermarking. *IEEE Transaction on Multimedia, 7*(4), 727-739.

Robinson, D. J. M., & Hawksford, M. J. (1999). Time-domain auditory model for the assessment of high-quality coded audio. *107th Convention of the Audio Engineering Society* - preprint 5071.

Rome Convention for the Protection of Performers, Producers of Phonograms and Broadcasting Organizations. (1961). Retrieved from http://www.wipo.int/treaties/en/ip/rome

Romeo, A., Romdotti, G., Mattavelli, M., & Mlynek, D. (1999). Cryptosystem architectures for very high throughput multimedia encryption: The RPK solution. In *Proceedings of the 6th IEEE International Conference on Electronics, Circuits and Systems, 1*, 5-8 Sept., 261 -264.

Rosenblatt, F. (1985). The perceptron: Probabilistic model for information storage and organization in the brain. *Psychology Review, 65*, 386-408.

Rowley, J., (1998). *The electronic library*. London: *Library Association Publishing*. 263.

Rudin, N., & Inman, K. (2001). *An introduction to forensic DNA analysis (2nd ed)*. CRC Press.

Rui, Y., Huang, T. S., & Chang, S. F. (1999). Image retrieval: Current techniques, promising directions and open issues. *Journal of Visual Communication and Image Representation, 10*(4), 39-62.

Ruley, J. D. (2001). The future of Moore's law, Part 1. Retrieved June 25, 2001, from http://www.byte.com

Rummelhart, D. E., McClelland, J. L,. & the PDP Research Group. (1986). *Parallel Distributed Processing, 1*. The MIT Press.

Rysman, M., & Simcoe, T. (2006). *Patents and the performance of voluntary standard setting organizations*. Unpublished Manuscript, Boston University.

Sahuguet, A., & Azavant, F. (2001). Building intelligent Web applications using lightweight wrappers. *Data & Knowledge Engineering, 36*(3), 283-316.

Said, A. (1996). A new fast and efficient image codec based on set partitioning in hierarchical trees. *IEEE Transactions on Circuits and Systems for Video Technology, 6*(3), 243-250.

Salop, S.C., & Scheffman, D.T. (1983). Raising rivals' costs. *American Economic Review, 73*(2), 267-271.

Salop, S.C., & Scheffman, D.T. (1987). Cost-raising strategies. *Journal of Industrial Economics, 36*(1), 19-34.

Samal, A., & Lyengar, P.A. (1992). Automatic recognition and analysis of human faces and facial expressions: *A survey. Pattern Recognition, 25*, 65-77.

Samuelson, P. (1996). Legally speaking: Legal protection for database content. *Communications of the ACM, 39*(12), 17-23.

Samuelson, P. (2003). DRM {and, or, vs.} the law. *Communications of the ACM, 46*(4), 41-45.

Sanchez-Reillo, R., Sanchez-Avila, C., & Gonzalez-Marcos, A. (2000). Biometric identification through hand geometry measurements. *IEEE Transactions on Pattern Analysis and Machine Intelligence, 22*(10), 1168-1171.

Sandirigama, M., Shimizu, A., & Noda, M. T. (2000). Simple and secure password authentication protocol (SAS). *IEICE Transactions on Communications, E83-B(6)*, 1363-1365.

Sarvas, R., & Soininen, A. (2002, October). *Differences in European and U.S. patent regulation affecting wireless standardization*. Paper presented at the International Workshop on Wireless Strategy in the Enterprise, Berkeley, California.

Sasaki, H., & Kiyoki, Y. (2002). A methodology to protect multimedia databases by patentable programs of indexing and retrieval based-on semantic similarity. *IPS of Japan Transactions on Databases, 43*(13), 108-127. (*in Japanese*).

Sasaki, H., & Kiyoki, Y. (2002). Patenting the processes for content-based retrieval in digital libraries. In E.-P. Lim, S. Foo, C. Khoo, H. Chen, E. Fox, S. Urs, & T. Costantino (eds.), *Proceedings of the Fifth International Conference on Asian Digital Libraries (ICADL)*, Digital Libraries: People, Knowledge, & Technology, LNCS, 2555 (p. 471-482).

Sasaki, H., & Kiyoki, Y. (2003). A proposal for digital library protection. In *Proceedings of the Third IEEE-CS/ACM Joint Conference on Digital Libraries (JCDL)* (p. 392).

Sasaki, H., & Kiyoki, Y. (2005). A formulation for patenting content-based retrieval processes in digital libraries. *Journal of Information Processing and Management, 41*(1), 57-74.

Sasaki, J., Yoneda, T., & Funyu, Y. (2006). A reliable and useful information distribution system: The "Kuchikomi

Network." *Information Modelling and Knowledge Bases XVII* (pp. 180-190).

Sasaki, J., Shimomukai, H., Yoneda, T., & Funyu, Y. (2006). Development of designed Q-R code. In *Proceedings of the 16th European-Japanese Conference (EJC) on Information Modelling and Knowledge Base.*

Sasaki, J., Yoneda, T., & Funyu, Y. (2005). A reliable and useful information distribution system: Kuchikomi Network. In *Proceedings of the 15th European-Japanese Conference (EJC) on Information Modelling and Knowledge Base.*

Scharinger, J. (1998). Kolmogorov systems: Internal time, irreversibity and cryptographic applications. In D. Dubois (Ed.), *Proceedings of the AIP Conference on Computing Anticipatory Systems, 437,* Woodbury, NY: Amer. Inst. of Phys.

Schauder, D., & Pang, N. (2006). *Keynote presentation: Digital storytelling.* Paper presented at the Museums Australia 2006 seminar: Storytelling through emerging technologies. Victoria, Australia.

Scherer, F.M., & Ross, D. (Eds.). (1990). *Industrial market structure and economic performance.* Dallas, Geneva: 3.A.

Schlachter, E. (1997). The intellectual property renaissance in cyberspace: Why copyright law could be unimportant on the Internet. *Berkeley Technology Law Journal, 12*(1). Retrieved October 12, 2006, from http://btlj.boalt.org/data/articles/12-1_spring_1997_symp_2-schlachter.pdf

Schmidt, M. B., Bekkering, E., & Warkentin, M. (2004, April 14-16). On the illicit use of steganography and its detection, In *Proceedings of the 2004 ISOneWorld International Conference,* Las Vegas, NV (pp. 1-10).

Schneier B. (1995) Applied cryptography (2nd. ed.). Wiley.

Schulman, J. (2005). Liability of Internet service providers for infringing activities of their customers: Will the INDUCE Act solve the problem? *Baltimore Intellectual Property Law Journal, 13.*

Servetti, A., Testa, C., Carlos, J., & Martin, D. (2003). *Frequency-selective partial encryption of compressed audio.* Paper presented at the International Conference on Audio, Speech and Signal Processing, Hong Kong, April, 5, 668-671.

Shamir, A. (1979). How to share a secret. *Communications of the ACM, 22*(1), 612-613.

Shamir, A. (1985). Identity-based cryptosystems and signature schemes. In Proceedings of CRYPTO'84. *Lecture Notes in Computer Science, 96,* 47-53.

Shapiro, C. (2001). Navigating the patent thicket: Cross licenses, patent pools and standard-setting. [Unpublished manuscript, on file with *Columbia Law Review*].

Shapiro, C., & Varian, H. (1999). *Information rules. A strategic guide to the network economy.* Boston, MA: Harvard Business School Press.

Shapiro, J. M. (1993). Embedded image coding using zerotrees of wavelet coding. *IEEE Transactions on Signal Processing, 41*(12), 3445-3462.

Shavell, S. & van Ypersele, T. (1999). *Rewards versus intellectual property rights.* National Bureau of Economics Research Working Paper, No. 6956.

Shi, C., & Bhargava, B. (1998). A fast MPEG video encryption algorithm. In *Proceedings of the 6th ACM International Multimedia Conference* (pp. 81-88). Bristol: UK, September.

Shi, C., Wang, S., & Bhargava, B. (1999). MPEG video encryption in real-time using secret key cryptography. In *Proceedings of PDPTA'99* (pp. 2822-2828). Las Vegas, NV: Computer Science Research, Education and Application Press,.

Shurmer, M., & Lea, G. (1995, June). Telecommunications standardization and intellectual property rights: A fundamental dilemma? *Standardview, 3*(2).

Simcoe, T. (2004). *Design by committee? The organization of technical standards development.* Dissertation, University of California at Berkeley.

Simon, C., & Goldstein, I. (1935). A new scientific method of identification. *New York State Journal of Medicine, 35*(18), 901-906.

Slater, J. B. (2005). When America sneezes. *Mute, 2*(1), 5.

Smeulders, A. W. M., Worring, M., Santini, S., Gupta, A., & Jain, R. (2000). Content-based image retrieval at the end of the early years. *IEEE Transactions on Pattern Analysis and Machine Intelligence, 22*(12), 1349-1380.

Smith & Abel (1999). *Bark and ERB Bilinear Transforms.*

Smith, I. (2005). Social-mobile applications. *IEEE Computer,* April.

Snapper, J. (1995). Intellectual property protections for computer software. In D. G. Johnson & H. Nissenbaum (Eds.), *Computing, ethics and social values,* (pp. 181-189). Englewood Cliffs, NJ: Prentice Hall.

Sobrado L., & Birget, J. C. (2002). Graphical passwords. *The Rutgers Scholar, 4.*

Soininen, A. H. (2005).Open Standards and the Problem with Submarine Patents. Proceedings SIIT 2005 pp. 231-244 4th International conference on standardization and innovation in information technology.

Sonera Plaza. (2002). *Digital Rights Management* white paper. Technical report, Sonera Plaza Ltd. Retrieved December 18, 2006, from http://www.medialab.sonera.fi

Song, S., (1999). *Electronic commerce and its impacts to library and information profession.* [Online] http://www.slis.ualberta.ca/538-99/ssong/termproj.htm.

Sony Corp of America v. Universal City Studios, Inc. (1984). 464 U.S. 417.

Spada, P. (1997). Banche dati e diritto d'autore, *AIDA,* pp. 5.

Spinello, R. (2004). Note on the DeCSS Case. In R. A. Spinello & H. Tavani (Eds.), *Readings in cyberethics (2ⁿᵈ ed.),* pp. 264-268. Sudbury, MA: Jones and Bartlett.

Sridharan, S., Dawson, E., & Goldburg, B. (1991). Fast Fourier transform based speech encryption system. *IEE*

Proceedings of Communications, Speech and Vision, 138(3), 215-223.

Stamatoudi, I. (2002). *Copyright and multimedia products. A comparative analysis.* Cambridge University Press.

State Street Bank & Trust Co. v. Signature Financial Group (1998). 149 F. 3d 1368 [Fed. Cir.].

Stazi, A. (2004). *La pubblicità commerciale on line.* Italy: Giuffrè.

Stroyd, A.H. (2000). *Lemelson bar coding patents: Attempting to sink the submariner.* Retrieved August 29, 2006, from http://www.mhia.org/PSC/pdf/Lemelson.PDF

SUAN (Secure User Authentication with Nijigen code). Retrieved from HYPERLINK "http://suan.asgTamaru, S., Nakazawa, J., Takashio, K. & Tokuda, H. (2003). PPNP: A privacy profile negotiation protocol for services in public spaces. In *Proceeding of fifth international conference on Ubiquitous Computing (UbiComp2003),* Seattle, WA., Oct. 2003.

Sugibuchi, T., Tanaka, Y. (2004). Integrated visualization framework for relational databases and Web resources. Intuitive Human Interfaces for Organizing and Accessing Intellectual Assets. *Lecture Notes in Computer Science, 3359,* 159-174

Sun, H. M., Lin, Y. H., & Wu, M. F. (2006). API monitoring system for defeating worms and exploits in MS-Windows system. *Proceedings of Information Security and Privacy, Lecture Notes in Computer Science, 4058,* 159-170.

Suo, X., Zhu, Y., & Owen, G. S. (2005). Graphical passwords: *A survey. 21ˢᵗ Annual Computer Security Applications Conference (ACSAC 2005),* Tucson AZ.

Surowiecki, J. (2006, December 26/January 2). Blackberry picking. *The New Yorker,* Financial Page.

Swann, P. (2000). *The economics of standardization.* Final Report for Standards and Technical Regulations, Directorate Department of Trade and Industry, University of Manchester.

Swanson, M. D., Bin, Z., & Tewfik, A. H. (1998). Multiresolution scene-based video watermarking using perceptual models. *IEEE Journal on Selected Areas, 16*(4), 540-550.

Swanson, M. D., Zhu, B., & Tewfil, A. H. (1996). Transparent robust image watermarking. *Proceedings of International Conference on Image Processing*, 3, 211-214.

Swanson, M.D., Zhu, B., & Tewfik, A.H. (1998, May). Multiresolution scene-based video watermarking using perceptual models. *IEEE Journal on Selected Areas in Communications, 16*(4), 540-550.

Symbol Technologies Inc. v. Lemelson Medical, Education & Research Foundation. 277 F.3d 1361, 1363. Federal Circuit, 2002.

Symbol Technologies, Inc et al. v. Lemelson Medical, Education & Research Foundation. LP et al., 422 F.3d 1378. Federal Circuit, 2005.

Tai, E. T. T. (2003). Exhaustion and online delivery of digital works. *EIPR, 25-5*, 207.

Takada, T., & Koike, H. (2003). Awase-E: Image-based authentication for mobile phones using user's favorite images. In *Proceedings of 5th International Symposium* (pp. 347-351), Mobile HCI 2003. Springer.

Takefuji, Y. (2003). Technical report of DRIVERWARE IMMUNE. *US Air Force Office of Scientific Research with Grant Number AOARD 03-4049*

Takefuji, Y. (2005). Nullification of unknown malicious code execution with buffer overflows. Driverware IMMUNE–Final Report. Technical report of DRIVERWARE IMMUNE, *US Air Force Office of Scientific Research with Grant Number AOARD 03-4049.*

Takefuji, Y., Lee, K., & Aiso, H. (1992). An artificial maximum neural network: A winner-take-all neuron model forcing the state of the system in a solution domain. *Biological Cybernetics, 67*, 243-251.

Tanaka Y, & Ito K. (2004b). Meme media architecture for the reediting and redistribution of Web resources. Flexible Query Answering Systems, FQAS 2004. *Lecture Notes in Computer Science, 3055*, 1-12

Tanaka Y, Ito K, & Kurosaki D. (2004a). Meme media architectures for re-editing and redistributing intellectual

assets over the Web. *International Journal of Hum. Comput. Stud., 60*(4), 489-526.

Tanaka, T., & Kubo, N. (2004). Biometric authentication by hand vein patterns. *SICE 2004 Annual Conference*, 1, 249-253.

Tanaka, Y. (1996). Meme media and a World-wide meme pool. In *Proceedings of MM'96*, (Boston, USA, 1996) (pp. 175-186).

Tanaka, Y. (2003). *Meme media and meme market architectures: Knowledge media for editing, distributing, and managing intellectual resources.* John Wiley & Sons.

Tanaka, Y., & Imataki, T. (1989). IntelligentPad: A hypermedia system allowing functional compositions of active media objects through direct manipulations. In *Proceedings of IFIP'89*, (San Francisco, USA, 1989) (pp. 541-546).

Tanaka, Y., Fujima, J., & Sugibuchi, T. (2001). Meme media and meme pools for re-editing and redistributing intellectual assets. In *Proceedings of OHS-7/SC-3/AH-3*, (Aarhus, Denmark, 2001). *Lecture Notes in Computer Science, 2266*, 28-46.

Tanaka, Y., Nagasaki, A., Akaishi, M., & Noguchi, T. (1992). A synthetic media architecture for an object-oriented open platform. In *Proceedings of IFIP'92*, (Madrid, Spain, 1992) (pp. 104-110).

Tang, L. (1996). Methods for encrypting and decrypting MPEG video data efficiently. In *Proceedings of the Fourth ACM International Multimedia Conference (ACM Multimedia'96)* (pp. 219-230), Boston, MA, November 1996.

Tavani, H. (2004). *Ethics & technology: Ethical issues in an age of information and communication technology.* Hoboken, NJ: John Wiley & Sons.

Teece, D.J. (2000). *Managing intellectual capital.* Oxford University Press.

Tennant, R., (1997). Digital potential and pitfalls. *Library Journal, 122*(19), 21-22. Also available in Library Journal Digital, InfoTech News: Digital Libraries, November 15. [Online] http://www.libraryjournal.com/articles/infotech/digitallibraries/19971115_2014.asp.

Tewari, G., Youll, J., & Maes, P. (2003). Personalized location-based brokering using an agent-based intermediary architecture. *Decision Support Systems, 34*(2), 127-137.

Tewfik, A.H., & Swanson, M. (1997, July). Data hiding for multimedia personalization, interaction, and protection. *IEEE Signal Processing Magazine, 14*(4), 41-44.

The Lemelson Foundation. (n.d.). Jerome H. Lemelson. Retrieved August 29, 2006, from http://www.lemelson.org/about/bio_jerry.php

Thumm, N. (2001). Management of intellectual property rights in European biotechnology firms. *Technological Forecasting and Social Change, 67*(July), 259-272.

Thumm, N. (2002). Europe's construction of a patent system for biotechnological inventions: An assessment of industry views. *Technological Forecasting and Social Change, 69*(December), 917-928.

Tilki, J. F., & Beex, A. A. (1996). Encoding a hidden digital signature onto an audio signal using psychoacoustic masking. In *Proceedings 1996 7ᵗʰ International Conference on Signal Processing.* 476-480.

Toivanen, O. (2005). *Choosing standards.* Unpublished Manuscript, University of Helsinki.

Torrubia, A., & Mora, F. (2002). Perceptual cryptography on MPEG Layer III bit-streams. *IEEE Transactions on Consumer Electronics, 48*(4), 1046-1050.

Torrubia, A., & Mora, F. (2003). Perceptual cryptography of JPEG compressed images on the JFIF bit-stream domain. In *Proceedings of the IEEE International Symposium on Consumer Electronics* (pp. 58-59), ISCE, 17-19 June 2003.

Tosun, A. S., & Feng, W. C. (2000). Efficient multi-layer coding and encryption of MPEG video streams. In *Proceedings of IEEE International Conference on Multimedia and Expo, 1,* 119-122.

Tosun, A. S., & Feng, W. C. (2001). Lightweight security mechanisms for wireless video transmission. In *Proceedings, International Conference on Information Technology: Coding and Computing* (pp. 157-161), 2-4 April.

Tosun, A. S., & Feng, W. C. (2001). On error preserving encryption algorithms for wireless video transmission. In *Proceedings of the ACM International Multimedia Conference and Exhibition* (pp. 302-308), IV, Ottawa, Ont.

Tovée, M. J. (1996). *An introduction to the visual system.* Cambridge University Press.

Townshend v. Rockwell International Corp. and Conexant Systems, Inc., 55 U.S.P.Q.2d 1011. Northern District of California, 2000.

Trade Related Aspects of Intellectual property rights (TRIPS) Agreement. (1994). Annex 1C

Trial Transcript (2000). *Universal City Studios v. Remeirdes* 111 F. Supp. 294 [S.D.N.Y.].

Trichili, H., Bouhlel, M.-S., Solaiman, B., & Kamoun, L. (2003). Exploitation of the HVS features for the enhancement of image watermarking techniques. *ISPA03, 2,* 1076-1081.

Trithemius, J. (1606). *Steganographia.* Retrieved November 17, 2005, from http://www.esotericarchives.com/tritheim/stegano.htm

Tyson, L., & Sherry, E. (1997). Statutory protection for databases: Economic and public policy issues. Retrieved August 25, 2006, from http://www.infoindustry.org/ppgrc/doclib/grdoc016.htm

U.S. Constitution, Article I, § 8, clause 8.

U.S. Copyright Act. (1976).17 U.S.C. sec. 101, & 103.

U.S. Department of Commerce. (2000). *Safe Harbor Privacy Principles.* Retrieved December 18, 2006, from http://www.export.gov/safeharbor/SHPRINCIPLESFINAL.htm

U.S. Department of Defense. (1985). *Trusted Computer System Evaluation Criteria.* Technical Report DoD 5200.28.

U.S. Patent and Trademark Office. (1996). *Examination guidelines for computer-related inventions, 61 Fed. Reg. 7478 (Feb. 28, 1996).*

Uchida, K. (2005). Fingerprint identification. *NEC Journal of Advanced Technology, 2*(1).

Uehara, T. (2001). *Combined encryption and source coding.* Retrieved from http://www.uow.edu.au/~tu01/CESC.html

United Christian Scientists v. Christian Science Board of Directors (1987). 829 F.2d 1152 [D.C. Cir.].

United States of America v. Microsoft Corporation (2001). 253 F. 3d 34 [D.C. Cir.].

Universal City Studios v. Corley (2001). 273 F. 3d 429 [2d Cir.].

Universal City Studios v. Remeirdes (2000). 111 F. Supp. 294 [S.D.N.Y.].

Universal City Studios v. Sony Corp of America (1979). 480 F. Supp. 429 [C.D. Cal.].

University of Washington. (2006). *Human subjects manual.* Retrieved December 18, 2006, from http://www.washington.edu/research/hsd/hsdman4.html

Unsworth, J. (1997). *New copyright and database regulations: USPTO, WIPO, and You.* London: University of London & Oxford University.

Vaidhyanathan, S. (2001). *Copyrights and copywrongs: The rise of intellectual property and how it threatens creativity.* New York: New York University Press.

Van Schyndel, R.G., Tirkel, A.Z., & Osborne, C.F. (1994, November). A digital watermark. *Proceedings of IEEE International Conference of Image Processing '94: Vol. 2* (pp. 86-90). Austin, TX.

Van Zandt, T. (2004). Information overload in a network of targeted communication. *RAND Journal of Economics, 35*(3), 542-560.

Varchaver, N. (2001, May 3). *Jerome Lemelson the patent king.* Retrieved August 29, 2006, from http://www.engin.brown.edu/courses/en90/fall/2003/Lemelson%20Fortune%20may%2014%202001%20article.pdf

Venugopal, S., Buyya, R., & Ramamohanarao, K. (2006) A taxonomy of data Grids for distributed data sharing, management, and processing. *ACM Computing Surveys, 38*(1), 3.

Vermont, S. (2002). The economics of patent litigation. In B. Berman (Ed.), *From ideas to assets. Investing wisely in intellectual property.* John Wiley & Sons.

Vervloesem, K. (2006). Croatian government adopts open source software policy. *News Forge.* Retrieved October 16, 2006, from http://www.newsforge.com/article.pl?sid=06/08/11/1855229

Visa. (2002). *3-D Secure™ Introduction* version 1.0.2.

Viskey. Retrieved from http://www.viskey.com

VisualPass. Retrieved from http://penguin.poly.edu/seminars/visualpass/visualpasswords.ppt

Viterbi, A. J. (1979). Spread spectrum communications—myths and realities. *IEEE Communication Magazine.*

Volokh, E. (1998). Freedom of speech and injunctions in intellectual property cases. *Duke Law Journal, 48,* 147.

Voloshynovskiy, S., Pereira, S., Iquise, V., & Pun, T. (2001, June). Attack modelling: Towards a second generation watermarking benchmark. *Signal Processing, 81*(6), 1177-1214.

W3C (2004). *Patent policy.*

W3C. (1999). *Removing data transfer from P3P.* Retrieved December 18, 2006, from http://www.w3c.org/P3P/data-transfer.html

W3C. (2006). *Platform for privacy preferences project.* Retrieved from http://www.w3.org/P3P/

Wagner, R. P. (2003). Information wants to be free: Intellectual property and the mythologies of control. *Columbia Law Review, 103,* 995.

Wakelin, K. (1998). Innovation and export behaviour at the firm level. *Research Policy, 26,* 829-841.

Walia, S. (2006). Battling e-commerce credit card fraud. In *e-Commerce Times,* May 25 2006, http://www.ecommercetimes.com/story/50558.html

Wang, R. D., Xu, D. W., & Qian, L. (2005). Audio watermarking algorithm based on wavelet packet and psychoacoustic model. *PDCAT 2005,* 812-814.

Warwick, S. (2004). Is copyright ethical? In R.A. Spinello & H.T. Tavani (Eds.), *Readings in cyberethics (2nd ed.),* pp. 305-321. Sudbury, MA: Jones and Bartlett Publishers.

Washington State Library Council (1999). *Issues in Digitization: A report prepared for the Washington State Library Council,* Jan 5.

Watson, A.B. (1987, December). Efficiency of an image code based on human vision. *Journal of Optical Society of America, 4*(12), 2401-2417.

Watson, A.B. (1993, February). Dct quantization matrices visually optimized for individual images. *Proceedings of SPIE: Vol. 1913. Human Vision, Visual Processing and Digital Display IV* (pp. 202-216). Bellingham, WA.

Watts, J.J.S., & Baigent, D.R. (2002). Intellectual property, standards and competition law: Navigating a minefield. *IEEE,* 837-842.

Wee, S. J., & Apostolopoulos, J. G. (2001). Secure scalable video streaming for wireless networks. In *Proceedings of the IEEE International Conference on Acoustics, Speech, and Signal Processing* (pp. 2049-2052), Salt Lake City UT, May, 4.

Wee, S. J., & Apostolopoulos, J. G. (2003). Secure scalable streaming and secure transcoding with JPEG-2000. In *Proceedings of IEEE International Conference on Image Processing, 1,* 205-208, Sept. 14-17.

Wei, L. (2002). Retrieved from http://wlu-share.tripod.com/ImgPasswd.htm

Weinshall, D. (2004). *Secure authentication schemes suitable for an associative memory.* Leibniz Center for Research in Computer Science, Technical Report 2004-00.

Weiser, P. (2003). The Internet, innovation, and intellectual property policy. *Columbia Law Review, 103,* 534.

Wen, J., Sevra, M., Luttrell, M., & Jin, W. (2001). A format-compliant configurable encryption framework for access control of multimedia. In *Proceedings of the IEEE Workshop on Multimedia Signal Proc.* (pp. 435-440), Cannes, France, Oct..

Westen, S. J. P., Lagendijk, R. L., & Biemond, J. (1996). Optimization of JPEG color image coding using a human visual system model. *Proceedings of the SPIE, 2657,* 370-381.

Westman, R. (1999, October). The battle of standards—And the road to peace. *On—The New World of Communication,* pp. 26-30.

Wheaton v. Peters (1834). 33 U.S. 591.

Wiil, U. K., & Leggett, J. J. (1996). The hyperdisco approach to open hypermedia systems. In *Proceedings of Hypertext'96,* (Washington, USA, 1996) (pp.140-148).

Wiil, U. K., Nürnberg, P. J., & Leggett, J. J. (1999). Hypermedia research directions: An infrastructure perspective. *ACM Computing Surveys, 31*(4).

Wikipedia. (2006). *Wikipedia: Copyrights.* Retrieved October 13, 2006, from http://en.wikipedia.org/wiki/Wikipedia:Copyrights

Winn, E. (2000). Who owns the customer? The emerging law of commercial transactions in electronic customer data. *Business Law, 56,* 213.

WIPO Copyright Treaty. (1996). Geneva December 20, from http://www.wipo.int/treaties/en/ip/wct/trtdocs_wo033.html

WIPO Performances and Phonograms Treaty. (1996). Geneva December 20. Retrieved from http://www.wipo.int/treaties/en/ip/wppt/trtdocs_wo034.html

Wireless Watch. (2005a, November 29). Mobile patents war shifts to email. *The Register.* Retrieved August 29, 2006, from http://www.theregister.co.uk/2005/11/29/mobile_email_patents_war/

Wireless Watch. (2005b, November 15). *The Register.* Qualcomm IP battle hots up. Retrieved August 29, 2006, from http://www.theregister.co.uk/2005/11/15/qualcomm_ip_battle/

Wolfe, P. J., & Godsill, S. J. (2000). Towards a perceptually optimal spectral amplitude estimator for audio signal enhancement. *Proceedings of the IEEE International Conference on Acoustics, Speech, and Signal Processing, 2,* 821-824.

Wolfgang, R.B., Podilchuk, C.I., & Delp, E.J. (1999, July). Perceptual watermarks for digital images and video. *Proceedings of IEEE, 87*(7), 1108-1126.

Wong, W. (2002, April 18). IBM ebMXL patent plan royalty-free. *Tech Update.*

World Wide Web Consortium. (1999). *XML path language (XPath).* Retrieved from http://www.w3.org/TR/xpath

World Wide Web Consortium. (2000). *Simple object access protocol (SOAP) 1.1.* Retrieved from http://www.w3.org/TR/SOAP/

World Wide Web Consortium. (2003). *Document object model (DOM) level 2 HTML specification.* Retrieved from http://www.w3.org/DOM/

Wos, L. (1998). The problem of explaining the disparate performance of hyperresolution and paramodulation. *J. Autom. Reasoning, 4*(2), 215-219.

Wos, L., Robinson, G.., & Carson, D. (1965). Efficiency and completeness of the set of support strategy in theorem proving. *J. ACM,* 536-541.

Wu, C. P., Su, P. C., & Kuo, C. C. J. (2000). Robust and efficient digital audio watermarking using audio content analysis. *Security and Watermarking of Multimedia Contents (SPIE), 3971,* 382-392.

Wu, C., & Kuo, C. C. (2000). Fast encryption methods for audiovisual data confidentiality. In SPIE International Symposia on Information Technologies 2000. Boston, MA, USA, Nov. 2000, *Proceedings of SPIE, 4209,* 284-295.

Wu, C., & Kuo, C. C. (2001). Efficient multimedia encryption via entropy codec design. In SPIE International Symposium on Electronic Imaging 2001. San Jose, CA, USA, Jan. 2001, *Proceedings of SPIE, 4314,* 128-138.

Wu, M., & Liu, B. (1998). Watermarking for image authentication. *Proceedings of 1998 IEEE International Conference on Image Processing, 2,* 437-441.

Wu, M., Miller, R., & Garfinkel, S.L.(2004). Secure Web authentication with mobile phones, *DIMACS symposium on usable privacy and security 2004.*

Xie, G., & Shen, H. (2005). Toward improved wavelet-based watermarking using the pixel-wise masking model. *ICICP2005, 1,* 689-692.

Xing, H., & Scordilis, M. S., (2005). Improved spread spectrum digital audio watermarking based on a modified perceptual entropy psychoacoustic model. *Proceedings of IEEE Southeast Conference,* 283-286.

Yahoo Corporation. *Currency Conversion.* Retrieved from http://quote.yahoo.com/m3?u

Yaqoob, N. (2006). My Ubuntu experience. *SPIDER, September 2006,* 10-12.

Ye, Y., Yang, Q., Wang, Y. (2003). Magic cube encryption for digital image using chaotic sequence, *Journal of Zhejiang University of Technology, 31*(2), 173-176.

Yen J. C. & Guo, J. I. (1999). A new MPEG encryption system and its VLSI architecture. *IEEE Workshop on Signal Processing Systems* (pp. 430-437), Taipei.

Yen, A. (1990). Restoring the natural law: Copyright as labor and possession. *Ohio State Law Journal,* 51, 517.

Yeo, I. K., & Kim, H. J. (2003). Modified patchwork algorithm: A novel audio watermarking scheme. *IEEE Transaction On Speech and Audio Processing, 11*(4).

Yoshitaka, A., & Ichikawa, T. (1999). A survey on content-based retrieval for multimedia databases. *IEEE Transactions on Knowledge and Data Engineering, 11*(1), 81-93.

Yu, H., & Yu, X. (2003). Progressive and scalable encryption for multimedia content access control. *Proceeding of IEEE International Conference on Communications* (pp. 547-550).

Yuan, C., Zhu, B., Wang, Y., Li, S., & Zhong, Y. (2003). Efficient and fully scalable encryption for MPEG-4 FGS. *IEEE Int. Symp. Circuits and Systems,* May, 620-623.

Yuhang, D. Dayan, Z. & Kejun, W. (2005). A study of hand vein recognition method. *IEEE International Conference Mechatronics and Automation, 4,* 2106-2110.

Yun, Y. W., (2002). The "123" of Biometric Technology. *Synthesis Journal.*

Zeng, W., & Lei, S. (2003). Efficient frequency domain selective scrambling of digital video. *IEEE Trans on Multimedia, 5*(1), 118-129.

Zhang, F., & Zhang, H. (2004). Applications of neural network to watermarking capacity. *IEEE International Symposium on Communications and Information Technology 2004, 1*, 340-343.

Zhang, J., Wang, N. C., & Xiong, F. (2002). Hiding a logo watermark into the multiwavelet domain using neural networks. *Proceedings of 14th IEEE International Conference on Tools with Artificial Intelligence*, 477-482.

Zhang, X., & Zhang, F. (2005). A blind watermarking algorithm based on neural network. *ICNN&B '05 International Conference on Neural Networks and Brain IEEE, 2*, 1073-1076.

Zhang, Z. M., Li, R. Y., & Wang, L. (2003). Adaptive watermark scheme with RBF neural networks. *Proceedings of the 2003 International Conference on Neural Networks and Signal Processing IEEE, 2*, 1517-1520.

Zhao, W., Chellappa, R., Rosenfeld, A., & Phillips, P. J. (2003). Face recognition: A literature survey. *ACM Computing Surveys*, 399-458.

Zhou, X., & Petrov, P. (20 control applications. In *Proceedings of the 43rd annual conference on Design automation* (pp.352-257).

Zittrain, J. (2006).The generative Internet. *The Harvard Law Review Association, 119,* Harv. L. Rev. 1974.

Zwicker, E., & Zwicker, U. T. (1991). Audio engineering and psychoacoustics: matching signals to the final receiver: The human auditory system. *Journal of Audio Engineering Society, 39*(3), 115-126.

About the Contributors

Hideyasu Sasaki, a graduate of the University of Tokyo in 1994, received an LL.M., from the University of Chicago Law School in 1999, an MS and a PhD in Cybernetic Knowledge Engineering (Media and Governance) with honors from Keio University in 2001, 2003, respectively. He is an associate professor at Department of Information Science and Engineering, Ritsumeikan University. He was an assistant professor at Keio University from 2003 to 2005. His research interests include content-based metadata indexing and image retrieval, digital libraries, multimedia databases, and intellectual property law and management. He has been admitted to practice as an Attorney-and-Counselor at Law in the New York State Bar, since 2000. He is active as an international program committee member at the International Society on Law and Technology (LawTech), the International Conference on Asian Digital Libraries (ICADL) and Euro-Japan Conference on Information Modeling and Knowledge Bases (EJC), respectively.

* * * *

Ruo Ando graduated the faculty of policy management at Keio University in 2000. He earned a master's degree and a PhD from the Graduate School of Media and Governance, Keio University (2002 and 2006). His major field of study is computer and information security. Currently, he is a researcher at the National Institute of Information and Communication Technology. Ando's main research topics are secure OS and virtual machine monitor, intrusion detection/prevention system, and automated reasoning.

Luigi Atzori (M'97) is an assistant professor in telecommunications at the University of Cagliari, Italy. He earned a PhD in EE and CS from the University of Cagliari (1999). Atzori's main research topics include error recovery and concealment, video postprocessing, IP telephony playout buffering, and video streaming. He has published more than 45 journal articles and refereed conference papers, and serves on the organizing and technical committees of leading multimedia communications conferences.

Shi-Cho Cha earned a BS and PhD in information management from the National Taiwan University (1996 and 2003, respectively). He is currently an assistant professor with the Department of Information, National Taiwan University of Science and Technology, where he has been a faculty member since 2006. He is a certified PMP and CISSP. From 2003-2006, he was a manager at PriceWaterhouseCoopers, Taiwan. His current research interests are in the area of information security management, with specific interests in risk assessment and information security investment evaluation.

Yutaka Funyu earned a BS from Tohoku University in 1962. Since then, he has been working with the Kawasaki Steel Co. Ltd. from 1962, CSK Co. Ltd. from 1987, and Yokogawa Co. Ltd. from 1990. He received PhD from Tohoku University, Japan. He is now working in Iwate Prefectural University as a vice president and professor. His recent research fields are software design method and construction methodology of information systems.

Giaime Ginesu graduated (MSc) in Electronic Engineering at the University of Cagliari in 2001, discussing a thesis on thermal image processing and pattern recognition. During 2001, he was (Erasmus grant) at the Institute for Telecommunications of the Technical University of Braunschweig and at the Fraunhofer Institute WKI (Germany), to work out his master thesis. In 2003, he spent a period of 6 months as Visiting Scholar at the Rensselaer Polytechnic Institute (Troy, NY), to work on volumetric data coding. In 2005, he achieved PhD in Electronic Engineering at the Dept. of Electronic Engineering, University of Cagliari, discussing a thesis on volumetric data processing and coding. His research interests are related to image processing and transmission, volumetric data processing and coding, error concealment for wavelet-based image transmission, image based authentication, and JPEG2000/MPEG standards. He is a member of IEEE and CNIT's Unit of Research in Cagliari.

Daniele Giusto is Director of CNIT@UniCA Lab of Multimedia Communications and Professor of Telecommunications at the Faculty of Engineering, University of Cagliari, Italy, where he teaches Communication Systems and Image Processing and Transmission. He is also a Visiting Professor of Image Processing at the International Advanced School of Optical Technologies, Nuoro, Italy. His research interests are in the area of video/image processing and communication. He is the recipient of the 1993 AEI Ottavio Bonazzi best paper award, and corecipient of a 1998 IEEE Chester Sall best paper award. Dr. Giusto is a senior member of IEEE, and a member of AEI, EURASIP, and SPIE; he is also a member of the board of CNIT, the Italian University Consortium for Telecommunications, an Evaluator/Auditor for the European Commission, and the Italian National Delegate in the ISO JTC_1/ SC_29/WG_1 (JPEG) standardization committee. He has been General Chair for the PACKET VIDEO 2000 International Workshop.

Kimihito Ito received his BA in 1992, his MA in 1994, and his PhD in 1999 all in electrical engineering, and all from Hokkaido University. After postdoctoral positions at Meme Media Laboratory at Hokkaido University, he worked as an Instructor at Graduate School of Information Science and Technology at Hokkaido University from 2004 to 2005. He is currently an Associate Professor at Hokkaido University Research Center for Zoonosis Control. His research interests focus on bioinformatics, artificial intelligence, and their application to zoonosis control. He is a member of Japanese Society of Artificial Intelligence, and a member of the editing committee.

Yuh-Jzer Joung received his BS in Electrical Engineering from the National Taiwan University in 1984, and his MS and PhD in Computer Science from the State University of New York at Stony Brook in 1988 and 1992, respectively. He is currently a professor at the Department of Information Management in the National Taiwan University, where he has been a faculty member since 1992. From 1999 to 2000, he was a visiting scientist at the Lab for Computer Science, Massachusetts Institute of Technology. He was the chair of his department from 2001 to 2005. His main research interests are in the area of distributed computing, with specific interests in multiparty interaction, fairness, (group) mutual exclusion, ad hoc and peer-to-peer computing, and personal data management.

Eleanna Kafeza has a PhD in Computer Science from Hong Kong University of Science and Technology. She is currently a Lecturer (tenure track) at the Department of Marketing and Communications of the Athens University of Economics and Business. Her research interests include workflows, grid scheduling, and Web services.

Irene Kafeza is an Attorney-at-Law, member of Athens Bar Association. She holds a Master of Laws in Chinese and Comparative Law from City University of Hong Kong and a Master of Laws in Information Technology Law from The University of Hong Kong. Her research interests include Intellectual Property and Information Technology issues and legal issues of electronic agents contracting.

Yasushi Kiyoki received his BEng, MEng, and PhD in electrical engineering from Keio University in 1978, 1980, and 1983, respectively. From 1984 to 1996, he was an assistant professor and an associate professor at Institute of Information Sciences and Electronics, University of Tsukuba. In 1996, he joined the faculty of Keio University, where he is a tenured professor at the Department of Environmental Information. His research addresses multidatabase systems, knowledge-base systems, semantic associative processing, and multimedia database systems. He serves as the editor-in-chief on Information Modeling and Knowledge Bases (IOS Press). He also served as the program chair for the 7th International Conference on Database Systems for Advanced Applications.

Shiguo Lian was born in Jiangsu, China, in 1979. He received the Bachelor and PhD degrees in information security from Nanjing University of Science & Technology in 2000 and 2005, respectively. He worked as a research assistant in EE Department of City University of Hong Kong in 2004. He is now a researcher in Service Anticipation Multimedia Innovation (SAMI) Lab of France Telecom R&D Beijing. He is the member of IEEE, SPIE, EURASIP, and Chinese Association of Graph and Image. His research interests include multimedia content protection, data encryption, data authentication, and image processing.

Mirko Luca Lobina (M'00) is a researcher in telecommunications at the University of Cagliari, Italy. He received PhD in EE and CS from the University of Cagliari in 2004. Main research topics: audio postprocessing and watermarking, IP telephony playout buffering.

Davide Mula (BSC'04) is a student-researcher in Digital Right Management (DRM) at LUISS Guido Carli - Rome. He will discuss his Master Thesis in June 06 on the applications of the concept of database in DRM. Main research topics: DRM and watermarking.

Kensuke Naoe graduated the faculty of environmental information at Keio University in 2002. He received the Master degree at Graduate School of Media and Governance at Keio University in 2004. His major is artificial neural network and information security. Interested in the area of research in watermark using neural network, network intrusion detection, cryptography and malware detection.

Takashi Nozaki, who is General Manager of SciencePark Corporation, is a visiting researcher of Takefuji Lab. at Keio University. He is a member of the DRIVERWARE IMMUNE project granted by US Air Force Office of Scientific Research with Grant Number AOARD 03-4049.

Natalie Pang is a PhD student in Monash University's Faculty of Information Technology. Her doctoral research investigates the interplay between user-centered design principles and the knowledge commons in communities. Prior to embarking on her PhD, she has been working in Monash University in Malaysia as a researcher in areas of telecommunications, digital libraries, and social computing. She has worked in various cross-disciplinary areas of information technology in Singapore, Malaysia, and Australia. Natalie is a key member of several research projects in Australia, Singapore, and China. Other than a part-time staff member of the Centre for Community Networking Research group and full-time doctoral student of the Faculty, she also serves as Research Associate for Museum Victoria.

Jun Sasaki received BS degree and MS degrees from Iwate University in 1979 and 1981, respectively. Then, he had been working in NTT Laboratories from 1981 to 1998. He received his PhD degree from Tohoku University Japan, in 1993, by researching on reliability of optical fiber networks. He is now working in Iwate Prefectural University as an associate professor. His recent research field is information system for life supporting of aged people.

Hiroaki Shimomukai received BS and MS degrees from Iwate Prefectural University in 2004 and 2006, respectively. Then, he is working as a system-developing engineer at Gingatsushin Co. Ltd.. His research field is application systems using cellular phone and the two dimensional code.

Koichiro Shoji, who is CEO of SciencePark Corporation, is a visiting researcher of Takefuji Lab. at Keio University. He is a member of the DRIVERWARE IMMUNE project granted by U.S. Air Force Office of Scientific Research with Grant Number AOARD 03-4049. Won a Kanagawa Industrial Technology Development Award for Information Leakage Monitoring Tool called "4th Eye".

Yoshiyasu Takefuji is a tenured professor on faculty of environmental information at Keio University since April 1992. He was an Editor of the Journal of Neural Network Computing, an associate editor of IEEE Trans. on Neural Networks, Neural/parallel/scientific computations, and Neurocomputing, and a guest editor of Journal Analog Integrated Circuits and Signal Processing in the special issue on analog VLSI neural networks and also guest editor of Neurocomputing in the special issue on neural network optimization.

Yuzuru Tanaka has been a professor of Computer Science in Graduate School of Information Science and Technology, Hokkaido University, Japan since 1990. He founded the Meme Media Laboratory at the university in 1995. He also worked as a professor of Digital Library at the Graduate School of Informatics, Kyoto University between 1998 and 2000. Since 2004, he is also a visiting professor of Natinal Institute of Informatics. He received his Master degree in electronics and PhD in computer science from Kyoto University and the University of Tokyo, respectively. His research area included database design theory, database machine architecture, and component-based media architecture. His current research focuses on meme media system architecture, IntelligentPad and IntelligentBox and their integration with Web technologies. IntelligentPad has been attracting Japanese industries and government organizations. This led to the establishment of the IntelligentPad Consortium in 1993, and later in 1995, to an alliance with CI Labs in United States. In 1994, Dr. Tanaka received the grand prize of annual technological achievement award from Nikkei BP.

Index

A

B

C

non-utilitarian 39
non iso-frequency masking 145
nonlinear 104
  adaptive
    system 398, 402, 404, 409
  behavior 405
  classification
    problems 122
  feature
    extraction
      scheme 117
    function 149
    system 405
nonuniform 104
notification mechanism 168
null hypothesis 101

O

OEM agreement 333
online brokerage house 189
online personal data licensing (OPDL) 162, 163, 181
online public access catalogue (OPAC) 286
open content licenses 260, 262, 263, 264, 266, 269, 270, 271, 272
Open hypermedia systems (OHSs) 221
open profiling standard (OPS) 166
open source 391
operating systems (OS) 62
optimal asymmetric encryption padding (OAEP) 193
Organization for Economic Cooperation and Development (OECD) 164
Organization for the Advancement of Structured Information Standards (OASIS) 321
organized techniques for theorem proving and effective research (OTTER) 245
Original Equipment Manufacturers (OEMs) 62
output layer 123

P

pairwise master key (PMK) 190
paradigm 387
parameters public 401
parametric values 11
password authentication protocol (PAP) 190, 191
patchwork 100, 101
  algorithm 108
  scheme 101
  strategy 103, 107
patent 39, 42, 305, 306, 310, 322
  applications 320

claiming
    technology 323
  intensity 293, 298
  portfolio 295, 338
  problems 338
  system 42, 325
Patent and Trademark Office (PTO) 43
patenting 296
  computer
    programs 43
  strategy 295
pedestal effect 149
peer-to-peer (P2P) 26, 168
  file-sharing
    technology 55
  networks 52, 53, 54, 65, 387
  sharing
    model 270
performance rights 263
permutation algorithms 75
personal
  channel
    agent (PCA) 167
  data 181
    licenser 168, 175, 179, 182
Personal Information Protection and Electronic Document Act of Canada 163
Personhood 31
philosophy of right 32
PHP: Hypertext Preprocessor (PHP) 220
Platform for Privacy Preferences (P3P) 166
political 319
preferences processor 169
primitive number 406
privacy 162, 163, 164, 166
  profile
    negotiation
      protocol (PPNP) 207
private
  key 400, 401
  personal
    identification
      data 189
probability density function (Pdf) 110
professional knowledge 1
programming by demonstrations (PBD) 221
property 31
  right 31, 33, 64
proposal model 408
proprietary model 65
protect intellectual propriety 399